State & Local Taxation

Fourth Edition
2001
Volume I

Richard D. Pomp
Alva P. Loiselle Professor of Law
University of Connecticut School of Law

Oliver Oldman
Learned Hand Professor of Law Emeritus
Harvard Law School

State & Local Taxation
Fourth Edition
2001

Cover Photo by Verenda Smith, who waited for the perfect storm (Washington style). In one of her other incarnations, she was a professional photographer, and as the cover indicates, she has not lost her eye.

Cover designed by Gagan Associates, who add class to whatever they touch, and are a delight to work with.

Photo of the trading floor of the Boston Stock Exchange, Chapter One, reprinted with the permission of the Boston Stock Exchange.

Photo of Mayor John Street in the studios of WHYY, Chapter Two, reprinted with the permission of WHYY, Inc.

Photo of Lake Shore Auto Parts and Irv Oppenheim, Chapter Two, reprinted with the permission of Irv Oppenheim.

Photo of Met Life advertisement, Chapter Two, reprinted with permission of United Media Licensing.

Photo of "Welcome to Delaware," Chapter Six, by Bill Remington, who risked his personal safety to take it.

Photo of roller coaster at Darien Lake, Chapter Seven, reprinted with permission of Six Flags, Darien Lake.

Photo of former Commissioner Janette Lohman, Chapter Nine, reprinted with permission of Janette Lohman and Associated Industries of Missouri.

Photo of International Harvester advertisement, Chapter Nine, reprinted with permission of the State Historical Society of Wisconsin.

Photo of one of the three building that make up the headquarters of the National Geographic Society, chapter Nine, by Joseph H. Bailey, reprinted with the permission of the National Geographic Society.

Photo of the headquarters of Moorman Manufacturing, Chapter Eleven, reprinted with permission of Moorman Manufacturing, Inc.

Photo of products of Colgate Palmolive, Chapter Eleven, reprinted with permission of Colgate-Palmolive Company.

Photo of Geoffrey and design, a mark of Geoffrey, Inc., Chapter Eleven, reprinted with permission of Geoffrey, Inc.

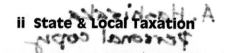

Inquiries about this book should be addressed to the publisher:

Prof. Richard D. Pomp
Alva P. Loiselle Professor of Law
Connecticut Law School
65 Elizabeth Street
Hartford, Conn.
06105-2290

Fax: (860) 570-5242

Phone: (860) 570-5251

E-Mail: rpomp@law.uconn.edu

Library of Congress Cataloging-in-Publication Data

Pomp, Richard D.
      State and local taxation : cases and materials / by Richard D. Pomp
      and Oliver Oldman — 4th ed. 2001
      Includes index
      ISBN # 0-9653722-0-0
      1. Taxation—United States—States—Law and legislation—Cases
2. Local taxation—Law and legislation—United States—Cases.
I. Pomp, Richard D. II. Title.
KF6720.P66 2001

In memory of my father
Morris Pomp

Contents

Volume I

Contents

Contents

Contents

Volume II

Contents

Contents

Contents

Volume III

Contents

Contents

Preface for Students

Once upon a time, issues of state and local taxation played to a small audience. Federal tax matters held center stage; state and local issues were relegated to the wings. Lately, however, state and local tax matters have emerged from their secondary status and have moved into the spotlight. The major accounting firms have expanded their state and local services and have organized special consulting divisions to work with state officials. Law firms have also begun competing for what was formerly the domain of accountants. Academics are discovering what a small but devoted number of their colleagues had already known: that state and local tax issues present all of the intellectual challenges inherent in the study of the federal corporate and personal income taxes and the wealth transfer tax, with the additional challenge of a constitutional dimension. Further, whereas many of the weaknesses in the federal tax system are well documented, intensely analyzed, and the subject of lively scholarly debate, state tax issues are, by comparison, an unexplored territory. Many fundamental questions remain unresolved. Some of you will find that exhilarating because you will participate in formulating the answers; others will find that frustrating and long for the highly embroidered Internal Revenue Code.

Most state tax systems are ripe for reexamination by policymakers, legislators, and academics. The premises that underlie a traditional state tax system are under severe attack. Many state tax systems developed in a far simpler time–a time when substantial sectors of the economy, such as transportation, communications, banking, and power generation were either regulated or subject to significant federal controls. State tax systems evolved when the economy was dominated by mercantile and manufacturing activities, and little thought had to be given to the tax treatment of services. Multinational corporations and conglomerates were yet to emerge, and few corporations had substantial amounts of foreign income. It was a world in which corporations did not electronically transfer funds around the globe, 800 telephone numbers were not widespread, large mail order houses had not yet proliferated, the Internet was not a household word, and the pace of federal tax reform was comfortingly slow. In addition, state taxes were typically low enough to discourage much litigation.

Today, the world is more complex and state tax systems have been overtaken by technological advances, new forms of business organizations, the globalization of business, changes in the judicial climate, the relaxation of federal controls over the economy, and the threat of significant federal tax reform.[1] Many states have organized some type of temporary commission to study their tax structures. Although in most cases these commissions were responding directly to a financial crisis, others, like New York's, were formed because of legislative concerns that the existing tax structure was atavistic.[2]

Federal tax changes have also helped move state tax issues onto center stage. The most significant change was the Economic Recovery Tax Act of 1981 (ERTA), which gutted the federal corporate income tax by revamping the treatment of depreciation and by introducing safe-harbor leasing. Many of the largest corporations in the United States paid no corporate income tax for several years as a consequence of ERTA.[3]

ERTA had a major impact upon the field of state taxation. Because no state wishes to reinvent the Internal Revenue Code, state personal and corporate income taxes are, with varying degrees of fidelity, based on federal concepts. If ERTA's rules on depreciation and safe-harbor leasing had been incorporated into state tax laws, however, many states would have suffered significant losses of tax revenue

---

1. These issues are more fully developed in Richard D. Pomp, State Tax Reform for the Eighties, 16 Conn. L. Rev. (1984). See also Gene Corrigan, Interstate Corporate Income Taxation–Recent Revolutions and a Modern Response, 29 Vand. L. Rev. 423 (1976).

2. See Richard D. Pomp, State Tax Reform New York Style, in 1985 Nat'l Tax Ass'n–Tax Inst. Am. Proc. 192 (1985); Richard D. Pomp, Reforming a State Corporate Income Tax, 51 Alb. L. Rev. 375 (1987). See also William Dodge, Structuring State and Local Tax Reform Commissions (1986).

3. See Citizens for Tax Justice, Corporate Income Taxes in the Reagan Years (1984).

without receiving commensurate benefits. Accordingly, many states refused to embrace fully the federal changes and "decoupled" from ERTA's rules on depreciation and safe-harbor leasing.[4] More fundamentally, many states started to question the degree to which other aspects of their tax laws should emulate and mimic the Internal Revenue Code.[5] The decoupling issue sharply focused both the revenue costs and the administrative benefits of conforming with the federal system.

ERTA also had severe repercussions for state and local tax practitioners. By decreasing the impact of the federal income tax on many corporations, ERTA substantially increased the relative significance of state income taxes, especially in states that had decoupled. In many cases, a corporation's state corporate tax was greater than its federal corporate tax—a situation that did not escape notice by CEOs or corporate tax managers. State and local tax practitioners became the object of new interest on the part of corporate management. Consciousness about state tax issues was also heightened by the U.S. Supreme Court's decisions in Complete Auto, Japan Line, Moorman, Commonwealth Edison, Maryland v. Louisiana, Westinghouse, Mobil, Exxon, Asarco, Woolworth, and Container (see Chapters 1 and 11), all of which were decided between 1977 and 1983. Corporations that had typically treated state issues as secondary to federal concerns reexamined their own priorities. Emphasis shifted from issues of compliance to those of planning.

The Tax Reform Act of 1986 also had a major effect on the state tax profession. By lowering federal marginal tax rates, the Act increased the after-tax cost of deductible state taxes. The Act generated additional pressure on lawyers and accountants to reduce state taxes through planning. This pressure was exacerbated by increases occurring in state taxes across the country.

New forms of doing business, such as limited liability companies (LLCs), the increased use of holding companies, more sophisticated tax minimization strategies, and the rise of electronic commerce are forcing tax administrations to become more aggressive. This combination of pressures has generated an unprecedented demand for legal and accounting services.

There is a fairly small number of well known, extremely capable law firms with active, full-time state tax practices. They are staffed with the luminaries in the field. These firms, however, are the exception. Many large, prominent firms with traditionally strong federal tax practices have been late in recognizing the potential of the state tax market. Such firms have displayed the common bias of federal tax lawyers who traditionally have looked down on their state counterparts as the Rodney Dangerfields of the

---

4. For a background discussion, see New York State Legislative Commission on the Modernization and Simplification of Tax Administration and the Tax Law, The Article 9-A Franchise Tax: Should New York Adopt ACRS? (Staff Report Dec. 31, 1984).

5. See, e.g., New York State Legislative Commission on the Modernization and Simplification of Tax Administration and the Tax Law, The New York State Personal Income Tax: An Overview (Staff Report May 29, 1985), revised as Richard D. Pomp, Restructuring a State Income Tax in Response to the Tax Reform Act of 1986, 36 Tax Notes 1195 (1987), reprinted in 1988 Nat'l Tax Ass'n -- Tax Inst. Am. Proc. (1988), a revision of Richard D. Pomp, Simplicity and Complexity in the Context of a State Tax System, in Reforming State Tax Systems (S. Gold ed. 1986).

profession.[6] But the times have changed and these firms are now playing catch up and competing with the accounting firms.

Meanwhile, the bigger accounting firms are no longer content to do compliance work and have dynamic and growing state practices geared to planning and tax minimization strategies. Actively recruiting from law firms, industry, and government, and wooing recent graduates with attractive starting salaries (often commensurate with those of law firms), these accounting firms now claim some of the brightest minds in the business, people who combine technical virtuosity with a creativity and a boldness that was more commonly associated in the past with the federal tax bar. With their extensive network of offices, their computer simulation models, their large staffs that can handle an array of state tax issues, and their increased willingness to be involved in dispute resolution, the accounting firms

have changed the nature of a state tax practice and have emerged as major players.[7] Over time, the states have increased their rates and expanded their bases; they continue to hire young, ambitious, and well-trained professionals who raise cutting edge issues. The ante has been upped, which means taxpayers are more willing to litigate because the stakes are now higher. It is also increasingly worthwhile for clients to spend more time and money on tax planning.

In short, by any measure—adoption of new taxes, changes in existing taxes, amount of litigation, number of court decisions, number of scholarly articles, or extent of job opportunities—the field of state and local taxation is in ferment.[8] Consequently, whether your interests run to the public or private sectors, are mercenary or intellectual, or any combination thereof, your timing in taking a course in state and local taxation is excellent.[9]

---

6. See David Brunori, Behind the Curve: State and Local Taxation in U.S. Law Schools, State Tax Notes, May 5, 1997.

7. See Richard D. Pomp, The Future of the State Corporate Income Tax: Reflections (and Confessions) of a State Tax Lawyer, in The Future of State Taxation 49 (D. Brunori ed. 1998).

8. For a taste of some of the excitement that awaits you in this course, see David Brunori, State Tax Policy: A Political Perspective (2001).

9. You are lucky that your school even offers a course on state taxation. See Brunori, supra note 6.

Preface for Teachers

We have provided more material (including questions) than can be taught (or answered) in a three or four credit course. (Shame on the schools that are still offering only a two credit course.) Our goal is to err on the side of over inclusion so that you will be able to pick and choose from our selections, depending on your tastes and interests.

We often use some of the cases as springboards to discuss taxes that are not covered in detail by any of the materials. For example, Shaffer (Ch. 4), Yale & Towne Mfg. Co. (Ch.4), Austin (Ch. 4), Lunding (Ch. 4), and J.C. Penney (Ch. 3), provide perfect opportunities to elaborate on personal income taxes. Those who are familiar with the federal rules on the taxation of residents and nonresidents might want to draw comparisons with the state approaches. The federal credit for foreign income taxes can be usefully compared with similar approaches in state personal income taxes. For those of you who wish to present a brief introduction to the taxation of LLCs and LLPs, we have added a short piece at the end of Chapter 10.

Jefferson Lines (Ch. 9), Tyler Pipe (Ch. 9), and Armco (Ch. 9), are logical places to discuss the differences between business activities taxes, such as gross receipts taxes, and retail sales taxes.

Japan Line (Ch. 1), Fulton (Ch. 1), Nordlinger (Ch. 2), Lake Shore Auto Parts (Ch. 2), Norfolk & Western (Ch. 3), and Michelin (Ch. 5), can be used to introduce real and personal property taxes. We find that most teachers do not have time or the inclination to teach a major unit on the property tax. As a substitute, some have had wonderful experiences bringing a local assessor, appraiser, or property tax practitioner to class. Both of the editors have a longstanding interest in the property tax, and Ollie has occasionally taught an entire course on it. Nonetheless, we also find that the typical two, three, or four credit course does not allow much time to be spent on the property tax. Those that wish to allocate more time, however, should contact Ollie for his teaching materials.

We have added two new Chapters in this edition: Chapter 14, Intergovernmental Immunities and Chapter 15, The Taxation of American Indians. These are complimentary, although either can be taught without the other.

Wherever possible, we inform the students about what happened after a case was decided. For example, did the legislature overrule the case by amending the statute? What happened on remand? We raise the issue of remedies throughout the Questions and Comments.

The materials are organized so that the basic constitutional building blocks are first explored in Chapters 1 through 5 and then applied in the context of the sales and use taxes (Ch. 6 through 9), the corporate income tax (Ch. 10 and 11), the deregulation of the utilities (Ch. 12), and electronic commerce (Ch. 13). Many of the sales and corporate tax cases raise commerce clause and due process issues and could have been discussed in Chapters 1 and 3, but we think pedagogically both taxes are best taught in their separate units. The chapter on electronic commerce is a fitting capstone for the course because the issues it raises cut across all of the earlier material. The material on the taxation of American Indians (Ch. 15) and on intergovernmental immunities (Ch. 14) is probably best taught toward the end of the course. If both chapters are taught, Chapter 14 should probably be taught before Chapter 15.

There is nothing sacrosanct about the order of the materials. No matter what the order, issues will inevitably come up that require background information not yet presented. We sometimes start the course with sales and use taxes, work back to the first five chapters and conclude with corporate taxes and electronic commerce. We found that this order provides a nice change of pace and rhythm, as students alternate between the details of two specific tax regimes and the more abstract principles of constitutional interpretation.

Within each chapter we have tended, with some exceptions, to arrange the cases chronologically. This order allows a student to see the incremental evolution of the law. It also alerts the student to attempts by the Court at revisionist history. A chronological arrangement ensures that the students are not reading a case that requires an understanding of doctrines yet to be studied. We have experimented over the years with arranging cases under topic headings, such as "discrimination against foreign commerce," or "the unitary business principle." The cases do not always come neatly pigeonholed, however, and often involve (or should have involved) other issues. Putting a label on on a case sometimes bridles creative thinking, and of course is not the way problems are presented in practice. A chronological order allows the student to understand the state of the law prior to the case at issue and illuminates the doctrinal tools (often limited) with which the Court had to work. A student is more apt to appreciate creative lawyering and to see why the Court embarked upon a shift in doctrines or paradigms. Sometimes we will revisit an earlier case after the students have had the benefit of reading a more recent one. Although editors often struggle with the knotty problem of how to arrange cases, in the end few professors follow the arrangement anyway. We ourselves (much to the amazement of our students) often experiment and deviate from the order of the cases in the materials.

We hope that our organization of the material, our emphasis on cases rather than summaries of cases, and our choice of questions and comments, teach the students the difference between rules and information, on the one hand, and wisdom and knowledge on the other. When it comes to U.S. Supreme Court cases, we have resisted the temptation to use squibs, which encourages a student to substitute information for analysis. The cases have been brutally edited to make them more readable by students and cannot substitute for the originals. String citations have been omitted without any indication to the reader. At the suggestion of our students, we have sometimes replaced the uninformative generic terms "Commissioner" or "Commission" with the name of the state involved. We have, however, left intact citations to the classic cases that are part of our shared tax heritage in this field.

We look forward to hearing your comments and suggestions for the next edition. The beauty of desktop publishing is that we can respond quickly, as we did in this edition, to your recommendations and make sure that we cover cutting edge developments (such as the expanded chapters on the sales tax, the new material on the taxation of American Indians, the new material on electronic commerce, the deregulation of the utilities, and the introduction to LLCs and LLPs), as well as correct errors. We would also like to hear your suggestions for cases to be included in the next edition (or ones that should be deleted).

Preface for Practitioners

Our experiences as expert witnesses, brief writers, consultants, and participants in Supreme Court litigation convince us that academics and practitioners each bring unique skills and perceptions to the table. We hope this book vindicates that belief.

Although this casebook is not intended to be a treatise or encyclopedic in coverage, we think that the background material in each chapter will provide a useful overview of the underlying structure of the taxes and of the constitutional provisions addressed. The questions and comments after each case may stimulate new thoughts about old material and provide tools for dealing with undeveloped and emerging issues.

Successful litigation and tax planning often require revisiting precedent from a different perspective. Our questions and comments are intended to serve that objective. We do not expect you necessarily to agree with our views, but we hope you will find the materials provocative and stimulating. Please let us know your disagreements. We and our readers want to benefit from the insights that can result when a practitioner's experiences and understandings are melded with an academic's perspective.

Having worked over the years with many of the luminaries in the field, we appreciate that one of the skills of any successful lawyer is a mastery of the record and a sensitivity to the differences in the factual setting among cases. To that end, we believe that students should read actual cases and not summaries thereof. Consequently, while we have brutally edited some of the cases to make them more readable, this work remains a casebook rather than a treatise.

In the past few years, there has been an explosion of material on state taxation, which reduces pressure on the coverage of a casebook. New journals, portfolios, firm newsletters, weekly publications, weekly commentary from legal publishers, and daily electronic information ensures that interested parties have access to much of the same information. The key is working creatively with that common pool of data. We hope our materials serve that goal rather than add to the information overload.

Acknowledgments

Many persons have contributed through the years to my thinking about issues of state taxation in general, and more recently to this work in particular. The list is long and the risk of overlooking someone is great. Accordingly, I have limited my thanks to those who have commented on drafts of this book with apologies to everyone else whose contributions may have been less focused, but just as valuable.

I am fortunate to have as my close friend for nearly three decades, Professor Michael J. McIntyre of Wayne State University. Professor McIntyre, one of the country's premier tax theorists, has consistently served as a collaborator on projects and as my intellectual provocateur throughout the years, and so it was with these materials. He is gracious with his support, tireless with his advice and suggestions, and always unselfish with his time. If he has any failings at all, they are left on the tennis court. I am privileged to have him as a trusted friend, and he makes my life richer by his presence.

Chapters One through Five had the benefit of two of the nation's leading constitutional law scholars. Professor Richard S. Kay, my close friend and colleague, has been a continual source of insight and support. His intellectual curiosity extends to even matters of state taxation and his wise counsel and extraordinary judgment added greatly to the book. Professor Jeremy R. Paul, currently Associate Dean of the Connecticut Law School, was never too busy to review a draft (or to resist the temptation to rewrite a sentence here or there) or to offer encouragement and perceptive advice.

Chapter Ten had a balanced review—Linda Fontaine from the private sector—and Paull Mines from the public sector. No author could ask for more. Linda is National Tax Advisor for Whole Foods Market, as well as a part-time student (and more recently, part owner) of the Academy of Oriental Medicine in Austin, Texas, where she studies Tax Chi. Paull is General Counsel for the Multistate Tax Commission and one of the great intellectuals in the field, the proverbial scholar's lawyer and lawyer's scholar. As this edition got close to its deadline, I barraged Paull with last minute e mails, all of which he answered promptly and with his inimitable humor and insight. He is too sweet a soul to have asked me to stop bothering him. Linda and Paull have years' of wisdom and an intellectual honesty and integrity that could not help but make for a more balanced finished product.

I was fortunate in the discussion of the tax consequences of deregulation in Chapter Twelve to have had reviews by both Craig B. Fields of Morrison and Foerster and Marilyn A. Wethekam of Horwood, Marcus and Berk Both are on the cutting edge of these issues and are making the law in this area. Earl Goldhammer of American Electric Power, and Mark Muchow, with the West Virginia Department of Taxation and Revenue, shared their breadth of experiences with helpful comments on the non-tax portions. As luck would have it, one of my former students, Philip Sussler (who met his wife in one of the first state tax courses I taught at UConn), is an internationally known consultant in the electric utility industry. He represents plant developers, municipalities, utilities, and large end users. He has tried very hard to educate me in this extremely fluid area.

Chapter Thirteen benefitted greatly from the learning of Michael Mazerov, currently with the Center on Budget Priorities, who is not a lawyer–but could easily be one–and watching his mind at work most assume that he is one. Others might well have turned cynical and jaded by now, but Michael is still going strong, fighting the good battles, no matter what the odds.

The new chapter on the taxation of American Indians was inspired by Dean Nell Newton. UConn is fortunate, as is the State of Connecticut, to have as its new dean one of the country's leading legal scholars on Native Americans and mentor to many who practice in the field. Under her leadership, the University of Connecticut Law School has become the center of a historic effort to revise Felix S. Cohen's classic work, Handbook of Federal Indian Law. Without her encouragement and support, both institutionally and personally, I would not have had the confidence to undertake that chapter.

In working on that chapter, I was fortunate enough to have had the counsel of Ted Spangler, Deputy Attorney General for the State of Idaho and Frank Katz, former

Chief Counsel for the New Mexico Revenue and Taxation Department. Both are experienced hands in this field, whose advice and guidance were most appreciated.

This edition of the casebook would not have been possible–quite literally–without the Herculean efforts of Joan Wood, or as she became known over time, Saint Joan. She combines the aesthetic judgment of an artist, the computer skills of a programmer, and the demeanor of a Zen master. She inherited this project cold and quickly climbed a steep learning curve without assistance. Not only did she climb it, but today she could be a beta tester for both Windows and Word Perfect. She survived lightning storms that disabled her computer, Microsoft goblins and gremlins, and other software idiosyncracies that were not for mortals to understand. She proved at each step of the way that at least for now humans are still a bit smarter than computers. Without being asked, Joan gave unselfishly of her evenings and weekends, with only release time to pursue tournament play in lawn bowling. Her wonderful upbeat attitude, calm demeanor, and keen mind were a soothing influence on those around her. Every overextended author working against a seemingly impossible deadline, should be similarly blessed by working with a Saint. I have worked with a lot of research assistants over the years, but none can surpass Tom Newman, who had just finished his first year at the law school when he made the ill-advised decision to work on the casebook. Nothing was too pedestrian–or intimidating–for Tom. His attention to detail and proofreading acumen are rare in a student (or in many law firm associates). His computer skills, reflecting his former career as a scientist, allowed him to resolve daily crises. When it seemed that the entire software industry was plotting against the completion of the book (perhaps because of the authors' views on the taxation of remote vendors), Tom's quiet self confidence was infectious and reassuring. He was extraordinary in negotiating computer databases and the Internet to track down obscure footnotes. He is a dedicated, hard working, highly motivated self starter and a joy to work with. Because of his analytical prowess, I came to rely on Tom for spotting substantive errors and weaknesses in the presentation. When one commitment after another took me away from this project, Tom was left in charge and I was left with peace of mind. Any law firm will be lucky to snag this rare talent.

Finally, please be assured that I appreciate all the e-mails, telephone calls, and conversations at conferences from those of you expressing words of encouragement, as well as suggestions for improving the casebook. If only there were more hours in the day.

Chapter 1

Commerce Clause

"The Congress shall have Power . . . To regulate Commerce with foreign Nations, and among the several States . . ."

U.S. Const., art. I, §8, cl. 3.

The Articles of Confederation reserved to the states–but did not grant to Congress–the power to regulate foreign and interstate commerce. This distribution of power proved unworkable because it allowed the states to continue their internecine feuding through trade wars and trade barriers. The states were also unable to deal cohesively with foreign trade relations. Trade with Great Britain, as well as with other countries, diminished with a resulting shortage of foreign currency. Political leaders feared that economic warfare would dissolve the union.[1]

One of the principal reasons for replacing the Articles of Confederation with the Federal Constitution was the need for national economic unity, unhampered by discriminatory and retaliatory state reprisals against commerce from other states and countries.[2] It was hoped that a national body such as the Congress, entrusted with the power to regulate interstate and foreign commerce, would be able to neutralize competing parochial economic interests.[3]

The Commerce Clause provides that "Congress shall have Power . . . To regulate Commerce with foreign Nations, and among the several States, and with the Indian Tribes."[4] The proposed Clause was relatively uncontroversial both during the Philadelphia convention and in the ratifying conventions. There was "nearly universal agreement that the federal government should be given the power of regulating commerce."[5] "The records disclose no constructive criticisms by the states of the commerce clause as proposed to them."[6] In the ratifying conventions, there was little opposition to the Commerce Clause, which "in its general substance was everybody's darling."[7] Madison described the Commerce Clause as an addition to the powers of the new federal government "which few oppose and from which no apprehensions are entertained."[8]

Despite its noncontroversial birth, the Clause has spawned much tax litigation.[9] "The Commerce Clause is one of the most prolific sources of national power

---

1. John E. Nowak & Ronald D. Rotunda, Constitutional Law 158-60 (6th ed. 2000). Camps Newfound/Owatonna, Inc. v. Town of Harrison, 520 U.S. 564, 571 (1997) ("Because each State was free to adopt measures fostering its own local interests without regard to possible prejudice to nonresidents . . . a 'conflict of commercial regulations, destructive to the harmony of the States' ensued.") This conflict of commercial regulations "was the immediate cause, that led to the forming of a [constitutional] convention." Id.

2. "[T]he generating source of the Constitution lay in the rising volume of restraints upon commerce which the Confederation could not check." Wiley Rutledge, A Declaration of Legal Faith 25 (1947). In 1786, Virginia proposed a meeting of the states "to consider how far a uniform system in their commercial regulations may be necessary to their common interest and their permanent harmony." Bittker On The Regulation of Interstate and Foreign Commerce (1999), p. 1-4. This 1786 meeting, the so-called Annapolis Convention, was the impetus for the Constitutional Convention of 1787.

3. Other constitutional provisions were also intended to prevent regional coalitions from asserting their power to attain preferential protective legislation. Bittker, supra note 2, p. xxi.

See, e.g., the federal export clause, forbidding Congress to tax exports, and the port preference clause, forbidding Congress to favor the ports of one state over those of another.

4. U.S. Const. art. I, § 8, cl. 3.

5. Albert S. Abel, The Commerce Clause in the Constitutional Convention and in Contemporary Comment, 25 Minn. L. Rev. 432, 443-44 (1941).

6. Felix Frankfurter, The Commerce Clause Under Marshall, Taney, and Waite 12 (1937).

7. Abel, supra note 5, at 446.

8. The Federalist No. 45, at 291 (James Madison) (Henry C. Lodge ed. 1923).

9. In 1959, the Court noted with frustration that there had been three hundred "full-dress" opinions dealing with state taxes that were challenged on Commerce Clause grounds, producing a "quagmire" of decisions that have been "not always clear. . . consistent or reconcilable."Northwestern States Portland Cement Co. v. Minn., 358 U.S. 450, 457, 458 (1959), quoting Miller Bros. v. Maryland, 347 U.S. 340, 344 (1954).

and an equally prolific source of conflict with legislation of the state. While the Constitution vests in Congress the power to regulate commerce among the states, it does not say what the states may or may not do in the absence of congressional action, nor how to draw the line between what is and what is not commerce among the states. Perhaps even more than by interpretation of its written word, this Court has advanced the solidarity and prosperity of this Nation by the meaning it has given to these great silences of the Constitution."[10]

Through the years, the Supreme Court has interpreted the Commerce Clause in three different ways regarding the issue of taxation and regulation: (1) all state regulation or taxation of interstate commerce is prohibited;[11] (2) the states have the power to regulate and tax interstate commerce unless prohibited or preempted by Congress;[12] or (3) even if not prohibited or preempted by Congress, the

states have the power to regulate or tax some, but not all, interstate commerce. Because the Commerce Clause does not explicitly proscribe state regulation or taxation of interstate commerce,[13] the first and third interpretations implement the "negative" or "dormant" Commerce Clause. This doctrine asserts that some constraint on state taxation or regulation is required by the policies underlying the Commerce Clause, notwithstanding that Congress has neither prohibited nor preempted the legislation at issue.

Most of the cases discussed in this Chapter deal with the negative Commerce Clause. Although Congress has sometimes prohibited state taxation of commerce,[14] the dormant commerce clause remains the major restraint on the states. As you read these cases, be aware that Justice Scalia rejects the negative Commerce Clause doctrine.[15] He would strike down state legislation only if it facially discriminates against interstate commerce or is indistinguishable from a type of law previously held unconstitutional.[16] Apparently, Justice Scalia, Justice Thomas and Chief Justice Rehnquist are willing to re-examine the

---

10. Hughes v. Oklahoma, 441 U.S. 322, 326 n.2 (1979), quoting H. P. Hood & Sons, Inc. v. Du Mond, 336 U.S. at 534-35 (1949).

11. Charles Pinckney's draft constitution provided for the exclusive grant of power to Congress to regulate interstate commerce, which would have pre-empted the states from also regulating the same commerce. See Abel, supra note 5, at 434 (1941); Leloup v. Port of Mobile, 127 U.S. 640, 648 (1888); Robbins v. Shelby County Taxing Dist., 120 U.S. 489 (1887).

12. For examples of Congressional prohibition or preemption, 15 U.S.C. §391 (states cannot levy taxes on electric energy that discriminate against out-of-state purchasers; 47 U.S.C. §251 (localities cannot tax providers of home satellite services); 47 U.S.C. §251 (states cannot tax the interstate transportation of passengers by motor carrier); 49 U.S.C §40116 (states cannot levy user charges on persons in air commerce); 29 U.S.C. §1144(a) (ERISA supersedes state taxes related to employee benefit plans); 49 U.S.C. §14501 (Railroad Revitalization and Regulatory Reform Act of 1975, also known as the "4R" Act) (states cannot tax railroad property more heavily than commercial and industrial property; similar protection subsequently extended to motor carriers, 49 U.S.C. §14501 and air carriers, 49 U.S.C. 40116); 15 U.S.C. 78bb(d) (restrictions on state's taxation of stock transfers); Internet Tax Freedom Act, 112 Stat. 2681 (1998), discussed in the chapter on electronic commerce, infra; Mobile Telecommunications Sourcing Act, 114 Stat. 626, providing groundrules for state taxation of mobile telecommunications services; 104 P.L. 95 (states cannot levy an income tax on nonresidents). The Court has not been sympathetic to claims of federal preemption based on general federal policies rather than on specific statutory provisions. See, e.g., Barclays Bank v. Franchise Tax Bd., 512 U.S. 298 (1994); Container Corp. v. Franchise Tax Bd., 463 U.S. 159 (1983); Commonwealth Edison Co. v. Mont., 453 U.S. 609 (1981); Maryland v. Louisiana, 451 U.S. 725 (1981); Mobil Oil Corp. v. Commissioner of Taxes, 445 U.S. 425 (1980).

---

13. The Constitution contains only two clauses that proscribe state taxation: one of general applicability–the Import-Export Clause, and one of narrow applicability–the Duty of Tonnage Clause. See U.S. Const. art. I, §10, cl. 2, cl. 3.

14. See supra note 12.

15. Of all the current members of the U.S. Supreme Court, Justice Scalia is the most vehement critic of the dormant commerce clause doctrine. His attack starts with the language of the Commerce Clause, whose text "is a charter for Congress, not the courts, to ensure 'an area of trade free from interference by the States.'" Tyler Pipe v. Wash. State Dep't of Revenue, 483 U.S. 232, 260, citing Boston Stock Exch. v. State Tax Comm'n, 429 U.S. 318, 328 (1977). The "language of the . . . Clause gives no indication of exclusivity . . . Nor can one assume generally that Congress' Article I powers are exclusive; many of them plainly coexist with concurrent authority in the States." 483 U.S. at 261. "Furthermore, there is no correlative denial of power over commerce to the States . . . as there is, for example, with the power to coin money or make treaties." Id.

For other attacks by Justice Scalia on the dormant commerce clause doctrine, see infra notes 22, 29. Justice Scalia endorses Justice Frankfurter's conclusion that "the doctrine that state authority must be subject to such limitations as the Court finds it necessary to apply for the protection of the national community . . . [is] an audacious doctrine, which, one may be sure, would hardly have been publicly avowed in support of the adoption of the Constitution." Frankfurter, supra note 6, at 19. Justice Black expressed similar views to Justice Scalia, but without the scholarly weaponry. See infra note 25.

16. See Tyler Pipe, 483 U.S. at 259-65; Oklahoma Tax Commission v. Jefferson Lines, 514 U.S. at 200 (1995).

doctrine,[17] but Justice O'Connor has recently stated that she is not.[18]

In Gibbons v. Ogden,[19] a non-tax case concerning the granting of a steamboat monopoly to a private company, Chief Justice Marshall in dictum advanced the third interpretation of the Commerce Clause, described above. Marshall supported a reading of the Clause that would grant Congress broad power to regulate "commerce which concerns more states than one,"[20] while allowing the states "to regulate its police, its domestic trade, and to govern its own citizens,"[21] even if that regulation had an impact on interstate commerce.[22]

Shortly after Gibbons v. Ogden, Chief Justice Marshall elaborated his views in a case striking down a Maryland statute requiring that importers pay for a special license:

"[T]he taxing power of the States must have some limits . . . . It cannot interfere with any regulation of commerce. If the States may tax all persons and property found on their territory, what shall restrain them from taxing goods in their transit through the State from one port to another. . .or from taxing the transportation of articles passing from the State itself to another State, for commercial purposes? These cases are all within the sovereign power of taxation, but would obviously derange the measures of Congress to regulate commerce, and affect materially the purpose for which that power was given."[23]

As characterized by Justice Frankfurter, Marshall's view "became central to our whole constitutional scheme: the doctrine that the commerce clause, by its own force and without national legislation, puts it into the power of the

---

17. See Camps Newfound/Owatonna, 520 U.S. 564 (dissenting opinion of Justice Thomas joined by Justice Scalia and Chief Justice Rehnquist.) Scholars have also been critical of the Court's negative commerce clause jurisprudence. See, e.g., David P. Currie, The Constitution in the Supreme Court: The First Hundred Years 1789-1888, p. 234 (1985) (referring to the negative commerce clause as "arbitrary, conclusory, and irreconcilable with the constitutional text"); Laurence H. Tribe, 1 American Constitutional Law 1102 (3rd ed. 2000) ("The Supreme Court's approach to Commerce Clause issues . . . often appears to turn more on ad hoc reactions to particular cases than on any consistent application of coherent principles"); Martin H. Redish and Shane V. Nugent, The Dormant Commerce Clause and the Constitutional Balance of Federalism, 1987 Duke L.J. 569, 573 ("[N]ot only is there no textual basis [for it but] the dormant Commerce Clause actually contradicts, and therefore directly undermines, the Constitution's carefully established textual structure for allocating power between federal and state sovereigns.").

18. South Cent. Bell Tel. Co. v. Alabama, 526 U.S. 160 (1999) (concurring opinion of Justice O'Connor).

19. 22 U.S. 1 (1824). See Frankfurter, supra note 6, at 15-17, 58 (1937).

20. 22 U.S. at 194. Chief Justice Marshall's views reflected those of Madison. See Tribe, supra note 17, at 1045.

21. 22 U.S. at 208. The federal government is not formally granted a general police power or the right to act in order to promote the health, safety, or welfare of the nation. During the Constitutional Convention there was an unsuccessful proposal to grant the federal government such a general police power. Nowak & Rotunda, supra note 1, at 158. Art. I, §8, however, provides that "Congress shall have Power to . . . provide for the common Defence and general Welfare of the United States . . . [and] To regulate Commerce . . . among the several states [and] To make all Laws which shall be necessary and proper for carrying into Execution the foregoing Powers, and all other Powers vested by this Constitution in the Government of the United States." A combination of these provisions has been employed to justify nearly all of the legislation that would be described at the state level as the exercise of general police powers.

22. Justice Scalia criticizes the attempt to distinguish between state laws intended to regulate commerce from those intended to promote, for example, health. "Distinguishing between laws with the *purpose* of regulating commerce and 'police power' statutes with that *effect* is, as Taney demonstrated in the License Cases . . . more interesting as a metaphysical exercise than useful as a practical technique for marking out the powers of separate sovereigns." Tyler Pipe, 483 U.S. at 262 (1987) (Scalia, J. concurring in part and dissenting in part). See also H. Biklé, The Silence of Congress, 41 Harv. L. Rev. 200 (1927).

23. Brown v. Maryland, 25 U.S. 419, 448-49 (1827). Chief Justice Marshall assumed that a state tax was a regulation of commerce. "This feature of his opinion could not have surprised his generation of lawyers, since taxes were the principal weapons used by the states in the commercial strife that led to the Philadelphia convention and to its adoption of the Commerce Clause itself." Bittker, supra note 2, at p. 2-30-31.

Court to place limits upon state authority."[24] Unfortunately, Marshall never had the opportunity to apply his views to a case involving a tax on interstate commerce.

The second of the three possible interpretations was endorsed by Chief Justice Taney, Marshall's successor. Reflecting a more literal interpretation of the Clause, a more expansive view of state power, and a view fundamentally opposing Marshall's, Taney argued that a state could regulate or tax interstate commerce unless its actions conflicted with those of Congress.[25] Throughout its early history, the Court vacillated between Marshall's and Taney's views.[26]

---

24. Frankfurter, supra note 6, at 18.

25. The License Cases, 46 U.S. at 578-80 (1847), rev'd on other grounds, Leisy v. Harding, 135 U.S. 100 (1890). For the clearest expression of Chief Justice's Taney's rejection of the dormant Commerce Clause, see his dissent in The Passenger Cases, 48 U.S. at 482 (1849) ("if it is hereinafter to be the law of this court, that the power to regulate commerce has abridged the taxing power of the States. . .I cannot foresee to what it may lead"). Taney's views represented those of Alexander Hamilton, who believed that the Constitution allowed the states the "absolute and unqualified" power to tax interstate commerce except for levying duties on imports and exports. The Federalist No. 32, at 185 (Alexander Hamilton) (Henry C. Lodge ed. 1923). See also 2 Joseph Story, Commentaries on The Constitution of The United States §§ 937-38 at 410-12 (1833). These views have been recently resurrected by Justice Scalia in Tyler Pipe, 483 U.S. 232. Similar views had been expressed earlier by Justices Douglas and Black. See, e.g., Southern Pac. Co. v. Arizona, 325 U.S. 761 (1945) (Douglas, J. dissenting); J.D. Adams Mfg. Co. v. Storen, 304 U.S. 307 (1938) (Black, J. dissenting in part). Taney would have upheld a tax that discriminated against interstate commerce; Scalia would not. See supra note 16 and accompanying text. See also Thomas R. Powell, Indirect Encroachment on Federal Authority by the Taxing Power of the States, 31 Harv. L. Rev. 321, 572, 721 (1918).

26. "Even after it was no longer accepted in its pure version, the Madisonian view left its legacy in the form of a pervasive suspicion of any state action seriously (especially if differentially) burdening individuals or enterprises outside the state and hence unable to influence its policies, as well as any state action threatening to revive interstate economic rivalries of the sort that had undermined the Articles of Confederation. And even after Taney's anti-Madisonian view had been rejected as doctrine, it too persisted in the form of a reluctance to treat subjects as exclusively within the regulatory authority of Congress unless those subjects were of such national concern as to make federal regulation very likely; this reluctance has been defended as necessary to avoid a regulatory vacuum in which states *cannot* regulate and Congress *will not* regulate. Flying in the face of Madison's conclusion that the Commerce Clause *should* cause precisely such a vacuum, this view has surfaced repeatedly throughout the history of Commerce Clause adjudication." Tribe, supra note 17, at 1046 (emphasis in original).

In 1851, in Cooley v. Board of Wardens,[27] a non-tax case described as an attempt "to reconcile all that had gone before in a formulation that laid the groundwork for nearly all that has come since,"[28] the Court rejected the first and second possible interpretations and held that the Commerce Clause prohibits some, but not all, state regulation. Cooley involved a Pennsylvania statute requiring ships entering or leaving the Philadelphia port to engage a local pilot. The Court characterized the statute as a regulation of commerce. In upholding the statute, the Court held that the states had the power to regulate some aspects of commerce. Congress had the exclusive power to regulate subjects of interstate commerce that were national in nature, or required a uniform system or plan of regulation.[29] Provided Congress has not preempted the area or adopted any conflicting regulation, the states could exercise concurrent powers over subjects that called for diverse treatment; these subjects were considered local.

---

27. 53 U.S. 299 (1851).

28. Tribe, supra note 17, at 1047. See also Currie, supra note 17, at 234 ("Taken by itself, Cooley may appear arbitrary, conclusory, and irreconcilable with the Constitutional text. Nevertheless, anyone who has slogged through the Augean agglomeration preceding [the Court's] labors must find them scarcely less impressive than those of the old stable-cleaner himself").

29. "[T]he power to regulate commerce, embraces a vast field, containing not only many, but exceedingly various subjects, quite unlike in their nature; some imperatively demanding a single uniform rule . . . and some, like the subject now in question, as imperatively demanding that diversity, which alone can meet the local necessities of navigation." Cooley v. Board of Wardens, 53 U.S. at 319 (1851). Justice Scalia criticizes the doctrine that judicial enforcement of the Commerce Clause is necessary in cases where the subject matter is national or admits of only one uniform system or plan of regulation. "That would perhaps be a wise rule to adopt (though it is hard to see why judges rather than legislators are fit to determine what areas of commerce 'in their nature' require national regulation), but it has the misfortune of finding no conceivable basis in the text of the Commerce Clause, which treats 'Commerce . . . among the several States' as a unitary subject." Tyler Pipe, 483 U.S. at 262 (Scalia, J. concurring in part and dissenting in part).

Justice Scalia argues that the dormant Commerce Clause lacks "any clear theoretical underpinning . . ." The Commerce Clause is "a charter for Congress, not the courts, to ensure 'an area of trade free from interference by the States.'" "The least plausible theoretical justification of all is the idea that in enforcing the negative Commerce Clause the Court is not applying a constitutional command at all, but is merely interpreting the will of Congress, whose silence in certain fields of interstate commerce (but not in others) is to be taken as a prohibition of regulation. There is no conceivable reason why congressional inaction under the Commerce Clause should be deemed to have the same pre-emptive effect elsewhere accorded only to congressional action. There, as elsewhere, 'Congress' silence is just that–silence. . . .'" Id. at 260, 262.

Penn. flat tax / tax on I/s Freight comm   *Railway Tax not tax in I/s com*

The Cooley criteria were first applied to a state tax in the Case of the State Freight Tax,[30] in which the Court invalidated as applied to interstate commerce a Pennsylvania flat tax levied on each ton of freight transported within the State, independent of distance traveled.[31] The statute on its face applied to companies transporting freight in Pennsylvania, whether in interstate or intrastate commerce.[32] The Court characterized the tax as "imposed upon freight carried,"[33] "in effect a regulation of interstate commerce,"[34] on a subject exclusively within the power of Congress.[35] The Court viewed the interstate transportation of freight as requiring "one regulating power" to avoid destroying "commercial intercourse between States remote from each other," which might be "crushed under the load of many" similar taxes.[36] The case made it clear that a state tax could violate the Commerce Clause, notwithstanding that Congress neither explicitly prohibited the tax nor preempted the area with its own tax or regulation. In other words, the Commerce Clause, by its own force, prohibited some types of state taxation.[37]

violate C.C. ✗ even if not explicit proh. tax nor preempt

The doctrinal quagmire that was to characterize this area for the next 100 years immediately started with the companion case to State Freight Tax, State Tax on Railway Gross Receipts,[38] involving the same parties. Here, the Court upheld a gross receipts tax applied to the receipts from a transportation business, part of which was conducted interstate. Unlike the tax on freight in State Freight Tax, the Court did not characterize the gross receipts tax as a tax on interstate transportation. "[E]very tax upon personal property, or upon occupations, business, or franchises, affects more or less the subjects, and the operations of commerce. Yet it is not everything that affects commerce that amounts to a regulation of it, within the meaning of the Constitution."[39] "[The gross receipts tax] is a tax upon the railroad company, measured in amount by the extent of its business, or the degree to which its franchise is exercised. That its ultimate effect may be to increase the cost of transportation must be admitted.... Still it is not a tax upon transportation, or upon commerce...."[40]

G.R. tax ok

In effect, the Court distinguished a tax on each ton of coal transported within a state from a tax on the receipts from transporting that coal. The former was imposed on interstate commerce whereas the latter was imposed after such commerce had ended. State Freight Tax and Railway Gross Receipts have been described as "a paradigm of the Court's commerce clause jurisprudence in the state tax field for nearly a century: two taxes that have a substantially similar impact on interstate commerce are accorded different constitutional treatment. The Court, conceding that the 'line is sometimes difficult to define with distinctness,' nevertheless drew one that was discernible, if at all, only to itself. The line drawn was then explained in terms that effectively assured the Court ample discretion to draw lines in the future as it deemed appropriate without

30. 82 U.S. 232 (1872). Earlier cases invalidating state taxes primarily relied on other clauses of the Constitution, although dicta could fairly be read as anticipating Case of the State Freight Tax. See, e.g., Hays v. Pacific Mail S.S. Co., 58 U.S. 596 (1854); Brown v. Maryland, 25 U.S. 419 (1827); Low v. Austin, 80 U.S. 29 (1871); Almy v. California, 65 U.S. 169 (1860); Crandall v. Nevada, 73 U.S. 35 (1867); Steamship Co. v. Portwardens, 73 U.S. 31 (1867); Ward v. Maryland, 79 U.S. 418 (1870); Wilmington R.R. v. Reid, 80 U.S. 264 (1871); State Tonnage Tax Cases, 79 U.S. 204 (1870). Marshall had suggested that a state tax could violate the Commerce Clause in Brown v. Maryland, 25 U.S. at 448-49.

31. Using modern concepts, the tax would be described as unfairly apportioned or internally inconsistent.

32. "The State may tax its internal commerce, but if an act to tax interstate or foreign commerce is unconstitutional, it is not cured by including in its provisions subjects within the domain of the State." 82 U.S. at 277.

33. Id. at 278.

34. Id. at 279.

35. Id. at 279-80 (citing Cooley, 53 U.S. 299).

36. Id. at 280. Although Case of the State Freight Tax referred to the tax being unapportioned, id. at 273, which would create the risk of multiple taxation, later cases read the opinion as holding that interstate commerce could not be taxed at all. Robbins v. Shelby County, 120 U.S. at 497 (1887). Presumably, this view would strike down a tax on interstate commerce, regardless of whether it was apportioned. The dissent in Case of State Freight would have upheld the tax on the grounds that the tax was imposed on the business, and that the tonnage transported was only the mode of ascertaining the extent of the business. Moreover, the statute did not discriminate against interstate commerce. The majority's fear that interstate commerce might be "crushed under the load of many" similar taxes anticipates the subsequent development of the multiple burden doctrine.

37. Justice Scalia describes the case as formally adopting the negative Commerce Clause doctrine, which was earlier alluded to in dicta in Cooley, 53 U.S. 299 and Gibbons, 22 U.S. 1. Tyler Pipe, 483 U.S. at 260 (Scalia, J. concurring and dissenting in part).

38. 82 U.S. 284 (1872); compare Philadelphia and S.S.S. Co. v. Penn., 122 U.S. 326 (1887).

39. 82 U.S. at 293.

40. Id. at 294. See also Maine v. Grand Trunk Ry. Co., 142 U.S. 217 (1891); United States Express Co. v. Minn., 223 U.S. 335 (1912).

providing any clear guidance whether a particular levy will fall on one side or the other."[41]

Put simply, ~~any state tax on an activity that the Court viewed as part of interstate commerce~~ was unconstitutional. The lack of analytical substance to this line drawing became apparent when 15 years after upholding the gross receipts tax in Railway Gross Receipts, the Court struck down a similar gross receipts tax on a steamship company engaged in interstate commerce.[42]

Underlying this line drawing was the fear that allowing the states to tax interstate commerce would lead to unmanageable burdens on commerce that the Court could not police.[43] "If the power [to tax interstate commerce] exists in the state at all, it has no limit but the discretion of the state, and might be exercised in such a manner as to drive away that commerce, or to load it with an intolerable burden, seriously affecting the business and prosperity of other states . . . ."[44] The Court was willing, however, to uphold taxes on activities that were "local," that is, activities that were sufficiently removed from interstate commerce, notwithstanding that the same type of burdens could result.

The Court formulated analytical touchstones for determining the boundaries between permitted and invalid state taxation, "but the absence of an adequate standard is evidenced by the plethora of cases that one cannot reconcile merely by applying the Cooley doctrine."[45] By the end of the 19th century, the Court commonly conceptualized state taxation in terms of its direct or indirect burdens on interstate commerce: taxes imposing direct burdens were invalid whereas taxes

imposing indirect burdens were upheld.[46] The test was a legal one, having no grounding in economics. The direct/indirect burden test was sometimes applied in non-tax cases, with the Court balancing the state purpose served by the regulation with the degree to which it impeded interstate commerce.[47]

Other times, the direct/indirect test was merely another way of describing the national-local dichotomy introduced by Cooley. A tax that indirectly, incidentally, or remotely burdened commerce was described as a tax on a local activity,[48] which the Court considered as separate from interstate commerce. The taxation of an interstate business often turned on whether there were local activities acceptable to the Court that could serve as the subject matter of the tax.[49]

Applying these distinctions, the Court upheld property taxes on instrumentalities of interstate commerce,[50] such as railroad property as well as gross receipts taxes levied in lieu of such property taxes.[51] "Although the transportation of the subjects of interstate commerce, or the receipts received therefrom, or the occupation or

---

41. Walter Hellerstein, State Taxation of Interstate Business: Perspectives on Two Centuries of Constitutional Adjudication, 41 Tax Law. 37, 44 (1987). Sometimes two taxes with the same economic effect should be treated differently, but not for the reasons discussed in the text. See Oklahoma Tax Comm'n v. Jefferson Lines, infra Chapter 9; Walter Hellerstein, Michael J. McIntyre, & Richard D. Pomp, Commerce Clause Restraints on State Taxation after Jefferson Lines, 51 Tax L. Rev. 47 (1995).

42. Philadelphia and S.S.S. Co., 122 U.S. 326 (1887). See also Gloucester Ferry Co. v. Penn., 114 U.S. 196 (1885).

43. William B. Lockhart, A Revolution in State Taxation of Commerce?, 65 Minn. L. Rev. 1025, 1031 (1981).

44. Philadelphia and S.S.S. Co., 122 U.S. at 346 (1887).

45. Nowak & Rotunda, supra note 1, at 316-317.

46. Southern Ry. v. King, 217 U.S. 524 (1910); Adams Express Co. v. Ohio, 165 U.S. 194 (1897); Pullman's Palace Car v. Penn., 141 U.S. 18 (1891).

47. See Tribe, supra note 17, at 1049.

48. See Richard L. Strecker, 'Local Incidents' of Interstate Business, 18 Ohio St. L. J. 69 (1957); David F. Shores, State Taxation of Interstate Commerce–Quiet Revolution or Much Ado About Nothing?, 38 Tax Law Rev. 127, 136 (1982). Professor Shores notes that the Court also used the "local-national" and "direct-indirect" rubrics in evaluating the constitutionality of state regulations under the Commerce Clause. An important difference, he observes, is that the state regulation cases were anchored in a more rational purpose and effect analysis. By contrast, in the tax cases the Court substituted the labels for analysis. Id.

49. Cf. Ficklen v. Shelby County, 145 U.S. 1 (1892), with Robbins v. Shelby County, 120 U.S. 489 (1887). "By the turn of the century the Court had laid the groundwork for the chaos and irrationality which were to become the characteristics of constitutional law on state taxation of interstate commerce." Shores, supra note 48, at 136.

50. The Delaware R.R. Tax, 85 U.S. 206 (1873); Adams Express, 165 U.S. 194; Postal Tel. Cable Co. v. Adams, 155 U.S. 688 (1895); Pullman's Palace, 141 U.S. 18.

51. Postal Tel., 155 U.S. 688; Maine v. Grand Trunk, 142 U.S. 217; United States Express, 223 U.S. at 346-348. The Court had to be convinced, however, that the tax on gross receipts was indeed a substitute for a property tax. The distinctions between the levies sustained and those invalidated were frequently based on formal differences.

business of carrying it on, cannot be directly subjected to state taxation, yet property belonging to corporations or companies engaged in such commerce may be. . ." [52] Property taxes on railroad track, rolling stock, telegraph wires and the like were not considered to be direct taxes on interstate commerce.

By contrast, the Court struck down franchise, privilege, and license taxes on foreign corporations or individuals conducting an exclusively interstate business,[53] taxes on the gross receipts from interstate commerce,[54] and taxes on transportation and communication companies.[55]

It was irrelevant that a tax did not discriminate against interstate commerce: "Interstate commerce cannot be taxed at all, even though the same amount of tax should be laid on domestic commerce. . ."[56] The reasoning in these cases has been vigorously criticized as mechanical, unpredictable, and divorced from economic realities.[57] "[T]he traditional test of the limit of state action by inquiring whether the interference with commerce is direct or indirect seems to me too mechanical, too uncertain in its application, and too remote from actualities, to be of value. In thus making use of the expressions, 'direct' and 'indirect interference' with commerce, we are doing little more than using labels to describe a result rather than any trustworthy formula by which it is reached."[58]

The narrower the interpretation of what constitutes interstate commerce the less the impact of the Court's prohibition against state taxation of such commerce. Manufacturing,[59] production of natural gas,[60] mining,[61] and the generation of electricity,[62] were all held to be local activities, separate from interstate commerce. The distinctions drawn were often Talmudic in nature.[63]

One of the less controversial doctrines has been the Court's view that the Commerce Clause prohibits state taxes that discriminate against interstate commerce, which has been "a central tenet of the Court's Commerce Clause case law throughout its history, and it commands particularly wide acceptance on a Court whose Commerce Clause jurisprudence has often been marked by disagreement."[64] Although the meaning of

---

52. Adams Express, 165 U.S. at 220.

53. See, e.g., Robbins v. Shelby County, 120 U.S. at 497; Leloup v. Port of Mobile, 127 U.S. at 648 (". . . no State has the right to lay a tax on interstate commerce in any form, whether by way of duties laid on the transportation of the subjects of that commerce, or on the receipts derived from that transportation, or on the occupation or business of carrying it on, and the reason is that such taxation is a burden on that commerce, and amounts to a regulation of it, which belongs solely to Congress."); Cheney Bros. Co. v. Mass., 246 U.S. 147 (1918); Alpha Portland Cement Co. v. Mass., 268 U.S. 203 (1925).

54. Philadelphia and S.S.S. Co., 122 U.S. 326 (1887).

55. Fargo v. Michigan, 121 U.S. 230 (1887); Pickard v. Pullman S. Car Co., 117 U.S. 34 (1886); Gloucester Ferry, 114 U.S. 196 (1885); Moran v. New Orleans, 112 U.S. 69 (1884); Leloup v. Port of Mobile, 127 U.S. 640 (1888); Telegraph Co. v. Texas, 105 U.S. 460 (1881).

56. Robbins v. Shelby County, 120 U.S. at 497; see also Leloup, 127 U.S. 640.

57. See, e.g. Paul J. Hartman, Federal Limitations on State and Local Taxation 283 (1981).

58. Di Santo v. Pennsylvania, 273 U.S. 34, 44 (1927) (Stone, J. dissenting). Justice Stone's dissent could be read as supporting the type of balancing test commonplace in commerce clause

---

cases involving state regulations. For Chief Justice Stone's application of such an approach, see Southern Pacific Co. v. Arizona, 325 U.S. 761 (1945). As described in the text, however, Chief Justice Stone developed an alternative approach for evaluating state taxes. For a discussion of the inadequacies of a balancing-type of approach in analyzing state taxes, see Bittker, supra note 2, at pp. 8-10 to 8-11.

59. American Mfg. Co. v. St. Louis, 250 U.S. 459 (1919), discussed infra.

60. Hope Natural Gas Co. v. Hall, 274 U.S. 284 (1927).

61. Oliver Iron Mining Co. v. Lord, 262 U.S. 172 (1923).

62. Utah Power & Light Co. v. Pfost, 286 U.S. 165 (1932).

63. In general, see Strecker, supra note 48. A tax could be upheld as not constituting a direct levy on interstate commerce even if the same activity could be regulated by Congress under its Commerce Clause powers. Cf. Minn. v. Blasius, 290 U.S. 1 (1933) (upholding property tax on cattle shipped into St. Paul stockyards from outside Minnesota), with Stafford v. Wallace, 258 U.S. 495 (1922) (upholding power of Congress to regulate stockyards). After Complete Auto Transit, 430 U.S. 274 (1977), discussed infra, which allows the states to tax directly interstate commerce, a finding that a transaction constitutes interstate commerce is not tantamount to striking down a state tax on such transaction. The expansion of state powers of taxation may have encouraged the Court to state two years after Complete Auto that "the definition of 'commerce' is the same when relied on to strike down or restrict state legislation as when relied on to support some exertion of federal control or regulation." Hughes, 441 U.S. at 326 n.2 (1979), (citing Philadelphia v. N.J., 437 U.S. at 621-623).

64. Peter D. Enrich, Saving the States from Themselves: Commerce Clause Constraints on State Tax Incentives for Business, 110 Harv. L. Rev. 377, 426 (1996).

[handwritten margin notes: "discrim tax to advantage local biz", "discrim effect"]

discrimination has not been rigorously developed,[65] a state cannot "discriminatorily tax the products manufactured or the business operations performed in any other State,"[66] or impose a tax that "provid[es] a direct commercial advantage to local business."[67] In the case of commodities, commerce clause protection applies "until the commodity has ceased to be the subject of discriminating legislation. . ."[68] Statutes that are facially discriminatory are "virtually per se invalid."[69] The Court will occasionally look behind a statute that is facially neutral and strike it down if it is discriminatory in effect.[70]

---

65. For the most part, the concept of discrimination is judicially-developed. The Internet Tax Freedom Act, see the chapter entitled, Taxation of Electronic Commerce, prohibits "discriminatory taxes," but does not define the concept. There is, however, one attempt to statutorily define discrimination. 15 U.S.C. § 391 prohibits discriminatory state taxation of out-of-state producers, distributors, and consumers of electricity. The statute defines a discriminatory tax as one that "results, either directly or indirectly, in a greater tax burden on electricity which is generated and transmitted in interstate commerce than on electricity which is generated and transmitted in intrastate commerce."

66. Boston Stock Exch., 429 U.S. at 337 (1977).

67. Id. at 329, quoting Northwestern States Portland Cement, 358 U.S. at 458.

68. Welton v. Missouri, 91 U.S. 275, 282 (1875). Welton invalidated a peddlers' license tax imposed only on dealers in out-of-state goods. Professor Shores states that the discrimination principle was probably first applied to invalidate a state tax in Welton. David F. Shores, State Taxation of Gross Receipts and the Negative Commerce Clause, 54 Mo. L. Rev. 555, 558 n.17 (1989). Welton would be described using today's vocabulary as involving a facially discriminatory statute, virtually per se unconstitutional.

69. Memphis Steam Laundry v. Stone, 342 U.S. 389 (1952); Fulton Corp. v. Faulkner, 516 U.S. at 331 (quoting Oregon Waste Sys., Inc. v. Dept. of Envtl. Quality, 511 U.S. at 99.

70. Robbins v. Shelby County, 120 U.S. 489 (1887); Caldwell v. N.C., 187 U.S. 622 (1903); Norfolk & Western v. Sims, 191 U.S. 441 (1903); Dozier v. Ala., 218 U.S. 124 (1910). Many of the early discrimination cases involving license fees, taxes, or permits arose from attempts by southern and western states after the Civil War to protect their merchants against traveling or itinerant persons selling products made in the industrial states. These cases sometimes involved statutes that were facially discriminatory. Welton, for example, involved a tax that applied to only out-of-state goods. See also Webber v. Virginia, 103 U.S. 344 (1880); Walling v. Mich., 116 U.S. 446 (1886). Other taxes were neutral on their face but discriminatory in impact, applying to all persons not having a place of business in the jurisdiction, or to specific goods which happened to not be made in the jurisdiction. Referring to Robbins, Professor

By 1938, the prevailing Commerce Clause doctrine in the case of nondiscriminatory taxes could be summarized as follows:

[Taxes] were sustained on the ground that they were levied on a "local" incident or event, or that the burden of the tax on the interstate commerce was "indirect" or "incidental." Although the particular activities or events, upon which the tax was imposed, was essential to the interstate commerce operation, they were taxable. The approach to the test of constitutionality of the tax was thus conceptual and mechanical. Generally, the economic consequences of a tax were not thought by the Court to be of any significance in determining whether the tax was forfended by the commerce clause. . . . "names were made to matter more than mathematics or economics."

The touchstone for a judicial condemnation of a tax was not any actual or probable hampering affect [sic] of the taxation on the commerce; the judicially declared vice of an invalid tax was simply its "direct" bearing or affect [sic] on interstate commerce. That brand of doctrinal declaration, of course, assumed a trustworthiness in the test of constitutionality which did not exist, and afforded but little guidance to the legislator, the lower courts, or the taxpaying businessman in predicting whether a particular tax would run afoul of the commerce clause. This test of constitutionality . . . described a result reached, not the reasons for that result. The Court was more concerned with captions than with consequences.[71]

Despite such criticism, the Court continued to use tenuous analytical approaches to analyzing Commerce Clause claims.

Perhaps in response to the pressing financial needs of the states during the Great Depression, and to the political climate of the Roosevelt Administration, a new phase of Commerce Clause interpretation rejecting the old formalism began in 1938. The turning point was Justice Stone's famous decision in Western Live Stock v. Bureau of Revenue,[72] upholding a New Mexico tax measured by

---

Bittker notes that "by according itinerant salesmen the same constitutional status as the railroads [in Case of the State Freight Tax], the Supreme Court came close to announcing that the nation's economy was a seamless web stretching from sea to shining sea–a legal vision that is usually credited to the New Deal." Bittker, supra note 2, at p. 8-6. A relatively more recent case involving a facially neutral but unconstitutional statute is Nippert v. City of Richmond, 327 U.S. 416 (1946). Nippert involved a license tax imposed by the City of Richmond, Virginia, on conducting business as a solicitor. In striking down the tax, Justice Rutledge emphasized that the tax had to be paid before any business could be conducted and underscored the burdens imposed on small businesses, especially the "casual or occasional" ones. Id. at 429. However, he also said that "[t]o ignore the variations in effect which follow from application of the tax, uniform on the face of the ordinance . . . is only to ignore those practical consequences." Id. at 431.

71. Hartman, supra note 57, at 62-63.

72. 303 U.S. 250 (1938). Justice Stone's views were foreshadowed by his well-known dissent in Di Santo, 273 U.S. at 43, a non-tax case striking down a Pennsylvania fee paid by non-

N.m Ad Sales Tax

Local adv.

gross receipts. The taxpayer challenged the application of the tax to the sale of advertising in a magazine published in New Mexico but distributed nationally. All the work in preparing the magazine took place in New Mexico.

Although part of the opinion upheld the tax using the orthodox approach of characterizing the tax as falling on the local activity of preparing, printing, and publishing magazine advertising,[73] Justice Stone articulated a cumulative burdens or multiple taxation analysis–an attempt to balance the revenue needs of the states with the underlying rationale of the Commerce Clause.[74] According to Justice Stone, "[i]t was not the purpose of the commerce clause to relieve those engaged in interstate commerce from their just share of state tax burden even though it increases the cost of doing the business."[75] "Even interstate business must pay its way,"[76] a position at odds with the then prevailing doctrine, but one that would ultimately be adopted by the Court.[77] "[T]he tax . . . here . . . must accommodate

itself to the double demand that interstate business shall pay its way, and that at the same time it shall not be burdened with cumulative exactions" not imposed on local commerce.[78]

Justice Stone summarized the earlier cases as follows:

The vice characteristic of those [taxes] which have been held invalid is that they have placed on the commerce burdens of such a nature as to be capable, in point of substance, of being imposed . . . or added to . . . with equal right by every state which the commerce touches, merely because interstate commerce is being done, so that without the protection of the commerce clause it would bear cumulative burdens not imposed on local commerce.[79]

Interstate business could be taxed, according to Justice Stone, provided there was no risk of multiple taxation not borne by local commerce. New Mexico's statute did not impose any risk of cumulative burdens because "[a]ll the events upon which the tax is conditioned–the preparation, printing and publication of the advertising matter, and the receipt of the sums paid for it–occur in New Mexico and not elsewhere. All are beyond any control and taxing power which, without the commerce clause, those states could exert through its dominion over the distribution of the magazine or its subscribers."[80] "So far as the value contributed to appellants' New Mexico business by circulation of the magazine interstate is taxed, it cannot again be taxed elsewhere any more than the value of railroad property taxed locally. The tax is not one which in form or substance can be repeated by other states in such manner as to lay an added burden on the interstate distribution of the magazine."[81]

On the one hand, Justice Stone's assertion that interstate commerce could be taxed and his emphasis on multiple taxation was a shift in doctrine; on the other hand, his emphasis on the local activities that took place in New

---

railroad or steamship companies selling tickets for transportation to or from foreign countries. The majority viewed the regulation as an unconstitutional interference with foreign commerce; Justice Stone took a more realistic approach. See also McGoldrick v. Berwind-White Coal Mining, 309 U.S. 33 (1940); International Harvester Co. v. Dept. of Treasury, 322 U.S. 340 (1944); International Harvester Co. v. Evatt, 329 U.S. 416 (1947).

73. This part of the opinion relied on American Mfg., 250 U.S. 459 (1919), and is essentially similar to Ficklen, 120 U.S. 489 (1887).

74. Perhaps the earliest version of the multiple tax doctrine was expressed by the Court in Case of the State Freight Tax, 82 U.S. 232, 280 (1872) ("It is of national importance that. . .there should be but one regulating power, for if one State can directly tax persons or property passing through it, or tax them indirectly by levying a tax upon their transportation, every other may, and thus commercial intercourse between States remote from each other may be destroyed. The produce of Western States may thus be effectually excluded from Eastern markets, for though it might bear the imposition of a single tax, it would be crushed under the load of many.")

75. 303 U.S. at 254.

76. Id., quoting Postal Tel.-Cable Co. v. Richmond, 249 U.S. 252, 259 (1919).

77. See, e.g., Northwestern States Portland Cement, 358 U.S. at 461-62 (1959) ("[I]t is axiomatic that the founders did not intend to immunize [interstate] commerce from carrying its fair share of the costs of the state government in return for the benefits it derives from within the State."); Complete Auto Transit, 430 U.S. at 278, 288; Department of Revenue v. Association of Wash. Stevedoring Cos., 435 U.S. at 738, 750.

For a similar philosophy in the context of imports, see Michelin Tire Corp. v. Wages, 423 U.S. 276 (1976).

78. 303 U.S. at 258.

79. Id. at 255-56.

80. Id. at 260. According to Professor Hartman, supra note 57, at 69-70, Western Live Stock is not the fountainhead of the 'cumulative burdens' approach. The rudiments of that approach can be found almost a century earlier in Hays, 58 U.S. at 599: "Now, it is quite apparent that if the State of California possessed the authority to impose the tax in question, any other State in the Union, into the ports of which the vessels entered in the prosecution of their trade and business, might also impose a like tax." Similarly, the dangers of multiple burdens had also been recognized in Case of the State Freight Tax, 82 U.S. at 280.

81. 303 U.S. at 260.

Mexico was quite orthodox and consistent with earlier cases.[82] Nor did Justice Stone reject the doctrine that a tax could not be imposed on the privilege of engaging in an exclusively interstate activity.

The Court's shift in emphasis under Justice Stone to the risk of multiple taxation can be illustrated by comparing J.D. Adams Manufacturing Co. v. Storen[83] decided in 1938, with American Manufacturing Co. v. St. Louis,[84] decided in 1919. American Manufacturing upheld a St. Louis license fee for pursuing the occupation of a manufacturer, measured by the total gross proceeds of sales of products manufactured in that City, regardless of where they were sold. The taxpayer challenged the application of the tax to goods manufactured in St. Louis, removed to an out-of-state warehouse and sold outside Missouri. The Court concluded that "the tax in question is a tax upon the privilege of pursuing the business of manufacturing these goods in the city of St. Louis. . ."[85] The tax was on a local manufacturing activity and was therefore not a direct tax on interstate commerce. The City merely postponed determining the tax until the goods were sold. "[T]he operation and effect of the [tax]. . . produces no direct burden on commerce. . . and only the same kind of incidental and indirect effect as that which results from the payment of property taxes. . ."[86]

By contrast, 20 years later in J.D. Adams Manufacturing Co., the Court struck down an Indiana gross income tax imposed on an Indiana manufacturer's unapportioned gross receipts from products manufactured in Indiana and shipped to purchasers in other states:

> The vice of the statute as applied to receipts from interstate sales is that the tax includes in its measure, without apportionment, receipts derived from activities in interstate commerce; and that the exaction is of such a character that if lawful it may in substance be laid to the fullest extent by States in which the goods are sold as well as those in which they are manufactured. Interstate commerce would thus be subjected to the risk of a double tax burden to which intrastate commerce is not exposed, and which the commerce clause forbids.[87]

Whether a tax was apportioned or not was to play a role in the Court's assessment of the risk of multiple taxation, but Adam's refusal to overrule American Manufacturing, which also involved an unapportioned tax, was unsatisfying. Adams described American Manufacturing as involving an excise "upon the privilege of manufacturing" and "it was permissible to measure the tax by the sales price of the goods produced rather than by their value at the date of manufacture."[88] Apparently equating the gross income tax in Adams with a sales tax, the Court further distinguished American Manufacturing by stating that "[i]f the [St. Louis] tax . . . had been a sales tax the city could not have measured it by sales consummated in another State."[89] Presumably, the Adams court would have upheld the Indiana tax if it had been levied on the exercise of the privilege of manufacturing, illustrating that the multiple burdens doctrine was malleable and capable of justifying ephemeral distinctions.[90] "Despite its emphasis on multiple taxation, the Court thus again invoked the empty distinction of earlier cases between a tax on doing business measured by gross receipts [American Manufacturing] and a tax on gross receipts [Adams Manufacturing]."[91]

One year after Adams Manufacturing, Justice Stone in Gwin, White & Prince, Inc.[92] invalidated a Washington tax on the act or privilege of engaging in business activities. The taxpayer was a marketing agent that sold Washington-grown fruit out-of-state on a commission basis. Justice Stone viewed the tax as reaching receipts attributable to marketing and sales activities outside Washington, which raised the possibility that those states in which such activities took place could also tax the sale. "[T]he tax, though nominally imposed upon [taxpayer's] activities in Washington, by the very method of its measurement reaches the entire interstate commerce service rendered both within and without the state and burdens the commerce in direct proportion to its

---

82. The case is similar to Ficklen, 145 U.S. 1, upon which it relied.

83. 304 U.S. 307 (1938).

84. 250 U.S. 459 (1919).

85. Id. at 462.

86. Id. at 464.

87. 304 U.S. at 311. In Freeman v. Hewit, 329 U.S. 249 (1946), involving the same Indiana tax, the Court apparently rejected Adams Mfg.'s concern with the lack of apportionment and held the tax unconstitutional when applied to gross receipts from interstate commerce.

88. Adams Mfg., 304 U.S. at 312-13. The Indiana tax, by contrast, was described as reaching "indiscriminately and without apportionment, the gross compensation for both interstate commerce and intrastate activities. . ." Id. at 314.

89. Id. at 313.

90. The very multiple taxation that the Court was concerned about when it struck down Adams Mfg., 304 U.S. 307, occurred with respect to the tax upheld in American Mfg., 250 U.S. 459. In General Motors Corp. v. Wash., 377 U.S. 436 (1964), the Court upheld a Washington gross receipts tax on the sale of goods that, ironically, were manufactured in St. Louis.

91. Shores, supra note 48, at 139.

92. Gwin, White & Prince, Inc. v. Henneford, 305 U.S. at 438.

volume."[93] "[T]he tax, measured by the entire volume of the interstate commerce in which [the taxpayer] participates, is not apportioned to its activities within the state . . . . The present tax, though nominally local, thus in its practical operation discriminates against interstate commerce, since it imposes upon it, merely because interstate commerce is being done, the risk of a multiple burden to which local commerce is not exposed."[94]

Adams Manufacturing and Gwin, White and Prince invalidated taxes imposed by the origin state. A tax levied by the destination state was upheld by Justice Stone in McGoldrick v. Berwind-White Coal Mining Co.,[95] which involved a New York City sales tax levied on the purchase of coal mined in Pennsylvania and delivered in New York City. The statute defined "sale" as "any transfer of title or possession."[96] Because the seller had an office in New York City, where the coal was delivered, the tax was viewed as falling on a local activity after interstate commerce had ended. The Court found no risk of multiple burdens, citing Adams for the proposition that Pennsylvania could not tax the transaction. The dissent would have invalidated the tax under the multiple tax burden doctrine. According to the dissent, if New York City could tax the act of delivery, Pennsylvania could tax the act of shipment; moreover, the states through which the coal was shipped could also levy a tax.[97]

After Justice Stone's death in 1946, the multiple tax burden doctrine was championed by Justice Rutledge until his own death a few years later. In a famous and powerful opinion,[98] Justice Rutledge formulated the governing principles as follows:

"[A] state may not single out interstate commerce for special tax burden . . . . Nor may it discriminate against interstate commerce and in favor of its local trade . . . . [T]he state may not impose cumulative burdens upon interstate trade or commerce . . . . Thus, the state may

not impose certain taxes on interstate commerce, its incidents or instrumentalities, which are no more in amount or burden than it places on its local business, not because this of itself is discriminatory, cumulative or special or would violate due process, but because other states also may have the right constitutionally, apart from the commerce clause, to tax the same thing and either the actuality or the risk of their doing so makes the total burden cumulative, discriminatory or special."[99]

Under Justices Stone and Rutledge, the Court attempted a more realistic approach to Commerce Clause issues, focusing on the impact of a tax on interstate commerce, while recognizing that interstate commerce must bear its fair share of state taxation.[100] Although exclusively interstate transactions were still exempt from taxation, the Court often resolved this tension in favor of the states by finding that a tax fell on a local aspect of a transaction that was distinct from interstate commerce.[101] The Court was willing to characterize unapportioned taxes that did not raise the risk of multiple taxation as falling on local incidents.[102]

Despite the powerful views of Chief Justice Stone and Justice Rutledge, the Court under the leadership of Justice Frankfurter started to back slide in McLeod v. J.E. Dilworth Co.,[103] at least in terms of its verbiage. Dilworth involved an Arkansas sales tax on a sale to Arkansas customers by a Tennessee corporation with offices in Memphis. The corporation solicited orders in Arkansas through traveling salespersons domiciled in Tennessee or through the mail or telephone. Orders were accepted in Memphis and the goods shipped from Tennessee, with title passing upon delivery to the carrier in Memphis. Justice Frankfurter described the transaction as a sale made by a Tennessee vendor that is consummated in Tennessee and held that Arkansas could not tax it. He

---

93. Id. at 438.

94. Id. at 439.

95. 309 U.S. 33 (1940). In dictum, Justice Stone stated that a tax on the privilege of conducting interstate commerce was unconstitutional. Id. at 48.

96. Id. at 43.

97. Id. at 68-69.

98. Concurring in International Harvester, 322 U.S. 340 (1944), and in General Trading Co. v. State Tax Comm'n, 322 U.S. 335 (1944), and dissenting in McLeod v. J.E. Dilworth Co., 322 U.S. 327 (1944). See the chapter entitled Use Taxes & Interstate Aspects of Sales, Use & Gross Receipts Taxes.

99. 322 U.S. at 358.

100. One difference between Justices Stone and Rutledge may have involved whether a tax could be imposed on the privilege of conducting a purely interstate business. Despite his expansive views on the taxing powers of the state, Justice Stone never renounced the doctrine that taxes could not be levied on the privilege of engaging in an exclusively interstate business. See, e.g., Berwind-White, 309 U.S. at 48. Justice Douglas apparently agreed with this view. See Joseph v. Carter & Weekes Stevedoring Co., 330 U.S. at 442-43 (Douglas, J. dissenting). Justice Rutledge never subscribed to this view. He did, however, concur in Douglas' dissent in Carter & Weekes, supra. But see Memphis Natural Gas Co. v. Stone, 335 U.S. at 96-99 (Rutledge, J. concurring).

101. See, e.g., Memphis Natural Gas, 335 U.S. 80.

102. See generally Adams Mfg., 304 U.S. 307 (1938); Berwind-White, 309 U.S. 33 (1940); General Trading, 322 U.S. 335 (1944).

103. 322 U.S. 327.

described the Commerce Clause as creating "an area of free trade among the several States. That clause vested the power of taxing a transaction forming an unbroken process of interstate commerce in the Congress, not in the States."[104] "For Arkansas to impose a tax on such transaction would be to project its powers beyond its boundaries and to tax an interstate transaction."[105]

Formal distinctions, rather than economic substance could still be determinative, however, even to a staunch defender of interstate commerce such as Justice Frankfurter. In a companion case to McLeod, Justice Frankfurter upheld an Iowa tax on an interstate sale under facts strikingly similar to those in McLeod. The difference was that Iowa levied a use tax, rather than a sales tax.[106] Iowa's tax had the same economic effect as Arkansas' tax: only the name was different. Justice Frankfurter's interest in a free trade zone was apparently more a reflection of a rigorous doctrinaire approach rather than any underlying coherent economic theory.

Justice Frankfurter applied his free trade philosophy in Freeman v. Hewit,[107] which involved the same Indiana tax dealt with in Adams Manufacturing. In Freeman, the Court invalidated the unapportioned Indiana gross income tax levied on the gross receipts from the sale by an Indiana trustee of stock on the N.Y. Stock Exchange; New York did not tax the transaction. Justice Frankfurter held that any state tax imposed directly on an interstate transaction is unconstitutional.[108] "[T]he aim of the Commerce Clause was precisely to prevent States from exacting toll from those engaged in national commerce."[109] The economic effect of the tax was irrelevant:

Nor is there any warrant in the constitutional principles heretofore

applied by this Court to support the notion that a State may be allowed one single-tax-worth of direct interference with the free flow of commerce. An exaction by a State from interstate commerce falls not because of a proven increase in the cost of the product. What makes the tax invalid is the fact that there is interference by a State with the freedom of interstate commerce.[110]

Using language reminiscent of the old "direct-indirect" test, which the Court seemed to have abandoned in Western Live Stock, Justice Frankfurter referred to the Indiana levy as a "direct tax," a "direct imposition on that very freedom of commercial flow which for more than a hundred and fifty years has been the ward of the Commerce Clause," a "levy upon the very process of commerce across State lines," and dismissed the multiple burdens test as "a fashion in judicial writing."[111] Justice Frankfurter reasserted his views that the Commerce Clause created "an area of trade free from interference by the States," and that it "is immaterial that local commerce is subjected to a similar encumbrance."[112] As usual, the Court did not explain how a tax on interstate commerce was different from a tax measured by interstate commerce that had identical economic effects.[113]

According to Professor Hartman, Freeman "marked a recrudescence of what was tantamount to the old, imprecise and unreliable 'direct-indirect' burdens test for

---

104. 322 U.S. at 330-31.

105. Id. at 330.

106. General Trading, 322 U.S. 335 (1944). Seven years earlier the Court had upheld a use tax, such as Iowa's, on the ground that it applied to use of the property, which occurred after interstate commerce had ended. Henneford v. Silas Mason Co., Inc., 300 U.S. 577 (1937).

107. 329 U.S. 249 (1946).

108. Not surprisingly, the Court relied on Adams Mfg., 304 U.S. 307, in striking down the tax. 329 U.S. at 255. Justice Frankfurter presumably would have upheld the tax if it were levied on a local incident, notwithstanding the tax would have had the same effect as the tax struck down. See id. at 255, where the Court cites with approval American Mfg., 250 U.S. 459 (1919).

109. Id. at 254.

110. Id. at 256-57. Complete Auto, 430 U.S. 274 (1977), described Freeman as announcing "a blanket prohibition against any state taxation imposed directly on an interstate transaction," and holding that "a direct tax on interstate sales, even if fairly apportioned and nondiscriminatory, was . . . unconstitutional per se." Id. at 280. Justice Rutledge in his concurring opinion in Freeman argued "that the tax should be judged by its economic effects rather than by its formal phrasing," id. at 280, a position endorsed in Complete Auto. Justice Rutledge set forth three considerations for evaluating the constitutionality of a tax, which are closely related to first three prongs of Complete Auto. Id. at 281. The fourth prong of Complete Auto is probably the least significant of that case's criteria. See Commonwealth Edison v. Montana, 453 U.S. 609 (1981).

111. 329 U.S. at 254-57.

112. Id. at 252.

113. Justice Rutledge would have struck the tax on the basis of J. D. Adams Manufacturing:
[The] opinion refuses to rest squarely on the Adams case, although that case would be completely controlling if no change in the law were intended. No basis for distinguishing the cases on the facts or the ultimate questions is found or stated. The Court takes them as identical. Yet it places no emphasis upon apportionment, the absence of which the Adams opinion held crucial. The Court also puts to one side as irrelevant the factor there most stressed, namely, the danger of multiple taxation, that is, of similar taxation by other states, if the Indiana tax should be upheld in the attempted application. Id. at 260 (Rutledge, J., concurring).

determining the constitutionality of a tax when questioned on commerce clause grounds. The Freeman criterion of tax validity under the commerce clause pretty much dredged up the discredited and discarded pre-Stone Age 'direct-indirect' burdens test, used when the Court was declaring that interstate commerce could not be taxed at all."[114] Freeman notwithstanding, the Court continued to allow interstate transactions to be taxed when the tax could be characterized as falling on "some local incident,"[115] a fiction that was still viable.

The resurgence of the old formalistic school of Commerce Clause interpretation crested with Spector Motor Service, Inc. v. O'Connor.[116] Spector struck down a fairly apportioned, nondiscriminatory Connecticut net income tax imposed on the privilege of "carrying on or doing business within the state,"[117] as applied to a business conducting exclusively interstate commerce.[118] The tax violated the Commerce Clause because the federal government had the exclusive power to tax the privilege of engaging in interstate commerce.[119] "The

constitutional infirmity of [the] tax persists no matter how fairly it is apportioned to business done within the state."[120]

Spector turned out not to have any severe effect on the states. A skillful draftsman could blunt the Spector doctrine.[121] For example, a Virginia statute levying a tax "for the privilege of doing business in this State" measured by gross receipts attributable to activities in Virginia was invalidated but subsequently upheld when a tax having the same economic effect was redrafted as a franchise tax on tangible property in the form of "going-concern value," as measured by gross receipts attributable to activities in Virginia.[122] Labels were still cloaked with constitutional dignity.[123]

The lack of any principled and coherent approach made it impossible to reconcile the conflicting cases except on the most metaphysical of criteria. By 1959, the Court itself was frustrated by this doctrinal muddle and described its opinions as leaving "much room for controversy and confusion and little in the way of precise guides to the States in the exercise of their indispensable

---

114. Hartman, supra note 57, at 77.

115. Norton Co. v. Dept. of Revenue, 340 U.S. at 537.

116. 340 U.S. 602 (1951), overruled by Complete Auto. In Complete Auto, the Court refers to Freeman as "[t]he modern origin of the Spector rule." 430 U.S. at 279.

117. 340 U.S. at 604 n.1.

118. Taxes on the privilege of conducting an exclusively interstate transportation or communication company were held unconstitutional as early as 1885. Gloucester Ferry, supra note 55. In Gloucester, the Court applied the Cooley doctrine and characterized the interstate transportation and communication as a subject of national character, requiring uniformity of regulation.

119. A state is barred from imposing a tax on an out-of-state corporation as a condition to its conducting an interstate business within the taxing state. Pensacola Tel. Co. v. Western Union Tel. Co., 96 U.S. 1, 12-13 (1877); Leloup, 127 U.S. at 645; Western Union Tel. Co. v. Kansas, 216 U.S. at 47-48. Extrapolating from this proposition, the Court held that a state could not tax the privilege of doing business as applied to an out-of-state corporation doing an exclusively interstate business in the state. Cheney Bros., 246 U.S. at 153-54. Likewise, the Court struck down taxes on the "carrying on" or "doing business" when applied to a corporation conducting an interstate business. Alpha Portland Cement, 268 U.S. 203; Spector Motor, 340 U.S. 602. Business license taxes on interstate companies (e.g., telegraph, transportation, or manufacturing) were also held unconstitutional. See, e.g., Western Union, supra, at 47-48 (1910); Crutcher v. Kentucky, 141 U.S. 47 (1891). "[W]here a taxpayer is engaged both in intrastate and interstate commerce, a state may tax the privilege of carrying on intrastate business and, within

reasonable limits, may compute the amount of the charge by applying the tax rate to a fair proportion of the taxpayer's business done within the state, including both interstate and intrastate." Spector Motor, 304 U.S. at 609-10. Presumably, the Court would have upheld Spector Motor if the taxpayer had been engaged in activity that could be characterized as "intrastate." Id. at 610-11 (Clark, J., Black, J., Douglas, J., dissenting). Cf. Robbins v. Shelby County, 120 U.S. 489 (invalidating a privilege tax on commissioned salesmen selling for out-of-state principals) with Ficklen, 145 U.S. 1 (upholding privilege tax on commissioned salesmen engaged in interstate business but licensed to engage in intrastate business).

120. 340 U.S. at 609. The Court did recognize, however, that the "State is not precluded from imposing taxes upon other activities . . . which, unlike the privilege of doing interstate business, are subject to the sovereign power of the State." Id.

121. For example, in Spector, 340 U.S. 602, Connecticut could have successfully taxed the income through a fairly apportioned net income tax. See Northwestern States Portland Cement, 358 U.S. 450.

122. Cf. Railway Express Agency, Inc. v. Virginia, 347 U.S. 359 (1954) with Railway Express Agency, Inc. v. Virginia, 358 U.S. 434 (1959).

123. Rather defensively, the Court attempted to justify its decisions in the Railway Express cases, supra note 122, with the explanation that "[o]ne must comprehend . . . the difference between the use of magic words or labels validating an otherwise invalid tax and their use to disable an otherwise constitutional levy." 358 U.S. at 441.

power of taxation," and acknowledged the "need for clearing up the tangled underbrush of past cases."[124]

In that year, Northwestern States Portland Cement Co. v. Minnesota[125] abandoned Justice Frankfurter's views and returning to its prior emphasis on multiple taxation, the Court upheld a state income tax imposed directly on an apportioned share of a corporation's net income earned within Minnesota, notwithstanding that the Minnesota activities were part of the corporation's exclusively interstate business. All of the taxpayer's manufacturing operations were in Iowa; 48% of its sales were in Minnesota, where it had a rented sales office with four salespersons. Orders were transmitted to Iowa for approval. Shipments were made directly from the plant to the purchasers.

The Court recognized that "[w]hile it is true that a State may not erect a wall around its borders preventing commerce an entry, it is axiomatic that the founders did not intend to immunize such [interstate] commerce from carrying its fair share of the costs of the state government in return for the benefits it derives from within the State."[126] Only taxes that discriminate against interstate commerce, or that expose commerce to the burdens of multiple taxation, or are privilege taxes based on the right to carry on business in the taxing state are unconstitutional.[127]

The Minnesota tax was upheld because it was apportioned, did not result in multiple taxation, and did not discriminate against interstate commerce. Northwestern States, however, did not indicate the

Court had abandoned its previous formalistic approach: "it is beyond dispute that a State may not lay a tax on the 'privilege' of engaging in interstate commerce."[128] Spector was distinguished on the grounds that Connecticut's tax was levied "on" the franchise of a corporation engaged exclusively in interstate commerce, albeit measured by net income, whereas the Minnesota tax was imposed directly "on" the net income of the corporation.[129]

Of course, a nondiscriminatory tax on the privilege of engaging in exclusively interstate commerce measured by apportioned net income could be redrafted as a tax imposed directly upon apportioned net income from interstate commerce.[130] This lesson was not lost upon the states. Many states that had franchise taxes levied on the privilege of engaging in business, measured by net income, which could not be applied to exclusively interstate businesses, adopted new net income taxes of the type upheld in Northwestern States.[131]

A series of cases involving unapportioned gross receipts taxes indicated that the Court would continue to uphold taxes if it could find a constitutionally proper "local" subject for taxation. In other words, the Court would expand state powers of taxation by finding some local "hook" upon which it could justify the tax. In 1964, for example, General Motors Corp. v. Washington[132] upheld a Washington State tax on the privilege of "making sales at wholesale"[133] within the State, measured by total unapportioned gross receipts. Ironically, some of the gross receipts that Washington sought to tax were from products manufactured in St. Louis that were subject to that City's doing business tax, also measured by unapportioned gross receipts, which was upheld in

---

124. Northwestern States Portland Cement, 358 U.S. at 457.

125. 358 U.S. 450 (1959).

126. Id. at 461-62. For a similar statement in Western Live Stock, see 303 U.S. at 254.

127. 358 U.S. at 458. Not surprisingly, Justice Frankfurter dissented:
I venture to say that every other decision–I say decision, not talk or dicta–on which reliance is placed, presented a situation where conjoined with the interstate commerce was severable local state business on the basis of which the state taxing power became constitutionally operative. The difference between those situations and this, as a matter of economics, involves the distinction between taking into account the total activity of the enterprise as a going business in determining a fairly apportioned tax based on locally derived revenues, and taxing a portion of revenue concededly produced by exclusively interstate commerce. To be sure, such a distinction is a nice one, but the last word on the necessity of nice distinctions in this area was said by Mr. Justice Holmes in Galveston, H. & S.A.R. Co. v. Texas, 210 U.S. 217, 225: "It being once admitted, as of course it must be, that not every law that affects commerce is a regulation of it in a constitutional sense, nice distinctions are to be expected." 358 U.S. at 473.

128. 358 U.S. at 458, citing Spector, 340 U.S. 602 (1951).

129. Congressional reaction to Northwestern States was swift. Less than a year after the decision, Congress enacted P.L. 86-272, 15 U.S.C. §§ 381-84, limiting a state's power to tax income from certain activities in interstate commerce. See Wisconsin Department of Revenue v. Wrigley Co., Chapter 11, The Corporate Income Tax: The Leading Cases.

130. In Complete Auto, 430 U.S. 274 (1977), the Court described the difference between Northwestern States and Spector as "only . . . a trap for the unwary draftsman." Id. at 279. See also Colonial Pipeline Co. v. Traigle, 421 U.S. 100 (1975), upholding an apportioned, nondiscriminatory franchise tax levied for the privilege of doing business in corporate form.

131. See Chapter 10 infra.

132. 377 U.S. 436 (1964).

133. Id. at 439.

American Manufacturing, discussed above.[134] Because the same gross receipts were taxed by St. Louis, General Motors argued that the Washington tax must fall because it would produce multiple taxation. The Court's response was unsatisfying: "[General Motors] has not demonstrated what definite burden, in a constitutional sense, the St. Louis tax places on the identical interstate shipments by which Washington measures its tax."[135] Apparently no unconstitutional multiple taxation resulted because both St. Louis and the State of Washington were taxing intrastate activities: St. Louis was taxing manufacturing whereas Washington was taxing the local activity of selling at wholesale.[136]

That General Motors was not an aberration became clear in 1975 in Standard Press Steel Co. v. Department of Revenue of Washington.[137] The taxpayer had a single resident employee who was not directly engaged in selling activities in Washington; nonresident engineers would visit the State for three days every six weeks. Sales negotiations occurred outside the State and orders from Washington customers were filled from inventories held outside the State and delivered by common carrier. In upholding the tax, the Court stated: "In the instant case . . . the tax is on the gross receipts from sales made to a local customer, which may have some impact on commerce. Yet . . . it is 'apportioned exactly to the activities taxed,' all of which are intrastate."[138]

The following 1977 case overrules Spector, disavows any notion that states cannot tax directly interstate commerce,[139] and sets forth in dicta what has become known as the four prong test for evaluating a tax's constitutionality under the Commerce Clause.

---

134. See supra notes 83-91 and accompanying text.

135. 377 U.S. at 449. The Court cited for its proposition International Harvester Co. v. Evatt, 329 U.S. at 421-23. That case concerned an Ohio franchise tax on foreign corporations doing business in Ohio, measured by capital stock allocable to Ohio. The allocation formula was based partly on "business done" in Ohio, which was determined on the basis of sales within Ohio as a percentage of the corporation's total sales. See 329 U.S. at 419. The State defined Ohio sales to include all sales of goods manufactured within Ohio, regardless of where they were actually sold. In addition, the statute further treated as Ohio sales the sale of goods manufactured outside the state provided they were sold through Ohio sales agencies. In effect, the Court allowed Ohio to tax both goods manufactured within the State but sold outside the State as well as goods manufactured outside the State and sold within Ohio. The Court viewed Ohio as taxing intrastate activities in either case: manufacturing that occurred within Ohio with respect to outbound shipments and sales activities that occurred within Ohio with respect to inbound shipments.

136. See 377 U.S. at 448-49. This type of approach is criticized in Walter Hellerstein, Michael J. McIntyre, and Richard D. Pomp, Commerce Clause Restraints on State Taxation After Jefferson Lines, 51 Tax Law Rev. 47, 94-102 (1995).

137. 419 U.S. 560 (1975), involving the same Washington gross receipts tax as in General Motors v. Washington.

138. Id. at 564 (quoting Gwin, White & Prince, 305 U.S. at 440).

139. The decision in Complete Auto was foreshadowed by Colonial Pipeline, 421 U.S. 100 (1975).

Complete Auto Transit, Inc.
v. Brady, Chairman, Mississippi Tax Commission
Supreme Court of the United States, 1977.
430 U.S. 274, 97 S. Ct. 1076, 51 L. Ed. 2d 326.

MR. JUSTICE BLACKMUN delivered the opinion of the Court.

Once again we are presented with "'the perennial problem of the validity of a state tax for the privilege of carrying on, within a state, certain activities' related to a corporation's operation of an interstate business." The issue in this case is whether Mississippi runs afoul of the Commerce Clause when it applies the tax it imposes on "the privilege of . . . doing business" within the State to appellant's activity in interstate commerce. The Supreme Court of Mississippi unanimously sustained the tax against appellant's constitutional challenge.

I

The taxes in question are sales taxes assessed by the Mississippi State Tax Commission against the appellant. . . . The assessments were made pursuant to the following Mississippi statutes:

"There is hereby levied and assessed and shall be collected, privilege taxes for the privilege of engaging or continuing in business or doing business within this state to be determined by the application of rates against gross proceeds of sales or gross income or values, as the case may be. . ."

"Upon every person operating a pipeline, railroad, airplane, bus, truck, or any other transportation business for the transportation of persons or property for compensation or hire between points within this State, there is hereby levied, assessed, and shall be collected, a tax equal to five per cent of the gross income of such business . . . ."

Any person liable for the tax is required to add it to the gross sales price and, "insofar as practicable," to collect it at the time the sales price is collected.

. . . .

Appellant is a Michigan corporation engaged in the business of transporting motor vehicles by motor carrier for General Motors Corporation. General Motors assembles outside Mississippi vehicles that are destined for dealers within the State. The vehicles are then shipped by rail to Jackson, Miss., where, usually within 48 hours, they are loaded onto appellant's trucks and transported by appellant to the Mississippi dealers. Appellant is paid on a contract basis for the transportation from the railhead to the dealers.[4]

Appellant claimed that its transportation was but one part of an interstate movement, and that the taxes assessed and paid were unconstitutional as applied to operations in interstate commerce. . . .

[In rejecting this argument] the Mississippi Supreme Court . . . concluded:

"It will be noted that Taxpayer has a large operation in this State. It is dependent upon the State for police protection and other State services the same as other citizens. It should pay its fair share of taxes so long, but only so long, as the tax does not discriminate against interstate commerce, and there is no danger of interstate commerce being smothered by cumulative taxes of several states. There is no possibility of any other state duplicating the tax involved in this case."

Appellant, in its complaint in Chancery Court, did *not* allege that its activity which Mississippi taxes does not have a sufficient nexus with the State; or that the tax discriminates against interstate commerce; or that the tax is unfairly apportioned; or that it is unrelated to services provided by the State.[6] No such claims were made before the Mississippi Supreme Court, and although appellant argues here that a tax on "the privilege of engaging in interstate commerce" creates an unacceptable risk of discrimination and undue burdens, it does not claim that discrimination or undue burdens exist in fact.

Appellant's attack is based solely on decisions of this Court holding that a tax on the "privilege" of engaging in an activity in the State may not be applied to an activity that is part of interstate commerce. See, e.g., Spector Motor Service v. O'Connor, 340 U.S. 602 (1951); Freeman v. Hewit, 329 U.S. 249 (1946). This rule looks only to the fact that the incidence of the tax is the "privilege of doing business"; it deems irrelevant any consideration of

transportation it provides from the railhead to the dealers is part of a movement in interstate commerce. Appellee argues that appellant's transportation is intrastate business, but further argues that even if the activity is part of interstate commerce, the tax is not unconstitutional. The Mississippi courts, in upholding the tax, assumed that the transportation is in interstate commerce. For present purposes, we make the same assumption.

6. See Boston Stock Exchange v. State Tax Comm'n, 429 U.S. 318 (1977); General Motors Corp. v. Washington, 377 U.S. 436 (1964); Illinois Cent. R. Co. v. Minnesota, 309 U.S. 157 (1940); Ingels v. Morf, 300 U.S. 290 (1937). See also Standard Steel Co. v. Washington Rev. Dept., 419 U.S. 560 (1975), and Clark v. Paul Gray, Inc., 306 U.S. 583 (1939).

4. The parties understandably go to great pains to describe the details of the bills of lading, and the responsibility of various entities for the vehicles as they travel from the assembly plant to the dealers. Appellant seeks to demonstrate that the

the practical effect of the tax. The rule reflects an underlying philosophy that interstate commerce should enjoy a sort of "free trade" immunity from state taxation.[7]

Appellee, in its turn, relies on decisions of this Court stating that "[i]t was not the purpose of the commerce clause to relieve those engaged in interstate commerce from their just share of state tax burden even though it increases the cost of doing the business," Western Live Stock v. Bureau of Revenue, 303 U.S. at 254. These decisions[8] have considered not the formal language of the tax statute but rather its practical effect, and have sustained a tax against Commerce Clause challenge when the tax is applied to an activity with a substantial nexus with the taxing State, is fairly apportioned, does not discriminate against interstate commerce, and is fairly related to the services provided by the State.

Over the years, the Court has applied this practical analysis in approving many types of tax that avoided running afoul of the prohibition against taxing the "privilege of doing business," but in each instance it has refused to overrule the prohibition. Under the present state of the law, the Spector rule, as it has come to be known, has no relationship to economic realities. Rather it stands only as a trap for the unwary draftsman.

II

The modern origin of the Spector rule may be found in Freeman v. Hewit, supra.[9] At issue in Freeman was the

application of an Indiana tax upon "the receipt of the entire gross income" of residents and domiciliaries. Indiana sought to impose this tax on income generated when a trustee of an Indiana estate instructed his local stockbroker to sell certain securities. The broker arranged with correspondents in New York to sell the securities on the New York Stock Exchange. The securities were sold, and the New York brokers, after deducting expenses and commission, transmitted the proceeds to the Indiana broker who in turn delivered them, less his commission, to the trustee. The Indiana Supreme Court sustained the tax, but this Court reversed.

Mr. Justice Frankfurter, speaking for five Members of the Court, announced a blanket prohibition against any state taxation imposed directly on an interstate transaction. He explicitly deemed unnecessary to the decision of the case any showing of discrimination against interstate commerce or error in apportionment of the tax. He recognized that a State could constitutionally tax local manufacture, impose license taxes on corporations doing business in the State, tax property within the State, and tax the privilege of residence in the State and measure the privilege by net income, including that derived from interstate commerce. Nevertheless, a direct tax on interstate sales, even if fairly apportioned and nondiscriminatory, was held to be unconstitutional per se.

Mr. Justice Rutledge, in a lengthy concurring opinion, argued that the tax should be judged by its economic effects rather than by its formal phrasing. After reviewing the Court's prior decisions, he concluded: "The fact is that 'direct incidence' of a state tax or regulation . . . has long since been discarded as being in itself sufficient to outlaw state legislation." In his view, a state tax is unconstitutional only if the activity lacks the necessary connection with the taxing state to give "jurisdiction to tax," or if the tax discriminates against interstate commerce, or if the activity is subject to multiple taxation.[10]

---

7. The Court summarized the "free trade" view in Freeman v. Hewit, 329 U.S. at 252:

"[T]he Commerce Clause was not merely an authorization to Congress to enact laws for the protection and encouragement of commerce among the States, but by its own force created an area of trade free from interference by the States. In short, the Commerce Clause even without implementing legislation by Congress is a limitation upon the power of the States. . . . This limitation on State power . . . does not merely forbid a State to single out interstate commerce for hostile action. A State is also precluded from taking any action which may fairly be deemed to have the effect of impeding the free flow of trade between States. It is immaterial that local commerce is subjected to a similar encumbrance."

8. See, e.g., General Motors Corp. v. Washington, supra; Northwestern Cement Co. v. Minnesota, 358 U.S. 450 (1959); Memphis Gas Co. v. Stone, 335 U.S. 80 (1948); Wisconsin v. J. C. Penney Co., 311 U.S. 435, 444 (1940).

9. Although we mention Freeman as the starting point, elements of the views expressed therein, and the positions that underlie that debate, were evident in prior opinions. Compare State Tax on Railway Gross Receipts, 15 Wall. 284 (1873), with Fargo v. Michigan, 121 U.S. 230 (1887); and compare Di Santo v. Pennsylvania, 273 U.S. 34 (1927), and Cooney v. Mountain

States Tel. Co., 294 U.S. 384 (1935), with Western Live Stock v. Bureau of Revenue, 303 U.S. 250 (1938). See generally P. Hartman, State Taxation of Interstate Commerce (1953); Barrett, State Taxation of Interstate Commerce—"Direct Burdens," "Multiple Burdens," or What Have You?, 4 Vand. L. Rev. 496 (1951), and writings cited therein at 496 n. 1; Dunham, Gross Receipts Taxes on Interstate Transactions, 47 Colum. L. Rev. 211 (1947).

10. Mr. Justice Rutledge agreed with the result the Court reached in Freeman because of his belief that the apportionment problem was best solved if States other than the market State were forbidden to impose unapportioned gross receipts taxes of the kind Indiana sought to exact.

The rule announced in Freeman was viewed in the commentary as a triumph of formalism over substance, providing little guidance even as to formal requirements. See P. Hartman, State Taxation of Interstate Commerce 200-204 (1953); Dunham, Gross Receipts Taxes on Interstate Transactions, 47 Colum. L. Rev. 211 (1947). Although the rule might have been utilized as the keystone of a movement toward absolute immunity of interstate commerce from state taxation,[11] the Court consistently has indicated that "interstate commerce may be made to pay its way," and has moved toward a standard of permissibility of state taxation based upon its actual effect rather than its legal terminology.

The narrowing of the rule to one of draftsmanship and phraseology began with another Mississippi case, Memphis Gas Co. v. Stone, 335 U.S. 80 (1948). Memphis Natural Gas Company owned and operated a pipeline running from Louisiana to Memphis. Approximately 135 miles of the line were in Mississippi. Mississippi imposed a "franchise or excise" tax measured by "the value of the capital used, invested or employed in the exercise of any power, privilege or right enjoyed by [a corporation] within this state." The Mississippi Supreme Court upheld the tax, and this Court affirmed.

In an opinion for himself and two others, Mr. Justice Reed noted that the tax was not discriminatory, that there was no possibility of multiple taxation, that the amount of the tax was reasonable, and that the tax was properly apportioned to the investment in Mississippi. He then went on to consider whether the tax was "upon the privilege of doing interstate business within the state." He drew a distinction between a tax on "the privilege of doing interstate business" and a tax on "the privilege of exercising corporate functions within the State," and held that while the former is unconstitutional, the latter is not barred by the Commerce Clause. He then approved the tax there at issue because

"there is no attempt to tax the privilege of doing an interstate business or to secure anything from the corporation by this statute except compensation for the protection of the enumerated local activities of 'maintaining, keeping in repair, and otherwise in manning the facilities.'"

Mr. Justice Black concurred in the judgment without opinion. Mr. Justice Rutledge provided the fifth vote, stating in his concurrence:

"[I]t is enough for me to sustain the tax imposed in this case that it is one clearly within the state's power to lay insofar as any limitation of due process or 'jurisdiction to tax' in that sense is concerned; it is nondiscriminatory, that is, places no greater burden upon interstate commerce than the state places upon competing intrastate commerce of like character; is duly apportioned, that is, does not undertake to tax any interstate activities carried on outside the state's borders; and cannot be repeated by any other state."

Four Justices dissented, on the grounds that it had not been shown that the State afforded any protection in return for the tax, and that, therefore, the tax must be viewed as one on the "privilege" of engaging in interstate commerce. The dissenters recognized that an identical effect could be achieved by an increase in the ad valorem property tax, but would have held, notwithstanding, that a tax on the "privilege" is unconstitutional.

The prohibition against state taxation of the "privilege" of engaging in commerce that is interstate was reaffirmed in Spector Motor Service v. O'Connor, 340 U.S. 602 (1951), a case similar on its facts to the instant case. The taxpayer there was a Missouri corporation engaged exclusively in interstate trucking. Some of its shipments originated or terminated in Connecticut. Connecticut imposed on a corporation a "tax or excise upon its franchise for the privilege of carrying on or doing business within the state," measured by apportioned net income.

The Court recognized that "where a taxpayer is engaged both in intrastate and interstate commerce, a state may tax the privilege of carrying on intrastate business and, within reasonable limits, may compute the amount of the charge by applying the tax rate to a fair proportion of the taxpayer's business done within the state, including both interstate and intrastate." It held, nevertheless, that a tax on the "privilege" of doing business is unconstitutional if applied against what is exclusively interstate commerce. The dissenters argued, on the other hand, that there is no constitutional difference between an "exclusively interstate" business and a "mixed" business, and that a fairly apportioned and nondiscriminatory tax on either type is not prohibited by the Commerce Clause.

The Spector rule was applied in Railway Express Agency v. Virginia, 347 U.S. 359 (1954) (Railway Express I), to declare unconstitutional a State's "annual license tax" levied on gross receipts for the "privilege of doing business in this State." The Court, by a 5-to-4 vote, held that the tax on gross receipts was a tax on the privilege of doing business rather than a tax on property in the State, as Virginia contended.

Virginia thereupon revised the wording of its statute to impose a "franchise tax" on "intangible property" in the

---

11. A consistent application of the doctrine of immunity for interstate commerce, of course, would have necessitated overruling the cases approved by the Freeman Court that upheld taxes whose burden, although indirect, fell on interstate commerce.

form of "going concern" value as measured by gross receipts. The tax was again asserted against the Agency which in Virginia was engaged exclusively in interstate commerce. This Court's opinion, buttressed by two concurring opinions and one concurrence in the result, upheld the reworded statute as not violative of the Spector rule. Railway Express Agency v. Virginia, 358 U.S. 434 (1959) (Railway Express II). In upholding the statute, the Court's opinion recognized that the rule against taxing the "privilege" of doing interstate business had created a situation where "the use of magic words or labels" could "disable an otherwise constitutional levy."

There was no real economic difference between the statutes in Railway Express I and Railway Express II. The Court long since had recognized that interstate commerce may be made to pay its way. Yet under the Spector rule, the economic realities in Railway Express I became irrelevant. The Spector rule had come to operate only as a rule of draftsmanship, and served only to distract the courts and parties from their inquiry into whether the challenged tax produced results forbidden by the Commerce Clause.

On the day it announced Railway Express II, the Court further confirmed that a State, with proper drafting, may tax exclusively interstate commerce so long as the tax does not create any effect forbidden by the Commerce Clause. In Northwestern Cement Co. v. Minnesota, 358 U.S. 450 (1959), the Court held that net income from the interstate operations of a foreign corporation may be subjected to state taxation, provided the levy is not discriminatory and is properly apportioned to local activities within the taxing State forming sufficient nexus to support the tax. Limited in that way, the tax could be levied even though the income was generated exclusively by interstate sales. Spector was distinguished, briefly and in passing, as a case in which "the incidence" of the tax "was the privilege of doing business." 358 U.S. at 464.

Thus, applying the rule of Northwestern Cement to the facts of Spector, it is clear that Connecticut could have taxed the apportioned net income derived from the exclusively interstate commerce. It could not, however, tax the "privilege" of doing business as measured by the apportioned net income. The reason for attaching constitutional significance to a semantic difference is difficult to discern.

The unsatisfactory operation of the Spector rule is well demonstrated by our recent case of Colonial Pipeline Co. v. Traigle, 421 U.S. 100 (1975). Colonial was a Delaware corporation with an interstate pipeline running through Louisiana for approximately 258 miles. It maintained a work force and pumping stations in Louisiana to keep the pipeline flowing, but it did no intrastate business in

that State. In 1962, Louisiana imposed on Colonial a franchise tax for "the privilege of carrying on or doing business" in the State. The Louisiana Court of Appeal invalidated the tax as violative of the rule of Spector. The Supreme Court of Louisiana refused review. The Louisiana Legislature, perhaps recognizing that it had run afoul of a rule of words rather than a rule of substance, then redrafted the statute to levy the tax, as an alternative incident, on the "qualification to carry on or do business in this state or the actual doing of business within this state in a corporate form." Again, the Court of Appeal held the tax unconstitutional as applied to the appellant. But this time the Louisiana Supreme Court upheld the new tax.

By a 7-to-1 vote, this Court affirmed. No question had been raised as to the propriety of the apportionment of the tax, and no claim was made that the tax was discriminatory. The Court noted that the tax was imposed on that aspect of interstate commerce to which the State bore a special relation, and that the State bestowed powers, privileges, and benefits sufficient to support a tax on doing business in the corporate form in Louisiana. Accordingly, on the authority of Memphis Gas, the tax was held to be constitutional. The Court distinguished Spector on the familiar ground that it involved a tax on the privilege of carrying on interstate commerce, while the Louisiana Legislature, in contrast, had worded the statute at issue "narrowly to confine the impost to one related to appellant's activities within the State in the corporate form."

. . . .

III

In this case, of course, we are confronted with a situation like that presented in Spector. The tax is labeled a privilege tax "for the privilege of . . . doing business" in Mississippi, and the activity taxed is, or has been assumed to be, interstate commerce. We note again that no claim is made that the activity is not sufficiently connected to the State to justify a tax, or that the tax is not fairly related to benefits provided the taxpayer, or that the tax discriminates against interstate commerce, or that the tax is not fairly apportioned.

The view of the Commerce Clause that gave rise to the rule of Spector perhaps was not without some substance. Nonetheless, the possibility of defending it in the abstract does not alter the fact that the Court has rejected the proposition that interstate commerce is immune from state taxation:

"It is a truism that the mere act of carrying on business in interstate commerce does not exempt a corporation from state taxation. 'It was not the purpose of the commerce clause to relieve those engaged in interstate commerce from their just share of state tax burden even though it increases the cost of doing business.' Western Live Stock v.

Bureau of Revenue, 303 U.S. at 254." Colonial Pipeline Co. v. Traigle, 421 U.S. at 108.

Not only has the philosophy underlying the rule been rejected, but the rule itself has been stripped of any practical significance. If Mississippi had called its tax one on "net income" or on the "going concern value" of appellant's business, the Spector rule could not invalidate it. There is no economic consequence that follows necessarily from the use of the particular words, "privilege of doing business," and a focus on that formalism merely obscures the question whether the tax produces a forbidden effect. Simply put, the Spector rule does not address the problems with which the Commerce Clause is concerned.[15] Accordingly, we now reject the rule of Spector Motor Service, Inc. v. O'Connor, that a state tax on the "privilege of doing business" is per se unconstitutional when it is applied to interstate commerce, and that case is overruled.

. . . .

15. It might be argued that "privilege" taxes, by focusing on the doing of business, are easily tailored to single out interstate businesses and subject them to effects forbidden by the Commerce Clause, and that, therefore, "privilege" taxes should be subjected to a per se rule against their imposition on interstate business. Yet property taxes also may be tailored to differentiate between property used in transportation and other types of property, see Railway Express II, 358 U.S. 434 (1959); an income tax could use different rates for different types of business; and a tax on the "privilege of doing business in corporate form" could be made to change with the nature of the corporate activity involved. Any tailored tax of this sort creates an increased danger of error in apportionment, of discrimination against interstate commerce, and of a lack of relationship to the services provided by the State. See Freeman v. Hewit, 329 U.S. at 265-266, n. 13 (concurring opinion). A tailored tax, however accomplished, must receive the careful scrutiny of the courts to determine whether it produces a forbidden effect on interstate commerce. We perceive no reason, however, why a tax on the "privilege of doing business" should be viewed as creating a qualitatively different danger so as to require a per se rule of unconstitutionality.

It might also be argued that adoption of a rule of absolute immunity for interstate commerce (a rule that would, of course, go beyond Spector) would relieve this Court of difficult judgments that on occasion will have to be made. We believe, however, that administrative convenience, in this instance, is insufficient justification for abandoning the principle that "interstate commerce may be made to pay its way."

Questions and Comments

1. The Mississippi statute taxes the gross proceeds of transportation from points within Mississippi. The statute does not purport to tax transportation activities outside Mississippi. Why, then, was the Commerce Clause implicated?

The taxpayer is being paid for the transportation from the railhead in Jackson, Mississippi, to dealers throughout Mississippi. Is the taxpayer arguing that the Mississippi statute is unconstitutional on its face or only unconstitutional as applied to its particular fact situation?

2. Examine the Court's statement in the last paragraph of footnote 15. What "difficult judgments" might be raised by a rule of absolute immunity for interstate commerce?

3. Before this case, was it possible for a tax that did not discriminate against interstate commerce, that was fairly apportioned, that was related to services provided by the state, and for which nexus existed, to be unconstitutional if it were imposed on interstate commerce? After this case?

4. *Complete Auto* is said to impose a four-prong test for determining whether a tax satisfies the Commerce Clause. What are those four tests? What is the rationale underlying these tests? Is the Court implying that its examination of the practical effect of a tax is limited to only these four criteria?

5. Does *Complete Auto* overrule *Freeman v. Hewit*?

6. Examine Justice Rutledge's concurrence in *Freeman v. Hewit*. How does the commerce clause analysis set forth in *Complete Auto* differ from Rutledge's analysis?

7. Which of the four prongs set forth in *Complete Auto* must also be satisfied for purposes of the Due Process Clause?

8. Is the fair apportionment requirement just another name for the multiple tax doctrine? See Shores, State Taxation of Gross Receipts and the Negative Commerce Clause, 54 Mo. L. Rev. 555, 565 (1989).

9. Did the taxpayer challenge the "fairly related" test? What is the nature of the inquiry under that test? Is the fairly related test similar to the nexus requirement? See *Wisconsin v. J.C. Penney Co.*, 311 U.S. 435, 444 (1940). Does the "fairly related" test invite a detailed inquiry into the benefits that a state provides a taxpayer?

10. What is the relationship between the nondiscrimination prong and the multiple tax doctrine?

11. What is the relationship between the first prong and the second prong? If a state taxes an activity over which it has no nexus, is it more or less likely that the tax is not fairly apportioned? If a tax is not apportioned, is it more or less likely that multiple taxation will occur?

12. Was the Court consistent in how it described the nexus requirement? Did it always refer to "substantial" nexus?

13. Did the Court view itself as announcing a new four-part test or only as abandoning a highly formalistic doctrine?

14. Examine footnote 15. Suppose a state levied a severance tax on coal and that all of the coal was shipped out-of-state. The legislative history makes it very clear that the state chose to tax coal precisely because it was all shipped out-of-state. Would such a tax be constitutional?

15. Why is the decision silent regarding the multiple taxation doctrine?

16. For critical commentary on *Complete Auto Transit*, see Neil M. Robinson, *Complete Auto Transit Test Applied to State Use Tax: D.H. Homes Co. v. McNamara*, 42 Tax Law. 391 (1989); R. Douglas Harmon, *Judicial Review Under Complete Auto Transit: When is a State Tax on Energy-Producing Resources "Fairly Related"?*, 1982 Duke L.J. 682; Richard L. Musick, *A Deferential Interpretation of the Complete Auto Transit Test for Determining Whether a State Tax Unconstitutionally Burdens Interstate Commerce*, 1982 B.Y.U. L. Rev. 765; Donald F. Santa, Jr., *The Incomplete Complete Auto Transit Test: Commerce Clause Analysis in Commonwealth Edison v. Montana*, 8 Colum. J. Envtl. L. 185 (1982); Jeanne M. Gode, *Labor Law - Caging the Wildcat Striker After Complete Auto Transit, Inc. v. Reis*, 7 J. Corp. L. 915 (1982); Robert Capel, *Taxation - State Taxation of Interstate Commerce: The Final Step: Complete Auto Transit, Inc. v. Brady*, 21 How. L.J. 661 (1978); Evalyn B. David, *Taxation - Constitutional Law - Application and Rejection of Per Se Unconstitutional Rule As Applied to State Taxation of Interstate Commerce - Complete Auto Transit, Inc. v. Brady, 430 U.S. 274 (1977)* 9 Seton Hall L. Rev. 910 (1978); Brandon F. White, *State Taxation on the Privilege of Doing Interstate Business; Complete Auto Transit, Inc. v. Brady*, 19 B.C. L. Rev. 312 (1978); Scott Specht, *State Taxation of Interstate Business: An End to the Privilege Tax Immunity: Complete Auto Transit, Inc. v. Brady, 97 S. Ct. 1076 (1977)*,

29 U. Fla. L. Rev. 752 (1977); Ken Jaray, *Recent Developments in State Taxation of Interstate Commerce: Complete Auto Transit, Inc. v. Brady and National Geographic*

Society v. California Board of Equalization, 7 Cap. U. L. Rev. 143 (1977).

Boston Stock Exchange et al. v. State Tax Commission et al.
Supreme Court of the United States, 1977.
429 U.S. 318, 97 S.Ct. 599, 50 L. Ed. 2d 514.

MR. JUSTICE WHITE delivered the opinion of the Court.

In this case we are asked to decide the constitutionality of a recent amendment to New York State's longstanding tax on securities transactions. Since 1905, New York has imposed a tax (transfer tax) on securities transactions, if part of the transaction occurs within the State. In 1968, the state legislature amended the transfer tax statute so that transactions involving an out-of-state sale are now taxed more heavily than most transactions involving a sale within the State. In 1972, appellants, six "regional" stock exchanges located outside New York, filed an action in state court against the State Tax Commission of New York and its members. The Exchanges' complaint alleged that the 1968 amendment unconstitutionally discriminates against interstate commerce by imposing a greater tax burden on securities transactions involving out-of-state sales than on transactions of the same magnitude involving in-state sales.

. . . .

I

New York Tax Law §270.1 provides that "all sales, or agreements to sell, or memoranda of sales and all deliveries or transfers of shares or certificates of stock" in any foreign or domestic corporation are subject to the transfer tax. Administrative regulations promulgated with respect to the transfer tax provide that the tax applies if any one of the five taxable events occurs within New York, regardless of where the rest of the transaction takes place, and that if more than one taxable event occurs in the State, only one tax is payable on the entire transaction. For transactions involving sales, the rate of tax depends on the selling price per share and the total tax liability is determined by the number of shares sold. Thus, under the unamended version of §270, a transaction involving a sale and a transfer of shares in New York was taxed the same as a transaction involving an in-state transfer but an out-of-state sale. In both instances, the occasion for the tax was the occurrence of at least one taxable event in the State, the rate of tax was based solely on the price of the securities, and the total tax was determined by the number of shares sold. The Exchanges do not challenge the constitutionality of §270.

None of the States in which the appellant Exchanges are located taxes the sale or transfer of securities. During the 1960's the New York Stock Exchange became concerned that the New York transfer tax created a competitive disadvantage for New York trading and was thus responsible for the growth of out-of-state exchanges. In response to this concern and fearful that the New York Stock Exchange would relocate outside New York, the legislature in 1968 enacted §270-a to

amend the transfer tax by providing for two deviations from the uniform application of §270 when one of the taxable events, a sale, takes place in New York. First, transactions by nonresidents of New York are afforded a 50% reduction ("nonresident reduction") in the rate of tax when the transaction involves an in-state sale. Taxable transactions by residents (regardless of where the sale is made)[8] and by nonresidents selling outside the State do not benefit from the rate decrease. Second, §270-a limits the total tax liability of any taxpayer (resident or nonresident) to $350 (maximum tax) for a single transaction when it involves a New York sale. If a sale is made out-of-state, the §270 tax rate applies to an in-state transfer (or other taxable event) without limitation.

. . . .

[The Court reviews the legislative history of §270-a and quotes Governor Rockefeller that the purpose of the change was to provide long-term relief from the

---

8. The Exchanges do not challenge New York's authority to tax residents in a greater amount than nonresidents as long as the extent of the tax burden does not depend on an out-of-state sale.

competitive pressures of the regional exchanges.] Appellant Exchanges contend that the legislative history states explicitly what is implicit in the operation of §270-a: The amendment imposes an unequal tax burden on out-of-state sales in order to protect an in-state business. They argue that this discrimination is impermissible under the Commerce Clause. Appellees do not dispute the statements of the legislature and the Governor that §270-a is a measure to reduce out-of-state competition with an in-state business. They agree, however, with the holding of the Court of Appeals that the legislature has chosen a nondiscriminatory, and therefore constitutionally permissible, means of "encouraging" sales on the New York Stock Exchange. We hold that §270-a discriminates against interstate commerce in violation of the Commerce Clause.

II

. . . .

[T]he fundamental principle that we find dispositive of the case now before us [is]: No State, consistent with the Commerce Clause, may "impose a tax which discriminates against interstate commerce . . . by providing a direct commercial advantage to local business." Northwestern States Portland Cement, 358 U.S. at 457. See also Halliburton Oil Well Co., 373 U.S. 64 (1963); Nippert v. Richmond, 327 U.S. 416 (1946). The prohibition against discriminatory treatment of interstate commerce follows inexorably from the basic purpose of the Clause. Permitting the individual States to enact laws that favor local enterprises at the expense of out-of-state businesses "would invite a multiplication of preferential trade areas destructive" of the free trade which the Clause protects. Dean Milk Co., 340 U.S. at 356.

Although apparently accepting the teaching of the prior cases, the Court of Appeals seemed to view §270-a as "compensatory legislation" enacted to "neutralize" the competitive advantage §270 conferred on stock exchanges outside New York. Thus, it analogized the New York statute to state use taxes which have survived Commerce Clause challenges. The statute will not support this characterization.

Prior to the 1968 amendment, the New York transfer tax was neutral as to in-state and out-of-state sales. Just like a use tax an in-state transfer or delivery of securities triggered the tax and the burden fell equally on all transactions regardless of the situs of sale. Thus, the choice of an exchange for the sale of securities that would be transferred or delivered in New York was not influenced by the transfer tax; wherever the sale was made, tax liability would arise. The flow of interstate commerce in securities was channeled neither into nor out of New York by the state tax.[11]

Section 270-a upset this equilibrium. After the amendment took effect, a nonresident contemplating the sale of securities that would be delivered or transferred in New York faced two possible tax burdens. If he elected to sell on an out-of-state exchange, the higher rates of §270 applied without limitation on the total tax liability; if he sold the securities on a New York exchange, the one-half rate of §270-a applied and then only up to a $350 tax liability. Similarly, residents engaging in large block transactions on the New York exchanges were subject to a maximum tax levy of $350; but if they sold out-of-State, their tax bill would be limited only by the number of shares sold. Thus, under §270-a the choice of exchange by all nonresidents and by residents engaging in large transactions is not made solely on the basis of nontax criteria. Because of the delivery or transfer in New York, the seller cannot escape tax liability by selling out of State, but he can substantially reduce his liability by selling in State. The obvious effect of the tax is to extend a financial advantage to sales on the New York exchanges at the expense of the regional exchanges. Rather than "compensating" New York for a supposed competitive disadvantage resulting from §270, the amendment forecloses tax-neutral decisions and creates both an advantage for the exchanges in New York and a discriminatory burden on commerce to its sister States.
. . . .

. . . In all the use-tax cases, an individual faced with the choice of an in-state or out-of-state purchase could make that choice without regard to the tax consequences. If he purchased in State, he paid a sales tax; if he purchased out of State but carried the article back for use in State, he paid a use tax of the same amount. The taxes treated both transactions in the same manner.

---

11. Of course, the unamended §270 did discourage sales in New York when no other taxable event would occur in that State, since out-of-state sales would not be taxed at all while in-state sales would be taxed at the full rate. Section 270-a, however, does not neutralize this competitive disadvantage of the New York exchanges. Although the reduced tax of the amendment decreases the disincentive to trade out of State, to the extent that any tax is imposed on transactions involving only an in-state sale, sales in New York are discouraged. Had New York sought to eliminate the only competitive edge enjoyed by the regional exchanges as a result of §270, it could have done so without burdening commerce to its sister States by simply declaring that sales would not be a taxable event. Under that system, sellers who would not otherwise be liable for the tax would not incur liability by electing to sell on a New York exchange.

Because it imposes a greater tax liability on out-of-state sales than on in-state sales, the New York transfer tax, as amended by §270-a, falls short of the substantially evenhanded treatment demanded by the Commerce Clause. The extra tax burden on out-of-state sales created by §270-a is not what the New York Court of Appeals holds it out to be; it neither compensates for a like burden on in-state sales, nor neutralizes an economic advantage previously enjoyed by the appellant Exchanges because of §270.[12]

III

The court below further attempted to save §270-a from invalidation under the Commerce Clause by finding that the effect the amendment might have on sales by residents and nonresidents did not amount to unconstitutional discrimination. As to New York residents, the court found that the higher tax on large out-of-state sales would have no "practical" effect since "it is more than likely . . . that the sale would be made on a New York exchange in any event." As to the discriminatory tax burden on all out-of-state sales by nonresidents, the court observed that because New York sales by nonresidents also involve interstate commerce, §270-a does not discriminate against interstate commerce in favor of intrastate commerce; rather, it discriminates between two kinds of interstate transactions. Although it did not so state, the Court of Appeals apparently believed that such discrimination was permissible under the Commerce Clause. We disagree with the Court of Appeals with respect to both residents and nonresidents.

The maximum tax discrimination against out-of-state sales by residents is not triggered until the taxed transaction involves a substantial number of shares. Investors, institutional and individual, engaging in such large-block transactions can be expected to choose an exchange on the basis of services, prices, and other market conditions rather than geographical proximity.

Even a small difference in price (of either the securities or the sales services) can, in a large sale, provide a substantial enough additional profit to outweigh whatever additional transaction costs might be incurred from trading on an out-of-state exchange. The New York Legislature, in its legislative findings in connection with §270-a, recognized that securities transactions by residents were not being conducted only on the New York exchanges; it therefore considered the amendment necessary to "[retain] within the state of New York . . . sales involving large blocks of stock." If, as the Court of Appeals assumed, it were "more than likely" that residents would sell in New York, there would have been no reason for the legislature to reduce the tax burden on in-state sales by residents in order to retain their sales in New York. Nor is the discriminatory burden of the maximum tax insubstantial. On a transaction of 30,000 shares selling at $20 or more, for example, the tax on an in-state sale is the maximum $350, while an out-of-state sale is taxed $1,500. The disparity between the two taxes increases with the number of shares sold. Such a large tax penalty for trading on out-of-state markets cannot be deemed to have no practical effect on interstate commerce.[13]

Both the maximum tax and the rate reduction provisions of §270-a discriminate against out-of-state sales by non-residents. The fact that this discrimination is in favor of nonresident, in-state sales which may also be considered as interstate commerce, see Freeman v. Hewit, 329 U.S. at 258-259, does not save §270-a from the restrictions of the Commerce Clause. A State may no more use discriminatory taxes to assure that nonresidents direct their commerce to businesses within the State than to assure that residents trade only in intrastate commerce. As we stated at the outset, the fundamental purpose of the Clause is to assure that there be free trade among the several States. This free trade purpose is not confined to the freedom to trade with only one State; it is a freedom to trade with any State, to engage in commerce across all state boundaries.

There has been no prior occasion expressly to address the question whether a State may tax in a manner that discriminates between two types of interstate

---

12. Because of the discrimination inherent in §270-a, we also reject the Commission's argument that the tax should be sustained because it is imposed on a local event at the end of interstate commerce. While it is true that, absent an undue burden on interstate commerce, the Commerce Clause does not prohibit the States from taxing the transfer of property within the State, the tax may not discriminate between transactions on the basis of some interstate element. International Harvester Co. v. Department of Treasury, 322 U.S. at 347-348. As was held in Welton v. Missouri, 91 U.S. 275, 282 (1876): "[T]he commercial power [of the Federal Government] continues until the commodity has ceased to be the subject of discriminating legislation by reason of its foreign character. That power protects it, even after it has entered the State, from any burdens imposed by reason of its foreign origin."

13. Even if we did not conclude that large-block sellers are likely to rely on economic rather than geographical factors in choosing an exchange, §270-a would fall before the Commerce Clause. Whatever the current inclinations of New York investors, the Clause protects out-of-state businesses from any discriminatory burden on their interstate commercial activities. Even if the tax is not now the sole cause of New York residents' refusal to trade on out-of-state exchanges, at the very least it reinforces their choice of an in-state exchange and is an inhibiting force to selling out of State; that inhibition is an unconstitutional barrier to the free flow of commerce.

transactions in order to favor local commercial interests over out-of-state businesses, but the clear import of our Commerce Clause cases is that such discrimination is constitutionally impermissible. Guy v. Baltimore, 100 U.S. at 443, held that no State, consistent with the Commerce Clause, may "build up its domestic commerce by means of unequal and oppressive burdens upon the industry and business of other States"; and in Baldwin v. G.A.F. Seelig, Inc., 294 U.S. 511 (1935), New York was prohibited from regulating the price of out-of-state milk purchases because the effect of that regulation would be "to suppress or mitigate the consequences of competition between the states."[14] More recently, we noted that this "Court has viewed with particular suspicion state statutes requiring business operations to be performed in the home State that could more efficiently be performed elsewhere. Even where the State is pursuing a clearly legitimate local interest, this particular burden on commerce has been declared to be virtually per se illegal." Pike v. Bruce Church, Inc., 397 U.S. at 145. Cf. Halliburton Oil Well Co., 373 U.S. at 72-73.

Although the statutes at issue in those cases had the primary effect of prohibiting or discriminatorily burdening a resident's purchase of out-of-state goods and services, the constitutional policy of free trade and competition that led to their demise is equally fatal to the New York transfer tax. New York's discriminatory treatment of out-of-state sales is made possible only because some other taxable event (transfer, delivery, or agreement to sell) takes place in the State. Thus, the State is using its power to tax an in-state operation as a means of "requiring [other] business operations to be performed in the home State." As a consequence, the flow of securities sales is diverted from the most economically efficient channels and directed to New York. This diversion of interstate commerce and diminution of free competition in securities sales are wholly inconsistent with the free trade purpose of the Commerce Clause.

IV

Our decision today does not prevent the States from structuring their tax systems to encourage the growth and development of intrastate commerce and industry. Nor do we hold that a State may not compete with other States for a share of interstate commerce; such competition lies at the heart of a free trade policy. We hold only that in the process of competition no State may discriminatorily tax the products manufactured or the business operations performed in any other State.

---

14. Baldwin is particularly relevant to this case. After holding that the Commerce Clause prohibits obstructions to competition between the States, Mr. Justice Cardozo expressly rejected the proposition that such obstructions may be justified as measures to assure the economic health of local industry:

"If New York, in order to promote the economic welfare of her farmers, may guard them against competition with the cheaper prices of Vermont, the door has been opened to rivalries and reprisals that were meant to be averted by subjecting commerce between the states to the power of the nation."

. . . .

"The Constitution was framed under the dominion of a political philosophy less parochial in range. It was framed upon the theory that the peoples of the several states must sink or swim together, and that in the long run prosperity and salvation are in union and not division." 294 U.S. at 522-523.

For the same reasons that Baldwin rejected New York's attempts to protect its dairy industry from competition from without, we now reject a similar attempt to protect New York's securities industry.

Questions and Comments

1. State A offers nonresidents a property tax exemption for five years for any property bought in State A after the enactment of the legislation. Constitutional? Cf. *Allied Stores*, in the Equal Protection Clause chapter.

2. Would it be constitutional for New York City to grant a property tax abatement to the New York Stock Exchange, which, by reducing an operating cost, would allow the Exchange to compete better with regional exchanges? Could New York grant a subsidy to the Exchange rather than an abatement?

3. As part of its corporate income tax, New York offers an investment tax credit for investment in property located in New York. Many states offer similar credits or other types of tax incentives to encourage taxpayers to move their operations to that state or to encourage existing businesses to expand within that state rather than expanding elsewhere. Would you characterize these provisions as "attempts to foreclose tax neutral decisions"? If so, are all of these incentives unconstitutional? If not, how would you define a tax neutral decision or distinguish these incentives?

4. Was the statute at issue internally consistent? Externally consistent?

5. Did the Court balance New York's interests with the burden imposed on interstate commerce? In non-tax cases involving a provision that is being challenged under the Commerce Clause, the Court has stated that when a state provision "regulates evenhandedly to effectuate a legitimate local public interest, and its effects on interstate commerce are only incidental, it will be upheld unless the burden imposed on such commerce is clearly excessive in relation to the putative local benefits. *Huron Cement Co. v. Detroit*, 362 U.S. 440, 443.

If a legitimate local purpose is found, then the question becomes one of degree. And the extent of the burden that will be tolerated will of course depend on the nature of the local interest involved, and on whether it could be promoted as well with a lesser impact on interstate activities. Occasionally the Court has candidly undertaken a balancing approach in resolving these issues, *Southern Pacific Co. v. Arizona*, 325 U.S. 761, but more frequently it has spoken in terms of 'direct' and 'indirect' effects and burdens." *Pike* v. *Bruce Church, Inc.*, 397 U.S. 137, 142 (1970). Did the Court adopt a similar approach in *Boston Stock*?

6. Is a tax that discriminates against interstate commerce constitutional if it is imposed on a local event preceding or subsequent to such commerce?

7. Could the challenged provisions be characterized as offsetting the preexisting tax's effect of diverting certain sales out of New York? See Peter D. Enrich, *Saving the States from Themselves: Commerce Clause Constraints on State Tax Incentives for Business*, 110 Harv. L. Rev. 378, 464-65 (1996).

8. While *Boston Stock* was on appeal, federal law was changed to prohibit a state from taxing a change in the beneficial or record ownership of securities merely because the transfer agent's facilities are located in the taxing state. 15 U.S.C. § 78bb(d)(1982).

9. Why did the plaintiffs have standing?

10. For critical commentary on *Boston Stock Exchange*, see David P. Falck, *Taxes and Bounties Burdening Interstate Commerce: Distinguishing Boston Stock Exchange from Alexandria Scrap*, 34 Wash & Lee L. Rev. 979 (1977).

Japan Line, Ltd., et al. v. County of Los Angeles et al.
Supreme Court of the United States, 1979.
441 U.S. 434, 99 S. Ct. 1813, 60 L. Ed. 2d 336.

MR. JUSTICE BLACKMUN delivered the opinion of the Court.

. . . .

This case presents the question whether a State, consistently with the Commerce Clause of the Constitution, may impose a nondiscriminatory ad valorem property tax on foreign-owned instrumentalities (cargo containers) of international commerce.

Appellants are six Japanese shipping companies; they are incorporated under the laws of Japan, and they have their principal places of business and commercial domiciles in that country. Appellants operate vessels used exclusively in foreign commerce; these vessels are registered in Japan and have their home ports there. The vessels are specifically designed and constructed to accommodate large cargo shipping containers. The containers, like the ships, are owned by appellants, have their home ports in Japan, and are used exclusively for hire in the transportation of cargo in foreign commerce. Each container is in constant transit save for time spent undergoing repair or awaiting loading and unloading of cargo. All appellants' containers are subject to property tax in Japan and, in fact, are taxed there.

. . . . Appellants' containers, in the course of their international journeys, pass through appellees' jurisdictions intermittently. Although none of appellants' containers stays permanently in California, some are there at any given time; a container's average stay in the State is less than three weeks. The containers engage in no intrastate or interstate transportation of cargo except as continuations of international voyages. Any movements or periods of nonmovement of containers in appellees' jurisdictions are essential to, and inseparable from, the containers' efficient use as instrumentalities of foreign commerce.

Property present in California on March 1, (the "lien date" under California law) of any year is subject to ad valorem property tax. A number of appellants' containers were physically present in appellees jurisdictions on the lien dates in 1970, 1971, and, 1972; this number was fairly representative of the containers' "average presence" during each year. Appellees levied property taxes in excess of $550,000 on the assessed value of the containers present on March 1 of the three years in question. During the same period, similar containers owned or controlled by steamship companies domiciled in the United States, that appeared from time to time in Japan during the course of international commerce, were not subject to property taxation in Japan, and therefore were not, in fact, taxed in that country.

. . . .

III

A

The "home port doctrine" was first alluded to in Hays v. Pacific Mail S. S. Co., 17 How. 596 (1855). In Hays, California sought to impose property taxes on oceangoing vessels intermittently touching its ports. The vessels' home port was New York City, where they were owned, registered, and based; they engaged in intercoastal commerce by way of the Isthmus of Panama, and remained in California briefly to unload cargo and undergo repairs. This Court held that the ships had established no tax situs in California:

"We are satisfied that the State of California had no jurisdiction over these vessels for the purpose of taxation; they were not, properly, abiding within its limits, so as to become incorporated with the other personal property of the State; they were there but

temporarily, engaged in lawful trade and commerce, with their situs at the home port, where the vessels belonged, and where the owners were liable to be taxed for the capital invested, and where the taxes had been paid." Id., at 599-600.

Because the vessels were properly taxable in their home port, this Court concluded, they could not be taxed in California at all.

The "home port doctrine" enunciated in Hays was a corollary of the medieval maxim mobilia sequuntur personam ("movables follow the person," and resulted in personal property being taxable in full at the domicile of the owner. This theory of taxation, of course, has fallen into desuetude, and the "home port doctrine," as a rule for taxation of moving equipment, has yielded to a rule of fair apportionment among the States. This Court, accordingly, has held that various instrumentalities of commerce may be taxed, on a properly apportioned basis, by the nondomiciliary States through which they travel. In discarding the "home port" theory for the theory of apportionment, however, the Court consistently has distinguished the case of oceangoing vessels. E.g., Pullman's Palace, 141 U.S. at 23-24 (approving apportioned tax on railroad rolling stock, but distinguishing vessels "engaged in interstate or foreign commerce upon the high seas"); Ott, 336 U.S. at 173-174 (approving apportioned tax on barges navigating inland waterways, but "not reach[ing] the question of taxability of ocean carriage"); Braniff, 347 U.S. at 600 (approving apportioned tax on domestic aircraft, but distinguishing vessels "used to plow the open seas"). Relying on these cases, appellants argue that the "home port doctrine," yet vital, continues to prescribe the proper rule for state taxation of oceangoing ships. Since containers are "functionally a part of the ship," Leather's Best, Inc. v. S. S. Mormaclynx, 451 F.2d 800, 815 (CA2 1971), appellants conclude, the containers, like the ships, may be taxed only at their home ports in Japan, and thus are immune from tax in California.

Although appellants' argument, as will be seen below, has an inner logic, we decline to cast our analysis of the present case in this mold. The "home port doctrine" can claim no unequivocal constitutional source; in assessing the legitimacy of California's tax, the Hays Court did not rely on the Commerce Clause, nor could it, in 1854, have relied on the Due Process Clause of the Fourteenth Amendment. The basis of the "home port doctrine," rather, was common-law jurisdiction to tax. Given its origins, the doctrine could be said to be "anachronistic"; given its underpinnings, it may indeed be said to have been "abandoned." Northwest Airlines, Inc. v. Minnesota, 322 U.S. at 320 (Stone, C.J., dissenting). As a theoretical matter, then, to rehabilitate the "home port doctrine" as a tool of Commerce Clause analysis would be somewhat odd. More importantly, to hold in this case that the "home port doctrine" survives would be to prove too much. If an oceangoing vessel could indeed be taxed only at its home port, taxation by a nondomiciliary State logically would be barred, regardless of whether the vessel were domestically or foreign owned, and regardless of whether it were engaged in domestic or foreign commerce. In Hays itself, the vessel was owned in New York and was engaged in interstate commerce through international waters. There is no need in this case to decide currently the broad proposition whether mere use of international routes is enough, under the "home port doctrine," to render an instrumentality immune from tax in a nondomiciliary State. The question here is a much more narrow one, that is, whether instrumentalities of commerce that are owned, based, and registered abroad and that are used exclusively in international commerce, may be subjected to apportioned ad valorem property taxation by a State.[7]

B

In construing Congress' power to "regulate Commerce . . . among the several States," the Court recently has affirmed that the Constitution confers no immunity from state taxation, and that "interstate commerce must bear its fair share of the state tax burden." Assn. of Wash. Stevedoring, 435 U.S. at 750. Instrumentalities of interstate commerce are no exception to this rule, and the Court regularly has sustained property taxes as applied to various forms of transportation equipment. See Pullman's Palace, supra (railroad rolling stock); Ott, supra (barges on inland waterways); Braniff, supra (domestic aircraft). Cf. Central Greyhound Lines, 334 U.S. at 663 (motor vehicles). If the state tax "is applied to an activity with a substantial nexus with the taxing State, is fairly apportioned, does not discriminate against interstate commerce, and is fairly related to the services provided by the State," no impermissible burden on interstate commerce will be found.

Appellees contend that cargo shipping containers, like other vehicles of commercial transport, are subject to property taxation, and that the taxes imposed here meet Complete Auto's fourfold requirements. The containers, they argue, have a "substantial nexus" with California

because some of them are present in that State at all times; jurisdiction to tax is based on "the habitual employment of the property within the State," Braniff, 347 U.S. at 601, and appellants' containers habitually are so employed. The tax, moreover, is "fairly apportioned," since it is levied only on the containers' "average presence" in California.[8] The tax "does not discriminate," thirdly, since it falls evenhandedly on all personal property in the State; indeed, as an ad valorem tax of general application, it is of necessity nondiscriminatory. The tax, finally, is "fairly related to the services provided by" California, services that include not only police and fire protection, but also the benefits of a trained work force and the advantages of a civilized society.

These observations are not without force. We may assume that, if the containers at issue here were instrumentalities of purely interstate commerce, Complete Auto would apply and be satisfied, and our Commerce Clause inquiry would be at an end. Appellants' containers, however, are instrumentalities of foreign commerce, both as a matter of fact and as a matter of law.[10] The premise of appellees' argument is that the Commerce Clause analysis is identical, regardless of whether interstate or foreign commerce is involved. This premise, we have concluded, must be rejected. When construing Congress' power to "regulate Commerce with foreign Nations," a more extensive constitutional inquiry is required.

---

8. By taxing property present on the "lien date," California roughly apportions its property tax for mobile goods like containers. For example, if each of appellants' containers is in California for three weeks a year, the number present on any arbitrarily selected date would be roughly 3/52 of the total entering the State that year. Taxing 3/52 of the containers at full value, however, is the same as taxing all the containers at 3/52 value. Thus, California effectively apportions its tax to reflect the containers' "average presence," i.e., the time each container spends in the State per year.

10. Appellants' containers entered the United States pursuant to the Customs Convention on Containers, which grants containers "temporary admission free of import duties and import taxes and free of import prohibitions and restrictions," provided they are used solely in foreign commerce and are subject to re-exportation. 20 U.S.T., at 304. Similarly, 19 CFR §10.41a(a)(3)(1978) designates containers "instruments of international traffic," with the result that they "may be released without entry or the payment of duty" under 19 U.S.C. § 1322 (a). See 19 CFR §10.41a (a)(1) (1978). A bilateral tax Convention between Japan and the United States associates containers with the vehicles that carry them, and provides that income "derived by a resident of a Contracting State . . . from the use, maintenance, and lease of containers and related equipment . . . in connection with the operation in international traffic of ships or aircraft . . . is exempt from tax in the other Contracting State." Convention Between the United States of America and Japan for the Avoidance of Double Taxation, Mar. 8, 1971.

---

7. Accordingly, we do not reach questions as to the taxability of foreign-owned instrumentalities engaged in interstate commerce, or of domestically owned instrumentalities engaged in foreign commerce. Cf. Sea-Land Service, Inc. v. County of Alameda, 528 P.2d 56 (1974) (domestically owned containers used in intercoastal and foreign commerce held subject to apportioned property tax); Flying Tiger Line, Inc. v. County of Los Angeles, 333 P.2d 323 (1958) (domestically owned aircraft used in foreign commerce held subject to apportioned property tax).

When a State seeks to tax the instrumentalities of foreign commerce, two additional considerations, beyond those articulated in Complete Auto, come into play. The first is the enhanced risk of multiple taxation. It is a commonplace of constitutional jurisprudence that multiple taxation may well be offensive to the Commerce Clause. In order to prevent multiple taxation of interstate commerce, this Court has required that taxes be apportioned among taxing jurisdictions, so that no instrumentality of commerce is subjected to more than one tax on its full value. The corollary of the apportionment principle, of course, is that no jurisdiction may tax the instrumentality in full. "The rule which permits taxation by two or more states on an apportionment basis precludes taxation of all of the property by the state of the domicile. . . . Otherwise there would be multiple taxation of interstate operations." Standard Oil Co. v. Peck, 342 U.S. at 384-385; Braniff, 347 U.S. at 601. The basis for this Court's approval of apportioned property taxation, in other words, has been its ability to enforce full apportionment by all potential taxing bodies.

Yet neither this Court nor this Nation can ensure full apportionment when one of the taxing entities is a foreign sovereign. If an instrumentality of commerce is domiciled abroad, the country of domicile may have the right, consistently with the custom of nations, to impose a tax on its full value.[11] If a State should seek to tax the same instrumentality on an apportioned basis, multiple taxation inevitably results. Hence, whereas the fact of apportionment in interstate commerce means that "multiple burdens logically cannot occur," Washington Revenue Dept., 435 U.S. at 746-747, the same conclusion, as to foreign commerce, logically cannot be drawn. Due to the absence of an authoritative tribunal capable of ensuring that the aggregation of taxes is computed on no more than one full value, a state tax, even though "fairly apportioned" to reflect an instrumentality's presence within the State, may subject foreign commerce "'to the risk of a double tax burden to which [domestic] commerce is not exposed, and which the commerce clause forbids.'" Evco v. Jones, 409 U.S. at 94, quoting J. D. Adams Mfg. Co., 304 U.S. at 311.

Second, a state tax on the instrumentalities of foreign commerce may impair federal uniformity in an area where federal uniformity is essential. Foreign commerce is preeminently a matter of national concern. "In international relations and with respect to foreign intercourse and trade the people of the United States act through a single government with unified and adequate national power." Board of Trustees v. United States, 289 U.S. 48, 59 (1933). Although the Constitution, Art. I, § 8, cl. 3, grants Congress power to regulate commerce "with foreign Nations" and "among the several States" in parallel phrases, there is evidence that the Founders intended the scope of the foreign commerce power to be the greater. Cases of this Court, stressing the need for uniformity in treating with other nations, echo this distinction. In approving state taxes on the instrumentalities of interstate commerce, the Court consistently has distinguished oceangoing traffic; these cases reflect an awareness that the taxation of foreign commerce may necessitate a uniform national rule. Indeed, in Pullman's Palace, the Court wrote that the "'vehicles of commerce by water being instruments of intercommunication with other nations, the regulation of them is assumed by the national legislature.'" 141 U.S. at 24, quoting Railroad Co. v. Maryland, 21 Wall. at 470. Finally, in discussing the Import-Export Clause, this Court, in Michelin Tire Corp., 423 U.S. at 285, spoke of the Framers' overriding concern that "the Federal Government must speak with one voice when regulating commercial relations with foreign governments." The need for federal uniformity is no less paramount in ascertaining the negative implications of Congress' power to "regulate Commerce with foreign Nations" under the Commerce Clause.[14]

---

11. Oceangoing vessels, for example, are generally taxed only in their nation of registry; this fact in part explains the phenomenon of "flags of convenience" (a term deemed derogatory in some quarters), whereby vessels are registered under the flags of countries that permit the operation of ships "at a nominal level of taxation." See B. Boczek, Flags of Convenience 5, 56-57 (1962). Aircraft engaged in international traffic, apparently, are likewise "subject to taxation on an unapportioned basis by their country of origin."

14. The policies animating the Import-Export Clause and the Commerce Clause are much the same. In Michelin, the Court noted that the Import-Export Clause met three main concerns: "[T]he Federal Government must speak with one voice when regulating commercial relations with foreign governments. . .; import revenues were to be the major source of revenue of the Federal Government and should not be diverted to the States; and harmony among the States might be disturbed unless seaboard States . . . were prohibited from levying taxes on [goods in transit]." 423 U.S. at 285-286 (footnotes omitted). See 25 Minn. L. Rev., at 448, and n. 67, 452, and n. 81, 456-457, and n. 110 (need to deal in unified manner with foreign nations); id., at 446-451 (need to preserve federal revenue); id., at 448-449, and nn. 69-70, 470-471, 472-473 (need to prevent disharmony among States on account of import duties). In Washington Revenue Dept. v. Association of Wash. Stevedoring Cos., 435 U.S. 734 (1978), we noted that the third Michelin factor–preserving harmony among the States–mandated the same inquiry as to the effect of a state tax as the Interstate Commerce Clause. See id., at 754-755. In this case, similarly, the first Michelin factor–the need to speak with one voice when regulating commercial relations with foreign governments–mandates the same inquiry as to the effect of a state tax as the Foreign Commerce Clause. In Washington Revenue Dept., the Court, holding that the state tax at issue did not prevent

A state tax on instrumentalities of foreign commerce may frustrate the achievement of federal uniformity in several ways. If the State imposes an apportioned tax, international disputes over reconciling apportionment formulae may arise. If a novel state tax creates an asymmetry in the international tax structure, foreign nations disadvantaged by the levy may retaliate against American-owned instrumentalities present in their jurisdictions. Such retaliation of necessity would be directed at American transportation equipment in general, not just that of the taxing State, so that the Nation as a whole would suffer. If other States followed the taxing State's example, various instrumentalities of commerce could be subjected to varying degrees of multiple taxation, a result that would plainly prevent this Nation from "speaking with one voice" in regulating foreign commerce.

For these reasons, we believe that an inquiry more elaborate than that mandated by Complete Auto is necessary when a State seeks to tax the instrumentalities of foreign, rather than of interstate, commerce. In addition to answering the nexus, apportionment, and nondiscrimination questions posed in Complete Auto, a court must also inquire, first, whether the tax, notwithstanding apportionment, creates a substantial risk of international multiple taxation, and, second, whether the tax prevents the Federal Government from "speaking with one voice when regulating commercial relations with foreign governments." If a state tax contravenes either of these precepts, it is unconstitutional under the Commerce Clause.

C

Analysis of California's tax under these principles dictates that the tax, as applied to appellants' containers, is impermissible. Assuming, arguendo, that the tax passes muster under Complete Auto, it cannot withstand scrutiny under either of the additional tests that a tax on foreign commerce must satisfy.

First, California's tax results in multiple taxation of the instrumentalities of foreign commerce. By stipulation, appellants' containers are owned, based, and registered in Japan; they are used exclusively in international commerce; and they remain outside Japan only so long as needed to complete their international missions. Under these circumstances, Japan has the right and the power to tax the containers in full. California's tax, however, creates more than the risk of multiple taxation; it produces multiple taxation in fact. Appellants' containers not only "are subject to property tax . . . in Japan," but, as

the trial court found, "are, in fact, taxed in Japan." Thus, if appellees' levies were sustained, appellants "would be paying a double tax."[17]

Second, California's tax prevents this Nation from "speaking with one voice" in regulating foreign trade. The desirability of uniform treatment of containers used exclusively in foreign commerce is evidenced by the Customs Convention on Containers, which the United States and Japan have signed. Under this Convention, containers temporarily imported are admitted free of "all duties and taxes whatsoever chargeable by reason of importation." 20 U.S.T., at 304. The Convention reflects a national policy to remove impediments to the use of containers as "instruments of international traffic." 19 U.S.C. § 1322(a). California's tax, however, will frustrate attainment of federal uniformity. It is stipulated that American-owned containers are not taxed in Japan. California's tax thus creates an asymmetry in international maritime taxation operating to Japan's disadvantage. The risk of retaliation by Japan, under these circumstances, is acute, and such retaliation of necessity would be felt by the Nation as a whole.[18] If other States follow California's

---

17. The stipulation of facts, like the trial court's finding, states that "[a]ll containers of [appellants] are subject to property tax and are, in fact, taxed in Japan." The record does not further elaborate on the nature of Japan's property tax. Appellants have uniformly insisted that Japan's property tax is unapportioned, i.e., that it is imposed on the containers' full value, and we so understand the trial court's finding. Although appellees do not seriously challenge this understanding, amicus curiae Multistate Tax Commission suggests that the record is inadequate to establish double taxation in fact: Japan, amicus says, may offer "credits . . . for taxes paid elsewhere." Amicus provides no evidence to support this theory. Both the Solicitor General, Brief for United States as Amicus Curiae and the Department of State assure us that Japan taxes appellants' containers at their "full value," and we accept this interpretation of the trial court's factual finding.

Because California's tax in this case creates multiple taxation in fact, we have no occasion here to decide under what circumstances the mere *risk* of multiple taxation would invalidate a state tax, or whether this risk would be evaluated differently in foreign, as opposed to interstate, commerce. Compare Moorman Mfg. Co., 437 U.S. at 276-277, and Assn. of Wash. Stevedoring, 435 U.S. at 746, with, e.g., Central R. Co. v. Pennsylvania, 370 U.S. at 615; Ott v. Mississippi Barge Line Co., 336 U.S. at 175; and Northwest Airlines, Inc., 322 U.S. at 326 (Stone, C.J., dissenting).

18. Retaliation by some nations could be automatic. West Germany's wealth tax statute, for example, provides an exemption for foreign-owned instrumentalities of commerce, but only if the owner's country grants a reciprocal exemption for German-owned instrumentalities. Vermogensteuergesetz (VStG), Art. 1, § 2(3), reprinted in I Bundesgesetzblatt (BGB1) 950 (Apr. 23, 1974). The European Economic Community (EEC), when apprised of California's tax on foreign-owned containers,

---

"speaking with one voice," noted: "No foreign business or vessel is taxed." 435 U.S. at 754.

example (Oregon already has done so), foreign-owned containers will be subjected to various degrees of multiple taxation, depending on which American ports they enter. This result, obviously, would make "speaking with one voice" impossible. California, by its unilateral act, cannot be permitted to place these impediments before this Nation's conduct of its foreign relations and its foreign trade.

Because California's ad valorem tax, as applied to appellants' containers, results in multiple taxation of the instrumentalities of foreign commerce, and because it prevents the Federal Government from "speaking with one voice" in international trade, the tax is inconsistent with Congress' power to "regulate Commerce with foreign Nations." We hold the tax, as applied, unconstitutional under the Commerce Clause.

D

Appellees proffer several objections to this holding. They contend, first, that any multiple taxation in this case is attributable, not to California, but to Japan. California, they say, is just trying to take its share; it should not be foreclosed by Japan's election to tax the containers in full. California's tax, however, must be evaluated in the realistic framework of the custom of nations. Japan has the right and the power to tax appellants' containers at their full value; nothing could prevent it from doing so. Appellees' argument may have force in the interstate commerce context. Cf. Moorman Mfg. Co., 437 U.S. at 277, and n.12 (1978). In interstate commerce, if the domiciliary State is "to blame" for exacting an excessive tax, this Court is able to insist upon rationalization of the apportionment. As noted above, however, this Court is powerless to correct malapportionment of taxes imposed from abroad in foreign commerce.

Appellees contend, secondly, that any multiple taxation created by California's tax can be cured by congressional action or by international agreement. We find no merit in this contention. The premise of appellees' argument is that a State is free to impose demonstrable burdens on commerce, so long as Congress has not pre-empted the field by affirmative regulation. But it long has been "accepted constitutional doctrine that the commerce clause, without the aid of Congressional legislation. . . affords some protection from state legislation inimical to the national commerce, and that in such cases, where Congress has not acted, this Court, and not the state legislature, is under the commerce clause the final arbiter of the competing demands of state and national

interests." Southern Pacific Co. v. Arizona ex rel. Sullivan, 325 U.S. at 769. Accord, Hughes v. Oklahoma, ante, at 326, and n. 2; Boston Stock Exchange, 429 U.S. at 328. Appellees' argument, moreover, defeats, rather than supports, the cause it aims to promote. For to say that California has created a problem susceptible only of congressional–indeed, only of international–solution is to concede that the taxation of foreign-owned containers is an area where a uniform federal rule is essential. California may not tell this Nation or Japan how to run their foreign policies.

Third, California appellees argue that, even if California's tax results in multiple taxation, that fact, after Moorman, is insufficient to condemn a state tax under the Commerce Clause. In Moorman, the Court refused to invalidate Iowa's single-factor income tax apportionment formula, even though it posed a credible threat of overlapping taxation because of the use of three-factor formulae by other States. See also the several opinions in Moorman in dissent. That case, however, is quite different from this one. In Moorman, the existence of multiple taxation, on the record then before the Court, was "speculative," id., at 276; on the record of the present case, multiple taxation is a fact. In Moorman, the problem arose, not from lack of apportionment, but from mathematical imprecision in apportionment formulae. Yet, this Court consistently had held that the Commerce Clause "does not call for mathematical exactness nor for the rigid application of a particular formula; only if the resulting valuation is palpably excessive will it be set aside." Northwest Airlines, 322 U.S. at 325 (Stone, C.J., dissenting). Accord, Moorman, 437 U.S. at 274 (citing cases). This case, by contrast, involves no mere mathematical imprecision in apportionment; it involves a situation where true apportionment does not exist and cannot be policed by this Court at all. Moorman, finally, concerned interstate commerce. This case concerns foreign commerce. Even a slight overlapping of tax–a problem that might be deemed de minimis in a domestic context–assumes importance when sensitive matters of foreign relations and national sovereignty are concerned.

Finally, appellees present policy arguments. If California cannot tax appellants' containers, they complain, the State will lose revenue, even though the containers plainly have a nexus with California; the State will go uncompensated for the services it undeniably renders the containers; and, by exempting appellants' containers from tax, the State in effect will be forced to discriminate against domestic, in favor of foreign, commerce. These arguments are not without weight, and, to the extent appellees cannot recoup the value of their services through user fees, they may indeed be disadvantaged by our decision today. These arguments, however, are directed to the wrong forum. "Whatever subjects of this [the commercial] power are in their nature national, or

apparently determined to consider "suitable counter-measures." Press Release, Council of the European Communities, 521st Council Meeting–Transport (Luxembourg, June 12, 1978), p. 21.

admit only of one uniform system, or plan of regulation, may justly be said to be of such a nature as to require exclusive legislation by Congress." Cooley v. Board of Wardens, 12 How. 299, 319 (1852). The problems to which appellees refer are problems that admit only of a federal remedy. They do not admit of a unilateral solution by a State. The judgment of the Supreme Court of California is reversed.

Questions and Comments

1. In *Wardair Canada, Inc. v. Florida Dept. of Revenue*, 477 U.S. 1 (1986), the Supreme Court held that Florida's sales tax on all aviation fuel sold within the state to airlines, regardless of whether the fuel is used to fly within or without the state, or whether the airline is engaged in a substantial or a nominal amount of business within the state, did not violate the Foreign Commerce Clause. The appellant was a Canadian airline that operated charter flights to and from the United States. The appellant conceded that Florida's tax satisfied the *Complete Auto* tests so that the only issue before the Court was whether *Japan Line* was violated.

2. Why didn't the County of Los Angeles levy its property tax on the ships themselves?

3. Examine footnote 8. What is the assumption underlying footnote 8?

4. Suppose the containers were loaded on trucks and shipped throughout the United States. Could a state levy an apportioned property tax on the containers if they only passed through the state, in transit to other states?

5. Would it have been a better result if the Court had upheld the tax and left it to Congress to intervene if required by foreign commerce concerns?

6. Suppose Japan Line has a Japanese employee who is in California for only part of the year. Assume California taxes such employee on an apportioned share of his income. Constitutional? Can California tax Japan Line on an apportioned share of its taxable income?

7. Does any U.S. treaty prohibit the Los Angeles County property tax? If not, what inference should be drawn about the importance of uniformity in this area?

8. Is there any merit in California's argument that "a state is free to impose demonstrable burdens on commerce, so long as Congress has not preempted the field by affirmative regulation"?

9. Suppose the County of Los Angeles exempted all containers from property taxation but instead imposed a user charge of a flat fee per container. Constitutional?

10. After this case, will it be easier or harder for the United States to convince a foreign country not to tax (or not to allow its subnational governments to tax) the containers of U.S. ships?

11. Is a domestically owned instrumentality of foreign commerce properly subject to an apportioned property tax?

12. Did the Los Angeles County property tax violate the Import-Export Clause?

13. Does the Court's requirement that the tax at issue not create the enhanced risk of multiple taxation suggest that such requirement is not part of *Complete Auto's* third prong?

14. Is the Court correct in its assertion in footnote 18?

15. Imagine that Japan Line competes with a U.S.-owned container shipping company for the lucrative California-Japan route. Does the decision place the U.S.-owned company at a competitive disadvantage?

16. Does the Court hold that a dormant foreign commerce clause exists?

17. What did the Court cite in support of its proposition that "the custom of nations" allowed Japan to tax the containers in full?

18. Did the taxpayer allege that the California tax discriminated against foreign commerce?

19. Can a state discriminate in favor of foreign commerce? See *Sears Roebuck & Co. v. County of Los Angeles*, 85 Cal. App. 3d 763 (1978) (property tax exemption for goods imported from abroad but not for goods brought into California from other states violates Commerce Clause), aff'd without opinion, 449 U.S. 1119 (1981); *Star-Kist Foods, Inc. v. County of Los Angeles* (same), 719 P.2d 987 (1986), cert. den., 480 U.S. 930 (1987).

20. As you read *Itel, Mobil, Container,* and *Barclays,* consider the extent to which *Japan Line* has been eviscerated.

21. For critical commentary on *Japan Line*, see Svetlana V. Petroff, *Constitutional Law–Commerce Clause–State Property Tax on Foreign Commerce–Japan Line, Ltd. v. County of Los Angeles*, 26 N.Y.L. Sch. L. Rev. 619 (1981); Marc W. Sargis, *Japan Line, Ltd. v. County of Los Angeles: The Foreign Commerce Clause: An Economic Approach to the Negative Effects of State Taxation*, 13 J. Marshall L. Rev. 793 (1980); Marguerite E. Howard, *Note, Japan Line, Ltd. v. County of Los Angeles, 441 U.S. 434 (1979)*, 5 Int'l Trade L.J. 319 (1980); Laura Treadgold Oles, *Constitutional Law - The Scope of the Commerce Clause in International Commerce - Japan Line, Ltd. v. County of Los Angeles, 441 U.S. 434 (1979)*, 55 Wash. L. Rev. 885 (1980); Jerome M. Balsam, *The Negative Commerce Clause - A Strict Test for State Taxation of Foreign Commerce - Japan Line, Ltd. v. County of Los Angeles*, N.Y.U. J. Int'l L. & Pol., Spring 1980, at 135; Gary Brookmyer, *Constitutional Limitations on State Taxation of Foreign Commerce: Japan Line, Ltd. v. County of Los Angeles*, 12 Law. Am. 227 (1980); Ann Schulman, *Taxation - State Property Taxation of Instrumentalities of Foreign Commerce - State Ad Valorem Property Taxation of Japanese Shipping Cargo Containers Used Exclusively in Foreign Commerce And Belonging to Companies Based, Registered, and Fully Taxed in Japan, Is Unconstitutional Under the Commerce Clause. Japan Line, Ltd. v. County of Los Angeles, 441 U.S. 434 (1979)*, 15 Tex. Int'l L.J. 213 (1980); William D. Johnson, *Taxation: Taxation of Goods in International Commerce - Japan Line, Ltd. v. County of Los Angeles, 99 S. Ct. 1813 (1979)*, 20 Harv. Int'l L.J. 725 (1979); Ginger S. Barum, *State Ad Valorem Taxes on Instrumentalities of International Commerce: Japan Line, Ltd. v. County of Los Angeles*, 11 Law & Pol'y Int'l Bus. 1213 (1979); Carl Gulliver, *Commerce Clause Limits on Direct Taxation of Foreign Containers: Japan Line, Ltd. v. County of Los Angeles*, 14 J. Int'l L. & Econ. 153 (1979).

Itel Containers Int'l Corp. v. Huddleston, Commissioner of Revenue of Tennessee
Supreme Court of the United States, 1993.
507 U.S. 60, 113 S.Ct. 1095, 122 L. Ed. 2d 421.

JUSTICE KENNEDY delivered the opinion of the Court.

In this case we consider the validity of a state tax affecting cargo containers used in international trade, a subject we have addressed once before. See Japan Line, 441 U.S. 434 (1979). We sustain Tennessee's sales tax on leases of containers owned by a domestic company and used in international shipping.

I

The use of large steel containers to transport goods by truck, rail and ocean-going carrier was a major innovation in transportation technology. In 1990, the United States shipped, by value, 60% of its marine imports and 52% of its marine exports in these containers. Itel Containers, the petitioner here, is a Delaware corporation with its principal place of business in California. Itel's primary business is leasing cargo containers to participants in the international shipping industry, and all its leases restrict use of its containers to international commerce. The leases are solicited and negotiated through Itel marketing offices in California, Illinois, New Jersey, South Carolina, Texas, and Washington, and the leased containers are delivered to lessees or their agents in many of the 50 States, including Tennessee. The Tennessee deliveries occur either at Itel's Memphis terminal or at several designated third-party terminals.

In December 1986, the Tennessee Department of Revenue assessed $382,465 in sales tax, penalties and interest on the proceeds Itel earned from leased containers delivered in Tennessee for the period of January 1983 through November 1986. Itel paid under protest and filed an action for a refund, challenging the constitutionality of the Tennessee tax under the Commerce Clause, the Import-Export Clause and the Supremacy Clause. The last challenge to the tax was based on an alleged conflict both with federal regulations and with two international conventions to which the United States is a signatory. Customs Convention on Containers, Dec. 2, 1972 (hereinafter 1972 Container Convention); Customs Convention on Containers, May 18, 1956 (hereinafter 1956 Container Convention). The Tennessee Chancery Court reduced the assessment to $158,012 on state-law grounds but rejected Itel's constitutional claims.

II

Itel's primary challenge is that the imposition of the Tennessee sales tax is proscribed by both the 1972 and 1956 Container Conventions. The Conventions restrict the authority of signatories to tax cargo containers by requiring signatory nations to grant the containers "temporary admission" into their borders, subject to exportation "within three months from the date of importation" unless this period is extended by Customs authorities. 1972 Container Convention, Arts. 3 and 4; 1956 Container Convention, Arts. 2 and 3. Temporary admission status permits the containers to enter a nation "free of import duties and taxes" under the 1972 Convention and "free of import duties and import taxes" under the 1956 Convention. 1972 Container Convention, Art. 1; 1956 Container Convention, Art. 2.

The Conventions define these key phrases in similar terms. The 1972 Convention defines "import duties and taxes" to mean "Customs duties and all other duties, taxes, fees and other charges which are collected on, or in connection with, the importation of goods, but not including fees and charges limited in amount to the approximate cost of services rendered." 1972 Container Convention, Art. 1. The 1956 Convention defines "import duties and import taxes" to mean "not only Customs duties but also all duties and taxes whatsoever chargeable by reason of importation." 1956 Container Convention, Art. 1. Itel does not claim the Tennessee sales taxes on its container leases is a "Customs dut[y]" under either Convention. Rather, it says that because its containers would not be available for lease, and hence taxation, in Tennessee but for their importation into the United States, the Tennessee tax must be a tax "collected on, or in connection with, the importation of goods" in contravention of the 1972 Convention and a tax "chargeable by reason of importation" in contravention of the 1956 Convention.

We cannot accept Itel's interpretation of the Container Conventions. Our interpretation must begin, as always, with the text of the Conventions. The text, instead of supporting Itel's broad construction, makes clear that it is the reason a State imposes a tax, not the reason for the presence of the containers within a State's jurisdiction, that determines whether a tax violates the Container Conventions. The Conventions thus disallow only those taxes imposed based on the act of importation itself. In contrast, Itel's interpretation would bar all taxes on containers covered by the Conventions, because each covered container is, by definition, in the United States as a result of its temporary importation. This reading makes superfluous the Conventions' qualifying language that the only taxes proscribed are those "collected on, or in connexion with, the importation of goods" and those "chargeable by reason of importation." 1972 Container Convention, Art. 1; 1956 Container Convention, Art. 1.

In an attempt to counteract the interpretation that the Conventions prohibit only those taxes based on the importation of containers, Itel asserts that the consistent practice of other signatory nations and a prior interpretation of the 1956 Convention by the United States prove that signatory nations read the Conventions to proscribe all taxes on containers within their borders. Itel, however, overstates the probative value of these actions.

As evidence that other signatory nations free cargo containers of all domestic taxation, Itel places primary reliance on the Economic Community Sixth Directive and the United Kingdom Value Added Tax (VAT), as illuminated in an amicus brief filed by the United Kingdom. Under the European VAT system, no direct tax, be it a VAT, sales or use tax, is imposed on the value of international container leases. See Sixth Council Directive of May 17, 1977, Arts. 14(1)(i) and 15(13).

The value of international container leases, however, is included in the cost of transporting goods, which in turn is added to the value of the goods when calculating VAT tax liability. Itel admits this is tantamount to an indirect tax on the value of international container leases, but claims the distinction between an indirect tax (paid by the consumer of import goods) and a direct tax on the container itself (paid by either the lessor or lessee of the container) is significant. Whether or not, in the abstract, there is a significant difference between direct and indirect taxation, the Container Conventions do not distinguish between the two methods or differentiate depending upon the legal incidence of a tax. For example, the first declaration in both Convention Protocols of Signature states that inclusion of the weight or value of containers in the weight or value of goods for calculating import duties and taxes upon those goods conflicts with the Conventions, even though this would be only an indirect tax on the containers and the legal incidence of the tax would not fall on the container lessor or lessee. 1972 Container Convention, Protocol of Signature; 1956 Container Convention, Protocol of Signature. The Conventions, in short, prohibit both direct and indirect taxes imposed based on the importation of a container, but permit direct and indirect taxes imposed on some other basis.

As further evidence in support of its position, Itel points to the statements of signatory nations objecting to Tennessee's taxation of container leases. With all due respect to those statements, we adhere to our interpretation. We are mindful that 11 nations (Denmark, Finland, France, Germany, Italy, Japan, the Netherlands, Norway, Spain, Sweden and the United Kingdom), each a signatory to at least one Container Convention, have sent a diplomatic note to the United States Department of State submitting that they do not "impose sales taxes (or equivalent taxes of different nomenclatures) on the lease of cargo containers that are used in international commerce among the Contracting Parties to the Conventions." App. to Brief for United Kingdom of Great Britain and Northern Ireland as Amicus Curiae 1a. The meaning these nations ascribe to the phrase "equivalent taxes" is not clear. For purposes of calculation and assessment, the European VAT system, enacted in most of the objecting nations, is by no means equivalent to a sales tax. See Trinova Corp. v. Michigan Dept. of Treasury,

498 U.S. 358, 365-366 (1991). But as we discussed above, for the purpose of determining whether a tax is one based on importation, the European VAT system is equivalent to Tennessee's sales tax system–that is, neither system imposes a tax based on the act of importation. Only this latter form of equivalence is relevant under the Container Conventions.

Directing our attention to the amicus brief filed by the United States in Japan Line, 441 U.S. 434 (1979), Itel next claims the United States Government once interpreted the 1956 Container Convention to prohibit all domestic taxes on international cargo containers. Even if this were true, the Government's current position is quite different; its amicus brief in this case expresses agreement with our interpretation of both the 1972 and the 1956 Container Conventions.

In its amicus brief in Japan Line, moreover, the United States did not say that the 1956 Container Convention prohibited the imposition of any domestic tax on international cargo containers. Its position was simply that under the 1956 Convention the United States gave containers "the same status it gives under the customs laws to articles admitted to a 'bonded manufacturing warehouse.'" Starting from this premise the Government argued that, like state taxes on goods in customs bonded warehouses destined for foreign trade, see McGoldrick v. Gulf Oil Corp., 309 U.S. 414, 428-429 (1940), state taxes on containers would frustrate a federal scheme designed to benefit international commerce. We declined, and continue to decline, to adopt this expansive view of McGoldrick and the pre-emptive effect of the Container Conventions. See infra. And, in any event, the Government's pre-emption argument in Japan Line does not conflict with its present interpretation that the Container Conventions themselves are violated only by a tax assessed upon the importation of containers.

Tennessee's sales tax is imposed upon the "transfer of title or possession, or both, exchange, barter, lease or rental, conditional, or otherwise, in any manner or by any means whatsoever of tangible personal property for a consideration." It is a sales tax of general application that does not discriminate against imported products either in its purpose or effect. Indeed, its assessment bears no relation to importation whatsoever. The tax is not pre-empted by the 1972 or 1956 Container Convention.

III

Itel next argues that the application of Tennessee's sales tax to its container leases is pre-empted because it would frustrate the federal objectives underlying the Container Conventions and the laws and regulations granting favored status to international containers. See Hines v. Davidowitz, 312 U.S. at 67 (state law pre-empted when it "stands as an obstacle to the accomplishment and execution of the full purposes and objectives of Congress"). The federal regulatory scheme for cargo containers, it claims, parallels the regulatory scheme creating customs bonded warehouses which we have found to pre-empt most state taxes on warehoused goods. R. J. Reynolds Tobacco Co. v. Durham County, 479 U.S. 130 (1986); Xerox Corp. v. County of Harris, 459 U.S. 145 (1982); McGoldrick v. Gulf Oil Corp., supra.

Itel's reliance on these decisions is misplaced. In McGoldrick and its progeny, we stated that Congress created a system for bonded warehouses where imports could be stored free of federal customs duties while under the continuous supervision of local customs officials "in order to encourage merchants here and abroad to make use of American ports." Xerox Corp., supra, at 103 S.Ct., at 527. By allowing importers to defer taxes on imported goods for a period of time and to escape taxes altogether on reexported goods, the bonded warehouse system "enabled the importer, without any threat of financial loss, to place his goods in domestic markets or to return them to foreign commerce and, by this flexibility, encouraged importers to use American facilities." R. J. Reynolds Tobacco Co., supra, at 107 S.Ct., at 510. This federal objective would be frustrated by the imposition of state sales and property taxes on goods not destined for domestic distribution, regardless of whether the taxes themselves discriminated against goods based on their destination. Xerox Corp., supra, at 103 S.Ct. at 526-528. See also R. J. Reynolds Tobacco Co., supra, at 107 S.Ct., at 509-510. McGoldrick, supra, at 60 S.Ct., at 669-670.

In contrast, the federal regulatory scheme for containers used in foreign commerce discloses no congressional intent to exempt those containers from all or most domestic taxation. In Japan Line we said that the 1956 Container Convention acknowledged "[t]he desirability of uniform treatment of containers used exclusively in foreign commerce" and "reflect[ed] a national policy to remove impediments to the use of containers." 441 U.S. at 452-453. But we did not hold that the Convention and the federal regulatory scheme for cargo containers expressed a national policy to exempt containers from all domestic taxation. Rather, we relied on the federal laws, along with proof of an international customary norm of home port taxation and California's creation of an asymmetry in international maritime taxation, for our conclusion that California's ad valorem property tax violated the foreign commerce clause by impeding the Government's ability to "'spea[k] with one voice'" in conducting our nation's foreign affairs. Ibid.

Itel does not better its pre-emption argument by claiming that the federal regulatory scheme for containers, like the customs bonded warehouse scheme, is so pervasive that it demonstrates a federal purpose to occupy the field of container regulation and taxation. We doubt that the container regulatory scheme can be considered as pervasive as the customs warehouse scheme. The latter provides for continual federal supervision of warehouses, strict bonding requirements and special taxing rules, whereas the former is limited more to the general certification and taxing of containers. Even if Itel were correct on this point, however, we have not held that state taxation of goods in bonded warehouses is pre-empted by Congress' intent to occupy the field of bonded warehouse regulation. In fact, in R. J. Reynolds we specifically held that the bonded warehouse statutes and regulations did not evidence such a purpose. 479 U.S. at 149. So, too, we cannot conclude that in adopting laws governing the importation of containers Congress intended to foreclose any and all concurrent state regulation or taxation of containers.

The precise federal policy regarding promotion of container use is satisfied by a proscription against taxes that are imposed upon or discriminate against the importation of containers. We find that Tennessee's general sales tax, which applies to domestic and foreign goods without differentiation, does not impede the federal objectives expressed in the 1972 and 1956 Container Conventions and related federal statutes and regulations.

IV

A

Itel's third challenge to Tennessee's tax on container leases is that the tax violates the foreign commerce clause as interpreted by Japan Line. U.S. Const, Art. I, § 8, cl. 3. We began our analysis in Japan Line with a reformulation of the foreign commerce clause test:

"In addition to answering the nexus, apportionment, and nondiscrimination questions posed in Complete Auto, a court must also inquire, first, whether the tax, notwithstanding apportionment, creates a substantial risk of international multiple taxation, and, second, whether the tax prevents the Federal Government from 'speaking with one voice when regulating commercial relations with foreign governments.'" Japan Line, supra, at 451.

Without passing on the point, we assumed the California property tax in question would have met the test of Complete Auto, see 441 U.S. at 451. Proceeding to the two foreign commerce requirements we had identified, we found the California tax incompatible with both. We held that because Japan had the established right, consistent with the custom of nations, see id., to tax the property value of the containers in full, California's tax

"produce[d] multiple taxation in fact." We held further that California's tax prevented the United States from speaking with one voice in foreign affairs, in that "[t]he risk of retaliation by Japan, under these circumstances, [was] acute, and such retaliation of necessity would be felt by the Nation as a whole."

Four years later we again addressed whether a California tax offended the foreign commerce clause, this time in the context of a unitary business income tax. Container Corp. of America v. Franchise Tax Bd., 463 U.S. 159 (1983). Although recognizing that California's income tax shared some of the same characteristics as the property tax involved in Japan Line, we nevertheless upheld it based on two distinguishing characteristics.

First, the problem of double taxing in Container Corp., "although real, [was] not the 'inevitabl[e]' result of the California [income] taxing scheme." On the other hand, "[i]n Japan Line, we relied strongly on the fact that one taxing jurisdiction claimed the right to tax a given value in full, and another taxing jurisdiction claimed the right to tax the same entity in part—a combination resulting necessarily in double taxation." That the Japan Line Court adopted a rule requiring States to forgo assessing property taxes against foreign-owned cargo containers "was by no means unfair, because the rule did no more than reflect consistent international practice and express federal policy."

Second, we noted that "in [Container Corp.], unlike Japan Line, the Executive Branch ha[d] decided not to file an amicus curiae brief in opposition to the state tax." Together with our conclusion that the California income tax did not result in automatic double taxation, the Government's nonintervention suggested that the tax presented no serious threat to United States foreign policy.

. . . .

C

We proceed to evaluate the tax under Japan Line's two foreign commerce clause factors. Left to decide whether Tennessee's tax rests on the Japan Line or the Container Corp. side of the scale, we have no doubt that the analysis and holding of Container Corp. control.

Itel asserts that Tennessee's law invites multiple taxation of container leases because numerous foreign nations have a sufficient taxing nexus with the leases to impose equivalent taxes, and many nations in fact would do so were it not for the Container Conventions' prohibitions. As an initial matter, of course, we have concluded that the Conventions do not prohibit Tennessee's sales tax or equivalent taxes imposed by other nations. To the extent Tennessee has invited others to tax cargo container leases, foreign sovereigns, in an exercise of their independent judgment, have chosen not to accept.

Furthermore, the foreign commerce clause cannot be interpreted to demand that a state refrain from taxing any business transaction that is also potentially subject to taxation by a foreign sovereign. "Japan Line does not require forbearance so extreme or so one-sided." Container Corp., supra, 463 U.S. at 193. Tennessee has decided to tax a discrete transaction occurring within the State. See Wardair Canada, 477 U.S. at 9. And, according to its interpretation of its revenue code, which we accept, Tennessee credits against its own tax any tax properly paid in another jurisdiction, foreign or domestic, on the same transaction. By these measures, Tennessee's sales tax reduces, if not eliminates, the risk of multiple international taxation. Absent a conflict with a "consistent international practice [or] . . . federal policy," Container Corp., 463 U.S. at 190, the careful apportionment of a state tax on business transactions conducted within state borders does not create the substantial risk of international multiple taxation that implicates foreign commerce clause concerns.

Itel further claims that if other States in this country follow Tennessee's lead and tax international container leases, the United States will be unable to speak with one voice in foreign trade because international container leases will be subject to various degrees of domestic taxation. As a consequence, Itel insists, container owners and users will be hit by retaliatory foreign taxes. To the extent Itel is arguing that the risk of double taxation violates the one voice test, our response is the same as above: Tennessee's tax does not create the substantial risk of international multiple taxation that implicates foreign commerce clause concerns.

To the extent Itel is arguing that taxes like Tennessee's engender foreign policy problems, the United States disagrees. The Federal Government, in adopting various conventions, statutes and regulations that restrict a State's ability to tax international cargo containers in defined circumstances, has acted on the subject of taxing cargo containers and their use. It has chosen to eliminate state taxes collected in connection with the importation of cargo containers. The state tax here does not fall within that proscription, and the most rational inference to be drawn is that this tax, one quite distinct from the general class of import duties, is permitted. Unlike in Japan Line or Container Corp., moreover, the United States has filed an amicus brief defending Tennessee's law: "Far from conflicting with international custom, the Tennessee tax appears to promote it. The Tennessee tax thus does not interfere with our ability 'to speak with one voice' on this issue involving foreign commerce." This submission "is by no means

dispositive." Container Corp., 463 U.S. at 195-196. But given the strong indications from Congress that Tennessee's method of taxation is allowable, and with due regard for the fact that the nuances of foreign policy "are much more the province of the Executive Branch and Congress than of this Court," id., at 196, we find no reason to disagree with the United States' submission that Tennessee's tax does not infringe the Government's ability to speak with one voice when regulating commercial relations with other nations. "It would turn dormant Commerce Clause analysis entirely upside down to apply it where the Federal Government has acted, and to apply it in such a way as to reverse the policy that the Federal Government has elected to follow." Wardair Canada, supra, at 12.

V

Itel's final avenue of attack on the Tennessee tax is that, as applied to international container leases, it violates the Import-Export Clause. Our modern Import-Export Clause test was first announced in Michelin Tire Corp. v. Wages, 423 U.S. 276, 285-286 (1976):

"The Framers of the Constitution . . . sought to alleviate three main concerns by committing sole power to lay imposts and duties on imports in the Federal Government, with no concurrent state power: [1] the Federal Government must speak with one voice when regulating commercial relations with foreign governments, and tariffs, which might affect foreign relations, could not be implemented by the States consistently with that exclusive power; [2] import revenues were to be the major source of revenue of the Federal Government and should not be diverted to the States; and [3] harmony among the States might be disturbed unless seaboard States, with their crucial ports of entry, were prohibited from levying taxes on citizens of other States by taxing goods merely flowing through their ports to the other States not situated as favorably geographically."

The first and third components in this formulation mirror inquiries we have already undertaken as part of our foreign commerce clause analysis. That is, the one voice component of the Michelin test is the same as the one voice component of our Japan Line test. Japan Line, 441 U.S. at 449-450, n. 14. And the state harmony component parallels the four Complete Auto requirements of the foreign and domestic commerce clause. Department of Revenue of Washington v. Association of Washington Stevedoring Cos., 435 U.S. 734, 754-755 (1978) ("The third Import-Export Clause policy . . . is vindicated if the tax falls upon a taxpayer with a reasonable nexus to the State, is properly apportioned, does not discriminate, and relates reasonably to services provided by the State"). Having concluded that the Tennessee tax survives Commerce Clause scrutiny, we must conclude the tax is consistent with the first and third component of our Michelin test.

This leaves only Michelin's second component: ensuring that import revenues are not being diverted from the Federal Government. We need not provide a detailed explanation of what, if any, substantive limits this aspect of Michelin places on state taxation of goods flowing through international channels, for the tax here is not a tax on importation or imported goods, but a tax on a business transaction occurring within the taxing State. The tax does not draw revenue from the importation process and so does not divert import revenue from the Federal Government. For similar reasons, we reject the argument that the tax violates the prohibition on the direct taxation of imports and exports "in transit," the rule we followed in Richfield Oil, 329 U.S. at 78-79, 84. Even assuming that rule has not been altered by the approach we adopted in Michelin, it is inapplicable here. Tennessee's sales tax is levied on leases transferring temporary possession of containers to third parties in Tennessee; it is not levied on the containers themselves or on the goods being imported in those containers. The tax thus does not divert import revenue from the Federal Government because "the taxation falls upon a service distinct from [import] goods and their value." Washington Stevedoring, supra, 435 U.S. at 757. See also Canton R. Co. v. Rogan, 340 U.S. at 513-514.

VI

For the reasons we have stated, we hold that Tennessee's sales tax, as applied to Itel's international container leases, does not violate the Commerce, Import-Export or Supremacy Clause. The judgment of the Supreme Court of Tennessee is affirmed.

REHNQUIST, C. J., and WHITE, STEVENS, O'CONNOR, SOUTER, and THOMAS, JJ., joined, and in all but Parts IV and V of which SCALIA, J., joined.

[Concurring Opinion of JUSTICE SCALIA omitted.]

JUSTICE BLACKMUN, dissenting.

It is established "that a treaty should generally be 'construe[d] . . . liberally to give effect to the purpose which animates it' and that '[e]ven where a provision of a treaty fairly admits of two constructions, one restricting, the other enlarging, rights which may be claimed under it, the more liberal interpretation is to be preferred.'" This Court recognized in Japan Line that the Container Conventions reflect a "national policy to remove impediments to the use of containers as 'instruments of international traffic.'" Tennessee's tax clearly frustrates that policy.

In concluding that Tennessee's tax is not prohibited, the majority studiously ignores the realities of container leasing. All petitioner's containers are dedicated to international commerce, which means that they spend no more than three months at a time in any one jurisdiction. See 1972 Convention, Art. 4; 1956 Convention, Art. 3. Furthermore, transferring containers to new lessees is an integral part of any container-leasing operation. A major advantage of leasing rather than owning a container is that a shipper may return the container to the lessor at or near the shipment destination without having to provide for the return transport of the container. J. Tan, Containers: The Lease-Buy Decision 13 (London, International Cargo Handling Coordination Association, 1983). The lessor then transfers the container to another shipper who needs to carry goods from that location or transports the container to another location where it is needed. Leased containers like those of petitioner are constantly crossing national boundaries and are constantly being transferred to new lessees at the ends of their journeys. Whether Tennessee taxes the act of importation or the act of transfer makes little difference with respect to leased containers. Each kind of tax imposes substantial "impediments to the use of containers as 'instruments of international traffic.'" Japan Line, 441 U.S. at 453, quoting 19 U.S.C. § 1322(a), and each, in my view, is prohibited by the Container Conventions.

This is also the view of the other signatory nations to the Conventions. Their consistent practice is persuasive evidence of the Conventions' meaning. See Air France v. Saks, 470 U.S. 392, 396 (1985), quoting Choctaw Nation of Indians v. United States, 318 U.S. 423, 431-432 (1943) ("'[T]reaties are construed more liberally than private agreements, and to ascertain their meaning we may look beyond the written words to . . . the practical construction adopted by the parties'"). Neither Tennessee nor the United States as amicus curiae can point to any other jurisdiction that directly taxes the lease of containers used in international commerce. Under the European Value Added Tax ("VAT") system, as the majority acknowledges, ante, no direct tax is imposed on the value of international container leases.

In an attempt to make international practice fit its reading of the Conventions, the majority mistakenly equates the European VAT on *goods* with Tennessee's tax on containers. See ante. The European VAT is analogous to an American sales tax but is imposed on the value added to goods at each stage of production or distribution rather than on their sale price. See Trinova Corp. v. Michigan Dept. of Treasury, 498 U.S. at 365-366. The act of transporting goods to their place of sale adds to their value and the cost of transportation is reflected in their price. An American sales tax reaches the cost of transportation as part of the sale price of goods. The European VAT taxes the cost of transportation as part of the value added to goods during their distribution.

Tennessee's analogue to the European VAT is its sales tax on goods imported by container, not its direct tax on the proceeds of container leases. Petitioner does not argue that Tennessee must refrain from imposing a sales tax on goods imported by container. It argues, instead, that like every other party to the Conventions Tennessee may not impose a direct tax on containers themselves.

Even if Tennessee's tax did not violate the Container Conventions, it would violate the Foreign Commerce Clause by preventing the United States from "speaking with one voice" with respect to the taxation of containers used in international commerce. This Court noted in Japan Line that the Conventions show "[t]he desirability of uniform treatment of containers used exclusively in foreign commerce." Tennessee's tax frustrates that uniformity.

The Court correctly notes that the Solicitor General's decision to file an amicus brief defending the tax "'is by no means dispositive.'" Indeed, such a submission, consistent with the separation of powers, may not be given any weight beyond its power to persuade. The constitutional power over foreign affairs is shared by Congress and the President, see, e. g., U.S. Const., Art. I, § 8, cl. 11 (Congress shall have the power to declare war); Art. II, § 2, cl. 2 (President shall have the power, by and with the advice and consent of the Senate, to make treaties); and Art. II, § 3 (President shall receive ambassadors), but the power to regulate commerce with foreign nations is textually delegated to Congress alone. "It is well established that *Congress* may authorize States to engage in regulation that the Commerce Clause would otherwise forbid," Maine v. Taylor, 477 U.S. 131, 138, (1986) (emphasis added), but the President may not authorize such regulation by the filing of an amicus brief. While the majority properly looks to see whether Congress intended to permit a tax like Tennessee's, it mistakenly infers permission for the tax from Congress' supposed failure to prohibit it. "[T]his Court has exempted state statutes from the implied limitations of the [Commerce] Clause only when the congressional direction to do so has been 'unmistakably clear.'" Taylor, 477 U.S. at 139, quoting South-Central Timber Development, Inc. v. Wunnicke, 467 U.S. 82, 91 (1984). "The need for affirmative approval is heightened by the fact that [Tennessee's tax] has substantial ramifications beyond the Nation's borders." Wunnicke, 467 U.S. at 92, n. 7. Not only does the majority invert this analysis by finding congressional authorization for the tax in congressional silence, but it finds silence only by imposing its own narrow reading on the Conventions.

The majority invites States that are constantly in need of new revenue to impose new taxes on containers. The result, I fear, will be a patchwork of state taxes that will burden international commerce and frustrate the purposes of the Container Conventions. I respectfully dissent.

Questions and Comments

1. Do sales taxes have to meet the four tests of *Complete Auto*? Do all sales taxes on transactions taking place within a state meet those tests?

2. What is left of *Japan Line* after *Itel Containers*? Does *Itel Containers* make it clear that *Container Corp.* severely restricted the scope of *Japan Line*?

3. Are the U.S. treaty partners claiming that the Tennessee sales tax violates the container agreements? Or are they simply arguing that they do not tax the containers directly? Does the direct/indirect distinction make any sense? Are the European countries giving a liberal reading to the container conventions in concluding that indirect taxation under the VAT is permissible?

4. Tennessee offers taxpayers a credit for other sales taxes imposed on their container leases. Is this credit necessary to sustain the tax? Do you expect that Tennessee will give the credit for a European VAT?

5. What is the significance of the amicus brief filed by the U.S. government? Do you think the case would have come out different if the U.S. government had failed to file? If it had filed a brief in opposition to the tax? After this case, do you think the taxpayer can ever win a foreign commerce case without getting a supporting amicus brief from the U.S. government?

6. In dissent, Justice Blackmun argues that it is primarily Congressional action, not action by the Executive, that is important for foreign commerce clause purposes. Is that view consistent with his opinion in *Japan Line*? With his joining the majority in *Container Corp.*?

7. Revisit *Itel* after reading *Washington Stevedoring*, in the Import-Export Clause chapter.

8. Is the Tennessee tax internally consistent?

9. For critical commentary on *Itel Containers*, see Douglas Patch, *Itel Containers v. Huddleston: The Downfall of the Customs Convention on Containers*, 13 Wis. Int'l L.J. 513

(1995); *Lessor Hit with Greater Tax: Itel Containers International Corp. v. Huddleston*, 27 Creighton L. Rev. 1131 (1994); Dianne Elizabeth Chipps, *Itel Containers International Corp. v. Huddleston: State Taxation of Foreign Commerce Instrumentalities*, 47 Tax Law. 479 (1994); Larry Lempert, *Examiner Sees Holes in Itel Safety Net*, 5 Legal Times 1 (1982).

Maryland et al. v. Louisiana
Supreme Court of the United States, 1981.
451 U.S. 725, 101 S. Ct. 2114, 68 L. Ed. 2d 576.

JUSTICE WHITE delivered the opinion of the Court.

In this original action, several States, joined by the United States and a number of pipeline companies, challenge the constitutionality of Louisiana's "First-Use Tax" imposed on certain uses of natural gas brought into Louisiana, principally from the Outer Continental Shelf (OCS), as violative of the Supremacy Clause and the Commerce Clause of the United States Constitution.

I

The lands beneath the Gulf of Mexico have large reserves of oil and natural gas. Initially, these reserves could not be developed due to technological difficulties associated with offshore drilling. In 1938, the first drilling rig was constructed off the coast of Louisiana, and with the advent of new technologies, offshore drilling has become commonplace. Exploration and development of the OCS in the Gulf of Mexico have become large industries providing a substantial percentage of the natural gas used in this country. Most of the gas being extracted from the lands underlying the Gulf is piped to refining plants located in coastal portions of Louisiana where the gas is "dried"– the liquefiable hydrocarbons gathered and removed– on its way to ultimate distribution to consumers in over 30 States. It is estimated that 98% of the OCS gas processed in Louisiana is eventually sold to out-of-state consumers with the 2% remainder consumed within Louisiana. The contractual arrangements between a producer of gas and the pipeline companies vary. Most often, the producer sells the gas to the pipeline companies at the wellhead, although the producer may retain an interest in any extractable components. Some producers, however, retain full ownership rights and simply pay a flat fee for the use of the pipeline companies' facilities.

. . . .

In 1978, the Louisiana Legislature enacted a tax of seven cents per thousand cubic feet of natural gas on the "first use" of any gas imported into Louisiana which was not previously subjected to taxation by another State or the United States. The Tax imposed is precisely equal to the severance tax the State imposes on Louisiana gas producers. The Tax is owed by the owner of the gas at the time the first taxable "use" occurs within Louisiana. About 85% of the OCS gas brought ashore is owned by the pipeline companies, the rest by the producers. Since most States impose their own severance tax, it is acknowledged that the primary effect of the First-Use Tax will be on gas produced in the federal OCS area and then piped to processing plants located within Louisiana. It has been estimated that Louisiana would receive at least $150 million in annual receipts from the First-Use Tax.

The stated purpose of the First-Use Tax was to reimburse the people of Louisiana for damages to the State's waterbottoms, barrier islands, and coastal areas resulting from the introduction of natural gas into Louisiana from areas not subject to state taxes as well as to compensate for the costs incurred by the State in protecting those resources. Moreover, the Tax was designed to equalize competition between gas produced in Louisiana and subject to the state severance tax of seven cents per thousand cubic feet, and gas produced elsewhere not subject to a severance tax such as OCS gas. The Act specified a number of different uses justifying imposition of the First-Use Tax including sale, processing, transportation, use in manufacturing, treatment, or "other ascertainable action at a point within the state."

The Act itself, as well as provisions found elsewhere in the state statutes, provided a number of exemptions from and credits for the First-Use Tax. The Severance Tax Credit provided that any taxpayer subject to the First-Use Tax was entitled to a direct tax credit on any Louisiana severance tax owed in connection with the extraction of natural resources within the State. Second, municipal or state-regulated electric generating plants and natural gas distributing services located within Louisiana, as well as any direct purchaser of gas used for consumption directly by that purchaser, were provided tax credits on other Louisiana taxes upon a showing that "fuel costs for electricity generation or natural gas distribution or consumption have increased as a direct result of increases in transportation and marketing costs of natural gas delivered from the federal domain of the outer continental shelf...," which implicitly includes any increases resulting from the First-Use Tax. Furthermore, imported natural gas used for drilling oil or gas within the State was exempted from the First-Use Tax. Thus, Louisiana consumers of OCS gas for the most part are not burdened by the Tax, but it does uniformly apply to gas moving out of the State. The Act also purported to establish the legal effect of the Tax in terms of defining the proper allocation of the Tax among potentially liable parties. Specifically, the Act declared that the "tax shall be deemed a cost associated with uses made by the owner in preparation of marketing of the natural gas." Any contract which attempted to allocate the cost of the Tax to any party except the ultimate consumer was declared to be "against public policy and unenforceable to that extent."

. . . .

Initially, it is clear to us that the flow of gas from the OCS wells, through processing plants in Louisiana, and through interstate pipelines to the ultimate consumers in over 30 States constitutes interstate commerce. Louisiana argues that the taxable "uses" within the State break the flow of commerce and are wholly local events. But although the Louisiana "uses" may possess a sufficient local nexus to support otherwise valid taxation,[27] we do not agree that the flow of gas from the

wellhead to the consumer, even though "interrupted" by certain events, is anything but a continual flow of gas in interstate commerce. Gas crossing a state line at any stage of its movement to the ultimate consumer is in interstate commerce during the entire journey.

A state tax must be assessed in light of its actual effect considered in conjunction with other provisions of the State's tax scheme. In this case, the Louisiana First-Use Tax unquestionably discriminates against interstate commerce in favor of local interests as the necessary result of various tax credits and exclusions. No further hearings are necessary to sustain this conclusion. Under the specific provisions of the First-Use Tax, OCS gas used for certain purposes within Louisiana is exempted from the Tax. OCS gas consumed in Louisiana for (1) producing oil, natural gas, or sulphur; (2) processing natural gas for the extraction of liquefiable hydrocarbons; or (3) manufacturing fertilizer and anhydrous ammonia, is exempt from the First-Use Tax. Competitive users in other States are burdened with the Tax. Other Louisiana statutes, enacted as part of the First-Use Tax package, provide important tax credits favoring local interests. Under the Severance Tax Credit, an owner paying the First-Use Tax on OCS gas receives an equivalent tax credit on any state severance tax owed in connection with production in Louisiana. On its face, this credit favors those who both own OCS gas and engage in Louisiana production.[28] The obvious economic effect of this Severance Tax Credit is to encourage natural gas owners involved in the production of OCS

---

27. The United States suggests that the uses enunciated in the Act do not have a sufficient local nexus to support the Tax under the Commerce Clause. See Michigan-Wisconsin Pipe Line Co. v. Calvert, 347 U.S. 157 (1954). While the local nexus of certain of the uses is suspect, other uses would appear to have a substantial local nexus so that on the present record it would be difficult to say that the entire Tax was unconstitutional on this ground. The Act contains a severability clause providing that if any use is found to be an unconstitutional basis for taxation, the next use would be taxed. Given our resolution on the discrimination charge, we find it unnecessary to reach the local nexus claim especially in light of the severability clause. . . .

The United States and the plaintiff States also argue that the First-Use Tax is not fairly apportioned. To be valid, a tax on interstate commerce must be reasonably apportioned to the value of the activities occurring within the State upon which the Tax is imposed. See Washington Revenue Dept. v. Washington Stevedoring Assn., 435 U.S. 734, 746-747 (1978). It is submitted that several factors suggest this principle is being violated. First, the Tax is imposed on each use as a function of the volume of the gas subject to the use, without attempting to tailor the amount of the Tax depending on the nature or extent of the actual use of the gas within Louisiana. Second, the use of the proceeds of the First-Use Tax demonstrates that the Tax is substantially in excess of the amount fairly associated with the local uses. Under the Act, 75% of the proceeds are used to service Louisiana's general debt, while only one-quarter is directly used to alleviate the alleged environmental damage caused by the pipeline activities. Third, the State has not demonstrated a sufficient relationship between other services provided by the State and the amount of the First-Use Taxes provided. In light of our determination that the Tax is

discriminatory, however, we need not determine the apportionment issue. . . .

28. The United States has provided an example which the Special Master used to illustrate the possible discrimination: "This difference can be illustrated by the following example. Owner A has 1000 mcf of OCS gas; owner B has 500 mcf of OCS gas and 500 mcf of gas subject to Louisiana's severance tax. A owes $70 of first use tax; B owes $35 of first use tax and $35 in severance tax. B, however, pays only $35 in first use taxes. He owes no severance tax because he can credit the first use payment against the severance tax liability." Second Report, at 34, n. 18.

It has been observed that the credit means that "gas extracted offshore and gas extracted in Louisiana will be treated the same for Louisiana tax purposes only when the First Use Taxpayer has no severance tax liability to absorb the First Use Taxes." As a result, First-Use Tax-payers have an incentive to "undertake mineral extraction activities in Louisiana so as to minimize their effective First Use Tax burden and to compete on equal terms with other First Use Taxpayers whose First Use Tax burden has already been so minimized." W. Hellerstein, State Taxation in the Federal System: Perspectives on Louisiana's First Use Tax on Natural Gas, Shell Foundation Lecture at Tulane University School of Law (Nov. 20, 1980), pp. 23-24.

gas to invest in mineral exploration and development within Louisiana rather than to invest in further OCS development or in production in other States. Finally, under the Louisiana statutes, any utility producing electricity with OCS gas, any natural gas distributor dealing in OCS gas, or any direct purchaser of OCS gas for consumption by the purchaser in Louisiana may recoup any increase in the cost of gas attributable to the First-Use Tax through credits against various taxes or a combination of taxes otherwise owed to the State of Louisiana. Louisiana consumers of OCS gas are thus substantially protected against the impact of the First-Use Tax and have the benefit of untaxed OCS gas which because it is not subject to either a severance tax or the First-Use Tax may be cheaper than locally produced gas. OCS gas moving out of the State, however, is burdened with the First-Use Tax.

. . . .

In our view, the First-Use Tax cannot be justified as a compensatory tax. The concept of a compensatory tax first requires identification of the burden for which the State is attempting to compensate. Here, Louisiana claims that the First-Use Tax compensates for the effect of the State's severance tax on local production of natural gas. To be sure, Louisiana has an interest in protecting its natural resources, and, like most States, has chosen to impose a severance tax on the privilege of severing resources from its soil. But the First-Use Tax is not designed to meet these same ends since Louisiana has no sovereign interest in being compensated for the severance of resources from the federally owned OCS land. The two events are not comparable in the same fashion as a use tax complements a sales tax. In that case, a State is attempting to impose a tax on a substantially equivalent event to assure uniform treatment of goods and materials to be consumed in the State. No such equality exists in this instance. The common thread

running through the cases upholding compensatory taxes is the equality of treatment between local and interstate commerce. See Boston Stock Exchange, 429 U.S. at 331-332; Silas Mason Co., 300 U.S. at 583-584. See generally Halliburton Oil, 373 U.S. at 70 ("equal treatment for in-state and out-of-state taxpayers similarly situated is the condition precedent for a valid use tax on goods imported from out-of-state"). As already demonstrated, however, the pattern of credits and exemptions allowed under the Louisiana statute undeniably violates this principle of equality. As we have said, OCS gas may generally be consumed in Louisiana without the burden of the First-Use Tax. Its principal application is to gas moving out of the State. Of course, it does equalize the tax burdens on OCS gas leaving the State and Louisiana gas going into the interstate market. But this sort of equalization is not the kind of "compensating" effect that our cases have recognized.

It may be true that further hearings would be required to provide a precise determination of the extent of the discrimination in this case, but this is an insufficient reason for not now declaring the Tax unconstitutional and eliminating the discrimination. We need not know how unequal the Tax is before concluding that it unconstitutionally discriminates. Accordingly, we grant plaintiffs' exception that the First-Use Tax is unconstitutional under the Commerce Clause because it unfairly discriminates against purchasers of gas moving through Louisiana in interstate commerce.

. . . .

JUSTICE POWELL took no part in the consideration or decision of this case.

[Concurring opinion by Chief Justice Burger and dissenting opinion by Justice Rehnquist omitted.]

Questions and Comments

1. Suppose Louisiana were to repeal its severance tax and first use tax and replace them with a traditional sales and use tax. Assume that Louisiana allowed as a credit any severance, use, or sales taxes paid to other jurisdictions and that this was the only credit allowed. Would the resulting tax regime be constitutional? Would your answer change if the sales or use tax were creditable against a resident's personal income tax?

2. The Court describes the Severance Tax Credit as encouraging "natural gas owners involved in the production of OCS gas to invest in mineral exploration and development within Louisiana rather than to invest in further OCS development or in production in other

States." Why couldn't the credit be described as encouraging those involved in the production of Louisiana gas to invest in mineral exploration and development within the OCS? Assuming this were a defensible characterization, would the Court's analysis be different?

3. Could Louisiana constitutionally levy a tax only on gas consumed by nonresidents? Does the first use tax substantially have that effect?

4. How does Louisiana's severance tax protect its natural resources? Did Louisiana's first use tax and

severance tax have the common goal of taxing the consumption and depletion of natural resources?

5. Did Louisiana's tax violate the Import-Export Clause?

6. Could the Louisiana tax be defended as equalizing the tax burdens on OCS gas leaving the State and Louisiana gas leaving the State?

7. Is the result in this case consistent with *Commonwealth Edison*?

8. Is a statute that discriminates against interstate commerce unconstitutional per se?

9. Why did Maryland and the rest of the plaintiff States (New York, Massachusetts, Rhode Island, Illinois, Indiana, Michigan, Wisconsin, and New Jersey) have standing? Why did the United States intervene?

10. For critical commentary on *Maryland v. Louisiana*, see James L. Rice III, *Constitutional Law-State Taxation-Louisiana First Use Tax on Natural Gas*, 57 Tul. L. Rev. 390 (1982).

Commonwealth Edison Co. v. Montana
Supreme Court of the United States, 1981.
453 U.S. 609, 101 S. Ct. 2946, 69 L. Ed. 2d 884.

JUSTICE MARSHALL delivered the opinion of the Court.

In this appeal, we consider whether the tax Montana levies on each ton of coal mined in the State violates the Commerce and Supremacy Clauses[*] of the United States Constitution.

I

Buried beneath Montana are large deposits of low-sulfur coal, most of it on federal land. Since 1921, Montana has imposed a severance tax on the output of Montana coal mines, including coal mined on federal land. After commissioning a study of coal production taxes in 1974, in 1975, the Montana Legislature enacted the tax schedule at issue in this case. The tax is levied at varying rates depending on the value, energy content, and method of extraction of the coal, and may equal, at a maximum, 30% of the "contract sales price." Under the terms of a 1976 amendment to the Montana Constitution, after December 31, 1979, at least 50% of the revenues generated by the tax must be paid into a permanent trust fund, the principal of which may be appropriated only by a vote of three-fourths of the members of each house of the legislature.

Appellants, 4 Montana coal producers and 11 of their out-of-state utility company customers, filed these suits in Montana state court in 1978. They sought refunds of over $ 5.4 million in severance taxes paid under protest, a declaration that the tax is invalid under the Supremacy and Commerce Clauses, and an injunction against further collection of the tax. Without receiving any

evidence, the court upheld the tax and dismissed the complaints.

II
A

As an initial matter, appellants assert that the Montana Supreme Court erred in concluding that the Montana tax is not subject to the strictures of the Commerce Clause. In appellants' view, Heisler's [Heisler v. Thomas Colliery Co., 260 U.S. 245 (1922)] "mechanical" approach, which looks to whether a state tax is levied on goods prior to their entry into interstate commerce, no longer accurately reflects the law. Appellants contend that the correct analysis focuses on whether the challenged tax substantially affects interstate commerce, in which case it must be scrutinized under the Complete Auto Transit test.

We agree that Heisler's reasoning has been undermined by more recent cases. The Heisler analysis evolved at a time when the Commerce Clause was thought to prohibit the States from imposing any direct taxes on interstate commerce. Consequently, the distinction between intrastate activities and interstate commerce was crucial to protecting the States' taxing power.

The Court has, however, long since rejected any suggestion that a state tax or regulation affecting interstate commerce is immune from Commerce Clause scrutiny because it attaches only to a "local" or intrastate activity. Correspondingly, the Court has rejected the notion that state taxes levied on interstate commerce are per se invalid. In reviewing Commerce Clause challenges to state taxes, our goal has instead been to "establish a consistent and rational method of inquiry" focusing on "the practical effect of a challenged tax." Mobil Oil Corp. v. Commissioner of Taxes, 445 U.S. 425, 443 (1980). We conclude that the same "practical" analysis should apply

---

[*]. [Ed. The Court rejected the appellant's Supremacy Clause argument, holding that the Mineral Lands Leasing Act, 30 U.S.C. § 181 et seq. authorized the imposition of Montana's severance tax.]

in reviewing Commerce Clause challenges to state severance taxes.

In the first place, there is no real distinction–in terms of economic effects–between severance taxes and other types of state taxes that have been subjected to Commerce Clause scrutiny. See, e.g., Michigan-Wisconsin Pipe Line Co., 347 U.S. 157 (1954); Carter & Weekes Stevedoring Co., 330 U.S. 422 (1947), Puget Sound Stevedoring Co., 302 U.S. 90 (1937), both overruled in Washington Revenue Dept. v. Association of Wash. Stevedoring Cos.[6] State taxes levied on a "local" activity preceding entry of the goods into interstate commerce may substantially affect interstate commerce, and this effect is the proper focus of Commerce Clause inquiry. Second, this Court has acknowledged that "a State has a significant interest in exacting from interstate commerce its fair share of the cost of state government," Washington Revenue Dept. v. Association of Wash. Stevedoring Cos., supra, at 748. As the Court has stated, "'[e]ven interstate business must pay its way.'" Western Live Stock, 303 U.S. 250, 254 (1938), quoting Postal Telegraph-Cable Co. v. Richmond, 249 U.S. 252, 259 (1919). Consequently, the Heisler Court's concern that a loss of state taxing authority would be an inevitable result of subjecting taxes on "local" activities to Commerce Clause scrutiny is no longer tenable.

We therefore hold that a state severance tax is not immunized from Commerce Clause scrutiny by a claim that the tax is imposed on goods prior to their entry into the stream of interstate commerce. Any contrary statements in Heisler and its progeny are disapproved. We agree with appellants that the Montana tax must be evaluated under Complete Auto Transit's four-part test. Under that test, a state tax does not offend the Commerce Clause if it "is applied to an activity with a substantial nexus with the taxing State, is fairly apportioned, does not discriminate against interstate commerce, and is fairly related to services provided by the State."

B

Appellants do not dispute that the Montana tax satisfies the first two prongs of the Complete Auto Transit test. As the Montana Supreme Court noted, "there can be no

argument here that a substantial, in fact, the only nexus of the severance of coal is established in Montana." Nor is there any question here regarding apportionment or potential multiple taxation, for as the state court observed, "the severance can occur in no other state" and "no other state can tax the severance." Appellants do contend, however, that the Montana tax is invalid under the third and fourth prongs of the Complete Auto Transit test.

Appellants assert that the Montana tax "discriminate[s] against interstate commerce" because 90% of Montana coal is shipped to other States under contracts that shift the tax burden primarily to non-Montana utility companies and thus to citizens of other States. But the Montana tax is computed at the same rate regardless of the final destination of the coal, and there is no suggestion here that the tax is administered in a manner that departs from this evenhanded formula. We are not, therefore, confronted here with the type of differential tax treatment of interstate and intrastate commerce that he Court has found in other "discrimination" cases. See, e.g., Maryland v. Louisiana, 451 U.S. 725 (1981); Boston Stock Exchange, 429 U.S. 318 (1977); cf. BT Investment Managers, Inc., 447 U.S. 27 (1980); Philadelphia v. New Jersey, 437 U.S. 617 (1978).

Instead, the gravamen of appellants' claim is that a state tax must be considered discriminatory for purposes of the Commerce Clause if the tax burden is borne primarily by out-of-state consumers. Appellants do not suggest that this assertion is based on any of this Court's prior discriminatory tax cases. In fact, a similar claim was considered and rejected in Heisler. There, it was argued that Pennsylvania had a virtual monopoly of anthracite coal and that, because 80% of the coal was shipped out of State, the tax discriminated against and impermissibly burdened interstate commerce. The Court, however, dismissed these factors as "adventitious considerations." We share the Heisler Court's misgivings about judging the validity of a state tax by assessing the State's "monopoly" position or its "exportation" of the tax burden out of State.

The premise of our discrimination cases is that "[t]he very purpose of the Commerce Clause was to create an area of free trade among the several States." McLeod v. J.E. Dilworth Co., 322 U.S. at 330 (1944). Under such a regime, the borders between the States are essentially irrelevant. As the Court stated in West v. Kansas Natural Gas Co., 221 U.S. at 255 (1911), "'in matters of foreign and interstate commerce there are no state lines.'" See Boston Stock Exchange v. State Tax Comm'n, supra, at 331-332. Consequently, to accept appellants' theory and invalidate the Montana tax solely because most of Montana's coal is shipped across the very state borders that ordinarily are to be considered irrelevant would

---

6. The Heisler approach has forced the Court to draw distinctions that can only be described as opaque. Compare, for example, East Ohio Gas Co., 283 U.S. 465 (1931) (movement of gas into local supply lines at reduced pressure constitutes local business), with Interstate Natural Gas Co., 284 U.S. 41 (1931) (movement of gas into local supply lines constitutes part of interstate business).

require a significant and, in our view, unwarranted departure from the rationale of our prior discrimination cases.

Furthermore, appellants' assertion that Montana may not "exploit" its "monopoly" position by exporting tax burdens to other States, cannot rest on a claim that there is need to protect the out-of-state consumers of Montana coal from discriminatory tax treatment. As previously noted, there is no real discrimination in this case; the tax burden is borne according to the amount of coal consumed and not according to any distinction between in-state and out-of-state consumers. Rather, appellants assume that the Commerce Clause gives residents of one State a right of access at "reasonable" prices to resources located in another State that is richly endowed with such resources, without regard to whether and on what terms residents of the resource-rich State have access to the resources. We are not convinced that the Commerce Clause, of its own force, gives the residents of one State the right to control in this fashion the terms of resource development and depletion in a sister State.[8]

In any event, appellants' discrimination theory ultimately collapses into their claim that the Montana tax is invalid under the fourth prong of the Complete Auto Transit test: that the tax is not "fairly related to the services provided by the State." Because appellants concede that Montana may impose some severance tax on coal mined in the State, the only remaining foundation for their discrimination theory is a claim that the tax burden borne by the out-of-state consumers of Montana coal is excessive. This is, of course, merely a variant of appellants' assertion that the Montana tax does not satisfy the "fairly related" prong of the Complete Auto Transit test, and it is to this contention that we now turn.

Appellants argue that they are entitled to an opportunity to prove that the amount collected under the Montana tax is not fairly related to the additional costs the State incurs because of coal mining.[10] Thus, appellants' objection is to the *rate* of the Montana tax, and even then, their only complaint is that the *amount* the State receives in taxes far exceeds the *value* of the services provided to the coal mining industry. In objecting to the tax on this ground, appellants may be assuming that the Montana tax is, in fact, intended to reimburse the State for the cost of specific services furnished to the coal mining industry. Alternatively, appellants could be arguing that a State's power to tax an activity connected to interstate commerce cannot exceed the value of the services specifically provided to the activity. Either way, the premise of appellants' argument is invalid. Furthermore, appellants have completely misunderstood the nature of the inquiry under the fourth prong of the Complete Auto Transit test.

The Montana Supreme Court held that the coal severance tax is "imposed for the general support of the government" and we have no reason to question this characterization of the Montana tax as a general revenue tax.[11] Consequently, in reviewing appellants' contentions, we put to one side those cases in which the Court reviewed challenges to "user" fees or "taxes" that were designed and defended as a specific charge imposed by the State for the use of state-owned or state-provided transportation or other facilities and services. See, e.g., Evansville-Vanderburgh Airport Authority Dist. v. Delta Airlines, Inc., 405 U.S. 707 (1972); Clark v. Paul

---

8. Nor do we share appellants' apparent view that the Commerce Clause injects principles of antitrust law into the relations between the States by reference to such imprecise standards as whether one State is "exploiting" its "monopoly" position with respect to a natural resource when the flow of commerce among them is not otherwise impeded. The threshold questions whether a State enjoys a "monopoly" position and whether the tax burden is shifted out of State, rather than borne by in-state producers and consumers, would require complex factual inquiries about such issues as elasticity of demand for the product and alternative sources of supply. Moreover, under this approach, the constitutionality of a state tax could well turn on whether the in-state producer is able, through sales contracts or otherwise, to shift the burden of the tax forward to its out-of-state customers. As the Supreme Court of Montana observed, "[i]t would be strange indeed if the legality of a tax could be made to depend on the vagaries of the terms of contracts."

10. Appellants expect to show that the "legitimate local impact costs [of coal mining]–for schools, roads, police, fire and health protection, and environmental protection and the like–might amount to approximately 2 [cents] per ton, compared to present average revenues from the severance tax alone of over $ 2.00 per ton." Appellants contend that inasmuch as 50% of the revenues generated by the Montana tax is "cached away, in effect, for unrelated and unknown purposes," it is clear that the tax is not fairly related to the services furnished by the State.

At oral argument before the Montana Supreme Court, appellants' counsel suggested that a tax of "perhaps twelve and a half to fifteen percent of the value of the coal" would be constitutional.

11. Contrary to appellants' suggestion, the fact that 50% of the proceeds of the severance tax is paid into a trust fund does not undermine the Montana court's conclusion that the tax is a general revenue tax. Nothing in the Constitution prohibits the people of Montana from choosing to allocate a portion of current tax revenues for use by future generations.

Gray, Inc., 306 U.S. 583 (1939); Ingels v. Morf, 300 U.S. 290 (1937).[12]

This Court has indicated that States have considerable latitude in imposing general revenue taxes. The Court has, for example, consistently rejected claims that the Due Process Clause of the Fourteenth Amendment stands as a barrier against taxes that are "unreasonable" or "unduly burdensome." See, e. g., Pittsburgh v. Alco Parking Corp., 417 U.S. 369 (1974); Magnano Co. v. Hamilton, 292 U.S. 40 (1934); Alaska Fish Salting & By-Products Co. v. Smith, 255 U.S. 44 (1921). Moreover, there is no requirement under the Due Process Clause that the amount of general revenue taxes collected from a particular activity must be reasonably related to the value of the services provided to the activity. Instead, our consistent rule has been:

"Nothing is more familiar in taxation than the imposition of a tax upon a class or upon individuals who enjoy no direct benefit from its expenditure, and who are not responsible for the condition to be remedied."

"A tax is not an assessment of benefits. It is, as we have said, a means of distributing the burden of the cost of government. The only benefit to which the taxpayer is constitutionally entitled is that derived from his enjoyment of the privileges of living in an organized society, established and safeguarded by the devotion of taxes to public purposes. Any other view would preclude the levying of taxes except as they are used to compensate for the burden on those who pay them, and would involve abandonment of the most fundamental principle of government–that it exists primarily to provide for the common good." Carmichael v. Southern Coal & Coke Co., 301 U.S. 495, 521-523 (1937) (citations and footnote omitted).

There is no reason to suppose that this latitude afforded the States under the Due Process Clause is somehow divested by the Commerce Clause merely because the taxed activity has some connection to interstate commerce; particularly when the tax is levied on an activity conducted within the State. "The exploitation by foreign corporations [or consumers] of intrastate opportunities under the protection and encouragement of local government offers a basis for taxation as unrestricted as that for domestic corporations." To accept appellants' apparent suggestion that the Commerce Clause prohibits the States from requiring an activity connected to interstate commerce to contribute

to the general cost of providing governmental services, as distinct from those costs attributable to the taxed activity, would place such commerce in a privileged position. But as we recently reiterated, "'[i]t was not the purpose of the commerce clause to relieve those engaged in interstate commerce from their just share of state tax burden even though it increases the cost of doing business.'" Colonial Pipeline Co. v. Traigle, 421 U.S. at 108, quoting Western Live Stock v. Bureau of Revenue, 303 U.S. at 254. The "just share of state tax burden" includes sharing in the cost of providing "police and fire protection, the benefit of a trained work force, and 'the advantages of a civilized society.'" Exxon Corp., 447 U.S. at 228 (1980), quoting Japan Line, 441 U.S. at 445. See Assn. of Wash. Stevedoring Cos., 435 U.S. at 750-751; id., at 764 (Powell, J., concurring in part and concurring in result); General Motors Corp. v. Washington, 377 U.S. at 440-441.

Furthermore, there can be no question that Montana may constitutionally raise general revenue by imposing a severance tax on coal mined in the State. The entire value of the coal, before transportation, originates in the State, and mining of the coal depletes the resource base and wealth of the State, thereby diminishing a future source of taxes and economic activity. In many respects, a severance tax is like a real property tax, which has never been doubted as a legitimate means of raising revenue by the situs State (quite apart from the right of that or any other State to tax income derived from use of the property). When, as here, a general revenue tax does not discriminate against interstate commerce and is apportioned to activities occurring within the State, the State "is free to pursue its own fiscal policies, unembarrassed by the Constitution, if by the practical operation of a tax the state has exerted its power in relation to opportunities which it has given, to protection which it has afforded, to benefits which it has conferred by the fact of being an orderly, civilized society." Wisconsin v. J.C. Penney Co., 311 U.S. at 444. As we explained in General Motors Corp v. Washington, supra, at 440-441:

"[T]he validity of the tax rests upon whether the State is exacting a constitutionally fair demand for that aspect of interstate commerce to which it bears a special relation. For our purposes, the decisive issue turns on the operating incidence of the tax. In other words, the question is whether the State has exerted its power in proper proportion to appellant's activities within the State and to appellant's consequent enjoyment of the opportunities and protections which the State has afforded. . . . As was said in Wisconsin v. J.C. Penney Co., 311 U.S. at 444, '[t]he simple but controlling question is whether the state has given anything for which it can ask return.'"

---

12. As the Court has stated, "such imposition, although termed a tax, cannot be tested by standards which generally determine the validity of taxes." Interstate Transit, Inc. v. Lindsey, 283 U.S. 183, 190 (1931). Because such charges are purportedly assessed to reimburse the State for costs incurred in providing specific quantifiable services, we have required a showing, based on factual evidence in the record, that "the fees charged do not appear to be manifestly disproportionate to the services rendered. . . ." Clark v. Paul Gray, Inc., 306 U.S. at 599. See id., at 598-600; Ingels v. Morf, 300 U.S. at 296-297.

. . . .

The relevant inquiry under the fourth prong of the Complete Auto Transit test[14] is not, as appellants suggest, the amount of the tax or the value of the benefits allegedly bestowed as measured by the costs the State incurs on account of the taxpayer's activities.[15] Rather, the test is closely connected to the first prong of the Complete Auto Transit test. Under this threshold test, the interstate business must have a substantial nexus with the State before any tax may be levied on it. See National Bellas Hess, Inc., 386 U.S. 753 (1967). Beyond that threshold requirement, the fourth prong of the Complete Auto Transit test imposes the additional limitation that the measure of the tax must be reasonably related to the extent of the contact, since it is the activities or presence of the taxpayer in the State that may properly be made to bear a "just share of state tax burden," Western Live Stock, 303 U.S. at 254. See National Geographic Society v. California Board of Equalization, 430 U.S. 551 (1977); Standard Pressed Steel Co. v. Washington Revenue Dept., 419 U.S. 560 (1975). As the Court explained in J.C. Penney Co., supra, at 446 (emphasis added), "the incidence of the tax *as well as its measure* [must be] tied to the earnings which the State . . . has made possible, insofar as government is the prerequisite for the fruits of civilization for which, as Mr. Justice Holmes was fond of saying, we pay taxes."

Against this background, we have little difficulty concluding that the Montana tax satisfies the fourth prong of the Complete Auto Transit test. The "operating incidence" of the tax, see General Motors Corp. v. Washington, 377 U.S. at 440-441, is on the mining of coal within Montana. Because it is measured as a percentage of the value of the coal taken, the Montana tax is in "proper proportion" to appellants' activities within the State and, therefore, to their "consequent enjoyment of the opportunities and protections which the State has afforded" in connection with those activities. Id., at 441. Cf. Nippert v. Richmond, 327 U.S. at 427. When a tax is assessed in proportion to a taxpayer's activities or presence in a State, the taxpayer is shouldering its fair share of supporting the State's provision of "police and fire protection, the benefit of a trained work force, and 'the advantages of a civilized society.'" Exxon Corp. v. Wisconsin Dept. of Revenue, 447 U.S. at 228, quoting Japan Line, 441 U.S. at 445.

Appellants argue, however, that the fourth prong of the Complete Auto Transit test must be construed as requiring a factual inquiry into the relationship between the revenues generated by a tax and costs incurred on account of the taxed activity, in order to provide a mechanism for judicial disapproval under the Commerce Clause of state taxes that are excessive. This assertion reveals that appellants labor under a misconception about a court's role in cases such as this.[16] The simple fact is that the appropriate level or rate of taxation is essentially a matter for legislative, and not judicial, resolution.[17] In essence, appellants ask this Court to prescribe a test for the validity of state taxes that would require state and federal courts, as a matter of federal constitutional law, to calculate acceptable rates or levels of taxation of activities that are conceded to be legitimate subjects of taxation. This we decline to do.

In the first place, it is doubtful whether any legal test could adequately reflect the numerous and competing economic, geographic, demographic, social, and political considerations that must inform a decision about an acceptable rate or level of state taxation, and yet be reasonably capable of application in a wide variety of individual cases. But even apart from the difficulty of the judicial undertaking, the nature of the fact-finding and judgment that would be required of the courts merely reinforces the conclusion that questions about the

---

14. The fourth prong of the Complete Auto Transit test is derived from General Motors, J.C. Penney, and similar cases. See 430 U.S. at 279, n. 8; see also National Geographic Society v. California Board of Equalization, 430 U.S. at 558.

15. Indeed, the words "amount" and "value" were not even used in Complete Auto Transit. See 430 U.S. at 279. Similarly, our cases applying the Complete Auto Transit test have not mentioned either of these words. See Exxon Corp. v. Wisconsin Dept. of Revenue, 447 U.S. at 228; Mobil Oil Corp. v. Commissioner of Taxes, 445 U.S. at 443; Japan Line, Ltd. v. County of Los Angeles, 441 U.S. at 444-445; Washington Revenue Dept. v. Association of Wash. Stevedoring Cos., 435 U.S. at 750; National Geographic Society v. California Board of Equalization, supra, at 558.

16. In any event, the linchpin of appellants' contention is the incorrect assumption that the amount of state taxes that may be levied on an activity connected to interstate commerce is limited by the costs incurred by the State on account of that activity. Only then does it make sense to advocate judicial examination of the relationship between taxes paid and benefits provided. But as we have previously noted, interstate commerce may be required to contribute to the cost of providing all governmental services, including those services from which it arguably receives no direct "benefit." In such circumstances, absent an equal protection challenge (which appellants do not raise), and unless a court is to second-guess legislative decisions about the amount or disposition of tax revenues, it is difficult to see how the court is to go about comparing costs and benefits in order to decide whether the tax burden on an activity connected to interstate commerce is excessive.

17. Of course, a taxing statute may be judicially disapproved if it is "so arbitrary as to compel the conclusion that it does not involve an exertion of the taxing power, but constitutes, in substance and effect, the direct exertion of a different and forbidden power, as, for example, the confiscation of property." Magnano Co. v. Hamilton, 292 U.S. at 44.

appropriate level of state taxes must be resolved through the political process. Under our federal system, the determination is to be made by state legislatures in the first instance and, if necessary, by Congress, when particular state taxes are thought to be contrary to federal interests.[18]

Furthermore, the reference in the cases to police and fire protection and other advantages of civilized society is not, as appellants suggest, a disingenuous incantation designed to avoid a more searching inquiry into the relationship between the value of the benefits conferred on the taxpayer and the amount of taxes it pays. Rather, when the measure of a tax is reasonably related to the taxpayer's activities or presence in the State–from which it derives some benefit such as the substantial privilege of mining coal–the taxpayer will realize, in proper proportion to the taxes it pays, "[t]he only benefit to which the taxpayer is constitutionally entitled. . . [:] that derived from his enjoyment of the privileges of living in an organized society, established and safeguarded by the devotion of taxes to public purposes." Carmichael v. Southern Coal & Coke Co., 301 U.S. at 522. Correspondingly, when the measure of a tax bears no relationship to the taxpayers' presence or activities in a State, a court may properly conclude under the fourth prong of the Complete Auto Transit test that the State is imposing an undue burden on interstate commerce. See Nippert v. Richmond, 327 U.S. at 427; cf. Michigan-Wisconsin Pipe Line Co., 347 U.S. 157 (1954). We are satisfied that the Montana tax, assessed under a formula that relates the tax liability to the value of appellant coal producers' activities within the State, comports with the requirements of Complete Auto Transit . . . .

. . . .

IV

In sum, we conclude that appellants have failed to demonstrate either that the Montana tax suffers from any of the constitutional defects alleged in their complaints, or that a trial is necessary to resolve the issue of the constitutionality of the tax. Consequently, the judgment of the Supreme Court of Montana is affirmed.

JUSTICE WHITE, concurring.

. . . Congress has the power to protect interstate commerce from intolerable or even undesirable burdens. It is also very much aware of the Nation's energy needs, of the Montana tax, and of the trend in the energy-rich States to aggrandize their position and perhaps lessen the tax burdens on their own citizens by imposing unusually high taxes on mineral extraction. Yet, Congress is so far content to let the matter rest, and we are counseled by the Executive Branch through the Solicitor General not to overturn the Montana tax as inconsistent with either the Commerce Clause or federal statutory policy in the field of energy or otherwise. The constitutional authority and the machinery to thwart efforts such as those of Montana, if thought unacceptable, are available to Congress, and surely Montana and other similarly situated States do not have the political power to impose their will on the rest of the country. As I presently see it, therefore, the better part of both wisdom and valor is to respect the judgment of the other branches of the Government. I join the opinion and the judgment of the Court.

JUSTICE BLACKMUN, with whom JUSTICE POWELL and JUSTICE STEVENS join, dissenting.

In Complete Auto Transit, a unanimous Court observed: "A tailored tax, however accomplished, must receive the careful scrutiny of the courts to determine whether it produces a forbidden effect on interstate commerce." 430 U.S. at 288-289, n. 15. In this case, appellants have alleged that Montana's severance tax on coal is tailored to single out interstate commerce, and that it produces a forbidden effect on that commerce because the tax bears no "relationship to the services provided by the State." Ibid. The Court today concludes that appellants are not entitled to a *trial* on this claim. Because I believe that the "careful scrutiny" due a tailored tax makes a trial here necessary, I respectfully dissent.

I

The State of Montana has approximately 25% of all known United States coal reserves, and more than 50% of the Nation's low-sulfur coal reserves. Approximately 70-75% of Montana's coal lies under land owned by the Federal Government in the State. The great bulk of the coal mined in Montana–indeed, allegedly as much as 90%–is exported to other States pursuant to long-term purchase contracts with out-of-state utilities. Those contracts typically provide that the costs of state taxation shall be passed on to the utilities; in turn, fuel adjustment clauses allow the utilities to pass the cost of taxation along to their consumers. Because federal environmental legislation has increased the demand for low-sulfur coal, and because the Montana coal fields occupy a "pivotal" geographic position in the Midwestern and northwestern energy markets, Montana has supplied an increasing percentage of the Nation's coal.

---

18. The controversy over the Montana tax has not escaped the attention of the Congress. Several bills were introduced during the 96th Congress to limit the rate of state severance taxes. See S. 2695, H.R. 6625, H.R. 6654 and H.R. 7163. Similar bills have been introduced in the 97th Congress. See S. 178, H.R. 1313.

. . . .

Appellants' complaint alleged that Montana's severance tax is ultimately borne by out-of-state consumers, and for the purposes of this appeal that allegation is to be treated as true. Appellants further alleged that the tax bears no reasonable relationship to the services or protection provided by the State. The issue here, of course, is whether they are entitled to a trial on that claim, not whether they will succeed on the merits. It should be noted, however, that Montana imposes numerous other taxes upon coal mining. . . . In light of these circumstances, the Interstate and Foreign Commerce Committee of the United States House of Representatives concluded that Montana's coal severance tax results in revenues "far in excess of the direct and indirect impact costs attributable to the coal production." Several commentators have agreed that Montana and other similarly situated Western States have pursued a policy of "OPEC-like revenue maximization," and that the Montana tax accordingly bears no reasonable relationship to the services and protection afforded by the State. These findings, of course, are not dispositive of the issue whether the Montana severance tax is "fairly related" to the services provided by the State within the meaning of our prior cases. They do suggest, however, that appellants' claim is a substantial one. . . .

. . . .

. . . The gravamen of appellants' complaint is that the severance tax does not satisfy the fourth prong of the Complete Auto Transit test because it is tailored to, and does, force interstate commerce to pay more than its way. Under our established precedents, appellants are entitled to a trial on this claim.

The Court's conclusion to the contrary rests on the premise that the relevant inquiry under the fourth prong of the Complete Auto Transit test is simply whether the measure of the tax is fixed as a percentage of the value of the coal taken. This interpretation emasculates the fourth prong. No trial will ever be necessary on the issue of fair relationship so long as a State is careful to impose a proportional rather than a flat tax rate; thus, the Court's rule is no less "mechanical" than the approach entertained in Heisler, disapproved today. Under the Court's reasoning, any ad valorem tax will satisfy the fourth prong; indeed, the Court implicitly ratifies Montana's contention that it is free to tax this coal at 100% or even 1,000% of value, should it choose to do so. Likewise, the Court's analysis indicates that Montana's severance tax would not run afoul of the Commerce

Clause even if it raised sufficient revenue to allow Montana to eliminate all other taxes upon its citizens.[11]

The Court's prior cases neither require nor support such a startling result.[12] The Court often has noted that "'[i]t was not the purpose of the commerce clause to relieve those engaged in interstate commerce from their *just share* of state tax burden even though it increases the cost of doing the business.'" Complete Auto Transit, 430 U.S. at 279 (emphasis added), quoting Western Live Stock, 303 U.S. at 254. Accordingly, interstate commerce cannot claim any exemption from a state tax that "is fairly related to the services provided by the State." We have not interpreted this requirement of "fair relation" in a narrow sense; interstate commerce may be required to share equally with intrastate commerce the cost of providing "police and fire protection, the benefit of a trained work force, and 'the advantages of a civilized society.'" Exxon Corp. v. Wisconsin Dept. of Revenue, 447 U.S. at 228, quoting Japan Line, Ltd. v. County of Los Angeles, 441 U.S. at 445. See, e.g., Nippert v. Richmond, 327 U.S. at 433. Moreover, interstate commerce can be required to "pay its own way" in a narrower sense as well: the State may tax interstate commerce for the

---

11. As the example of Alaska illustrates, this prospect is not a fanciful one. Ninety percent of Alaska's revenue derives from petroleum taxes and royalties; because of the massive sums that have been so raised, that State's income tax has been eliminated. As noted above, Montana's severance tax already allegedly accounts for 20% of its total tax revenue, and the State has enacted property and income tax relief.

12. The Court apparently derives its interpretation of the fourth prong of the Complete Auto Transit test primarily from Wisconsin v. J.C. Penney Co., 311 U.S. 435 (1940), and General Motors Corp. v. Washington, 377 U.S. 436 (1964). In neither of those cases, however, did the Court consider the question presented here. J.C. Penney involved a Fourteenth Amendment challenge brought by a foreign corporation to a Wisconsin tax imposed on domestic and foreign corporations "for the privilege of declaring. . . dividends" out of income from property located and business transacted in Wisconsin. The corporation argued that because the income from the Wisconsin transactions had been transferred to New York, Wisconsin had "no jurisdiction to tax" those amounts. 311 U.S. at 436. The Court rejected that argument, holding that "[t]he fact that a tax is contingent upon events brought to pass without a state does not destroy the nexus between such a tax and transactions within a state for which the tax is an exaction," Id., at 445. In General Motors, the question before the Court was the validity of an unapportioned tax on the gross receipts of a corporation in interstate commerce. The Court concluded that there was a sufficient nexus to uphold the tax. 377 U.S. at 448. See id., at 449-450 (BRENNAN, J., dissenting).

purpose of recovering those costs attributable to the activity itself.[13]

. . . .

Thus, the Court has been particularly vigilant to review taxes that "single out interstate business," since "[a]ny tailored tax of this sort creates an increased danger of error in apportionment, of discrimination against interstate commerce, and of a lack of relationship to the services provided by the State."[14] Moreover, the Court's vigilance has not been limited to taxes that discriminate upon their face: "Not the tax in a vacuum of words, but its practical consequences for the doing of interstate commerce in applications to concrete facts are our concern." Nippert, 327 U.S. at 431. See Maryland v. Louisiana, 451 U.S. at 756. This is particularly true when the challenged tax, while facially neutral, falls so heavily upon interstate commerce that its burden "is not likely

---

13. . . . .

The Court has continued to scrutinize carefully taxes on interstate commerce that are designed to reimburse the State for the particular costs imposed by that commerce. See, e.g., Evansville-Vanderburgh Airport Authority Dist. v. Delta Airlines, Inc., 405 U.S. 707 (1972); Clark v. Paul Gray, Inc., 306 U.S. 583 (1939); Ingels v. Morf, 300 U.S. 290 (1937). In analyzing such taxes, it has required that there be factual evidence in the record that "the fees charged do not appear to be manifestly disproportionate to the services rendered." Clark, 306 U.S. at 599. The Court concludes that this test has no bearing here because the Montana Supreme Court held that the coal severance tax was "'imposed for the general support of the government.'" In fact, however, the matter is not nearly so clear as the Court suggests. The Montana court also implied that the tax was designed at least in part to compensate the State for the special costs attributable to coal mining, as have appellees here.

Indeed, the stated objectives of the 1975 amendment were to: "(a) preserve or modestly increase revenues going to the general fund, (b) to respond to current social impacts attributable to coal development, and (c) to invest in the future, when new energy technologies reduce our dependence on coal and mining activity may decline." Statement to Accompany the Report of the Free Joint Conference Committees on Coal Taxation 1 (1975). Since the tax was designed only to "preserve or modestly increase" general revenues, it is appropriate for a court to inquire here whether the "surplus" revenue Montana has received from this severance tax is "manifestly disproportionate" to the present or future costs attributable to coal development.

14. Complete Auto Transit gave several examples of "tailored" taxes: property taxes designed to differentiate between property used in transportation and other types of property; an income tax using different rates for different types of business; and a tax on the "privilege of doing business in corporate form" that changed with the nature of the corporate activity involved. 430 U.S. at 288, n. 15. A severance tax using different rates for different minerals, is of course, directly analogous to these examples.

---

to be alleviated by those political restraints which are normally exerted on legislation where it affects adversely interests within the state." McGoldrick v. Berwind-White Co., 309 U.S. at 46, n. 2. Cf. Raymond Motor Transportation, Inc. v. Rice, 434 U.S. at 446-447. In sum, then, when a tax has been "tailored" to reach interstate commerce, the Court's cases suggest that we require a closer "fit" under the fourth prong of the Complete Auto Transit test than when interstate commerce has not been singled out by the challenged tax.

As a number of commentators have noted, state severance taxes upon minerals are particularly susceptible to "tailoring." "Like a tollgate lying athwart a trade route, a severance or processing tax conditions access to natural resources." Developments in the Law: Federal Limitations on State Taxation of Interstate Business, 75 Harv. L. Rev. 953, 970 (1962). Thus, to the extent that the taxing jurisdiction approaches a monopoly position in the mineral, and consumption is largely outside the State, such taxes are "[e]conomically and politically analogous to transportation taxes exploiting geographical position." Brown, The Open Economy: Justice Frankfurter and the Position of the Judiciary, 67 Yale L.J. 219, 232 (1957). But just as a port State may require that imports pay their own way even though the tax levied increases the cost of goods purchased by inland customers, see Michelin Tire Corp., 423 U.S. at 288 (1976), so also may a mineral-rich State require that those who consume its resources pay a fair share of the general costs of government, as well as the specific costs attributable to the commerce itself. Thus, the mere fact that the burden of a severance tax is largely shifted forward to out-of-state consumers does not, standing alone, make out a Commerce Clause violation. But the Clause *is* violated when, as appellants allege is the case here, the State effectively selects "a class of out-of-state taxpayers to shoulder a tax burden grossly in excess of any costs imposed directly or indirectly by such taxpayers on the State."

III

It is true that a trial in this case would require "complex factual inquiries" into whether economic conditions are such that Montana is in fact able to export the burden of its severance tax. I do not believe, however, that this threshold inquiry is beyond judicial competence.[17] If the

---

17. There is no basis for the conclusion that the issues presented would be more difficult than those routinely dealt with in complex civil litigation. See, e.g., Milwaukee v. Illinois, 451 U.S. at 349 (dissenting opinion). "The complexity of a properly presented federal question is hardly a suitable basis for denying federal courts the power to adjudicate." Id., at 349, n. 25.

trial court were to determine that the tax is exported, it would then have to determine whether the tax is "fairly related," within the meaning of Complete Auto Transit. The Court to the contrary, this would not require the trial court "to second-guess legislative decisions about the amount or disposition of tax revenues." If the tax is in fact a legitimate general revenue measure identical or roughly comparable to taxes imposed upon similar industries, a court's inquiry is at an end; on the other hand, if the tax singles out this particular interstate activity and charges it with a grossly disproportionate share of the general costs of government, the court must determine whether there is some reasonable basis for the legislative judgment that the tax is necessary to compensate the State for the particular costs imposed by the activity.

To be sure, the task is likely to prove to be a formidable one; but its difficulty does not excuse our failure to undertake it. This case poses extremely grave issues that threaten both to "polarize the Nation," and to reawaken "the tendencies toward economic Balkanization" that the Commerce Clause was designed to remedy. See Hughes v. Oklahoma, 441 U.S. at 325-326. It is no answer to say that the matter is better left to Congress:[19]

"While the Constitution vests in Congress the power to regulate commerce among the states, it does not say what the states may or may not do in the absence of congressional action. . . . Perhaps even more than by interpretation of its written word, this Court has advanced the solidarity and prosperity of this Nation by the meaning it has given to these great silences of the Constitution." H. P. Hood & Sons, Inc. v. Du Mond, 336 U.S. at 534-535.

I would not lightly abandon that role.[20] Because I believe that appellants are entitled to an opportunity to prove that, in Holmes' words, Montana's severance tax "embodies what the Commerce Clause was meant to end," I dissent.

---

19. As the Court notes, the issue has not escaped congressional attention. Ante, n. 18. No bill, however, has yet been passed, and this Court is not disabled to act in the interim; to the contrary, strong policy and institutional considerations suggest that it is appropriate that the Court consider this issue. Indeed, whereas Montana argues that the question presented here is one better left to Congress, in 1980 hearings before the Senate Committee on Energy and Natural Resources, the then Governor of Montana took the position that the reasonableness of this tax was "a question most properly left to the court," not a congressional committee. See Hearing on S. 2695 before the Senate Committee on Energy and Natural Resources, 96th Cong., 2d Sess., 237 (1980).

---

20. Justice Holmes' words are relevant:

"I do not think the United States would come to an end if we lost our power to declare an Act of Congress void. I do think the Union would be imperilled if we could not make that declaration as to the laws of the several States. For one in my place sees how often a local policy prevails with those who are not trained to national views and how often action is taken that embodies what the Commerce Clause was meant to end." O. Holmes, Law and the Court, in Collected Legal Papers 291, 295-296 (reprint, 1952).

Questions and Comments

1. A state that levies an income tax on salaries and wages will typically apply the same rate to both residents and nonresident commuters. Yet nonresident commuters do not receive the same level of public services and benefits that residents receive. Compare, for example, A, a nonresident commuter who works for thirty years in State X paying the same income tax each year as B, a resident of State X and A's co-worker. B's children are able to go to X's State University and pay a lower in-state tuition than A's children. Moreover, B has the benefits of X's infrastructure, social programs, and so forth. Is it taxation without representation when a state taxes nonresidents?

Does State X export its income tax when it is paid by nonresidents such as A? What about Nevada's tax on gambling? Delaware's fees on incorporations? New York's old stock transfer tax? A rate of sales tax at a state's major airport that is higher than the rate that applies elsewhere in the state? A special tax on the rental of hotel rooms? A special tax on the rental of cars? How would Justice Blackmun analyze these situations? See *American Ass'n v. Levitt*, 279 F. Supp. 40 (S.D.N.Y. 1967), aff'd, 405 F.2d 1148 (2d Cir. 1969).

In *Utah Power & Light Co. v. Pfost*, 286 U.S. 165 (1932), the Court upheld an Idaho tax on a public utility's generation of electric power at its hydroelectric plants within Idaho even though it sold about 85% of its output to consumers in Utah and Wyoming. Should Montana have cited *Utah Power* in support of its position in *Commonwealth Edison?*

2. In defending North Dakota's severance tax, then Governor Arthur A. Link set forth the following costs imposed on his State from mining: the removal of fertile top soil, the consumption of vast amounts of scarce water, and the interference with water aquifers. See Link, Political Constraint in North Dakota's Coal Severance Tax, 31 Nat'l Tax J. 207, 263 (1978). More fundamentally, unlike most other industries, the natural resource industry irreparably depletes an asset of a state. More ecological and aesthetic costs may be also imposed compared with other industries. How should these factors influence a court's analysis of a severance tax? Could these factors be quantified for purposes of evaluating a severance tax's constitutionality under *Complete Auto's* fourth prong?

Although Montana in this case argued that the issue of its severance tax was best left to Congress, in hearings before Congress the then Governor of Montana argued that the severance tax was best left to the courts. See

Hearing on S. 2695 before the Senate Committee on Energy and Natural Resources, 96th Cong., 2d Sess., 237 (1980).

3. Does the case emasculate the fourth prong of *Complete Auto*? Does the fourth prong play a different role when a user fee is at issue rather than a general revenue tax? Would a severance tax that was levied as a fixed amount per ton of coal mined satisfy the fourth prong? What type of tax would satisfy the first three prongs of *Complete Auto* but not the fourth?

One commentator concludes that none of the cases cited by Justice Blackmun in support of the fourth prong of *Complete Auto Transit* actually support his position. See I Jerome Hellerstein, State Taxation: Corporate Income and Franchise Taxes at 156 n.266 (1983). Having created the test in *Complete Auto Transit*, perhaps Justice Blackmun had incentive to breathe life into it, as suggested by his dissent in *Commonwealth Edison.*

For an earlier version of the fourth prong of *Complete Auto* see *Union Refrigerator Transit Co. v. Kentucky*, 199 U.S. 194, 202 (1905):

The power of taxation, indispensable to the existence of every civilized government, is exercised upon the assumption of an equivalent rendered to the taxpayer in the protection of his person and property, or in the creation and maintenance of public conveniences in which he shares–such, for instance, as roads, bridges, sidewalks, pavements, and schools for the education of his children.

4. Under Justice Blackmun's approach, would a court determine the proper rate of severance tax or only strike down as unconstitutional a state's actual rate? Suppose, under Justice Blackmun's view, a 30% rate was unconstitutional. Assume that Montana then lowered its rate to 28%. Would a new round of litigation be triggered? Or would the evidence a trial court received in determining the constitutionality of the 30% rate suggest what rate would be acceptable? How often would such a trial have to be held? Under the majority's view of the fourth prong, what test would a court apply in determining how the costs of maintaining a civilized society should be distributed?

Compare Justice Blackmun's views with that of Justice Frankfurter:

At best, this Court can only act negatively; it can determine whether a specific state tax is imposed in violation of the Commerce Clause. Such decisions must necessarily depend on the application of rough and ready legal concepts. We cannot make a detailed inquiry into the incidence of diverse economic burdens in order to determine the extent to which such burdens conflict with the necessities of national economic life. Neither can we devise appropriate standards for dividing up national revenue on the basis of more or less abstract principles of constitutional law, which cannot be responsive to the subtleties of the interrelated economies of Nation and State. *Northwestern States Portland Cement Co. v. Minnesota*, 358 U.S. at 476 (Frankfurter, J. dissenting).

Also compare:

Judicial control of national commerce–unlike legislative regulations–must from inherent limitations of the judicial process treat the subject by the hit-and-miss method of deciding single local controversies upon evidence and information limited by the narrow rules of litigation. Spasmodic and unrelated instances of litigation cannot afford an adequate basis for the creation of integrated national rules which alone can afford that full protection for interstate commerce intended by the Constitution . . . Unconfined by "the narrow scope of judicial proceedings" Congress alone can, in the exercise of its plenary constitutional control over interstate commerce, not only consider whether . . . a tax . . . is consistent with the best interests of our national economy, but can also on the basis of full exploration of the many aspects of a complicated problem devise a national policy fair alike to the States and our Union. *McCarroll*, 309 U.S. at 188-89 (Black, J., and Douglas, J., dissenting).

5. Realistically, can't a single "excessive" tax be as burdensome to interstate commerce as multiple taxes on the same commerce? Why should the latter be prohibited by the Commerce Clause but not the former?

6. The taxpayers repeatedly refer to the amount of Montana's tax or to the value of the benefits bestowed by Montana whereas the Court refers to the measure of the tax. Whose interpretation is more in keeping with the fourth prong of *Complete Auto*?

7. The Court states that in many respects a severance tax is like a real property tax. Is a severance tax more like a real property tax or more like a sales tax? Does it matter how a severance tax is characterized? Once the Court characterized the severance tax as a property tax, was the result in the case predictable? Was there a reason the Court preferred the property tax analog to a sales tax analog?

8. The taxpayers did not challenge whether the Montana tax was properly apportioned. 453 U.S. at 617. Should they have? Suppose the taxpayers sell their coal to a utility in the State of Washington through a sales office in that State. Could Washington tax the receipts from the sale of the coal? *See General Motors Corp. v. Washington*, 377 U.S. 436 (1964) and *Standard Pressed Steel Company v. Department of Revenue*, 419 U.S. 560 (1975). See Shores, State Taxation of Interstate Commerce–Quiet Revolution or Much Ado About Nothing? 38 Tax Law Rev. 127, 152, 157-58 (1982).

9. Suppose the tax at issue is not the Montana severance tax but a property tax on coal. Would the Court's approach be the same?

10. Is the Court's analysis of the discrimination issue consistent with *Maryland v. Louisiana*?

11. Is the opinion helpful in deciding whether a state-imposed charge is a user fee or a tax? What turns on whether a charge is a user fee or a tax? If a user charge is struck down as excessive, can a state reinstitute it as a tax and have it tested by the more generous standard that applies to general revenue raising measures?

12. Assume that Montana was the only state in which low-sulphur coal was mined. Does it necessarily follow that Montana's severance tax will be exported?

13. Suppose the State of Montana had only one tax: a severance tax on coal. Suppose further that all of the coal subject to the severance tax was exported. Would the tax be constitutional? Is this the type of targeted tax that is referred to in footnote 15 of *Complete Auto*?

14. Suppose that Montana exported all of its coal to foreign countries. Would the Court's analysis be the same?

15. Did the Montana Legislature have protectionist motives in imposing the severance tax? Does a severance tax have protectionist effects? Is a severance tax similar to a tariff? Was the Court influenced by these considerations?

16. Is it fair to characterize the difference between the majority and the dissent as basically involving conflicting views about the nature and scope of judicial review? The oversight role of Congress in this area? Why aren't the types of issues raised in this case best left to Congress to evaluate?

17. Is this case inconsistent with the "new realism" exhibited by the Court in *Complete Auto Transit*?

18. During the early, formative days of constitutional interpretation, the Court was actively involved in trying to formulate a workable definition of interstate commerce. *Commonwealth Edison* makes it clear that the Court is taking a broad view of the activities that will be analyzed under the Commerce Clause. The Court's approach in tax cases mirrors the approach it has taken in evaluating whether federal legislation can be upheld under the Commerce Clause. See, e.g., *Wickard v. Filburn*, 317 U.S. 111 (1942) (wheat grown by a farmer for self-consumption affects interstate commerce); *Heart of Atlanta Hotel v. U.S.*, 379 U.S. 241 (1964) (discrimination by a hotel can impede interstate commerce in the form of travel). The parallel developments between the tax cases and the regulatory cases is not surprising because the Court has stated that "the definition of 'commerce' is the same when relied on to strike down or restrict state

legislation as when relied on to support some exertion of federal control or regulation." *Hughes v. Oklahoma*, 441 U.S. at 326 (citing *Philadelphia v. New Jersey*, 437 U.S. at 621-23).

In *Wickard v. Filburn*, supra, the Court upheld the application of the Agricultural Adjustment Act of 1938 to the wheat produced by a family farm, including the part consumed by the family itself in the form of flour. Even if the activity "be local and though it may not be regarded as commerce," 317 U.S. at 126, when taken into account with the other farms, "it exerts a substantial economic effect on interstate commerce." 317 U.S. at 120 n. 16. Congress could "properly have considered the wheat consumed on the farm where grown, if wholly outside the scheme of regulation, would have a substantial effect in defeating and obstructing its purpose to stimulate trade therein at increased prices." Id. at 129.

The Court has recently balked, however, at a completely open ended approach to what constitutes interstate commerce. In *United States v. Lopez*, 514 U.S. 549 (1995), the Court refused to accept a Commerce Clause defense for a federal statute prohibiting possession of firearms in school zones. It is too early to tell whether *Lopez* will be viewed as an aberration, limited to its unusual facts, or whether it signals a retrenchment by the Court, although *Camps Newfound/Owatonna, Inc. v. Town of Harrison, Maine*, infra, decided two years after *Lopez*, suggests the Court is still taking an expansive view of what constitutes interstate commerce.

19. A brief review of the leading cases on the definition of interstate commerce is found in the chapter on the Import-Export Clause, where the question of what constitutes interstate commerce, especially whether a good has entered or left the stream of commerce, may still be relevant.

20. The definition of interstate commerce may be relevant under state law. For example, many states provide that they will not levy a sales tax on a sale in interstate commerce. See, e.g., La. R.S. 47:305(E). These provisions date from the early days of the sales tax, several decades before the U.S. Supreme Court's landmark decision in *Complete Auto*. During that earlier period, the Court prohibited states from taxing what it characterized as "interstate commerce" but generally allowed them to tax various cross-border transactions as long as the taxing statute was not discriminatory and made some in-state aspect of the transaction the focus of the tax. *Complete Auto* marked the end of that period of formalism. Under current constitutional doctrines, states generally may tax interstate commerce provided the tax meets the four-prong test of *Complete Auto*.

Because of the changes in constitutional doctrines, state statutes that exempt sales made in interstate commerce are ambiguous. At the heart of the matter is whether the exemption should be interpreted in accordance with constitutional doctrines at the time of enactment (the "static" approach) or whether the exemption should be interpreted in light of current constitutional doctrines (the "ambulatory" approach). Both the static approach and the ambulatory approach have validity under some circumstances.[1]

The following four interpretations of a state exemption for interstate commerce are possible:

Approach #1 (Static). The state will not tax interstate commerce in violation of the Constitution as determined under the federal jurisprudence that existed at the time of the provision's enactment.

Approach #2 (Ambulatory). The state will not tax interstate commerce in violation of the Constitution as determined under *existing* federal jurisprudence.

Approach #3 (Static). The state cannot tax *any* interstate commerce regardless of what its powers might be under the Constitution, but the determination of what constitutes interstate commerce would be made under the federal jurisprudence existing at the time the provision was enacted.

Approach #4 (Ambulatory). Same as three above, except that the determination regarding what constitutes interstate commerce would be made under existing federal jurisprudence.

Which of these four approaches set forth above should be followed by a state is initially a matter of legislative intent. In most states, little or no legislative history exists with respect to older statutes (or in some cases, even with respect to new statutes). The two static approaches–approaches one and three–are identical, or nearly so, in practice. Before 1977, it was black letter law that a state could not impose any tax on interstate commerce under federal constitutional jurisprudence. Consequently, an outright ban on the taxation of

---

1. The static/ambulatory language is sometimes used in the context of tax treaties. Tax treaties frequently incorporate by reference some of the domestic laws of the signatory countries (Contracting States). As a result, the issue arises as to whether the incorporated law is the law at the time the treaty was ratified or the law as amended by subsequent domestic legislation. In the treaty context, the static approach was once favored, but the modern trend is to favor the ambulatory approach in most circumstances.

This note was prepared in conjunction with Professor Michael J. McIntyre.

interstate commerce, as defined under federal constitutional doctrines before 1977 (*Approach #3*), is the practical equivalent of a ban on the taxation of interstate commerce to the extent prohibited by the Constitution prior to 1977 (*Approach #1*). An exemption for interstate commerce would have had no practical effect prior to 1977 because it merely stated the constraints already imposed on a state by the Constitution, as interpreted by the Supreme Court. After *Complete Auto* in 1977, however, the static approaches would limit a state from exercising to the fullest extent its powers to tax interstate commerce.

The ambulatory approaches–approaches two and four–could produce very different results in practice. *Approach #2* conforms state law with post-*Complete Auto* jurisprudence. Under *Approach #2*, a state may tax interstate commerce provided the *Complete Auto* tests are satisfied. *Approach #4*, however, would require a tax department to derive from federal cases the contemporary federal constitutional definition of interstate commerce, notwithstanding that such definition has largely become irrelevant since 1977, when *Complete Auto* allowed the states to tax cross-border transactions regardless of whether interstate commerce was involved. *Approach #4* would require the formulation of a definition of interstate commerce, and cross-border transactions falling within that definition would not be taxable by the state even if they met the *Complete Auto* tests.

Approach #4 is inconsistent with the theory of statutory interpretation underlying the ambulatory approach. Under that theory, statutes that incorporate legal rules of another jurisdiction by reference (implicitly or explicitly) should be updated automatically as they are updated by the jurisdiction whose rules are being incorporated. When that jurisdiction no longer applies the incorporated rules, however, the reason for updating them is eliminated. Accordingly, because federal jurisprudence is no longer concerned with the definition of interstate commerce, the case for adopting *Approach #4* is weak.

Because static *Approaches #1* and *#3* are essentially equivalent, and ambulatory *Approaches #2* and *#4* can be made essentially equivalent, the above discussion suggests that the main issue for debate is whether the static approach or the ambulatory approach should be followed in interpreting an exemption for interstate commerce. Adopting the static approach would mean, as a practical matter, that a state would be prevented from taxing cross-border transactions, regardless of what its powers might be after *Complete Auto*, if those transactions constituted "interstate commerce" under pre-1977 law. Adopting the ambulatory approach would mean that a state would be permitted to tax cross-

border transactions to the fullest extent of its constitutional powers.[2]

The difference between the static approach and the ambulatory approach is not as great as it might appear at first blush. Even before the Court's 1977 landmark decision in *Complete Auto*, the Court had made clear that a state could tax cross-border transactions if the tax was levied on a "local incident" of a cross-border transaction and not levied on "interstate commerce" as such. The Court also upheld taxes on cross-border transactions if they were levied before interstate commerce began or after it had ended. In combination, these Court doctrines allowed states, with careful drafting, to tax much of what can now be taxed under the tests of *Complete Auto*.

The old doctrines produced results that rested on the most rarified of distinctions. The Court itself acknowledged on more than one occasion that its dormant Commerce Clause jurisprudence "is something of a 'quagmire' and the 'application of constitutional principles to specific state statutes leaves much room for controversy and confusion and little in the way of precise guides to States in the exercise of their indispensable power of taxation.'" *Quill Corp. v. North Dakota*, 504 U.S. at 315-316, quoting *Northwestern Portland Cement Co. v. Minnesota*, 358 U.S. at 457-58. Many of the strained distinctions that contributed to the quagmire, however, were abandoned after the *Complete Auto* decision in 1977.

21. For critical commentary on *Commonwealth Edison*, see John R. Sagan, *Severance Taxes and the Commerce Clause: Commonwealth Edison v. Montana*, 1983 Wis. L. Rev. 427; Jerry R. Fish, *Commonwealth Edison Co. v. Montana: Leading the Severance Tax Stampede*, 12 Envtl. L. 1031 (1982); Carol L. Powers, *State Taxation of Energy Resources: Affirmation of Commonwealth Edison Company v. Montana*, 10 B.C. Envtl. Aff. L. Rev. 503 (1982); John T. Bradford, *Beyond Commonwealth Edison Co. v. Montana - Direct Congressional Limitations on State Taxation of Natural Resources*, 9 J. Corp. Tax'n 253 (1982); Lucy Gamon, *Constitutional Law - Commonwealth Edison Co. v. Montana - the Constitutional and Public Policy Implications of State Taxation of Coal*, 8 J. Corp. L. 202 (1982); Donald F. Santa, Jr., *The Incomplete Complete Auto Transit Test: Commerce Clause Analysis in Commonwealth Edison v. Montana*, 8 Colum. J. Envtl. L.185 (1982); Mark Shepherd, *Commonwealth Edison Co. v. Montana*, 10 Ecology L.Q. 97 (1982); Mike McGrath and Walter Hellerstein, *Reflections on Commonwealth Edison Co. v. Montana*, 43 Mont. L. Rev. 165 (1982); Nancy K.

---

2. In effect, the ambulatory approach would mean that the exemption would impose no effective limits on state taxing power after 1977 because the statute would merely impose a limitation on state powers that was coterminous with the limitation imposed by the Constitution.

Stalcup, *Commonwealth Edison Co. v. State of Montana: Constitutional Limitations on State Energy Resource Taxation*, 9 Pepp. L. Rev. 487 (1982); Christine Chute, *Constitutional Law - Commerce Clause Standards for State*

Taxation of Mineral Severance: Commonwealth Edison, et al. v. State of Montana, et al., 17 Land & Water L. Rev. 169 (1982).

Westinghouse Electric Corp. v. Tully et al.
Supreme Court of the United States, 1984.
466 U.S. 388, 104 S. Ct. 1856, 80 L. Ed. 2d 388.

JUSTICE BLACKMUN delivered the opinion of the Court.

In this case, we are confronted with the question of the constitutionality of a franchise tax credit afforded by the State of New York to certain income of Domestic International Sales Corporations.

I

The tax credit in issue was enacted as part of the New York Legislature's response to additions to and changes in the United States Internal Revenue Code of 1954. In an effort to "provide tax incentives for U.S. firms to increase their exports," Congress gave special recognition to a corporate entity it described as a "Domestic International Sales Corporation" or "DISC." §§ 991-997 of the Code. A corporation qualifies as a DISC if substantially all its assets and gross receipts are export-related. Under federal law, a DISC is not taxed on its income. Instead, a portion of the DISC's income–labeled "deemed distributions"–is attributed to the DISC's shareholders on a current basis, whether or not that portion is actually paid or distributed to them. Under the statutory provisions in effect during the calendar years 1972 and 1973 (the tax years in question in this case), 50% of a DISC's income was deemed distributed to its shareholders. Taxes on the remaining income of the DISC–labeled "accumulated DISC income"–are *deferred* until either that accumulated income is actually distributed to the shareholders or the DISC no longer qualifies for special tax treatment.

Enactment of the federal DISC legislation caused revenue officials in the State of New York some concern. New York does not generally impose its franchise tax on distributions received by a parent from a subsidiary; instead, the subsidiary is taxed directly to the extent it does business in the State. Given the State's tax structure, had New York followed the federal lead in not taxing DISCs, a DISC's income would not have been taxed by the State. A budget analyst reported to the legislature that if no provision were made to tax DISCs, New York might suffer revenue losses of as much as $20-$30 million annually. On the other hand, the analyst warned that state taxation of DISCs would discourage their formation in New York and also discourage the manufacture of export goods within the State.

With these conflicting considerations in mind, New York enacted legislation pertaining to the taxation of DISCs. The enacted provisions require the consolidation of the receipts, assets, expenses, and liabilities of the DISC with those of its parent. The franchise tax is then assessed against the parent on the basis of the consolidated amounts. In an attempt to "provide a positive incentive for increased business activity in New York State," however, the legislature provided a "partially offsetting tax credit." The result of the credit is to lower the effective tax rate on the accumulated DISC income reflected in the consolidated return to 30% of the otherwise applicable franchise tax rate. The DISC credit, significantly, is limited to gross receipts from export products "shipped from a regular place of business of the taxpayer within [New York]." The credit is computed by (1) dividing the gross receipts of the DISC derived from export property shipped from a regular place of business within New York by the DISC's total gross receipts derived from the sale of export property; (2) multiplying that quotient (the DISC's New York export ratio) by the parent's New York business allocation percentage;[5] (3) multiplying that product by the New York tax rate applicable to the parent; (4) multiplying that product by 70%; and (5) multiplying that product by the parent's attributable share of the accumulated income of the DISC for the year.

II

The basic facts are stipulated. Appellant Westinghouse Electric Corporation (Westinghouse) is a Pennsylvania corporation engaged in the manufacture and sale of electrical equipment, parts, and appliances. Westinghouse is qualified to do business in New York, and it regularly pays corporate income and franchise taxes to that State. Among Westinghouse's subsidiaries is Westinghouse Electric Export Corporation (Westinghouse Export), a Delaware corporation wholly owned by Westinghouse, that qualifies as a federally tax-exempt DISC. Westinghouse Export acts as a commission

---

5. A corporation's business allocation percentage for New York tax purposes is computed according to a formula set forth in N.Y. Tax Law § 210.3. The percentage is, basically, the average of the percentages of the corporation's property situated, income earned, and payroll distributed within the State.

agent on behalf of both Westinghouse and Westinghouse's other affiliates for export sales of products manufactured in the United States and services related to those products. All of Westinghouse Export's income in 1972 and 1973 consisted of commissions on export sales. On both its 1972 and 1973 federal income and New York State franchise tax returns, Westinghouse included as income, and paid taxes on, an amount of deemed distributed income equal to about half of Westinghouse Export's income. In 1972, Westinghouse Export's income was about $26 million, and Westinghouse included in its consolidated return approximately $13 million of income deemed distributed from Westinghouse Export. In 1973, the income of Westinghouse Export was approximately $58 million; Westinghouse reported almost $30 million of that amount as deemed distributed income. Westinghouse, however, did not include the DISC's *accumulated* income in its consolidated returns.

The appellees, as the New York State Tax Commission (Tax Commission), sought to include in Westinghouse's consolidated income the accumulated DISC income; that is, the Tax Commission computed Westinghouse's taxable income by first combining all of Westinghouse Export's income with that of Westinghouse. The Commission gave Westinghouse the benefit of the DISC export credit for the approximately 5% of Westinghouse Export's receipts each year that could be attributed to New York shipments. After applying the relevant allocation and tax percentages, the Tax Commission asserted deficiencies in Westinghouse's franchise tax of $73,970 (later corrected to $71,970) plus interest for 1972 and $151,437 plus interest for 1973.

Westinghouse filed a petition for redetermination of the proposed deficiencies. By its petition, as later perfected, Westinghouse contended that by requiring it to compute its franchise tax liability on a consolidated basis with Westinghouse Export, the Tax Commission was taxing income that did not have a jurisdictional nexus to the State, in violation of the Commerce and Due Process Clauses of the United States Constitution. Westinghouse further contended that limiting the tax benefit of the DISC export credit to gross receipts from shipments attributable to a New York place of business violated the Commerce, Due Process, and Equal Protection Clauses. The Commission declined to entertain Westinghouse's contentions, on the ground that, as an administrative agency, it lacked jurisdiction to pass upon "the constitutionality of the laws of the State of New York."
. . . .

III

The Tax Commission seeks to convince us that the DISC tax credit forgives merely a portion of the tax that New York has jurisdiction to levy. All the accumulated income of a DISC is attributed to its parent for tax purposes. Under unitary tax principles, however, if the parent has a regular place of business outside New York, the State will not actually tax the full amount of the accumulated income. Only a portion of the parent's net income (which includes the accumulated DISC income) will be subject to tax in New York. That portion is determined by reference to a business allocation percentage determined by averaging the percentages of in-state property, payroll, and receipts. This Court long has upheld, subject to certain restraints, the use of a formula-apportionment method to determine the percentage of a business' income taxable in a given jurisdiction. Container Corp., 463 U.S. at 169-171 (1983); see Illinois Central R. Co. v. Minnesota, 309 U.S. 157 (1940); Hans Rees' Sons, 283 U.S. 123 (1931); Bass, Ratcliff & Gretton, 266 U.S. 271 (1924); Underwood Typewriter Co., 254 U.S. 113 (1920).

The Tax Commission's argument that New York employs a constitutionally acceptable allocation formula, in our view, serves only to obscure the issue in this case. The acceptability of the allocation formula employed by the State of New York is not relevant to the question before us. The fact that New York is attempting to tax only a fairly apportioned percentage of a DISC's accumulated income does not insulate from constitutional challenge the State's method of allowing the DISC export credit. New York's apportionment procedure determines what portion of a business' income is within the jurisdiction of New York. Nothing about the apportionment process releases the State from the constitutional restraints that limit the way in which it exercises its taxing power over the income within its jurisdiction.

Here, Westinghouse argues that the State of New York has sought to exercise its taxing power over accumulated DISC income in a manner that offends the Commerce Clause and the Equal Protection Clause of the Fourteenth Amendment. This challenge is not foreclosed by our holding that New York's allocation of DISC income is constitutionally acceptable. "Fairly apportioned" and "nondiscriminatory" are not synonymous terms. It is to the question whether the method of allowing the credit is discriminatory in a manner that violates the Commerce Clause that we now turn.

The Tax Commission argues that multiplying the allowable credit by the New York export ratio of the DISC merely ensures that the State is not allowing a parent corporation to claim a tax credit with respect to DISC income that is not taxable by the State of New York. This argument ignores the fact that the percentage of the DISC's accumulated income that is subject to New York franchise tax is determined by the parent's business allocation percentage, not by the export ratio. In computing the allowable credit, the statute requires the parent to factor in its business allocation percentage. This procedure alleviates the State's fears that it will be overly generous with its tax credit, for once the adjustment of multiplying the allowable DISC export credit by the parent's business allocation percentage has been accomplished, the tax credit has been fairly apportioned to apply only to the amount of the accumulated DISC income taxable to New York. From the standpoint of fair apportionment of the credit, the additional adjustment of the credit to reflect the DISC's New York export ratio is both inaccurate and duplicative.

It is this second adjustment, made only to the credit and not to the base taxable income figure, that has the effect of treating differently parent corporations that are similarly situated in all respects except for the percentage of their DISCs' shipping activities conducted from New York. This adjustment has the effect of allowing a parent a greater tax credit on its accumulated DISC income as its subsidiary DISC moves a greater percentage of its shipping activities into the State of New York. Conversely, the adjustment decreases the tax credit allowed to the parent for a given amount of its DISC's shipping activity conducted from New York as the

DISC increases its shipping activities their States.[9]

---

9. Hypothetical examples demonstrate that similarly situated corporations, each operating a wholly owned DISC, would face different tax assessments in New York depending on the location from which the DISC shipped its exports. For a parent corporation that has an income of $10,000, a wholly owned DISC with accumulated income of $500, and a New York business allocation percentage of 40%, and assuming an applicable New York tax rate of 10%, Table A shows the difference in New York tax liability in situations where the DISC ships 100%, 50%, or 0% of its exports from locations in New York:

TABLE A

	100%	50%	0%
% of DISC Shipment from New York	100%	50%	0%
Parent's Income	$10,000	$10,000	$10,000
DISC Accumulated Income	500	500	500
Consolidated Income	10,500	10,500	10,500
New York Business Allocation %	40%	40%	40%
Income Taxable by New York	4,200	4,200	4,200
New York Tax Rate	10%	10%	10%
Tax Liability (Pre-Credit)	420	420	420
DISC Credit Allowed	14	7	0
Final Tax Assessment	406	413	420

The DISC credit allowed is computed by multiplying the percentage of the DISC's export revenues derived from New York shipments (100%, 50% or 0%) by the parent's New York business allocation percentage (40%); multiplying that product by the parent's New York tax rate (10%); multiplying that product by the credit percentage (70%); and, finally, multiplying that product by the amount of the accumulated DISC income attributable to the parent ($500).

We are not unmindful of one factor that results when a corporation is induced to move more of its export business into the State of New York: the parent's business allocation percentage will be adjusted upward to reflect the increased percentage of DISC activity in the State. The increased tax liability will more than offset the increased credit, so that the parent's tax liability to the State of New York, in absolute terms, increases. The parent's effective New York tax rate, however, decreases as its DISC does a greater percentage of its shipping from New York. In the next example, each parent is assumed to do 40% of its own business from New York, so that $4,000 of its income is attributable to New York activity. Each DISC has $500 of accumulated income, but differs from the others in terms of the percentage of its income that results from shipping exports from New York ports. Assuming that the same amount of payroll and property are required to generate each dollar of the DISC's income, the business allocation percentage increases proportionately as the percentage of the DISC's income derived from New York shipping activity increases:

TABLE B

% of DISC Shipment from New York	100%	50%	0%
Parent's Income	$10,000	$10,000	$10,000
DISC Accumulated Income	500	500	500
Consolidated Income	10,500	10,500	10,500
New York Business Allocation %	42.86%	40.48%	38.10%
Income Taxable by New York	4,500	4,250	4,000
New York Tax Rate	10%	10%	10%
Tax Liability (Pre-Credit)	450	425	400
DISC Credit Allowed	15	7	0
Final Tax Assessment	435	418	400
Effective Tax Rate on Income Taxable in New York	9.67%	9.84%	10%

The third example demonstrates the most pernicious effect of the credit scheme. In this example, each parent and its DISC maintain the same amount of business in New York as do the other parent-DISC organizations, but the DISCs differ with respect to the amount of export shipping they do from outside New York. Each parent has $10,000 of income and each does 40% of its own business in New York. In addition, each DISC ships the goods that account for $3,000 of its income from New York. The only difference among the three parent-DISC organizations is the amount of DISC activity each conducts outside New York. As the DISC conducts a greater amount of shipping from outside New York, the DISC export credit allowed the parent decreases. Thus, New York lowers the incentive it awards for in-state DISC activity as the DISC increases its out-of-state activity:

Thus, not only does the New York tax scheme "provide a positive incentive for increased business activity in New York State," Budget Report, at 18, but also it penalizes increases in the DISC's shipping activities in other States.

In determining whether New York's method of allowing a DISC export credit violates the Commerce Clause, the foundation of our analysis is the basic principle that "'[t]he very purpose of the Commerce Clause was to create an area of free trade among the several States.'" Boston Stock Exchange v. State Tax Comm'n, 429 U.S. at 328, quoting McLeod v. J. E. Dilworth Co., 322 U.S. at 330; accord, Great Atlantic & Pacific Tea Co. v. Cottrell, 424 U.S. 366 (1976). The undisputed corollary of that principle is that "'the Commerce Clause was not merely an authorization to Congress to enact laws for the protection and encouragement of commerce among the States, but by its own force created an area of trade free from interference by the States. . . . [T]he Commerce Clause even without implementing legislation by

TABLE C

% of DISC Shipment from New York DISC Accumulated Income from New York Shipments	100%	75%	60%
	$3,000	$3,000	$3,000
DISC Accumulated Income from Shipments from Other States	0	1,000	2,000
Total DISC Accumulated Income	3,000	4,000	5,000
Parent's Income	10,000	10,000	10,000
Consolidated Income	13,000	14,000	15,000
New York Business Allocation %	53.85%	50%	46.67%
Income Taxable by New York	7,000	7,000	7,000
New York Tax Rate	10%	10%	10%
Tax Liability (Pre-credit)	700	700	700
DISC Credit Allowed	113	105	98
Final Tax Assessment	587	595	602

These examples illustrate what is inherent in the method devised by the New York Legislature for computing the DISC credit: the credit is awarded in a discriminatory manner on the basis of the percentage of a DISC's shipping conducted from within the State of New York.

Congress is a limitation upon the power of the States,'" including the States' power to tax. Boston Stock Exchange, 429 U.S. at 328, quoting Freeman v. Hewit, 329 U.S. at 252. For that reason, "[n]o State, consistent with the Commerce Clause, may 'impose a tax which discriminates against interstate commerce . . . by providing a direct commercial advantage to local business.'" Boston Stock Exchange, 429 U.S. at 329, quoting Northwestern States Portland Cement Co., 358 U.S. at 458. See also Halliburton Oil Well Cementing Co., 373 U.S. 64 (1963); Nippert v. Richmond, 327 U.S. 416 (1946); I.M. Darnell & Son Co., 208 U.S. 113 (1908); Guy v. Baltimore, 100 U.S. 434 (1880); Welton v. Missouri, 91 U.S. 275 (1876).

We have acknowledged that the delicate balancing of the national interest in free and open trade and a State's interest in exercising its taxing powers requires a case-by-case analysis and that such analysis has left "'much room for controversy and confusion and little in the way of precise guides to the States in the exercise of their indispensable power of taxation.'" Boston Stock Exchange, 429 U.S. at 329, quoting Northwestern States, 358 U.S. at 457. In light of our decision in Boston Stock Exchange, however, we think that there is little room for such "controversy and confusion" in the present litigation. The lessons of that case, as explicated further in Maryland v. Louisiana, 451 U.S. 725 (1981), are controlling.

In both Maryland v. Louisiana and Boston Stock Exchange, the Court struck down state tax statutes that encouraged the development of local industry by means of taxing measures that imposed greater burdens on economic activities taking place outside the State than were placed on similar activities within the State. In Maryland v. Louisiana, the Court held that Louisiana's "First-Use" tax–which imposed a tax on natural gas brought into the State while giving local users a series of exemptions and credits–violated the Commerce Clause because it "unquestionably discriminate[d] against interstate commerce in favor of local interests." 451 U.S. at 756. Similarly, in Boston Stock Exchange, the Court held unconstitutional a New York stock-transfer tax that reduced the tax payable by nonresidents when the tax involved an in-state (rather than an out-of-state) sale and applied a maximum limit to the tax payable on any in-state (but not out-of-state) sale. See 429 U.S. at 332. The stock-transfer tax was declared unconstitutional because it violated the principle that "no State may discriminatorily tax the products manufactured or the business operations performed in any other State." Id. at 337. The tax schemes rejected by this Court in both Maryland v. Louisiana and Boston Stock Exchange involved transactional taxes rather than taxes on general income. That distinction, however, is irrelevant to our analysis. The franchise tax is a tax on the income of a

business from its aggregated business transactions. It cannot be that a State can circumvent the prohibition of the Commerce Clause against placing burdensome taxes on out-of-state transactions by burdening those transactions with a tax that is levied in the aggregate–as is the franchise tax–rather than on individual transactions.

Nor is it relevant that New York discriminates against business carried on outside the State by disallowing a tax credit rather than by imposing a higher tax. The discriminatory economic effect of these two measures would be identical. New York allows a 70% credit against tax liability for all shipments made from within the State. This provision is indistinguishable from one that would apply to New York shipments a tax rate that is 30% of that applied to shipments from other States. We have declined to attach any constitutional significance to such formal distinctions that lack economic substance. See, e.g., Maryland v. Louisiana, 451 U.S. at 756 (tax scheme imposing tax at uniform rate on in-state and out-of-state sales held to be unconstitutional because discrimination against interstate commerce was "the necessary result of various tax credits and exclusions" that benefitted only in-state consumers of gas).

The Tax Commission contends that the DISC export credit is a subsidy to American export business generally, and as such, is consistent with congressional intent in establishing DISCs and with the Commerce Clause. We find no merit in this argument. While the Federal Government may seek to increase domestic employment and improve our balance-of-payments by offering tax advantages to those who produce in the United States rather than abroad, a State may not encourage the development of local industry by means of taxing measures that "invite a multiplication of preferential trade areas" within the United States, in contravention of the Commerce Clause. Dean Milk Co. v. Madison, 340 U.S. at 356. We note, also, that if the credit were truly intended to promote exports from the United States in general, there would be no reason to limit it to exports from within New York.

The Tax Commission argues that even if the tax is discriminatory, the burden it places on interstate commerce is not of constitutional significance. It points to the facts that New York is a State with a relatively high franchise tax and that the actual effect of the credit, when viewed in terms of the whole New York tax scheme, is slight. It argues that the credit was not intended to divert new activity into New York, but, rather, to prevent the loss of economic activity already in the State at the time the tax on accumulated DISC income was enacted. Whether the discriminatory tax diverts new business into the State or merely prevents current business from being diverted elsewhere, it is still a discriminatory tax that "forecloses tax-neutral decisions and . . . creates . . . an advantage" for firms operating in New York by placing "a discriminatory burden on commerce to its sister States." Boston Stock Exchange, 429 U.S. at 331. The State has violated the prohibition in Boston Stock Exchange against using discriminatory state taxes to burden commerce in other States in an attempt to induce "'business operations to be performed in the home State that could more efficiently be performed elsewhere.'" id., at 336, quoting Pike v. Bruce Church, Inc., 397 U.S. at 145, and to "'impose an artificial rigidity on the economic pattern of the industry,'" id., at 146, quoting Toomer v. Witsell, 334 U.S. at 404.[12] When a tax, on its face, is designed to have discriminatory economic effects, the Court "need not know how un-equal the Tax is before concluding that it unconstitutionally discriminates." Maryland v. Louisiana, 451 U.S. at 760.

The manner in which New York allows corporations a tax credit on the accumulated income of their subsidiary DISCs discriminates against export shipping from other States, in violation of the Commerce Clause. The contrary judgment of the New York Court of Appeals is therefore reversed.

---

12. The Tax Commission seeks to classify the tax credit at issue here as an indirect subsidy to export commerce, similar to provision and maintenance of ports, airports, waterways, and highways; to provision of police and fire protection; and to enactment of job-incentive credits and investment-tax credits. Id., at 21-22. We reiterate that it is not the provision of the credit that offends the Commerce Clause, but the fact that it is allowed on an impermissible basis, i.e., the percentage of a specific segment of the corporation's business that is conducted in New York. As in Boston Stock Exchange, we do not "hold that a State may not compete with other States for a share of interstate commerce; such competition lies at the heart of a free trade policy. We hold only that in the process of competition no State may discriminatorily tax the products manufactured or the business operations performed in any other State." 429 U.S. at 336-337.

Questions and Comments

1. It may be unclear from the opinion why the federal creation of DISCs in 1971 created an immediate problem for New York. Had the State not responded with special legislation, some revenue loss would have resulted for three reasons. First, a corporation's federal taxable income is the starting point in calculating its New York tax. Because DISCs are not taxable entities for federal purposes and thus have no taxable income, they would not have been taxable for New York purposes. Second, distributions to shareholders from a DISC would have constituted either investment income or income from a subsidiary; such income would have been either fully exempt or 50% exempt under New York law. In addition, the 50% of dividends that would have been included in income would have been subject to the State's very favorable rules on the allocation of investment income. In many cases, a very low percentage of the dividends would have been allocated to New York, resulting in only a nominal tax. Third, because DISCs can use artificial intercompany pricing rules to shift income away from a controlling shareholder to the DISC, New York shareholders could reduce their State taxable income by receiving less than fair market value for the sale of their products to the DISC.

The State could have protected itself fully against any revenue loss by requiring a shareholder to file a consolidated report with its DISC. In this way, the DISC would have been treated basically as a branch of the shareholder and its creation would have had no tax consequences in New York. This approach was viewed as unacceptable because of the fear that it would discourage the manufacturing of export goods in New York. The fear was that manufacturers would shift their activities to states offering more favorable treatment of DISCs. Nonetheless, because of the loss in revenue, the New York Legislature was unwilling to adopt the federal approach in toto. The legislative compromise, as discussed in the case, was to adopt a consolidated return for most DISCs but then to rebate part of the tax through the use of the export credit, which was held unconstitutional in this case.

Westinghouse was remanded to the New York Court of Appeals to determine what part of the State scheme for the taxation of DISCs remained in force. That court eliminated only the unconstitutional portion of the credit: the ratio of New York export receipts to total export receipts. *Westinghouse v. Tully,* 63 N.Y.2d 191 (1984).

In 1984 Congress created a new incentive for exporters–the Foreign Sales Corporation (FSC)–to replace DISCs. The only type of DISCs allowed after 1984 is the "interest charge DISC," intended for use by small exporters. FSCs were intended to mute criticism leveled against DISCs, which were attacked by foreign countries as an illegal export subsidy that violated the General Agreement on Tariff and Trade (GATT).

FSCs also pose a problem for New York and most other states because income can be allocated between a parent and its FSC using artificial pricing formulas. For an exhaustive study of the New York taxation of DISCs and FSCs, suggesting that New York should consider taxing FSCs and interest charge DISCs in the same manner as other corporations, see Legislative Commission on the Modernization and Simplification of Tax Administration and the Tax Law, The New York Tax Treatment of DISCs and FSCs, (October 17, 1986). Although the report deals with the New York tax system, the analysis and recommendations are applicable to other state systems.

2. Although it is not clear from the facts, it would not be unusual if Westinghouse Export Corporation were basically a paper corporation. In a typical situation involving DISCs, the export goods are produced by a parent corporation and transferred to the DISC for export. Commonly, the transfer is merely a paper transaction. In these situations, the DISC provisions are functionally no more than a requirement that separate books be kept that permit the computation of a cash subsidy paid through the tax system on certain profits labeled export profits. Moreover, one of the significant features of the old federal tax regime for DISCs was the liberal intercompany transfer pricing rules. These rules were mechanical, unrelated to, and more favorable than the normal fair market value (arm's length pricing) rule used to value an item transferred among related parties.

3. *Westinghouse* arises in the context of New York's treatment of DISCs but that fact pattern is essentially irrelevant. The same issue would have been presented if New York had simply granted a credit against its corporate income tax which was based on the ratio of in-state sales to out-of-state sales. It may be easier to understand *Westinghouse* if you read the case as if that were the only relevant provision at issue.

4. Is the key to understanding *Westinghouse* the fact that an increase in a corporation's New York exports would decrease a corporation's tax? Or, is the key that an increase in non-New York exports would increase its tax? Compare a provision that grants a credit for in-state investment (e.g., an investment tax credit). A corporation will receive a larger credit the more that it invests in the

state. But a corporation will not increase its tax if it holds its in-state investment constant and increases its out-of-state investment. Is that a sufficient basis upon which to uphold the constitutionality of a state investment tax credit?

Two commentators have suggested that provisions that confer a benefit on the basis of in-state activity can be distinguished from those which penalize out-of-state activity. Philip M. Tatarowicz and Rebecca F. Mims-Velarde, An Analytical Approach to State Tax Discrimination Under the Commerce Clause, 39 Vand. L. Rev. 879, 933-34 (1986). Does this suggestion explain *Westinghouse*? What about *Boston Stock*, *Bacchus*, or *New Energy*? Does *Westinghouse* involve a protectionist measure like that involved in *Bacchus*, *Boston Stock*, or *New Energy*?

5. Under a typical state corporate income tax, a taxpayer's liability will be inversely proportional to the amount of its sales that take place out-of-state. Is this what happened under New York's scheme?

6. Does *Westinghouse* suggest that a state can use a carrot (a tax reduction), such as an investment tax credit, to

induce investment but cannot use a stick (a tax increase) to penalize taxpayers that invest in other states?

7. Would a credit that was a function only of a corporation's New York exports be constitutional? How would such a credit be any different from an investment tax credit?

8. The State classified the tax credit in *Westinghouse* as an indirect subsidy to exports. Suppose that instead of a tax credit the State actually adopted a spending program that was equal in amount to the value of the credit. In other words, suppose the New York Department of Commerce sent Westinghouse a check equal to the amount that it otherwise would have claimed as a credit. Would it be constitutional for New York to reduce the amount of that check in proportion to Westinghouse's activities outside New York? Would it be constitutional for New York to increase the amount of the check in proportion to Westinghouse's New York activities?

9. For critical commentary on *Westinghouse*, see Lee A. Sheppard, *Westinghouse Prevails in Challenge to New York DISC Tax Credit*, 23 Tax Notes 454 (1984).

American Trucking Ass'n, v. Scheiner, Secretary, Dept. of Revenue of PA.
Supreme Court of the United States, 1987.
483 U.S. 266, 107 S. Ct. 2829, 97 L. Ed. 2d 226

JUSTICE STEVENS delivered the opinion of the Court.

[Pennsylvania's highway] expenditures are financed, in substantial part, by three types of levies on users of Pennsylvania's highways: vehicle registration fees, fuel consumption taxes, and lump-sum annual fees which we will describe as "flat taxes." Although the two taxes at issue in this litigation are both flat taxes–a $25 "marker fee" assessed from August 18, 1980, through March 31, 1983, and an "axle tax" imposed thereafter–registration fees and fuel taxes are principal sources of revenue for road-related purposes and therefore the mechanics of their collection provide necessary background for our analysis of the economic significance and constitutional validity of the challenged flat taxes.

Registration Fees

Owners of motor vehicles that are based in Pennsylvania must register them with the Department of Transportation and pay an annual registration fee. The weight of a truck or truck tractor determines the amount of the annual fee. Prior to 1980, there were 20 weight classifications, and the corresponding fees ranged from $39 to $606 per vehicle. In 1980, the registration fees were increased and five new weight classes for heavier vehicles were added to the statutory

schedule; from 1980 to 1982 the maximum registration fee was $1125, for a vehicle weighing 79,001 to 80,000 pounds. In 1982, the registration fees for vehicles weighing more than 26,000 pounds (classes 9-25) were reduced by multiples of $36 ranging up to a $180 reduction; thereafter, the maximum fee was $945.

Pennsylvania, many other States, and Provinces of Canada participate in an apportioned registration scheme called the "International Registration Plan" (IRP). Participants in this plan share the registration fees for vehicles based in their States with other IRP States in which the vehicles travel. The percentage of each vehicle's total registration fee that is allocated to each IRP State other than the State in which the vehicle is based is determined by dividing the total number of miles the vehicle traveled within the IRP State during the preceding year by its total mileage. The total fee payable to each State is the product of each State's total fee for full registration of each vehicle and that State's percentage share of the vehicle's mileage. Thus, if 30% of the mileage of a Pennsylvania-based vehicle was accrued in other States, Pennsylvania's share of the registration fee would be 70% of the full amount specified in its statutory schedule. On the other hand, if a vehicle based in another IRP State logged 40% of its mileage in Pennsylvania, its owner would be required to pay that portion of the Pennsylvania fee schedule to Pennsylvania. Pennsylvania collects no registration fees from motor carriers based in non-IRP States and, conversely, Pennsylvania-based vehicles pay no registration fees to non-IRP States.[7]

In sum, the amount of each truck's registration fee is determined by the weight of the vehicle and, if the truck travels in other IRP States, in part by its in-state mileage. No vehicle is required to pay more than one full registration fee.

Fuel Consumption Taxes

Pennsylvania collects a fuel consumption tax in two ways. It imposes a per-gallon fuel tax on fuel purchased within the State. The State also requires trucks that travel less than 90% of their miles in Pennsylvania to pay a tax based on their miles traveled in Pennsylvania, reduced by the amount of the tax actually paid through fuel purchased at Pennsylvania pumps. The amount of these taxes does not depend on the vehicle's State of registration.

The Flat Taxes

Pennsylvania requires an identification marker issued by the Department of Revenue to be affixed to every motor carrier vehicle. A motor carrier vehicle is a "truck, truck tractor or combination having a gross weight or registered gross weight in excess of 17,000 pounds." Until 1980, the fee for the issuance of this marker was $2. In that year the fee was increased to $25, but vehicles registered in Pennsylvania were exempted from the fee. The statute effected this exemption by providing that for each vehicle registered in Pennsylvania the "marker fee shall be deemed a part of and included in the vehicle registration fee."

The parties have stipulated that the administrative costs associated with the issuance of the identification markers total approximately $5 per vehicle. In 1982, when it enacted the axle tax, Pennsylvania reduced the annual marker fee from $25 to $5 per vehicle. Since

---

7. . . . .

  Pennsylvania also has nonapportioned reciprocity agreements with non-IRP States. A Pennsylvania-based carrier that pays a registration fee to Pennsylvania obtains the privilege of operating the vehicle over the highways of "all other states with which Pennsylvania has registration reciprocity respecting that vehicle registration." Likewise, carriers that pay registration fees to States with which Pennsylvania has reciprocity agreements receive the privilege of operating their vehicles on the roads of their home state and "the roads of all other states, including Pennsylvania, with which the home state has registration reciprocity."

1982, then, the marker fee is sufficient only to meet the specific cost of issuing the marker, but the effect of the $25 marker fee from 1980 to 1982 was to impose a flat tax on vehicles registered in other States. This tax was, at least nominally, not imposed on Pennsylvania-registered vehicles. It should be noted, however, that the same statute that increased the marker fee in 1980 to $25 for out-of-state vehicles weighing more than 17,000 pounds also increased Pennsylvania's registration fees for such vehicles by amounts substantially larger than $25.

In 1982, Pennsylvania enacted its axle tax and, as noted, reduced the marker fee to $5 per vehicle. The axle tax applies to all trucks, truck tractors, and combinations weighing more than 26,000 pounds, whether registered in Pennsylvania or elsewhere; it requires an annual payment of $36 per vehicle axle. For example, the tax is $72 for a two-axle vehicle and $180 for a five-axle vehicle. If a truck travels less than 2,000 miles in Pennsylvania, however, it is entitled to a rebate: the axle tax paid multiplied by the ratio of the amount by which the vehicle's in-state mileage was short of 2,000 miles to 2,000 determines the rebate amount. Moreover, the axle tax is excused when a trucker pays $25 for a trip permit for a period not exceeding five days.

The same statute that enacted the axle tax in 1982 also reduced the registration fees for all weight classes of vehicles of more than 26,000 pounds. In classes 9-12, which generally include two-axle vehicles required to pay a $72 axle tax, the reduction amounted to $72; in classes 13-17, which usually include three-axle vehicles subject to a $108 axle tax, it amounted to $108; in classes 18, 19, and 20, usually four-axle vehicles subject to a $144 axle tax, it amounted to $144, and in the five heaviest classes–vehicle weights exceeding the permissible weight for four-axle vehicles–it amounted to $180.[8] In brief, the amounts of the reductions in all classes were a

---

8. The explanation for the substantial congruence between the amount of the reductions in registration fee and the amount of axle tax imposed lies in the statutory requirement that a truck with a given number of axles may not exceed a specified weight. As Chief Justice Nix explained in his dissent, the registration fee "reductions correspond to the number of axles most commonly used and minimally required by law in each weight class. . . . Except in a few instances, the [registration fee] reductions created by the Act were intended to and did exactly offset the impact of the Axle Tax upon motor carrier vehicles registered in Pennsylvania." 509 A. 2d 838, 858, n. 1 (1986). The Commonwealth Court had also found that the reductions in registration fees "generally offset the tax owed based on the number of axles ordinarily required of vehicles within each affected weight class." American Trucking Assns., Inc. v. Bloom, 487 A. 2d 465, 467 (1985).

multiple of the $36 per axle which is used as the measure for the axle tax.

II

Appellants represent a class of interstate motor carriers whose vehicles are registered outside of Pennsylvania and who paid the $25 marker fee while it was in effect and who have thereafter been subject to the axle tax. They brought separate actions in the Commonwealth Court of Pennsylvania challenging the constitutionality of the $25 marker fee and of the axle tax. In each case, appellants made two separate arguments based on the Commerce Clause of the Federal Constitution.

First, they argued that the entire economic burden of each tax fell on out-of-state vehicles because the 1980 statute "deemed" the marker fee for Pennsylvania vehicles to be a part of the registration fee, and the 1982 legislation granted Pennsylvania vehicles a reduction in registration fees that neatly offset the newly imposed axle tax. Second, they argued that even if owners of vehicles registered in Pennsylvania, through payment of registration fees, shared the burden of the two flat taxes with owners of vehicles based elsewhere, the taxes were nevertheless discriminatory because both taxes imposed a much heavier charge per mile of highway usage by out-of-state vehicles. On the average, the Pennsylvania-based vehicles subject to the flat taxes travel about five times as many miles on Pennsylvania roads as do the out-of-state vehicles; correspondingly, the cost per mile of each of the flat taxes is approximately five times as high for out-of-state vehicles as for local vehicles.[9] Although out-of-state and in-state vehicles subject to the axle tax traveled approximately the same number of miles on Pennsylvania's highways, less than 1/6 of the State's total axle tax revenues were generated by Pennsylvania-based vehicles in fiscal years 1982-1983 and 1983-1984.

. . . .

III

Although we have described our own decisions in this area as a "quagmire" of judicial responses to specific state tax measures, Northwestern Cement Co., 358 U.S. at 457-458, we have steadfastly adhered to the central tenet that the Commerce Clause "by its own force created an area of trade free from interference by the States." Boston Stock Exchange, 429 U.S. at 328. One primary consequence of this constitutional restriction

on state taxing powers, frequently asserted in litigation, is that "a State may not tax a transaction or incident more heavily when it crosses state lines than when it occurs entirely within the State." In its guarantee of a free trade area among States, however, the Commerce Clause has a deeper meaning that may be implicated even though state provisions, such as the ones reviewed here, do not allocate tax burdens between insiders and outsiders in a manner that is facially discriminatory.[12]

The parties broadly state the constitutional question in this appeal as whether Pennsylvania's flat taxes result in a blanket discrimination against interstate commerce. The operator of a Pennsylvania-based vehicle that engages in interstate commerce, however, has no apparent quarrel with the challenged flat taxes; he is "deemed" to pay the $25 marker fee through his registration fee, and the axle taxes he paid beginning in 1982 were generally offset by the statutory reduction in vehicle registration fees. But some operators of vehicles based in other States or Provinces have neither consolation, for they have paid registration fees to their own jurisdictions and still face Pennsylvania's axle taxes. The precise issue is therefore more subtle: do the methods by which the flat taxes are assessed discriminate against some participants in interstate commerce in a way that contradicts the central purpose of the Commerce Clause? We find dispositive those of our precedents which make it clear that the Commerce Clause prohibits a State from imposing a heavier tax burden on out-of-state businesses that compete in an interstate market than it imposes on its own residents who also engage in commerce among States.

The way in which a tax levied on participants in interstate commerce is measured and assessed bears directly on whether it implicates central Commerce Clause values. The method of assessing the marker and axle taxes in this case on Pennsylvania-based vehicles and

---

12. Our more recent cases repeat a theme that recurred in an early series of decisions invalidating facially neutral taxes on nonresident solicitors, or "drummers," seeking to engage in business within the taxing jurisdiction. In Nippert v. Richmond, 327 U.S. 416 (1946), we explained:

"As has been so often stated but nevertheless seems to require constant repetition, not all burdens upon commerce, but only undue or discriminatory ones, are forbidden. For, though 'interstate business must pay its way,' a State consistently with the commerce clause cannot put a barrier around its borders to bar out trade from other States and thus bring to naught the great constitutional purpose of the fathers in giving to Congress the power 'To regulate Commerce with foreign Nations, and among the several States. . .[.] Nor may the prohibition be accomplished in the guise of taxation which produces the excluding or discriminatory effect." Id., at 425-426.

. . . .

---

9. In 1981, the cost of the marker fee was more than ½ cent per mile for all foreign-based motor carrier vehicles and about 1/10 cent per mile for all Pennsylvania-based motor carrier vehicles.

on other vehicles establishes that the State is not treating the two types of vehicles with an even hand. There are important and obvious differences of a constitutional magnitude between the State's registration fees and fuel taxes, on the one hand, and its flat taxes, on the other.

The State's vehicle registration fee has its counterpart in every other State and the District of Columbia. It is a tax that readily satisfies the test of "internal consistency" that we have applied in other contexts. Under this test, even though the registration fee is assessed, as indeed it has been, by every jurisdiction, it causes no impermissible interference with free trade because every State respects the registration of every other State. Payment of one registration fee enables a carrier to operate a vehicle either locally or in the interstate market. Having paid one registration fee, a vehicle may pass among the States as freely as it may roam the State in which it is based; the Commerce Clause is not offended when state boundaries are economically irrelevant.

Yet even if more than one jurisdiction applies a charge to participants in interstate commerce, the Commerce Clause may be satisfied if the revenue measures maintain state boundaries as a neutral factor in economic decisionmaking. Pennsylvania's fuel consumption taxes, for example, do not hinder the maintenance of a free trade area among States. The fuel consumption taxes are directly apportioned to the mileage traveled in Pennsylvania; they are therefore simply payments for traveling a certain distance that happens to be within Pennsylvania. When a vehicle uses other States' roads, it may be subject to their fuel taxes, but the free trade area is unimpaired; if one sovereign controlled the entire free trade area, it would have the equivalent authority to impose a charge for the use of all of its roads.[15]

---

15. It might be objected that if other States impose lower fuel taxes or forgo them entirely, then Pennsylvania's tax is inconsistent with a free trade area because it furnishes a disincentive to travel throughout that State. But the disincentive affects local and out-of-state vehicles in precisely the same way, and thus does not implicate the Commerce Clause. When a tax does establish a difference in treatment, however, the "immunities implicit in the Commerce Clause and the potential taxing power of a State can hardly be made to depend, in the world of practical affairs, on the shifting incidence of the varying tax laws of the various States at a particular moment." Freeman v. Hewitt, 329 U.S. at 256 (1946). The adverse economic impact in dollars and cents upon a participant in interstate commerce for crossing a state boundary and thus becoming subject to another State's taxing jurisdiction is neither necessary to establish a Commerce Clause violation, see Armco Inc. v. Hardesty, 467 U.S. at 644,

The unapportioned flat taxes, however, penalize some travel within the free trade area. Whether the full brunt, or only a major portion, of their burden is imposed on the out-of-state carriers, their inevitable effect is to threaten the free movement of commerce by placing a financial barrier around the State of Pennsylvania. To pass the "internal consistency" test, a state tax must be of a kind that, "if applied by every jurisdiction, there would be no impermissible interference with free trade." Armco, 467 U.S. at 644. If each State imposed flat taxes for the privilege of making commercial entrances into its territory, there is no conceivable doubt that commerce among the States would be deterred.[16]

Although the actual imposition of flat taxes by other jurisdictions is not necessary to sustain the Commerce Clause challenge to Pennsylvania's flat taxes under the "internal consistency" test, the adoption of these flat taxes by other jurisdictions even before the Pennsylvania suits were resolved surely suggests that acquiescence in these flat taxes would occasion manifold threats to the national free trade area. Since 1980 when Pennsylvania authorized the $25 marker fee, six other States have also adopted flat taxes and seven States have adopted retaliatory levies that are assessed on motor carrier vehicles that are based in Pennsylvania or another flat-tax

---

nor sufficient, see Complete Auto Transit, Inc. v. Brady, 430 U.S. at 289 (1977) (taxes on interstate business are not invalid per se).

16. A line of cases invalidating unapportioned flat taxes that provided general revenue also illustrates the principle that the very nature of the market that interstate operators serve prevents them from making full use of the privilege of doing business for which they have paid the State. Thus, we found that a tax on drummers in the city of Memphis for the privilege of doing business there on behalf of out-of-state firms discriminated against out-of-state manufacturers. We reasoned that their local competitors, "having regular licensed houses of business [in Memphis], have no occasion for such agents, and, if they had, they are not subject to any tax therefor. They are taxed for their licensed houses, it is true; but so, it is presumable, are the merchants and manufacturers of other states in the places where they reside; and the tax on drummers operates greatly to their disadvantage in comparison with the merchants and manufacturers of Memphis." Robbins v. Shelby County Taxing District, 120 U.S. at 498. See also Best & Co. v. Maxwell, 311 U.S. at 456-457 (annual flat tax on those who were not regular retail merchants in the State invalid because its actual effect "is to discriminate in favor of intrastate businesses, whatever may be the ostensible reach of the language"); Nippert v. Richmond, 327 U.S. 416 (1946). As one commentator observed almost half a century ago: "True, each fee is imposed upon the use of different states' highways, but the cumulative effect does not result from the mileage or distance traveled, but from the interstate character of the journey. The same mileage in one state would result in only one tax." Lockhart, State Tax Barriers to Interstate Trade, 53 Harv. L. Rev. 1253, 1269 (1940).

State. Such taxes can obviously divide and disrupt the market for interstate transportation services. In practical effect, since they impose a cost per mile on appellants' trucks that is approximately five times as heavy as the cost per mile borne by local trucks, the taxes are plainly discriminatory.[21] Under our consistent course of decisions in recent years a state tax that favors in-state business over out-of-state business for no other reason than the location of its business is prohibited by the Commerce Clause. Nor is the axle tax saved because some out-of-state carriers which accrue high mileage in Pennsylvania pay the axle tax at a lower per-mile rate than some Pennsylvania based carriers; it makes no difference that the axle tax, on its face, does not exact a lower per mile charge from Pennsylvania based carriers than from out-of-state carriers. Like the exemption from wholesaling tax for goods manufactured in Washington that we struck down in Tyler Pipe Industries, Inc., the axle tax has a forbidden impact on interstate commerce because it exerts an inexorable hydraulic pressure on interstate businesses to ply their trade within the State that enacted the measure rather than "among the several States."

IV

Notwithstanding our recent precedents invalidating various state taxation measures that failed the "internal consistency" test, Pennsylvania advances three arguments in defense of its flat taxes. They are said to reflect a reasonable charge for the privilege of using its roads when considered alongside the high price that Pennsylvania-based trucks pay in registration fees. Appellees also argue that the flat taxes are no different from the flat user fees this Court has recently upheld. Finally, talismanically invoking decisions in which we upheld flat taxes for the privilege of doing business within a State, appellees contend that a mere disparity in per-mile costs between interstate and intrastate truckers provides no basis upon which to strike down a tax. We are persuaded, however, that none of the cases relied upon by appellees controls our disposition.

---

21. "It is true also that a State may impose, even on motor vehicles engaged exclusively in interstate commerce, a reasonable charge as their fair contribution to the cost of constructing and maintaining the public highways . . . . But no part of the license fee here in question may be assumed to have been prescribed for that purpose. A flat tax, substantial in amount and the same for busses plying the streets continuously in local service and for busses making, as do many interstate busses, only a single trip daily, could hardly have been designed as a measure of the cost or value of the use of the highways." Sprout v. South Bend, 277 U.S. at 170.

The "Rational Restructuring" Defense

[Appellees] argue that the axle tax does not discriminate against interstate commerce because "it is but a small part of Pennsylvania's multi-tiered scheme of taxes and fees designed to finance an extensive highway system." Appellees contend that domestic trucks pay a higher price to use Pennsylvania's highways than those registered in other States, and specifically, that the totality of the tax and fee changes since 1980 has resulted in higher relative taxes on trucks registered in Pennsylvania. The registration fee reductions in 1982 only partially offset these increases. We find this argument unavailing.

Appellees' reasoning is based on the erroneous premise that relief for Pennsylvania-based trucks is constitutionally permissible because they are subject to a higher financial burden for their use of Pennsylvania's roads than trucks based in other States must pay for use of the same roads. This premise is flawed for three reasons. Pennsylvania-based trucks are allowed to travel throughout the United States without paying more than one registration fee; the registration fees they pay are not solely for the use of Pennsylvania's highways. In addition, while it is true that registration fees are lower in some States, they are also higher in some other States. Most importantly, even if the relative amounts of the States' registration fees confer a competitive advantage on trucks based in other States, the Commerce Clause does not permit compensatory measures for the disparities that result from each State's choice of tax levels. To the extent that a competitive disadvantage is conferred on Pennsylvania carriers by the relative amounts of the States' registration fees, the remedy lies in a change in their level, the enlargement of participation in the IRP, or the collection of revenues through valid taxes. The axle tax cannot be vindicated as a "rational restructuring of burdens" simply because it arguably benefits a class of truckers that pays more to use the State's highways than does another class of highway users. As one commentator has observed, "[i]mplementation of a rule of law that a tax is nondiscriminatory because other taxes of at least the same magnitude are imposed by the taxing State on other taxpayers engaging in different transactions would plunge the Court into the morass of weighing comparative tax burdens." The flat taxes must stand or fall on their own.

The User Fee Defense

Taken on their own, the marker fee and axle tax are wholly unlike the user fees we upheld in Evansville-Vanderburgh Airport Authority District v. Delta Airlines, Inc., 405 U.S. 707 (1972), a case relied upon by the Pennsylvania Supreme Court. Evansville-Vanderburgh involved the question whether a municipal airport authority could collect a flat service fee of $1 for each passenger boarding a commercial aircraft operating from the airport.[23] After reviewing our decisions concerning highway tolls, as well as the cases holding that a State may impose a flat fee for the privilege of using its roads without regard to the actual use by particular vehicles, so long as the fee is not excessive, we stated:

"At least so long as the toll is based on some fair approximation of use or privilege for use, as was that before us in Capitol Greyhound [Lines v. Brice, 339 U.S. 542 (1950)], and is neither discriminatory against interstate commerce nor excessive in comparison with the governmental benefit conferred, it will pass constitutional muster, even though some other formula might reflect more exactly the relative use of the state facilities by individual users." Id., at 716-717.

We then explained why the $1 fee satisfied the two essential conditions that it be neither discriminatory nor excessive:

"The Indiana and New Hampshire charges meet those standards. *First*, neither fee discriminates against interstate commerce and travel. While the vast majority of passengers who board flights at the airports involved are traveling interstate, both interstate and intrastate flights are subject to the same charges. Furthermore, there is no showing of any inherent difference between these two classes of flights, such that the application of the same fee to both would amount to discrimination against one or the other. See Nippert v. Richmond, 327 U.S. 416 (1946).

"*Second*, these charges reflect a fair, if imperfect, approximation of the use of facilities for whose benefit they are imposed." Id., at 717.

Pennsylvania's flat taxes satisfy neither of these conditions: They discriminate against out-of-state vehicles by subjecting them to a much higher charge per mile traveled in the State, and they do not even purport to approximate fairly the cost or value of the use of Pennsylvania's roads.

The Pennsylvania Supreme Court also relied on Commonwealth Edison Co. v. Montana, 453 U.S. 609 (1981). The State of Montana imposed a severance tax on coal at the same rate whether the final destination of the coal was local or interstate. We rejected the taxpayer's discrimination claim, which was premised on the fact that 90% of Montana coal was shipped to other States under contracts that shifted the tax burden principally to utility companies outside of Montana and that therefore imposed the bulk of the tax burden on out-of-state consumers of Montana coal. We held that "there is no real discrimination in this case; the tax

burden is borne according to the amount of coal consumed and not according to any distinction between in-state and out-of-state consumers." Because the tax was a percentage of the value of the contract, and because only Montana could impose the tax, every holder of an equivalently valued contract paid the same tax; whether the shipment crossed a state border was irrelevant to the magnitude of the tax burden imposed by Montana. The flat taxes in this case are distinguishable in two ways. First, the amount of Pennsylvania's marker and axle taxes owed by a trucker does not vary directly with miles traveled or with some other proxy for value obtained from the State. "[W]hen the measure of a tax bears no relationship to the taxpayers' presence or activities in a State, a court may properly conclude under the fourth prong of the Complete Auto Transit test that the State is imposing an undue burden on interstate commerce." Id., at 629. As Justice Frankfurter argued in his dissent in Capitol Greyhound Lines, 339 U.S. at 557 (1950):

"So long as a State bases its tax on a relevant measure of actual road use, obviously both interstate and intrastate carriers pay according to the facilities in fact provided by the State. But a tax levied for the privilege of using roads, and not their actual use, may, in the normal course of operations and not as a fanciful hypothesis, involve an undue burden on interstate carriers. While the privilege extended by a State is unlimited in form, and thus theoretically the same for all vehicles, whether interstate or intrastate, the intrastate vehicle can and will exercise the privilege whenever it is in operation, while the interstate vehicle must necessarily forego the privilege some of the time simply because of its interstate character, i.e., because it operates in other States as well. In the general average of instances, the privilege is not as valuable to the interstate as to the intrastate carrier."

Second, unlike the Montana coal tax, highway use taxes can be imposed by other States.

"And because it operates in other States there is danger—and not a fanciful danger—that the interstate carrier will be subject to the privilege taxes of several States, even though his entire use of the highways is not significantly greater than that of intrastate operators who are subject to only one privilege tax." Ibid. (footnote omitted).

Justice Frankfurter thus illuminated the reason that a State's imposition of an unapportioned flat tax, unlike the neutral user fee in Evansville-Vanderburgh and the neutral severance tax in Commonwealth Edison Co., discriminates against interstate commerce.

The Flat Tax Defense

Third, the cases in support of the State's authority to impose flat use taxes, while lending support to appellees' argument, can no longer suffice to uphold flat taxes with the blatantly discriminatory consequences associated with the marker fee and axle tax.

In Clark v. Poor, 274 U.S. 554 (1927), the Court held that users of a State's highways, "although engaged

---

23. In response Congress prohibited any "tax, fee, head charge, or other charge" on air travel. 49 U.S.C. App. § 1513(a). If Congress should disagree with this decision, it would, of course, have the power to authorize flat taxes of this kind. See Prudential Insurance Co. v. Benjamin, 328 U.S. 408, 434 (1946).

exclusively in interstate commerce, may be required to contribute to their cost and upkeep. . . . There is no suggestion that the tax discriminates against interstate commerce." Id., at 557. A few years later in Aero Mayflower Transit Co. v. Georgia Public Service Comm'n, 295 U.S. 285 (1935), the Court sustained an annual license fee of $25 imposed on both out-of-state and domestic vehicles, concluding that the case was so similar to Clark v. Poor, supra, "as to apply a closure to debate." 295 U.S. at 289. Unlike the Clark case, however, the Court considered and rejected an argument that it was unfair to impose the same charge upon an interstate carrier as upon a local carrier that used the roads more. The Court reasoned that the fee covered the same privilege for both carriers:

"The appellant urges the objection that its use of roads in Georgia is less than that by other carriers engaged in local business, yet they pay the same charge. The fee is not for the mileage covered by a vehicle. There would be administrative difficulties in collecting on that basis. The fee is for the privilege of a use as extensive as the carrier wills that it shall be. There is nothing unreasonable or oppressive in a burden so imposed. Cf. Clark v. Poor, supra; Hicklin v. Coney, [290 U.S. 169 (1933)]. One who receives a privilege without limit is not wronged by his own refusal to enjoy it as freely as he may." 295 U.S. at 289.

In a second case brought by the same interstate carrier, the Court again relied on the principle of Clark v. Poor to support the proposition that "a state, consistently with the commerce clause, may lay upon motor vehicles engaged exclusively in interstate commerce, or upon those who own and so operate them, a fair and reasonable nondiscriminatory tax as compensation for the use of its highways." Aero Mayflower Transit Co. v. Board of Railroad Comm'rs, 332 U.S. at 503. Aero Mayflower held that two flat taxes imposed by Montana on each commercial vehicle operated on its highways did not discriminate against interstate commerce; "[b]oth levies apply exclusively to operations wholly within the state or the proceeds of such operations, although those operations are interstate in character." Id., at 502. The Court was careful to identify the consideration for the taxes as the privilege of using the State's highways, and to point out that the appellant had erred by failing to distinguish between a tax on that privilege and a tax on the privilege of engaging in interstate commerce:

"Appellant therefore confuses a tax 'assessed for a proper purpose and . . . not objectionable in amount,' Clark v. Poor, supra, at 557, that is, a tax affirmatively laid for the privilege of using the state's highways, with a tax not imposed on that privilege but upon some other such as the privilege of doing the interstate business. Though necessarily related, in view of the nature of interstate motor traffic, the two privileges are not identical, and it is useless to confuse them. . . ." Id., at 504.

Later in the opinion, the Court again emphasized the fact that the gross revenue fee was exacted in consideration for the privilege of using the State's highways, not for the privilege of doing interstate business. Id., at 506.

The distinction between a tax on the privilege of using a State's highways and a tax on the privilege of engaging in interstate commerce was also dispositive in Spector Motor Service, Inc. v. O'Connor, 340 U.S. 602 (1951), decided just four years later. Again addressing a tax on an interstate motor carrier, the Court this time invalidated it, distinguishing Aero Mayflower Transit Co. v. Board of Railroad Comm'rs because the Spector tax was "not levied as compensation for the use of highways," 340 U.S. at 607, and was not a tax on sales or use. "It is a 'tax or excise' placed unequivocally upon the corporation's franchise for the privilege of carrying on exclusively interstate transportation in the State." We explained:

"Even though the financial burden on interstate commerce might be the same, the question whether a state may validly make interstate commerce pay its way depends first of all upon the constitutional channel through which it attempts to do so. Freeman v. Hewit, 329 U.S. 249 [1946]; McLeod v. Dilworth Co., 322 U.S. 327 [1944]." Id., at 608.

In our more recent decisions we have rejected this somewhat metaphysical approach to the Commerce Clause that focused primarily on the character of the privilege rather than the practical consequences of the tax. In 1977, while we recognized that we had invalidated privilege taxes on in-state activity deemed to be part of interstate commerce, we also noted that we had "moved toward a standard of permissibility of state taxation based upon its actual effect rather than its legal terminology." Complete Auto Transit, Inc. v. Brady, 430 U.S. at 281. "These decisions have considered not the formal language of the tax statute but rather its practical effect, and have sustained a tax against Commerce Clause challenge when the tax is applied to an activity with a substantial nexus with the taxing State, is fairly apportioned, does not discriminate against interstate commerce, and is fairly related to the services provided by the State." Id., at 279. In Complete Auto Transit, Inc., we not only observed that the Spector rule against a tax on the privilege of interstate commerce "has no relationship to economic realities," id., at 279, and expressly overruled the Spector case itself, id., at 289, but also concluded that "the philosophy underlying the rule [that interstate commerce is immune from state taxation has] been rejected." Id., at 288. In ruling that the theoretical underpinnings of this rule had been eroded, we necessarily called into question the future vitality of earlier cases that had upheld facially neutral flat taxes against challenges premised on the rule of immunity for interstate commerce. Unsuccessful challenges had then been turned away on the theory that the State was not taxing the conduct of interstate commerce, but instead was taxing a unitary, formally defined privilege that was sometimes part of intrastate commerce and sometimes part of interstate commerce. Now that it has been firmly established that interstate commerce as such has no immunity from state taxation, it is no longer appropriate to uphold a flat tax merely because the particular formula by which its charges are reckoned extends the same nominal privilege to interstate commerce that it extends to in-state activities. Such formalism "merely obscures the question whether the tax produces a forbidden effect." Ibid.

Thus, the precedents upholding flat taxes can no longer support the broad proposition, advanced by appellees, that every flat tax for the privilege of using a State's highways must be upheld even if it has a clearly discriminatory effect on commerce by reason of that commerce's interstate character. Although out-of-state carriers obtain a privilege to use Pennsylvania's highways that is nominally equivalent to that which local carriers receive, imposition of the flat taxes for a privilege that is several times more valuable to a local business than to its out-of-state competitors is unquestionably discriminatory and thus offends the Commerce Clause. The great constitutional purpose of the Fathers cannot be defeated by using an apparently neutral "guise of taxation which produces the excluding or discriminatory effect." Nippert v. Richmond, 327 U.S. at 426. Those precedents are still valid, however, in their recognition that the Commerce Clause does not require the States to avoid flat taxes when they are the only practicable means of collecting revenues from users and the use of a more finely graduated user fee schedule would pose genuine administrative burdens.[26]

---

26. In Aero Mayflower Transit Co. v. Board of Railroad Comm'rs, 332 U.S. 495 (1947), after disposing of the appellant's main claims, the Court in a footnote summarily rejected appellant's alternative claim that the minimum fee of $15 on gross receipts was unreasonable because it imposed a tax roughly 10 times greater than would be required if the percentage standard set forth in the statute (0.5% of gross operating revenues) were used. We observed that the :

"Federal Constitution does not require the state to elaborate a system of motor vehicle taxation which will reflect with exact precision every gradation in use. In return for the $15 fee appellant can do business grossing $3,000 per vehicle annually for operations on Montana roads. Appellant was not wronged by its failure to make the full use of the highways permitted." Id., at 506, n. 19. Our disposition was thus based on the costs the State would encounter in collecting taxes for vehicles that earned less than $3,000 annually in Montana. We also emphasized the administrative impossibility of precise apportionment according to road use in Capitol Greyhound Lines v. Brice, 339 U.S. at 546. In that case we upheld a 2% tax on the fair market value of motor vehicles for the use of state highways as a rough approximation of use because of the administrative burden of applying a tax formula that would vary "with every factor affecting appropriate compensation for road use."

The administrative machinery of revenue collection for highways is now obviously capable of taking into account at least the gross variations in cost per unit of highway usage between Pennsylvania-based and out-of-state carriers that are presented by these facts. Pennsylvania, as noted, uses mileage figures to apportion motor carriers' registration fees among IRP jurisdictions, to collect fuel taxes from trucks that travel less than 90% of their miles in Pennsylvania, and to calculate axle tax rebates. Pennsylvania also apportions the corporate income tax it imposes on interstate carriers by the carrier's total miles traveled in the State. While flat taxes may be perfectly valid when administrative difficulties make collection of more finely calibrated user charges impracticable, we conclude that this justification is unavailable in the case of Pennsylvania's unapportioned marker fee and axle tax.

V

Appellees request that in the event of an adverse decision, the Court remand the case to the Pennsylvania Supreme Court to consider whether our ruling should be applied retroactively and to decide other remedial issues. We agree that having decided the constitutional issue presented to us, we should remand for further proceedings in the marker fee, axle tax, and marker fee refund suits. See Tyler Pipe Industries, Inc. v. Washington Dept. of Revenue, 483 U. S. at 251-253.

JUSTICE O'CONNOR, with whom THE CHIEF JUSTICE and JUSTICE POWELL join, dissenting.

In finding Pennsylvania's "flat" highway use taxes unconstitutional under the Commerce Clause, the Court today directly overrules the holdings of at least three cases: Capitol Greyhound Lines v. Brice, 339 U.S. 542 (1950); Aero Mayflower Transit Corp. v. Board of Railroad Comm'rs, 332 U.S. 495 (1947); and, Aero Mayflower Transit Co. v. Georgia Public Service Comm'n, 295 U.S. 285 (1935). . . . Certainly, as a matter of first impression the constitutionality of flat highway use taxes could have been resolved differently. Nonetheless, this particular issue has been settled now for over 50 years and Congress has not seen fit to pre-empt these taxes by exercising its commerce power, though, of course, it has had recent occasion to consider and reconsider the problems of the trucking industry.

. . . .

In the meantime, the reliance interest sought to be protected by the doctrine of stare decisis has grown up around the settled rule. For example, Pennsylvania has collected some $300 million in axle taxes to be spent on highway improvements that, of course, largely benefit the interstate trucking industry. In my view, Pennsylvania, in structuring its program for financing highway construction and repair, had every reason to rely upon the settled understanding that flat highway taxes reasonably related to the extent of the benefit conferred do not violate the Commerce Clause. . . .

. . . .

Neither does Armco dictate a different result. The West Virginia taxation scheme in that case on its face discriminated against out-of-state manufacturers: "if the property was manufactured in the State, no tax on the sale is imposed. If the property was manufactured out of the State and imported for sale, a tax of 0.27% is imposed on the sale price." Since this facially discriminatory tax could not be justified under the compensatory tax doctrine, it was held unconstitutional. See Maryland v. Louisiana. There is nothing in Armco to suggest that the Aero Mayflower line of cases was being implicitly disapproved or even that these cases were considered at all relevant to the case before the Court. Nor do I read Armco as establishing a grandiose version of the "internal consistency test" as the constitutional measure of all state taxes under the Commerce Clause. In my view, the fact that the tax in Armco was facially discriminatory sufficiently supports holding that tax invalid under the Commerce Clause. At most, Armco may be read for the proposition that a tax that is facially discriminatory is unconstitutional if it is not "internally consistent." In no way does it stand for the proposition that *nondiscriminatory* state taxes must also generally be "internally consistent" to pass constitutional muster. Creating an "internal consistency" rule of general application is an entirely novel enterprise that the Court undertakes for the first time in this case. Yet the Court gives no reason why such a rule is necessary or desirable, nor does it discuss the views of the lower courts or commentators. Indeed, the limited scholarly work on general application of the internal consistency test is largely negative. See, e.g., Judson & Duffy, An Opportunity Missed: Armco, Inc. v. Hardesty, A Retreat From Economic Reality in Analysis of State Taxes, 87 W. Va. L. Rev. 723, 739-740 (1985); Lathrop, Armco–A Narrow and Puzzling Test for Discriminatory State Taxes Under the Commerce Clause, 63 Taxes 551, 557 (1985). I am simply unwilling to follow the Court down this path without some greater understanding of the need, and authority, for doing so. I respectfully dissent.

JUSTICE SCALIA, with whom THE CHIEF JUSTICE joins, dissenting.

I agree with the Court that the "internal consistency" test it adopts requires invalidation of the Pennsylvania axle tax and marker fee–as it would any unapportioned flat tax involving multi-state activities. For the reasons given in my dissent in Tyler Pipe, I do not believe that test can be derived from the Constitution or is compelled by our past decisions. The same tax is imposed on in-state as on out-of-state trucks; that is all I would require. See Capitol Greyhound Lines v. Brice, 339 U.S. 542 (1950); Aero Mayflower Transit Co. v. Board of Railroad Comm'rs, 332 U.S. 495 (1947); Aero Mayflower Transit Co. v. Georgia Public Service Comm'n, 295 U.S. 285 (1935).

The Court's disposition relieves it of the need to address appellants' narrower contention that the axle tax is facially discriminatory because the same law that introduced it reduced registration fees for Pennsylvania-based trucks by, for all practical purposes, precisely the amount of the axle taxes. I would reject that challenge as well. The axle tax is imposed uniformly on both in-state and out-of-state vehicles, and is therefore not facially discriminatory. The registration fee is imposed only on in-state trucks, and its reduction likewise does not facially discriminate against interstate commerce. Since both the axle tax and the reduction in registration fees are independently nondiscriminatory, I would sustain them.

Appellants rely on Maryland v. Louisiana, in which we invalidated Louisiana's use tax on offshore gas because the State credited payments of that tax against other taxes imposed on local commerce, such as the severance tax on in-state production, and exempted gas used for certain in-state activities from the tax. That case is readily distinguishable. Pennsylvania provides no exemption from its axle tax for in-state truckers, and does not permit axle tax payments to be used as credits against the registration fee. The axle tax alone–unlike the gas tax in Maryland v. Louisiana–is on its face nondiscriminatory.

It may well be that the lowering of the exclusively intrastate registration fee has the same net effect as would a tax credit for the axle tax. But so would have the establishment of the registration fee and the axle tax at their current levels in the first place. To determine the facially discriminatory character of a tax not on the basis of the tax alone, but on the basis of the structure of a State's tax code, is to extend our case law into a new field, and one in which principled distinctions become impossible. What if, for example, the registration fees for Pennsylvania-based barges, rather than trucks, had been reduced in an amount that precisely compensated for the additional revenues to be derived from the increased axle fees? Or what if Pennsylvania had enacted the axle tax without reducing registration fees, and then one year later made a corresponding reduction in truck registration fees? This case, of course, is more difficult than those examples, because the tax reduction and axle tax both apply to the same mode of transport and were enacted simultaneously. However, to inquire whether a tax reduction is close enough in time or in mode to another tax so that "in effect" the latter should be treated as facially discriminatory is to ask a question that has no answer.

Legislative action adjusting taxes on interstate and intrastate activities spans a spectrum, ranging from the obviously discriminatory to the manipulative to the ambiguous to the wholly innocent. Courts can avoid arbitrariness in their review only by policing the entire spectrum (which is impossible), by policing none of it, or by adopting rules which subject to scrutiny certain well-defined classes of actions thought likely to come at or near the discriminatory end of the spectrum. We have traditionally followed the last course, confining our disapproval to forms of tax that seem clearly designed to discriminate,* and accepting the fact that some amount of discrimination may slip through our net. A credit against intrastate taxes falls readily within the highly suspect category; a reduction of intrastate taxes to take account of increased revenue from a nondiscriminatory axle tax does not.

I acknowledge that the distinction between a credit and a straight reduction is a purely formal one, but it seems to me less absurd than what we will be driven to if we abandon it. The axle tax and registration fee reduction in this case appeared in the same bill. Extend the rule to treat that as "in effect" a tax credit, and the next case will involve two different bills enacted the same day, or a week apart, or at the beginning and end of the same session. A line must be drawn somewhere, and (in the absence of direction from any authoritative text) I would draw it here.

---

*. There is one area where we seem to have based our decisions less on the form of the tax than on the character of the activity taxed: the "drumming" cases, where we have invalidated, without elaborate inquiry, facially neutral taxes on soliciting activities. See, e.g., Nippert v. Richmond, 327 U.S. 416 (1946). "Everybody knows" that these laws have but a single purpose, to protect local merchants from out-of-town (and hence out-of-state) competition. The temptation was great to presume that whole class of taxes, regardless of their nondiscriminatory form, guilty until proved innocent. I do not think those cases are an attractive model on which to base a more general Commerce Clause jurisprudence.

Questions and Comments

1. The Court evaluates the Pennsylvania flat tax by examining the amount of the flat tax per mile traveled in the state by both Pennsylvania-based trucks and out-of-state trucks. How did the Court defend using a "charge per mile traveled in the state" as the standard for evaluating the flat tax? Why not some alternative measure such as charge "per dollar of gross receipts for transportation attributable to the state," charge "per dollar of profit earned in the state," charge "per time spent in the state," or charge "per damage done to the roads"?

2. The Court states that the "imposition of the flat taxes for a privilege that is several times more valuable to a local business than to its out-of-state competitors is unquestionably discriminatory and thus offends the Commerce Clause." Presumably, the privilege referred to is the use of Pennsylvania roads, but that is valuable only because it is a means to an end: making a profit. Accordingly, in evaluating the Pennsylvania statute why couldn't the Court use as its standard the flat charge divided by profit rather than by miles?

3. Why didn't the Court characterize the recent Pennsylvania changes as a legislative attempt to exempt Pennsylvania-registered motor carriers from payment of the $25 marker fee?

Why didn't the Court characterize the axle tax, together with the simultaneous reduction in registration fees that offset the axle tax for Pennsylvania registered vehicles, as facially discriminatory because it imposed the axle tax only on interstate motor carriers registered outside of Pennsylvania? Is the Court's analysis of this issue consistent with its approach in *Maryland v. Louisiana*?

4. What was the significance of the stipulation that the administrative costs associated with the issuance of the identification markers were approximately five dollars per vehicle?

5. Since 1982, the Pennsylvania marker fee is only five dollars per vehicle. Why does the State bother levying a fee this small?

6. Under what conditions is a flat tax constitutional?

7. The Court states that "the Commerce Clause does not permit compensatory measures for the disparities that result from each State's choice of tax levels." Does this statement apply to the use tax, commonly called the *compensatory* use tax?

8. Consider the *Evansville-Vanderburgh* case, involving a departure fee of one dollar, which was relied upon by the Pennsylvania Supreme Court. Suppose the airport that charged the fee was geographically situated so that most interstate flights left the state's airspace almost immediately upon takeoff while most intrastate flights flew entirely over the state's airspace. Under those facts, would the departure fee discriminate against interstate commerce for the same reasons that the unapportioned axle tax was discriminatory? Does the airport departure fee satisfy the internal consistency test? Does the internal consistency doctrine apply to user charges? Should it?

9. The Pennsylvania fuel consumption tax provides a credit for fuel purchased at Pennsylvania pumps. Does the statute's failure to provide a credit for fuel purchased outside the State render it unconstitutional?

10. Which prongs of *Complete Auto* did the Pennsylvania statute violate? Can a tax violate the fourth prong without violating any of the other prongs?

11. Is the Court's approach consistent with its approach in *Commonwealth Edison*? *Austin*?

12. State A is separated from State B by a narrow body of water. A bridge connects State A and State B. A toll is charged for use of this bridge, with States A and B sharing the revenue. Is the toll constitutional?

Suppose that States C and D were connected by a highway and that this was the only road connecting C and D. Could State C build a toll booth on its side of the border? Assume that the toll charged is independent of the number of miles traveled in State C.

13. Suppose that out-of-state vehicles traveled five times as many miles on Pennsylvania roads as do Pennsylvania-based vehicles, and that the cost per mile of the flat taxes was five times as high for in-state vehicles as for out-of-state vehicles. Would the Pennsylvania flat taxes be constitutional?

14. Does Pennsylvania's registration fee have to be apportioned to be constitutional?

15. Could Pennsylvania restrict access to its State highways only to vehicles registered in Pennsylvania or in states having reciprocity agreements with Pennsylvania?

16. Owners or operators of commercial vehicles often pay different taxes, e.g., fuel consumption or road use, based on estimated distances traveled through different states, which have varying taxes and tax rates. Traditionally, owners or operators of commercial vehicles make painstaking comparisons of mileage logs and charts with regional maps and routes.

A new process uses satellite or land-based transceivers to track a vehicle. A vehicle carries a microprocessor, a data base of geographic information, and a positioning sensor. The sensor receives and records positioning information from satellite or land-based receivers, which marks the vehicle's location along its route. The microprocessor determines the distance traveled in each tax region by comparing the geographic data with the vehicle's location. N.Y. Times, Mar. 23, 1998, p. D2.

17. Three months after Pennsylvania levied its axle tax and reduced the registration fee pro tanto on in-state trucks, the New Jersey Legislature denounced the tax for "causing great hardship" to owners of trucks registered in New Jersey and called on all states to take "retaliatory measures." A year later, Maine accepted this invitation and adopted "reciprocal taxes," designed to mirror those imposed by Pennsylvania on trucks registered in Maine. See Borello, American Trucking Association v. Scheiner: Truckers Challenge Pennsylvania's Highway User Fees Under the Dormant Commerce Clause, 41 U. Miami L. Rev. 1117, 1118 (1987).

18. *American Trucking Associations* was relied upon in *City of Tampa v. Carolina Freight Carriers Corp.*, 529 So.2d 324 (Fla. Dist. Ct. App. 1988), holding that Tampa's flat occupational tax on a trucking company's transfer facility violated the Commerce Clause.

19. In *American Trucking Associations, Inc. v. Smith*, the Court held that *Scheiner* should be applied prospectively and that taxpayers were entitled to relief only for taxes levied after June 23, 1987, the day *Scheiner* was decided.

20. Federal law prohibits state taxes on persons traveling in air commerce but allows "reasonable rental charges, landing fees, and other service charges from aircraft operators for the use of airport facilities." 49 U.S.C. §40116(e)(2). In *Northwest Airlines v. County of Kent*, 510 U.S. 355 (1994), the Court rejected the argument that airport user fees were an invalid tax on persons traveling in air commerce. The Court held that a levy is reasonable if "it (1) is based on some fair approximation of use of the facilities, (2) is not excessive in relation to the benefits conferred, and (3) does not discriminate against interstate commerce." 510 U.S. at 364.

21. The Massachusetts Supreme Judicial Court upheld that State's minimum tax of $228 on out-of-state truckers, which was imposed on a per corporation basis and which contained an exclusion for companies making less than 13 pickups, deliveries, or trips through Massachusetts. *Aloha Freightways v. Mass.*, 701 N.E.2d 961 (1998).

22. For critical commentary on *American Trucking*, see *American Trucking Associations v. Scheiner: Truckers Challenge Pennsylvania's Highway User Fees Under the Dormant Commerce Clause*, 41 U. Miami L. Rev. 1117 (1987).

Bacchus Imports, Ltd., et al. v. Dias, Director of Taxation of Hawaii, et al.

Supreme Court of the United States, 1984.
468 U.S. 263, 104 S. Ct. 3049, 82 L. Ed. 2d 200.

JUSTICE WHITE delivered the opinion of the Court.

Appellants challenge the constitutionality of the Hawaii liquor tax, which is a 20% excise tax imposed on sales of liquor at wholesale. Specifically at issue are exemptions from the tax for certain locally produced alcoholic beverages. . . .

I

The Hawaii liquor tax was originally enacted in 1939 to defray the costs of police and other governmental services that the Hawaii Legislature concluded had been increased due to the consumption of liquor. At its inception the statute contained no exemptions. However, because the legislature sought to encourage development of the Hawaiian liquor industry, it enacted

an exemption for okolehao from 1971 until 1981, and an exemption for fruit wine from 1976 until 1981.* Okolehao is a brandy distilled from the root of the ti plant, an indigenous shrub of Hawaii. The only fruit wine manufactured in Hawaii during the relevant time was pineapple wine. Locally produced sake and fruit liqueurs are not exempted from the tax.

Appellants–Bacchus Imports, Ltd., and Eagle Distributors, Inc.–are liquor wholesalers who sell to licensed retailers. They sell the liquor at their wholesale price plus the 20% excise tax . . . . Their complaint alleged that the Hawaii

---

*. [Ed. The exemption applied to "Okolehao manufactured in the State" and "fruit wine manufactured in the State from products grown in the State." Ha. Rev. Stat. § 244-4.]

liquor tax was unconstitutional because it violates both the Import-Export Clause and the Commerce Clause of the United States Constitution. The wholesalers sought a refund of approximately $45 million, representing all of the liquor tax paid by them for the years in question.

. . . .

II

The State presents a claim not made below that the wholesalers have no standing to challenge the tax because they have shown no economic injury from the claimed discriminatory tax. The wholesalers are, however, liable for the tax. Although they may pass it on to their customers, and attempt to do so, they must return the tax to the State whether or not their customers pay their bills. Furthermore, even if the tax is completely and successfully passed on, it increases the price of their products as compared to the exempted beverages, and the wholesalers are surely entitled to litigate whether the discriminatory tax has had an adverse competitive impact on their business. The wholesalers plainly have standing to challenge the tax in this Court.*

III

A cardinal rule of Commerce Clause jurisprudence is that "[n]o State, consistent with the Commerce Clause, may 'impose a tax which discriminates against interstate commerce . . . by providing a direct commercial advantage to local business.'" Boston Stock Exchange, 429 U.S. at 329 (quoting Northwestern States Portland Cement Co., 358 U.S. at 458). Despite the fact that the tax exemption here at issue seems clearly to discriminate on its face against interstate commerce by bestowing a commercial advantage on okolehao and pineapple wine, the State argues—and the Hawaii Supreme Court held—that there is no improper discrimination.

A

Much of the State's argument centers on its contention that okolehao and pineapple wine do not compete with the other products sold by the wholesalers. The State relies in part on statistics showing that for the years in question sales of okolehao and pineapple wine constituted well under one percent of the total liquor sales in Hawaii. It also relies on the statement by the Hawaii Supreme Court that "[w]e believe we can safely assume these products pose no competitive threat to

---

**. [Ed. Of the four plaintiffs, one actually sold okolehao and pineapple wine. This plaintiff argued that its volume of sales of the exempted product was relatively insubstantial. In re Bacchus Imports, Ltd., 656 P. 2d 724, 727, n. 9 (1982).]

other liquors produced elsewhere and consumed in Hawaii," as well as the court's comment that it had "good reason to believe neither okolehao nor pineapple wine is produced elsewhere." However, neither the small volume of sales of exempted liquor nor the fact that the exempted liquors do not constitute a present "competitive threat" to other liquors is dispositive of the question whether competition exists between the locally produced beverages and foreign beverages; instead, they go only to the extent of such competition. It is well settled that "[w]e need not know how unequal the Tax is before concluding that it unconstitutionally discriminates." Maryland v. Louisiana, 451 U.S. at 760.

The State's position that there is no competition is belied by its purported justification of the exemption in the first place. The legislature originally exempted the locally produced beverages in order to foster the local industries by encouraging increased consumption of their product. Surely one way that the tax exemption might produce that result is that drinkers of other alcoholic beverages might give up or consume less of their customary drinks in favor of the exempted products because of the price differential that the exemption will permit. Similarly, nondrinkers, such as the maturing young, might be attracted by the low prices of okolehao and pineapple wine. On the stipulated facts in this case, we are unwilling to conclude that no competition exists between the exempted and the non-exempted liquors.

B

The State contends that a more flexible approach, taking into account the practical effect and relative burden on commerce, must be employed in this case because (1) legitimate state objectives are credibly advanced, (2) there is no patent discrimination against interstate trade, and (3) the effect on interstate commerce is incidental. See Philadelphia v. New Jersey, 437 U.S. at 624. On the other hand, it acknowledges that where simple economic protectionism is effected by state legislation, a stricter rule of invalidity has been erected. Ibid.

A finding that state legislation constitutes "economic protectionism" may be made on the basis of either discriminatory purpose, see Hunt v. Washington Apple Advertising Comm'n, 432 U.S. at 352-353, or discriminatory effect, see Philadelphia v. New Jersey, supra. See also Minnesota v. Clover Leaf Creamery Co., supra, at 471, n. 15. Examination of the State's purpose in this case is sufficient to demonstrate the State's lack of entitlement to a more flexible approach permitting inquiry into the balance between local benefits and the burden on interstate commerce. See Pike v. Bruce Church, Inc., 397 U.S. at 142. The Hawaii Supreme Court described the legislature's motivation in enacting the exemptions as follows:

"The legislature's reason for exempting 'ti root okolehao' from the 'alcohol tax' was to 'encourage and promote the establishment of a new industry,' and the exemption of 'fruit wine manufactured in the State from products grown in the State' was intended 'to help' in stimulating 'the local fruit wine industry.'"

Thus, we need not guess at the legislature's motivation, for it is undisputed that the purpose of the exemption was to aid Hawaiian industry. Likewise, the effect of the exemption is clearly discriminatory, in that it applies only to locally produced beverages, even though it does not apply to all such products. Consequently, as long as there is some competition between the locally produced exempt products and nonexempt products from outside the State, there is a discriminatory effect.

No one disputes that a State may enact laws pursuant to its police powers that have the purpose and effect of encouraging domestic industry. However, the Commerce Clause stands as a limitation on the means by which a State can constitutionally seek to achieve that goal. One of the fundamental purposes of the Clause "was to insure . . . against discriminating State legislation." Welton v. Missouri, 91 U.S. at 280. In Welton, the Court struck down a Missouri statute that "discriminat[ed] in favor of goods, wares, and merchandise which are the growth, product, or manufacture of the State, and against those which are the growth, product, or manufacture of other states or countries. . . ." Id., at 277. Similarly, in Walling v. Michigan, 116 U.S. at 455, the Court struck down a law imposing a tax on the sale of alcoholic beverages produced outside the State, declaring:

"A discriminating tax imposed by a State operating to the disadvantage of the products of other States when introduced into the first mentioned State, is, in effect, a regulation in restraint of commerce among the States, and as such is a usurpation of the power conferred by the Constitution upon the Congress of the United States."

More recently, in Boston Stock Exchange, the Court struck down a New York law that imposed a higher tax on transfers of stock occurring outside the State than on transfers involving a sale within the State. We observed that competition among the States for a share of interstate commerce is a central element of our free-trade policy but held that a State may not tax interstate transactions in order to favor local businesses over out-of-state businesses. Thus, the Commerce Clause limits the manner in which States may legitimately compete for interstate trade, for "in the process of competition no State may discriminatorily tax the products manufactured or the business operations performed in any other State." It is therefore apparent that the Hawaii Supreme Court erred in concluding that there was no improper discrimination against interstate commerce merely because the burden of the tax was borne by consumers in Hawaii.

The State attempts to put aside this Court's cases that have invalidated discriminatory state statutes enacted for protectionist purposes. See Minnesota v. Clover Leaf Creamery Co., supra, at 471; Lewis v. BT Investment Managers, Inc., supra, at 36-37. The State would distinguish these cases because they all involved attempts "to enhance thriving and substantial business enterprises at the expense of any foreign competitors." Hawaii's attempt, on the other hand, was "to subsidize non-existent (pineapple wine) and financially troubled (okolehao) liquor industries peculiar to Hawaii." However, we perceive no principle of Commerce Clause jurisprudence supporting a distinction between thriving and struggling enterprises under these circumstances, and the State cites no authority for its proposed distinction. In either event, the legislation constitutes "economic protectionism" in every sense of the phrase. It has long been the law that States may not "build up [their] domestic commerce by means of unequal and oppressive burdens upon the industry and business of other States." Guy v. Baltimore, 100 U.S. at 443. Were it otherwise, "the trade and business of the country [would be] at the mercy of local regulations, having for their object to secure exclusive benefits to the citizens and products of particular States." Id., at 442. It was to prohibit such a "multiplication of preferential trade areas" that the Commerce Clause was adopted. Dean Milk Co., 340 U.S. at 356. Consequently, the propriety of economic protectionism may not be allowed to hinge upon the State's–or this Court's–characterization of the industry as either "thriving" or "struggling."

We also find unpersuasive the State's contention that there was no discriminatory intent on the part of the legislature because "the exemptions in question were not enacted to discriminate against foreign products, but rather, to promote a local industry." If we were to accept that justification, we would have little occasion ever to find a statute unconstitutionally discriminatory. Virtually every discriminatory statute allocates benefits or burdens unequally; each can be viewed as conferring a benefit on one party and a detriment on the other, in either an absolute or relative sense. The determination of constitutionality does not depend upon whether one focuses upon the benefitted or the burdened party. A discrimination claim, by its nature, requires a comparison of the two classifications, and it could always be said that there was no intent to impose a burden on one party, but rather the intent was to confer a benefit on the other. Consequently, it is irrelevant to the Commerce Clause inquiry that the motivation of the legislature was the desire to aid the makers of the locally produced beverage rather than to harm out-of-state producers.

We therefore conclude that the Hawaii liquor tax exemption for okolehao and pineapple wine violated the

Commerce Clause because it had both the purpose and effect of discriminating in favor of local products.

. . . .

V

The State further contends that even if the challenged tax is adjudged to have been unconstitutionally discriminatory and should not have been collected from the wholesalers as long as the exemptions for local products were in force, the wholesalers are not entitled to refunds since they did not bear the economic incidence of the tax but passed it on as a separate addition to the price that their customers were legally obligated to pay within a certain time. Relying on United States v. Jefferson Electric Mfg. Co., 291 U.S. 386 (1934), a case involving interpretation of a federal tax refund statute, the State asserts that only the parties bearing the economic incidence of the tax are constitutionally entitled to a refund of an illegal tax. It further asserts that the wholesalers, at least arguably, do not even bear the legal obligation for the tax and that they have shown no competitive injury from the alleged discrimination. The wholesalers assert, on the other hand, that they were liable to pay the tax whether or not their customers paid their bills on time and that if the tax was illegally discriminatory the Commerce Clause requires that the taxes collected be refunded to them. Their position is also that the discrimination has worked a competitive injury on their business that entitles them to a refund.

These refund issues, which are essentially issues of remedy for the imposition of a tax that unconstitutionally discriminated against interstate commerce, were not addressed by the state courts. Also, the federal constitutional issues involved may well be intertwined with, or their consideration obviated by, issues of state law.[14] Also, resolution of those issues, if required at all, may necessitate more of a record than so far has been made in this case. We are reluctant, therefore, to address them in the first instance. Accordingly, we reverse the judgment of the Supreme Court of Hawaii and remand for further proceedings not inconsistent with this opinion.

[The court also held that the twenty-first amendment did not save the exemption from a Commerce Clause challenge.]

[Dissenting opinion by JUSTICE STEVENS, who would have upheld the tax on the basis of the twenty-first amendment, with whom JUSTICE REHNQUIST and JUSTICE O'CONNOR joined.]

---

14. It may be, for example, that given an unconstitutional discrimination, a full refund is mandated by state law.

Questions and Comments

1. How were the plaintiffs damaged by the exemption for okolehao and fruit wines? Weren't they free to distribute such wines?

2. If Hawaii could have proven that no competition existed between the local wines and other beverages sold by the wholesalers, would the statute have been upheld? What if the only competition was between the exempted products and other beverages produced only in Hawaii? Compare *General Motors Corp. v. Tracy* in the chapter on the deregulation of utilities.

3. The statute limited the exemption to only okolehao or fruit wine manufactured in Hawaii. What if the exemption applied to okolehao or fruit wine regardless of where they were manufactured? See *Div. of Alcoholic Beverages and Tobacco v. McKesson*, 524 So. 2d 1000 (1988), rev'd on other grounds, 496 U.S. 18 (1990).

4. Would the case have been more difficult if there had been no legislative history declaring the purpose of the statute? Did the statutory scheme have the effect of a tariff?

5. Was the State's position that there was no competition between okolehao and other alcoholic beverages belied by the Legislature's purposes in enacting the exemption? Might the exemption keep the local okolehao industry alive even if it did not increase consumption of such wine?

6. In analyzing Hawaii's statute, did the Court apply a balancing test? Did the Court apply a balancing test in *Boston Stock*?

7. Suppose in order to encourage its domestic industry, Hawaii granted interest-free loans to certain manufacturers. Would it be unconstitutional for Hawaii to grant an interest-free loan to the manufacturers of okolehao or fruit wine?

8. Suppose Hawaii had a program to encourage indigenous culture. As part of this program, it made a grant to the manufacturers of okolehao and fruit wine. Constitutional?

9. Suppose Hawaii had drafted its tax so that it applied to liquor and wines made from grapes. There was no specific exemption for fruit wines because they were not subject to the tax in the first place. Would such a statute be constitutional?

10. The Court dealt with the issue of whether *Bacchus* should be applied prospectively only in *James B. Beam Distilling Co. v. Georgia*, 501 U.S. 529 (1991). The Court held that because *Bacchus* had been applied to the taxpayer in that case, the decision had to apply to all taxpayers with open claims, that is, taxpayers whose claims were not barred by statute of limitations or other procedural barriers.

11. What is the proper remedy in this case? Should the plaintiffs receive a refund of all the tax they paid or should the refund be paid only to those who purchased the products sold by the wholesalers? Or, should the State collect tax from the distributors of okolehao and fruit wine? Do the plaintiffs have to prove the extent to which they were damaged?

The majority stated that the "wholesalers are surely entitled to litigate whether the discriminatory tax has had an adverse competitive impact on their business." 468 U.S. at 267. In dicta, the dissent expressed skepticism about whether the wholesalers could prove that the exemptions harmed their businesses, partly because their customers have reimbursed them for the excise tax and partly because they were able to sell the exempted products themselves. 468 U.S. at 278.

Upon remand of *Bacchus*, the State took the position that the taxpayers were entitled to a refund in an amount equal to the economic harm they had actually suffered. Under this theory, the taxpayers would have to prove their lost profits rather than automatically receive a refund of the discriminatory tax. The State's position was apparently endorsed by the Hawaii Supreme Court. Was the State's position consistent with the majority's views in *Bacchus*? The dissent's views? Rather than litigate the amount of economic harm, the parties in *Bacchus* settled the case. See also *West Virginia v. Canady*, 434 S.E.2d 10 (1993), discussed after *Armco*, in Chapter Nine.

In *McKesson Corp. v. Div. of Alcoholic Beverages & Tobacco*, 496 U.S. 18 (1990), decided one year before *Beam*, the Supreme Court expounded on the issue of remedies. That case involved a successful challenge to Florida's excise tax on liquor. Prior to *Bacchus*, Florida granted tax preferred treatment to alcoholic beverages made from certain agricultural crops grown in Florida and manufactured and bottled in Florida. In response to *Bacchus*, the statute was amended to grant exemptions or tax preferences to wine and distilled spirits manufactured from citrus, sugar cane, and certain grapes, all of which grow in Florida, no matter where manufactured. The Florida Supreme Court held that the preferences violated the commerce clause, but applied its holding prospectively only. *Div. of Alcoholic Beverages and Tobacco v. McKesson*, 524 So. 2d 1000 (1988). The U.S. Supreme Court held that "if a State places a taxpayer under duress promptly to pay a tax when due and relegates him to a postpayment refund action in which he can challenge the tax's legality, the Due Process Clause of the Fourteenth Amendment obligates the State to provide meaningful backward-looking relief to rectify any unconstitutional deprivation." 496 U.S. at 31. The taxpayer is not automatically entitled to a refund. Florida, could, for example, collect back taxes from those who were the beneficiaries of the unconstitutional exemptions, although this approach would have to be consistent with federal and Florida law on retroactive taxation. Id. at 40. By contrast, a state that, unlike Florida, provided an opportunity to protest a tax prior to payment would have discharged its due process responsibilities and would not have to provide backward-looking relief.

12. Counties in Pennsylvania impose a personal property tax that applies to stocks. An exemption is provided for domestic corporations or corporations doing business in Pennsylvania. The exemption was held to be unconstitutional in *Annenberg v. Commonwealth*, 757 A.2d 338 (Pa. 2000) because it discriminated against out-of-state corporations. In order to cure the statute, some counties are attempting to retroactively collect the tax on stock that was subject to the exemption. The plaintiffs are challenging the validity of that remedy. See *Annenberg v. County of Montgomery*, No. 01-03713, Court of Common Pleas, Montgomery County, Pennsylvania. For a very thoughtful analysis of the remedy issue, see John F. Coverdale, *Remedies for Unconstitutional State Taxes*, 32 Conn. L. Rev. 73 (2000).

13. For critical commentary on *Bacchus Imports*, see Susan M. Johnson, *From Bacchus to Our House: Taxation of the Oregon Wine Industry Under Current Twenty-First Amendment and Commerce Clause Jurisprudence*, 73 Or. L. Rev. 711 (1994); Christopher J. Ohmes, *Recent Triumphs Against Discrimination in Interstate Commerce: The Armco and Bacchus Imports Decisions*, 5 J. St. Tax'n 131 (1986); Eric T. Freeman, *The Twenty-first Amendment and the Commerce Clause: What Rationale Supports Bacchus Imports*, 13 Hastings Const. L.Q. 361 (1986); Gisele M. Sutherland, *Commerce Clause Reigns Over Twenty-first Amendment: Bacchus I port, Ltd. v. Dias*, 38 Tax Law. 527 (1985).

New Energy Company of Indiana v. Limbach
Supreme Court of the United States, 1988.
486 U.S. 269, 108 S. Ct. 1803, 100 L. Ed. 2d 302.

JUSTICE SCALIA delivered the opinion of the Court.

Appellant New Energy Company of Indiana has challenged the constitutionality of Ohio Rev. Code Ann. section 5735.145(B), a provision that awards a tax credit against the Ohio motor vehicle fuel sales tax for each gallon of ethanol sold (as a component of gasohol) by fuel dealers, but only if the ethanol is produced in Ohio or in a State that grants similar tax advantages to ethanol produced in Ohio. The question presented is whether section 5735.145(B) discriminates against interstate commerce in violation of the Commerce Clause.

I

Ethanol, or ethyl alcohol, is usually made from corn. In the last decade it has come into widespread use as an automotive fuel, mixed with gasoline in a ratio of 1:9 to produce what is called gasohol. The interest in ethanol emerged in reaction to the petroleum market dislocations of the early 1970's. The product was originally promoted as a means of achieving energy independence while providing a market for surplus corn; more recently, emphasis has shifted to its environmental advantages as a replacement for lead in enhancing fuel octane. Ethanol was, however (and continues to be), more expensive than gasoline, and the emergence of ethanol production on a commercial scale dates from enactment of the first federal subsidy, in the form of an exemption from federal motor fuel excise taxes, in 1978. Since then, many States, particularly those in the grain-producing areas of the country, have enacted their own ethanol subsidies. Ohio first passed such a measure in 1981, providing Ohio gasohol dealers a credit of so many cents per gallon of ethanol used in their product against the Ohio motor vehicle fuel sales tax payable on both ethanol and gasoline. This credit was originally available without regard to the source of the ethanol. In 1984, however, Ohio enacted section 5735.145(B), which denies the credit to ethanol coming from States that do not grant a tax credit, exemption, or refund to ethanol from Ohio, or, if a State grants a smaller tax advantage than Ohio's, granting only an equivalent credit to ethanol from that State.

Appellant is an Indiana limited partnership that manufactures ethanol in South Bend, Indiana, for sale in several States, including Ohio. Indiana repealed its tax exemption for ethanol, at which time it also passed legislation providing a direct subsidy to Indiana ethanol producers (the sole one of which was appellant). Thus, by reason of Ohio's reciprocity provision, appellant's ethanol sold in Ohio became ineligible for the Ohio tax credit. . . .

II

It has long been accepted that the Commerce Clause not only grants Congress the authority to regulate commerce among the States, but also directly limits the power of the States to discriminate against interstate commerce. This "negative" aspect of the Commerce Clause prohibits economic protectionism–that is, regulatory measures designed to benefit in-state economic interests by burdening out-of-state competitors. See, e.g., Bacchus Imports, 468 U.S. at 270-273; H.P. Hood & Sons, supra, at 532-533; Guy v. Baltimore, 100 U.S. at 443 (1880). Thus, state statutes that clearly discriminate against interstate commerce are routinely struck down, see, e.g., Sporhase v. Nebraska ex rel. Douglas, 458 U.S. 941 (1982); Lewis v. BT Investment Managers, Inc., 447 U.S. 27 (1980); Dean Milk Co., 340 U.S. 349 (1951), unless the discrimination is demonstrably justified by a valid factor unrelated to economic protectionism, see, e.g., Maine v. Taylor, 477 U.S. 131 (1986).

The Ohio provision at issue here explicitly deprives certain products of generally available beneficial tax treatment because they are made in certain other States, and thus on its face appears to violate the cardinal requirement of nondiscrimination. Appellees argue, however, that the availability of the tax credit to some out-of-state manufacturers (those in States that give tax advantages to Ohio-produced ethanol) shows that the Ohio provision, far from discriminating against interstate commerce, is likely to promote it, by encouraging other States to enact similar tax advantages that will spur the interstate sale of ethanol. We rejected a similar contention in an earlier "reciprocity" case, Great Atlantic & Pacific Tea Co. v. Cottrell, 424 U.S. 366 (1976). The regulation at issue there permitted milk from out of State to be sold in Mississippi only if the State of origin accepted Mississippi milk on a reciprocal basis. Mississippi put forward, among other arguments, the assertion that "the reciprocity requirement is in effect a free-trade provision, advancing the identical national interest that is served by the Commerce Clause." Id., at 378. In response, we said that "Mississippi may not use the threat of economic isolation as a weapon to force sister States to enter into even a desirable reciprocity agreement." Id., at 379. More recently, we characterized a Nebraska reciprocity requirement for the export of ground water from the State as "facially discriminatory legislation" which merited "'strictest scrutiny.'" Sporhase v. Nebraska ex rel. Douglas, supra, at 958, quoting Hughes v. Oklahoma, supra, at 337.

It is true that in Cottrell and Sporhase the effect of a State's refusal to accept the offered reciprocity was total

elimination of all transport of the subject product into or out of the offering State; whereas in the present case the only effect of refusal is that the out-of-state product is placed at a substantial commercial disadvantage through discriminatory tax treatment. That makes no difference for purposes of Commerce Clause analysis. In the leading case of Baldwin v. G.A.F. Seelig, Inc., 294 U.S. 511 (1935), the New York law excluding out-of-state milk did not impose an absolute ban, but rather allowed importation and sale so long as the initial purchase from the dairy farmer was made at or above the New York State-mandated price. In other words, just as the appellant here, in order to sell its product in Ohio, only has to cut its profits by reducing its sales price below the market price sufficiently to compensate the Ohio purchaser-retailer for the forgone tax credit, so also the milk wholesaler-distributor in Baldwin, in order to sell its product in New York, only had to cut its profits by increasing its purchase price above the market price sufficiently to meet the New York-prescribed minimum. We viewed the New York law as "an economic barrier against competition" that was "equivalent to a rampart of customs duties." Id., at 527. Similarly, in Hunt v. Washington Apple Advertising Comm'n, 432 U.S. 333, 349-351 (1977), we found invalid under the Commerce Clause a North Carolina statute that did not exclude apples from other States, but merely imposed additional costs upon Washington sellers and deprived them of the commercial advantage of their distinctive grading system. The present law likewise imposes an economic disadvantage upon out-of-state sellers; and the promise to remove that if reciprocity is accepted no more justifies disparity of treatment than it would justify categorical exclusion. We have indicated that reciprocity requirements are not per se unlawful. See Cottrell, supra, at 378. But the case we cited for that proposition, Kane v. New Jersey, 242 U.S. at 167-168, discussed a context in which, if a State offered the reciprocity did not accept it, the consequence was, to be sure, *less favored* treatment for its citizens, but nonetheless treatment that complied with the minimum requirements of the Commerce Clause. Here, quite to the contrary, the threat used to induce Indiana's acceptance is, in effect, taxing a product made by its manufacturers at a rate higher than the same product made by Ohio manufacturers, without (as we shall see) justification for the disparity.

. . . .

Appellees contend that even if section 5735.145(B) is discriminatory, the discrimination is not covered by the Commerce Clause because of the so-called market-participant doctrine. That doctrine differentiates between a State's acting in its distinctive governmental capacity, and a State's acting in the more general capacity of a market participant; only the former is subject to the limitations of the negative Commerce Clause. See Hughes v. Alexandria Scrap Corp., 426 U.S.

794, 806-810 (1976). Thus, for example, when a State chooses to manufacture and sell cement, its business methods, including those that favor its residents, are of no greater constitutional concern than those of a private business. See Reeves, Inc. v. Stake, 447 U.S. at 438-439.

The market-participant doctrine has no application here. The Ohio action ultimately at issue is neither its purchase nor its sale of ethanol, but its assessment and computation of taxes–a primeval governmental activity. To be sure, the tax credit scheme has the purpose and effect of subsidizing a particular industry, as do many dispositions of the tax laws. That does not transform it into a form of state participation in the free market. Our opinion in Alexandria Scrap, supra, a case on which appellees place great reliance, does not remotely establish such a proposition. There we examined, and upheld against Commerce Clause attack on the basis of the market-participant doctrine, a Maryland cash subsidy program that discriminated in favor of in-state auto-hulk processors. The purpose of the program was to achieve the removal of unsightly abandoned autos from the State, 426 U.S. at 796-797, and the Court characterized it as proprietary rather than regulatory activity, based on the analogy of the State to a private purchaser of the auto hulks, id., at 808-810. We have subsequently observed that subsidy programs unlike that of Alexandria Scrap might not be characterized as proprietary. See Reeves, Inc., 447 U.S. 429, at 440, n. 14. We think it clear that Ohio's assessment and computation of its fuel sales tax, regardless of whether it produces a subsidy, cannot plausibly be analogized to the activity of a private purchaser.

It has not escaped our notice that the appellant here, which is eligible to receive a cash subsidy under Indiana's program for in-state ethanol producers, is the potential beneficiary of a scheme no less discriminatory than the one that it attacks, and no less effective in conferring a commercial advantage over out-of-state competitors. To believe the Indiana scheme is valid, however, is not to believe that the Ohio scheme must be valid as well. The Commerce Clause does not prohibit all state action designed to give its residents an advantage in the marketplace, but only action of that description *in connection with the state's regulation of interstate commerce.* Direct subsidization of domestic industry does not ordinarily run afoul of that prohibition; discriminatory taxation of out-of-state manufactures does. Of course, even if the Indiana subsidy were invalid, retaliatory violation of the Commerce Clause by Ohio would not be acceptable. Cottrell, 424 U.S. at 379-380.

III

Our cases leave open the possibility that a State may validate a statute that discriminates against interstate commerce by showing that it advances a legitimate local purpose that cannot be adequately served by reasonable nondiscriminatory alternatives. See, e.g., Maine v. Taylor, 477 U.S. at 138, 151; Sporhase v. Nebraska ex rel. Douglas, 458 U.S. at 958; Hughes v. Oklahoma, 441 U.S. at 336-337; Dean Milk Co., 340 U.S. at 354. This is perhaps just another way of saying that what may appear to be a "discriminatory" provision in the constitutionally prohibited sense–that is, a protectionist enactment–may on closer analysis not be so. However it be put, the standards for such justification are high. Cf. Philadelphia v. New Jersey, 437 U.S. at 624 (1978) ("[W]here simple economic protectionism is effected by state legislation, a virtually per se rule of invalidity has been erected"); Hughes v. Oklahoma, 441 U.S. at 337 ("[F]acial discrimination by itself may be a fatal defect" and "[a]t a minimum . . . invokes the strictest scrutiny").

Appellees advance two justifications for the clear discrimination in the present case: health and commerce. As to the first, they argue that the provision encourages use of ethanol (in replacement of lead as a gasoline octane-enhancer) to reduce harmful exhaust emissions, both in Ohio itself and in surrounding States whose polluted atmosphere may reach Ohio. Certainly the protection of health is a legitimate state goal, and we assume for purposes of this argument that use of ethanol generally furthers it. But section 5735.145(B) obviously does not, except perhaps by accident. As far as ethanol use in Ohio itself is concerned, there is no reason to suppose that ethanol produced in a State that does not offer tax advantages to ethanol produced in Ohio is less healthy, and thus should have its importation into Ohio suppressed by denial of the otherwise standard tax credit. And as far as ethanol use outside Ohio is concerned, surely that is just as effectively fostered by other States' subsidizing ethanol production or sale in some fashion other than giving a tax credit to Ohio-produced ethanol; but these helpful expedients do not qualify for the tax credit. It could not be clearer that health is not the purpose of the provision, but is merely an occasional and accidental effect of achieving what is its purpose, favorable tax treatment for *Ohio*-produced ethanol.[3] Essentially the same reasoning also responds to appellees' second (and related) justification for the discrimination, that the reciprocity requirement is designed to increase commerce in ethanol by encouraging other States to enact ethanol subsidies.

___

3. We do not interpret the trial court's acceptance of appellees' proposed finding of fact of April 10, 1985, as a judicial finding that protecting health was in fact a purpose of the Ohio General Assembly, rather than merely one of several conceivable purposes for the enactment. In any event, a subjective purpose that has so little rational relationship to the provision in question is not merely implausible but, even if true, inadequate to validate patent discrimination against interstate commerce.

What is encouraged is not ethanol subsidies in general, but only favorable treatment for Ohio-produced ethanol. In sum, appellees' health and commerce justifications amount to no more than implausible speculation, which does not suffice to validate this plain discrimination against products of out- of-state manufacture.

Questions and Comments

1. Under what conditions can a state statute that discriminates against interstate commerce be upheld?

2. Could Ohio provide a cash subsidy to Ohio producers of ethanol?

3. Is the Court's treatment of the discrimination issue consistent with its approach in *Boston Stock Exchange, Maryland v. Louisiana*, or *Bacchus*?

4. For a discussion of the market participation doctrine, see Dan T. Coenen, *Untangling the Market–Participation Exemption to the Dormant Commerce Clause*, 88 Mich. L. Rev. 395 (1989).

5. For critical commentary on *New Energy*, see Susan Brom, *Tax Credit for Ohio-Produced Ethanol: Forced Reciprocity or Promotion of Health and Commerce? New Energy Company of Indiana v. Limbach*, 42 Tax Law. 401 (1989).

West Lynn Creamery, Inc. v. Healy
Supreme Court of the United States, 1994.
512 U.S. 186, 114 S. Ct. 2205, 129 L. Ed. 2d 157.

JUSTICE STEVENS delivered the opinion of the Court.

A Massachusetts pricing order imposes an assessment on all fluid milk sold by dealers to Massachusetts retailers. About two-thirds of that milk is produced out of State. The entire assessment, however, is distributed to Massachusetts dairy farmers. The question presented is whether the pricing order unconstitutionally discriminates against interstate commerce. We hold that it does.

I

Petitioner West Lynn Creamery, Inc., is a milk dealer licensed to do business in Massachusetts. It purchases raw milk, which it processes, packages, and sells to wholesalers, retailers, and other milk dealers. About 97% of the raw milk it purchases is produced by out-of-state farmers. Petitioner LeComte's Dairy, Inc., is also a licensed Massachusetts milk dealer. It purchases all of its milk from West Lynn and distributes it to retail outlets in Massachusetts.

Since 1937, the Agricultural Marketing Agreement has authorized the Secretary of Agriculture to regulate the minimum prices paid to producers of raw milk by issuing marketing orders for particular geographic areas. While the Federal Government sets minimum prices based on local conditions, those prices have not been so high as to prevent substantial competition among producers in different States. In the 1980's and early 1990's, Massachusetts dairy farmers began to lose market share to lower cost producers in neighboring States. In response, the Governor of Massachusetts appointed a Special Commission to study the dairy industry. The Commission found that many producers had sold their dairy farms during the past decade and that if prices paid to farmers for their milk were not significantly increased, a majority of the remaining farmers in Massachusetts would be "forced out of business within the year." On January 28, 1992, relying on the Commission's Report, the Commissioner of the Massachusetts Department of Food and Agriculture (respondent) declared a State of Emergency. In his declaration he noted that the average federal blend price had declined from $14.67 per hundred pounds (cwt) of raw milk in 1990 to $12.64/cwt in 1991, while costs of production for Massachusetts farmers had risen to an estimated average of $15.50/cwt. Id., at 27. He concluded:

"Regionally, the industry is in serious trouble and ultimately, a federal solution will be required. In the meantime, we must act on the state level to preserve our local industry, maintain reasonable minimum prices for the dairy farmers, thereby ensure a continuous and adequate supply of fresh milk for our market, and protect the public health."

Promptly after his declaration of emergency, respondent issued the pricing order that is challenged in this proceeding.

The order requires every "dealer"[4] in Massachusetts to make a monthly "premium payment" into the "Massachusetts Dairy Equalization Fund." The amount of those payments is computed in two steps. First, the monthly "order premium" is determined by subtracting the federal blend price for that month from $15 and dividing the difference by three; thus if the federal price is $12/cwt, the order premium is $1/cwt.[5] Second, the premium is multiplied by the amount (in pounds) of the dealer's sales in Massachusetts. Each month the fund is distributed to Massachusetts producers. Each Massachusetts producer receives a share of the total fund equal to his proportionate contribution to the State's total production of raw milk.

. . . .

II

The Commerce Clause vests Congress with ample power to enact legislation providing for the regulation of prices paid to farmers for their products. An affirmative exercise of that power led to the promulgation of the federal order setting minimum milk prices. The Commerce Clause also limits the power of the Commonwealth of Massachusetts to adopt regulations that discriminate against interstate commerce. "This 'negative' aspect of the Commerce Clause prohibits economic protectionism–that is, regulatory measures designed to benefit in-state economic interests by burdening out-of-state competitors. . . . Thus, state statutes that clearly discriminate against interstate commerce are routinely struck down . . . unless the discrimination is demonstrably justified by a valid factor

unrelated to economic protectionism . . ." New Energy Co. of Indiana v. Limbach, 486 U.S. at 273-274.[9]

The paradigmatic example of a law discriminating against interstate commerce is the protective tariff or customs duty, which taxes goods imported from other States, but does not tax similar products produced in State. A tariff is an attractive measure because it simultaneously raises revenue and benefits local producers by burdening their out-of-state competitors. Nevertheless, it violates the principle of the unitary national market by handicapping out-of-state competitors, thus artificially encouraging in-state production even when the same goods could be produced at lower cost in other States.

Because of their distorting effects on the geography of production, tariffs have long been recognized as violative of the Commerce Clause. In fact, tariffs against the products of other States are so patently unconstitutional that our cases reveal not a single attempt by any State to enact one. Instead, the cases are filled with state laws that aspire to reap some of the benefits of tariffs by other means. In Baldwin v. G. A. F. Seelig, Inc., 294 U.S. 511 (1935), the State of New York attempted to protect its dairy farmers from the adverse effects of Vermont competition by establishing a single minimum price for all milk, whether produced in New York or elsewhere. This Court did not hesitate, however, to strike it down. Writing for a unanimous Court, Justice Cardozo reasoned:

"Neither the power to tax nor the police power may be used by the state of destination with the aim and effect of establishing an economic barrier against competition with the products of another state or the labor of its residents. Restrictions so contrived are an unreasonable clog upon the mobility of commerce. They set up what is equivalent to a rampart of customs duties designed to neutralize advantages belonging to the place of origin."

Thus, because the minimum price regulation had the same effect as a tariff or customs duty–neutralizing the advantage possessed by lower cost out-of-state producers–it was held unconstitutional. Similarly, in Bacchus, this Court invalidated a law which advantaged local production by granting a tax exemption to certain liquors produced in Hawaii. Other cases of this kind are legion. Welton v. Missouri, 91 U.S. 275 (1876); Guy v. Baltimore, 100 U.S. 434 (1880); Toomer v. Witsell, 334

---

4. A "dealer" is defined as "any person who is engaged within the Commonwealth in the business of receiving, purchasing, pasteurizing, bottling, processing, distributing, or otherwise handling milk, purchases or receives milk for sale as the consignee or agent of a producer, and shall include a producer-dealer, dealer-retailer, and sub-dealer."

5. The Commissioner appears to have set the order premium at only a third of the difference between the federal price and $15 because Massachusetts farmers produce only about one-third of the milk sold as fluid milk in the State. Since Massachusetts dairy farmers produce one-third of the milk, an assessment of one-third the difference between $15 and the federal minimum price generates enough revenue to give Massachusetts dairy farmers the entire difference between $15 and the federal minimum price without leaving any surplus. By paying Massachusetts dairy farmers the entire difference between $15 and the federal minimum price, the order premium allows Massachusetts farmers whose cost of production is $15/cwt to sell their milk without loss at the federal minimum price.

---

9. The "negative" aspect of the Commerce Clause was considered the more important by the "father of the Constitution," James Madison. In one of his letters, Madison wrote that the Commerce Clause "grew out of the abuse of the power by the importing States in taxing the non-importing, and was intended as a negative and preventive provision against injustice among the States themselves, rather than as a power to be used for the positive purposes of the General Government." 3 M. Farrand, Records of the Federal Convention of 1787, p. 478 (1911).

U.S. 385 (1948); Polar Ice Cream & Creamery Co., 375 U.S. 361 (1964); Chemical Waste Management, Inc. v. Hunt, 504 U.S. 334 (1992); see also, Washington State Apple Advertising Comm'n, 432 U.S. at 351 (invalidating statute, because it "has the effect of stripping away from the Washington apple industry the competitive and economic advantages it has earned . . .").

Under these cases, Massachusetts' pricing order is clearly unconstitutional. Its avowed purpose and its undisputed effect are to enable higher cost Massachusetts dairy farmers to compete with lower cost dairy farmers in other States. The "premium payments" are effectively a tax which makes milk produced out of State more expensive. Although the tax also applies to milk produced in Massachusetts, its effect on Massachusetts producers is entirely (indeed more than) offset by the subsidy provided exclusively to Massachusetts dairy farmers. Like an ordinary tariff, the tax is thus effectively imposed only on out-of-state products. The pricing order thus allows Massachusetts dairy farmers who produce at higher cost to sell at or below the price charged by lower cost out-of-state producers.[10] If there were no federal minimum prices for milk, out-of-state producers might still be able to retain their market share by lowering their prices. Nevertheless, out-of-staters' ability to remain competitive by lowering their prices would not immunize a discriminatory measure. New Energy Co., 486 U.S. at 275. In this case, because the Federal Government sets minimum prices, out-of-state producers may not even have the option of reducing prices in order to retain market share. The Massachusetts pricing order thus will almost certainly "cause local goods to constitute a larger share, and goods with an out-of-state

source to constitute a smaller share, of the total sales in the market."[12] Exxon Corp. v. Governor of Maryland, 437 U.S. at 126, n.16 (1978). In fact, this effect was the motive behind the promulgation of the pricing order. This effect renders the program unconstitutional, because it, like a tariff, "neutralizes advantages belonging to the place of origin." Baldwin, 294 U.S. at 527.

In some ways, the Massachusetts pricing order is most similar to the law at issue in Bacchus. Both involve a broad-based tax on a single kind of good and special provisions for in-state producers. Bacchus involved a 20% excise tax on all liquor sales, coupled with an exemption for fruit wine manufactured in Hawaii and for okolehao, a brandy distilled from the root of a shrub indigenous to Hawaii. The Court held that Hawaii's law was unconstitutional because it "had both the purpose and effect of discriminating in favor of local products." See also I. M. Darnell & Son Co. v. Memphis, 208 U.S. 113 (1908) (invalidating property tax exemption favoring local manufacturers). By granting a tax exemption for local products, Hawaii in effect created a protective tariff. Goods produced out of State were taxed, but those produced in State were subject to no net tax. It is obvious that the result in Bacchus would have been the same if instead of exempting certain Hawaiian liquors from tax, Hawaii had rebated the amount of tax collected from the sale of those liquors. See New Energy (discriminatory tax credit). And if a discriminatory tax rebate is unconstitutional, Massachusetts' pricing order is surely invalid; for Massachusetts not only rebates to domestic milk producers the tax paid on the sale of Massachusetts milk, but also the tax paid on the sale of milk produced elsewhere. The additional rebate of the tax paid on the sale of milk produced elsewhere in no way reduces the danger to the national market posed by tariff-like barriers, but instead exacerbates the danger by giving

---

10. A numerical example may make this effect clearer. Suppose the federal minimum price is $12/cwt, that out-of-state producers can sell milk profitably at that price, but that in-state producers need a price of $15/cwt in order to break even. Under the pricing order, the tax or "order premium" will be $1/cwt (one-third the difference between the $15/cwt target price and the $12/cwt federal minimum price). Assuming the tax generates sufficient funds (which will be the case as long as two-thirds of milk is produced out of State, which appears to be the case), the Massachusetts farmers will receive a subsidy of $3/cwt. This subsidy will allow them to lower their prices from $15/cwt to $12/cwt while still breaking even. Selling at $12/cwt, Massachusetts dairy farmers will now be able to compete with out-of-state producers. The net effect of the tax and subsidy, like that of a tariff, is to raise the after-tax price paid by the dealers. If exactly two-thirds of the milk sold in Massachusetts is produced out of State, net prices will rise by $1/cwt. If out-of-state farmers produce more than two-thirds of the raw milk, the Dairy Equalization Fund will have a surplus, which will be refunded to the milk dealers. This refund will mitigate the price increase, although it will have no effect on the ability of the program to enable higher-cost Massachusetts dairy farmers to compete with lower-cost out-of-staters.

---

12. That is not to say that the Massachusetts dairy industry may not continue to shrink and that the market share of Massachusetts dairy producers may not continue its fall. It may be the case that Massachusetts producers' costs are so high that, even with the pricing order, many of them will be unable to compete. Nevertheless, the pricing order will certainly allow more Massachusetts dairy farmers to remain in business than would have had the pricing order not been imposed. For Commerce Clause purposes, it does not matter whether the challenged regulation actually increases the market share of local producers or whether it merely mitigates a projected decline. See Bacchus Imports, Ltd., 468 U.S. at 272 ("We perceive no principle of Commerce Clause jurisprudence supporting a distinction between thriving and struggling enterprises . . ."); Baldwin v. G. A. F. Seelig, Inc., 294 U.S. at 523.

domestic producers an additional tool with which to shore up their competitive position.[14]

III

Respondent advances four arguments against the conclusion that its pricing order imposes an unconstitutional burden on interstate commerce: (A) Because each component of the program–a local subsidy and a non-discriminatory tax–is valid, the combination of the two is equally valid; (B) The dealers who pay the order premiums (the tax) are not competitors of the farmers who receive disbursements from the Dairy Equalization Fund, so the pricing order is not discriminatory; (C) The pricing order is not protectionist, because the costs of the program are borne only by Massachusetts dealers and consumers, and the benefits are distributed exclusively to Massachusetts farmers; and (D) the order's incidental burden on commerce is justified by the local benefit of saving the dairy industry from collapse. We discuss each of these arguments in turn.

A

Respondent's principal argument is that, because "the milk order achieves its goals through lawful means," the order as a whole is constitutional. He argues that the payments to Massachusetts dairy farmers from the Dairy Equalization Fund are valid, because subsidies are constitutional exercises of state power, and that the order premium which provides money for the Fund is valid, because it is a nondiscriminatory tax. Therefore the pricing order is constitutional, because it is merely the combination of two independently lawful regulations. In effect, respondent argues, if the State may impose a valid tax on dealers, it is free to use the proceeds of the tax as it chooses; and if it may independently subsidize its farmers, it is free to finance the subsidy by means of any legitimate tax.

Even granting respondent's assertion that both components of the pricing order would be constitutional

---

14. One might attempt to distinguish Bacchus by noting that the rebate in this case goes not to the entity which pays the tax (milk dealers) but to the dairy farmers themselves. Rebating the taxes directly to producers rather than to the dealers, however, merely reinforces the conclusion that the pricing order will favor local producers. If the taxes were refunded only to the dealers, there might be no impact on interstate commerce, because the dealers might not use the funds to increase the price or quantity of milk purchased from Massachusetts dairy farmers. The refund to the dealers might, therefore, result in no advantage to in-state producers. On the other hand, by refunding monies directly to the dairy farmers, the pricing order ensures that Massachusetts producers will benefit.

standing alone,[15] the pricing order nevertheless must fall. A pure subsidy funded out of general revenue ordinarily imposes no burden on interstate commerce, but merely assists local business. The pricing order in this case, however, is funded principally from taxes on the sale of milk produced in other States. By so funding the subsidy, respondent not only assists local farmers, but burdens interstate commerce. The pricing order thus violates the cardinal principle that a State may not "benefit in-state economic interests by burdening out-of-state competitors." New Energy , 486 U.S. at 273-274; see also Bacchus, 468 U.S. at 272; Guy v. Baltimore, 100 U.S. at 443.

More fundamentally, respondent errs in assuming that the constitutionality of the pricing order follows logically from the constitutionality of its component parts. By conjoining a tax and a subsidy, Massachusetts has created a program more dangerous to interstate commerce than either part alone. Nondiscriminatory measures, like the evenhanded tax at issue here, are generally upheld, in spite of any adverse effects on interstate commerce, in part because "the existence of major in-state interests adversely affected . . . is a powerful safeguard against legislative abuse." Minnesota v. Clover Leaf Creamery Co., 449 U.S. at 473, n.17; see also Raymond Motor Transportation, Inc. v. Rice, 434 U.S. at 444, n.18 (special deference to state highway regulations because "their burden usually falls on local economic interests as well as other States' economic interests, thus insuring that a State's own political processes will serve as a check against unduly burdensome regulations"); South Carolina State Highway Dept. v. Barnwell Bros., Inc., 303 U.S. at 187; Goldberg v. Sweet, 488 U.S. at 266.[17] However, when

---

15. We have never squarely confronted the constitutionality of subsidies, and we need not do so now. We have, however, noted that "direct subsidization of domestic industry does not ordinarily run afoul" of the negative Commerce Clause. New Energy Co. of Indiana v. Limbach, 486 U.S. at 278; see also Hughes v. Alexandria Scrap Corp., 426 U.S. at 815 (STEVENS, J., concurring). In addition, it is undisputed that States may try to attract business by creating an environment conducive to economic activity, as by maintaining good roads, sound public education, or low taxes. Zobel v. Williams, 457 U.S. at 67 (Brennan, J., concurring); Bacchus Imports, Ltd. v. Dias, 468 U.S. at 271; Metropolitan Life Ins. Co. v. Ward, 470 U.S. at 876-878.

17. The same principle is recognized in the conceptually similar field of intergovernmental taxation, where nondiscrimination also plays a central role in setting the boundary between the permissible and the impermissible. Washington v. United States, 460 U.S. at 545 ("A 'political check' is provided when a state tax falls on a significant group of state citizens who can be counted upon to use their votes to keep the State from raising the tax excessively, and thus placing an unfair burden on the Federal Government"); South Carolina v. Baker, 485 U.S. at 525-526, n. 13; United States v. County of Fresno, 429 U.S. at 462-464.

a nondiscriminatory tax is coupled with a subsidy to one of the groups hurt by the tax, a state's political processes can no longer be relied upon to prevent legislative abuse, because one of the in-state interests which would otherwise lobby against the tax has been mollified by the subsidy. So, in this case, one would ordinarily have expected at least three groups to lobby against the order premium, which, as a tax, raises the price (and hence lowers demand) for milk: dairy farmers, milk dealers, and consumers. But because the tax was coupled with a subsidy, one of the most powerful of these groups, Massachusetts dairy farmers, instead of exerting their influence against the tax, were in fact its primary supporters.[18]

Respondent's argument would require us to analyze separately two parts of an integrated regulation, but we cannot divorce the premium payments from the use to which the payments are put. It is the entire program–not just the contributions to the fund or the distributions from that fund–that simultaneously burdens interstate commerce and discriminates in favor of local producers. The choice of constitutional means–nondiscriminatory tax and local subsidy–cannot guarantee the constitutionality of the program as a whole. New York's minimum price order also used constitutional means–a State's power to regulate prices–but was held unconstitutional because of its deleterious effects. Baldwin v. G. A. F. Seelig, Inc., 294 U.S. 511(1935). Similarly, the law held unconstitutional in Bacchus, 468 U.S. 263 (1984), involved the exercise of Hawaii's undisputed power to tax and to grant tax exemptions.

Our Commerce Clause jurisprudence is not so rigid as to be controlled by the form by which a State erects barriers to commerce. Rather our cases have eschewed formalism for a sensitive, case-by-case analysis of purposes and effects. As the Court declared over 50 years ago: "The commerce clause forbids discrimination, whether forthright or ingenious. In each case it is our duty to determine whether the statute under attack, whatever its name may be, will in its practical operation work discrimination against interstate commerce." Best & Co. v. Maxwell, 311 U.S. 454 (1940); Maryland v. Louisiana, 451 U.S. 725 (1981); Exxon Corp. v. Governor of Maryland, 437 U.S. at 147; see also Guy v. Baltimore, 100 U.S. at 443 (invalidating discriminatory wharfage fees which were "mere expedient or device to accomplish, by

indirection, what the State could not accomplish by a direct tax, viz., build up its domestic commerce by means of unequal and oppressive burdens upon the industry and business of other States"); Baldwin v. G. A. F. Seelig, Inc., 294 U.S. at 527 ("What is ultimate is the principle that one state in its dealings with another may not put itself in a position of economic isolation. Formulas and catchwords are subordinate to this overmastering requirement"); Dean Milk Co., 340 U.S. at 354; New Energy Co., 486 U.S. at 275, 276 (invalidating reciprocal tax credit because it, "in effect, taxes a product made by [Indiana] manufacturers at a rate higher than the same product made by Ohio manufacturers . . .").

B

Respondent also argues that since the Massachusetts milk dealers who pay the order premiums are not competitors of the Massachusetts farmers, the pricing order imposes no discriminatory burden on commerce. This argument cannot withstand scrutiny. Is it possible to doubt that if Massachusetts imposed a higher sales tax on milk produced in Maine than milk produced in Massachusetts that the tax would be struck down, in spite of the fact that the sales tax was imposed on consumers, and consumers do not compete with dairy farmers? For over 150 years, our cases have rightly concluded that the imposition of a differential burden on any part of the stream of commerce —from wholesaler to retailer to consumer—is invalid, because a burden placed at any point will result in a disadvantage to the out-of-state producer. Brown v. Maryland, 25 U.S. 419 (1827) ("So, a tax on the occupation of the importer is, in like manner, a tax on importation. It must add to the price of the article, and be paid by the consumer, or by the importer himself, in like manner as a direct duty on the article itself would be made." "The distinction between a tax on the thing imported, and on the person of the importer, can have no influence on this part of the subject. It is too obvious for controversy that they interfere equally with the power to regulate commerce"); I. M. Darnell & Son Co., 208 U.S. 113 (1908) (differential burden on intermediate stage manufacturer); Bacchus Imports, 468 U.S. 263 (1984) (differential burden on wholesaler); Webber v. Virginia, 103 U.S. at 350 (differential burden on sales agent); New Energy Co. of Indiana v. Limbach, 486 U.S. at 273-274 (differential burden on retailer).

C

Respondent also argues that "the operation of the Order disproves any claim of protectionism," because "*only* in-state consumers feel the effect of any retail price increase . . . . [and] the dealers themselves . . . have a substantial in-state presence." This argument, if accepted, would undermine almost every discriminatory tax case. State taxes are ordinarily paid by in-state businesses and

---

18. As the Governor's Special Commission Relative to the Establishment of a Dairy Stabilization Fund realized, consumers would be unlikely to organize effectively to oppose the pricing order. The Commission's report remarked, "the estimated two cent increase per quart of milk would not be noticed by the consuming public," because the price of milk varies so often and for so many reasons that consumers would be unlikely to feel the price increases or to attribute them to the pricing order.

consumers, yet if they discriminate against out-of-state products, they are unconstitutional. The idea that a discriminatory tax does not interfere with interstate commerce "merely because the burden of the tax was borne by consumers" in the taxing State was thoroughly repudiated in Bacchus Imports, Ltd. v. Dias, 468 U.S. at 272. The cost of a tariff is also borne primarily by local consumers, yet a tariff is the paradigmatic Commerce Clause violation.

More fundamentally, respondent ignores the fact that Massachusetts dairy farmers are part of an integrated interstate market. As noted above, the purpose and effect of the pricing order are to divert market share to Massachusetts dairy farmers. This diversion necessarily injures the dairy farmers in neighboring States. Furthermore, the Massachusetts order regulates a portion of the same interstate market in milk that is more broadly regulated by a federal milk marketing order which covers most of New England. The Massachusetts producers who deliver milk to dealers in that regulated market are participants in the same interstate milk market as the out-of-state producers who sell in the same market and are guaranteed the same minimum blend price by the federal order. The fact that the Massachusetts order imposes assessments only on Massachusetts sales and distributes them only to Massachusetts producers does not exclude either the assessments or the payments from the interstate market . . . The obvious impact of the order on out-of-state production demonstrates that it is simply wrong to assume that the pricing order burdens only Massachusetts consumers and dealers.

D

Finally, respondent argues that any incidental burden on interstate commerce "is outweighed by the 'local benefits' of preserving the Massachusetts dairy industry." In a closely related argument, respondent urges that "the purpose of the order, to save an industry from collapse, is not protectionist." If we were to accept these arguments, we would make a virtue of the vice that the rule against discrimination condemns. Preservation of local industry by protecting it from the rigors of interstate competition is the hallmark of the economic protectionism that the Commerce Clause prohibits. In Bacchus Imports, Ltd. v. Dias, 468 U.S. at 272, we explicitly rejected any distinction "between thriving and struggling enterprises." Whether a State is attempting to "enhance thriving and substantial business enterprises" or to "subsidize . . . financially troubled" ones is irrelevant to Commerce Clause analysis. With his characteristic eloquence, Justice Cardozo responded to an argument that respondent echoes today:

"The argument is pressed upon us, however, that the end to be served by the Milk Control Act is something more than the economic welfare of the farmers or of any other class or classes. The end to be served is the maintenance of a regular and adequate supply of pure and wholesome milk, the supply being put in jeopardy when the farmers of the state are unable to earn a living income. Let such an exception be admitted, and all that a state will have to do in times of stress and strain is to say that its farmers and merchants and workmen must be protected against competition from without, lest they go upon the poor relief lists or perish altogether. To give entrance to that excuse would be to invite a speedy end of our national solidarity. The Constitution was framed under the dominion of a political philosophy less parochial in range. It was framed upon the theory that the peoples of the several states must sink or swim together, and that in the long run prosperity and salvation are in union and not division". Baldwin v. G. A. F. Seelig, 294 U.S. at 522-523.

In a later case, also involving the welfare of Massachusetts dairy farmers, Justice Jackson described the same overriding interest in the free flow of commerce across state lines:

"Our system, fostered by the Commerce Clause, is that every farmer and every craftsman shall be encouraged to produce by the certainty that he will have free access to every market in the Nation, that no home embargoes will withhold his exports, and no foreign state will by customs duties or regulations exclude them. Likewise, every consumer may look to the free competition from every producing area in the Nation to protect him from exploitation by any. Such was the vision of the Founders; such has been the doctrine of this Court which has given it reality." H. P. Hood & Sons, Inc. v. Du Mond, 336 U.S. at 539.

The judgment of the Supreme Judicial Court of Massachusetts is reversed.

JUSTICE SCALIA, with whom JUSTICE THOMAS joins, concurring in judgment.

In my view the challenged Massachusetts pricing order is invalid under our negative-Commerce-Clause jurisprudence, for the reasons explained in Part II below. I do not agree with the reasons assigned by the Court, which seem to me, as explained in Part I, a broad expansion of current law. Accordingly, I concur only in the judgment of the Court.

I

The purpose of the negative Commerce Clause, we have often said, is to create a national market. It does not follow from that, however, and we have never held, that every state law which obstructs a national market violates the Commerce Clause. Yet that is what the Court says today. It seems to have canvassed the entire corpus of negative-Commerce-Clause opinions, culled out every free-market snippet of reasoning, and melded them into the sweeping principle that the Constitution is violated by any state law or regulation that "artificially encourages in-state production even when the same goods could be produced at lower cost in other States." See ante (the law here is unconstitutional because it "neutralizes the advantage possessed by lower cost out-of-state producers"); (price order is unconstitutional because it allows in-state producers "who produce at higher cost to sell at or below the price charged by lower cost out-of-state producers"); (a state program is unconstitutional where it "'neutralizes advantages belonging to the place of origin'"); ("Preservation of local industry by protecting it from the rigors of interstate competition is the hallmark of the economic protectionism that the Commerce Clause prohibits").

As the Court seems to appreciate by its eagerness expressly to reserve the question of the constitutionality of subsidies for in-state industry, ante, n.15, this expansive view of the Commerce Clause calls into question a wide variety of state laws that have hitherto been thought permissible. It seems to me that a State subsidy would clearly be invalid under any formulation of the Court's guiding principle identified above. The Court guardedly asserts that a "pure subsidy funded out of general revenue *ordinarily* imposes no burden on interstate commerce, but merely assists local business," ante, (emphasis added), but under its analysis that must be taken to be true only because most local businesses (e.g., the local hardware store) are not competing with businesses out of State. The Court notes that, in funding this subsidy, Massachusetts has taxed milk produced in other States, and thus "not only assists local farmers, but burdens interstate commerce." But the same could be said of almost all subsidies funded from general state revenues, which almost invariably include monies from use taxes on out-of-state products. And even where the funding does not come in any part from taxes on out-of-state goods, "merely assisting" in-state businesses, unquestionably neutralizes advantages possessed by out-of-state enterprises. Such subsidies, particularly where they are in the form of cash or (what comes to the same thing) tax forgiveness, are often admitted to have as their purpose–indeed, are nationally advertised as having as their purpose–making it more profitable to conduct business in-state than elsewhere, i.e., distorting normal market incentives.

The Court's guiding principle also appears to call into question many garden-variety state laws heretofore permissible under the negative Commerce Clause. A state law, for example, which requires, contrary to the industry practice, the use of recyclable packaging materials, favors local non-exporting producers, who do not have to establish an additional, separate packaging operation for in-state sales. If the Court's analysis is to be believed, such a law would be unconstitutional without regard to whether disruption of the "national market" is the real purpose of the restriction, and without the need

to "balance" the importance of the state interests thereby pursued, see Pike v. Bruce Church, Inc., 397 U.S. 137 (1970). These results would greatly extend the negative Commerce Clause beyond its current scope. If the Court does not intend these consequences, and does not want to foster needless litigation concerning them, it should not have adopted its expansive rationale. Another basis for deciding the case is available, which I proceed to discuss.

II

"The historical record provides no grounds for reading the Commerce Clause to be other than what it says–an authorization for Congress to regulate commerce." Tyler Pipe, 483 U.S. at 263 (SCALIA, J., concurring in part and dissenting in part). Nonetheless, we formally adopted the doctrine of the negative Commerce Clause 121 years ago, see Case of the State Freight Tax, 82 U.S. 232 (1873), and since then have decided a vast number of negative-Commerce-Clause cases, engendering considerable reliance interests. As a result, I will, on stare decisis grounds, enforce a self-executing "negative" Commerce Clause in two situations: (1) against a state law that facially discriminates against interstate commerce, and (2) against a state law that is indistinguishable from a type of law previously held unconstitutional by this Court. See Itel Containers Int'l Corp., 507 U.S. 60 (SCALIA, J., concurring in judgment) (collecting cases). Applying this approach–or at least the second part of it–is not always easy, since once one gets beyond facial discrimination our negative-Commerce-Clause jurisprudence becomes (and long has been) a "quagmire." Northwestern States Portland Cement Co., 358 U.S. at 458 (1959). See generally D. Currie, The Constitution in the Supreme Court: The First Hundred Years 1789-1888, pp. 168-181, 222-236, 330-342, 403-416 (1985). The object should be, however, to produce a clear rule that honors the holdings of our past decisions but declines to extend the rationale that produced those decisions any further. See American Trucking, 483 U.S. at 305-306 (SCALIA, J., dissenting).

There are at least four possible devices that would enable a State to produce the economic effect that Massachusetts has produced here: (1) a discriminatory tax upon the industry, imposing a higher liability on out-of-state members than on their in-state competitors; (2) a tax upon the industry that is nondiscriminatory in its assessment, but that has an "exemption" or "credit" for in-state members; (3) a nondiscriminatory tax upon the industry, the revenues from which are placed into a segregated fund, which fund is disbursed as "rebates" or "subsidies" to in-state members of the industry (the situation at issue in this case); and (4) with or without nondiscriminatory taxation of the industry, a subsidy for the in-state members of the industry, funded from the State's general revenues. It is long settled that the first of these methodologies is unconstitutional under the negative Commerce Clause. See, e.g., Guy v. Baltimore, 100 U.S. at 443. The second of them, "exemption" from or "credit" against a "neutral" tax, is no different in principle from the first, and has likewise been held invalid. See Maryland v. Louisiana, 451 U.S. at 756; Westinghouse, 466 U.S. at 399-400. The fourth methodology, application of a state subsidy from general revenues, is so far removed from what we have hitherto held to be unconstitutional, that prohibiting it must be regarded as an extension of our negative-Commerce-Clause jurisprudence and therefore, to me, unacceptable. See New Energy, 486 U.S. at 278 (1988). Indeed, in my view our negative-Commerce Clause cases have already approved the use of such subsidies. See Hughes v. Alexandria Scrap Corp., 426 U.S. at 809-810 (1976).

The issue before us in the present case is whether the third of these methodologies must fall. Although the question is close, I conclude it would not be a principled point at which to disembark from the negative-Commerce-Clause train. The only difference between methodology (2) (discriminatory "exemption" from nondiscriminatory tax) and methodology (3) (discriminatory refund of nondiscriminatory tax) is that the money is taken and returned rather than simply left with the favored in-state taxpayer in the first place. The difference between (3) and (4), on the other hand, is the difference between assisting in-state industry through discriminatory taxation, and assisting in-state industry by other means.

I would therefore allow a State to subsidize its domestic industry so long as it does so from nondiscriminatory taxes that go into the State's general revenue fund. Perhaps, as some commentators contend, that line comports with an important economic reality: a State is less likely to maintain a subsidy when its citizens perceive that the money (in the general fund) is available for any number of competing, non-protectionist, purposes. See Coenen, Untangling the Market-Participant Exemption to the Dormant Commerce Clause, 88 Mich. L. Rev. 395, 479 (1989); Collins, Economic Union as a Constitutional Value, 63 N. Y. U. L. Rev. 43, 103 (1988); Gergen, The Selfish State and the Market, 66 Tex. L. Rev. 1097, 1138 (1988); see also ante n. 17. That is not, however, the basis for my position, for as THE CHIEF JUSTICE explains, "analysis of interest group participation in the political process may serve many useful purposes, but serving as a basis for interpreting the dormant Commerce Clause is not one of them." Post (dissenting opinion). Instead, I draw the line where I do because it is Clause jurisprudence.

CHIEF JUSTICE REHNQUIST, with whom JUSTICE BLACKMUN joins, dissenting.

The Court is less than just in its description of the reasons which lay behind the Massachusetts law which it strikes down. The law undoubtedly sought to aid struggling Massachusetts dairy farmers, beset by steady or declining prices and escalating costs. This situation is apparently not unique to Massachusetts; New Jersey has filed an amicus brief in support of respondent because New Jersey has enacted a similar law. Both States lie in the northeastern metropolitan corridor, which is the most urbanized area in the United States, and has every prospect of becoming more so. The value of agricultural land located near metropolitan areas is driven up by the demand for housing and similar urban uses; distressed farmers eventually sell out to developers. Not merely farm produce is lost, as is the milk production in this case, but, as the Massachusetts Special Commission whose report was the basis for the order in question here found:

"Without the continued existence of dairy farmers, the Commonwealth will lose its supply of locally produced fresh milk, together with the open lands that are used as wildlife refuges, for recreation, hunting, fishing, tourism, and education."

Massachusetts has dealt with this problem by providing a subsidy to aid its beleaguered dairy farmers. In case after case, we have approved the validity under the Commerce Clause of such enactments. "No one disputes that a State may enact laws pursuant to its police powers that have the purpose and effect of encouraging domestic industry." Bacchus, 468 U.S. at 271. "Direct subsidization of domestic industry does not ordinarily run afoul of the [dormant Commerce Clause]; discriminatory taxation of out-of-state manufacturers does." New Energy, 486 U.S. at 278 (1988). But today the Court relegates these well-established principles to a footnote and, at the same time, gratuitously casts doubt on the validity of state subsidies, observing that "we have never squarely confronted" their constitutionality. Ante, n.15.

But in Milk Control Bd. v. Eisenberg Farm Products, 306 U.S. 346 (1939), the Court upheld a Pennsylvania statute establishing minimum prices to be paid to Pennsylvania dairy farmers against a Commerce Clause challenge by a Pennsylvania milk dealer which shipped all of its milk purchased in Pennsylvania to New York to be sold there. The Court observed that "the purpose of the statute . . . is to reach a domestic situation in the interest of the welfare of the producers and consumers of milk in Pennsylvania." It went on to say:

"One of the commonest forms of state action is the exercise of police power directed to the control of local conditions and exerted in the interest of the welfare of the state's citizens. Every state police statute necessarily will affect interstate commerce in some degree, but such a statute does not run counter to the grant of Congressional power merely because it incidentally or indirectly involves or burdens interstate commerce. . . . These principles have guided judicial decision for more than a century."

The Massachusetts subsidy under consideration is similar in many respects to the Pennsylvania statute described in Eisenberg, supra. Massachusetts taxes all dealers of milk within its borders. The tax is evenhanded on its face, i.e., it affects all dealers regardless of the point of origin of the milk, ("the tax also applies to milk produced in Massachusetts . . . "); (". . . the evenhanded tax at issue here . . ."). The State has not acted to strong-arm sister States as in Limbach; rather, its motives are purely local. As the Supreme Judicial Court of Massachusetts aptly described it: "The premiums represent one of the costs of doing business in the Commonwealth, a cost all milk dealers must pay."

Consistent with precedent, the Court observes: "A pure subsidy funded out of general revenue ordinarily imposes no burden on interstate commerce, but merely assists local business." And the Court correctly recognizes that "nondiscriminatory measures, like the evenhanded tax at issue here, are generally upheld" due to the deference normally accorded to a State's political process in passing legislation in light of various competing interest groups. Minnesota v. Clover Leaf Creamery Co., 449 U.S. at 473, n.17, and Raymond Motor Transportation Inc. v. Rice, 434 U.S. at 444, n.18. But the Court strikes down this method of state subsidization because the non-discriminatory tax levied against all milk dealers is coupled with a subsidy to milk producers. The Court does this because of its view that the method of imposing the tax and subsidy distorts the State's political process: the dairy farmers, who would otherwise lobby against the tax, have been mollified by the subsidy. But as the Court itself points out, there are still at least two strong interest groups opposed to the milk order–consumers and milk dealers. More importantly, nothing in the dormant Commerce Clause suggests that the fate of state regulation should turn upon the particular lawful manner in which the state subsidy is enacted or promulgated. Analysis of interest group participation in the political process may serve many useful purposes, but serving as a basis for interpreting the dormant Commerce Clause is not one of them.

The Court concludes that the combined effect of the milk order "simultaneously burdens interstate commerce and discriminates in favor of local producers." In support of this conclusion, the Court cites Baldwin v. G. A. F. Seelig, Inc., 294 U.S. 511 (1935), and Bacchus Imports, Ltd. v.

Dias, supra, as two examples in which constitutional means were held to have unconstitutional effects on interstate commerce. But both Baldwin and Bacchus are a far cry from this case.

In Baldwin, supra, in order to sell bottled milk in New York, milk dealers were required to pay a minimum price for milk, even though they could have purchased milk from Vermont farmers at a lower price. This scheme was found to be an effort to prevent Vermont milk producers from selling to New York dealers at their lower market price. As Justice Cardozo explained, under the New York statute, "the importer . . . may keep his milk or drink it, but sell it he may not." 294 U.S. at 521. Such a scheme clearly made it less attractive for New York dealers to purchase milk from Vermont farmers, for the disputed law negated any economic advantage in so doing. Under the Massachusetts milk order, there is no such adverse effect. Milk dealers have the same incentives to purchase lower priced milk from out-of-state farmers; dealers of all milk are taxed equally. To borrow Justice Cardozo's description, milk dealers in Massachusetts are free to keep their milk, drink their milk, and sell it–on equal terms as local milk.

In Bacchus, the State of Hawaii combined its undisputed power to tax and grant exemptions in a manner that the Court found violative of the Commerce Clause. There, the State exempted a local wine from the burdens of an excise tax levied on all other liquor sales. Despite the Court's strained attempt to compare the scheme in Bacchus to the milk order in this case, it is clear that the milk order does not produce the same effect on interstate commerce as the tax exemption in Bacchus. I agree with the Court's statement that Bacchus can be distinguished "by noting that the rebate in this case goes not to the entity which pays the tax (milk dealers) but to the dairy farmers themselves." This is not only a distinction, but a significant difference. No decided case supports the Court's conclusion that the negative Commerce Clause prohibits the State from using money that it has lawfully obtained through a neutral tax on milk dealers and distributing it as a subsidy to dairy farmers. Indeed, the case which comes closest to supporting the result the Court reaches is the ill-starred opinion in United States v. Butler, 297 U.S. 1 (1936), in which the Court held unconstitutional what would have been an otherwise valid tax on the processing of agricultural products because of the use to which the revenue raised by the tax was put.

. . . .

Questions and Comments

1. The federal government began regulating the dairy industry during the Great Depression, when many dairy farmers could not survive. Congress passed the Agriculture Act of 1933, which authorized the USDA to regulate the price of milk in order to ensure an adequate supply and reduce farm failures. These regulations were intended to be temporary until the industry recovered, but as is often the case, constituencies develop with a vested interest in continuing the regulatory scheme.

Critics characterize the regulations as anti-competitive, as increasing the cost of milk to the consumer, for preventing the dairy industry from becoming more efficient, and for subsidizing inefficient farmers. In this era of deregulation, there have been calls for phasing out these price supports, but no progress has occurred to date. In 1966, Congress enacted the Freedom to Farm Act, with one goal being the reexamination of Depression-era federal agricultural subsidies, including milk price supports. Congress also mandated that the USDA promulgate regulations for a new pilot program designed to help wean farmers from subsidies, but subsequent legislation terminated these efforts.

In response to losing *West Lynn Creamery*, Massachusetts abandoned its pricing order/subsidy scheme. In 1996, the U.S. Secretary of Agriculture gave the six New England states the power to set the price paid to dairy farmers. Supporters of this action claimed it would help stabilize prices at both the farm and retail levels, but dairy executives warned that retail prices would rise. Litigation has been threatened. Boston Globe, Aug. 10, 1996, p. E1.

Maine passed the Maine Dairy Farm Stabilization Act, which imposed a tax on packaged fluid milk sold in Maine, whether produced in or out-of-state and gave a rebate of the funds collected to in-state dairy farmers. The tax revenue was kept out of general revenue and used to finance the rebate. After *West Lynn Creamery*, this scheme was held unconstitutional. The Maine Legislature then enacted a surcharge on milk handlers that was nearly identical to the prior Act except that the revenues were deposited in the State's general funds. A federal district court upheld the Act. On appeal, the first circuit held that the Tax Injunction Act deprives the federal courts (other than the Supreme Court) of jurisdiction to decide the merits of the constitutional issue and dismissed the case. The court viewed the milk handling surcharge as more of a tax than a fee. Cumberland Farms, Inc. v. Maine, No. 96-2353, reported in BNA, Daily Tax Report, p. K-4 (6/25/97).

2. Did the Massachusetts scheme have the effect of a tariff? Did the premium payments apply only to imported milk? Did milk produced in Massachusetts sell for a different price than milk produced out-of-state? Were the premium payments a tax?

3. Suppose Massachusetts had not earmarked the premium payments for use by Massachusetts milk producers. Would the statute then have been constitutional? What if Massachusetts follows this strategy after this decision? Why do you think Massachusetts did not follow this strategy? What was gained by earmarking the tax?

4. According to Massachusetts officials, the pricing order did not increase the price of milk to consumers. Stores often keep the price of milk as low as possible in order to generate floor traffic. This goal would have been undercut by a price increase. These officials noted, however, that some dealers did increase their prices to their customers in response to the pricing order. Refunds to these dealers after the Court's decision were apparently not passed on to their customers.

5. Is the majority right that "[i]t is obvious that the result in *Bacchus* would have been the same if instead of exempting certain Hawaiian liquors from tax, Hawaii had rebated the amount of tax collected from the sale of those liquors?" Does *New Energy* support the majority's statement?

6. The Court stated that nondiscriminatory measures are generally upheld because the existence of major in-state interests adversely affected is a powerful safeguard against legislative abuse. Did such safeguards exist in *Commonwealth Edison*, supra? In *Moorman*, discussed in the chapter entitled, State Corporate Incomes Taxes: The Leading Cases?

7. City X grants a 5 year property tax exemption for all new manufacturing facilities. Constitutional?

8. State Y grants an investment tax credit in its corporate income tax for investment in manufacturing machinery. Constitutional?

9. How critical to the majority's reasoning was the earmarking of the revenue in a segregated fund?

10. How convincing is Justice Scalia's reasoning? After identifying four points on the continuum, he concludes that "[t]he difference between (3) and (4) . . . is the difference between assisting in-state industry through discriminatory taxation, and assisting in-state industry by

other means." Why does "(3)" involve discriminatory taxation? Consider that he also describes (3) as "a nondiscriminatory tax upon the industry, the revenues from which are placed into a segregated fund . . ."

Justice Scalia describes situation (2) as "a tax upon the industry that is nondiscriminatory in its assessment, but that has an 'exemption' or 'credit' for in-state members." Does that statement describe *Bacchus*?

11. For a general discussion of the constitutionality of state tax incentives, see Peter Enrich, *Saving the States from Themselves: Commerce Clause Constraints on State Tax Incentives for Business*, 110 Harvard L. Rev. 378 (1996); Walter Hellerstein and Dan T. Coenen, *Commerce Clause Restraints on State Business Development Incentives*, 81 Cornell L. Rev. 789 (1996).

12. For critical commentary on *West Lynn*, see Brian C. Newberry, *Recent Decision: Constitutional Law - Taking the Dormant Commerce Clause Too Far? - West Lynn Creamery, Inc. v. Healy,* 69 Temple L. Rev. 547 (1996); Jennifer Erdman Shirkey, *The Constitutionality of Multistate Antitakeover "Schemes" Under the Commerce Clause: Potential Consequences of the West Lynn Creamery Decision,* 52 Wash. & Lee L. Rev. 1475 (1995); Christopher P. La Puma, *Massachusetts Tax and Subsidy Scheme Violates Commerce Clause: West Lynn Creamery, Inc. v. Healy*, 48 Tax Law. 641 (1995); William L. Oemichen, *Milk, State Taxes, State Subsidies, and the Commerce Clause: When States Cannot Tax an Agricultural Commodity to Fund a Subsidy for Its Struggling Industries, West Lynn Creamery, Inc. v. Healy, 114 S. Ct. 2205 (1994)*, 18 Hamline L. Rev. 415 (1995); George P. Patterson, *Does the Commerce Clause Value Public Goods?: West Lynn Creamery v. Healy,* 44 Cath. U. L. Rev. 977 (1995); Walter Hellerstein, *West Lynn Creamery and the Constitutionality of State Tax Incentives*, 65 Tax Notes 619 (1994).

Fulton Corporation v. Faulkner, Secretary of Revenue of North Carolina
Supreme Court of the United States, 1996.
516 U.S. 325, 116 S. Ct. 848, 133 L. Ed. 2d 796.

JUSTICE SOUTER delivered the opinion of the Court.

In this case we decide whether North Carolina's "intangibles tax" on a fraction of the value of corporate stock owned by North Carolina residents inversely proportional to the corporation's exposure to the State's income tax violates the Commerce Clause. We hold that it does.

I

During the period in question here, North Carolina levied an "intangibles tax" on the fair market value of corporate stock owned by North Carolina residents or having a "business, commercial, or taxable situs" in the State. Although the tax was assessed at a stated rate of one quarter of one percent, residents were entitled to calculate their tax liability by taking a taxable percentage deduction equal to the fraction of the issuing corporation's income subject to tax in North Carolina. This figure was set by applying a corporate income tax apportionment formula averaging the portion of the issuing corporation's sales, payroll, and property located in the State.

Thus, a corporation doing all of its business within the state would pay corporate income tax on 100% of its income, and the taxable percentage deduction allowed to resident owners of that corporation's stock under the intangibles tax would likewise be 100%. Stock in a corporation doing no business in North Carolina, on the other hand, would be taxable on 100% of its value. For the intermediate cases, holders of stock were able to look up the taxable percentage for a large number of corporations as determined and published annually by the North Carolina Secretary of Revenue. . . .

. . . .

II

. . . .

In evaluating state regulatory measures under the dormant Commerce Clause, we have held that "the first step . . . is to determine whether it 'regulates evenhandedly with only 'incidental' effects on interstate commerce, or discriminates against interstate commerce.'" Oregon Waste Systems, Inc. v. Department of Environmental Quality of Ore., 511 U.S. at 99 (quoting Hughes v. Oklahoma, 441 U.S. at 336). With respect to state taxation, one element of the protocol summarized in Complete Auto, treats a law as discriminatory if it "'tax[es] a transaction or incident more heavily when it crosses state lines than when it occurs entirely within the State.'" Chemical Waste Management, 504 U.S. at 342 (1992) (quoting Armco, 467 U.S. at 642); see also Boston Stock Exchange, 429 U.S. at 332, n.12 (1977) (noting that a State "may not discriminate between transactions on the basis of some interstate element"). State laws discriminating against interstate commerce on their face are "virtually per se invalid." Oregon Waste, supra, at 99, see also Philadelphia v. New Jersey, 437 U.S. at 624.

We have also recognized, however, that a facially discriminatory tax may still survive Commerce Clause scrutiny if it is a truly "'compensatory tax' designed simply to make interstate commerce bear a burden already borne by intrastate commerce." Associated Industries, 511 U.S. at 647.[2] Thus, in Silas Mason Co., 300 U.S. 577 (1937), we upheld the State of Washington's tax on the privilege of using any article of tangible personal property within the State. The statute exempted the use of any article that had already been subjected to a sales tax equal to the use tax or greater, so that the use tax effectively applied only to goods purchased out of state. Although the use tax was itself facially discriminatory, we held that the combined effect of the sales and use taxes was to subject intrastate and interstate commerce to equivalent burdens. "'There is no demand in . . . [the] Constitution that the State shall put its requirements in any one statute,'" we said; rather, "'[i]t may distribute them as it sees fit, if the result, taken in its totality, is within the State's constitutional power.'" Id., at 584 (quoting Gregg Dyeing Co., 286 U.S. at 480). As Justice Cardozo explained for the Court, the complementary arrangement assures that "[w]hen the account is made up, the stranger from afar is subject to no greater burdens as a consequence of ownership than the dweller within the gates. The one pays upon one activity or incident, and the other upon another, but the sum is the same when the reckoning is closed." 300 U.S. at 584.

Since Silas Mason, our cases have distilled three conditions necessary for a valid compensatory tax. First, "a State must, as a threshold matter, 'identif[y] . . . the [intrastate tax] burden for which the State is attempting to compensate.'" Oregon Waste, 511 U.S. at 103 (quoting Maryland v. Louisiana, 451 U.S. at 758). Second, "the tax on interstate commerce must be shown roughly to approximate–but not exceed–the amount of the tax on intrastate commerce." Oregon Waste, supra, at 103. "Finally, the events on which the interstate and intrastate taxes are imposed must be 'substantially equivalent'; that is, they must be sufficiently similar in substance to serve

as mutually exclusive 'prox[ies]' for each other" (quoting Armco, supra, at 643).

III

There is no doubt that the intangibles tax facially discriminates against interstate commerce. A regime that taxes stock only to the degree that its issuing corporation participates in interstate commerce favors domestic corporations over their foreign competitors in raising capital among North Carolina residents and tends, at least, to discourage domestic corporations from plying their trades in interstate commerce. The Secretary practically concedes as much, and relies instead on the compensatory tax defense.[3] The only issue, then, is whether the taxable percentage deduction can be sustained as compensatory.

A

As we have said, a State that invokes the compensatory tax defense must identify the intrastate tax for which it seeks to compensate, and it should go without saying that this intrastate tax must serve some purpose for which the State may otherwise impose a burden on interstate commerce. In Maryland v. Louisiana, 451 U.S. 725 (1981), for example, we rejected Louisiana's argument that, because it imposed a severance tax on natural resources extracted from its own soil, it could impose a compensating "first use" tax on resources produced out of state but used within Louisiana. Because "Louisiana has no sovereign interest in being compensated for the severance of resources from the federally owned [Outer Continental Shelf] land," we held

---

2. We use the terms "compensatory" tax and "complementary" tax as two ways of describing the same phenomenon: a tax on interstate commerce "complements" a tax on intrastate commerce to the extent that it "compensates" for the burdens imposed on intrastate commerce by imposing a similar burden on interstate commerce. We have also described taxes on interstate commerce as being imposed "in lieu" of taxes on intrastate commerce. See, e.g., Railway Express Agency, Inc. v. Virginia, 358 U.S. at 436; Postal Telegraph Cable Co. v. Adams, 155 U.S. at 700. This last class of cases, however, has involved taxes which were at least arguably not facially discriminatory, and we have evaluated these cases under a somewhat different standard.

3. Although the Secretary does suggest that the tax is so small in amount as to have no practical impact at all, we have never recognized a "de minimis" defense to a charge of discriminatory taxation under the Commerce Clause. See, e.g., Associated Industries, 511 U.S. 641 ("[A]ctual discrimination, wherever it is found, is impermissible, and the magnitude and scope of the discrimination have no bearing on the determinative question whether discrimination has occurred"); Maryland v. Louisiana, 451 U.S. at 760 ("We need not know how unequal the Tax is before concluding that it unconstitutionally discriminates"). We likewise reject the Secretary's speculation that the most likely effect, if any, of the taxable percentage deduction is to encourage out-of-state firms to compete in the North Carolina market so that their North Carolina shareholders may take advantage of the deduction. As we explain further, infra, such promotion of in-state markets at the expense of out-of-state ones furthers the "economic Balkanization" that our jurisprudence has long sought to prevent. Hughes v. Oklahoma, 441 U.S. at 325-326; see also Halliburton Oil, 373 U.S. at 72 (a state may not impose "a tax which is discriminatory in favor of the local merchant" so as to "encourag[e] an out-of-state operator to become a resident in order to compete on equal terms") (internal quotation marks and citation omitted).

that "[t]he two events are not comparable in the same fashion as a use tax complements a sales tax."

In this case, the Secretary suggests that the intangibles tax, with its taxable percentage deduction, compensates for the burden of the general corporate income tax paid by corporations doing business in North Carolina. But because North Carolina has no general sovereign interest in taxing income earned out of state, Maryland v. Louisiana teaches that the Secretary must identify some in-state activity or benefit in order to justify the compensatory levy. Indeed, we have repeatedly held that "no state tax may be sustained unless the tax . . . has a substantial nexus with the State . . . [and] is fairly related to the services provided by the State." Id., at 754; see also Jefferson Lines, Inc., 514 U.S. at 183-184; Complete Auto Transit, Inc., 430 U.S. at 279. The Secretary does not disagree, but rather insists that North Carolina may impose a compensatory tax upon foreign corporations because they may avail themselves of access to North Carolina's capital markets.

The Secretary's theory is that one of the services provided by the State, and supported through its general corporate income tax, is the maintenance of a capital market for corporations wishing to sell stock to North Carolina residents. Since those corporations escape North Carolina's income tax to the extent those corporations do business in other States, the Secretary says, the State may require those companies to pay for the privilege of access to the State's capital markets by a tax on the value of the shares sold. So, the Secretary concludes, the intangibles tax "rests squarely on 'the settled principle that interstate commerce may be made to pay its way.'"

The argument is unconvincing, and we rejected a counterpart of it in Oregon Waste, where we held that Oregon could not charge an increased fee for disposal of waste generated out of state on the theory that in-state waste generators supported the cost of waste disposal facilities through general income taxes. Although we relied primarily upon the conclusion that earning income and disposing of waste are not "substantially equivalent taxable events," we also spoke of the danger of treating general revenue measures as relevant intrastate burdens for purposes of the compensatory tax doctrine. "[P]ermitting discriminatory taxes on interstate commerce to compensate for charges purportedly included in general forms of intrastate taxation would allow a state to tax interstate commerce more heavily than in-state commerce anytime the entities involved in interstate commerce happened to use facilities supported by general state tax funds." We declined then, as we do now, "to open such an expansive loophole in our carefully confined compensatory tax jurisprudence."

Even shutting our eyes to that loophole, we are unpersuaded that North Carolina's corporate income tax is designed to support the maintenance of an intrastate capital market. North Carolina, like most States, regulates access to its capital markets by means of Blue Sky laws, which prescribe who may sell securities in North Carolina, the procedures that must be followed to do so, and the fees imposed for the privilege. Absent probative evidence to the contrary, which the Secretary has not supplied, we can reasonably assume that North Carolina has provided for the upkeep of its capital market through these provisions, not through the general corporate income tax.

If the corporate income tax does not support the maintenance of North Carolina's capital market, then the State has not justified imposition of a compensating levy on the ownership of shares in corporations not subject to the income tax. While we need not hold that a State may never justify a compensatory tax by an intrastate burden included in a general form of taxation, the linkage in this case between the intrastate burden and the benefit shared by out-of-staters is far too tenuous to overcome the risk posed by recognizing a general levy as a complementary twin.

B

The second prong of our analysis requires that "the tax on interstate commerce . . . be shown roughly to approximate–but not exceed–the amount of the tax on intrastate commerce." Oregon Waste, supra, at 1352. The Secretary argues that the relative magnitudes of the corporate income tax and the intangibles tax can be evaluated best by reference to the price/earnings (P/E) ratios of taxpayer firms. This ratio represents the relationship of the value of a corporation's stock, the target of the intangibles tax, to the corporation's earnings, which are subjected to the income tax. North Carolina taxes corporate income and ownership of stock at rates of 7.75% and .25%, respectively. Given these rates, the State Supreme Court found that "a North Carolina corporation need only have a P/E ratio less than 31 (7.75/.25) in order to have the tax against its income exceed the intangibles tax against the stockholders of a comparable corporation doing business only in [other States] and having all its shareholders in North Carolina. Since P/E ratios are only rarely greater than 31, most out-of-state corporations will in fact be paying less taxes to North Carolina . . . than a similar North Carolina corporation."

The math is fine, but even leaving aside the issue of who is really paying the taxes the example compares apples to oranges. When a corporation doing business in a State pays its general corporate income tax, it pays for a wide range of things: construction and maintenance of a transportation network, institutions that educate the workforce, local police and fire protection, and so on. The Secretary's justification for the intangibles tax, however, rests on only one of the many services funded by the corporate income tax, the maintenance of a capital market for the shares of both foreign and domestic corporations. To the extent that corporations do their business outside North Carolina, after all, they get little else from the State. Even, then, if we suppressed our suspicion that North Carolina actually funds its capital market through its Blue Sky fees, not its general corporate taxation, the relevant comparison for our analysis has to be between the size of the intangibles tax and that of the corporate income taxes component that purportedly funds the capital market.

That comparison, of course, is for the present practical purpose impossible. The corporate income tax is a general form of taxation, not assessed according to the taxpayer's use of particular services, and before its revenues are earmarked for particular purposes they have been commingled with funds from other sources. As a result, the Secretary cannot tell us what proportion of the corporate income tax goes to support the capital market, or whether that proportion represents a burden greater than the one imposed on interstate commerce by the intangibles tax. True, it is not inconceivable, however unlikely, that a capital markets component of the corporate income tax exceeds the intangibles tax in magnitude, but the Secretary cannot carry her burden of demonstrating this on the record in front of us.

This difficulty simply confirms our general unwillingness to "permi[t] discriminatory taxes on interstate commerce to compensate for charges purportedly included in general forms of intrastate taxation." Oregon Waste, 511 U.S. at 105, n.8. Where general forms of taxation are involved, we ordinarily cannot even begin to make the sorts of quantitative assessments that the compensatory tax doctrine requires. See also infra.

C

The tax, finally, fails even the third prong of compensatory tax analysis, which requires the compensating taxes to fall on substantially equivalent events. Although we found such equivalence in the sales/use tax combination at issue in Silas Mason, our more recent cases have shown extreme reluctance to recognize new compensatory categories. In Oregon Waste, we even pointed out that "use taxes on products purchased out of state are the only taxes we have upheld in recent memory under the compensatory tax doctrine." On the other hand, we have rejected equivalence arguments for pairing taxes upon the earning of income and the disposing of waste, ibid., the severance of natural resources from the soil and the use of resources

imported from other states, Maryland v. Louisiana, 451 U.S. at 759, and the manufacturing and wholesaling of tangible goods. Tyler Pipe, 483 U.S. at 244; Armco, 467 U.S. at 642. In each case, we held that the paired activities were not "sufficiently similar in substance to serve as mutually exclusive prox[ies] for each other." Oregon Waste, supra, at 103.

In the face of this trend, the Secretary argues that North Carolina has assured substantial equivalence by employing the same apportionment formula to tie the percentage of share value subject to the intangibles tax directly to the percentage of income earned within the state. The Secretary further contends that the intangibles tax and the corporate income tax fall on substantially equivalent "events" because they fall on economically equivalent "values": the value of a corporation's stock and the value of a corporation's income, respectively. Even assuming the truth of both these assertions, however, we find that the intangibles tax is not functionally equivalent to the corporate income tax.

By equivalence of value, the Secretary means that the value reached by the intangibles tax reflects that targeted by the income tax to a substantial degree because of the influence of corporate earnings on the price of stock. While that may be true enough,[5] it does not explain away the fact that the taxes are apparently different (quite apart from stated rates) in a number of obvious respects, including the parties ostensibly taxed. Something more than mere influence of the one stated tax base on the value of the other would therefore be necessary before we could conclude that equivalent events (or "values") are taxed. The nature of that something more flows from the objective of the equivalent-event requirement, which is to enable in-state and out-of-state businesses to compete on a footing of equality. In Silas Mason, for example, we observed that "[t]he practical effect" of Washington's sales/use tax regime "must be that retail sellers in Washington will be helped to compete upon terms of equality with retail dealers in other states who are exempt from a sales tax or any corresponding burden." 300 U.S. at 581; see also Halliburton Oil Well Cementing Co. v. Reily, 373 U.S. at 70 ("[E]qual treatment for in-state and out-of-state

---

5. It is generally well accepted that corporate income will ordinarily be a good indicator of the stock's value. See, e.g., J. Weston & E. Brigham, Essentials of Managerial Finance 254-257 (10th ed. 1993). While there may be cases in which other factors will play a more significant role, and while the past corporate earnings that the income tax reaches may be an imperfect proxy for the anticipated future earnings upon which stock price is actually based, we are willing to accept the Secretary's judgment that the taxed values correspond for purposes of this case.

taxpayers similarly situated is the condition precedent for a valid use tax on goods imported from out-of-state"). This equality of treatment does not appear when the allegedly compensating taxes fall respectively on taxpayers who are differently described, as, for example, resident shareholders and corporations doing business out of state. A State defending such a scheme as one of complementary taxation, therefore, has the burden of showing that the actual incidences of the two tax burdens are different enough from their nominal incidences so that the real taxpayers are within the same class, and that therefore a finding of combined neutrality on interstate competition would at least be possible.[6]

In principle, the door may be open for such an argument. It is well established that "the ultimate distribution of the burden of taxes [may] be quite different from the distribution of statutory liability," McLure, Incidence Analysis and the Supreme Court: An Examination of Four Cases from the 1980 Term, 1 Sup. Ct. Econ. Rev. 69, 72 (1982), with such divergence occurring when the nominal taxpayer can pass it through to other parties, like consumers. The Secretary's equivalence argument might work in the present case, then, if we could find that the economic impact of North Carolina's corporate income tax is passed through to shareholders of corporations doing business in state in a way that offsets the disincentive imposed by the intangibles tax to buying stock in corporations doing business out of state.

But there is a problem with this line of argument, and it lies in the frequently extreme complexity of economic incidence analysis. The actual incidence of a tax may depend on elasticities of supply and demand, the ability of producers and consumers to substitute one product for another, the structure of the relevant market, the time frame over which the tax is imposed and evaluated, and so on. See, e.g., Commonwealth Edison, 453 U.S. at 619, n. 8 (determining "whether the tax burden is shifted out of State, rather than borne by in-state producers and consumers, would require complex factual inquiries about such issues as elasticity of demand for the product and alternative sources of supply"). We declined to shoulder any such analysis in Minneapolis Star & Tribune Co. v. Minnesota Comm'r of Revenue, 460 U.S. at 589-590, noting that "courts as institutions are poorly equipped to evaluate with precision the relative burdens of various methods of taxation. The complexities of

factual economic proof always present a certain potential for error, and courts have little familiarity with the process of evaluating the relative economic burden of taxes" (footnote omitted). We were likewise unwilling to "plunge . . . into the morass of weighing comparative tax burdens by comparing taxes on dissimilar events" in Oregon Waste. 511 U.S. at 105. Indeed, the general difficulty of comparing the economic incidence of state taxes paid by different taxpayers upon different transactions goes a long way toward explaining why we have so seldom recognized a valid compensatory tax outside the context of sales and use taxes.[8]

In this case, not only has the State failed to proffer any analysis addressing the complexity of its burden, but we have particular reason to doubt the Secretary's suggestion that domestic corporate income taxes are so reflected in the stock values of corporations doing business in state as to offset the effects of the intangibles tax. . . .

. . . .

V

North Carolina's intangibles tax facially discriminates against interstate commerce, it fails justification as a valid compensatory tax, and, accordingly, it cannot stand. At the same time, of course, it is true that "a State found to have imposed an impermissibly discriminatory tax retains flexibility in responding to this determination." McKesson, 496 U.S. at 39-40. In McKesson, for example, we said that a State might refund the additional taxes imposed upon the victims of its discrimination or, to the extent consistent with other

---

6. Silas Mason makes clear that actual incidence upon the same class of taxpayers is a necessary condition for a finding that two taxes are complementary. Our analysis has sometimes focused upon other factors, however, see, e.g., Armco, 467 U.S. at 643, and we need not decide today whether identity of tax incidence is *sufficient* to compel the conclusion that two taxes fall upon substantially equivalent events.

8. The only exception of which we are aware is Hinson v. Lott, 75 U.S. 148 (1869). In that case, we upheld an Alabama tax on each gallon of liquor imported into the State on the ground that it complemented a tax of equal magnitude on each gallon of liquor distilled in the State. We noted that this tax scheme was "necessary to make the tax equal on all liquors sold in the State," id., at 153, a rationale consistent with our conclusion that the compensatory tax doctrine is fundamentally concerned with equalizing competition between in-staters and out-of-staters. Indeed, we cited Hinson in support of a similar proposition in Silas Mason. See 300 U.S. at 585. In determining that a tax on importers and distillers would actually equalize competition in the liquor market, the Hinson court made a good common-sense estimate of the likely incidence of the two taxes. Simply because modern economic tools may indicate that the incidence question is more complex, moreover, does not undermine the basic principle of equal competition established in Hinson. By the same token, however, Hinson does not alter our conclusion today that courts will ordinarily be unable to evaluate the economic equivalence of allegedly complementary tax schemes that go beyond traditional sales/use taxes. See infra. So much for Hinson in theory; for Hinson in practice, compare it with Armco, supra.

constitutional provisions (notably due process), retroactively impose equal burdens the tax's former beneficiaries. A State may also combine these two approaches. These options are available because the Constitution requires only that "the resultant tax actually assessed during the contested period reflec[t] a scheme that does not discriminate against interstate commerce." Id., at 41.[11]

In this case, that choice may well be dictated by the severability clause enacted as part of the intangibles tax statute. That issue, however, as well as the question whether Fulton has properly complied with the procedural requirements of North Carolina's tax refund statute, ought to come before the state courts in the first instance. Where "the federal constitutional issues involved [in the remedial determination] may well be intertwined with, or their consideration obviated by, issues of state law," our practice is to leave the remedy for the state supreme court to fashion on remand. Bacchus Imports, 468 U.S. at 277 (1984);see also Tyler Pipe Industries, 483 U.S. at 252; Williams v. Vermont, 472 U.S. at 28 (1985). We do that here.[Concurring opinion of CHIEF JUSTICE REHNQUIST omitted.]

---

11. We have also suggested that a "'meaningful opportunity for taxpayers to withhold contested tax assessments and to challenge their validity in a predeprivation hearing' is itself sufficient to satisfy constitutional concerns." Associated Industries, supra, 511 U.S. at 656 (quoting McKesson, 496 U.S. at 38, n. 21). The Secretary has not asserted that such an opportunity was afforded to Fulton under North Carolina's remedial scheme.

Questions and Comments

1. On remand, Fulton argued that the Supreme Court had held that the entire intangibles tax was unconstitutional. The State Supreme Court disagreed and severed the taxable percentage deduction. Fulton Corp. v. Faulkner, 481 S.E.2d 8, 9-10 (1997). Accordingly, Fulton received no refunds. The State court invited the Legislature to intervene.

The Legislature responded by repealing the tax and by prohibiting the Secretary of Revenue from enforcing the tax for one or more of the tax years from 1990 through 1994. Accordingly, refunds were granted to Fulton.

In a subsequent class action suit, refunds were also granted to all taxpayers that paid the intangibles tax for any of the tax years from 1990 through 1994, regardless of whether they had filed timely refund claims. Approximately $440 million in refunds were paid. See Smith v. State of North Carolina, 95 CVS 06715 (Wake County), Shaver v. State of North Carolina, 98 CVS 00625 (Wake County), Smith v. Offerman, 349 N.C. 332 (1998), and N.C. Session Law 1999-0327.

2. *Oregon Waste*, referred to in the opinion involved an Oregon fee imposed for the in-state disposal of waste. The fee was $.85/ton of waste generated in Oregon and $2.25/ton for waste generated out-of-state. Oregon contended that intrastate commerce "through general taxation" paid taxes that were equivalent to the additional levy imposed on out-of-state garbage. The Court stated that even if the State were right, the argument "fails because the in-state and out-of-state levies are not imposed on substantially equivalent events." *Oregon Waste*, 511 U. S. at 104.

3. Did the North Carolina statute have the effect of discouraging local corporations (intrastate corporations) from conducting interstate commerce?

4. Other than the sales and use taxes, what other compensating taxes can you think of?

5. Was the tax at issue internally consistent?

6. Why was the North Carolina statute facially discriminatory when it did not distinguish between corporations incorporated in North Carolina and all others? Did the statute confer a direct competitive advantage to local business?

7. What is the definition of facial discrimination? Does the discrimination have to be apparent from the face of the statute, making it unnecessary for a court to take into account behavioral or economic considerations? Is an exemption for pineapple wine facially discriminatory if such wine is made only in Hawaii? See *Bacchus*, supra. What if no one on the court knew that, but the parties stipulated to it? What if everyone knew that?

8. What evidence did the State offer to show that the intangibles tax on stock was intended to make multistate corporations pay for the privilege of participating in North Carolina's capital markets?

9. How would you determine a corporation's "fair share" of the cost of maintaining North Carolina's capital market?

10. Did the North Carolina tax regime encourage out-of-state corporations to sell their goods in North Carolina, in competition with in-state corporations? If so, is that the type of "economic protectionism" that violates the Commerce Clause?

11. Is it likely that large interstate corporations whose shares are taxable nearly in full by North Carolina compete for capital with purely intrastate corporations?

12. Does this case support the proposition that the flow of capital constitutes interstate commerce? Is it constitutional for a state to exempt the interest paid on securities that it issues but to tax the interest paid on securities issued by other states? See *Shaper v. Tracy*, 647 N.E.2d 550 (Ohio App. 1994); *Dominion National Bank v. Olsen*, 771 F.2d 108 (6th Cir. 1985). Can a state tax interest from out-of-state banks at a higher rate than interest received from in-state banks? See *Aronson v. Commonwealth*, 516 N.E.2d 137 (1982), cert. denied, 488 U. S. 818 (1989).

13. Is it constitutional for a state to exempt from its personal income tax interest from in-state banks? In analyzing the discrimination, what classes of income should be compared: interest from in-state banks compared to interest from out-of-state banks, or interest from in-state banks compared to all other interest paying investments? See *Smith et al. v. N. H. Dept. of Rev. Admin.*, 692 A.2d 486 (N.H. 1997). *Smith* is discussed after *G.M. v. Tracy* in Chapter 12.

14. Consider the State Supreme Court's statement that most P/E ratios are less than 31. Is that statement as true today as when made by the court in 1994? What is the P/E ratio of a hot Internet stock that has never made a profit? Is the definition of earnings for purposes of the

P/E ratio the same as the definition of taxable income in a typical state corporate income tax?

15. In *Perini Corporation v. Commissioner of Revenue*, 419 Mass. 763, cert. denied sub nom., *Adams v. Perini Corp.*, 116 S. Ct. 83 (1995), the Massachusetts Supreme Judicial Court held that portions of the State corporate excise tax unconstitutionally discriminated against interstate commerce. The invalid portions allowed a domestic intangible property corporation to deduct from its taxable net worth the value of a subsidiary of which it owned 80% or more of the voting stock, but only if that subsidiary was incorporated in Massachusetts. A foreign intangible property corporation could deduct from its taxable net worth the value of a subsidiary of which it owned 80% or more of the voting stock, but only if that subsidiary was incorporated outside of Massachusetts and did no business in Massachusetts. The court held that this statutory scheme was facially discriminatory because the statute classified corporations based on place of incorporation. The issue of remedies was left open. In *Perini Corp. et al. v. Commissioner of Revenue,* Mass. Supreme Judicial Ct., Suffolk Cty., SJC-06657 (May 13, 1996), the court held that any intangible property corporation can exclude the value of all 80% or more owned subsidiaries from the calculation of their net worth.

16. Consider a state that taxes dividends under its corporate income tax. Assume that the state does not wish to tax twice the same profits. That is, once a corporation is taxed on an apportionable share of its profits, the state does not wish to tax those same profits when they are distributed as dividends. Consequently, a corporation receiving dividends can deduct an amount that represents the profits of the payor that have already been subject to taxation by the state. Is this approach to eliminating double taxation constitutional after *Fulton*?

Arizona allows a deduction for dividends received from corporations whose apportionment factors are at least 50% in Arizona. Rhode Island allows a deduction for dividends if the payor is subject to Rhode Island tax. South Dakota has a similar rule for dividends received from financial institutions. Are these approaches constitutional? See *Ceridian Corp. v. Franchise Tax Board*, 2001 Ca. App. Lexis 27.

17. Kentucky levies an ad valorem tax upon intangibles, which include bank deposits and corporate shares, at the rate of .25%. For bank accounts held by banks incorporated in Kentucky, the rate is reduced to .001%. For shares, an exemption is provided for shareholders of corporations that "pay taxe[s] to [Kentucky] on at least 75% of its property, wherever located." Is this tax scheme constitutional? See *Herschel St. Ledger v. Kentucky*, 1997 Ky. Lexis 17.

18. Is it constitutional for a state to provide accelerated depreciation for in-state investment but provide only straight line depreciation for out-of-state investment? See *R.J. Reynolds Tobacco v. City of New York*, 237 A.D. 2d 6 (N.Y. 1997); *Beatrice Cheese v. Wis. Dept. of Rev.*, 1993 Wisc. Tax Lexis 5.

19. Alabama requires each corporation doing business in the State to pay a franchise tax based on the firm's capital. A domestic corporation pays tax in an amount equal to 1% of the par value of the firm's stock. A foreign corporation pays tax in an amount equal to 0.3% of the value of the actual amount of capital employed in Alabama. Under Alabama law, a domestic firm may set its stock's par value at a level well below its book or market value. Foreign corporations have no similar flexibility.

Alabama also imposes a domestic shares tax, which is a property tax on shares of domestic stock. It is assessed against shareholders based upon the value of the shares they hold, but in practice it is normally paid by the corporation itself.

In *South Central Bell Telephone Co. v. Alabama*, 526 U.S. 160 (1999), the Court had a very easy time in striking down the Alabama statute. The State conceded that domestic corporations could reduce their franchise tax liability simply by reducing the par value of their stock, while foreign corporations did not have that same flexibility. The State did not argue that the different tax rates for foreign and domestic corporations offset the difference in the tax base.

The Court concluded that the statute facially discriminated against interstate commerce. The Court rejected the argument that the foreign franchise tax was a complementary or compensatory tax that offsets the domestic shares tax on domestic corporations. The franchise tax on foreign corporations was not "roughly approximate" to the special burden on domestic corporations, nor were the two taxes similar in substance.

Was the discrimination apparent from the face of the statute?

20. For critical commentary on *Fulton Corporation*, see Michael Haag & Michael Boekhaus, *The Final Nail in the Compensatory Tax Coffin? The Impact of the Supreme Court's Decision in Fulton Corp. v. Faulkner on the Doctrine of Compensatory Taxes*, 21 Hamline L. Rev. 451 (1998);Christopher J. Hess, *The Constitutionality of Taxing the "Stranger within the Gates": The Impact of Fulton v. Faulkner on the Pennsylvania County Personal Property Tax*, 16 J.L. & Com. 233 (1997).

Camps Newfound/Owatonna, Inc. v. Town of Harrison, Maine, et al.
Supreme Court of the United States, 1997.
520 U.S. 564, 117 S. Ct. 1590, 137 L. Ed. 2d 852.

JUSTICE STEVENS delivered the opinion of the Court.

The question presented is whether an otherwise generally applicable state property tax violates the Commerce Clause of the United States Constitution because its exemption for property owned by charitable institutions excludes organizations operated principally for the benefit of nonresidents.

I

Petitioner is a Maine nonprofit corporation that operates a summer camp for the benefit of children of the Christian Science faith. . . . About 95% of the campers are not residents of Maine.

. . . Petitioner's revenues include camper tuition averaging about $400 per week for each student, contributions from private donors, and income from a "modest endowment." In recent years, the camp has had an annual operating deficit of approximately $175,000. From 1989 to 1991, it paid over $20,000 in real estate and personal property taxes each year.

The Maine statute at issue provides a general exemption from real estate and personal property taxes for "benevolent and charitable institutions incorporated" in the State. With respect to institutions that are "in fact conducted or operated principally for the benefit of persons who are not residents of Maine," however, a charity may only qualify for a more limited tax benefit, and then only if the weekly charge for services provided does not exceed $30 per person. Because most of the campers come from out of State, petitioner could not qualify for a complete exemption. And, since the weekly tuition was roughly $400, petitioner was ineligible for any charitable tax exemption at all.

II

. . . .

This case involves an issue that we have not previously addressed–the disparate real estate tax treatment of a nonprofit service provider based on the residence of the consumers that it serves. The Town argues that our dormant Commerce Clause jurisprudence is wholly inapplicable to this case, because interstate commerce is not implicated here . . . We first reject these arguments, and then explain why we think our prior cases make it clear that if profit-making enterprises were at issue, Maine could not tax petitioner more heavily than other camp operators simply because its campers come principally from other States. We next address the

novel question whether a different rule should apply to a discriminatory tax exemption for charitable and benevolent institutions. Finally, we reject the Town's argument that the exemption should either be viewed as a permissible subsidy or as a purchase of services by the State acting as a "market participant."

III

We are unpersuaded by the Town's argument that the dormant Commerce Clause is inapplicable here, either because campers are not "articles of commerce," or more generally because the camp's "product is delivered and 'consumed' entirely within Maine." Even though petitioner's camp does not make a profit, it is unquestionably engaged in commerce, not only as a purchaser, see Katzenbach v. McClung, 379 U.S. at 300-301; United States v. Lopez, 514 U.S. 549, but also as a provider of goods and services. It markets those services, together with an opportunity to enjoy the natural beauty of an inland lake in Maine, to campers who are attracted to its facility from all parts of the Nation. The record reflects that petitioner "advertises for campers in [out-of-state] periodicals . . . and sends its Executive Director annually on camper recruiting trips across the country." Petitioner's efforts are quite successful; 95 percent of its campers come from out of State. The attendance of these campers necessarily generates the transportation of persons across state lines that has long been recognized as a form of "commerce." Edwards v. California, 314 U.S. at 172; see also Caminetti v. United States, 242 U.S. at 491; Hoke v. United States, 227 U.S. at 320.

Summer camps are comparable to hotels that offer their guests goods and services that are consumed locally. In Heart of Atlanta Motel, Inc. v. United States, 379 U.S. 241 (1964), we recognized that interstate commerce is substantially affected by the activities of a hotel that "solicits patronage from outside the State of Georgia through various national advertising media, including magazines of national circulation." Id., at 243. In that case, we held that commerce was substantially affected by private race discrimination that limited access to the hotel and thereby impeded interstate commerce in the form of travel. Id., at 244, 258; see Lopez, 514 U.S. at 359. Official discrimination that limits the access of nonresidents to summer camps creates a similar impediment. Even when business activities are purely local, if "'it is interstate commerce that feels the pinch, it does not matter how local the operation which applies the squeeze.'" Heart of Atlanta, 379 U.S. at 258 (quoting

United States v. Women's Sportswear Mfrs. Assn., 336 U.S. at 464).

Although Heart of Atlanta involved Congress' affirmative Commerce Clause powers, its reasoning is applicable here. As we stated in Hughes v. Oklahoma, 441 U.S. 322 (1979), "The definition of 'commerce' is the same when relied on to strike down or restrict state legislation as when relied on to support some exertion of federal control or regulation." That case in turn rested upon our reasoning in Philadelphia v. New Jersey, 437 U.S. 617 (1978), in which we rejected a "two-tiered definition of commerce." "Just as Congress ha[d] power to regulate the interstate movement of [the] wastes" at issue in that case, so too we held were States "not free from constitutional scrutiny when they restrict that movement." Id., at 622-623. See also Sporhase v. Nebraska ex rel. Douglas, 458 U.S. at 953.

The Town's arguments that the dormant Commerce Clause is inapplicable to petitioner because the campers are not "articles of commerce," or more generally that interstate commerce is not at issue here, are therefore unpersuasive. The services that petitioner provides to its principally out-of-state campers clearly have a substantial effect on commerce, as do state restrictions on making those services available to nonresidents. Cf. C & A Carbone, Inc. v. Clarkstown, 511 U.S. at 391.

. . . .

We therefore turn to the question whether our prior cases preclude a State from imposing a higher tax on a camp that serves principally nonresidents than on one that limits its services primarily to residents.

IV

There is no question that were this statute targeted at profit-making entities, it would violate the dormant Commerce Clause. "State laws discriminating against interstate commerce on their face are 'virtually per se invalid.'" Fulton Corp. v. Faulkner, 516 U.S. at 326 (quoting Oregon Waste Systems, Inc. v. Department of Environmental Quality of Ore., 511 U.S. 93 (1994)). It is not necessary to look beyond the text of this statute to determine that it discriminates against interstate commerce. The Maine law expressly distinguishes between entities that serve a principally interstate clientele and those that primarily serve an intrastate market, singling out camps that serve mostly in-staters for beneficial tax treatment, and penalizing those camps that do a principally interstate business. As a practical matter, the statute encourages affected entities to limit their out-of-state clientele, and penalizes the principally nonresident customers of businesses catering to a primarily interstate market.

If such a policy were implemented by a statutory prohibition against providing camp services to nonresidents, the statute would almost certainly be invalid. We have "consistently . . . held that the Commerce Clause . . . precludes a state from mandating that its residents be given a preferred right of access, over out-of-state consumers, to natural resources located within its borders or to the products derived therefrom." New England Power Co. v. New Hampshire, 455 U.S. 331, 338 (1982). . . .

Avoiding this sort of "economic Balkanization," Hughes v. Oklahoma, 441 U.S. at 325, and the retaliatory acts of other States that may follow, is one of the central purposes of our negative Commerce Clause jurisprudence. See ibid.; West v. Kansas Natural Gas Co., 221 U.S. at 255 (expressing concern that "embargo may be retaliated by embargo, and commerce will be halted at state lines"). And, as we noted in Brown-Forman Distillers Corp. v. New York State Liquor Authority, 476 U.S. at 580: "Economic protectionism is not limited to attempts to convey advantages on local merchants; it may include attempts to give local consumers an advantage over consumers in other States." By encouraging economic isolationism, prohibitions on out-of-state access to in-state resources serve the very evil that the dormant Commerce Clause was designed to prevent.

Of course, this case does not involve a total prohibition. Rather, the statute provides a strong incentive for affected entities not to do business with nonresidents if they are able to so avoid the discriminatory tax. In this way, the statute is similar to the North Carolina "intangibles tax" that we struck down in Fulton Corp. v. Faulkner, 516 U.S. 325. That case involved the constitutionality under the Commerce Clause of a State "regime that taxe[d] stock [held by in-State shareholders] only to the degree its issuing corporation participates in interstate commerce." We held the statute facially discriminatory, in part because it tended "to discourage domestic corporations from plying their trades in interstate commerce." Maine's statute has a like effect.

To the extent that affected Maine organizations are not deterred by the statute from doing a principally interstate business, it is clear that discriminatory burdens on interstate commerce imposed by regulation or taxation may also violate the Commerce Clause. We have held that special fees assessed on nonresidents directly by the State when they attempt to use local services impose an impermissible burden on interstate commerce. See, e.g., Chemical Waste, 504 U.S. at 342 (discriminatory tax imposed on disposal of out-of-state hazardous waste). That the tax discrimination comes in the form of a deprivation of a generally available tax benefit, rather than a specific penalty on the activity itself, is of no moment. Thus, in New Energy Co. of Ind. v. Limbach, 486 U.S. at 274, the Court invalidated an Ohio statute that provided a tax credit for sales of ethanol produced in State, but not ethanol produced in certain other States; the law "deprive[d] certain products of generally available beneficial tax treatment because they are made in certain other States, and thus on its face appear[ed] to violate the cardinal requirement of nondiscrimination." Given the fact that the burden of Maine's facially discriminatory tax scheme falls by design in a predictably disproportionate way on out-of-staters,[13] the pernicious effect on interstate commerce is the same as in our cases involving taxes targeting out-of-staters alone.

Unlike in Chemical Waste, we recognize that here the discriminatory burden is imposed on the out-of-state customer indirectly by means of a tax on the entity transacting business with the non-Maine customer. This distinction makes no analytic difference. As we noted in West Lynn Creamery discussing the general phenomenon of import tariffs: "For over 150 years, our cases have rightly concluded that the imposition of a differential burden on any part of the stream of commerce–from wholesaler to retailer to consumer–is invalid, because a burden placed at any point will result in a disadvantage to the out-of-state producer." 512 U.S. at 202 (citing cases). So too here, it matters little that it is the camp that is taxed rather than the campers. The record demonstrates that the economic incidence of the tax falls at least in part on the campers, the Town has

not contested the point, and the courts below based their decision on this presumption.[**]

With respect to those businesses–like petitioner's–that continue to engage in a primarily interstate trade, the Maine statute therefore functionally serves as an export tariff that targets out-of-state consumers by taxing the businesses that principally serve them. As our cases make clear, this sort of discrimination is at the very core of activities forbidden by the dormant commerce clause. " '[A] State may not tax a transaction or incident more heavily when it crosses state lines than when it occurs entirely within the State.' " Chemical Waste, 504 U.S. at 342 (quoting Armco, 467 U.S. at 642 (1984)); see West Lynn Creamery, 512 U.S. at 193 (tariffs forbidden by the dormant Commerce Clause).

Ninety-five percent of petitioner's campers come from out of state. Insofar as Maine's discriminatory tax has increased tuition, that burden is felt almost entirely by out-of-staters, deterring them from enjoying the benefits of camping in Maine.[15] In sum, the Maine statute facially discriminates against interstate commerce, and is all but per se invalid. See, e.g., Oregon Waste, 511 U.S. at 100-101.

We recognize that the Town might have attempted to defend the Maine law under the per se rule by demonstrating that it " 'advances a legitimate local

---

13. Because the Maine tax is facially discriminatory, this case is unlike Commonwealth Edison Co., 453 U.S. 609 (1981). There, we held permissible under the Commerce Clause a generally applicable Montana severance tax on coal extracted from in-state mines. Appellants challenged the tax arguing, inter alia, that it discriminated against interstate commerce because 90% of the coal happened to be shipped to out-of-state users, and the tax burden was therefore borne principally by nonresidents. We rejected this claim, noting that "there is no real discrimination in this case; the tax burden is borne according to the amount of coal consumed and not according to any distinction between in-state and out-of-state consumers." Id., at 619. We recognized that an approach to the dormant Commerce Clause requiring an assessment of the likely demand for a particular good by nonresidents and a State's ability to shift its tax burden out of State "would require complex factual inquiries about such issues as elasticity of demand for the product and alternative sources of supply," id., at 619, n. 8, and declined to adopt such a difficult to police test. Here, in contrast, the tax scheme functions by design and on its face to burden out-of-state users disproportionately. Our analysis in Commonwealth Edison is therefore inapplicable.
. . . .

**. [Ed. In upholding the statute, the Maine Supreme Court concluded that nothing in the record suggested that the taxpayers competed with other summer camps outside of or within Maine or that the taxpayers lost business to competitors. The taxpayers did not claim that the exemption placed them at a competitive disadvantage. According to the Maine court, the "record suggests that the denial of a tax exemption results in increased costs that are passed along 'to some extent' to the campers in the form of increased tuition. . ." 655 A.2d at 879.]

15. The Town argues that these effects are entirely speculative, because the record does not reflect any decision by a potential camper not to attend petitioner's camp as a result of the burden imposed. The Supreme Judicial Court appears to have adopted similar reasoning. 655 A. 2d, at 879. This misconstrues the proper analysis. As we made clear most recently in Fulton Corp., 516 U.S. at 330-331, there is no "'de minimis' defense to a charge of discriminatory taxation under the Commerce Clause." A particularized showing of the sort respondent seeks is not required. See Associated Industries of Mo., 511 U.S. at 650 (1994) ("Actual discrimination, wherever it is found, is impermissible, and the magnitude and scope of the discrimination have no bearing on the determinative question whether discrimination has occurred"); Maryland v. Louisiana, 451 U.S. at 756; see also Boston Stock Exchange, 429 U.S. at 334, n.13 (1977).

purpose that cannot be adequately served by reasonable nondiscriminatory alternatives.' " Id., at 101 (quoting New Energy Co., 486 U.S. at 278). In assessing respondents' arguments, we would have applied our "strictest scrutiny." Hughes v. Oklahoma, 441 U.S. at 337. This is an extremely difficult burden, "so heavy that 'facial discrimination by itself may be a fatal defect.'" Oregon Waste, 511 U.S. at 101 (quoting Hughes, 441 U.S. at 337); see Chemical Waste Management, Inc. v. Hunt, 504 U.S. at 342 ("Once a state tax is found to discriminate against out-of-state commerce, it is typically struck down without further inquiry"). Perhaps realizing the weight of its burden, the Town has made no effort to defend the statute under the per se rule, and so we do not address this question. See Fulton Corp. v. Faulkner, 516 U.S. at (slip op., at 7-8).[16] We have no

[margin handwriting: Strict scrut. but no defense ∴ no issue]

doubt that if petitioner's camp were a profit-making entity, the discriminatory tax exemption would be impermissible.

V

The unresolved question presented by this case is whether a different rule should apply to tax exemptions for charitable and benevolent institutions. Though we have never had cause to address the issue directly, the applicability of the dormant Commerce Clause to the nonprofit sector of the economy follows from our prior decisions.

. . . .

A nonprofit entity is ordinarily understood to differ from a for-profit corporation principally because it "is barred from distributing its net earnings, if any, to individuals who exercise control over it, such as members, officers, directors, or trustees." Id., at 838. Nothing intrinsic to the nature of nonprofit entities prevents them from engaging in interstate commerce. Summer camps may be operated as for-profit or nonprofit entities; nonprofits may depend—as here—in substantial part on fees charged for their services. Clotfelter, The Distributional Consequences of Nonprofit Activities, in Who Benefits from the Nonprofit Sector? 1, 6 (C. Clotfelter ed., 1992) (nonprofits in some sectors are "heavily dependent on fees by paying customers, with private payments accounting for at least half of total revenues"). Whether operated on a for-profit or nonprofit basis, they purchase goods and services in competitive markets, offer their facilities to a variety of patrons, and derive revenues from a variety of sources, some of which are local and some out of State.

[margin handwriting: non distrib. not non interst comm]

---

16. JUSTICE SCALIA submits that we err by following our precedent in Fulton and declining to address an argument that the Town itself did not think worthy of pressing. But even if there were reason to consider the State's compliance with the per se rule, the Town would not prevail. In the single case JUSTICE SCALIA points to in which we found the per se standard to have been met, Maine v. Taylor, 477 U.S. 131 (1986), the State had no "'reasonable nondiscriminatory alternatives,'" Oregon Waste, 511 U.S. at 101 (quoting New Energy Co., 486 U.S. at 278), to the action it had taken. Absent a bar on the import of certain minnows, there was no way for Maine to protect its natural environment from the hazard of parasites and nonnative species that might have been accidentally introduced into the State's waters. Taylor, 477 U.S. at 141.

In contrast, here Maine has ample alternatives short of a facially discriminatory property tax exemption to achieve its apparent goal of subsidizing the attendance of the State's children at summer camp. Maine could, for example, achieve this end by offering direct financial support to parents of resident children. Cf. Shapiro v. Thompson, 394 U.S. 618 (1969). Though we have not had the occasion to address the issue, it might also be permissible for the State to subsidize Maine camps directly to the extent that they serve residents. See West Lynn Creamery, Inc. v. Healy, 512 U.S. at 199, n. 15; New Energy Co. of Ind. v. Limbach, 486 U.S. at 278 (noting that "[d]irect subsidization of domestic industry does not ordinarily run afoul" of the Commerce Clause); Hughes v. Alexandria Scrap Corp., 426 U.S. at 816 (STEVENS, J., concurring).

While the Town does argue its case under the less exacting analysis set forth in, e.g., Pike v. Bruce Church, Inc., 397 U.S. at 142, "this lesser scrutiny is only available 'where other [nondiscriminatory] legislative objectives are credibly advanced *and* there is *no* patent discrimination against interstate trade.'" Chemical Waste, 504 U.S. at 343, n. 5 (quoting Philadelphia v. New Jersey, 437 U.S. at 624 (emphasis added)). Because the Maine statute is facially discriminatory, the more deferential standard is inapplicable. Contrary to JUSTICE SCALIA's suggestion, this case is quite unlike General Motors Corp. v. Tracy, 519 U.S. 278 (1997). There, the Court premised its holding that the statute at issue was not facially discriminatory on the view that sellers of "bundled" and "unbundled" natural gas were principally competing in

For purposes of Commerce Clause analysis, any categorical distinction between the activities of profit-making enterprises and not-for-profit entities is therefore wholly illusory. Entities in both categories are major participants in interstate markets. And, although the summer camp involved in this case may have a relatively insignificant impact on the commerce of the entire Nation, the interstate commercial activities of nonprofit entities as a class are unquestionably

[margin handwriting: C.C. analysis no distinction fp + NP]

---

different markets. See id., at 280 ("dormant Commerce Clause protects markets and participants in markets, not taxpayers as such"). While it may be true that "disparate treatment constitutes discrimination only if the objects of the disparate treatment are . . . similarly situated," there is no question that the statute at issue here is facially discriminatory because it disparately treats identically situated Maine nonprofit camps depending upon whether they favor in-state, as opposed to out-of-state, campers.

significant.[18] See Wickard v. Filburn, 317 U.S. at 127-128; Lopez, 514 U.S. at (slip op., at 6, 10).

From the State's standpoint it may well be reasonable to use tax exemptions as a means of encouraging nonprofit institutions to favor local citizens, notwithstanding any possible adverse impact on the larger markets in which those institutions participate. Indeed, if we view the issue solely from the State's perspective, it is equally reasonable to use discriminatory tax exemptions as a means of encouraging the growth of local trade. But as our cases clearly hold, such exemptions are impermissible. See, e.g., Bacchus, 468 U.S. at 273. Protectionism, whether targeted at for-profit entities or serving, as here, to encourage nonprofits to keep their efforts close to home, is forbidden under the dormant Commerce Clause.[19] If there is need for a special exception for nonprofits, Congress not only has the

---

18. We are informed by amici that "the nonprofit sector spends over $389 billion each year in operating expenses–approximately seven percent of the gross national product." Brief for American Council on Education et al. as Amici Curiae 19. In recent years, nonprofits have employed approximately seven percent of the Nation's paid workers, roughly 9.3 million people in 1990. V. Hodgkinson, M. Weitzman, C. Toppe, & S. Noga, Nonprofit Almanac 1992-1993: Dimensions of the Independent Sector 29 (1992) (Table 1.5).

JUSTICE SCALIA wrongly suggests that Maine's law offers only a "narrow tax exemption," which he implies has no substantial effect on interstate commerce and serves only "to relieve the State of its burden of caring for its residents". This characterization is quite misleading. The statute expressly exempts from tax property used by such important nonprofit service industries as nursing homes and child care centers. Nonprofit participation in these sectors is substantial. Nationally, nonprofit nursing homes had estimated revenues of $18 billion in 1994. These entities compete with a sizeable for-profit nursing home sector, which had revenues of approximately $40 billion in 1994. Similarly, the $5 billion nonprofit market in child day care services competes with an $11 billion for-profit industry.

Nonprofit hospitals and health maintenance organizations also receive an exemption from Maine's property tax. While operating as nonprofit entities, their activities are serious business. . . . Nonprofit hospitals had national revenues of roughly $305 billion in 1994, considerably more than the $34 billion in revenues collected by hospitals operated on a for-profit basis.

Maine law further permits qualifying nonprofits to rent out their property on a commercial basis at market rates in order to support other activities, so long as that use of the property is only incidental to their own purposes. . . .

19. Contrary to JUSTICE SCALIA's suggestion, nothing in our holding today "prevent[s] a State from giving a tax break to charities that benefit the State's inhabitants." The States are, of course, free to provide generally applicable nondiscriminatory tax exemptions without running afoul of the dormant Commerce Clause.

---

power to create it, but also is in a far better position than we to determine its dimensions.[21]

VI

Rather than urging us to create a categorical exception for nonprofit entities, the Town argues that Maine's exemption statute should be viewed as an expenditure of government money designed to lessen its social service burden and to foster the societal benefits provided by charitable organizations. So characterized, the Town submits that its tax exemption scheme is either a legitimate discriminatory subsidy of only those charities that choose to focus their activities on local concerns, or alternatively a governmental "purchase" of charitable services falling within the narrow exception to the dormant Commerce Clause for States in their role as "market participants," see, e.g., Hughes v. Alexandria Scrap Corp., 426 U.S. 794 (1976); Reeves, Inc. v. Stake, 447 U.S. 429 (1980). We find these arguments unpersuasive. Although tax exemptions and subsidies serve similar ends, they differ in important and relevant respects, and our cases have recognized these distinctions. As for the "market participant" argument, we have already rejected the Town's position in a prior case, and in any event respondents' open-ended exemption for charitable and benevolent institutions is not analogous to the industry-specific state actions that we reviewed in Alexandria Scrap and Reeves.

The Town argues that its discriminatory tax exemption is, in economic reality, no different from a discriminatory subsidy of those charities that cater principally to local needs. Noting our statement in West Lynn Creamery that "[a] pure subsidy funded out of general revenue ordinarily imposes no burden on interstate commerce, but merely assists local business," 512 U.S. at 199, the Town submits that since a discriminatory subsidy may be permissible, a discriminatory exemption must be too. We have "never squarely confronted the constitutionality of subsidies," id., at 199, n. 15, and we need not address these questions today. Assuming, arguendo, that the Town is correct that a direct subsidy benefitting only those

---

21. We must admit to some puzzlement as to the force of the argument underlying JUSTICE SCALIA's dissent. On the one hand, he suggests that a categorical exemption of nonprofit activities from dormant Commerce Clause scrutiny would be proper. Yet at the same time, he makes a great effort to characterize *this* statute as being so narrow that, whatever the appropriate generally applicable rule, the dormant Commerce Clause ought not to apply here. As we have explained, the argument in favor of a *categorical* exemption for nonprofits is unpersuasive, and we disagree with JUSTICE SCALIA's characterization of this statute's effects. Accordingly, we reject his position on either of these theories.

nonprofits serving principally Maine residents would be permissible, our cases do not sanction a tax exemption serving similar ends.[22]

In Walz v. Tax Comm'n of City of New York, 397 U.S. 664 (1970), notwithstanding our assumption that a direct subsidy of religious activity would be invalid,[23] we held that New York's tax exemption for church property did not violate the Establishment Clause of the First Amendment.[24] That holding rested, in part, on the premise that there is a constitutionally significant difference between subsidies and tax exemptions.[25] We have expressly recognized that this distinction is also applicable to claims that certain state action designed to give residents an advantage in the market place is prohibited by the Commerce Clause.

In New Energy, 486 U.S. 269 (1988), we found unconstitutional under the Commerce Clause an Ohio tax scheme that provided a sales tax credit for ethanol produced in State, or manufactured in another State to the extent that State gave similar tax advantages to ethanol produced in Ohio. We recognized that the party challenging the Ohio scheme was "eligible to receive a cash subsidy" from its home State, and was therefore "the potential beneficiary of a scheme no less discriminatory than the one that it attacks, and no less effective in conferring a commercial advantage over out-of-state competitors." That was of no importance. We noted: "The Commerce Clause does not prohibit all state action designed to give its residents an advantage in the marketplace, but only action of that description *in connection with the State's regulation of interstate commerce.* Direct subsidization of domestic industry does not ordinarily run afoul of that prohibition; discriminatory taxation . . . does." (emphasis in original). See also West Lynn, 512 U.S. at 210 (SCALIA, J., concurring in judgment) (drawing similar distinction between forbidden generally applicable tax with discriminatory "exemption" and permissible "subsidy . . . funded from the State's general revenues"). This distinction is supported by scholarly commentary as well as precedent, and we see no reason to depart from it. See Enrich, Saving the States from Themselves: Commerce Clause Constraints on State Tax Incentives for Business, 110 Harv. L. Rev. 377, 442-443 (1996); Hellerstein & Coenen, Commerce Clause Restraints on State Business Development Incentives, 81 Cornell L. Rev. 789, 846-848 (1996).[26] The Town's claim that its discriminatory tax scheme should be viewed as a permissible subsidy is therefore unpersuasive.[27]

. . . .

Maine's tax exemption statute cannot be characterized as a proprietary activity falling within the

---

22. As the Supreme Judicial Court made clear, 655 A. 2d, at 878, under Maine law an exemption is categorized as a "tax expenditure." Me. Rev. Stat. Ann., Tit. 36, § 196 (1990). The Town's effort to argue that this state statutory categorization allows it to elide the Federal constitutional distinction between tax exemptions and subsidies is unavailing. We recognized long ago that a tax exemption can be viewed as a form of government spending. See Regan v. Taxation with Representation of Wash., 461 U.S. 540, 544 (1983). The distinction we have drawn for dormant Commerce Clause purposes does not turn on this point.

23. We noted, "[o]bviously a direct money subsidy would be a relationship pregnant with involvement and, as with most governmental grant programs, could encompass sustained and detailed administrative relationships for enforcement of statutory or administrative standards, but that is not this case." Walz, 397 U.S. at 675.

24. We reasoned that "New York's statute [cannot be read] as attempting to establish religion; it . . . simply spar[es] the exercise of religion from the burden of property taxation levied on private profit institutions." Id., at 673.

25. "The grant of a tax exemption is not sponsorship since the government does not transfer part of its revenue to churches but simply abstains from demanding that the church support the state. No one has ever suggested that tax exemption has converted libraries, art galleries, or hospitals into arms of the state or put employees 'on the public payroll.'" Id., at 675. As Justice Brennan noted: "Tax exemptions and general subsidies . . . are qualitatively different." Id., at 690 (concurring opinion).

26. The distinction provides a sufficient response to the Town's argument that our ruling today would invalidate a State's subsidization of all or part of its residents' tuition at State-owned universities.

27. JUSTICE SCALIA, would distinguish this line of authority by holding that it should not apply where a State is giving tax relief to charitable enterprises. As explained in Part V, supra, we see no categorical reason to treat for-profit and nonprofit entities differently under the dormant Commerce Clause. JUSTICE SCALIA's heavy reliance upon Board of Ed. of Ky. Annual Conference of Methodist Episcopal Church v. Illinois, 203 U.S. 553 (1906), is misplaced. In that case, a bequest to a Kentucky charitable corporation did not qualify for an exemption from the Illinois inheritance tax because the corporate legatee was not incorporated in Illinois. In this case, the petitioner is a Maine corporation, and the validity of the portion of the Maine statute that denies the exemption to out-of-state corporations is not at issue. Moreover, unlike the situation in Board of Ed. of Ky., in which none of the charitable activities of the legatee were performed in Illinois, all of the benefits of attending petitioner's camp in Maine are "bestowed within her borders." Id., at 563. While the dictum that JUSTICE SCALIA quotes is consistent with his analysis, it does not purport to address the applicability of the dormant Commerce Clause to charities in general, to resident charities, or to nonresident charities that provide benefits for both residents and nonresidents.

market-participant exception. In New Energy Co., Ohio argued similarly that a discriminatory tax credit program fell within the exception. We noted that the tax program had "the purpose and effect of subsidizing a particular industry, as do many dispositions of the tax laws." 486 U.S. at 277. "That," we explained, "does not transform it into a form of state participation in the free market." "The Ohio action ultimately at issue is neither its purchase nor its sale of ethanol, but its assessment and computation of taxes–a primeval governmental activity." As we indicated in White: "In this kind of case there is 'a single inquiry: whether the challenged "program constituted direct state participation in the market." '" 460 U.S. at 208 (quoting Reeves, 447 U.S. at 436, n. 7). A tax exemption is not the sort of direct state involvement in the market that falls within the market-participation doctrine.

Even if we were prepared to expand the exception in the manner suggested by the Town, the Maine tax statute at issue here would be a poor candidate. Like the tax exemption upheld in Walz–which applied to libraries, art galleries, and hospitals as well as churches–the exemption that has been denied to petitioner is available to a broad category of charitable and benevolent institutions. For that reason, nothing short of a dramatic expansion of the "market participant" exception would support its application to this case. Alexandria Scrap involved Maryland's entry into the market for automobile hulks, a discrete activity focused on a single industry. Similarly, [in Reeves] South Dakota's participation in the market for cement was–in part because of its narrow scope–readily conceived as a proprietary action of the State. In contrast, Maine's tax exemption–which sweeps to cover broad swathes of the nonprofit sector–must be viewed as action taken in the State's sovereign capacity rather than a proprietary decision to make an entry into all of the markets in which the exempted charities function. See White, 460 U.S. at 211, n. 7 (noting that "there are some limits on a state or local government's ability to impose restrictions that reach beyond the immediate parties with which the government transacts business"). The Town's version of the "market participant" exception would swallow the rule against discriminatory tax schemes. Contrary to the Town's submission, the notion that whenever a State provides a discriminatory tax abatement it is "purchasing" some service in its proprietary capacity is not readily confined to the charitable context. A special tax concession for liquors indigenous to Hawaii, for example, might be conceived as a "purchase" of the jobs produced by local industry, or an investment in the unique local cultural value provided by these beverages. Cf. Bacchus, 468 U.S. at 270-271. Discriminatory schemes favoring local farmers might be seen as the "purchase" of agricultural services in order to ensure that the State's citizens will have a steady local supply of

the product. Cf. West Lynn, 512 U.S. at 190 (striking down statute protecting in-state milk producers designed to "preserve . . . local industry" "thereby ensur[ing] a continuous and adequate supply of fresh milk for our market" (internal quotation marks omitted)). Our cases provide no support for the Town's radical effort to expand the market-participant doctrine.

VII

As was true in Bacchus Imports, the facts of this particular case, viewed in isolation, do not appear to pose any threat to the health of the national economy. Nevertheless, history, including the history of commercial conflict that preceded the constitutional convention as well as the uniform course of Commerce Clause jurisprudence animated and enlightened by that early history, provides the context in which each individual controversy must be judged. The history of our Commerce Clause jurisprudence has shown that even the smallest scale discrimination can interfere with the project of our federal Union. As Justice Cardozo recognized, to countenance discrimination of the sort that Maine's statute represents would invite significant inroads on our "national solidarity":

"The Constitution was framed under the dominion of a political philosophy less parochial in range. It was framed upon the theory that the peoples of the several states must sink or swim together, and that in the long run prosperity and salvation are in union and not division." Baldwin v. G. A. F. Seelig, Inc., 294 U.S. at 523.

The judgment of the Maine Supreme Judicial Court is reversed.

JUSTICE SCALIA, with whom THE CHIEF JUSTICE, JUSTICE THOMAS and JUSTICE GINSBURG join, dissenting.

The Court's negative-commerce-clause jurisprudence has drifted far from its moorings. Originally designed to create a national market for commercial activity, it is today invoked to prevent a State from giving a tax break to charities that benefit the State's inhabitants. In my view, Maine's tax exemption, which excuses from taxation only that property used to relieve the State of its burden of caring for its residents, survives even our most demanding commerce-clause scrutiny.

I

We have often said that the purpose of our negative-commerce-clause jurisprudence is to create a national market. As Justice Jackson once observed, the "vision of the Founders" was "that every farmer and every craftsman shall be encouraged to produce by the certainty that he will have free access to every market in the Nation, that no home embargoes will withhold his exports, and no foreign state will by customs duties or regulations exclude them." H. P. Hood & Sons, Inc. v. Du Mond, 336 U.S. at 539. In our zeal to advance this policy, however, we must take care not to overstep our mandate, for the Commerce Clause was not intended "to cut the States off from legislating on all subjects relating to the health, life, and safety of their citizens, though the legislation might indirectly affect the commerce of the country." Huron Portland Cement Co. v. Detroit, 362 U.S. at 443-444.

Our cases have struggled (to put it nicely) to develop a set of rules by which we may preserve a national market powers, each exercise of which no doubt has some effect on the commerce of the Nation. See Oklahoma Tax Comm'n v. Jefferson Lines, Inc., 514 U.S. at 180-183. The rules that we currently use can be simply stated, if not simply applied: Where a State law facially discriminates against interstate commerce, we observe what has sometimes been referred to as a "virtually per se rule of invalidity;" where, on the other hand, a state law is nondiscriminatory, but nonetheless adversely affects interstate commerce, we employ a deferential "balancing test," under which the law will be sustained unless "the burden imposed on [interstate] commerce is clearly excessive in relation to the putative local benefits," Pike v. Bruce Church, Inc., 397 U.S. at 142. See Oregon Waste Systems, Inc. v. Department of Environmental Quality of Ore., 511 U.S. at 99.

While the "virtually per se rule of invalidity" entails application of the "strictest scrutiny," Hughes v. Oklahoma, 441 U.S. at 337, it does not necessarily result in the invalidation of facially discriminatory State legislation, see, e.g., Maine v. Taylor, 477 U.S. 131 (1986) (upholding absolute ban on the importation of baitfish into Maine), for "what may appear to be a 'discriminatory' provision in the constitutionally prohibited sense–that is, a protectionist enactment–may on closer analysis not be so," New Energy Co. of Ind. v. Limbach, 486 U.S. at 278. Thus, even a statute that erects an absolute barrier to the movement of goods across state lines will be upheld if "the discrimination is demonstrably justified by a valid factor unrelated to economic protectionism," id., at 274, or to put a finer point on it, if the State law "advances a legitimate local purpose that cannot be adequately served by reasonable nondiscriminatory alternatives," id., at 278.

In addition to laws that employ suspect means as a necessary expedient to the advancement of legitimate State ends, we have also preserved from judicial invalidation laws that confer advantages upon the State's residents but do so without *regulating* interstate commerce. We have therefore excepted the State from scrutiny when it participates in markets rather than

regulates them–by selling cement, for example, see Reeves, Inc. v. Stake, 447 U.S. 429 (1980), or purchasing auto hulks, see Hughes v. Alexandria Scrap Corp., 426 U.S. (1976), or hiring contractors, see White v. Massachusetts Council of Construction Employees, 460 U.S. 204 (1983). Likewise, we have said that direct subsidies to domestic industry do not run afoul of the Commerce Clause. See New Energy Co., 486 U.S. at 278. In sum, we have declared that "[t]he Commerce Clause does not prohibit all state action designed to give its residents an advantage in the marketplace, but only action of that description *in connection with the State's regulation of interstate commerce*." Ibid. (emphasis in original).

II

In applying the foregoing principles to the case before us, it is of course important to understand the precise scope of the exemption. The Court's analysis suffers from the misapprehension that [the exemption] "sweeps to cover broad swathes of the nonprofit sector," including nonprofit corporations engaged in quintessentially commercial activities. That is not so. A review of Maine law demonstrates that the provision at issue here is a narrow tax exemption, designed merely to compensate or subsidize those organizations that contribute to the public fisc by dispensing public benefits the State might otherwise provide.

Although Maine allows nonprofit corporations to be organized "for any lawful purpose," the exemption does not extend to all nonprofit organizations, but only to those "benevolent and charitable institutions," which are "organized and conducted *exclusively* for benevolent and charitable purposes," (emphasis added), and only to those parcels of real property and items of personal property that are used "solely," "to further the organization's charitable purposes." The Maine Supreme Judicial Court has defined the statutory term "benevolent and charitable institutions" to include only those nonprofits that dispense "charity," which is in turn defined to include only those acts which are "'for the benefit of an indefinite number of persons, either by bringing their minds or hearts under the influence of education or religion, by relieving their bodies from disease, suffering, or constraint, by assisting them to establish themselves in life, or by erecting or maintaining public buildings or works *or otherwise lessening the burdens of government*.'" Lewiston v. Marcotte Congregate Housing, Inc., 673 A. 2d 209, 211 (1996) (emphasis added).

Moreover, the Maine Supreme Judicial Court has further limited the exemption by insisting that the party claiming its benefit "bring its claim unmistakably within the spirit and intent of the act creating the exemption," and by proclaiming that the spirit and intent of [the exemption] is to compensate charitable organizations for their contribution to the public fisc. As the Court has explained:

"'[A]ny institution which by its charitable activities relieves the government of part of [its] burden is conferring a pecuniary benefit upon the body politic, and in receiving exemption from taxation it is merely being given a "quid pro quo" for its services in providing something which otherwise the government would have to provide.'" Episcopal Camp Foundation, Inc. v. Hope, 666 A. 2d 108, 110 (1995) (quoting Young Men's Christian Assn. of Germantown v. Philadelphia, 187 A. 204, 210 (1936)).

. . . .

That [the exemption] serves to compensate private charities for helping to relieve the State of its burden of caring for its residents should not be obscured by the fact that this particular case involves a summer camp rather than a more traditional form of social service. The statute that the Court strikes down does not speak of "camps" at all, but rather lists as examples of "benevolent and charitable institutions" nonprofit nursing homes, boarding homes, community mental health service facilities and child care centers. . . . What is at issue in this case is not whether a summer camp can properly be regarded as relieving the State of social costs, but rather whether, *assuming it can*, a distinction between charities serving mainly residents and charities operated principally for the benefit of nonresidents is constitutional.[1]

_____

1. The Court protests that "there is no 'de minimis' defense to a charge of discriminatory taxation under the Commerce Clause," ante, at n. 15 as though that were the point of our emphasizing in this Part II the narrowness of the challenged limitation. It is not. Rather, the point is (1) that Maine's limitation focuses upon a particular state interest that is deserving of exemption from negative-commerce-clause invalidation, and (2) that acknowledging the principle of such an exemption (as developed in Part III below) will not place the "national market" in any peril. What the Court should have gleaned from our discussion, it did not: It persists in misdescribing the exemption we defend as "a categorical exemption of nonprofit activities from dormant Commerce Clause scrutiny." Ante, at n. 21; see also ante, at n. 27.

The Court also makes an attempt to contest on the merits the narrowness of the exemption, suggesting a massive effect upon interstate commerce by reciting the multi-billion-dollar annual revenues of nonprofit nursing homes, child care centers, hospitals and health maintenance organizations. See ante, at n. 18. But of course most of the services provided by those institutions are provided locally, to local beneficiaries. (In that regard the summer camp that is the subject of the present suit is most atypical.) The record does not show the number of nonprofit nursing homes, child care centers, hospitals and

III

I turn next to the validity of this focused tax exemption–applicable only to property used solely for charitable purposes by organizations devoted exclusively to charity–under the negative commerce clause principles discussed earlier. The Court readily concludes that, by limiting the class of eligible property to that which is used "principally for the benefit of persons who are Maine residents," the statute "facially discriminates" against interstate commerce. That seems to me not necessarily true. Disparate treatment constitutes discrimination only if the objects of the disparate treatment are, for the relevant purposes, similarly situated. See General Motors Corp. v. Tracy (slip. op., at 18-20). And for purposes of entitlement to a tax subsidy from the State, it is certainly reasonable to think that property gratuitously devoted to relieving the State of some of its welfare burden is not similarly situated to property used "principally for the benefit of persons who are not residents of [the State]." As we have seen, the theory underlying the exemption is that it is a quid pro quo for uncompensated expenditures that lessen the State's burden of providing assistance to its residents.

The Court seeks to establish "facial discrimination" by showing that the effect of treating disparate property disparately is to produce higher costs for those users of the property who come from out of State. But that could be regarded as an *indirect* effect upon interstate commerce produced by a tax scheme that is *not* facially discriminatory, which means that the proper mode of analysis would be the more lenient "balancing" standard discussed above. We follow precisely this mode of analysis in Tracy, upholding an Ohio law that provides preferential tax treatment to domestic public utilities. Such entities, we conclude, are not "similarly situated" to other fuel distributors; their insulation from out-of-state competition does not violate the negative Commerce Clause because it "serves important interests in health and safety." The Court in Tracy paints a compelling image of people shivering in their homes in the dead of winter without the assured service that competition-sheltered public utilities provide. No less important, however, is the availability of many of the benefits provided by Maine's private charities and facilitated not by total insulation from competition but by favorable tax treatment: care for the sick and dying, for example, or nursing services for the elderly.

_____

HMOs in Maine that have been denied the charitable exemption because their property is not used "principally for the benefit of persons who are Maine residents"; but it would be a good bet that the number is zero.

Even if, however, the Maine statute displays "facial discrimination" against interstate commerce, that is not the end of the analysis. The most remarkable thing about today's judgment is that it is rendered without inquiry into whether the purposes of the tax exemption *justify* its favoritism. Once having concluded that the statute is facially discriminatory, the Court rests. "[T]he Town," it asserts, "has made no effort to defend the statute under the per se rule." This seems to me a pointless technicality. The Town has asserted that the State's interest in encouraging private entities to shoulder part of its social-welfare burden validates this provision under the negative Commerce Clause. Whether it does so because the presence of that interest causes the resident-benefiting charities not to be "similarly situated" to the non-resident-benefiting charities, and hence *negates* "facial discrimination," or rather because the presence of that interest *justifies* "facial discrimination," is a question that is not only of no consequence but is also probably unanswerable. To strike down this statute because the Town's lawyers put the argument in one form rather than the other is truly senseless.[2]

If the Court were to proceed with that further analysis it would have to conclude, in my view, that this is one of those cases in which the "virtually per se rule of invalidity" does not apply. Facially discriminatory or not, the exemption is no more an artifice of economic protectionism than any state law which dispenses public assistance only to the State's residents.[3] Our cases have always recognized the legitimacy of limiting state-provided welfare benefits to bona fide residents. As JUSTICE STEVENS once wrote for a unanimous Court: "Neither the overnight visitor, the unfriendly agent of a hostile power, the resident diplomat, nor the illegal entrant, can advance even a colorable claim to a share in the bounty that a conscientious sovereign makes available to its own citizens." Mathews v. Diaz, 426 U.S. 67 (1976). States have restricted public assistance to their own bona fide residents since colonial times, see, M. Ierley, With Charity For All, Welfare and Society, Ancient Times to the Present 41 (1984), and such self-interested behavior (or, put more benignly, application of the principle that charity begins at home) is inherent in the very structure of our federal system, cf. Edgar v. MITE Corp., 457 U.S. at 644 ("the State has no legitimate interest in protecting nonresident[s]"). We have therefore upheld against equal protection challenge continuing residency requirements for municipal employment, see McCarthy v. Philadelphia Civil Serv. Comm'n, 424 U.S. 645 (1976), and bona fide residency requirements for free primary and secondary schooling, see Martinez v. Bynum, 461 U.S. 321 (1983).

If the negative Commerce Clause requires the invalidation of a law such as [the exemption], as a logical matter it also requires invalidation of the laws involved in those cases. After all, the Court today relies not on any discrimination against out-of-state nonprofits, but on the supposed discrimination against nonresident would-be *recipients* of charity (the nonprofits' "customers"); surely those individuals are similarly discriminated against in the direct distribution of state benefits. The problem, of course, is not limited to municipal employment and free public schooling, but extends also to libraries, orphanages, homeless shelters and refuges for battered women. One could hardly explain the constitutionality of a State's limiting its provision of these to its own residents on the theory that the State is a "market participant." These are traditional governmental functions, far removed from commercial activity and utterly unconnected to any genuine private market.

2. I do not understand the Court's contention, ante, & n. 16, that Fulton Corp. v. Faulkner, 516 U.S. 325 (1996), provides precedent for such a course. In Fulton, the arguments left unaddressed had not been made in another form, but had not been made at all. There (unlike here) the State *conceded* facial discrimination, and relied exclusively on the compensatory tax defense, see id., which the Court found had not been made out, see id. That narrow defense could not possibly have been regarded as an invocation of broader policy justifications such as those asserted here.

3. In a footnote responding to this dissent, the Court does briefly address whether the statute fails the "virtually per se rule of invalidity." It concludes that it does fail because "Maine has ample alternatives short of a facially discriminatory property tax exemption," such as offering direct cash subsidies to parents of resident children or to camps that serve residents. Ante, n. 16. These are *nonregulatory* alternatives (and hence immune from negative-commerce-clause attack), but they are not *nondiscriminatory* alternatives, which is what the exception to the "virtually per se rule of invalidity" requires. See Oregon Waste, 511 U.S. at 101 (quoting New Energy Co., 486 U.S. at 278). Surely, for example, our decision in Maine v. Taylor, which upheld Maine's regulatory ban on the importation of baitfish, would not have come out the other way if it had been shown that a state *subsidy* of sales of in-state baitfish could have achieved the same goal—by making the out-of-state fish noncompetitive and thereby excluding them from the market even more effectively than a difficult-to-police ban on importation. Where regulatory discrimination against out-of-state interests is appropriate, the negative Commerce Clause is not designed to push a State into nonregulatory discrimination instead. It permits State regulatory action disfavoring out-of-staters where disfavoring them is indispensable to the achievement of an important and nonprotectionist State objective. As applied to the present case: it is obviously impossible for a State to distribute social welfare benefits only to its residents without discriminating against nonresidents.

If, however, a State that provides social services directly *may* limit its largesse to its own residents, I see no reason why a State that chooses to provide some of its social services indirectly–by compensating or subsidizing private charitable providers–cannot be similarly restrictive.[4] In fact, we have already approved it. In Board of Ed. of Ky. Annual Conference of Methodist Episcopal Church v. Illinois, 203 U.S. 553 (1906), we upheld a state law providing an inheritance tax exemption to in-state charities but denying a similar exemption to out-of-state charities. We recognized that such exemptions are nothing but compensation to private organizations for their assistance in alleviating the State's burden of caring for its less fortunate residents, see id., at 561. "[I]t cannot be said," we wrote, "that if a State exempts property bequeathed for charitable or educational purposes from taxation it is unreasonable or arbitrary to require the charity to be exercised or the education to be bestowed within her borders and for her people," id., at 563.[5]

It is true that the opinion in Board of Education addressed only the Equal Protection and Privileges and Immunities Clauses of the Fourteenth Amendment, and not the Commerce Clause. A commerce-clause argument was unquestionably raised by the plaintiff in error, however, in both brief, and oral argument, and the Court could not have reached the disposition it did without

rejecting it. "[T]he Court implicitly rejected [the] argumen[t] . . . by refusing to address [it]." Clemons v. Mississippi, 494 U.S. at 747-748, n. 3. The Commerce Clause objection went undiscussed, I think, because it was (as it is here) utterly contrived: the State's legislated distinction between charity "bestowed within her borders and for her people" and charity bestowed elsewhere or for others did not implicate commerce at all, except to the indirect and permissible extent that innumerable state laws do.

Finally, even if Maine's property tax exemption for local charities constituted facial discrimination against out-of-state commerce, and even if its policy justification (unrelated to economic protectionism) were insufficient to survive our "virtually per se rule of invalidity," cf. Maine v. Taylor, 477 U.S. 131 (1986), there would remain the question whether we should not recognize an additional exception to the negative Commerce Clause, as we have in Tracy. As that case explains, just as a public health justification unrelated to economic protectionism may justify an overt discrimination against goods moving in interstate commerce, "so may health and safety considerations be weighed in the process of deciding the threshold question whether the conditions entailing application of the dormant Commerce Clause are present." 519 U.S. at 307. Today's opinion goes to great length to reject the Town's contention that Maine's property tax exemption does not fall squarely within either the "market participant" or "subsidy" exceptions to the negative Commerce Clause, but never stops to ask whether those exceptions are the only ones that may apply. As we explicitly acknowledge in Tracy–which effectively creates what might be called a "public utilities" exception to the negative Commerce Clause–the "subsidy" and "market participant" exceptions do not exhaust the realm of state actions that we should abstain from scrutinizing under the Commerce Clause. In my view, the provision by a State of free public schooling, public assistance, and other forms of social welfare to only (or principally) its own residents–whether it be accomplished directly or by providing tax exemptions, cash or other property to private organizations that perform the work for the State–implicates none of the concerns underlying our negative-commerce clause jurisprudence. That is, I think, self-evidently true, despite the Court's effort to label the recipients of the State's philanthropy as "customers," or "clientele". Because [the exemption] clearly serves these purposes and has nothing to do with economic protectionism, I believe that it is beyond scrutiny under the negative Commerce Clause.

---

4. It is true, of course, that the legitimacy of a State's subsidizing domestic commercial enterprises out of general funds does not establish the legitimacy of a State's giving domestic commercial enterprises preferential tax treatment. See West Lynn Creamery, Inc. v. Healy, 512 U.S. at 210-212 (SCALIA, J., concurring in judgment). But there is no valid comparison between, on the one hand, the State's giving tax relief to an enterprise devoted to the making of profit and, on the other hand, the State's giving tax relief to an enterprise which, for the purpose at hand, has the same objective as the State itself (the expenditure of funds for social welfare).

5. The Court attempts to distinguish Board of Education on the ground that the statute upheld in that case treated charities differently based on whether they were incorporated within the State, rather than on whether they dispensed charity within the State, see ante, at n. 27. That is quite impossible, inasmuch as we have *held* that out-of-state incorporation is *not* a constitutional basis for discriminating between charities. And in the case that announced that holding (invalidating the denial of a property tax exemption to a nonprofit corporation incorporated in another State), we distinguished Board of Education on the ground that the statute at issue there withheld the exemption "by reason of the foreign corporation's failure or inability to benefit the State in the same measure as do domestic nonprofit corporations." WHYY, Inc. v. Glassboro, 393 U.S. at 120. The Court's analysis contradicts both the holding of this case and its reading of Board of Education–which is obviously the correct one.

* * *

As I have discussed, there are various routes by which the Court could validate the statute at issue here: on the ground that it does not constitute "facial discrimination" against interstate commerce and readily survives the Pike v. Bruce Church balancing test; on the ground that it does constitute "facial discrimination" but is supported by such traditional and important state interests that it survives scrutiny under the "virtually per se rule of invalidity"; or on the ground that there is a "domestic charity" exception (just as there is a "public utility" exception) to the negative Commerce Clause. Whichever route is selected, it seems to me that the quid pro quo exemption at issue here is such a reasonable exercise of the State's taxing power that it is not prohibited by the Commerce Clause in the absence of congressional action. We held as much in Board of Education, and should not overrule that decision.

The State of Maine may have special need for a charitable-exemption limitation of the sort at issue here: its lands and lakes are attractive to various charities of more densely populated Eastern States, which would (if the limitation did not exist) compel the taxpayers of Maine to subsidize their generosity. But the principle involved in our disapproval of Maine's exemption limitation has broad application elsewhere. A State will be unable, for example, to exempt private schools that serve its citizens from State and local real estate taxes unless it exempts as well private schools attended predominantly or entirely by students from out-of-state. A State that provides a tax exemption for real property used exclusively for the purpose of feeding the poor must provide an exemption for the facilities of an organization devoted exclusively to feeding the poor in another country. These results may well be in accord with the parable of the Good Samaritan, but they have nothing to do with the Commerce Clause.

JUSTICE THOMAS, with whom JUSTICE SCALIA joins, and with whom CHIEF JUSTICE REHNQUIST joins as to Part I, dissenting.

The tax at issue here is a tax on real estate, the quintessential asset that does not move in interstate commerce. Maine exempts from its otherwise generally applicable property tax, and thereby subsidizes, certain charitable organizations that provide the bulk of their charity to Maine's own residents. By invalidating Maine's tax assessment on the real property of charitable organizations primarily serving non-Maine residents, because of the tax's alleged *indirect* effect on interstate commerce, the majority has essentially created a "dormant" Necessary and Proper Clause to supplement the "dormant" Commerce Clause. This move works a

significant, unwarranted, and, in my view, improvident expansion in our "dormant," or "negative," Commerce Clause jurisprudence.[1] For that reason, I join JUSTICE SCALIA's dissenting opinion.

I write separately, however, because I believe that the improper expansion undertaken today is possible only because our negative Commerce Clause jurisprudence, developed primarily to invalidate discriminatory state taxation of interstate commerce, was already both overbroad and unnecessary. It was overbroad because, unmoored from any constitutional text, it brought within the supervisory authority of the federal courts state action far afield from the discriminatory taxes it was primarily designed to check. It was unnecessary because the Constitution would seem to provide an *express* check on the States' power to levy certain discriminatory taxes on the commerce of other States–not in the judicially created negative Commerce Clause, but in the Article I, § 10 Import-Export Clause, our decision in Woodruff v. Parham, 75 U.S. 123 (1869), notwithstanding. That the expansion effected by today's decision finds some support in the morass of our negative Commerce Clause case law only serves to highlight the need to abandon that failed jurisprudence and to consider restoring the original Import-Export Clause check on discriminatory state taxation to what appears to be its proper role. As I explain in Part III, the tax (and tax exemption) at issue in this case seems easily to survive Import-Export Clause scrutiny; I would therefore, in all likelihood, sustain Maine's tax under that Clause as well, were we to apply it instead of the judicially created negative Commerce Clause.

I

The negative Commerce Clause has no basis in the text of the Constitution, makes little sense, and has proved virtually unworkable in application. See, e.g., Tyler Pipe Industries, Inc. v. Washington State Dept. of Revenue, 483 U.S. at 259-265 (SCALIA, J., dissenting); Bendix Autolite Corp. v. Midwesco Enterprises, Inc., 486 U.S. at 895-898 (SCALIA, J., concurring in judgment). In one fashion or another, every Member of the current Court and a goodly number of our predecessors have at least

---

1. Although the terms "dormant" and "negative" have often been used interchangeably to describe our jurisprudence in this area, I believe "negative" is the more appropriate term. See Oklahoma Tax Comm'n v. Jefferson Lines, Inc., 514 U.S. at 200 (SCALIA, J., joined by THOMAS, J., concurring in judgment) ("[T]he 'negative Commerce Clause' . . . is 'negative' not only because it negates state regulation of commerce, but also because it does *not* appear in the Constitution"). There is, quite frankly, nothing "dormant" about our jurisprudence in this area. See Eule, Laying the Dormant Commerce Clause to Rest, 91 Yale L. J. 425, 425, n. 1 (1982).

recognized these problems, if not been troubled by them.[4] Because the expansion effected by today's holding further undermines the delicate balance in what we have termed "Our Federalism," Younger v. Harris, 401 U.S. at 44, I think it worth revisiting the underlying justifications for our involvement in the negative aspects of the Commerce Clause, and the compelling arguments demonstrating why those justifications are illusory.

To cover its exercise of judicial power in an area for which there is no textual basis, the Court has historically offered two different theories in support of its negative Commerce Clause jurisprudence. The first theory posited was that the Commerce Clause itself constituted an *exclusive* grant of power to Congress. The "exclusivity" rationale was likely wrong from the outset, however.[6] It was seriously questioned even in early cases. See License Cases, 5 How. 504, 583, 615, 618, 624 (1847) (Four, and arguably five, of the seven participating Justices contending that the Commerce Clause was not exclusive). And, in any event, the Court has long since "repudiated" the notion that the Commerce Clause

---

4. Scholarly commentary, too, has been critical of our negative Commerce Clause jurisprudence. See D. Currie, The Constitution in the Supreme Court: The First Hundred Years 1789-1888, p. 234 (1985) (describing the negative Commerce Clause as "arbitrary, conclusory, and irreconcilable with the constitutional text"); see also, e.g., L. Tribe, American Constitutional Law 439 (2d ed. 1988) ("The Supreme Court's approach to commerce clause issues . . . often appears to turn more on ad hoc reactions to particular cases than on any consistent application of coherent principles"); Redish & Nugent, "The Dormant Commerce Clause and the Constitutional Balance of Federalism," 1987 Duke L. J. 569, 573 ("[N]ot only is there no textual basis [for it], the dormant Commerce Clause actually contradicts, and therefore directly undermines, the Constitution's carefully established textual structure for allocating power between federal and state sovereigns"); B. Gavit, The Commerce Clause of the United States Constitution 22 (1932) (noting that the Court has set "no conscious standard" but has rather, "in an imperial way," decided whether each particular state action presented to it "was or was not an invalid regulation of interstate commerce").

6. See also F. Frankfurter, The Commerce Clause Under Marshall, Taney and Waite 13 (1937) ("The conception that the mere grant of the commerce power to Congress dislodged state power finds no expression" in the records of the Philadelphia Convention nor the discussions preceding ratification); id., at 17-19 (noting that Chief Justice Marshall's discussion of the "exclusiveness" doctrine in Gibbons v. Ogden, 22 U.S. 1 (1824), "was logically irrelevant to [his] holding," and adding that "[i]t was an audacious doctrine, which, one may be sure, would hardly have been publicly avowed in support of the adoption of the Constitution. Indeed, The Federalist in effect denied it, by assuring that only express prohibitions in the Constitution limited the taxing power of the states" (citing The Federalist No. 32)).

operates as an exclusive grant of power to Congress, and thereby forecloses state action respecting interstate commerce. . . .

. . . .

The second theory offered to justify creation of a negative Commerce Clause is that Congress, by its silence, pre-empts state legislation. See Robbins v. Shelby County Taxing Dist., 120 U.S. at 493 (asserting that congressional silence evidences congressional intent that there be no state regulation of commerce). In other words, we presumed that congressional "inaction" was "equivalent to a declaration that inter-State commerce shall be free and untrammeled." Welton v. Missouri, 91 U.S. at 282. To the extent that the "preemption-by-silence" rationale ever made sense, it too has long since been rejected by this Court in virtually every analogous area of the law.

. . . .

Similarly, even where Congress has legislated in an area subject to its authority, our pre-emption jurisprudence explicitly rejects the notion that mere congressional silence on a particular issue may be read as pre-empting state law . . .

To be sure, we have overcome our reluctance to pre-empt state law in two types of situations: (1) where a state law directly conflicts with a federal law; and (2) where Congress, through extensive legislation, can be said to have pre-empted the field. But those two forms of pre-emption provide little aid to defenders of the negative Commerce Clause. Conflict pre-emption only applies when there is a direct clash between an Act of Congress and a state statute, but the very premise of the negative Commerce Clause is the *absence* of congressional action.

Field pre-emption likewise is of little use in areas where Congress has failed to enter the field, and certainly does not support the general proposition of "preemption-by-silence" that is used to provide a veneer of legitimacy to our negative Commerce Clause forays. Furthermore, field pre-emption is itself suspect, at least as applied in the absence of a congressional command that a particular field be pre-empted. Perhaps recognizing this problem, our recent cases have frequently rejected field pre-emption in the absence of statutory language expressly requiring it. Even when an express pre-emption provision has been enacted by Congress, we have narrowly defined the area to be pre-empted.

. . . .

In sum, neither of the Court's proffered theoretical justifications—exclusivity or preemption-by-silence–currently supports our negative Commerce Clause jurisprudence, if either ever did. Despite the collapse of its theoretical foundation, I suspect we have nonetheless adhered to the negative Commerce Clause because we believed it necessary to check state measures contrary to the perceived *spirit*, if not the actual letter, of the Constitution. Thus, in one of our early uses of the negative Commerce Clause, we invalidated a state tax on the privilege of selling goods "which are not the growth, produce, or manufacture of the State." Welton v. Missouri, 91 U.S. at 278. And in Cook v. Pennsylvania, 97 U.S. 566 (1878), we struck down a state tax on out-of-state goods sold at auction. To this day, we find discriminatory state taxes on out-of-state goods to be "virtually per se invalid" under our negative Commerce Clause. See, e.g., West Lynn Creamery, 512 U.S. 186 (1994); Associated Industries, 511 U.S. 641 (1994); New Energy, 486 U.S. 269 (1988); Maryland v. Louisiana, 451 U.S. 725 (1981). Though each of these cases reached what intuitively seemed to be a desirable result–and in some cases arguably was the constitutionally *correct* result, as I describe below–the negative Commerce Clause rationale upon which they rested remains unsettling because of that rationale's lack of a textual basis.

Moreover, our negative Commerce Clause jurisprudence has taken us well beyond the invalidation of obviously discriminatory taxes on interstate commerce. We have used the Clause to make policy-laden judgments that we are ill-equipped and arguably unauthorized to make. See Moorman Mfg., 437 U.S. at 278-280 (recognizing that establishing a formula for apportioning taxes on multistate corporations would require "extensive judicial lawmaking" for which the courts are ill-suited). In so doing, we have developed multifactor tests in order to assess the perceived "effect" any particular state tax or regulation has on interstate commerce. See Complete Auto; see also Quill. And in an unabashedly legislative manner, we have balanced that "effect" against the perceived interests of the taxing or regulating State, as the very description of our "general rule" indicates:

"Where the statute regulates even-handedly to effectuate a legitimate local public interest, and its effects on interstate commerce are only incidental, it will be upheld unless the burden imposed on such commerce is clearly excessive in relation to the putative local benefits. Huron Portland Cement Co. v. Detroit, 362 U.S. 440 (1960). If a legitimate local purpose is found, then the question becomes one of degree. And the extent of the burden that will be tolerated will of course depend on the nature of the local interest involved, and on whether it could be promoted as well with a lesser impact on interstate activities." Pike v. Bruce Church, Inc., 397 U.S. at 142.

Any test that requires us to assess (1) whether a particular statute serves a "legitimate" local public

interest; (2) whether the effects of the statute on interstate commerce are merely "incidental" or "clearly excessive in relation to the putative benefits"; (3) the "nature" of the local interest; and (4) whether there are alternative means of furthering the local interest that have a "lesser impact" on interstate commerce, and even then makes the question "one of degree," surely invites us, if not compels us, to function more as legislators than as judges. See Bendix Autolite Corp. v. Midwesco Enterprises, Inc., 486 U.S. at 897-898 (SCALIA, J., concurring in judgment) (urging abandonment of the Pike balancing test so as to "leave essentially legislative judgments to the Congress").

Moreover, our open-ended balancing tests in this area have allowed us to reach different results based merely "on differing assessments of the force of competing analogies." Oklahoma Tax Comm'n v. Jefferson Lines, Inc., 514 U.S. at 197, n. 7. . . .

. . . .

In my view, none of this policy-laden decision making is proper. Rather, the Court should confine itself to interpreting the text of the Constitution, which itself seems to prohibit in plain terms certain of the more egregious state taxes on interstate commerce described above, and leaves to Congress the policy choices necessary for any further regulation of interstate commerce.

II

Article I, § 10, cl. 2 of the Constitution provides that "[n]o State shall, without the Consent of the Congress, lay any Imposts or Duties on Imports or Exports . . . ." To the 20-century reader, the Clause appears only to prohibit States from levying certain kinds of taxes on goods imported from or exported to *foreign* nations. But a strong argument can be made that for the Constitution's Framers and ratifiers–representatives of States which still viewed themselves as semi-independent sovereigns–the terms "imports" and "exports" encompassed not just trade with foreign nations, but trade with *other States* as well.

The late Professor William Crosskey, in a persuasive treatment of this subject nearly a half-century ago, unearthed numerous Founding-era examples in which the word "import" referred to goods produced in other States. See W. Crosskey, The True Meaning of the Imports and Exports Clause: Herein of "Interstate Trade Barriers" in 1787, 1 Politics and the Constitution in the History of the United States 295-323 (1953). . . .

More significantly, the early statute books are replete with examples of these commonplace 18th-century understandings of the terms "import" and "export Act. . . ."

. . . .

In fact, when state legislators of the founding generation intended to limit the term "imports" only to goods of foreign origin, they were quite adept at so indicating. . . . Thus, based on this common 18th-century usage of the words "import" and "export," and the lack of any textual indication that the Clause was intended to apply exclusively to foreign goods, it seems likely that those who drafted the Constitution sought, through the Import-Export Clause, to prohibit States from levying duties and imposts on goods imported from or exported to other States as well as foreign nations, and that those who ratified the Constitution would have so understood the Clause.

Our Civil War era decision in Woodruff v. Parham, 75 U.S. 123 (1869), of course, held that the Import-Export Clause applied only to foreign trade. None of the parties to these proceedings have challenged that holding, but given that the common 18th-century understanding of the words used in the Clause extended to interstate as well as foreign trade, it is worth assessing the Woodruff Court's reasoning with an eye toward reconsidering that decision in an appropriate case.

The Woodruff Court began with a textual argument, contending that the power to levy "imposts" given to Congress in Art. I, § 8, cl. 1 applied only to foreign imports. Such a limited reading of the word "imposts" in that Clause was necessary, the Court claimed, because any other reading would be nonsensical: Goods "imported" by one State from another State, explained the Court, would be an "export" of the State where the goods were produced or grown, and the supposed power given to Congress in Art. I, § 8 to levy an "impost" on such "imports" would be prohibited by the Art. I, § 9 provision that "[n]o Tax or Duty shall be laid on Articles exported from any State." This apparent tension between § 8 and § 9 led the Court to believe that the word "imposts" in § 8 must be read as applying only to foreign imports in order to avoid a partial negation of the Art. I, § 8 power. The Court then extrapolated from this reading that the word "impost" in Art. I, § 10 similarly had the same limited application to foreign imports. As we have already seen, however, the word "import" derived its meaning from the jurisdiction into which goods were imported; consequently, it does not necessarily follow that the imports on which Congress was given the power to lay "imposts" in Art. I, § 8 were identical to the imports and exports on which the

several States were prohibited from levying "Imposts or Duties" by Art. I, § 10.[12]

The Woodruff Court bolstered its textual argument with two further arguments, neither of which appear still to be valid, if ever they were: First, that in the history of the Constitution's formation and adoption, "the words imports and imposts were used with *exclusive* reference to articles imported from foreign countries," id., at 133 (emphasis added), and second, the policy concern that goods imported from other States would be forever exempt from tax if the Clause were read to apply to interstate imports.

. . . .

There is, of course, no question that the ability of seaport States to tax the foreign imports of their neighbors was a source of discord between the States, and continued to be so through the Constitutional Convention itself. In order to support its contention, however, the Woodruff Court was obligated to show not merely that the words "duty," "impost," and "imports" were used in reference to foreign goods, but that foreign goods were the *exclusive* reference. Contrary to the Woodruff Court's claim, the historical record does not appear to support such an exclusive use of the words.

. . . .

Justice Nelson, of course, pointed out in his Woodruff dissent that a lack of "security or protection" against "obstructions and interruptions of commerce among the States" was "one of the principal grievances that led to the Convention of 1787, and to the adoption of the Federal Constitution." Woodruff, 8 Wall., at 140-141. But he seems not to have had in his arsenal many of the historical materials . . . which indicate that the *words* used in the Import-Export Clause encompassed, at the time the Constitution was written, both interstate and foreign trade. Indeed, the Woodruff majority itself felt compelled to note that its "research [had] extended" only so far as permitted by "the discussions on this subject, as they have come down to us from that time." Id., at 136; see also id., at 134 (referring to the "imperfectly . . . preserved" discussions of the Continental Congress). Whatever the cause, the

---

12. Even assuming that the word "impost" in the two Clauses applied to the same class of "imports," there is nothing nonsensical in reading "impost" in Art. I, § 8 as applicable to interstate as well as foreign trade. It is frequently the case that a broad grant of power in one Clause is restricted by another Clause. Moreover, a State could also import goods from a federal territory, and the congressional power to lay an impost on such (non-foreign) trade would not run afoul of the Art. I, § 9 prohibition.

Woodruff Court's analysis of the historical usage of the words overlooked many contrary examples and is thus not especially compelling.

The second contention that the Woodruff Court used to bolster its textual argument was a policy concern based on an unnecessarily broad view of the Import-Export Clause's prohibition. The Woodruff Court believed that the prohibition on "Duties or Imposts on Exports or Imports" exempted imported articles, and the merchants who traded in them, from state taxation of *any* kind, at least so long as they remained in their original packages. Id., at 137. This view of the Clause's prohibition would result in "the grossest injustice," said the Court, were the Clause to be read as applying to "articles brought from one State into another," for "[n]either the State nor the city which protects [the import merchant's] life and property [could] make him contribute a dollar to support its government." Ibid.

Woodruff's broad reading of the Clause's prohibition was explicitly adopted three years later in Low v. Austin, 80 U.S. 29 (1872), a case involving foreign imports. But we expressly overruled Low 20 years ago, in Michelin Tire Corp. v. Wages, 423 U.S. at 279, holding that the Import-Export Clause "cannot be read to accord imported goods preferential treatment that permits escape from uniform taxes imposed without regard to foreign origin for services which the State supplies," id., at 287; cf. United States v. International Business Machines Corp., 517 U.S. at 858 (distinguishing Art. I, § 9, cl. 5 Export Clause, which bars the United States from imposing any *tax* on exports, from the Import-Export Clause, which prohibits States from levying only *duties* and *imposts*). While Michelin and Low dealt with foreign imports, the expansive interpretation of the Import-Export Clause's prohibition rejected by Michelin was the same interpretation that gave the Woodruff Court pause and that seems to have been an impetus to its refusal to read the Clause as applying to imports from other States. Thus, after Michelin, the second argument the Woodruff Court used to bolster its weak textual analysis--that it would be a gross injustice to prohibit States from <u>levying</u> *any* taxes on goods which were produced in other States--no longer has any force.

. . . .

In sum, it would seem that Woodruff was, in all likelihood, wrongly decided. Of course, much of what the Import-Export Clause appears to have been designed to protect against has since been addressed under the negative Commerce Clause. As the majority recognizes, discriminatory State taxation of interstate commerce is one of the core pieces of our negative Commerce Clause jurisprudence. Were it simply a matter of invalidating state laws under one clause of the Constitution rather than another, I might be inclined to leave well enough alone. Indeed, our rule that state taxes that discriminate against interstate commerce are virtually per se invalid under the negative Commerce Clause may well approximate the apparent prohibition of the Import-Export Clause itself. But, as already described, without the proper textual roots, our negative Commerce Clause has gone far afield of its core–and we have yet to articulate either a coherent rationale for permitting the courts effectively to legislate in this field, or a workable test for assessing which state laws pass negative Commerce Clause muster. Precedent as unworkable as our negative Commerce Clause jurisprudence has become is simply not entitled to the weight of stare decisis. And it is quite possible that, were we to revisit Woodruff, we might find that the Constitution already affords us a textual mechanism with which to address the more egregious of State actions discriminating against interstate commerce.

III

Were we thus to shed ourselves of our nontextual negative Commerce Clause and all the accompanying multi-factor balancing tests we have employed, and instead merely apply what appears to me to be the relevant provision of the Constitution, this would seem to be a fairly straightforward case (although I reserve final judgment of the matter for a case when the Import-Export Clause is specifically addressed by the parties). Unlike the Export Clause of Art. I, § 9, which prohibits the Congress from levying *any* tax on exports, the Import-Export Clause only prohibits States from levying "duties" and "imposts."

The Maine property tax at issue here is almost certainly not an impost, for, as 18th-century usage of the word indicates, an impost was a tax levied on *goods* at the time of *importation*. Because the tax at issue here is levied on real property–property that cannot possibly have been "imported"–the tax would not seem to fit within any of the commonly accepted definitions of "impost."

"Duty," however, though frequently used like "impost" to denote "money paid for custom of goods," An Universal Etymological English Dictionary, does not appear to have been limited to taxes assessed at portside. In fact, "imposts" seems to have been viewed as a particular subclass of duties; the fact that the two words are used disjunctively in the Import-Export Clause suggests, therefore, that something broader than portside customs was within the constitutional prohibition.

. . . .

The tax at issue here is nothing more than a tax on real property. Such taxes were classified as "direct" taxes at the time of the Framing, and were not within the class of "indirect" taxes encompassed by the common understanding of the word "duties." The amount of the Maine tax is tied to the value of the real property on which it is imposed, not to any particular goods, and not even to the number of campers served. It does not appear, therefore, to be a "duty" on "imports" in any sense of the words. Even when coupled with the tax exemption for certain Maine charities (which is, in truth, no different than a subsidy paid out of the State's general revenues), Maine's property tax would not seem to be a "Duty or Impost on Imports or Exports" within the meaning of the Import-Export Clause. Thus, were we to overrule Woodruff and apply the Import-Export Clause to this case, I would in all likelihood sustain this tax under that Clause as well.

Questions and Comments

1. Consider the effect of this case on the definition of interstate commerce. Do residents of State A working in State B constitute interstate commerce? For purposes of the federal income tax, would such persons get to deduct their cost of commuting or would their decision to live in State A be viewed as an inherently personal one? Does the answer to that question have any bearing on how commuters should be viewed for purposes of the Commerce Clause? See *Tamagini v. N.Y. Tax Appeals Tribunal*, 695 N.E.2d 1125 (1998). See also *Luther v. Minn.*, 588 N.W.2d 502, cert. den., 528 U.S. 821 (1999).

2. Was the Maine statute internally consistent? Was it facially discriminatory?

3. Could the exemption be viewed as a subsidy favoring Maine residents? If so, would the exemption have been upheld under *New Energy* ("[d]irect subsidization of domestic industry does not ordinarily run afoul" of the Commerce Clause)?

4. One commentator compared Justice Stevens' describing the Maine statute as an export tariff to describing the New York City bridge and tunnel tolls as impermissibly burdening N.J. residents' access to entertainment in Manhattan. See Lee A. Sheppard, *Supreme Court Overextends the Negative Commerce Clause*, State Tax Notes, June 4, 1997. Do you agree?

In what sense was the Maine statute an export tariff? Do tariffs normally apply to exports?

5. Suppose after this case Maine were to limit its exemption to camps that charged less than $100 per week and it turned out that these camps disproportionately catered to Maine residents. Would this revised statute be constitutional?

6. Will this case have the effect of requiring Maine taxpayers to subsidize campers from other states? Would it be constitutional if Maine were to subsidize with a cash grant its low-income residents that went to camp in Maine?

7. Is this case consistent with *GM v. Tracy*? Are Maine charities catering to residents similarly situated to the plaintiffs in *GM*? Does it matter? How should a court decide whether two groups are similarly situated?

8. Did the *GM* majority think it was creating a public utilities exception to the negative Commerce Clause, as Justice Scalia suggests?

9. Did the plaintiffs merely package an equal protection argument in the cloak of the Commerce Clause?

10. During oral argument, Justice Scalia was reported as saying: "It seems to me [the statute] is more trouble than it's worth. Maybe we should strike it down for foolishness." State Tax Notes, Oct. 11, 1996. Is his opinion consistent with this view? Would Justice Scalia allow Illinois to deny a property tax exemption to the University of Chicago because so many of its students are from out-of-state?

11. What is the remedy the State should pursue after this case? Does the exemption apply to all camps or to no camps?

12. Suppose a state allows taxpayers to deduct a charitable contribution in calculating their state income tax. Could the deduction be granted only for contributions to Maine charities?

13. Is there any doubt that the Commerce Clause applies to nonprofits? Doesn't the Commerce Clause apply to the states? Aren't the states nonprofits?

14. Should the plaintiffs have cited *United States v. Sirois*, 87 F 3d. 34 (2nd Cir. 1996)?

15. Writing in the New York Times, columnist Anthony Lewis described Justice Thomas' dissent as an example of judicial activism. "Conservatives attack 'judicial activists' as if that breed consisted of liberal judges. In fact, some of the most radical, precedent-breaking ideas these days come from judges called conservative. As Thomas'

opinion shows, they may not stop short of ideas that could Balkanize the United States." N.Y. Times, June 2, 1997, p. 15A. Is this a fair characterization of Justice Thomas' dissent?

16. *Heart of Atlanta Motel,* referred to by the majority, upheld the constitutionality of the Civil Rights Act of 1964. Attorney General Kennedy began his argument by stating that the public accommodations provisions of the Act "were addressed to a commercial problem of grave national significance." Quoted in Bittker On The Regulation of Interstate and Foreign Commerce (1999), p. 2-21. He referred to the "the overwhelming evidence of the disruptive effect that racial discrimination has had on commercial intercourse." Id. Rather than the government's approach of relying on the Commerce Clause, some of the advocates of the Act preferred resting its constitutionality on Section 5 of the Fourteenth Amendment.

The Civil Rights Act of 1964 prohibits racial discrimination by any restaurant "if it serves or offers to serve interstate travelers or if a substantial portion of the food which it serves has moved in commerce." In *Katzenbach v. McClung,* 379 U.S. 294 (1964), the Court upheld the enforcement of the Act against Ollie's Barbecue. Ollie's was a local restaurant in Birmingham, Alabama, located about eleven blocks from an interstate highway. The Court conceded that "viewed in isolation, the volume of goods purchased by Ollie's Barbecue from sources supplied from out of state was insignificant when compared with the total food stuffs moving in commerce," nonetheless, a customer's contribution to interstate commerce "taken together with that of many others similarly situated, is far from trivial." Id. at 382, quoting Wickard, 317 U.S. at 127-128. These cases suggest that Congress has virtually unlimited powers under the Commerce Clause. Recent cases raise some doubts, albeit not involving taxation. For example, in *U.S. v. Morrison,* 529 U.S. 598 (2000), the Court held that Congress could not provide under the Commerce Clause a remedy for victims of gender-motivated crimes because there was not substantial effect on interstate commerce. See also *U.S. v. Lopez,* 514 U.S. 549 (1995) (Congress cannot prohibit under the Commerce Clause possession of firearms in school zones).

17. *Camps NewFound/Owatonna* was cited by *American Libraries Ass'n v. Pataki,* 969 F. Supp. 160 (S.D.N.Y. 1997) in support of the proposition that the Internet was an instrument of interstate commerce, albeit an innovative one. Id. at 173.

18. Revisit the cases invoking the negative Commerce Clause to strike down a state statute. How many of these would come out differently under Justice Thomas' approach?

19. For critical commentary on *Camps Newfound/Owatonna,* see Brannon P. Denning, *Justice Thomas, The Import-Export Clause, and Camps Newfound/Owatonna v. Harrison,* 70 U. Colo. L. Rev. 155 (1998); Karin J. Kysilka, *Recent Development: A Jurisdictional Vacuum in the Wake of Camps Newfound/Owatonna?: Camps Newfound/Owatonna v. Town of Harrison,* 21 Harv. J.L. & Pub. Pol'y 288 (1997); Evelyn Brody, *Nonprofit Symposium: Hocking the Halo: Implications of the Charities' Winning Briefs in Camps Newfound/Owatonna, Inc.,* 27 Stetson L. Rev. 433 (1997).

Chapter 2

Equal Protection

"[Nor] shall any State . . . deny to any person within its jurisdiction the equal protection of the laws."U.S. Const., amend. XIV, §1.

Law cannot function without drawing distinctions. To impose a speed limit, for example, those who drive above the limit must be treated differently from those who drive within the limit. The tax laws are replete with distinctions and classifications. An income tax treats high-income individuals differently from those with low incomes. Capital gains are taxed differently from other types of income. A sales tax treats tangible property differently from intangible property and from services.[1]

Because the law must draw lines, the Equal Protection Clause generally does not prohibit state legislatures from crafting legislation that draws distinctions among classes of individuals. Unless a classification scheme implicates the exercise of a fundamental right or categorizes persons on the basis of an inherently suspect characteristic, the Court has interpreted the Equal Protection Clause as requiring only that the distinctions drawn by a statute rationally further a legitimate state interest. A statute will be upheld under the Equal Protection Clause provided: a plausible policy reason exists for the classification; a rational legislator could have considered the facts on which the classification is based to be true; and the classification used to further the statutory goal is not so tenuous as to be arbitrary or irrational.[2]

The Court is especially deferential to a legislature in applying these standards to tax laws. The Court generally does not wish to second-guess a legislature on the innumerable exemptions, deductions, special rates, and other differential treatment, often highly technical in nature, which characterize most tax law. Nevertheless, statutes that distinguish between residents and nonresidents or between persons engaged in in-state and out-of-state activities are likely to receive special scrutiny, even though these have not been held to constitute suspect classes.

To be sure, statutes that facially discriminate against persons engaged in out-of-state activities are usually struck down under the Commerce Clause.[3] In striking down these discriminatory statutes, the commerce clause cases probably reach the same results that would have been reached under the Equal Protection Clause if the class of persons engaged in out-of-state activities were treated as a suspect group.[4]

Sometimes, however, the Commerce Clause does not apply to the taxpayer. For example, under federal legislation the Commerce Clause is inapplicable to the insurance industry.[5] In this situation, the Court has seemed to use the Equal Protection Clause as a surrogate Commerce Clause.[6] In addition, some of the older cases involving discrimination against persons engaged in out-of-state activities were brought by the taxpayer under the Equal Protection Clause, perhaps because of doubts about whether the facts at issue would fall within the Court's evolving commerce clause doctrine.[7]

---

3. See, e.g., Boston Stock Exchange v. State Tax Commission, Maryland v. Louisiana, Bacchus Imports v. Dias, New Energy Co. v. Limbach, in the Commerce Clause chapter.

4. A taxpayer asserting a claim that the Commerce Clause is violated can typically reformulate it as a claim that the Equal Protection Clause is violated. Nothing would be gained from this reformulation because of the lower level of scrutiny that would usually accompany the Court's equal protection analysis.

5. See Western & Southern Life Insurance Co. v. State Board of Equalization, infra this chapter.

6. See Metropolitan Life Insurance Co. v. Ward, infra this chapter. But compare Western & Southern Life, supra note 5.

7. See, e.g., Wheeling Steel Corp. v. Glander, infra this chapter. In a recent case, MCI successfully argued that Ohio denied it equal protection of the laws by assessing its equipment for personal property taxes at 100% of true value while assessing its competitor's at 31% of true value. MCI Telecommunications Corp. v. Limbach, 625 N.E. 2d 597 (1994). Both MCI and its competitors were conducting an interstate business. The Court has previously held that a state cannot discriminate between two kinds of interstate businesses, Boston Stock Exchange et al.

---

1. See the chapter entitled, Sales Taxes: Introduction.

2. Nordlinger v. Hahn, infra this chapter.

Perhaps for similar reasons, taxpayers have challenged classifications that discriminated against nonresidents under the Equal Protection Clause and not the Commerce Clause.[8] In these cases, the Court also seems to have applied an equal protection analysis as a substitute for a commerce clause analysis.

Although the Court has not explicitly defined nonresidents as a suspect class, its holdings are consistent with that approach.[9] Moreover, the implicit treatment of nonresidents as a suspect class is also consistent with the Court's analysis under the Privileges and Immunities Clause. [10]

v. State Tax Commission, 429 U.S. 318 (1977), but that opinion involved a facially discriminatory statute. The Pennsylvania statutes challenged by MCI did not distinguish between two kinds of interstate businesses. Rather, the statutes classified MCI's property as public utility property whereas its competitor's property was classified as general business property. Accordingly, the statutory scheme did not facially discriminate between two types of interstate businesses, although that was the result of the differences in classification.

8. See, e.g., WHYY, Inc. v. Borough of Glassboro, infra this chapter.

9. See, e.g., Wheeling Steel Corp. v. Glander; WHYY, Inc. v. Borough of Glassboro; Williams v. Vermont; infra this chapter.

10. See, e.g., Travis v. Yale & Towne Manufacturing Co., Austin v. New Hampshire, and Lunding v. New York in the Privileges & Immunities Clause chapter.

Wheeling Steel Corp. v.
Glander, Tax Commissioner of Ohio

Supreme Court of the United States, 1949.
337 U.S. 562, 69 S. Ct. 1291, 93 L. Ed. 1544.

MR. JUSTICE JACKSON delivered the opinion of the Court.

The State of Ohio has laid an ad valorem tax against certain intangible property, consisting of notes, accounts receivable and prepaid insurance, owned by foreign corporations. As applied to appellants in these two cases, the tax is challenged as violating the Federal Constitution on several grounds which may conveniently be considered in a single opinion. Facts are not in dispute.

Appellant Wheeling Steel Corporation is organized under the laws of Delaware, where it maintains a statutory office. Ohio has authorized it to do business in that State and four of its eight manufacturing plants are located there. General offices, from which its entire business is controlled and conducted, are in Wheeling, West Virginia. Its officers there have custody of its money, notes and books of account. In twelve other states, including Ohio, it maintains sales offices which solicit and receive orders for its products subject to acceptance or rejection at the Wheeling office, to which all are forwarded. From this office only may credit be extended to purchasers. Accounts are billed and collected from the Wheeling office and the sales offices have no powers or duties with respect to collection. All accounts or notes receivable are payable at Wheeling, where the written evidences thereof are kept. Proceeds from receivables are taken into appellant's treasury at Wheeling and there applied to general purposes of the business.

. . . .

The Ohio Tax Commissioner, applying §§ 5328-1 and 5328-2 of the General Code of Ohio,[1] assessed for taxation in Ohio a large amount of notes and accounts receivable which each appellant derived from shipments originating at Ohio manufacturing plants. The specific ground stated for assessment was that such receivables "result from the sale of property from a stock of goods maintained within this state."

. . . .

The Ohio statutory scheme assimilates its own corporate creations to natural residents and all others to nonresidents. While this classification is a permissible basis for some different rights and liabilities, we have held, as to taxation of intangibles, that the federal right of a nonresident "is the right to equal treatment." Hillsborough v. Cromwell, 326 U.S. at 623.

The certificate of the Tax Commissioner discloses how fundamentally discriminatory is the application of this ad valorem tax to intangibles when owned by a resident or a domestic corporation as contrasted with its application when those are owned by a domesticated corporation or a nonresident. If on the taxing date one of these petitioners and an Ohio competitor each owns an account receivable of the same amount from the same out-of-state customer for the same kind of commodity, both shipped from a manufacturing plant in Ohio and both sold out of Ohio by an agent having an office out of the State, appellant's account receivable would be subject to Ohio's ad valorem tax and the one held by the competing domestic corporation would not. It seems

---

1. Pertinent parts of the Ohio law read as follows:

"SEC. 5328-1. . . . Property of the kinds and classes mentioned in section 5328-2 of the General Code, used in and arising out of business transacted in this state by, for or on behalf of a non-resident person . . . shall be subject to taxation; and all such property of persons residing in this state used in and arising out of business transacted outside of this state by, for or on behalf of such persons . . . shall not be subject to taxation.

. . . .

"SEC. 5328-2. . . . Property of the kinds and classes herein mentioned, when used in business, shall be considered to arise out of business transacted in a state other than that in which the owner thereof resides in the cases and under the circumstances following:

"In the case of accounts receivable, when resulting from the sale of property sold by an agent having an office in such other state or from a stock of goods maintained therein, or from services performed by an officer, agent or employee connected with, sent from, or reporting to any officer or at any office located in such other state.

. . . .

"The provisions of this section shall be reciprocally applied, to the end that all property of the kinds and classes mentioned in this section having a business situs in this state shall be taxed herein and no property of such kinds and classes belonging to a person residing in this state and having a business situs outside of this state shall be taxed. It is hereby declared that the assignment of a business situs outside of this state to property of a person residing in this state in any case and under any circumstances mentioned in this section is inseparable from the assignment of such situs in this state to property of a person residing outside of this state in a like case and under similar circumstances. . . ."

. . . .

obvious that appellants are not accorded equal treatment, and the inequality is not because of the slightest difference in Ohio's relation to the decisive transaction, but solely because of the different residence of the owner.

The State does not seriously deny this unequal application of its own tax but claims that reciprocity provisions of the statute reestablish equality. Those provisions therefore require scrutiny.

This entire taxing plan rests on a statutory formula for fixing situs of intangible property both within and without the State. This is provided by § 5328-2 of the Code. These intangibles "shall be considered to arise out of business transacted *in a state other than that in which the owner thereof resides*" under certain circumstances. (Emphasis supplied.) This basic rule separates the situs of intangibles from the residence of their owner whereas it has traditionally been at such residence, though with some exceptions. The effect is that intangibles of nonresident owners are assigned a situs within the taxing reach of Ohio while those of its residents are assigned a situs without. The plan may be said to be logically consistent in that, while it draws all such intangibles of non-residents within the taxing power of Ohio, it by the same formula excludes those of residents. The exempted intangibles of residents are offered up to the taxing power of other states which may embrace this doctrine of a tax situs separate from residence. This is what is meant here by reciprocity, and the two provisions are declared inseparable; so that if the formula by which Ohio takes unto itself the accounts of nonresidents is held invalid, "such decision shall be deemed also to affect such provision as applied to property of a resident."

It is hard to see that this offer of reciprocity restores to appellants any of the equality which the application of the Ohio tax, considered alone, so obviously denies. There is no indication of a readiness by other states to copy Ohio's situs scheme so as to tax that which Ohio exempts. The proffered exchange of residents for intangible tax purposes may not commend itself as an even bargain between states. Ohio, being large, populous and highly industrialized, with heavy and basic industries, may well have much more to gain from a plan the effect of which is to tax credit exports to other states, than most states would have from a privilege to tax its own exports into Ohio. In the several years that the Ohio statute has been on the books, no other state has sought to take advantage of the "reciprocity" proffer. And if it did, the equality of rates which would also be necessary to equalize the burden between nonresidents and their resident competitors could be hardly expected nor is it provided for. Far from acceding to the situs doctrine which allocates these receivables to Ohio, the State of West Virginia stands on the very different situs doctrine approved by this Court in Wheeling Steel Corp. v. Fox, 298 U.S. 193, and under its authority has for the year in question taxed *all* of the receivables of the Wheeling Company, including those Ohio seeks to claim as having situs in Ohio. It is clear that this plan of "reciprocity" is not one which by credits or otherwise protects the nonresident or foreign corporation against the discriminations apparent in the Ohio statute. We think these discriminations deny appellants equal protection of Ohio law.

The judgments are reversed and the causes remanded for proceedings not inconsistent herewith.

[Concurring opinion by Mr. Justice Jackson and dissenting opinion by Mr. Justice Douglas, with whom Mr. Justice Black concurs, omitted.]

Questions and Comments

1. Does this case hold that the business situs of accounts receivables for purposes of an ad valorem tax cannot be a state other than the state of residence of the taxpayer? What is the state of residence of a corporation?

2. As a normative matter, where should intangibles be taxable?

3. Under the Ohio statute, does the ad valorem tax apply to the accounts receivable generated by an Ohio corporation shipping goods from Ohio that were sold by an agent with an office outside Ohio? Does the tax apply to an Ohio corporation shipping goods from outside Ohio that were sold by an agent with an office in Ohio? Would a corporation incorporated outside of Ohio be taxable in these situations?

4. Does the Ohio tax apply to a nonresident corporation shipping goods from Ohio that were sold by an agent outside Ohio? That shipped goods from out-of-state that were sold by an agent having an

office in Ohio?

5. Would the Ohio statute have been held constitutional if by the time the case had reached the Supreme Court all other states had adopted similar statutes? Why did no other state adopt the Ohio approach?

Should the constitutionality of a state's tax statute ever be contingent on the tax laws of other states?

6. If all states adopted the Ohio statute, would any double taxation of account receivables result? Consider a corporation resident in New York shipping goods from Ohio that were sold by an agent with an office in Pennsylvania. Would Ohio have taxed the receivables? Would Pennsylvania? How critical was it to the Court's analysis that West Virginia was also taxing these account receivables? What was West Virginia's claim to tax the account receivables?

7. Was the Ohio statute internally consistent? Externally consistent? Did the Ohio statute violate the Commerce Clause?

8. Why didn't Ohio tax resident corporations on their account receivables under the same circumstances in which it taxed nonresidents?

9. Could Ohio's statute be defended as a tax incentive for corporations to incorporate in Ohio? Why does Ohio care whether corporations are incorporated in Ohio or elsewhere? Was the Court wrong in not determining whether there were any other conceivable purposes that might have provided a rationale for the Ohio statute?

10. For critical commentary on *Wheeling Steel*, see Edward K. Halaby, *Another Chapter in the Wheeling Steel Litigation*, 18 U. Cin. L. Rev. 489 (1949).

Allied Stores of Ohio, Inc. v. Bowers, Tax Commissioner of Ohio
Supreme Court of the United States, 1959.
358 U.S. 522, 79 S. Ct. 437, 3 L. Ed. 2d 480.

MR. JUSTICE WHITTAKER delivered the opinion of the Court.

. . . Allied Stores of Ohio, Inc., an Ohio corporation, owns and operates a department store in each of four Ohio cities. It also maintains in each of those cities a private warehouse where it stores stocks of merchandise of the kinds sold in its stores. As needed, merchandise is transferred from the warehouse to the store, and when merchandise is sold by sample in the store–usually a heavy or bulky article–it is delivered from the warehouse directly to the customer.

Ohio Rev. Code Ann., § 5709. 01, provides, inter alia, that "All personal property located and *used in business* in this state [shall be] subject to taxation, regardless of the residence of the owners thereof. . . ."(Emphasis added.) During the tax year involved, § 5701. 08 (A), provided, in pertinent part, that:

"(A) Personal property is 'used' within the meaning of 'used in business' . . . when stored or kept on hand as material, parts, products, or merchandise; *but merchandise or agricultural products belonging to a nonresident of this state is not used in business in this state if held in a storage warehouse for storage only. . . .*"[1] (We have

added the italics, and, as was done by the Supreme Court of Ohio, we will refer to the italicized portion as the "proviso.")

Acting under those statutes, appellee, as Tax Commissioner of Ohio, proposed the assessment of an ad valorem tax against appellant based on the average value of the merchandise that it had stored in its four Ohio warehouses during the tax year ending January 31, 1954. Appellant petitioned the Board of Tax Appeals of Ohio for a redetermination, contending that the property stored in its four warehouses in the tax year involved was "merchandise . . . held in a storage warehouse for storage only," and that because the section exempted nonresidents,[3] but taxed residents, on stocks of merchandise so held, it denied to appellant, a resident of Ohio, the equal protection of the laws guaranteed by the Fourteenth Amendment of the Constitution. . . .

. . . .

. . . Does the proviso exempting "merchandise or agricultural products belonging to a nonresident . . . if

---

1. The unitalicized portion of the statute was enacted in 1931. The italicized clause was added by the Ohio Legislature at its next session in 1933. In September 1955 the section was amended by deleting the italicized clause and inserting the following: "and merchandise or agricultural products shipped

---

from outside of this state and held in this state in a warehouse or a place of storage for storage only and for shipment outside of this state are not used in business in this state."

3. The Supreme Court of Ohio has held that a foreign corporation, although authorized to do and doing a local business in Ohio, is a nonresident within the meaning of the proviso here in question.

held in a storage warehouse for storage only" deny to appellant, a resident of the State, the equal protection of the laws within the meaning of the Fourteenth Amendment? The applicable principles have been often stated and are entirely familiar. The States have a very wide discretion in the laying of their taxes. When dealing with their proper domestic concerns, and not trenching upon the prerogatives of the National Government or violating the guaranties of the Federal Constitution, the States have the attribute of sovereign powers in devising their fiscal systems to ensure revenue and foster their local interests. Of course, the States, in the exercise of their taxing power, are subject to the requirements of the Equal Protection Clause of the Fourteenth Amendment. But that clause imposes no iron rule of equality, prohibiting the flexibility and variety that are appropriate to reasonable schemes of state taxation. The State may impose different specific taxes upon different trades and professions and may vary the rate of excise upon various products. It is not required to resort to close distinctions or to maintain a precise, scientific uniformity with reference to composition, use or value. "To hold otherwise would be to subject the essential taxing power of the State to an intolerable supervision, hostile to the basic principles of our Government and wholly beyond the protection which the general clause of the Fourteenth Amendment was intended to assure." Ohio Oil Co. v. Conway, supra, 281 U.S. at 159.

But there is a point beyond which the State cannot go without violating the Equal Protection Clause. The State must proceed upon a rational basis and may not resort to a classification that is palpably arbitrary. The rule often has been stated to be that the classification "must rest upon some ground of difference having a fair and substantial relation to the object of the legislation." Royster Guano Co. v. Virginia, 253 U.S. at 415. "If the selection or classification is neither capricious nor arbitrary, and rests upon some reasonable consideration of difference or policy, there is no denial of the equal protection of the law." Brown-Forman Co. v. Kentucky, 217 U.S. at 573. That a statute may discriminate in favor of a certain class does not render it arbitrary if the discrimination is founded upon a reasonable distinction, or difference in state policy.

Coming directly to the concrete problem now before us, it has repeatedly been held and appears to be entirely settled that a statute which encourages the location within the State of needed and useful industries by exempting them, though not also others, from its taxes is not arbitrary and does not violate the Equal Protection Clause of the Fourteenth Amendment. Similarly, it has long been settled that a classification, though discriminatory, is not arbitrary nor violative of the Equal Protection Clause of the Fourteenth Amendment if any state of facts reasonably can be conceived that would sustain it.

In the light of the law thus well settled, how stands appellant's case? We cannot assume that state legislative enactments were adopted arbitrarily or without good reason to further some legitimate policy of the State. What were the special reasons, motives or policies of the Ohio Legislature for adopting the questioned proviso we do not know with certainty, nor is it important that we should, for a state legislature need not explicitly declare its purpose. But it is obvious that it may reasonably have been the purpose and policy of the State Legislature, in adopting the proviso, to encourage the construction or leasing and operation of warehouses in Ohio by nonresidents with the attendant benefits to the State's economy, or to stimulate the market for merchandise and agricultural products produced in Ohio by enabling nonresidents to purchase and hold them in the State for storage only, free from taxes, in anticipation of future needs. Other similar purposes reasonably may be conceived.

Therefore, we cannot say that the discrimination. . . was not founded upon a reasonable distinction, or difference in state policy, or that no state of facts reasonably can be conceived to sustain it. For those reasons, it cannot be said, in the light of the settled law as shown by the cases cited, that the questioned proviso was invidious or palpably arbitrary and denied appellant the equal protection of the laws within the meaning of the Fourteenth Amendment.

Appellant heavily relies on Wheeling Steel Corp. v. Glander, 337 U.S. 562. We think that case is not apposite. There Ohio statutes exempted from taxation certain accounts receivable owned by residents of the State but taxed those owned by nonresidents. The statutes, on their face admittedly discriminatory against nonresidents, themselves declared their purpose. That purpose was to proffer to other States a scheme of "reciprocity" for taxing accounts receivable. Ohio argued that the reciprocal character of its statutes eliminated the discriminatory effects against nonresidents, but this Court held that it did not. Having themselves specifically declared their purpose, the Ohio statutes left no room to conceive of any other purpose for their existence. And the declared purpose having been found arbitrarily discriminatory against nonresidents, the Court could hardly escape the conclusion that "the inequality [was] not because of the slightest difference in Ohio's relation to the decisive transaction, but solely because of the different residence of the owner." As we have shown, that is not the situation here. Here the discrimination against residents is not invidious nor palpably arbitrary because, as shown, it rests not upon the "different residence of the owner," but upon a state of facts that reasonably can be conceived to constitute a distinction, or difference in state policy, which the State is not prohibited from separately classifying for purposes of taxation by the Equal Protection Clause of the Fourteenth Amendment.

MR. JUSTICE BRENNAN, with whom MR. JUSTICE HARLAN joins, concurring.

We hold today that Ohio's ad valorem tax law does not violate the Equal Protection Clause in subjecting the property of Ohio corporations to a tax not applied to identical property of non-Ohio corporations. Yet in Wheeling Steel, the Court struck down, as violating the Equal Protection Clause, another provision of Ohio's ad valorem tax law which subjected the property of non-Ohio corporations to a tax not applied to identical property of Ohio corporations.

The question presented in the two cases, if stated generally, and as I shall show, somewhat superficially, is: Measured by the demands of the Equal Protection Clause, is a State constitutionally permitted separately to classify domestic and foreign corporations for the purposes of payment of or exemption from an ad valorem tax? In both cases the distinction complained of as denying equal protection of the laws is that the incidence of the tax in fact turns on "the different residence of the owner." With due respect to my Brethren's view, I think that if this were all that the matter was, Wheeling and this case would be indistinguishable.[3] Therefore, while I agree with my Brethren that the classification is valid in this case, I cannot reach that conclusion without developing the ground on which Wheeling is distinguishable.

Why is the "different residence of the owner" a constitutionally valid basis for Ohio's freeing the property of the foreign corporation from the tax in this case and an invalid basis for its freeing the property of the domestic corporation from the tax involved in the Wheeling case?

I think that the answer lies in remembering that our Constitution is an instrument of federalism. The Constitution furnishes the structure for the operation of the States with respect to the National Government and with respect to each other. The maintenance of the

principles of federalism is a foremost consideration in interpreting any of the pertinent constitutional provisions under which this Court examines state action. Because there are 49 States and much of the Nation's commercial activity is carried on by enterprises having contacts with more States than one, a common and continuing problem of constitutional interpretation has been that of adjusting the demands of individual States to regulate and tax these enterprises in light of the multistate nature of our federation. While the most ready examples of the Court's function in this field are furnished by the innumerable cases in which the Court has examined state taxation and regulation under the Commerce and Due Process Clauses, still the Equal Protection Clause, among its other roles, operates to maintain this principle of federalism.

Viewing the Equal Protection Clause as an instrument of federalism, the distinction between Wheeling and this case seems to me to be apparent. My Brethren's opinion today demonstrates that in dealing with as practical and complex a matter as taxation, the utmost latitude, under the Equal Protection Clause, must be afforded a State in defining categories of classification. But in the case of an ad valorem property tax, Wheeling teaches that a distinction which burdens the property of nonresidents but not like property of residents is outside the constitutional pale. But this is not because no rational ground can be conceived for a classification which discriminates against nonresidents solely because they are nonresidents: could not such a ground be found in the State's benign and beneficent desire to favor its own residents, to increase their prosperity at the expense of outlanders, to protect them from, and give them an advantage over, "foreign" competition? These bases of legislative distinction are adopted in the national policies of too many countries, including from time to time our own, to say that, absolutely considered, they are arbitrary or irrational. The proper analysis, it seems to me, is that Wheeling applied the Equal Protection Clause to give effect to its role to protect our federalism by denying Ohio the power constitutionally to discriminate in favor of its own residents against the residents of other state members of our federation. On the other hand, in the present case, Ohio's classification based on residence operates *against* Ohio residents and clearly presents no state action disruptive of the federal pattern. There is, therefore, no reason to judge the state action mechanically by the same principles as state efforts to favor residents. As my Brethren's opinion makes clear, a rational basis can be found for this exercise by Ohio of the latitude permitted it to define classifications under the Equal Protection Clause. One could, in fact, be found in the concept that it is proper that those who are bound to a State by the tie of residence and accordingly the more permanently receive its benefits are proper persons to bear the

---

3. The statute in Wheeling "discriminated" against nonresidents in the same way that the present statute "discriminates" against residents. What my Brethren describe as the forbidden purpose of the distinction in Wheeling seems to me clearly to be only a rejected argument made by the State to show that there was no discrimination in fact. I see no indication in Wheeling that the Court's condemnation of the tax was based solely on its rejection of the "reciprocity" argument.

primary share of its costs. Accordingly, in this context, it is proper to say that any relief forthcoming must be

obtained from the State Legislature.

Questions and Comments

1. What is the interpretation of "held in a storage warehouse for storage only"? Would another department store, located one block away from Allied and doing business in exactly the same manner as Allied, but incorporated in Delaware, be exempt under the statute?

2. What would have been the remedy if Allied had prevailed in its suit?

3. Why was the statute amended in 1955? Why did Allied continue to litigate this suit after the statute was amended?

4. Why didn't Allied switch its state of incorporation to become eligible for the exemption?

5. Does the exemption inure to the benefit of the owner of the warehouse or to the person storing goods in the warehouse? How does the exemption encourage "the construction or leasing and operation of warehouses in Ohio by nonresidents . . ."?

6. Would the Court have reached the same decision if the Ohio statute had exempted Ohio corporations but taxed nonresident corporations?

7. What standard does the Court apply in evaluating an equal protection challenge? That the classification must have a fair and substantial relation to the object of the legislation? Not be capricious or arbitrary? Must rest upon some reasonable distinction or difference in policy? Not be invidious? Have a rational basis? Not be palpably arbitrary?

8. Would it be fair to summarize Justice Brennan's concurrence as stating that nonresidents, having no representation in a state's legislature, need greater protection against discriminatory legislation than do residents? In other words, the Court should be more

vigilant when reviewing legislation that levies a higher tax burden on nonresidents than when reviewing legislation levying a higher burden on residents.

Is there more force to this view if the taxpayers of concern are individuals? If the suspect legislation affects corporations, is there any reason to think that a corporation incorporated in Delaware is less able to have its views represented at the Ohio Legislature in Columbus than is a corporation incorporated in Ohio? What if most of the largest corporations in the United States are incorporated in Delaware and that primarily smaller, intrastate corporations doing business only in Ohio tend to incorporate in Ohio? Under those facts, which group of corporations is likely to have more access to legislators at the Capitol? Who needs protection from whom?

9. Would Justice Brennan support Justice Marshall's views in *Goldberg v. Sweet*, that the Commerce Clause does not protect state residents from discriminatory taxes?

10. A New Mexico statute granted a tax exemption to Vietnam veterans only if they had resided in the State prior to May 8, 1976, one year and one day after the date designated by President Ford as the last day of the Vietnam era. Constitutional? See *Hooper v. Bernalillo County Assessor*, 472 U.S. 612 (1985).

11. At one time, four justices would have rejected the position endorsed in *Allied* that the Court should accept any conceivable bases for upholding a statute against an equal protection challenge. These justices would have rejected post hoc justifications and would have accepted only those bases that actually did motivate a legislature. See *United States Railroad Retirement Board v. Fritz*, 449 U.S. at 184 (Brennan, J. dissenting); *Schweiker v. Wilson*, 450 U. S. at 245 (Powell, J. dissenting, joined by Brennan, Marshall and Stevens, JJ).

[handwritten: Nonprofit corp - TV station USSC reversed b/c violn EPC - diff residence of owner]

WHYY, Inc. v. Borough of Glassboro et al.
Supreme Court of the United States, 1968.
393 U.S. 117, 89 S. Ct. 286, 21 L. Ed. 2d 242.

PER CURIAM.

The appellant is a nonprofit corporation organized under the laws of Pennsylvania. Under a license issued by the

Federal Communications Commission, it operates a noncommercial television station which broadcasts cultural, recreational, and educational programs. The broadcasting facilities for one of the television channels allocated to the appellant are in New Jersey; on its 50-acre plot in the Borough of Glassboro in that State appellant has erected a transmittal station and a tower. Signals on this channel reach approximately 8,000,000 people in the Delaware Valley area, of whom 29.5% are estimated to live in New Jersey. Some of the programs are designed to appeal especially to the residents of New Jersey. In accordance with New Jersey law, the appellant has registered and qualified to transact business in the State.

In November of 1963 the appellant wrote to the Glassboro Council requesting exemption, as a nonprofit organization, for state real and personal property taxes on its land and facilities for 1964. The request was denied, as was a similar petition to the Gloucester County Tax Board. The Division of Tax Appeals upheld the County Board, and the appellant took a further appeal to the Superior Court. That court held that while the appellant qualified for the exemption in all other respects, the statute exempted only those nonprofit corporations which were incorporated in New Jersey. 91 N. J. Super. 269, 219 A. 2d 893. On appeal to the Supreme Court of New Jersey, the appellant argued for the first time that the statute denied it equal protection of the laws in violation of the Fourteenth Amendment to the Constitution by discriminating against it solely on the basis of its foreign incorporation. The Supreme Court noted that it had discretion not to consider a question not raised in the lower court, but nevertheless proceeded to decide the constitutional question because of its widespread importance. It concluded that the classification was not wholly irrational and sustained the denial of exemption.

. . . .

This Court has consistently held that while a State may impose conditions on the entry of foreign corporations to do business in the State, once it has permitted them to enter, "the adopted corporations are entitled to equal protection with the state's own corporate progeny, at least to the extent that their property is entitled to an equally favorable ad valorem tax basis." Wheeling Steel Corp. v. Glander, 337 U.S. at 571-572. See Reserve Life Ins. Co. v. Bowers, 380 U.S. 258; Hanover Fire Ins. Co. v.

Harding, 272 U.S. 494; Southern R. Co. v. Greene, 216 U.S. 400. Yet New Jersey has denied the appellant a tax exemption which it accords other nonprofit corporations solely because of the appellant's foreign incorporation. This is not a case in which the exemption was withheld by reason of the foreign corporation's failure or inability to benefit the State in the same measure as do domestic nonprofit corporations. Compare Board of Education v. Illinois, 203 U.S. 553. Nor have the appellees advanced any other distinction between this appellant and domestic nonprofit corporations which would justify the inequality of treatment.

The New Jersey Supreme Court concluded that the legislative purpose could reasonably have been to avoid the administrative burden which the taxing authorities would bear if they had to examine the laws of other jurisdictions in order to determine whether a corporation with nonprofit status under those laws would also satisfy New Jersey requirements. But this burden would exist only if a foreign corporation sought exemption in New Jersey on the basis of its nonprofit status at home. It is one thing for a State to avoid this extra burden by refusing to grant such an automatic exemption. It is quite another to deny a foreign corporation an opportunity equivalent to that of a domestic corporation to demonstrate that it meets the requirements for a nonprofit corporation under local law. Neither the New Jersey Supreme Court nor the appellees have suggested that there is any greater administrative burden in evaluating a foreign than a domestic corporation under

Philadelphia Mayor John Street (r) in a forum recorded in the studios of WHYY.

New Jersey law. We must therefore conclude, as we did in Wheeling, that the appellant has not been "accorded equal treatment, and the inequality is not because of the slightest difference in [New Jersey's] relation to the decisive transaction, but solely because of the different

---

*. [Ed. The N. J. statute exempted N. J. nonprofit corporations owning property provided such corporations are authorized to carry out the purposes on account of which the exemption is claimed. The N. J. court stated that WHYY owns property and was authorized to carry out the purposes on account of which the exemption was claimed. If WHYY were incorporated or organized under N. J. law, the court said that it would have qualified for an exemption.]

residence of the owner." 337 U.S. at 572. The judgment of the New Jersey Supreme Court is reversed, and the case is remanded for further proceedings not inconsistent with this opinion.

MR. JUSTICE BLACK dissents from the reversal of this case and would affirm it.

Questions and Comments

1. According to the lower court decision, WHYY did not apply for a tax exemption pursuant to the procedures set forth in New Jersey law, which requires the property owner to submit a statement showing its right to an exemption. Instead, WHYY forwarded to the Glassboro Council a copy of its annual report and charter to demonstrate its nonprofit and educational character. It then requested an exemption from the Glassboro Council, which denied its claim. In the lower court, WHYY argued, *inter alia*, that because it had qualified to transact business in New Jersey by registering with the Secretary of State, it was, in effect, organized under the laws of New Jersey and thus was entitled to an exemption, and that it would be useless for it to go through the meaningless act of incorporating in New Jersey. In upholding the constitutionality of the New Jersey statute, the lower court stated:

The corporation laws of sister states may be less exacting than New Jersey with respect to what organizations qualify as nonprofit. If New Jersey were to grant tax exemptions to foreign non-profit corporations because the state of incorporation deemed them to be nonprofit in nature, it may well be that exemptions would thereby be granted to corporations which, if formed here, would not have a tax exempt status. The Legislature could validly decide that the State should not be burdened with the administrative problem of checking the status of foreign corporations under foreign laws and evaluating them with our requirements. 231 A. 2d 608, 612 (1967).

2. What opportunity was WHYY denied that was available to a N. J. corporation? Exempth from state personal + real prop taxes

3. What arguments can be made to support the proposition that greater administrative burdens are imposed in evaluating whether a foreign rather than a domestic corporation satisfies the nonprofit requirements of New Jersey law? Can Glassboro avoid examining Pennsylvania law?

4. Rather than litigating this suit, should WHYY have incorporated its New Jersey operations?

5. Did the N. J. statute violate the Commerce Clause?

6. In *Board of Education v. Illinois*, referred to in *WHYY*, the Court held that a tax exemption in the Illinois inheritance tax could be limited to Illinois charities. A Kentucky charity challenged Illinois' law. The Court determined that the Kentucky charity was differently situated from Illinois charities because the charter of the former required that its funds be expended solely in Kentucky and because it did not maintain an office or engage in charitable work in Illinois. Does this reasoning add force to the reasoning of the New Jersey lower court in *WHYY*? Does the Illinois statute violate the Commerce Clause?

7. In 1967, New Jersey amended its statute to provide an exemption for "buildings and structures located in this State and used exclusively by a nonprofit association or corporation organized under the law of this or another State for the production and broadcasting of educational television. . ." N. J. Stat. Ann. § 54:4-3. 6a.

Lehnhausen, Director, Department of Local Government Affairs of Illinois v. Lake Shore Auto Parts Co. et al.
Supreme Court of the United States, 1973.
410 U.S. 356, 93 S. Ct. 1001, 35 L. Ed. 2d 351.

MR. JUSTICE DOUGLAS delivered the opinion of the Court. In 1970 the people of Illinois amended its constitution adding Art. IX-A to become effective January 1, 1971, and reading:

"Notwithstanding any other provision of this Constitution, the taxation of personal property by valuation is prohibited as to individuals.

There apparently appeared on the ballot when Art. IX-A was approved the following:

"The amendment would abolish the personal property tax by valuation levied against individuals. It would not affect the same tax levied against corporations and other entities not considered in law to be individuals. The amendment would achieve this result by adding a new article to the Constitution of 1870, Article IX-A, thus setting aside existing provisions of Article IX, Section 1, that require the taxation by valuation of all forms of property, real and personal or other, owned by individuals and corporations."

Respondent Lake Shore Auto Parts Co., a corporation, brought an action against Illinois officials on its behalf and on behalf of all other corporations and "non-individuals" subject to the personal property tax, claiming it violated the Equal Protection Clause of the Fourteenth Amendment since it exempts from personal property taxes all personal property owned by individuals but retains such taxes as to personal property owned by corporations and other "non-individuals." The Circuit Court held the Revenue Act of Illinois, as amended by Art. IX-A, unconstitutional as respects corporations by reason of the Equal Protection Clause of the Fourteenth Amendment.

. . . .

The Equal Protection Clause does not mean that a State may not draw lines that treat one class of individuals or entities differently from the others. The test is whether the difference in treatment is an invidious discrimination. Harper v. Virginia Board of Elections, 383 U.S. at 666. Where taxation is concerned and no specific federal right, apart from equal protection, is imperiled,[3] the States have large leeway in making classifications and drawing lines which in their judgment produce reasonable systems of taxation. As stated in Allied Stores of Ohio v. Bowers, 358 U.S. at 526-527:

"The States have a very wide discretion in the laying of their taxes. When dealing with their proper domestic concerns, and not trenching upon the prerogatives of the National Government or violating the guaranties of the Federal Constitution, the States have the attribute of sovereign powers in devising their fiscal systems to ensure revenue and foster their local interests. Of course, the States, in the exercise of their taxing power, are subject to the requirements of the Equal Protection Clause of the Fourteenth Amendment. But that clause imposes no iron rule of equality, prohibiting the flexibility and variety that are appropriate to reasonable schemes of state taxation. The State may impose different specific taxes upon different trades and professions and may vary the rate of excise upon various products. It is not required to resort to close distinctions or to maintain a precise, scientific uniformity with reference to composition, use or value."

---

3. Classic examples are the taxes that discriminated against newspapers, struck down under the First Amendment (Grosjean v. American Press Co., 297 U.S. 233) or that discriminated against interstate commerce (see Michigan-Wisconsin Pipe Line Co. v. Calvert, 347 U.S. 157) or required license taxes to engage in interstate commerce.

In that case we used the phrase "palpably arbitrary" or "invidious" as defining the limits placed by the Equal Protection Clause on state power. Id., at 530. State taxes which have the collateral effect of restricting or even destroying an occupation or a business have been sustained, so long as the regulatory power asserted is properly within the limits of the federal-state regime created by the Constitution. Magnano Co. v. Hamilton, 292 U.S. at 44-47. When it comes to taxes on corporations and taxes on individuals, great leeway is permissible so far as equal protection is concerned. They may be classified differently with respect to their right to receive or earn income. In Lawrence v. State Tax Comm'n, 286 U.S. at 283, a state statute relieved domestic corporations of an income tax derived from activities carried on outside the State, but imposed the tax on individuals obtaining such income. We upheld the tax against the claim that it violated the Equal Protection Clause, saying:

"We cannot say that investigation in these fields would not disclose a basis for the legislation which would lead reasonable men to conclude that there is just ground for the difference here made. The existence, unchallenged, of differences between the taxation of incomes of individuals and of corporations in every federal revenue act since the adoption of the Sixteenth Amendment, demonstrates that there may be." Id., at 283-284.

It is true that in Quaker City Cab Co. v. Pennsylvania, 277 U.S. 389, the Court held that a gross receipts tax levied on corporations doing a taxi business violated the Equal Protection Clause of the Fourteenth Amendment, when no such tax was levied on individuals and partnerships operating taxicabs in competition with the corporate taxpayers. Justices Holmes, Brandeis, and Stone dissented. Id., at 403-412. Mr. Justice Holmes stated:

"If usually there is an important difference of degree between the business done by corporations and that done by individuals, I see no reason why the larger businesses may not be taxed and the small ones disregarded, and I think it would be immaterial if here and there exceptions were found to the general rule. . . . Furthermore if the State desired to discourage this form of activity in corporate form and expressed its desire by a special tax I think that there is nothing in the Fourteenth Amendment to prevent it." Id., at 403.

Each of these dissenters thought Flint v. Stone Tracy Co., 220 U.S. 107, should govern Quaker City Cab. The Flint case involved a federal tax upon the privilege of doing business in a corporate capacity, but it was not laid on businesses carried on by a partnership or private individual. It was, therefore, contended that the tax was "so unequal and arbitrary" as to be beyond the power of Congress. Id., at 158. We had not yet held that the Fifth Amendment in its use of due process carries a mandate of equal protection.[4] But the Court in dictum stated:

Irv Oppenheim, owner of Lake Shore Auto Parts

"[I]t could not be said, even if the principles of the Fourteenth Amendment were applicable to the present case, that there is no substantial difference between the carrying on of business by the corporations taxed, and the same business when conducted by a private firm or individual. The thing taxed is not the mere dealing in merchandise, in which the actual transactions may be the same, whether conducted by individuals or corporations, but the tax is laid upon the privileges which exist in conducting business with the advantages which inhere in the corporate capacity of those taxed, and which are not enjoyed by private firms or individuals. These advantages are obvious, and have led to the formation of such companies in nearly all branches of trade. The continuity of the business, without interruption by death or dissolution, the transfer of property interests by the disposition of shares of stock, the advantages of business controlled and managed by corporate directors, the general absence of individual liability, these and other things inhere in the advantages of business thus conducted, which do not exist when the same business is conducted by private individuals or partnerships. It is this distinctive privilege which is the subject of taxation, not the mere buying or selling or handling of goods which may be the same, whether done by corporations or individuals." Id., at 161-162.

While Quaker City Cab came after Flint, cases following Quaker City Cab have somewhat undermined it. White River Co. v. Arkansas, 279 U.S. 692, involved a state statute for collection of back taxes on lands owned by corporations but not individuals. The Court sustained the statute. Mr. Justice Butler, Mr, Chief Justice Taft, and Mr. Justice Van Devanter dissented, asserting that Quaker City Cab was not distinguishable. The majority made no effort to distinguish Quaker City Cab beyond saying that it did not involve, as did White River, back taxes. Id., at 696.

In Rapid Transit Co. v. New York, 303 U.S. 573, an excise tax was levied on every utility but not on other business units. In sustaining the tax against the claim of lack of

equal protection, the Court said:

"Since carriers or other utilities with the right of eminent domain, the use of public property, special franchises or public contracts, have many points of distinction from other businesses, including relative freedom from competition, especially significant with increasing density of population and municipal expansion, these public service organizations have no valid ground by virtue of the equal protection clause to object to separate treatment related to such distinctions." Id., at 579.

We reached the same result in Nashville, C. & St. L. R. Co. v. Browning, 310 U.S. 362, where Tennessee had used one system for making assessments under its ad valorem tax law as respects most taxpayers and a totally different one for public service corporations. So far as equal protection was concerned, we said that the grievance of the particular complainant was" common to the whole class" and not "invidious to a particular taxpayer."[5] Id., at 368.

Approval of the treatment "with that separateness" which distinguishes public service corporations from others, ibid., leads us to conclude in the present cases that making corporations and like entities liable for ad valorem taxes on personal property does not transcend the requirements of equal protection.

In Madden v. Kentucky, 309 U.S. 83, a State laid an ad valorem tax of 50¢ per $100 on deposits in banks outside the State and only 10¢ per $1,000 on deposits within the State. The classification was sustained against the charge of invidious discrimination, the Court noting that "in taxation, even more than in other fields, legislatures possess the greatest freedom in classification." Id., at 88. There is a presumption of constitutionality which can be overcome "only by the most explicit demonstration that a classification is a hostile and oppressive discrimination against particular persons and classes." Ibid. And the Court added, "The burden is on the one attacking the legislative arrangement to negative every conceivable

---

4. See Bolling v. Sharpe, 347 U.S. 497, decided May 17, 1954, which held that federal discrimination (in that case racial in nature) may be so arbitrary as to be violative of due process as the term is used in the Fifth Amendment.

5. In Atlantic & Pacific Tea Co. v. Grosjean, 301 U.S. 412, a State classified chain stores for purposes of a chain store tax according to the number of stores–inside and outside the State. The Court sustained the tax, saying:
"The statute bears equally upon all who fall into the same class, and this satisfies the guaranty of equal protection." Id., at 424. In Carmichael v. Southern Coal Co., 301 U.S. 495, a State laid an unemployment tax on employers, excluding, inter alia, agriculture, domestic service, crews of vessels on navigable waters, and eleemosynary institutions. The Court sustained the tax, saying: "This Court has repeatedly held that inequalities which result from a singling out of one particular class for taxation or exemption, infringe no constitutional limitation." Id., at 509. And it added:
"A legislature is not bound to tax every member of a class or none. It may make distinctions of degree having a rational basis, and when subjected to judicial scrutiny they must be presumed to rest on that basis if there is any conceivable state of facts which would support it."

basis which might support it." Ibid. That idea has been elaborated. Thus, in Carmichael v. Southern Coal Co., 301 U.S. 495, the Court, in sustaining an unemployment tax on employers, said:

"A state legislature, in the enactment of laws, has the widest possible latitude within the limits of the Constitution. In the nature of the case it cannot record a complete catalogue of the considerations which move its members to enact laws. In the absence of such a record courts cannot assume that its action is capricious, or that, with its informed acquaintance with local conditions to which the legislation is to be applied, it was not aware of facts which afford reasonable basis for its action. Only by faithful adherence to this guiding principle of judicial review of legislation is it possible to preserve to the legislative branch its rightful independence and its ability to function." Id., at 510.

Illinois tells us that the individual personal property tax was discriminatory, unfair, almost impossible to administer, and economically unsound. Assessment practices varied from district to district. About a third of the individuals paid no personal property taxes at all,

while the rest paid on their bank accounts, automobiles, household furniture, and other resources, and in rural areas they paid on their livestock, grain, and farm implements as well. As respects corporations, the State says, the tax is uniformly enforceable. Illinois says, moreover, that Art. IX-A is only the first step in totally eliminating the ad valorem personal property tax by 1979 but for fiscal reasons it was impossible to abolish the tax all at once.

We could strike down this tax as discriminatory only if we substituted our judgment on facts of which we can be only dimly aware for a legislative judgment that reflects a vivid reaction to pressing fiscal problems. Quaker City Cab Co. v. Pennsylvania is only a relic of a bygone era. We cannot follow it and stay within the narrow confines of judicial review, which is an important part of our constitutional tradition.

Reversed.

Questions and Comments

1. In *Quaker City Cab Co.*, referred to in the opinion, the Pennsylvania statute taxed the gross receipts derived by foreign or domestic corporations from their operation of taxicabs in interstate transportation of passengers. The Court said, "[t]he gross receipts of incorporated operators are taxed while those of natural persons and partnerships carrying on the same business are not. The character of the owner is the sole fact on which the distinction and discrimination are made to depend. The tax is imposed merely because the owner is a corporation. The discrimination is not justified by any difference in the source of the receipts or in the situation or the character of the property employed. It follows that the section fails to meet the requirement that a classification to be consistent with the equal protection clause must be based on a real and substantial difference having reasonable relation to the subject of the legislation." 277 U.S. 402.

2. Could the taxpayer have argued that the tax discrimi-

nated against interstate commerce?

3. Consider a state that has a corporate income tax but no personal income tax. Could a restaurant operating as a corporation successfully argue that the tax violates the Equal Protection Clause because its competitors on the same block operate as proprietorships and therefore have a competitive tax advantage?

4. If the plaintiffs had prevailed, would the constitutionality of the federal corporate income tax have been in jeopardy?

5. For critical commentary on *Lake Shore Auto Parts*, see Rodney J. Blackman, *The Implication of Lehnhausen v. Lake Shore Auto Parts Co. : Weakening or Eliminating Equal Protection for Corporations as a Class*, 16 Ariz. L. Rev. 41 (1974); Shane H. Anderson, *Personal Property Taxes– Lehnhausen v. Lake Shore Auto Parts Co.*, 22 DePaul L. Rev. 630 (1973).

Western & Southern Life Insurance Co. v. State Board of Equalization of California
Supreme Court of the United States, 1981.
451 U.S. 648, 101 S. Ct. 2070, 68 L. Ed. 2d 514.

JUSTICE BRENNAN delivered the opinion of the Court.

California imposes two insurance taxes on insurance

companies doing business in the State. A premiums tax, set at a fixed percentage of premiums paid on insurance policies issued in the State, is imposed on both foreign and domestic insurance companies and a "retaliatory" tax, set in response to the insurance tax laws of the insurer's home State, is imposed on some foreign insurance companies. This case presents the question of the constitutionality of retaliatory taxes assessed by the State of California against appellant Western & Southern Life Insurance Co., an Ohio corporation, and paid under protest for the years 1965 through 1971.

I

Section 685 of the California Insurance Code imposes a retaliatory tax on out-of-state insurers doing business in California, when the insurer's State of incorporation imposes higher taxes on California insurers doing business in that State than California would otherwise impose on that State's insurers doing business in California.[1] In computing the retaliatory tax owed by a given out-of-state insurer, California subtracts the California taxes otherwise due from the total taxes that would be imposed on a hypothetical similar California company doing business in the out-of-state insurer's State of incorporation. If the other State's taxes on the

---

1. "When by or pursuant to the laws of any other state or foreign country any taxes, licenses and other fees, in the aggregate, and any fines, penalties, deposit requirements or other material obligations, prohibitions or restrictions are or would be imposed upon California insurers, or upon the agents or representatives of such insurers, which are in excess of such taxes, licenses and other fees, in the aggregate, or which are in excess of the fines, penalties, deposit requirements or other obligations, prohibitions, or restrictions directly imposed upon similar insurers, or upon the agents or representatives of such insurers, of such other state or country under the statutes of this State, so long as such laws of such other state or country continue in force or are so applied, the same taxes, licenses and other fees, in the aggregate, or fines, penalties or deposit requirements or other material obligations, prohibitions, or restrictions, of whatever kind shall be imposed upon the insurers, or upon the agents or representatives of such insurers, of such other state or country doing business or seeking to do business in California. Any tax, license or other fee or other obligation imposed by any city, county, or other political subdivision or agency of such other state or country on California insurers or their agents or representatives shall be deemed to be imposed by such state or country within the meaning of this article."

This provision was enacted in present form in 1959, pursuant to the California Constitution, Art. XIII, § 14-4/5 (f)(3). At that time, the California Constitution permitted imposition of the retaliatory tax only when the other State taxed California insurers at a higher rate than it taxed its own insurers. See Cal. Const., Art. XIII, § 14-4/5 (f)(3) (West Supp. 1964). In 1964, however, the California Constitution was amended to permit the imposition of the retaliatory tax whenever the other State's taxes on California insurers are higher than California taxes on similar insurers. Cal. Const., Art. XIII, § 14-4/5 (f)(3).

hypothetical California insurer would be greater than California's taxes on the other State's insurer, a retaliatory tax in the amount of the difference is imposed. If the other State's taxes on the hypothetical California insurer would be less than or equal to California's taxes, however, California exacts no retaliatory tax from the other State's insurer.

Western & Southern, an Ohio corporation headquartered in Ohio, has engaged in the business of insurance in California since 1955. During the years in question, the company paid a total of $977,853. 57 to the State in retaliatory taxes. After unsuccessfully filing claims for refunds with appellee Board of Equalization, Western & Southern initiated this refund suit in Superior Court, arguing that California's retaliatory tax violates the Commerce and Equal Protection Clauses of the United States Constitution.

. . . .

III

Ordinarily, there are three provisions of the Constitution under which a taxpayer may challenge an allegedly discriminatory state tax: the Commerce Clause, see, e.g., Complete Auto Transit; the Privileges and Immunities Clause of Art. IV, § 2, see, e.g., Toomer v. Witsell, 334 U.S. 385 (1948); and the Equal Protection Clause, see, e.g., Wheeling Steel Corp. v. Glander, 337 U.S. 562 (1949). This case assumes an unusual posture, however, because the Commerce Clause is inapplicable to the business of insurance, [because of the McCarran Ferguson Act] and the Privileges and Immunities Clause is inapplicable to corporations. Only the Equal Protection Clause remains as a possible ground for invalidation of the California tax.

The Fourteenth Amendment forbids the States to "deny to any person within [their] jurisdiction the equal protection of the laws," but does not prevent the States from making reasonable classifications among such persons. See Lehnhausen v. Lake Shore Auto Parts Co., 410 U.S. at 359-360; Allied Stores of Ohio v. Bowers, 358 U.S. at 526-527. Thus, California's retaliatory insurance tax should be sustained if we find that its classification is rationally related to achievement of a legitimate state purpose.

But as appellee points out, state tax provisions directed against out-of-state parties have not always been subjected to such scrutiny. Rather, a line of Supreme Court cases most recently exemplified by Lincoln National Life Ins. Co. v. Read, 325 U.S. 673 (1945), holds that a State may impose a tax on out-of-state corporations for the "privilege" of doing business in the State, without any requirement of a rational basis. Since the California

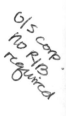

courts have defined the retaliatory tax as a "privilege" tax, application of the reasoning of these cases would require us to sustain the tax without further inquiry into its rational basis. We must therefore decide first whether California's retaliatory tax is subject to such further inquiry.

Some past decisions of this Court have held that a State may exclude a foreign corporation from doing business or acquiring or holding property within its borders. From this principle has arisen the theory that a State may attach such conditions as it chooses upon the grant of the privilege to do business within the State. Paul v. Virginia, 8 Wall., at 181. While this theory would suggest that a State may exact any condition, no matter how onerous or otherwise unconstitutional, from a foreign corporation desiring to do business within it, this Court has also held that a State may not impose *unconstitutional* conditions on the grant of a privilege.[*]

These two principles are in obvious tension. If a State cannot impose unconstitutional conditions on the grant of a privilege, then its right to withhold the privilege is less than absolute. But if the State's right to withhold the privilege is absolute, then no one has the right to challenge the terms under which the State chooses to exercise that right. In view of this tension, it is not surprising that the Court's attempt to accommodate both principles has produced results that seem inconsistent or illogical. Compare Doyle v. Continental Ins. Co., 94 U.S. 535 (1877), with Insurance Co. v. Morse, 20 Wall. 445 (1874); and compare Lincoln National Life Ins. Co. v. Read, supra, with Hanover Fire Ins. Co. v. Harding, 272 U.S. 494 (1926).

The doctrine that a State may impose taxes and conditions at its unfettered discretion on foreign corporations, in return for granting the "privilege" of doing business within the State, originated in Paul v. Virginia, supra, a case decided only 15 months after the effective date of the Fourteenth Amendment. . . .

. . . Viewing corporations as recipients of "special privileges," 8 Wall., at 181, and believing that "it might be of the highest public interest that the number of corporations in the State should be limited," id., at 182, the Court held that a State's assent to the creation of a domestic corporation or the entry of a foreign corporation "may be granted upon such terms and conditions as those States may think proper to impose."

Id., at 181.[10] Under this view, there was no need for the Court to consider whether the statute was arbitrary, irrational, or discriminatory. "[The States] may exclude the foreign corporation entirely; they may restrict its business to particular localities, or they may exact such security for the performance of its contracts with their citizens as in their judgment will best promote the public interest. The whole matter rests in their discretion." Ibid.

In two important respects, the legal underpinnings of Paul v. Virginia were soon eroded. First, the advent of laws of general incorporation, which swept the country in the late 19th century, altered the very nature of the corporation. Such laws, stimulated largely by "the desire for equality and the dread of special privilege[s]," permitted persons to form corporations freely, subject only to generally applicable requirements and limitations. Incorporation lost its status as a special privilege.[11] Second, the Fourteenth Amendment, ratified in 1868, introduced the constitutional requirement of equal protection, prohibiting the States from acting arbitrarily or treating similarly situated persons differently, even *with respect to privileges formerly dispensed at the State's discretion.* The combination of general incorporation laws and equal protection necessarily undermined the doctrine of Paul v. Virginia. If the right to incorporate or to do business within a State ceases to be a privilege to be dispensed by the State as it sees fit, and becomes a right generally available to all on equal terms, then the argument for special exactions as "privilege taxes" is destroyed.

The Court was slow to recognize the consequences of these developments. In Philadelphia Fire Assn. v. New York, 119 U.S. 110 (1886), the first relevant decision governed by the Fourteenth Amendment, the Court unhesitatingly applied the doctrine of Paul v. Virginia to sustain a New York retaliatory insurance tax against an equal protection challenge. . . .

---

10. This view of the corporation reflected the common understanding through the first three-quarters of the 19th century. As Justice Brandeis has noted, "at first, the corporate privilege was granted sparingly; and only when the grant seemed necessary in order to procure for the community some specific benefit otherwise unavailable." Louis K. Liggett Co. v. Lee, 288 U.S. at 549 (dissenting opinion).

11. In 1869, the year Paul v. Virginia was decided, the Commonwealth of Virginia did not permit general incorporation of insurance companies. Thus, the Court's conception of the corporate franchise in that case as a "grant of special privileges to the corporators, was an accurate portrayal of the corporation as it existed at that time. This was not to last for long. See Act of Mar. 30, 1871, 1870 Va. Acts, ch. 277 (general incorporation law made applicable to insurance companies).

---

[*]. [Ed. A state cannot exclude foreign corporations from conducting an interstate business. Western Union Telegraph v. Kansas, 216 U.S. at 33-34, 38-45 (1910).]

[The Court then reviewed the erosion of the Paul v. Virginia doctrine, culminating with Hanover Fire Ins. Co.]

....

After Hanover Fire Ins. Co., little was left of the doctrine of Paul v. Virginia and Philadelphia Fire Assn. v. New York, 119 U.S. 110 (1886). It was replaced by a new doctrine:

> "It is not necessary to challenge the proposition that, as a general rule, the state, having power to deny a privilege altogether, may grant it upon such conditions as it sees fit to impose. But the power of the state in that respect is not unlimited; and one of the limitations is that it may not impose conditions which require the relinquishment of constitutional rights. If the state may compel the surrender of one constitutional right as a condition of its favor, it may, in like manner, compel a surrender of all. It is inconceivable that guaranties embedded in the Constitution of the United States may thus be manipulated out of existence." Frost & Frost Trucking Co. v. Railroad Comm'n, 271 U.S. at 593-594.

The decision in Lincoln National Life Ins. Co. v. Read, 325 U.S. 673 (1945), thus stands as a surprising throwback to the doctrine of Paul v. Virginia and Philadelphia Fire Assn. v. New York. There, the Court seemed to adopt precisely the argument that was rejected in Hanover Fire Ins. Co. : "that a State may discriminate against foreign corporations by admitting them under more onerous conditions than it exacts from domestic companies. . . ." 325 U.S. at 677; cf. 272 U.S. at 507. The Court stated that the argument that a State may not impose unconstitutional conditions to entry "proves too much." 325 U.S. at 677. "If it were adopted," the Court said, "then the long-established rule that a State may discriminate against foreign corporations by admitting them under more onerous conditions than it exacts from domestic companies would go into the discard." Ibid. So long as a tax is "levied upon the privilege of entering the State and engaging in business there," it may not be challenged under the Equal Protection Clause, even though it may impose a burden greater and more discriminatory than was imposed at the date of the corporation's entry into the State. Id., at 678.

The holding in Lincoln National has been implicitly rejected in at least three subsequent cases. In Wheeling Steel Corp. v. Glander, 337 U.S. 562 (1949), the Court struck down a provision of Ohio's ad valorem tax law that subjected certain intangible property of non-Ohio corporations to a tax not applied to identical property of Ohio corporations. The Court concluded that the provision violated the Equal Protection Clause on the ground that the inequality of treatment was "not because of the slightest difference in Ohio's relation to the decisive transaction, but solely because of the

different residence of the owner." Id., at 572.[20] The decision in Wheeling Steel was not directly in conflict with that in Lincoln National, because the Ohio courts had held the tax in Wheeling Steel an "ad valorem property tax . . . and in no sense a franchise, privilege, occupation, or income tax." 337 U.S. at 572. However, the Wheeling Steel decision rejected the *principle* of Lincoln National: the opinion declared that a State's power to exclude out-of-state corporations is limited by the Constitution; the State may not "exac[t] surrender of rights derived from the Constitution of the United States." 337 U.S. at 571 (citing Hanover Fire Ins. Co. v. Harding, supra, at 507).

In Allied Stores of Ohio, Inc. v. Bowers, 358 U.S. 522 (1959), this Court sustained an Ohio statute exempting nonresidents from an ad valorem tax on certain property held in a storage warehouse, but not exempting Ohio residents from the tax. Without alluding to any possibility that legislative classifications based on State of incorporation should be subject to a different standard from other classifications, the Court held that state tax laws "must proceed upon a rational basis and may not resort to a classification that is palpably arbitrary." Id., at 527.[21]

Finally, in WHYY, Inc. v. Glassboro, 393 U.S. 117 (1968), this Court struck down a New Jersey statute exempting nonprofit corporations incorporated in New Jersey from tax, but denying a similar exemption to nonprofit corporations incorporated in other States. Disregarding Lincoln National, the Court stated that applicable principle of law as follows:

> "This Court has consistently held that while a State may impose

---

20. The State argued that other States could enact similar provisions, and thereby eliminate any inequality. This Court concluded, however, that "[i]t is hard to see that this offer of reciprocity restores to appellants any of the equality which the application of the Ohio tax, considered alone, so obviously denies." 337 U.S. at 573.

21. Justice Harlan and I, concurring, went still further. Arguing that the Equal Protection Clause must be used as "an instrument of federalism," 358 U.S. at 532, we rejected the Court's analysis as insufficiently protective of out-of-state interests. We stated that the Equal Protection Clause denies a State "the power constitutionally to discriminate in favor of its own residents against the residents of other state members of our federation." Id., at 533. Our position has not been adopted by the Court, which has subsequently required no more than a rational basis for discrimination by States against out-of-state interests in the context of equal protection litigation. E.g., Baldwin v. Montana Fish and Game Comm'n, 436 U.S. at 388-391; Hughes v. Alexandria Scrap Corp., 426 U.S. at 810-814.

conditions on the entry of foreign corporations to do business in the State, once it has permitted them to enter, 'the adopted corporations are entitled to equal protection with the state's own corporate progeny, at least to the extent that their property is entitled to an equally favorable ad valorem tax basis. ' Wheeling Steel Corp. v. Glander, 337 U.S. 562, 571-572. See Reserve Life Ins. Co. v. Bowers, 380 U.S. 258; Hanover Fire Ins. Co. v. Harding, 272 U.S. 494; Southern R. Co. v. Greene, 216 U.S. 400." 393 U.S. at 119-120.

In view of the decisions of this Court both before and after Lincoln National, it is difficult to view that decision as other than an anachronism. We consider it now established that, whatever the extent of a State's authority to exclude foreign corporations from doing business within its boundaries, that authority does not justify imposition of more onerous taxes or other burdens on foreign corporations than those imposed on domestic corporations, unless the discrimination between foreign and domestic corporations bears a rational relation to a legitimate state purpose. As we held in Power Manufacturing Co. v. Saunders, 274 U.S. at 493-494:

"No doubt there are. . . subjects as to which foreign corporations may be classified separately from both individuals and domestic corporations and dealt with differently. But there are other subjects as to which such a course is not admissible, the distinguishing principle being that classification must rest on differences pertinent to the subject in respect of which the classification is made."

IV

In determining whether a challenged classification is rationally related to achievement of a legitimate state purpose, we must answer two questions: (1) Does the challenged legislation have a legitimate purpose? and (2) Was it reasonable for the lawmakers to believe that use of the challenged classification would promote that purpose? See Minnesota v. Clover Leaf Creamery Co., 449 U.S. at 461-463; Vance v. Bradley, 440 U.S. at 97-98.

The legislative purpose of California's retaliatory tax is not difficult to discern, for such taxes have been a common feature of insurance taxation for over a century. Although variously expressed, the principal purpose of retaliatory tax laws is to promote the interstate business of domestic insurers by deterring other States from enacting discriminatory or excessive taxes. A survey of state retaliatory tax laws summarized:

"[W]hatever their character, it is obvious. . . that their ultimate object is not to punish foreign corporations doing business in the state, or retort the action of the foreign state in placing upon corporations of the enacting state doing business therein burdens heavier than those imposed upon corporations of such foreign state doing business in the enacting state, but to induce such foreign state to show the same consideration to corporations of

the enacting state doing business therein as is shown to corporations of such foreign state doing business in the enacting state." [22]

California's retaliatory tax is based upon a model statute drafted by the insurance industry, and is virtually identical to that enacted by many other States. Since the amount of revenue raised by the retaliatory tax is relatively modest, and the impetus for passage of the tax comes from the nationwide insurance industry, it is clear that the purpose is not to generate revenue at the expense of out-of-state insurers, but to apply pressure on other States to maintain low taxes on California insurers. As a committee of the California Assembly has said: "The actual rationale for the provision is that the application of the retaliatory laws acts as a deterrent to state taxation on the insurance industry."[23]

Decisions by the California courts lend weight to this analysis. The Court of Appeal in the instant case held that the purpose of the retaliatory tax "is to put pressure on the several states to impose the same tax burden on all insurance companies, foreign or domestic, and thereby encourage the doing of interstate business."

Many may doubt the wisdom of California's retaliatory tax; indeed, the retaliatory tax has often been criticized as a distortion of the tax system and an impediment to the raising of revenue from the taxation of insurance. But the courts are not empowered to second-guess the wisdom of state policies. Our review is confined to the *legitimacy* of the purpose.

There can be no doubt that promotion of domestic industry by deterring barriers to interstate business is a legitimate state purpose. This Court has recognized the legitimacy of state efforts to maintain the profit level of a domestic industry, and of efforts to "protect and enhance the reputation" of a domestic industry so that it might compete more effectively in the interstate market, Pike v. Bruce Church, Inc., 397 U.S. at 143. California's effort on behalf of its domestic insurance industry is no less legitimate.

---

22. Although the retaliatory tax is an imposition on interstate insurance companies, it is supported by the industry as a means of fostering uniform and moderate levels of taxation nationwide.

23. The nature of the classification supports this conclusion as well. The retaliatory tax is not imposed on foreign corporations qua foreign corporations, as would be expected were the purpose of the tax to raise revenue from noncitizens; rather, it is imposed only on corporations whose home States impose more onerous burdens on California insurers than California otherwise would impose on those corporations.

The mere fact that California seeks to promote its insurance industry by influencing the policies of other States does not render the purpose illegitimate. As we said in United States Steel Corp. v. Multistate Tax Comm'n, 434 U.S. at 478:

"Any time a State adopts a fiscal or administrative policy that affects the programs of a sister State, pressure to modify those programs may result. Unless that pressure transgresses the bounds of the Commerce Clause or the Privileges and Immunities Clause of Art. IV, § 2, see, e.g., Austin v. New Hampshire, 420 U.S. 656 (1975), it is not clear how our federal structure is implicated."

Having established that the purpose of California's lawmakers in enacting the retaliatory tax was legitimate, we turn to the second element in our analysis: whether it was reasonable for California's lawmakers to believe that use of the challenged classification would promote that purpose. We acknowledge at the outset that many persons believe that retaliatory taxes are not an effective means for accomplishment of the goal of deterring discriminatory and excessive taxation of insurance companies by the various States. See, e.g., Bodily, The Effects of Retaliation on the State Taxation of Life Insurers, 44 J. of Risk & Ins. 21 (1977); Pelletier, Insurance Retaliatory Laws, 39 Notre Dame Law. 243, 268-269 (1964); Task Force Report, supra, at 71. But whether *in fact* the provision will accomplish its objectives is not the question: the Equal Protection Clause is satisfied if we conclude that the California Legislature *rationally could have believed* that the retaliatory tax would promote its objective. Minnesota v. Clover Leaf Creamery Co., 449 U.S. at 466; Vance v. Bradley, 440 U.S. at 111; United States v. Carolene Products Co., 304 U.S. 144, 154 (1938).

The Interim Committee on Revenue and Taxation of the California Assembly conducted a major study of the State's tax system before recommending passage of a constitutional amendment permitting enforcement of the present retaliatory tax. That study found:

"It is true that insurers are disadvantaged by retaliatory taxation provisions in the short run, for they usually result in some insurers paying more in taxes in retaliating states. But, in the long run, insurers as a group pay less in taxes because of these provisions, since legislators, when considering measures affecting insurers, do consider retaliatory effects in instance after instance."

The study concluded that retaliatory taxes "have kept premiums lower and insurers' profits higher than would otherwise have been the case." It therefore recommended passage of the proposed constitutional amendment.

We cannot say that the California Legislature's conclusions were irrational, or even unreasonable.

Assuming that the lawmakers of each State are motivated in part by a desire to promote the interests of their domestic insurance industry, it is reasonable to suppose that California's retaliatory tax will induce other States to lower the burdens on California insurers in order to spare their domestic insurers the cost of the retaliatory tax in California.

In any event, we do not find the evidence against the retaliatory tax overwhelming. The California Department of Finance evaluated the effect of the retaliatory laws:

"Whether the insurance companies have sponsored this legislation or not, in their resistance to tax change they have benefitted by it. The home-owned companies in all but a half dozen states are able to say, 'Don't raise our taxes. If you do, we will have to pay more in other states.' The effectiveness of this barrier is demonstrated by the fact that of the 48 states, only 9 increased their insurance tax rates in the last twelve years. . . . None of these is an outstanding insurance state."

The California courts examined the issue, and found:

"The common purpose of [retaliatory tax] legislation in the several states has been to discourage any state from imposing discriminatory taxes or other burdens upon out-of-state companies. The effort seems to have been very largely successful; in any event taxes on insurance premiums have stayed close to 2 percent in most states, for both domestic and out-of-state insurers."

Authorities in the field have found the evidence mixed. The leading empirical study of the effect of retaliatory tax laws examined tax rates on life insurance premiums from 1935 through 1972, and found: (1) that tax rates have not increased significantly in absolute terms over the period; (2) that life insurance premiums taxes have declined as a percentage of total state tax revenues;[25] and (3) that discrimination against foreign insurance companies has declined over the period. Bodily, 44 J. of Risk & Ins. at 27-32. These results are precisely those that advocates of the retaliatory tax would predict, and thus provide some support for that theory. Statistical analysis of the available data, however, failed to verify this conclusion: the correlation between retaliatory tax laws and the observed results was not found to be statistically significant. Id., at 30-31. The author therefore concluded

---

25. A large part of this decline may be accounted for by the general decline in the States' reliance on business taxes. From 1957 to 1972, the proportion of total state tax revenues attributable to general business taxes fell by 17.7%, while the proportion attributable to life insurance premiums taxes fell by 20.0%. Bodily, The Effects of Retaliation on the State Taxation of Life Insurers, 44 J. of Risk & Ins. 21, 31-32 (1977). But see State Department of Finance, Budget Div., Highlights of Proposal for Quarterly Insurance Tax Payments 3-4 (1963) (showing that since 1950, the proportion of California tax revenues attributable to insurance taxes has decreased substantially relative to that attributable to bank and corporate taxes).

that retaliatory taxes have been "of questionable value." Id., at 34. Cf. Pelletier, 39 Notre Dame Law., at 267-269; Felton, Retaliatory Insurance Company Taxation: An Evaluation, 28 J. of Ins. 71, 77-78 (1961).

[handwritten: quest. value]

Parties challenging legislation under the Equal Protection Clause cannot prevail so long as "it is evident from all the considerations presented to [the legislature], and those of which we may take judicial notice, that the question is at least debatable." United States v. Carolene Products Co., supra, at 154. On this standard, we cannot but conclude that the California retaliatory insurance tax withstands the strictures of the Fourteenth Amendment.

Affirmed.

JUSTICE STEVENS, with whom JUSTICE BLACKMUN joins, dissenting. *[handwritten: Not legitimate to enact legisl. favor own corp to coerce other State]*

The practice of holding hostages to coerce another sovereign to change its policies is not new; nor, in my opinion, is it legitimate. California acknowledges that its discrimination against Ohio citizens within its jurisdiction is specifically intended to coerce the Ohio Legislature into enacting legislation favored by California. Today the Court holds that this state purpose is legitimate. In my opinion that coercive motivation is not an acceptable justification for California's discriminatory treatment of nonresidents.

The discrimination disclosed by this record is much more irregular than a simple preference for domestic corporations over foreign corporations. Some foreign insurance companies pay the same tax that domestic companies pay. Those that pay higher taxes than California companies do not all pay the same tax. Thus, for example, California taxes insurance companies incorporated in Ohio at a 2.5% rate, Montana companies at a 2.75% rate, and West Virginia and Idaho companies at a 3% rate. The prevailing tax rate in California for domestic companies and most foreign companies is 2.35%. Thus the insurance companies competing in the California market are subjected to flagrant discrimination.

A desire to eliminate discrimination in other States does not justify the discrimination practiced by California. All insurance companies that do business in Ohio are taxed at the 2.5% rate and all those that compete in the West Virginia market pay the 3% rate. Neither of those States has meddled in California's affairs or taken any action that has a special impact in California. California's justification for its retaliatory tax scheme is simply to apply pressure on other States to lower their tax rates to

the level that California considers acceptable. The possibility that different States may have different fiscal needs is a matter of no concern to California.[3]

Furthermore, the discrimination is not justified by any actions taken in California. The State has not pointed to any significant difference in the way different taxpayers conduct their business in California. No administrative problems justify charging residents of some States higher taxes than others. The mere difference in residence is admittedly an insufficient reason for disparate treatment, and the incremental tax collected from out-of-state companies is not justified as a revenue measure. Thus the retaliatory increment is in the nature of a monetary penalty imposed on foreign citizens to apply pressure to their sovereign. Analytically, pressure of that kind is comparable to ransom.[6]

The Fourteenth Amendment to the United States Constitution provides that no State may "deny to any person within its jurisdiction the equal protection of the laws." The federal interest vindicated by this provision requires every State to respect the individuality and the essential equality of every person subject to its jurisdiction; it forbids disparate treatment that is unrelated to any difference in the character or the behavior of persons subject to the State's jurisdiction.

---

3. The United States, as amicus curiae, takes the position that California has no legitimate interest in Ohio's level of taxation or fiscal structure when no discriminatory action against California citizens or corporations is involved. It states:
"The several states have different resources, populations, social and economic conditions, levels of public service, fiscal structures, methods and sources of raising revenue, and tax burdens, both in gross and per capita. With respect to other states, where no discriminatory or hostile action is involved, the states are largely autonomous in these matters. And even if another state has engaged in discriminatory action, the Constitution, as this Court has pointed out, does not contemplate the economic warfare of reprisal and retaliation. A&P Tea Co. v. Cottrell, 424 U.S. 366 (1976)."

6. California's objective is to confer a limited benefit on a limited group of companies that are incorporated under its law. This case involves the special interest of insurance companies in paying taxes at a rate no higher than the rate California requires for its budgetary purposes. The next case may involve a different industry with a different special interest. Thus, for example, the trucking industry or the motorcoach industry might favor high speed limits, loose safety inspection laws, and lax emission standards. If their lobbyists could persuade the legislature of a powerful State to adopt rules favorable to their interests, then under today's holding they may also seek retaliatory programs that would apply pressure to neighboring States to adopt similar rules. Although such a statute might violate other constitutional provisions, such as the Commerce Clause, under today's holding the Equal Protection Clause would present no impediment.

California's disapproval of the official policies of the State of Ohio cannot justify the exaction of special payments from individuals who come from that State, even though such exactions may cause them to plead with their legislature to conform to California's will.[7]

In my opinion the federal interest in the impartial administration of the laws of the several States is unquestionably paramount to any one State's parochial interest in applying pressure to its neighbors by use of "retaliatory" legislation. This discriminatory legislation is not justified by a legitimate purpose and therefore violates the Equal Protection Clause.

---

7. In holding that California's purpose in enacting the discriminatory tax is legitimate, the Court compares this case to state attempts to maintain the profit level of a domestic industry, Parker v. Brown, 317 U.S. at 363-367, and efforts to "protect and enhance the reputation" of a domestic industry, enabling it to compete more effectively in the interstate market. Pike v. Bruce Church, Inc., 397 U.S. at 143. The enactment of a statute designed to confer a direct benefit or to provide protection for domestic corporations is surely not comparable to California's imposition of a burden on foreign corporations designed to coerce foreign States to enact legislation which will benefit California corporations at the expense of the interest which motivated the foreign State's original tax rate.

Questions and Comments

1. We read *Western & Southern* for three purposes. First, to learn something about the unique state rules for taxing the insurance industry. Second, to witness the interment of the doctrine that approved discriminatory taxes based upon a state's power to condition a corporation's entry into the state in order to conduct an intrastate business. Finally, to dissect the Court's equal protection analysis.

The Court's historical survey regarding the treatment of the "privilege of doing business" may help explain why so many state taxes are imposed on "privileges" that, by today's standards, hardly seem like privileges at all; for example, the privilege of selling at retail, or the privilege of using property within a state.

2. The earliest retaliatory legislation was enacted in Massachusetts in 1832. That law provided that if any state enacted a tax or fee on Massachusetts' companies selling insurance within that state then any agent of an insurance company domiciled in that other state would have to pay a tax of 1/2 of 1% of the face amount of the insurance written in Massachusetts. Until 1944, there was little doubt about a state's right to levy retaliatory taxes. In *Paul v. Virginia*, 75 U.S. 168 (1869), the Court held that insurance did not constitute commerce because "[i]ssuing a policy of insurance is not a transaction of commerce" and insurance "contracts are not articles of commerce within any proper meaning of the word." Id. at 183. Accordingly, retaliatory taxes were immune from a Commerce Clause challenge. With the exception of Alabama, such legislation withstood challenge in every state.

In 1944, however, *United States v. South-Eastern Underwriters Association*, 322 U.S. 533 (1944), overruling *Paul v. Virginia*, held that the business of insurance was interstate commerce. Shortly thereafter, fourteen states repealed their retaliatory laws. This situation was soon reversed when the McCarran-Ferguson Act, 15 U.S.C. §§ 1011-1015 (1982), was enacted in 1945, which provided that it was the intention of Congress that the business of insurance and all persons engaged in that business were subject to the laws of the states in regard to regulation and taxation. The Act further provided that no act of Congress should be interpreted as applying to the insurance industry unless the act specifically stated that it was to apply.

In 1946, *Prudential Company of America v. Benjamin* upheld South Carolina's right to impose a discriminatory tax on foreign insurance companies as a condition of their doing business in that State. The legislation had been challenged primarily under the Commerce Clause. The Court interpreted the McCarran-Ferguson Act as removing Commerce Clause barriers to discriminatory taxation. In passing, the Court noted that the Equal Protection Clause did not forbid the South Carolina statute, but *Western & Southern* viewed the equal protection issue as not having been resolved in *Prudential*. After *Prudential*, states re-enacted retaliatory statutes that had been repealed after *South-Eastern Underwriters*. In general, see Matthew J. Zinn and Steve Reed, *Equal Protection and State Taxation of Interstate Business*, 41 Tax Law. 83 (1987).

3. According to a report issued by the Council of State Governments, initially the taxation of foreign insurance companies was motivated by the desire to encourage the creation of insurance companies domiciled within the borders of the individual states. Eventually, however, states began imposing insurance premium taxes for the purpose of retaliation with the intent to protect their domestic insurance companies from excessive taxation by other states. See The Council of State Governments, State Retaliatory Taxation of the Insurance Industry (1978).

4. X is an insurance company incorporated in California. X does business in State A. State A taxes all insurance companies, whether incorporated in State A or elsewhere, at a 3% rate. Assume that California would normally tax foreign insurance companies at 2%. If a company incorporated in State A is taxed by California, what rate will California apply?

Does California's tax only apply to residents of a state that imposes a discriminatory tax on outsiders? Is State A's tax, supra, discriminatory? Is California's?

5. If you are a multistate insurance company, are you a supporter of or an opponent of retaliatory tax laws? If retaliatory laws have kept insurance taxes low and are supported by the industry, why did the plaintiff– an insurance company–challenge the California statute?

6. Suppose a state has a very small domestic insurance industry. Should such a state worry about whether its tax on insurance premiums is out-of-line with that used by other states? Does such a state have any inducement to adopt a retaliatory tax law? Any reason not to do so? Could such a state be better off in terms of revenue raised if it were to levy a high tax on premiums and grant a

credit to its domestic insurance companies that holds them harmless from the retaliatory taxes of other states? Would such a credit be constitutional?

Under what conditions might it make good sense from the perspective of both a state and its domestic insurance companies for the state to practice reverse discrimination, that is, impose a higher tax on domestic insurance companies than on foreign insurance companies? Would such an approach survive an Equal Protection challenge?

7. Why is the amount of revenue raised by the retaliatory tax in California relatively modest? Did that influence the Court?

8. The Court states that the principal purpose of retaliatory tax laws is to promote the interstate business of domestic insurers by deterring other states from enacting discriminatory or excessive taxes. Do you think this was the actual reason the California Legislature adopted its retaliatory tax law? What does any legislature have to lose by adopting retaliatory tax laws on insurance companies? What does it have to gain?

Does the California statute have anything to do with deterring other states from enacting discriminatory taxes? Excessive taxes? What is the definition of discriminatory? Of excessive?

9. Does it matter what the California Legislature actually believed about the efficacy of its retaliatory tax or only what they might have rationally believed? Because a majority of the Court agreed that California's actual purpose in adopting its discriminatory legislation was legitimate, the Court did not have to decide whether any "conceivable" legitimate purpose would have sufficed. How does a court determine what a legislature actually believed?

10. What standards did the Court apply in distinguishing legitimate from illegitimate state goals? Was the Court influenced by the fact that the retaliatory tax was supported by the nationwide insurance industry?

11. Consider the various ways in which the purpose of California's statute could be characterized: a) promoting domestic industry by inducing other states to lower their taxes; b) promoting domestic industry; c) putting foreign corporations at a competitive disadvantage. How does a court know which of these characterizations should be used for purposes of its analysis? Is it important which one a court uses? Do you agree that the more general the characterization of a statute's purpose, the more likely it will be found legitimate?

Do you agree with the analysis of a law review note commenting on *Western & Southern*:

The problem that lower courts face in deciding equal protection challenges to discriminatory taxes goes beyond choosing a level of scrutiny. The courts usually assume that they can determine the state's purpose and then assess it for legitimacy; and they assume that they can determine means and assess them for congruence with purpose. Unfortunately, the definitions of purpose and means are fundamentally arbitrary. There is no clear division between means and ends. Any end can be recast as a means to a more general end; similarly, statutory means can be defined as the end that the statute is designed to achieve. These linguistic characterizations can change the result of equal protection cases, yet the existence and influence of this recharacterization problem has been slighted by Court and commentators alike.

. . . .

Any state scheme can be described in the form: "to do A by doing B by doing C by doing D" and so on. The number of sublevels is limited only by a court's diligence in subcategorizing. The court can draw a line between purpose and means anywhere below the first, most general level, and above the last, most specific level. Any discriminatory tax necessarily favors domestic corporations; thus, the illegitimate element "to provide domestic corporations with competitive advantages" will appear somewhere in the chain of levels. If a court draws the purpose-means line below this illegitimate element, the purpose is illegitimate and the law must fail. If a court draws the line above that phrase, the purpose is likely to be legitimate, and the law is likely to survive equal protection challenge. Note, "Taxing Out-of-State Corporations After *Western & Southern*: An Equal Protection Analysis," 34 *Stanford Law Review* 877, 891-2 (1982).

Compare Haller, Within the States' Jurisdiction: *Metropolitan, Northeast Bancorp*, and the Equal Protection Clause, 96 Yale L. J. 2110, 2124 n. 47:

The necessary "means" by which the classification employed by California effects its purpose is inseparable from that purpose. *It is, in fact, part of the purpose itself.* California's intention was to coerce other states into lowering their taxes and thereby to help the interstate business to California insurers. The statute does not aid domestic insurers unless it coerces other states' legislatures. *Western & Southern*, then, should be read as having held that the entire statutory purpose presented by the state–to promote the interstate business of domestic insurers by deterring other states from enacting discriminatory or excessive taxes– was legitimate, and not that aiding the interstate business of domestic insurers alone was legitimate. (Emphasis in original.)

12. Is it irrational for a legislature to impose heavier taxes on foreign companies than on domestic companies? Unfair–perhaps, unwise– maybe, but irrational? Can't a legislature reasonably believe that this policy will benefit its citizens and residents?

If nonresidents have less representation in a state legislature than do residents, then without Constitutional protection won't most states seek ways to raise revenue from the former in order to provide for the latter? Given Justice Brennan's concurrence in *Allied*, is it surprising that he did not join the dissent? Was Justice Brennan influenced by the fact that the California statute was adopted at the urging of the insurance industry and that it did not raise much money?

13. Justice Brennan uses both the terms "rational" and "reasonable" in testing whether the means adopted by California are related to the achievement of its purpose. Does Justice Brennan use these terms interchangeably or does he mean something different for each of them?

14. Would the California statute survive a Commerce Clause challenge? What is the significance of footnote 6 in the dissent?

15. Can a state levy an initial entrance fee for foreign insurance corporations that is more than the franchise taxes levied upon domestic corporations?

16. Some recent cases have interpreted the application of retaliatory tax provisions. See, e.g., *Prudential Ins. v. Mass.*, 709 N.E. 2d 1096 (1999) (taxes are compared on an insurance-line basis, not in the aggregate); *TIG Ins. v. Mich.*, 602 N.W. 2d 839 (1999) (mandatory payments to insurance associations should be taken into account in comparing burdens); *State Farm Ins. v. N.C.*, 497 S.E. 2d 451 (1998) (regulatory charge based on premiums does not have to be taken into account in comparing burdens).

17. In *Paul v. Virginia*, 75 U.S. (8 Wall.) 168 (1869), the Court argued that because a state may exclude a foreign corporation entirely, it may, therefore, grant entry upon conditions it chooses to impose. Id. at 181. This view has been replaced by the doctrine of unconstitutional conditions. See Kirk D. McQuiddy, *Taxing Out-of-State Corporations after Western & Southern: An Equal Protection Analysis*, 34 Stan. L. Rev. 877 note 11, 13-18 (1982).

18. Are retaliatory taxes constitutional under the Commerce Clause? See *Private Truck Council of America v. Quinn*, 503 A. 2d 214 (1986), where the Maine Supreme Court struck down that state's retaliatory tax on out-of-state truckers. Other courts have reached similar results. See *Florida v. Private Truck Council of America*, 531 So. 2d 367 (1988); *State v. Private Truck Council of America*, 258 Ga. 531, 371 S. E. 2d 378 (1988); *Private Truck Council of America v. State*, 128 N. H. 466, 517 A. 2d 1150 (1986); *Private Truck Council v. State*, 221 N. J. Super. 89, 534 A. 2d 13 (1987), aff'd, 111 N. J. 214, 544 A. 2d 33 (1988).

19. For critical commentary on *Western & Southern*, see Kirk D. McQuiddy, *Taxing Out-of-State Corporations After Western & Southern: An Equal Protection Analysis*, 34 Stan. L. Rev. 877 (1982); Glenn S. Hansen, *Constitutional Law - Insurance - A Retaliatory State Tax Assessed Against Insurers From States Imposing Higher Tax Burdens on All Insurance Companies Transacting Business Within Their Borders Is Not Subject to Challenge Under the Commerce Clause and Is Rationally Related to the Achievement of a Legitimate State Purpose Consistent With the Equal Protection Clause of the Fourteenth Amendment. - Western & Southern Life Insurance Co. v. State Board of Equalization*, 31 Drake L. Rev. 215 (1981-82).

Metropolitan Life Insurance Co. et al. v. Ward et al.
Supreme Court of the United States, 1985.
470 U.S. 869, 105 S. Ct. 1676, 84 L. Ed. 2d 751.

JUSTICE POWELL delivered the opinion of the Court.

This case presents the question whether Alabama's domestic preference tax statute, that taxes out-of-state insurance companies at a higher rate than domestic insurance companies, violates the Equal Protection Clause.

I

Since 1955, the State of Alabama has granted a preference to its domestic insurance companies by imposing a substantially lower gross premiums tax rate on them than on out-of-state (foreign) companies.[2] Under the current statutory provisions, foreign life insurance companies pay a tax on their gross premiums received from business conducted in Alabama at a rate of three percent, and foreign companies selling other types of

---

2. For domestic preference tax purposes, Alabama defines a domestic insurer as a company that both is incorporated in Alabama and has its principal office and chief place of business within the State. A corporation that does not meet both of these criteria is characterized as a foreign insurer.

insurance pay at a rate of four percent. All domestic insurance companies, in contrast, pay at a rate of only one percent on all types of insurance premiums. § 27-4-5(a). As a result, a foreign insurance company doing the same type and volume of business in Alabama as a domestic company generally will pay three to four times as much in gross premiums taxes as its domestic competitor.

Alabama's domestic preference tax statute does provide that foreign companies may reduce the differential in gross premiums taxes by investing prescribed percentages of their worldwide assets in specified Alabama assets and securities. By investing 10 percent or more of its total assets in Alabama investments, for example, a foreign life insurer may reduce its gross premiums tax rate from 3 to 2 percent. Similarly, a foreign property and casualty insurer may reduce its tax rate from four to three percent. Smaller tax reductions are available based on investment of smaller percentages of a company's assets. Ibid. Regardless of how much of its total assets a foreign company places in Alabama investments, it can never reduce its gross premiums tax rate to the same level paid by comparable domestic companies. These are entitled to the one-percent tax rate even if they have no investments in the State. Thus, the investment provision permits foreign insurance companies to reduce, but never to eliminate, the discrimination inherent in the domestic preference tax statute.

II

Appellants, a group of insurance companies incorporated outside of the State of Alabama, filed claims with the Alabama Department of Insurance in 1981, contending that the domestic preference tax statute, as applied to them, violated the Equal Protection Clause. They sought refunds of taxes paid for the tax years 1977 through 1980. The Commissioner of Insurance denied all of their claims on July 8, 1981.

Appellants appealed to the Circuit Court for Montgomery County, seeking a judgment declaring the statute to be unconstitutional and requiring the Commissioner to make the appropriate refunds. . . . Relying on this Court's opinion in Western & Southern Life Ins. Co. v. State Board of Equalization of California, 451 U.S. 648 (1981), the court ruled that the Alabama statute did not violate the Equal Protection Clause because it served "at least two purposes, in addition to raising revenue: (1) encouraging the formation of new insurance companies in Alabama, and (2) encouraging capital investment by foreign insurance companies in the Alabama assets and governmental securities set

forth in the statute." The court also found that the distinction the statute created between foreign and domestic companies was rationally related to those two purposes and that the Alabama Legislature reasonably could have believed that the classification would have promoted those purposes. After their motion for a new trial was denied, appellants appealed to the Court of Civil Appeals. It affirmed the Circuit Court's rulings as to the existence of the two legitimate state purposes, but remanded for an evidentiary hearing on the issue of rational relationship, concluding that summary judgment was inappropriate on that question because the evidence was in conflict.

GET MET. IT PAYS.
1-800-MetLife

Appellants petitioned the Supreme Court of Alabama for certiorari on the affirmance of the legitimate state purpose issue, and the State and the intervenors petitioned for review of the remand order. Appellants then waived their right to an evidentiary hearing on the issue whether the statute's classification bore a rational relationship to the two purposes found by the Circuit Court to be legitimate, and they requested a final determination of the legal issues with respect to their equal protection challenge to the statute. The Supreme Court denied certiorari on all claims. Appellants again waived their rights to an evidentiary hearing on the rational relationship issue and filed a joint motion with the other parties seeking rehearing and entry of a final judgment. The motion was granted, and judgment was entered for the State and the intervenors. This appeal followed, and we now reverse.

III

. . . .

Because appellants waived their right to an evidentiary hearing on the issue whether the classification in the Alabama domestic preference tax statute bears a rational relation to the two purposes upheld by the Circuit Court, the only question before us it whether those purposes are legitimate.[5]

A

(1) *encourages formation of new Ala.*

The first of the purposes found by the trial court to be a *Corp* legitimate reason for the statute's classification between foreign and domestic corporations is that it encourages the formation of new domestic insurance companies in Alabama. The State, agreeing with the Court of Civil Appeals, contends that this Court has long held that the promotion of domestic industry, in and of itself, is a legitimate state purpose that will survive equal protection scrutiny. In so contending, it relies on a series of cases, including Western & Southern, that are said to have upheld discriminatory taxes. See Bacchus Imports, Ltd. v. Dias, 468 U.S. 263 (1984); Pike v. Bruce Church, Inc., 397 U.S. 137 (1970); Allied Stores of Ohio, Inc. v. Bowers, infra; Parker v. Brown, 317 U.S. 341 (1943); Carmichael v. Southern Coal & Coke Co., 301 U.S. 495 (1937); Board of Education v. Illinois, 203 U.S. 553 (1906).

The cases cited lend little or no support to the State's contention. In Western & Southern, the case principally relied upon, we did not hold as a general rule that promotion of domestic industry is a legitimate state

purpose under equal protection analysis.[6] Rather, we held that California's purpose in enacting the retaliatory tax–to promote the *interstate* business of domestic insurers by deterring *other States* from enacting discriminatory or excessive taxes–was a legitimate one. 451 U.S. at 668. In contrast, Alabama asks us to approve its purpose of promoting the business of its domestic insurers *in Alabama* by penalizing foreign insurers who also want to do business in the State. Alabama has made no attempt, as California did, to influence the policies of other States in order to enhance its domestic companies' ability to operate interstate; rather, it has erected barriers to foreign companies who wish to do interstate business in order to improve its domestic insurers' ability to compete at home.

The crucial distinction between the two cases lies in the fact that Alabama's aim to promote domestic industry is purely and completely discriminatory, designed only to favor domestic industry within the State, no matter what

---

5. The State and the intervenors advanced some 15 additional purposes in support of the Alabama statute. As neither the Circuit Court nor the Court of Civil Appeals ruled on the legitimacy of those purposes, that question is not before us, and we express no view as to it. On remand, the State will be free to advance again its arguments relating to the legitimacy of those purposes.

As the dissent finds our failure to resolve whether Alabama may continue to collect its tax "baffling," we reemphasize the procedural posture of the case: it arose on a motion for summary judgment. The Court of Civil Appeals upheld the Circuit Court's ruling that the two purposes identified by it were legitimate, but the appellate court remanded on the issue of rational relationship as to those purposes because it found the evidence in conflict. In order to obtain an expedited ruling, appellants waived their right to an evidentiary hearing only as to the purposes "which the lower courts have determined to be legitimate." Thus, for this Court to resolve whether Alabama may continue to collect the tax, it would have to decide de novo whether any of the other purposes was legitimate, and also whether the statute's classification bore a rational relationship to any of these purposes–all this, on a record that the Court of Civil Appeals deemed inadequate.

6. We find the other cases on which the State relies also to be inapposite to this inquiry. Bacchus Imports, Pike, and Parker discussed whether promotion of local industry is a valid state purpose under the Commerce Clause. The Commerce Clause, unlike the Equal Protection Clause, is integrally concerned with whether a state purpose implicates local or national interests. The Equal Protection Clause, in contrast, is concerned with whether a state purpose is impermissibly discriminatory; whether the discrimination involves local or other interests is not central to the inquiry to be made. Thus, the fact that promotion of local industry is a legitimate state interest in the Commerce Clause context says nothing about its validity under equal protection analysis.

Moreover, neither Bacchus nor Pike ruled that a State's ability to promote domestic industry was unlimited, even under the Commerce Clause. Thus, in Bacchus, although we observed as a general matter that "a State may enact laws pursuant to its police powers that have the purpose and effect of encouraging domestic industry," we held that in so doing, a State may not constitutionally impose a discriminatory burden upon the business of other States, merely to protect and promote local business. Accord, Armco Inc. v. Hardesty, 467 U.S. at 642. Likewise, in Pike, the Court held that the state statute promoting a legitimate local interest must "regulat[e] evenhandedly."

Other cases cited by the State are simply irrelevant to the legitimacy of promoting local business at all. Carmichael relates primarily to the validity of a state unemployment compensation scheme, and Board of Education deals with the State's ability to regulate matters relating to probate. Bowers is the only one of the State's cases that involves the validity under the Equal Protection Clause of a tax that discriminates on the basis of residence of domestic *versus* foreign corporations. That case does little, however, to support the State's contention that promotion of domestic business is a legitimate state purpose. It was concerned with encouraging nonresidents–who are not competitors of residents–to build warehouses within the State.

the cost to foreign corporations also seeking to do business there. Alabama's purpose, contrary to California's, constitutes the very sort of parochial discrimination that the Equal Protection Clause was intended to prevent. As Justice Brennan, joined by Justice Harlan, observed in his concurrence in Allied Stores of Ohio, Inc. v. Bowers, 358 U.S. 522 (1959), this Court always has held that the Equal Protection Clause forbids a State to discriminate in favor of its own residents solely by burdening "the residents of other state members of our federation." Unlike the retaliatory tax involved in Western & Southern, which only burdens residents of a State that imposes its own discriminatory tax on outsiders, the domestic preference tax gives the "home team" an advantage by burdening *all* foreign corporations seeking to do business within the State, no matter what they or their States do.

The validity of the view that a State may not constitutionally favor its own residents by taxing foreign corporations at a higher rate solely because of their residence is confirmed by a long line of this Court's cases so holding. WHYY, Inc. v. Glassboro, 393 U.S. at 119-120; Wheeling Steel Corp. v. Glander, 337 U.S. at 571; Hanover Fire Ins. Co. v. Harding, 272 U.S. at 511; Southern R. Co. v. Greene, 216 U.S. at 417. See Reserve Life Ins. Co. v. Bowers, 380 U.S. 258 (1965) (per curiam). As the Court stated in Hanover Fire Ins. Co., with respect to general tax burdens on business, "the foreign corporation stands equal, and is to be classified with domestic corporations of the same kind." 272 U.S. at 511. In all of these cases, the discriminatory tax was imposed by the State on foreign corporations doing business within the State solely because of their residence, presumably to promote domestic industry within the State.[7] In relying on these cases and rejecting Lincoln in Western & Southern, we reaffirmed the continuing viability of the Equal Protection Clause as a means of challenging a statute that seeks to benefit domestic industry within the State only by grossly discriminating against foreign competitors.

The State contends that Allied Stores of Ohio, Inc. v. Bowers, supra, shows that this principle has not always held true. In that case, a domestic merchandiser challenged on equal protection grounds an Ohio statute that exempted foreign corporations from a tax on the value of merchandise held for storage within the State. The Court upheld the tax, finding that the purpose of

encouraging foreign companies to build warehouses within Ohio was a legitimate state purpose. The State contends that this case shows that promotion of domestic business *is* a legitimate state purpose under equal protection analysis. We disagree with the State's interpretation of Allied Stores and find that the case is not inconsistent with the other cases on which we rely. We agree with the holding of Allied Stores that a State's goal of bringing in new business is legitimate and often admirable. Allied Stores does not, however, hold that promotion of domestic business by *discriminating* against foreign corporations is legitimate. The case involves instead a statute that *encourages nonresidents—who are* not *competitors of residents*—to build warehouses within the State. The discriminatory tax involved did not favor residents by burdening outsiders; rather, it granted the nonresident businesses an exemption that residents did not share. Since the foreign and domestic companies involved were not competing to provide warehousing services, granting the former an exemption did not even directly affect adversely the domestic companies subject to the tax. On its facts, then, Allied Stores is not inconsistent with our holding here that promotion of domestic business within a State, by discriminating against foreign corporations that wish to compete by doing business there, is not a legitimate state purpose. See 358 U.S. at 532-533 (BRENNAN, J., concurring).

(2)

The State argues nonetheless that it is impermissible to view a discriminatory tax such as the one at issue here as violative of the Equal Protection Clause. This approach, it contends, amounts to no more than "Commerce Clause rhetoric in equal protection clothing." The State maintains that because Congress, in enacting the McCarran-Ferguson Act, 15 U.S.C. §§ 1011-1015, intended to authorize States to impose taxes that burden interstate commerce in the insurance field, the tax at issue here must stand. Our concerns are much more fundamental than as characterized by the State. Although the McCarran-Ferguson Act exempts the insurance industry from Commerce Clause restrictions, it does not purport to limit in any way the applicability of the Equal Protection Clause. As noted above, our opinion in Western & Southern expressly reaffirmed the viability of equal protection restraints on discriminatory taxes in the insurance context.[8]

---

7. Although the promotion of domestic business was not a purpose advanced by the States in support of their taxes in these cases, such promotion is logically the primary reason for enacting discriminatory taxes such as those at issue there.

---

8. In fact, as we note in Western & Southern, the legislative history of the McCarran-Ferguson Act reveals that the Act was Congress' response only to United States v. South-Eastern Underwriters Assn., 322 U.S. 533 (1944), and that Congress did not intend thereby to give the States any power to tax or regulate the insurance industry other than what they had

Moreover, the State's view ignores the differences between Commerce Clause and equal protection analysis and the consequent different purposes those two constitutional provisions serve. Under Commerce Clause analysis, the State's interest, if legitimate, is weighed against the burden the state law would impose on interstate commerce. In the equal protection context, however, if the State's purpose is found to be legitimate, the state law stands as long as the burden it imposes is found to be rationally related to that purpose, a relationship that is not difficult to establish. See Western & Southern, 451 U.S. at 674 (if purpose is legitimate, equal protection challenge may not prevail so long as the question of rational relationship is "'at least debatable'" (quoting United States v. Carolene Products Co., 304 U.S. at 154 (1938)).

The two constitutional provisions perform different functions in the analysis of the permissible scope of a State's power—one protects interstate commerce, and the other protects persons[9] from unconstitutional discrimination by the States. The effect of the statute at issue here is to place a discriminatory tax burden on foreign insurers who desire to do business within the State, thereby also incidentally placing a burden on interstate commerce. Equal protection restraints are applicable even though the *effect* of the discrimination in this case is similar to the type of burden with which the Commerce Clause also would be concerned. We reaffirmed the importance of the Equal Protection Clause in the insurance context in Western & Southern and see no reason now for reassessing that view.

In whatever light the State's position is cast, acceptance of its contention that promotion of domestic industry is always a legitimate state purpose under equal protection analysis would eviscerate the Equal Protection Clause in this context. A State's natural inclination frequently would be to prefer domestic business over foreign. If we accept the State's view here, then any discriminatory tax would be valid if the State could show it reasonably was intended to benefit

domestic business.[10] A discriminatory tax would stand or fall depending primarily on how a State framed its purpose—as benefitting one group or as harming another. This is a distinction without a difference, and one that we rejected last Term in an analogous context arising under the Commerce Clause. Bacchus Imports, Ltd. v. Dias, 468 U.S. at 273. See n. 6, supra. We hold that under the circumstances of this case, promotion of domestic business by discriminating against nonresident competitors is not a legitimate state purpose.

B

The second purpose found by the courts below to be legitimate was the encouragement of capital investment in the Alabama assets and governmental securities specified in the statute. We do not agree that this is a legitimate state purpose when furthered by discrimination. Domestic insurers remain entitled to the more favorable rate of tax regardless of whether they invest in Alabama assets. Moreover, the investment incentive provision of the Alabama statute does not enable foreign insurance companies to eliminate the discriminatory effect of the statute. No matter how much of their assets they invest in Alabama, foreign insurance companies are still required to pay a higher gross premiums tax than domestic companies. The State's investment incentive provision therefore does not cure, but reaffirms, the statute's impermissible classification based solely on residence. We hold that encouraging investment in Alabama assets and securities in this plainly discriminatory manner serves no legitimate state purpose.

IV

We conclude that neither of the two purposes furthered by the Alabama domestic preference tax statute and addressed by the Circuit Court for Montgomery County, see supra, is legitimate under the Equal Protection Clause to justify the imposition of the discriminatory tax at issue here. The judgment of the Alabama Supreme Court accordingly is reversed, and the case is remanded for further proceedings not inconsistent with this opinion.

It is so ordered.

---

previously possessed. Thus Congress expressly left undisturbed this Court's decisions holding that the Equal Protection Clause places limits on a State's ability to tax out-of-state corporations. See 451 U.S. at 655, n. 6.

9. It is well established that a corporation is a "person" within the meaning of the Fourteenth Amendment. E.g., Western & Southern, 451 U.S. at 660, n.12.

10. Indeed, under the State's analysis, *any* discrimination subject to the rational relation level of scrutiny could be justified simply on the ground that it favored one group at the expense of another. This case does not involve or question, as the dissent suggests, the broad authority of a State to promote and regulate its own economy. We hold only that such regulation may not be accomplished by imposing discriminatorily higher taxes on nonresident corporations solely because they are nonresidents.

JUSTICE O'CONNOR, with whom JUSTICE BRENNAN, JUSTICE MARSHALL, and JUSTICE REHNQUIST join, dissenting.

This case presents a simple question: Is it legitimate for a State to use its taxing power to promote a domestic insurance industry and to encourage capital investment within its borders? In a holding that can only be characterized as astonishing, the Court determines that these purposes are illegitimate. This holding is unsupported by precedent and subtly distorts the constitutional balance, threatening the freedom of both state and federal legislative bodies to fashion appropriate classifications in economic legislation. Because I disagree with both the Court's method of analysis and its conclusion, I respectfully dissent.

I

. . . .

Our precedents impose a heavy burden on those who challenge local economic regulation solely on Equal Protection Clause grounds. In this context, our long-established jurisprudence requires us to defer to a legislature's judgment if the classification is rationally related to a legitimate state purpose. Yet the Court evades this careful framework for analysis, melding the proper two-step inquiry regarding the State's purpose and the classification's relationship to that purpose into a single unarticulated judgment. This tactic enables the Court to characterize state goals that have been legitimated by Congress itself as improper solely because it disagrees with the concededly rational means of differential taxation selected by the legislature. This unorthodox approach leads to further error. The Court gives only the most cursory attention to the factual and legal bases supporting the State's purposes and ignores both precedent and significant evidence in the record establishing their legitimacy. Most troubling, the Court discovers in the Equal Protection Clause an implied prohibition against classifications whose purpose is to give the "home team" an advantage over interstate competitors even where Congress has authorized such advantages.

The Court overlooks the unequivocal language of our prior decisions. "Unless a classification trammels fundamental personal rights or is drawn upon inherently suspect distinctions such as race, religion, or alienage, our decisions presume the constitutionality of the statutory discriminations and require only that the classification challenged be rationally related to a legitimate state interest." New Orleans v. Dukes, 427 U.S. at 303. See, e.g., Lehnhausen v. Lake Shore Auto Parts Co., 410 U.S. 356 (1973). Judicial deference is strongest where a tax classification is alleged to infringe the right to equal protection. "[I]n taxation, even more than in other fields, legislatures possess the greatest freedom in classification." Madden v. Kentucky, 309 U.S. at 88. "Where the public interest is served one business may be left untaxed and another taxed, in order to promote the one or to restrict or suppress the other." Carmichael v. Southern Coal & Coke Co., 301 U.S. at 512 (citations omitted). As the Court emphatically noted in Allied Stores of Ohio, Inc. v. Bowers, 358 U.S. at 528 (citations omitted):

"[I]t has repeatedly been held and appears to be entirely settled that a statute which encourages the location within the State of needed and useful industries by exempting them, though not also others, from its taxes is not arbitrary and does not violate the Equal Protection Clause of the Fourteenth Amendment. Similarly, it has long been settled that a classification, though discriminatory, is not arbitrary or violative of the Equal Protection Clause of the Fourteenth Amendment if any state of facts reasonably can be conceived that would sustain it."

Appellants waived their right to an evidentiary hearing and conceded that Alabama's classification was rationally related to its purposes of encouraging the formation of domestic insurance companies and bringing needed services and capital to the State. Thus the only issue in dispute is the legitimacy of these purposes. Yet it is obviously legitimate for a State to seek to promote local business and attract capital investment, and surely those purposes animate a wide range of legislation in all 50 States.

The majority evades the obvious by refusing to acknowledge the factual background bearing on the legitimacy of the State's purpose or to address the many collateral public benefits advanced by Alabama. Instead, the Court dismisses appellees' arguments by merely stating that they were not ruled on by the courts below. In point of fact, the full range of purposes documented before this Court was also argued and documented before the Alabama Circuit Court. That court found "*at least* two purposes, in addition to raising revenue: (1) encouraging the formation of new insurance companies in Alabama, and (2) encouraging capital investment by foreign insurance companies in the Alabama assets and governmental securities set forth in the statute." As appellants concede, these purposes are simply a step in achieving the "larger set of purposes [whose] premise . . . is that domestic insurance companies, on the whole, benefit the state in ways which foreign companies do not."

In any event, it is settled law that the appellee may assert any argument in support of the judgment in his favor, regardless of whether it was relied upon by the court below. Dandridge v. Williams, 397 U.S. at 475, n. 6 . The

Court's failure actually to resolve whether Alabama may continue to collect its tax, is all the more baffling, since appellants took the exceptional step of conceding the factual issues to assure a speedy resolution of numerous pending lawsuits disruptive of industry stability. Our precedents do not condone such a miserly approach to review of statutes adjusting economic burdens. See, e.g., Allied Stores of Ohio, Inc. v. Bowers, supra, at 528-529; McGowan v. Maryland, 366 U.S. at 425; United States v. Carolene Products Co., 304 U.S. at 152-153; Borden's Farm Products Co. v. Baldwin, 293 U.S. at 209. The Court has consistently reviewed the validity of such statutes based on whatever "may reasonably have been the purpose and policy of the State Legislature, in adopting the proviso." Allied Stores of Ohio, Inc. v. Bowers, supra, at 528-529. It is to that inquiry that I now turn.

Appellees claim that Alabama's insurance tax, in addition to raising revenue and promoting investment, promotes the formation of new domestic insurance companies and enables them to compete with the many large multistate insurers that currently occupy some 75% to 85% of the Alabama insurance market. Economic studies submitted by the State document differences between the two classes of insurers that are directly relevant to the well-being of Alabama's citizens. Foreign insurers typically concentrate on affluent, high volume, urban markets and offer standardized national policies. In contrast, domestic insurers such as intervenors American Educators Life Insurance Company and Booker T. Washington Life Insurance Company are more likely to serve Alabama's rural areas, and to write low-cost industrial and burial policies not offered by the larger national companies.[1] Additionally, appellees argue persuasively that Alabama can more readily regulate domestic insurers and more effectively safeguard their solvency than that of insurers domiciled and having their principal places of business in other States.

Ignoring these policy considerations, the Court insists that Alabama seeks only to benefit local business, a purpose the Court labels invidious. Yet if the classification chosen by the State can be shown *actually*

---

1. "Industrial insurance" is the trade term for a low face-value policy typically sold door-to-door and maintained through home collection of monthly or weekly premiums. Alabama currently has more industrial insurance in force than any other State. Burial insurance is another form of insurance popular in rural Alabama that is offered exclusively by local insurers. By contrast, Metropolitan Life, like many multistate insurers, has discontinued writing even whole-life policies with face values below $15,000.

to promote the public welfare, this is strong evidence of a legitimate state purpose. See Note, Taxing Out-of-State Corporations After Western & Southern: An Equal Protection Analysis, 34 Stan. L. Rev. 877, 896 (1982). In this regard, Justice Frankfurter wisely observed:

"[T]he great divide in the [equal protection] decisions lies in the difference between emphasizing the actualities or the abstractions of legislation.

". . . To recognize marked differences that exist in fact is living law; to disregard practical differences and concentrate on some abstract identities is lifeless logic." Morey v. Doud, 354 U.S. 472 (dissenting).

A thoughtful look at the "actualities of [this] legislation" compels the conclusion that the State's goals are legitimate by any test.

II

. . . .

The majority opinion correctly notes that Congress did not intend the McCarran-Ferguson Act to give the States any power to tax or regulate the insurance industry other than they already possessed. But the legislative history cited by the majority relates not to differential taxation but to decisions of this Court that had invalidated state taxes on contracts of insurance entered into outside the State's jurisdiction. The Court fails to mention that at the time the Act was under consideration the taxing schemes of Alabama, Arizona, Arkansas, Illinois, Kansas, Kentucky, Maine, Michigan, Mississippi, Ohio, Oklahoma, Oregon, South Dakota, Tennessee, Texas, Washington, and Wisconsin all incorporated tax differentials favoring domestic insurers.

Any doubt that Congress' intent encompassed taxes that discriminate in favor of local insurers was dispelled in Prudential Insurance Co. v. Benjamin, 328 U.S. 408 (1946). Cf. Note, Congressional Consent to Discriminatory State Legislation, 45 Colum. L. Rev. 927 (1945) (discussing the issues of constitutional power posed by the Act.) There a foreign insurer challenged a tax on annual gross premiums imposed on foreign but not domestic insurers as a condition for renewal of its license to do business. Congress, the foreign insurer argued, was powerless to sanction the tax at issue because "the commerce clause 'by its own force' forbids discriminatory state taxation." 328 U.S. at 426. A unanimous Court rejected the argument that exacting a 3% gross premium tax from foreign insurers was invalid as "somehow technically of an inherently discriminatory character." Id., at 432. The Court concluded that the McCarran-Ferguson Act's effect was "clearly to sustain the exaction and that this can be done without violating *any* constitutional provision." Id., at 427 (emphasis added).

Benjamin expressly noted that nothing in the Equal Protection Clause forbade the State to enact a law such as the tax at issue. Id., at 438, and n. 50. In this regard the Court relied in part on Hanover Fire Ins. Co. v. Harding, 272 U.S. 494 (1926), a decision that explicitly recognized that differential taxation of revenues of foreign corporations may not be arbitrary or without reasonable basis. See Western & Southern Life Ins. Co. v. State Board of Equalization of California, 451 U.S. at 664, n.17. The Commerce Clause, Benjamin emphasized, is not a "one-way street" but encompasses congressional power "to discriminate against interstate commerce and in favor of local trade," "subject only to the restrictions placed upon its authority by other constitutional provisions." 328 U.S. at 434. Where the States and Congress have acted in concert to effect a policy favoring local concerns, their action must be upheld unless it unequivocally exceeds "some explicit and compelling limitation imposed by a constitutional provision or provisions designed and intended to outlaw the action taken entirely from our constitutional framework." Id., at 435-436.

Our more recent decision in Western & Southern in no way undermines the force of the analysis in [Prudential Insurance Co. v. Benjamin, 328 U.S. 408 (1946)]. Western & Southern confirms that differential premium taxes are not immune from review as "privilege" taxes, but it also teaches that the Constitution requires only that discrimination between domestic and foreign corporations bear a rational relationship to a legitimate state purpose. Benjamin clearly recognized that differentially taxing foreign insurers to promote a local insurance industry was a legitimate state purpose completely consonant with Congress' purpose in the McCarran-Ferguson Act.

The contemporary realities of insurance regulation and taxation continue to justify a uniquely local perspective. . . .

State insurance commissions vary widely in manpower and expertise. . . .

III

Despite abundant evidence of a legitimate state purpose, the majority condemns Alabama's tax as "purely and completely discriminatory" and "the very sort of parochial discrimination that the Equal Protection Clause was intended to prevent." Apparently, the majority views any favoritism of domestic commercial entities as inherently suspect. The majority ignores a long line of our decision. In the past this Court has not hesitated to apply the rational basis test to regulatory classifications that distinguish between domestic and out-of-state corporations or burden foreign interests to protect local concerns. The Court has always recognized that there are certain legitimate restrictions or policies in which, "[b]y definition, discrimination against nonresidents would inhere." Arlington County Board v. Richards, 434 U.S. at 7 (per curiam). For example, where State of incorporation or principal place of business affect the State's ability to regulate or exercise its jurisdiction, a State may validly discriminate between foreign and domestic entities. See G. D. Searle & Co. v. Cohn, 455 U.S. 404 (1982) (difficulty of obtaining jurisdiction over nonresident corporation provides a rational basis for excepting such corporations from statute of limitations); Metropolitan Casualty Ins. Co. v. Brownell, 294 U.S. 580 (1935) (domicile of insurer relevant to statute of limitations as foreign insurers' offices and funds generally located outside State); Board of Education v. Illinois, 203 U.S. at 562 (State's greater control over domestic than foreign nonprofit corporations justifies discriminatory tax).

A State may use its taxing power to entice useful foreign industry, see Allied Stores of Ohio, Inc. v. Bowers, 358 U.S. at 528, or to make residence within its boundaries more attractive, see Zobel v. Williams, 457 U.S. at 67-68 (BRENNAN, J., concurring). Though such measures might run afoul of the Commerce Clause, "[n]o one disputes that a State may enact laws pursuant to its police powers that have the purpose and effect of encouraging domestic industry." Bacchus Imports, Ltd. v. Dias, 468 U.S. at 271; Western & Southern Life Ins. Co. v. State Board of Equalization of California, supra, at 668. Cf. Edgar v. MITE Corp., 457 U.S. at 646 (Powell, J., concurring in part) (noting State's interest in protecting regionally based corporations from acquisition by foreign corporations).

Moreover, the Court has held in the dormant Commerce clause context that a State may provide subsidies or rebates to domestic but not to foreign enterprises if it rationally believes that the former contribute to the State's welfare in ways that the latter do not. Hughes v. Alexandria Scrap Corp., 426 U.S. 794 (1976). Although the Court has divided on the circumstances in which the dormant Commerce Clause allows such measures, see id., at 817 (BRENNAN, J., dissenting), surely there can be no dispute that they are constitutionally permitted where Congress itself has affirmatively authorized the States to promote local business concerns free of Commerce Clause constraints. Neither the Commerce Clause nor the Equal Protection Clause bars Congress from enacting or authorizing the States to enact legislation to protect industry in one State "from disadvantageous competition" with less stringently regulated businesses in other States. Hodel v. Indiana, 452 U.S. at 329. See also

Western & Southern, supra, at 669 (with congressional approval, States may promote domestic insurers by seeking to deter other States from enacting discriminatory or excessive taxes).

The majority's attempts to distinguish these precedents are unconvincing. First the majority suggests that a state purpose might be legitimate for purposes of the Commerce Clause but somehow illegitimate for purposes of the Equal Protection Clause. No basis is advanced for this theory because no basis exists. The test of a legitimate state purpose must be whether it addresses valid state concerns. To suggest that the purpose's legitimacy, chameleon-like, changes according to the constitutional clause cited in the complaint is merely another pretext to escape the clear message of this Court's precedents.

Next the majority asserts that "a State may not constitutionally favor its own residents by taxing foreign corporations at a higher rate solely because of their residence," citing cases that rejected discriminatory ad valorem property taxes, defended as taxes on the "privilege" of doing business. See, e.g., WHYY, Inc. v. Glassboro, 393 U.S. 117 (1968); Wheeling Steel Corp. v. Glander, 337 U.S. 562 (1949); Hanover Fire Ins. Co. v. Harding, 272 U.S. 494 (1926); Southern R. Co. v. Greene, 216 U.S. 400 (1910). These decisions were addressed in Western & Southern, and the classifications were characterized as impermissibly discriminatory because they did not "'rest on differences pertinent to the subject in respect of which the classification is made.'" 451 U.S. at 668, quoting Power Manufacturing Co. v. Saunders, 274 U.S. at 494. As the majority concedes, none of these decisions intimates that the tax statutes at issue in the decisions rested on relevant differences between domestic and foreign corporations or had purposes other than the raising of revenue at the out-of-state corporations' expense.

In fact, the Court noted in several of these opinions that foreign corporations *may* validly be taxed at a higher rate if the classification is based on some relevant distinction. No such distinction, however, had been demonstrated or even alleged. See WHYY, Inc. v. Glassboro, supra, at 120 ("This is not a case in which the exemption was withheld by reason of the foreign corporation's failure or inability to benefit the State in the same measure as do domestic nonprofit corporations"); Wheeling Steel Corp. v. Glander, supra, at 572 ("[T]he inequality is not because of the slightest difference in Ohio's relation to the decisive transaction"); Southern R. Co. v. Greene, supra, at 416-417 (parties conceded that the business of the foreign and domestic corporations was precisely the

distinction relevant to an asserted purpose, the classifications at issue in these decisions could never have survived rational basis scrutiny and no such analysis was even attempted. These precedents do not answer the question posed by this case: whether a legislature may adopt differential tax treatment of domestic and foreign insurers not simply to raise additional revenue but with the purpose of affecting the market as an "instrument of economic and social engineering." P. Hartman, Federal Limitations on State and Local Taxation § 3:2 (1981). The majority's suggestion that these cases necessarily decided the issue before us, as promotion of domestic business is "logically the primary reason for enacting discriminatory taxes such as those at issue [in the cited cases]," is mere speculation.

In treating these cases as apposite authority, the majority again closes its eyes to the facts. Alabama does *not* tax at a higher rate solely on the basis of residence; it taxes insurers, domestic as well as foreign, who do not maintain a principal place of business or substantial assets in Alabama, based on conceded distinctions in the contributions of these insurers *as a class* to the State's insurance objectives. The majority obscures the issue by observing that a given "foreign insurance company doing the same type and volume of business in Alabama as a domestic company" will pay a higher tax. Under our precedents, tax classifications need merely "res[t] upon some reasonable consideration of difference or policy." Allied Stores of Ohio, Inc. v. Bowers, 358 U.S. at 527. Rational basis scrutiny does not require that the classification be mathematically precise or that *every* foreign insurer or *every* domestic company fit to perfection the general profile on which the classification is based. "[T]he Equal Protection Clause does not demand a surveyor's precision" in fashioning classifications. Hughes v. Alexandria Scrap Corp., 426 U.S. at 814.

IV

Because Alabama's classification bears a rational relationship to a legitimate purpose, our precedents demand that it be sustained. The Court avoids this clear directive by a remarkable evasive tactic. It simply declares that the ends of promoting a domestic insurance industry and attracting investments to the State *when accomplished through the means of discriminatory taxation* are not legitimate state purposes. This bold assertion marks a drastic and unfortunate departure from established equal protection doctrine. By collapsing the two prongs of the rational basis test into one, the Court arrives at the ultimate issue—whether the *means* are constitutional—without ever engaging in the deferential inquiry we have adopted as a brake on judicial impeachment of legislative policy choices. In addition to unleashing an undisciplined form of Equal Protection Clause scrutiny, the Court's approach today has serious implications for the authority of Congress under the Commerce Clause. Groping for some basis for this radical departure from equal protection analysis, the Court draws heavily on Justice Brennan's concurring opinion in Allied Stores of Ohio, Inc. v. Bowers, supra, at 530, as support for its argument that "the Equal Protection Clause forbids a State to discriminate in favor of its own residents solely by burdening 'the residents of other state members of our federation.'"

As noted in Western & Southern, Justice Brennan's interpretation has not been adopted by the Court, "which has subsequently required no more than a rational basis for discrimination by States against out-of-state interests in the context of equal protection litigation." 451 U.S. at 667, n. 21. More importantly, to the extent the Court today purports to find in the Equal Protection Clause an instrument of federalism, it entirely misses the point of Justice Brennan's analysis. Justice Brennan reasoned that "[t]he Constitution furnishes the structure for the operation of the States with respect to the National Government and with respect to each other" and that "the Equal Protection Clause, among its other roles, operates to maintain this principle of federalism." 358 U.S. at 532. Favoring local business as an end in itself might be "rational" but would be antithetical to federalism. Accepting arguendo this interpretation, we have shown that the measure at issue here does not benefit local business as an end in itself but serves important ulterior goals. Moreover, any federalism component of equal protection is fully vindicated where Congress has explicitly validated a parochial focus. Surely the Equal Protection Clause was not intended to supplant the Commerce Clause, foiling Congress' decision under its commerce powers to "affirmatively permit [some measure of] parochial favoritism" when necessary to a healthy federation. White v. Massachusetts Council of Construction Employers, Inc., 460 U.S. at 213. Such a view of the Equal Protection Clause cannot be reconciled with the McCarran-Ferguson Act and our decisions in Western & Southern and Benjamin.

Western & Southern established that a State may validly tax out-of-state corporations at a higher rate if its goal is to promote the ability of its domestic businesses to compete in interstate markets. Nevertheless, the Court today concludes that the converse policy is forbidden, striking down legislation whose purpose is to encourage the intrastate activities of local business concerns by permitting them to compete effectively on their home turf. In essence, the Court declares: "We will excuse an unequal burden on foreign insurers if the State's purpose is to foster its domestic insurers' activities in other States, but the same unequal burden will be unconstitutional when employed to further a policy that places a higher social value on the domestic insurer's home State than interstate activities." This conclusion is not drawn from the Commerce Clause, the textual source of constitutional restrictions on state interference with interstate competition. Reliance on the Commerce Clause would, of course, be unavailing here in view of the McCarran-Ferguson Act. Instead the Court engrafts its own economic values on the Equal Protection Clause. Beyond guarding against arbitrary or irrational discrimination, as interpreted by the Court today this Clause now prohibits the effectuation of economic policies, even where sanctioned by Congress, that elevate local concerns over interstate competition. "But a constitution is not intended to embody a particular economic theory. . . . It is made for people of fundamentally differing views." Lochner v. New York, 198 U.S. at 75-76 (Holmes, J., dissenting). In the heyday of economic due process, Justice Holmes warned:

"Courts should be careful not to extend [the express] prohibitions [of the Constitution] beyond their obvious meaning by reading into them conceptions of public policy that the particular Court may happen to entertain." Tyson & Brother v. Banton, 273 U.S. at 445-446 (Holmes, J., dissenting, joined by Brandeis, J.).

Ignoring the wisdom of this observation, the Court fashions its own brand of economic equal protection. In so doing, it supplants a legislative policy endorsed by both Congress and the individual States that explicitly sanctioned the very parochialism in regulation and taxation of insurance that the Court's decision holds illegitimate.

The doctrine adopted by the majority threatens the freedom not only of the States but also of the Federal Government to formulate economic policy. The dangers in discerning in the Equal Protection Clause a prohibition against barriers to interstate business irrespective of the Commerce Clause should be self-evident. The Commerce Clause is a flexible tool of economic policy that Congress may use as it sees fit, letting it lie dormant or invoking it to limit as well as promote the free flow of commerce. Doctrines of equal protection are constitutional limits that constrain the acts of federal and state legislatures alike. See, e.g., Califano v. Webster, 430 U.S. 313 (1977); Cohen, Congressional Power to Validate Unconstitutional State Laws: A Forgotten Solution to an Old Enigma, 35 Stan. L. Rev. 387, 400-413 (1983). The Court's analysis casts a shadow over numerous congressional enactments that adopted as federal policy "the type of parochial favoritism" the Court today finds unconstitutional. White v. Massachusetts Council of Construction Employers, Inc., supra, at 213. Contrary to the reasoning in Benjamin, the

Court today indicates the Equal Protection Clause stands as an independent barrier if courts should determine that either Congress or a State has ventured the "wrong" direction down what has become, by judicial fiat, the one-way street of the Commerce Clause. Nothing in the Constitution or our past decisions supports forcing such an economic straitjacket on the federal system.

V

Today's opinion charts an ominous course. I can only hope this unfortunate adventure away from the safety of our precedents will be an isolated episode. I had thought the Court had finally accepted that "the judiciary may not sit as a superlegislature to judge the wisdom or desirability of legislative policy determinations made in areas that neither affect fundamental rights nor proceed along suspect lines; in the local economic sphere, it is only the invidious discrimination, the wholly arbitrary act, which cannot stand consistently with the Fourteenth Amendment." New Orleans v. Dukes, 427 U.S. at 303-304 (citations omitted).

Because I believe that the Alabama law at issue here serves legitimate state purposes through concededly rational means, and thus is neither invidious nor arbitrary, I would affirm the court below. I respectfully dissent.

Questions and Comments

1. The Court states that *Western & Southern* held that California's promotion of the interstate business of its domestic insurers was a legitimate purpose. How is California's promotion of the interstate business of its domestic insurers different from Alabama's promotion of its domestic insurance industry?

In *Western & Southern*, California taxed some, but not all foreign insurance companies at a higher rate than it taxed domestic companies. In *Metropolitan*, Alabama taxed all foreign companies at a higher rate. Did that influence the Court at all?

2. The Court says that the only question before it is whether the purposes of the Alabama statute are legitimate. Does this statement comport with its analysis?

3. Does the Court's analysis blur "means" with "ends"? The appellants waived their right to an evidentiary hearing on the means used by Alabama to achieve the statute's ends. Presumably, the only issue before the Court was the legitimacy of the ends. In addressing that issue, does the Court examine the means the Legislature adopted? Given the Court's analysis, is it likely to rule differently on any of the issues that will be decided upon remand?

Does the Court's treatment of *Allied Stores* confuse means with ends? The Court says that *Allied Stores* does not hold that promotion of domestic business by discriminating against foreign corporations is legitimate. But isn't the only question before the Court in *Metropolitan* whether the promotion of domestic business is legitimate?

4. Presumably, the promotion of domestic business is a legitimate state purpose under certain circumstances. Is the means the Alabama Legislature chose to implement that goal irrational? What could be more rational than promoting domestic business by discriminating against foreign businesses? If promoting domestic business is a legitimate state purpose, and if the rational relationship issue is not before the Court, why was the Alabama statute unconstitutional?

5. What if Alabama's purpose was described as inducing foreign insurers to incorporate and maintain their principal place of business in Alabama in order to better serve the needs of Alabama residents? Or, what if its purpose was described as making it economically feasible for its small domestic insurance companies to compete with large out-of-state companies in the interstate market? Would either of these descriptions strengthen Alabama's case? What constraints exist in describing a state's purpose?

6. The Circuit Court for Montgomery County ruled that the Alabama statute served the purpose of encouraging the formation of new insurance companies in Alabama. The Circuit Court also ruled that the statute encouraged capital investment by foreign insurance companies in Alabama assets. Did the Supreme Court hold that these are not legitimate state purposes? What is the defect in the Alabama statute? Is promotion of its domestic industry an illegitimate state purpose? Is the way Alabama sought to promote the industry not rational? Is discrimination against foreign insurers an irrational means of promoting its domestic insurance industry?

7. Could California's purpose in *Western & Southern* be

described as promoting its domestic insurance industry through taxes discriminating against out-of-state companies?

8. The trial court found that the encouragement of the formation of new domestic insurance companies in Alabama was a legitimate reason for the statute's classification. The State argued that the formation of new domestic insurance companies promoted domestic industry. What is the relationship between the formation of a domestic insurance company and the promotion of domestic industry?

9. Is Alabama's scheme whereby it reduces a foreign insurance company's tax if that company invests in Alabama assets similar to or different from an investment tax credit, whereby a corporation can reduce its tax liability by investing in qualifying assets?

10. Constitutionally, can Alabama offer a tax reduction to all corporations, domestic and foreign, that invest in Alabama assets? Could Alabama limit that reduction to only foreign corporations?

11. Is the Court's treatment of *Allied Stores* disingenuous? The Court describes that case as involving a statute that encourages nonresidents who are not competitors of residents to build warehouses within Ohio. Is there anything in the actual case that refers to whether the nonresidents are competitors of residents?

Allied Stores involved a situation where a nonresident corporation received a benefit that a resident corporation did not. How strong a precedent is *Allied Stores* for *Metropolitan*? What is left of *Allied Stores* after this case?

12. Suppose that a foreign insurance company decided to sell industrial insurance in Alabama. It rents a small office in Mobile and hires a team of part-time sales persons, who sell door-to-door. Would such an insurance company qualify for the lower rate under the Alabama statute? How does your answer affect the Court's reasoning?

13. Would the Alabama statute be constitutional if it provided a tax incentive to corporations whose principal office and chief place of business were within Alabama regardless of where they were incorporated?

14. Under O'Connor's view, could a well-advised legislature provide a rationale that would immunize against equal protection attack almost any tax statute that discriminated against "out-of-state" corporations?

15. Would the opinion have been different if foreign insurance companies could have fully eliminated the discrimination inherent in the domestic preference tax statute by investing in Alabama assets?

16. Justice Powell distinguishes equal protection analysis from commerce clause analysis by noting that not every law that violates the Commerce Clause will necessarily violate the Equal Protection Clause because of the different standards of review. The Commerce Clause invalidates a law, even if rational, if the burden imposed is excessive, whereas the Equal Protection Clause invalidates a law only if it is not rationally related to a legitimate purpose. In addition, the Commerce Clause applies to "commerce" while the Equal Protection Clause applies "persons".

According to Professor Cohen, "The kindest comments that can be made about these two arguments is that they are, respectively, irrelevant and silly." Cohen, Federalism in Equality Clothing: A Comment on *Metropolitan Life Insurance Company v. Ward*, 38 Stan. L. Rev. 1, 11 (1985). Professor Cohen argues that *Metropolitan Life* incorporated a watered down version of the Commerce Clause into its equal protection analysis and thus any measure that can pass commerce clause scrutiny should also satisfy the constitutional requirement of equal protection.

As framed by Justice Powell's opinion, the issue in *[Metropolitan]* did not concern whether the tax's structure "fit" its asserted purposes, but whether those purposes were forbidden by the Constitution. Different standards of judicial review were not relevant to the outcome in *[Metropolitan]*. As in *Western & Southern Life*, it was still necessary to identify a constitutional source for the proposition that benefitting local business by burdening out-of-state business is an impermissible purpose.

. . . .

The Court's second argument attempts to identify an equality value distinct from that flowing from the commerce clause. The equal protection clause, Justice Powell argued, supplies a distinct constitutional value forbidding discrimination against persons, while the commerce clause concerns only discrimination against commerce. Until, however, technology creates a world where out-of-state businesses are run and owned by something other than persons, any discrimination against out-of-state commerce must discriminate against persons.

Can every Due Process objection to a tax be restated as an Equal Protection objection? Can every Equal Protection objection to a tax be restated as a Due Process objection?

17. Is it useful to characterize *Western & Southern* as an attempt by California to generate a more level national playing field whereas Alabama's attempt was purposely to

make the playing field full of potholes and mounds? Does this sound like equal protection analysis or commerce clause analysis?

18. The Court states that "unlike the retaliatory tax involved in *Western & Southern*, which only burdens residents of a State that imposes its own *discriminatory* tax on outsiders, the domestic preference tax gives the 'home team' an advantage by burdening all foreign corporations seeking to do business within the State, no matter what they or their States do." Is the Court's understanding of the California statute correct? Did California retaliate only against residents of a state that imposed its own discriminatory tax on outsiders?

19. Given the nature of Justice Brennan's concurrence in *Allied*, is his dissent in *Metropolitan* unexpected?

20. Would the Alabama statute survive a Commerce Clause challenge?

21. If foreign insurance companies have no interest in writing industrial or burial policies, why do domestic insurance companies need any help whatsoever in competing in this market?

22. Could Congress overturn *Metropolitan Life* by legislation approving discriminatory insurance taxes?

23. The State asserted that the encouragement of capital investment in Alabama assets was a legitimate purpose. The Court rejected this argument on the grounds that investment in the specified assets would never reduce the premiums tax of foreign companies to the same rate as that imposed on domestic companies. Be that as it may, why is Alabama's goal illegitimate?

24. Suppose Alabama levied a discriminatory tax on only domestic corporations. How much of this case would be relevant to that tax?

25. In the short time since *Metropolitan Life* was decided, state courts have struck down their state's discriminatory insurance premiums tax. See *State v.*

American Bankers Ins. Co., 374 N.W. 2d 609 (S. D. 1985); *Metropolitan Life Ins. Co. v. Comm'r.*, 373 N.W.2d 399 (N. D. 1985); *Penn Mut. Ins. Co. v. Mich.*, 412 N.W.2d 669 (1987); *Principal Mut. Life v. Alaska*, 780 P2d 1023 (1989); but see *Gallagher v. Motors Ins. Corp.*, 605 So.2d 62 (Fla. 1992); *Harbor Ins. v. Conn.*, 544 A.2d 1221 (1988).

26. Insurance is not the only industry denied Commerce Clause protection. The Douglas Amendment to the Bank Holding Company Act, 12 U.S. C. Section 1842(d) (1982), prohibits a bank holding company or bank in one state from acquiring a bank in another state, unless the acquisition is "specifically authorized by the statute laws of the State in which such bank is located, by language to that effect and not merely by implication." In *Northeast Bancorp v. Board of Governors of the Federal Reserve System*, 472 U.S. 159 (1985), the Court upheld Massachusetts and Connecticut statutes permitting out-of-state bank holding companies based in one of the other New England states to acquire in-state banks, but prohibiting non-New England companies from acquiring in-state banks. Can you reconcile this case with *Metropolitan Life*? Justice O'Connor wrote in *Northeast Bancorp* "It is not clear to me why completely barring the banks of 44 States from doing business is less discriminatory than Alabama's scheme of taxing the insurance companies from 49 States at a slightly higher rate. Nor is it clear why the Equal Protection Clause should tolerate a regional 'home team' when it condemns a state 'home team.'" 472 U.S. at 179 (O'Connor, J. concurring).

27. For critical commentary on *Metropolitan Life*, see William Cohen, *Federalism in Equality Clothing: A Comment on Metropolitan Life Insurance Company v. Ward*, 38 Stan. L. Rev. 1 (1985); David W. Haller, *Within the States' Jurisdiction: Metropolitan, Northeast Bancorp, and the Equal Protection Clause*, 96 Yale L. J. 2110 (1987); Edward M. Burgh, *Metropolitan v. Ward: A Timely Second Look*, Nat'l Underwriter - Prop. & Casualty Ins. Ed., Feb. 7, 1986, at 19; William Cohen, *Federalism in Equality Clothing: A Comment on Metropolitan Life Insurance Company v. Ward*, 38 Stan. L. Rev. 1 (1985); Walter Hellerstein & Ruurd Leegstra, *Sup. Court in Metropolitan Life Strikes Down Discriminatory State Insurance Tax*, 63 J. Tax'n 108 (1985).

Williams v. Vermont
Supreme Court of the United States, 1985.
472 U.S. 14, 105 S. Ct. 2465, 86 L. Ed. 2d 11.

Car Regist. Tax
credits

JUSTICE WHITE delivered the opinion of the Court.

The State of Vermont collects a use tax when cars are registered with it. The tax is not imposed if the car was purchased in Vermont and a sales tax has been paid. The

tax is also reduced by the amount of any sales or use tax paid to another State if that State would afford a credit for taxes paid to Vermont in similar circumstances. The credit is available, however, only if the registrant was a Vermont resident at the time he paid the taxes.

Appellants, who bought cars outside of Vermont before becoming residents of that State, challenge the failure to grant them a similar credit. We agree that this failure denies them the equal protection of the laws.

. . . .

II

The Vermont Motor Vehicle Purchase and Use Tax is distinct from the State's general sales and use taxes. It is intended to "improve and maintain the state and interstate highway systems, to pay the principal and interest on bonds issued for the improvement and maintenance of those systems and to pay the cost of administering this chapter." The revenue from the tax goes into a distinct "transportation fund.". . .

[The Purchase and Use Tax] provides that the tax does not apply to

"pleasure cars acquired outside the state by a resident of Vermont on which a state sales or use tax has been paid by the person applying for a registration in Vermont, providing that the state or province collecting such tax would grant the same pro-rata credit for Vermont tax paid under similar circumstances. If the tax paid in another state is less than the Vermont tax the tax due shall be the difference."

. . . .

III

This Court has expressly reserved the question whether a State must credit a sales tax paid to another State against its own use tax. Southern Pacific Co. v. Gallagher, 306 U.S. at 172; Henneford v. Silas Mason Co., 300 U.S. at 587. The District of Columbia and all but three States with sales and use taxes do provide such a credit, although reciprocity may be required. CCH, State Tax Guide 6013 (1984). . . . Once again, however, we find it unnecessary to reach this question. Whatever the general rule may be, to provide a credit only to those who were residents at the time they paid the sales tax to another State is an arbitrary distinction that violates the Equal Protection Clause.

This Court has many times pointed out that in structuring internal taxation schemes "the States have large leeway in making classifications and drawing lines which in their judgment produce reasonable systems of taxation." Lehnhausen v. Lake Shore Auto Parts Co., 410 U.S. at 359. It has been reluctant to interfere with legislative policy decisions in this area. See Regan v. Taxation with Representation of Washington, 461 U.S.

---

*. [Ed. The tax at issue for both appellants was $282. Williams, a lawyer, argued the case pro se.]

at 547-548; San Antonio Independent School District v. Rodriguez, 411 U.S. 1, 40-41 (1973); Allied Stores of Ohio, Inc. v. Bowers, 358 U.S. at 526-527. An exemption such as that challenged here "will be sustained if the legislature could have reasonably concluded that the challenged classification would promote a legitimate state purpose." Exxon Corp. v. Eagerton, 462 U.S. at 196. See generally Schweiker v. Wilson, 450 U.S. at 234-235.

We perceive no legitimate purpose, however, that is furthered by this discriminatory exemption. As we said in holding that the use tax base cannot be broader than the sales tax base, "equal treatment for in-state and out-of-state taxpayers similarly situated is the condition precedent for a valid use tax on goods imported from out-of-state." Halliburton Oil Well Co. v. Reily, 373 U.S. at 70.[7] A State may not treat those within its borders unequally solely on the basis of their different residences or States of incorporation. WHYY v. Glassboro, 393 U.S. at 119; Wheeling Steel Corp. v. Glander, 337 U.S. at 571-572. In the present case, residence at the time of purchase is a wholly arbitrary basis on which to distinguish among present Vermont registrants—at least among those who used their cars elsewhere before coming to Vermont.[8] Having registered a car in Vermont they are similarly situated for all relevant purposes. Each is a Vermont resident, using a car in Vermont, with an equal obligation to pay for the maintenance and improvement of Vermont's roads. The purposes of the statute would be identically served, and with an identical burden, by taxing each. The distinction between them bears no relation to the statutory purpose. See Zobel v. Williams, 457 U.S. at 61; cf. Texaco, Inc. v. Short, 454 U.S. at 540. As the Court said in Wheeling, appellants have not been "accorded equal treatment, and the inequality is not because of the slightest difference in [Vermont's] relation to the decisive transaction, but solely because of the[ir] different residence." 337 U.S. at 572.

---

7. Halliburton was decided under the Commerce Clause and is not dispositive. We do not consider in what way, if any, the failure to give appellants a credit might burden interstate commerce. The critical point is the Court's emphasis on the need for equal treatment of taxpayers who can be distinguished only on the basis of residence. See also Henneford v. Silas Mason Co., 300 U.S. at 583-584.

8. The dissent does not disagree that such people are similarly situated, nor does it identify any justification for preferential treatment of the resident. It merely argues that the inequity is the acceptable result of the imprecision of a generally rational classification. Under rational-basis scrutiny, legislative classifications are of course allowed some play in the joints. But the choice of a proxy criterion—here, residence for State of use—cannot be so casual as this, particularly when a more precise and direct classification is easily drawn.

. . . .

Applied to those such as appellants, the use tax exceeds the usual justifications for such a tax. A use tax is generally perceived as a necessary complement to the sales tax, designed to "'protect a state's revenues by taking away the advantages to residents of traveling out of state to make untaxed purchases, and to protect local merchants from out-of-state competition which, because of its lower or nonexistent tax burdens, can offer lower prices.'" [Leverson v. Conway, 481 A. 2d 1029, at 1032] quoting Rowe-Genereux, Inc. v. Department of Taxes, 411 A. 2d 1345, 1347 (1980); see Henneford v. Silas Mason Co., supra, at 581. This customary rationale for the use tax has no application to purchases made out-of-state by those who were not residents of the taxing State at the time of purchase. These home-state transactions cannot be seen as lost Vermont sales, and are certainly not ones lost as a result of Vermont's sales tax. Imposing a use tax on them in no way protects local business. In short, in its structure, this sales and use tax combination is exactly the opposite of the customary provisions: there is no disincentive to the Vermont resident's purchasing outside the State, and there is a penalty on those who bought out-of-state but could not have been expected to do otherwise. The first provision limits local commerce, the second does not help it.

Despite Leverson's passing reference to the standard rationale for use taxes, then, the only plausible justification for imposing the tax on those in appellants' position in the first place—apart from the simple desire to raise funds—is the principle that those using the roads should pay for them. In Leverson, the Vermont Supreme Court supported the tax by reference to "Vermont's basic policy" of making those who use the highways contribute to their maintenance and improvement. 481 A. 2d, at 1034.[9] Yet this does not explain the exemption

for a resident who bought a car elsewhere and paid a tax to another State, which, as the dissent points out . . . is "directly contrary" to the user-pays principle. This "basic policy" arguably supports imposition of the use tax on appellants, and the denial of a credit to them; but it provides no rational reason to spare Vermont residents an equal burden. The same response applies to the Vermont court's statement that to allow an exemption for people in appellants' position, or for Vermonters who purchase in nonreciprocal States, "would run counter to the state's present policies of requiring user contributions and encouraging purchases within the state, and would result in the loss of tax revenues to the state." 481 A. 2d, at 1035. This is no less true with regard to the Vermonter who purchases a car in a reciprocal State. Granting the resident a credit for sales tax paid to the other State is similarly "counter to the state's policies of requiring user contributions and encouraging purchases within the state." Ibid.

. . . .

Appellees take a different tack, suggesting that the exemption is designed to encourage interstate commerce by enabling Vermont residents, faced with limited automobile offerings at home . . . to shop outside the State without penalty. . . . This justification may sound plausible, but it fails to support the classification at issue. Those in appellants' position pay exactly the penalty for purchasing out-of-state that Vermont spares its own residents. The credit may rationally further Vermont's legitimate interest in facilitating Vermonters' out-of-state purchases, but this interest does not extend to the facilitation of Vermonters' out-of-state use. Vermont may choose not to penalize old residents who used their cars in other States, but it cannot extend that benefit to old residents and deny it to new ones. The fact that it may be rational or beneficent to spare some the burden of double taxation does not mean that the beneficence can be distributed arbitrarily.

. . . .

In sum, we can see no relevant difference between motor vehicle registrants who purchased their cars out-of-state while they were Vermont residents and those who only came to Vermont after buying a car elsewhere. To free one group and not the other from the otherwise applicable tax burden violates the Equal Protection Clause.

IV

Our holding is quite narrow, and we conclude by emphasizing what we do not decide. We need not consider appellants' various arguments based on the right to travel, the Privileges and Immunities Clause, and the

---

9. A nonrecurring use tax pegged to the value of the car is an exceedingly loosely tailored means to this end. The amount of such a payment has no relation to the extent of use, includes the irrelevant variable of the luxury value of the car, and fails to account for the possibility of the owner moving out of the State or selling the car during its useful life. Reliance on annual registration fees would provide a more accurate measure of current use and would seem to be more closely related to the stated purpose. However, appellants do not challenge the tax itself as an equal protection violation. And despite the looseness of the fit, we would be hard pressed to say that this manner of funding highway maintenance and construction is irrational. "If the classification has some 'reasonable basis,' it does not offend the Constitution simply because the classification 'is not made with mathematical nicety or because in practice it results in some inequality.'" Dandridge v. Williams, 397 U.S. at 485, quoting Lindsley v. Natural Carbonic Gas Co., 220 U.S. at 78.

Commerce Clause. We again put to one side the question whether a State must in all circumstances credit sales or use taxes paid to another State against its own use tax. In addition, we note that this action was dismissed [below] for failure to state a claim before an answer was filed. The "dominant theme running through all state taxation cases" is the "concern with the actuality of operation." Halliburton, 373 U.S. at 69. It is conceivable that, were a full record developed, it would turn out that in practice the statute does not operate in a discriminatory fashion. Finally, in light of the fact that the action was dismissed on the pleadings, and given the possible relevance of state law, see Bacchus Imports, Ltd. v. Dias, 468 U.S. at 277, we express no opinion as to the appropriate remedy.

We hold only that, when the statute is viewed on its face, appellants have stated a claim of unconstitutional discrimination. The decision below is accordingly reversed, and the case is remanded for further proceedings not inconsistent with this opinion.

JUSTICE POWELL took no part in the decision of this case.

JUSTICE BRENNAN, concurring.

I join the Court's opinion for the reasons stated therein and in my concurring opinion in Zobel v. Williams, 457 U.S. at 65. General application of distinctions of the kind made by the Vermont statute would clearly, though indirectly, threaten the "federal interest in free interstate migration." Id., at 66. In addition, the statute makes distinctions among residents that are not "supported by a valid state interest independent of the discrimination itself." Id., at 70.

JUSTICE BLACKMUN, with whom JUSTICE REHNQUIST and JUSTICE O'CONNOR join, dissenting.

The Court in this case draws into question the constitutionality of a statute that was not intended to discriminate against anyone, does not discriminate against appellants, and, for all that appears, never has been applied in a discriminatory fashion against anyone else. Nevertheless, the Court has imagined a fanciful hypothetical discrimination, and then has threatened that the statute will violate equal protection unless the Vermont Supreme Court or the Vermont Legislature rejects the Court's conjecture.

As the Court recognizes, Vermont's use tax is designed to help defray the State's cost for building and maintaining its roads. Generally speaking, if one purchases an automobile in Vermont, one pays a sales

tax on the purchase. If one purchases a car elsewhere but registers it in Vermont, the use tax is assessed. The end result is that likely users of the State's roads are assessed a tax for their use. The overlapping series of credits and exemptions built into this vehicle tax system are designed to resolve a number of less common cases that fall outside the typical pattern of a Vermonter's purchase of a car either in Vermont or elsewhere. However complex and redundant, the exceptions and credits accomplish two related legitimate purposes: they facilitate the flow of interstate commerce by ensuring that residents and nonresidents alike are not penalized for purchasing cars in a foreign State, and they protect against the possibility that someone using the roads primarily in only one State will be forced to pay taxes in two States.

Thus Vermont, along with apparently every other State, will not charge a sales tax to an out-of-state purchaser of an automobile. This exemption ensures that out-of-state purchasers who do not use Vermont roads except to leave the State will not be made to pay for their use. The credit at issue in this litigation accomplishes much the same purpose. If a Vermont resident, for whatever reason, *does* pay an out-of-state sales tax, then, when he returns to Vermont with his car, he will be excused from payment of Vermont's use tax to the extent of the amount paid by way of the sales tax, if the other State provides a reciprocal credit. Again, the credit facilitates the interstate purchase of automobiles, and helps ensure that a car buyer is not paying for the use of two States' roads when using only one.[1]

A

Vermont's tax credit system worked exactly as it was intended to work in the cases of [appellants]. Each purchased his or her car and used it for a time in another State, and so paid a tax to that State for the use of its roads. When each subsequently moved to Vermont and registered the cars there, he or she paid a second tax for the use of the roads in their new State. Each used his or her car in two States, and each paid two States' use or

---

1. In the rare event that the use-tax credit is used because the out-of-state sales tax for some reason was paid, the State that receives the tax will not be the State whose roads are used, but the State where the car was purchased. Because the statute is reciprocal, however, it is hardly irrational to assume that the reciprocal payments will even out. The exemptions, thus, are entirely consistent with the user-pays principle of the tax. And from the point of view of the purchaser, as with these appellants, it matters little to whom he is paying a tax. He is using the car primarily in only one State, and paying a use or sales tax in one State.

sales taxes. Thus, appellants are not situated similarly to a Vermont resident who buys his car in Illinois or New York, is exempted from sales taxes there, drives it to Vermont, and pays Vermont's use tax. Such an individual uses a car only in Vermont, and pays only Vermont's use tax. As the Superior Court most appropriately found, any difference in treatment between appellants and the typical Vermont out-of-state automobile purchaser "is supported by [appellants'] use of the highways of more than one state." Nor would it have furthered the commerce-facilitating purposes of the tax to extend a credit to persons in appellants' situation. Having *already* purchased their cars, they are beyond the reach of any credit designed to facilitate the purchase of cars across state lines.

Vermont's asserted purposes being concededly legitimate, and the means used to achieve those purposes rational in the abstract and effective in these particular instances, the tax exemption should easily pass the minimal scrutiny this Court routinely applies to tax statutes. See, e.g., Regan v. Taxation with Representation of Washington, 461 U.S. at 547-548. The Court, however, has subjected Vermont's motor vehicle tax laws to a kind of microscopic scrutiny that few enactments could survive, and has managed, it feels, to find a way in which the statute can be understood to discriminate against appellants. The Court seems to have adopted a new level of scrutiny that is neither minimal nor strict, but strange unto itself. Out there somewhere, the Court imagines, is someone whom Vermont wishes to treat better than it treated [appellants].

This phantom beneficiary of Vermont's discrimination is a Vermont resident who leaves the State to purchase an automobile, pays the sales tax and registers the car in the foreign State of purchase, lives there for a while, and then returns to Vermont and registers the car there. This resident is said to be entitled to the [exemption and credit] while the similarly situated nonresident such as Mr. Williams is not. The phantom's car is said to be entitled to the credit because it is "acquired outside the state by a resident of Vermont" under the terms of the statute. . . . .

C

Even if the Court is correct in its understanding of [the statute], however, the identified discrimination still is created by a classification rationally related to a legitimate governmental purpose sufficient to satisfy the minimal scrutiny the Court routinely applies in similar equal protection challenges to tax provisions. The Court admits that it is a legitimate governmental purpose to assess taxes on people who use roads to provide for their upkeep. The question then becomes whether the identified discrimination worked by [the statute] is designed rationally to further this purpose. And I would have thought the answer was not even close.

The reason nonresidents who purchase cars out-of-state are taxed if they subsequently relocate in Vermont, while resident out-of-state purchasers are not, is that it was presumed that people will use their cars primarily in the States in which they reside. Most people who do not reside in Vermont and do not purchase their cars in that State, will not use their cars primarily in Vermont. If at some time in the future they move to Vermont and register their automobiles there, the assumption is that they will have used their cars in two different States. On the other hand, most people who reside in Vermont and purchase their cars out-of-state will return to Vermont immediately with their cars. Thus, the out-of-state purchaser is taxed, while the Vermont purchaser is exempted to the extent that he already has paid a sales tax. This distinction is hardly irrational, and the fact that there may be a Vermont resident who both purchases and uses his car out-of-state, and is therefore situated similarly to Mr. Williams, surely does not render the scheme irrational. A tax classification does not violate the demands of equal protection simply because it may not perfectly identify the class of people it wishes to single out. A State "is not required to resort to close distinctions or to maintain a precise, scientific uniformity with reference to composition, use or value." Allied Stores of Ohio, Inc. v. Bowers, 358 U.S. at 527.[4]

The Court disagrees, and finds that "residence at the time of purchase is a wholly arbitrary basis on which to distinguish among present Vermont registrants–at least among those who used their cars elsewhere before coming to Vermont.". . . The Court, however, ignores the purpose of the tax and of the classification. Vermont does not wish to "distinguish among present Vermont registrants," but to distinguish those who will likely use Vermont's roads immediately after they have purchased cars out-of-state from those who will not. Residency is not an irrational way to enact such a classification.

---

4. "States have large leeway in making classifications and drawing lines which in their judgment produce reasonable systems of taxation." Lehnhausen v. Lake Shore Auto Parts Co., 410 U.S. at 359. Were it otherwise, it would be an easy task to ferret out inconsistencies in taxation schemes. After all, even if Vermont's statute were worded in terms of the State of first registration, rather than the State of residency, as the Court wishes, it would still be possible to imagine some hypothetical Vermont registrant who uses his car initially exclusively in some other State. He, too, is situated similarly to Mr. Williams in that neither initially is using Vermont roads.

Moreover, the Court's qualification misstates the language of the statute, for [it] does not distinguish among residents depending upon where they first *used* their cars, but upon where they *acquired* their cars. A classification based on the assumption that people will use their cars in the States where they live, rather than in the States where they acquire them, is far from the kind of "palpably arbitrary" classification that the Court previously has struck down on equal protection grounds. See Allied Stores of Ohio, Inc. v. Bowers, 358 U.S. at 527. . . . .

Questions and Comments

1. Was it relevant that the Motor Vehicle and Use Tax is separate from Vermont's general sales and use tax? Would the opinion have been different if motor vehicles were subject to the general Vermont sales tax?

2. In the proceedings below, the State asserted that the exemption and credit applied only to Vermont residents who registered their cars in Vermont without first having registered them elsewhere. Assuming the Court had accepted this interpretation, would the statute have been constitutional?

3. Is Justice Blackmun's dissent limited to situations such as transportation, in which theoretically, at least, some relationship exists between the item and the use of services provided by the state?

4. Is a use tax a genuine tax upon use? If a consumer uses an object in several states, should a tax be paid upon its use in each state? If a consumer pays a use tax in one state and uses the object in another, does the second state have to allow a credit for the first state's use tax?

5. Should a use tax ever be applied to a nonresident who purchases an item out-of-state without intending at the time of purchase to use the item within the taxing state?

6. How should the use tax be applied to moveable property (e.g., heavy machinery, construction equipment), which is used in various states for a few months at a time? See, e.g., *Whitecomb Constr. v. Comm'r of Taxes*, 479 A. 2d 164 (1984).

7. In the case of automobiles, suppose the state of use credits sales taxes paid to other jurisdictions. What should the measure of the sales tax be if the automobile has been driven out-of-state for any length of time? Original purchase price or current fair market value? Considering how rapidly new cars lose their value upon being driven off the dealer's lot, would a state ever receive any net revenue on the registration of new cars purchased out-of-state if it were to grant a credit based on original cost rather than fair market value?

8. The dissent notes that "Vermont, along with apparently every other state, will not charge a sales tax to an out-of-state purchaser of an automobile." Why not? Could a state constitutionally levy a sales tax in such a case? If an out-of-state purchaser will pay a use tax upon registering the car in his or her state of residence, and if the state of residence grants a credit for sales taxes paid to other states, what does the state of sale gain by exempting the transaction? Does your answer depend on whether the tax in the state of sale is greater than the tax in the state of residence?

9. What is the definition of a Vermont resident? Is that definition important in evaluating the issues involved in *Williams*? Is it also relevant to know when a person is required to register a car in Vermont? Can a nonresident of Vermont be required to register a car?

10. Did Vermont's statute violate the Privileges and Immunities Clause? The Commerce Clause? Is the decision best understood as the covert application of a heightened scrutiny standard because the statute discriminated on the grounds of residency?

11. What kind of facts would show "that in practice the statute does not operate in a discriminatory fashion?"

12. In the case of a trade-in allowance on the purchase of a new car, many states impose a sales tax on only the difference between the price of the new car and the amount of the trade-in allowance. Assume that Vermont follows this approach. Suppose that Williams purchased a new car outside Vermont, receiving a trade-in allowance for his old car. When he registers his new car in Vermont, can the State levy its use tax on the cost of the new car or does it have to take into account the trade-in allowance? See *Commonwealth v. Smith*, 75 Dauph. 22 (Pa. C. Dauphin County 1960); *Matthews v. State Dep't of Revenue*, 562 P.2d 415 (1977).

13. In response to *Williams*, Vermont issued an administrative ruling that denied a sales tax credit to Vermont residents who buy and register their cars in other states before registering them in Vermont.

Residents who purchase a car but do not register it out-of-state are allowed the credit. A suit was brought by a couple who purchased and registered a car in another state and who subsequently moved to Vermont. They registered their car in Vermont, paid the Vermont use tax, and were denied a credit for the sales tax they paid on their out-of-state purchase of the car. In *Barringer v. Griffes*, 1 F. 3d 1331 (1993), the Second Circuit held that the Vermont statute violated the Commerce Clause.

14. Suppose Vermont redrafted its statute to deny a credit to anyone who used his or her car outside Vermont for more than six months before registering the car in Vermont. Would this revised statute violate the Equal Protection Clause?

15. Can a state discriminate among classes of residents? See *Zobel v. Williams*, 457 U.S. 55 (1982) (state cannot make cash distributions to residents that varies in amount based on years of residency); Hooper v. Bernalillo County, 472 U.S. 612 (1985) (tax exemption for Vietnam veterans who were residents before May 8, 1976 violates Equal Protection Clause).

16. For critical commentary on *Williams*, see Lee A. Sheppard, *Williams v. Vermont; Supreme Court Assumes Discrimination*, 27 Tax Notes 1325 (1985).

Nordlinger v. Hahn
Supreme Court of the United States, 1992.
505 U.S. 1, 112 S. Ct. 2326, 120 L. Ed. 2d 1.

Prop. 13
Amend CA Constn.
EPC challenge

JUSTICE BLACKMUN delivered the opinion of the Court.

In 1978, California voters staged what has been described as a property tax revolt by approving a statewide ballot initiative known as Proposition 13. The adoption of Proposition 13 served to amend the California Constitution to impose strict limits on the rate at which real property is taxed and on the rate at which real property assessments are increased from year to year. In this litigation, we consider a challenge under the Equal Protection Clause of the Fourteenth Amendment to the manner in which real property now is assessed under the California Constitution.

I

A

Proposition 13 followed many years of rapidly rising real property taxes in California. From fiscal years 1967-1968 to 1971-1972, revenues from these taxes increased on an average of 11.5 percent per year. In response, the California Legislature enacted several property tax relief measures, including a cap on tax rates in 1972. The boom in the State's real estate market persevered, however, and the median price of an existing home doubled from $31,530 in 1973 to $62,430 in 1977. As a result, tax levies continued to rise because of sharply increasing assessment values. Some homeowners saw their tax bills double or triple during this period, well outpacing any growth in their income and ability to pay.

By 1978, property tax relief had emerged as a major political issue in California. In only one month's time, tax relief advocates collected over 1.2 million signatures to qualify Proposition 13 for the June 1978 ballot. On election day, Proposition 13 received a favorable vote of 64.8 percent and carried 55 of the State's 58 counties. California thus had a novel constitutional amendment that led to a property tax cut of approximately $7 billion in the first year. A California homeowner with a $50,000 home enjoyed an immediate reduction of about $750 per year in property taxes.

As enacted by Proposition 13, Article XIIIA of the California Constitution caps real property taxes at 1% of a property's "full cash value." § 1(a). "Full cash value" is defined as the assessed valuation as of the 1975-1976 tax year or, "thereafter, the appraised value of real property when purchased, newly constructed, or a change in ownership has occurred after the 1975 assessment." § 2(a). The assessment "may reflect from year to year the inflationary rate not to exceed 2 percent for any given year." § 2(b).

Article XIIIA also contains several exemptions from this reassessment provision. One exemption authorizes the legislature to allow homeowners over the age of 55 who sell their principal residences to carry their previous base-year assessments with them to replacement residences of equal or lesser value. § 2(a). A second exemption applies to transfers of a principal residence (and up to $1 million of other real property) between parents and children. § 2(h).

In short, Article XIIIA combines a 1% ceiling on the property tax rate with a 2% cap on annual increases in assessed valuations. The assessment limitation, however, is subject to the exception that new construction or a change of ownership triggers a reassessment up to current appraised value. Thus, the assessment provisions of Article XIIIA essentially embody an "acquisition value" system of taxation rather than the more commonplace "current value" taxation. Real property is assessed at values related to the value of the property at the time it is acquired by the taxpayer rather than to the value it has in the current real estate market.

Over time, this acquisition value system has created dramatic disparities in the taxes paid by persons owning similar pieces of property. Property values in California have inflated far in excess of the allowed 2% cap on increases in assessments for property that is not newly constructed or that has not changed hands. As a result, longer-term property owners pay lower property taxes reflecting historic property values, while newer owners pay higher property taxes reflecting more recent values. For that reason, Proposition 13 has been labeled by some as a "welcome stranger" system—the newcomer to an established community is "welcome" in anticipation that he will contribute a larger percentage of support for local government than his settled neighbor who owns a comparable home. Indeed, in dollar terms, the differences in tax burdens are staggering. By 1989, the 44% of California home owners who have owned their homes since enactment of Proposition 13 in 1978 shouldered only 25% of the more than $4 billion in residential property taxes paid by homeowners statewide. If property values continue to rise more than the annual 2% inflationary cap, this disparity will continue to grow.

B

According to her amended complaint, petitioner Stephanie Nordlinger in November 1988 purchased a house in the Baldwin Hills neighborhood of Los Angeles County for $170,000. The prior owners bought the home just two years before for $121,500. Before her purchase, petitioner had lived in a rented apartment in Los Angeles and had not owned any real property in California.

In early 1989, petitioner received a notice from the Los Angeles County Tax Assessor, who is a respondent here, informing her that her home had been reassessed upward to $170,100 on account of its change in ownership. She learned that the reassessment resulted in a property tax increase of $453.60, up 36% to $1,701, for the 1988-1989 fiscal year.

Petitioner later discovered she was paying about five times more in taxes than some of her neighbors who owned comparable homes since 1975 within the same

residential development. For example, one block away, a house of identical size on a lot slightly larger than petitioner's was subject to a general tax levy of only $358.20 (based on an assessed valuation of $35,820, which reflected the home's value in 1975 plus the up-to-2% per year inflation factor).[2] According to petitioner, her total property taxes over the first 10 years in her home will approach $19,000, while any neighbor who bought a comparable home in 1975 stands to pay just $4,100. The general tax levied against her modest home is only a few dollars short of that paid by a pre-1976 owner of a $2.1 million Malibu beach-front home.

. . . .

II

The Equal Protection Clause of the Fourteenth Amendment, § 1, commands that no State shall "deny to any person within its jurisdiction the equal protection of the laws." Of course, most laws differentiate in some fashion between classes of persons. The Equal Protection Clause does not forbid classifications. It simply keeps governmental decision-makers from treating differently persons who are in all relevant respects alike. F. S. Royster Guano Co. v. Virginia, 253 U.S. at 415.

As a general rule, "legislatures are presumed to have acted within their constitutional power despite the fact that, in practice, their laws result in some inequality." McGowan v. Maryland, 366 U.S. at 425-426. Accordingly, this Court's cases are clear that, unless a classification warrants some form of heightened review because it jeopardizes exercise of a fundamental right or categorizes on the basis of an inherently suspect characteristic, the Equal Protection Clause requires only that the classification rationally further a legitimate state interest.

. . . .

B

The appropriate standard of review is whether the difference in treatment between newer and older owners rationally furthers a legitimate state interest. In general,

---

2. Petitioner proffered to the trial court additional evidence suggesting that the disparities in residential tax burdens were greater in other Los Angeles County neighborhoods. For example, a small 2-bedroom house in Santa Monica that was previously assessed at $27,000 and that was sold for $465,000 in 1989 would be subject to a tax levy of $4,650, a bill 17 times more than the $270 paid the year before by the previous owner. Petitioner also proffered evidence suggesting that similar disparities obtained with respect to apartment buildings and commercial and industrial income-producing properties.

the Equal Protection Clause is satisfied so long as there is a plausible policy reason for the classification, see United States Railroad Retirement Bd. v. Fritz, 449 U.S. at 174, 179, the legislative facts on which the classification is apparently based rationally may have been considered to be true by the governmental decisionmaker, see Minnesota v. Clover Leaf Creamery Co., 449 U.S. at 464, and the relationship of the classification to its goal is not so attenuated as to render the distinction arbitrary or irrational, see Cleburne v. Cleburne Living Center, Inc., 473 U.S. at 446. This standard is especially deferential in the context of classifications made by complex tax laws. "[I]n structuring internal taxation schemes 'the States have large leeway in making classifications and drawing lines which in their judgment produce reasonable systems of taxation.'" Williams v. Vermont, 472 U.S. at 22, quoting Lehnhausen v. Lake Shore Auto Parts Co., 410 U.S. at 359. See also Regan v. Taxation with Representation of Washington, 461 U.S. at 547 ("Legislatures have especially broad latitude in creating classifications and distinctions in tax statutes").

As between newer and older owners, Article XIIIA does not discriminate with respect to either the tax rate or the annual rate of adjustment in assessments. Newer and older owners alike benefit in both the short and long run from the protections of a 1% tax rate ceiling and no more than a 2% increase in assessment value per year. New owners and old owners are treated differently with respect to one factor only–the basis on which their property is initially assessed. Petitioner's true complaint is that the State has denied her–a new owner–the benefit of the same assessment value that her neighbors–older owners–enjoy.

We have no difficulty in ascertaining at least two rational or reasonable considerations of difference or policy that justify denying petitioner the benefits of her neighbors' lower assessments. First, the State has a legitimate interest in local neighborhood preservation, continuity, and stability. The State therefore legitimately can decide to structure its tax system to discourage rapid turnover in ownership of homes and businesses, for example, in order to inhibit displacement of lower income families by the forces of gentrification or of established, "mom-and-pop" businesses by newer chain operations. By permitting older owners to pay progressively less in taxes than new owners of comparable property, the Article XIIIA assessment scheme rationally furthers this interest.

Second, the State legitimately can conclude that a new owner at the time of acquiring his property does not have the same reliance interest warranting protection

against higher taxes as does an existing owner. The State may deny a new owner at the point of purchase the right to "lock in" to the same assessed value as is enjoyed by an existing owner of comparable property, because an existing owner rationally may be thought to have vested expectations in his property or home that are more deserving of protection than the anticipatory expectations of a new owner at the point of purchase. A new owner has full information about the scope of future tax liability before acquiring the property, and if he thinks the future tax burden is too demanding, he can decide not to complete the purchase at all. By contrast, the existing owner, already saddled with his purchase, does not have the option of deciding not to buy his home if taxes become prohibitively high. To meet his tax obligations, he might be forced to sell his home or to divert his income away from the purchase of food, clothing, and other necessities. In short, the State may decide that it is worse to have owned and lost, than never to have owned at all.

This Court previously has acknowledged that classifications serving to protect legitimate expectation and reliance interests do not deny equal protection of the laws. "The protection of reasonable reliance interests is not only a legitimate governmental objective: it provides an exceedingly persuasive justification. . . ."

. . . .

Petitioner argues that Article XIIIA cannot be distinguished from the tax assessment practice found to violate the Equal Protection Clause in Allegheny Pittsburgh. Like Article XIIIA, the practice at issue in Allegheny Pittsburgh resulted in dramatic disparities in taxation of properties of comparable value. But an obvious and critical factual difference between this case and Allegheny Pittsburgh is the absence of any indication in Allegheny Pittsburgh that the policies underlying an acquisition-value taxation scheme could conceivably have been the purpose for the Webster County tax assessor's unequal assessment scheme. In the first place, Webster County argued that "its assessment scheme is rationally related to its purpose of assessing properties *at true current value*" (emphasis added). 488 U.S. at 343. Moreover, the West Virginia "Constitution and laws provide that all property of the kind held by petitioners shall be taxed at a rate uniform throughout the State according to its estimated market value," and the Court found "no suggestion" that "the State may have adopted a different system in practice from that specified by statute." Id., at 345.

To be sure, the Equal Protection Clause does not demand for purposes of rational-basis review that a legislature or governing decisionmaker actually articulate at any time the purpose or rationale supporting its classification. United States Railroad Retirement Bd. v. Fritz, 449 U.S. at 179. See also McDonald v. Board of Election Comm'rs of Chicago, 394 U.S. at 809 (legitimate state purpose may be ascertained even when the legislative or administrative history is silent). Nevertheless, this Court's review does require that a purpose may conceivably or "may reasonably have been the purpose and policy" of the relevant governmental decision-maker. Allied Stores of Ohio, Inc. v. Bowers, 358 U.S. at 528-529. See also Schweiker v. Wilson, 450 U.S. at 235 (classificatory scheme must "rationally advanc[e] a reasonable and *identifiable* governmental objective" (emphasis added)). Allegheny Pittsburgh was the rare case where the facts precluded any plausible inference that the reason for the unequal assessment practice was to achieve the benefits of an acquisition-value tax scheme.[7] By contrast, Article XIIIA was enacted precisely to achieve the benefits of an acquisition-value system. Allegheny Pittsburgh is not controlling here.

Finally, petitioner contends that the unfairness of Article XIIIA is made worse by its exemptions from reassessment for two special classes of new owners: persons aged 55 and older, who exchange principal residences, and children who acquire property from their parents. This Court previously has declined to hold that narrow exemptions from a general scheme of taxation necessarily render the overall scheme invidiously discriminatory. See, e.g., Regan v. Taxation with Representation of Washington, 461 U.S. at 550-551 (denial of tax exemption to nonprofit lobbying organizations, but with an exception for veterans' groups, does not violate equal protection). For purposes of rational-basis review, the "latitude of discretion is notably wide in . . . the granting of partial or total exemptions upon grounds of policy." F.S. Royster Guano Co. v. Virginia, 253 U.S. at 415.

The two exemptions at issue here rationally further legitimate purposes. The people of California reasonably could have concluded that older persons in general

should not be discouraged from moving to a residence more suitable to their changing family size or income. Similarly, the people of California reasonably could have concluded that the interests of family and neighborhood continuity and stability are furthered by and warrant an exemption for transfers between parents and children. Petitioner has not demonstrated that no rational bases lie for either of these exemptions.

III

Petitioner and amici argue with some appeal that Article XIIIA frustrates the "American dream" of home ownership for many younger and poorer California families. They argue that Article XIIIA places startup businesses that depend on ownership of property at a severe disadvantage in competing with established businesses. They argue that Article XIIIA dampens demand for and construction of new housing and buildings. And they argue that Article XIIIA constricts local tax revenues at the expense of public education and vital services.

Time and again, however, this Court has made clear in the rational-basis context that the "Constitution presumes that, absent some reason to infer antipathy, even improvident decisions will eventually be rectified by the democratic process and that judicial intervention is generally unwarranted no matter how unwisely we may think a political branch has acted" (footnote omitted). Vance v. Bradley, 440 U.S. at 97. Certainly, California's grand experiment appears to vest benefits in a broad, powerful, and entrenched segment of society, and, as the Court of Appeal surmised, ordinary democratic processes may be unlikely to prompt its reconsideration or repeal. Yet many wise and well-intentioned laws suffer from the same malady. Article XIIIA is not palpably arbitrary, and we must decline petitioner's request to upset the will of the people of California.

[Concurring opinion by JUSTICE THOMAS omitted.]

JUSTICE STEVENS, dissenting.

During the two past decades, California property owners have enjoyed extraordinary prosperity. As the State's population has mushroomed, so has the value of its real estate. Between 1976 and 1986 alone, the total assessed value of California property subject to property taxation increased tenfold. Simply put, those who invested in California real estate in the 1970s are among the most fortunate capitalists in the world.

Proposition 13 has provided these successful investors with a tremendous windfall and, in doing so, has created severe inequities in California's property tax scheme.

---

7. In Allied Stores of Ohio, Inc. v. Bowers, 358 U.S. 522 (1959), the Court distinguished on similar grounds its decision in Wheeling Steel Corp. v. Glander, 337 U.S. 562 (1949), which invalidated a state statutory scheme exempting from taxation certain notes and accounts receivable owned by residents of the State but not notes and accounts receivable owned by nonresidents. 358 U.S. at 529. After the Court in Wheeling Steel determined that the statutory scheme's stated purpose was not legitimate, the other purposes did not need to be considered because "[h]aving themselves specifically declared their purpose, the Ohio statutes left no room to conceive of any other purpose for their existence." Id., at 530.

These property owners (hereinafter Squires) are guaranteed that, so long as they retain their property and do not improve it, their taxes will not increase more than 2% in any given year. As a direct result of this windfall for the Squires, later purchasers must pay far more than their fair share of property taxes.

The specific disparity that prompted petitioner to challenge the constitutionality of Proposition 13 is the fact that her annual property tax bill is almost 5 times as large as that of her neighbors who own comparable homes: While her neighbors' 1989 taxes averaged less than $400, petitioner was taxed $1,700. This disparity is not unusual under Proposition 13. Indeed, some homeowners pay 17 times as much in taxes as their neighbors with comparable property. For vacant land, the disparities may be as great as 500 to 1. Moreover, as Proposition 13 controls the taxation of commercial property as well as residential property, the regime greatly favors the commercial enterprises of the Squires, placing new businesses at a substantial disadvantage.

As a result of Proposition 13, the Squires, who own 44% of the owner-occupied residences, paid only 25% of the total taxes collected from homeowners in 1989. These disparities are aggravated by § 2 of Proposition 13, which exempts from reappraisal a property owner's home and up to $1 million of other real property when that property is transferred to a child of the owner. This exemption can be invoked repeatedly and indefinitely, allowing the Proposition 13 windfall to be passed from generation to generation. As the California Senate Commission on Property Tax Equity and Revenue observed:

"The inequity is clear. One young family buys a new home and is assessed at full market value. Another young family inherits its home, but pays taxes based on their parents' date of acquisition even though both homes are of identical value. Not only does this constitutional provision offend a policy of equal tax treatment for taxpayers in similar situations, it appears to favor the housing needs of children with homeowner-parents over children with non-homeowner-parents. With the repeal of the state's gift and inheritance tax in 1982, the rationale for this exemption is negligible."

The Commission was too generous. To my mind, the rationale for such disparity is not merely "negligible," it is nonexistent. Such a law establishes a privilege of a medieval character: Two families with equal needs and equal resources are treated differently solely because of their different heritage.

In my opinion, such disparate treatment of similarly situated taxpayers is arbitrary and unreasonable. Although the Court today recognizes these gross inequities, see ante, n.2, its analysis of the justification for those inequities consists largely of a restatement of the benefits that accrue to long-time property owners. That a law benefits those it benefits cannot be an adequate justification for severe inequalities such as those created by Proposition 13.

I

The standard by which we review equal protection challenges to state tax regimes is well established and properly deferential. "Where taxation is concerned and no specific federal right, apart from equal protection, is imperiled, the States have large leeway in making classifications and drawing lines which in their judgment produce reasonable systems of taxation." Lehnhausen v. Lake Shore Auto Parts Co., 410 U.S. 356, 359 (1973). Thus, as the Court today notes, the issue in this case is "whether the difference in treatment between newer and older owners rationally furthers a legitimate state interest."

But deference is not abdication and "rational basis scrutiny" is still scrutiny. Thus we have, on several recent occasions, invalidated tax schemes under such a standard of review. See e.g., Allegheny Pittsburgh Coal Co. v. County Comm'n of Webster County, 488 U.S. 336 (1989); Hooper v. Bernalillo County Assessor, 472 U.S. at 618; Williams v. Vermont, 472 U.S. 14 (1985); Metropolitan Life Ins. Co. v. Ward, 470 U.S. 869 (1985); cf. Zobel v. Williams, 457 U.S. 55, 60-61 (1982).

Just three Terms ago, this Court unanimously invalidated Webster County, West Virginia's assessment scheme under rational-basis scrutiny. Webster County employed a de facto Proposition 13 assessment system: The County assessed recently purchased property on the basis of its purchase price but made only occasional adjustments (averaging 3-4% per year) to the assessments of other properties. Just as in this case, "[t]his approach systematically produced dramatic differences in valuation between . . . recently transferred property and otherwise comparable surrounding land." Allegheny Pittsburgh, 488 U.S. at 341.

The "'[i]ntentional systematic undervaluation,'" id., at 345, found constitutionally infirm in Allegheny Pittsburgh has been codified in California by Proposition 13. That the discrimination in Allegheny Pittsburgh was de facto and the discrimination in this case de jure makes little difference. "The purpose of the equal protection clause of the Fourteenth Amendment is to secure every person within the State's jurisdiction against intentional and arbitrary discrimination, *whether occasioned by express terms of a statute or by its improper execution through duly constituted agents."* Sunday Lake Iron Co. v. Wakefield, 247 U.S. at 352-353 (emphasis added). If anything, the inequality created by Proposition 13 is constitutionally more problematic because it is the product of a state-wide policy rather than the result of an individual assessor's mal-administration.

Nor can Allegheny Pittsburgh be distinguished because West Virginia law established a market-value assessment regime. Webster County's scheme was constitutionally invalid not because it was a departure from *state law*, but because it involved the relative "'systematic undervaluation . . . [of] property *in the same class*'" (as that class was defined by state law). Allegheny Pittsburgh, 488 U.S. at 345 (emphasis added). Our decisions have established that the Equal Protection Clause is offended as much by the arbitrary delineation of classes of property (as in this case) as by the arbitrary treatment of properties within the same class (as in Allegheny Pittsburgh). Thus, if our unanimous holding in Allegheny Pittsburgh was sound--and I remain convinced that it was--it follows inexorably that Proposition 13, like Webster County's assessment scheme, violates the Equal Protection Clause. Indeed, in my opinion, state-wide discrimination is far more invidious than a local aberration that creates a tax disparity.

The States, of course, have broad power to classify property in their taxing schemes and if the "classification is neither capricious nor arbitrary, and rests upon some reasonable consideration of difference or policy, there is no denial of the equal protection of the law." Brown-Forman Co. v. Kentucky, 217 U.S. at 573. As we stated in Allegheny Pittsburgh, a "State may divide different kinds of property into classes and assign to each class a different tax burden so long as those divisions and burdens are reasonable." 488 U.S. at 344.

Consistent with this standard, the Court has long upheld tax classes based on the taxpayer's ability to pay, see, e.g., Fox v. Standard Oil Co. of New Jersey, 294 U.S. at 101; the nature (tangible or intangible) of the property, see, e.g., Klein v. Jefferson County Board of Tax Supervisors, 282 U.S. at 23-24; the use of the property, see, e.g., Clark v. Kansas City, 176 U.S. 114 (1900); and the status (corporate or individual) of the property owner, see, e.g., Lehnhausen v. Lake Shore Auto Parts Co., 410 U.S. 356 (1973). Proposition 13 employs none of these familiar classifications. Instead, it classifies property based on its nominal purchase price: All property purchased for the same price is taxed the same amount (leaving aside the 2% annual adjustment). That this scheme can be named (an "acquisition value" system) does not render it any less arbitrary or unreasonable. Under Proposition 13, a majestic estate

purchased for $150,000 in 1975 (and now worth more than $2 million) is placed in the same tax class as a humble cottage purchased today for $150,000. The only feature those two properties have in common is that somewhere, sometime a sale contract for each was executed that contained the price "$150,000." Particularly in an environment of phenomenal real property appreciation, to classify property based on its purchase price is "palpably arbitrary." Allied Stores of Ohio, Inc. v. Bowers, 358 U.S. 522, 530 (1959).

II

Under contemporary equal protection doctrine, the test of whether a classification is arbitrary is "whether the difference in treatment between [earlier and later purchasers] rationally furthers a legitimate state interest." The adjectives and adverbs in this standard are more important than the nouns and verbs.

A *legitimate* state interest must encompass the interests of members of the disadvantaged class and the community at large as well as the direct interests of the members of the favored class. It must have a purpose or goal independent of the direct effect of the legislation and one "'that we may reasonably presume to have motivated an impartial legislature.'" That a classification must find justification outside itself saves judicial review of such classifications from becoming an exercise in tautological reasoning.

"A State cannot deflect an equal protection challenge by observing that in light of the statutory classification all those within the burdened class are similarly situated. The classification must reflect pre-existing differences; it cannot create new ones that are supported by only their own bootstraps. 'The Equal Protection Clause requires more of a state law than nondiscriminatory application within the class it establishes. 'Rinaldi v. Yeager, 384 U.S. at 308." Williams v. Vermont, 472 U.S. 14, 27 (1985).

If the goal of the discriminatory classification is not independent from the policy itself, "each choice [of classification] will import its own goal, each goal will count as acceptable, and the requirement of a 'rational choice-goal relation will be satisfied by the very making of the choice." Ely, Legislative and Administrative Motivation in Constitutional Law, 79 Yale L.J. 1205, 1247 (1970).

A classification *rationally* furthers a state interest when there is some fit between the disparate treatment and the legislative purpose. As noted above, in the review of tax statutes we have allowed such fit to be generous and approximate, recognizing that "rational distinctions may be made with substantially less than mathematical exactitude." New Orleans v. Dukes, 427 U.S. at 303. Nonetheless, in some cases the underinclusiveness or the overinclusiveness of a classification will be so severe that it cannot be said that the legislative distinction "rationally furthers" the posited state interest. See, e.g., Jimenez v. Weinberger, 417 U.S. at 636-638.

The Court's cursory analysis of Proposition 13 pays little attention to either of these aspects of the controlling standard of review. The first state interest identified by the Court is California's "interest in local neighborhood preservation, continuity, and stability." It is beyond question that "inhibit[ing the] displacement of lower income families by the forces of gentrification," is a legitimate state interest; the central issue is whether the disparate treatment of earlier and later purchasers *rationally furthers* this goal. Here the Court offers not an analysis, but only a conclusion: "By permitting older owners to pay progressively less in taxes than new owners of comparable property, [Proposition 13] rationally furthers this interest."

I disagree. In my opinion, Proposition 13 sweeps too broadly and operates too indiscriminately to "rationally further" the State's interest in neighborhood preservation. No doubt there are some early purchasers living on fixed or limited incomes who could not afford to pay higher taxes and still maintain their homes. California has enacted special legislation to respond to their plight.[5] Those concerns cannot provide an adequate justification for Proposition 13. A statewide, across-the-board tax windfall for *all* property owners and their descendants is no more a "rational" means for protecting this small subgroup than a blanket tax exemption for all taxpayers named Smith would be a rational means to protect a particular taxpayer named Smith who demonstrated difficulty paying her tax bill.

Even within densely populated Los Angeles County, residential property comprises less than half of the market value of the property tax roll. It cannot be said that the legitimate state interest in preserving

neighborhood character is "rationally furthered" by tax benefits for owners of commercial, industrial, vacant, and other nonresidential properties.[6] It is just short of absurd to conclude that the legitimate state interest in protecting a relatively small number of economically vulnerable families is "rationally furthered" by a tax windfall for all 9,787,887 property owners in California.

The Court's conclusion is unsound not only because of the lack of numerical fit between the posited state interest and Proposition 13's inequities but also because of the lack of logical fit between ends and means. Although the State may have a valid interest in preserving some neighborhoods,[8] Proposition 13 not only "inhibit[s the] displacement" of settled families, it also inhibits the transfer of unimproved land, abandoned buildings, and substandard uses. Thus, contrary to the Court's suggestion, Proposition 13 is not like a zoning system. A zoning system functions by recognizing different uses of property and treating those different uses differently. See Euclid v. Ambler Realty Co., 272 U.S. at 388-390. Proposition 13 treats all property alike, giving *all* owners tax breaks, and discouraging the transfer or improvement of *all* property–the developed and the dilapidated, the neighborly and the nuisance.

In short, although I agree with the Court that "neighborhood preservation" is a legitimate state interest, I cannot agree that a tax windfall for all persons who purchased property before 1978 *rationally* furthers

---

5. As pointed out in the Commission Report, California has addressed this specific problem with specific legislation. The State has established two programs:
"Senior Citizens Property Tax Assistance. Provides refunds of up to ninety-six percent of property taxes to low income homeowners over age 62.
. . . .
"Senior Citizens Property Tax Postponement. Allows senior citizens with incomes under $20,000 to postpone all or part of the taxes on their homes until an ownership change occurs." Commission Report 23.

---

6. The Court's rationale for upholding Proposition 13 does not even arguably apply to vacant property. That, as the Court recognizes, Proposition 13 discourages changes of ownership means that the law creates an impediment to the transfer and development of such property no matter now [sic] socially desirable its improvement might be. It is equally plain that the competitive advantage enjoyed by the Squires who own commercial property is wholly unjustified. There is no rational state interest in providing those entrepreneurs with a special privilege that tends to discourage otherwise desirable transfers of income-producing property. In a free economy, the entry of new competitors should be encouraged, not arbitrarily hampered by unfavorable tax treatment.

8. The ambiguous character of this interest is illustrated by the options faced by a married couple that owns a three- or four-bedroom home that suited their family needs while their children lived at home. After the children have moved out, increased taxes and maintenance expenses would--absent Proposition 13–tend to motivate the sale of the home to a younger family needing a home of that size, or perhaps the rental of a room or two to generate the income necessary to pay taxes. Proposition 13, however, subsidizes the wasteful retention of unused housing capacity, making the sale of the home unwise and the rental of the extra space unnecessary.

that interest. To my mind, Proposition 13 is too blunt a tool to accomplish such a specialized goal. The severe inequalities created by Proposition 13 cannot be justified by such an interest.[9]

The second state interest identified by the Court is the "reliance interests" of the earlier purchasers. Here I find the Court's reasoning difficult to follow. Although the protection of reasonable reliance interests is a legitimate governmental purpose, see Heckler v. Mathews, 465 U.S. at 746, this case does not implicate such interests. A reliance interest is created when an individual justifiably acts under the assumption that an existing legal condition will persist; thus reliance interests are most often implicated when the government provides some benefit and then acts to eliminate the benefit. See, e.g., New Orleans v. Dukes, 427 U.S. 297 (1976). In this case, those who purchased property before Proposition 13 was enacted received no assurances that assessments would only increase at a limited rate; indeed, to the contrary, many purchased property in the hope that property values (and assessments) would appreciate substantially and quickly. It cannot be said, therefore, that the earlier purchasers of property somehow have a reliance interest in limited tax increases.

Perhaps what the Court means is that post-Proposition 13 purchasers have less reliance interests than pre-Proposition 13 purchasers. The Court reasons that the State may tax earlier and later purchasers differently because:

"an existing owner rationally may be thought to have vested expectations in his property or home that are more deserving of protection than the anticipatory expectations of a new owner at the point of purchase. A new owner has full information about the scope of future tax liability before acquiring the property, and if he thinks the future tax burden is too demanding, he can decide not to complete the purchase at all. By contrast, the existing owner, already saddled with his purchase, does not have the option of deciding not to buy his home if taxes become prohibitively high."[10]

This simply restates the effects of Proposition 13. A pre-Proposition 13 owner has "vested expectations" in reduced taxes *only* because Proposition 13 gave her such expectations; a later purchaser has no such expectations because Proposition 13 does not provide her such expectations. But the same can be said of any arbitrary protection for an existing class of taxpayers. Consider a law that establishes that homes with even street numbers would be taxed at twice the rate of homes with odd street numbers. It is certainly true that the even-numbered homeowners could not decide to "unpurchase" their homes and that those considering buying an even-numbered home would know that it came with an extra tax burden, but certainly that would not justify the arbitrary imposition of disparate tax burdens based on house numbers. So it is in this case. Proposition 13 provides a benefit for earlier purchasers and imposes a burden on later purchasers. To say that the later purchasers know what they are getting into does not answer the critical question: Is it reasonable and constitutional to tax early purchasers less than late purchasers when at the time of taxation their properties are comparable? This question the Court does not answer.

Distilled to its essence, the Court seems to be saying that earlier purchasers can benefit under Proposition 13 because earlier purchasers benefit under Proposition 13. If, however, a law creates a disparity, the State's interest preserving that disparity cannot be a "*legitimate* state interest" justifying that inequity. As noted above, a statute's disparate treatment must be justified by a purpose *distinct* from the very effects created by that statute. Thus, I disagree with the Court that the severe inequities wrought by Proposition 13 can be justified by what the Court calls the "reliance interests" of those who benefit from that scheme.[11] In my opinion, it is irrational

_____

9. Respondent contends that the inequities created by Proposition 13 are justified by the State's interest in protecting property owners from taxation on unrealized appreciation. The California Supreme Court relied on a similar state interest. See Amador Valley Joint Union High School Dist. v. State Bd. of Equalization, 583 P. 2d 1281, 1309-1311 (1978). This argument is closely related to the Court's reasoning concerning "neighborhood preservation"; respondent claims the State has an interest in preventing the situation in which "skyrocketing real estate prices . . . driv[e] property taxes beyond some taxpayers' ability to pay." As demonstrated above, whatever the connection between acquisition price and "ability to pay," a blanket tax windfall for all early purchasers of property (and their descendants) is simply too overinclusive to "rationally further" the State's posited interest in protecting vulnerable taxpayers.

_____

10. The Court's sympathetic reference to "existing owner[s] already saddled" with their property should not obscure the fact that these early purchasers have already seen their property increase in value more than tenfold.

11. Respondent, drawing on the analysis of the California Supreme Court, contends that the inequities created by Proposition 13 are also justified by the State's interest in "permitting the taxpayer to make more careful and accurate predictions of future tax liability. " Amador Valley, 583 P. 2d, at 1312. This analysis suffers from the same infirmity as the Court's "reliance" analysis. I agree that Proposition 13 permits greater predictability of tax liability; the relevant question, however, is whether the inequities between earlier and later purchasers

to treat similarly situated persons differently on the basis of the date they joined the class of property owners. Until today, I would have thought this proposition far from controversial. In Zobel v. Williams, 457 U.S. 55 (1982), we ruled that Alaska's program of distributing cash dividends on the basis of the recipient's years of residency in the State violated the Equal Protection Clause. The Court wrote:

"If the states can make the amount of a cash dividend depend on length of residence, what would preclude varying university tuition on a sliding scale based on years of residence--or even limiting access of finite public facilities, eligibility for student loans, for civil service jobs, or for government contracts by length of domicile? *Could states impose different taxes based on length of residence?* Alaska's reasoning could open the door to state apportionment of other rights, benefits, and services according to length of residency. It would permit the states to divide citizens into expanding numbers of permanent classes. Such a result would be clearly impermissible." Id., at 64 (emphasis added) (footnotes omitted).

Similarly, the Court invalidated on equal protection grounds New Mexico's policy of providing a permanent tax exemption for Vietnam veterans who had been state residents before May 8, 1976, but not to more recent arrivals. Hooper v. Bernalillo County Assessor, 472 U.S.

612 (1985). The Court expressly rejected the State's claim that it had a legitimate interest in providing special rewards to veterans who lived in the State before 1976 and concluded that "[n]either the Equal Protection Clause, nor this Court's precedents, permit the State to prefer established resident veterans over newcomers in the retroactive apportionment of an economic benefit."

As these decisions demonstrate, the selective provision of benefits based on the timing of one's membership in a class (whether that class be the class of residents or the class of property owners) is rarely a "legitimate state interest." Similarly situated neighbors have an equal right to share in the benefits of local government. It would obviously be unconstitutional to provide one with more or better fire or police protection than the other; it is just as plainly unconstitutional to require one to pay five times as much in property taxes as the other for the same government services. In my opinion, the severe inequalities created by Proposition 13 are arbitrary and unreasonable and do not rationally further a legitimate state interest.

Accordingly, I respectfully dissent.

---

created by Proposition 13 can be justified by something other than the benefit to the early purchasers. I do not believe that they can.

Questions and Comments

1. How does *Allegheny*'s rational basis test differ from the test applied in *Nordlinger*? Are the two cases consistent? Did the *Allegheny* Court consider the possibility that property owners could be treated as members of different classes based on when they bought their property? Was the assessor in *Allegheny* purposely discriminating against recently sold properties or just attempting to maintain current valuations for all taxpayers without engaging in the impossible task of assessing all properties annually? What is left of *Allegheny* after *Nordlinger*?

How would you describe the classes that were defined by Proposition 13? How did Justice Blackmun define such classes?

2. Taxpayer concedes that the Constitution permits property to be assessed at its market value during some base period fixed in the past provided that the same base year is used for all properties. Does that undermine her claim? Assuming that values appreciate at different rates, wouldn't the same disparities result among homeowners that the plaintiff challenged in *Nordlinger*?

3. How did Proposition 13 affect property values? Did Proposition 13 increase or decrease the supply of housing in California? How will the revaluation that will occur at the time of the sale affect the amount a buyer is willing to pay for a home? Generally speaking, how does an increase in property taxes affect home values?

4. As a tenant, would you have favored Proposition 13?

5. The Court concluded that existing homeowners had a reliance interest in the amount of their property taxes. Do taxpayers have a reliance interest in other aspects of the California tax structure? Did taxpayers buying a home in 1976 have a reliance interest in the rate at which California would tax gain on the sale of that home? What distinguishes the property tax from the income tax or sales tax? Indeed, until Proposition 13, did homeowners have any reason to think their property taxes would increase only slowly?

Why did the Court not protect the reliance interests of those who bought homes with the expectation of selling them with no tax detriment?

6. The Court notes that by 1989, forty-four percent of all homeowners paid only twenty-five percent of all residential property taxes. What portion of homes by fair market value was owned by the forty-four percent?

7. Was it relevant to the Court's analysis that Proposition 13 was passed by referendum rather than by the Legislature? What if the Proposition completely exempted current property owners but not future property owners from tax? Would the opinion be the same? Should it?

8. Was the Court correct that Proposition 13 will benefit low-income, long-time residents? What did the Court assume about the effects of Proposition 13 on housing values?

9. What was the majority's implicit definition of "stable neighborhood?" Were other definitions available that might be more relevant? Is a forest "stable" if all the trees are long-term residents?

10. Does this case support the constitutionality of a classified property tax?

11. Does Proposition 13 violate the Commerce Clause? Who would be in a position to allege a Commerce Clause violation?

12. The Supreme Court had granted certiorari in *R. H. Macy & Co., Inc. v. Contra Costa County*, 500 U.S. 951 (1991). In that case, the taxpayer argued that Proposition 13 violated the Commerce Clause because businesses moving to California were forced to pay higher taxes than businesses already established there. The California Court of Appeal rejected this argument: [Proposition 13] does not restrict interstate commerce because it taxes only real property within the state. 276 Cal. Rptr. 541 (1990). The court went on to define interstate commerce as including only "the flow of goods and services between and among the several states." Id. After the Court had granted certiorari, Macy's withdrew its suit. 501 U.S. 1245 (1991). Apparently, the company feared a consumer backlash if it were to win its case and if its victory were to lead to higher taxes in California, especially on homeowners. Part of Macy's fear was rational because it was deluged with letters from customers complaining about its challenge to Proposition 13; some of the letters contained cut up Macy's credit cards. 3 State Tax Notes 565 (1992).

13. Does acquisition-cost assessments deprive the property tax of its "moral foundation?" See John A.

Miller, *Rationalizing Injustice: The Supreme Court and the Property Tax*, 22 Hofstra L. Rev. 79 (1993).

14. According to Justice Stevens, is Proposition 13 underinclusive or overinclusive?

15. Is it a violation of the Equal Protection Clause for a state to tax single persons at a higher rate than married couples having the same income? See *Peden v. State*, 930 P.2d 1 (Kan. 1996).

16. For critical commentary on *Nordlinger*, see Robert C. Farrell, *Classifications that Disadvantage Newcomers and the Problem of Equality*, 28 U. Rich. L. Rev. 547 (1994); Steven T. Lawrence, *Solving the Proposition 13 Puzzle: from Amador to Nordlinger - Judicial Challenges and Alternatives*, 24 Pac. L. J. 1769 (1993); Andrew J. Hoerner, *When States Choose Inequality: High Court Mulls Proposition 13. (Nordlinger v. Hahn)*, 54 Tax Notes 1055 (1992); Mary LaFrance, *Constitutional Implications of Acquisition Value Real Property Taxation: The Elusive Rational Basis*, 1994 Utah L. Rev. 817; Mary LaFrance, *Constitutional Implications of Acquisition-Value Real Property Taxation: Assessing Burdens on Travel and Commerce*, 1994 Utah L. Rev. 1027 (1994); David Hilker, *Prologue. (U.S. Supreme Court Upholds Proposition 13, part 1)*, 11 J. State Tax'n 9(1) (1992); Samuel A. Mandarino, *Nordlinger to Allegheny: "This Town ain't Big Enough for the Both of Us,"* 1993 Wis. L. Rev. 1195 (1993); Michael D. Rawlings, *Taxation, Equal Protection, and Inquiry Into the Purpose of a Law*, 1993 B.Y.U.L. Rev. 1001 (1993); Andrew S. Johnston, *Tax Law: Constitutionality of "Welcome Stranger" Laws Under the Equal Protection Clause of the Fourteenth Amendment*, 23 Mem. St. L. Rev. 891 (1993); Hugh D. Rauscher, *Constitutional Law- "Welcome, Stranger": California's Acquisition Value Property Tax Survives an Equal Protection Challenge*, 27 Suffolk U. L. Rev. 961 (1993); John A. Miller, *Rationalizing Injustice: the Supreme Court and the Property Tax*, 22 Hofstra L. Rev. 79 (1993).

State Constitutional Provisions on Uniformity and Equality

The preceding cases all dealt with the Equal Protection Clause in the U.S. Constitution. State constitutions typically have provisions requiring uniformity or equality in taxation. These provisions are not necessarily interpreted in a manner identical to the federal Equal Protection Clause. In many cases, a state statute has been held to violate a uniformity or equality provision even though it would have been upheld under the Federal Equal Protection Clause. This situation may become more common after *Nordlinger*, which certainly set a very low standard for upholding state statutes challenged under the Federal Equal Protection Clause. For an exhaustive treatment of state uniformity and equal protection provisions see Wade J. Newhouse, Constitutional Uniformity and Equality in State Taxation (2d ed. 1984).

<table>
<tr><td>

Chapter

3

</td><td>

Due Process Clause

"[Nor] shall any State deprive any person of life, liberty, or property, without due process of law." U.S. Const., amend. XIV, §1.

</td></tr>
</table>

Due process is a multifaceted concept, having procedural, substantive, and jurisdictional aspects. Like many concepts in the law, these issues are about relationships, connections, and contacts. This chapter concerns the relationship between the state and the object or person over which the state is wishing to assert jurisdiction. The state may seek to tax a sale made by that person, tax income earned or property owned by that person, or require that person to collect a tax imposed by the state on a third party.

Relationships, connections, and contacts come in many sizes and shapes, from the diffused, attenuated, casual, and fleeting to the concrete, physical, regular, and sustained. Contacts can have both a quantitative and qualitative dimension. Whether a state can assert tax jurisdiction requires determining the nature and degree of these relationships, connections, and contacts. According to the Court, tax jurisdiction requires "some definite link, some minimum connection,"[1] often referred to as nexus, between the state and the person, object, or activity over which it is asserting jurisdiction. When such a link or minimum connection exists, then presumably the person is benefitting from the "protection, opportunities, and benefits"[2] provided by the state, for which a tax is levied as the quid pro quo.

The issues surrounding the existence of nexus have very much the flavor of the Court's "minimum contacts" approach to personal jurisdiction.[3] Until fairly recently, there was uncertainty about whether the Court would apply its personal jurisdiction learning to the issue of tax jurisdiction. The personal jurisdiction cases had evolved from requiring that the defendant have a "presence" in the forum state as a condition for suit, to a more flexible test of whether

a person's contacts with the forum state make it reasonable to require it to defend a suit there.

The Court's tax nexus cases had developed independently of its personal jurisdiction cases and required a physical presence of some sort (people or property) in the taxing state. There was intense speculation among commentators about whether the Court would allow these two doctrines to develop independently of each other.[4] Moreover, the stakes were large because whole industries, especially the direct marketing industry, structured themselves in order to avoid having a physical presence in a state and thus avoid being required to collect that state's use tax.

In a closely watched case involving an out-of-state direct marketer, *Quill v. North Dakota*,[5] the Court essentially applied its personal jurisdiction standards to tax nexus. "[I]f a foreign corporation purposefully avails itself of the benefits of an economic market in the forum State, it may subject itself to the State's in personam jurisdiction even if it has no physical presence in the State."[6] "[I]t is an inescapable fact of modern commercial life that a substantial amount of business is transacted solely by mail and wire communication across state lines, thus obviating the need for physical presence within a State in which business is conducted."[7] "Comparable reasoning justifies the imposition of the collection duty on a mail-order house that is engaged in continuous and

---

1. Miller Bros. v. Maryland, in the chapter entitled Use Taxes and Interstate Aspects of Sales, Use, and Gross Receipts Taxes.

2. Wisconsin v. J.C. Penney Co., 311 U.S. at 444, infra this chapter.

3. See Milliken v. Meyer, 311 U.S. at 463; International Shoe Co. v. Washington, 326 U.S. 310 (1945).

---

4. See, e.g., Jerome R. Hellerstein, Significant Sales and Use Tax Developments During the Past Half Century, 39 Vand. L. Rev. 961, 984-85 (1986); Charles Rothfeld, Mail Order Sales and State Jurisdiction to Tax, 53 Tax Notes 1405, 1414-18 (1991); Richard D. Pomp, Are the Standards for Tax Jurisdiction and Personal Jurisdiction Identical?, 54 Tax Notes 333 (1992), reprinted in 2 State Tax Notes 86 (1992).

5. 504 U.S. 298 (1992), infra this chapter.

6. Id. at 307.

7. Id. at 308, quoting Burger King Corp. v. Rudzewicz, 471 U.S. 462, 476 (1985).

widespread solicitation of business within a State."[8] The Court overruled its earlier tax due process decisions that required physical presence in a state.[9]

What is left of the nexus requirement after *Quill*? Perhaps everything. For in a novel approach unsupported by the case law, the *Quill* Court bifurcated the concept of nexus into a due process component, discussed above, and a commerce clause component, each with its own requirements.[10] The physical presence requirement is apparently alive and well, at least for the collection of the use tax, although it is now imposed by the Commerce Clause rather than the Due Process Clause. Many of the Court's earlier cases on physical presence may still be relevant in giving content to that term.

Applying the physical presence test to corporations raises special difficulties. The "physical presence" requirement cannot be applied literally to a corporation, which is a legal construct with no physical attributes. Unlike an individual, who can be physically present in a state and engaged in profit-seeking activities, a corporation can be physically present only indirectly, through, for example, persons with whom it has a legal relationship. A corporation that has employees in a state pursuing its business interests would likely have a physical presence in that state.[11]

Employer-employee, however, is only one type of relationship. As corporate America restructures, other relationships are replacing the traditional employer-employee relationship. The use of agents, jobbers, independent contractors, representatives, contract manufacturers, temps, and the like are becoming increasingly common. Indeed, corporations will sometimes eliminate an in-house function and then "outsource" that function to its former employees. Whether these types of relationships constitute nexus under the Commerce Clause will inevitably be the subject of future litigation. Moreover, *Quill* involved only the collection of the use tax. What the Commerce Clause will require as a nexus standard for the imposition of a use tax, a sales tax, an income tax, or other taxes is unclear. Cases involving whether the use of intangible property in a state provides nexus under a corporate income tax will eventually reach the Court.[12] The nexus standard for sales taxes is likely to be raised in the context of electronic commerce. See the chapter entitled, The Taxation of Electronic Commerce.

Quill involved only one aspect of the Due Process Clause. But it is not enough that a state can assert tax jurisdiction; it must exercise that jurisdiction in a manner that ensures that the tax is "rationally related to 'values connected with the taxing State.'"[13] This requirement, which has an analog under the Commerce Clause,[14] does not have sharp contours and the states have been given much latitude in fashioning their tax regimes. Applying this requirement in the context of an apportioned corporate income tax, which the Court has described as bearing "some resemblance . . . to slicing a shadow,"[15] is especially hard. Taxpayers have had better luck challenging an apportioned property tax, which unlike an income tax, is levied on assets that can be identified and physically located.

---

8. Id. at 308.

9. Id.

10. What was novel was not that a nexus requirement could be found in both the Commerce Clause and the Due Process Clause. The Court has not always clearly distinguished between the two clauses, making it difficult to ground a particular doctrine uniquely in one of these two clauses. Further, many doctrines address both commerce clause and due process concerns. For example, a tax that is unfairly apportioned under the Court's commerce clause analysis, see Complete Auto Transit v. Brady, 430 U.S. 274 (1977), in the Commerce Clause chapter, will tax out-of-state values and thus violate the Due Process Clause as well. But before Quill the Court never even intimated that the requirements of nexus were different under the Due Process Clause from the requirements under the Commerce Clause. See Richard D. Pomp and Michael J. McIntyre, State Taxation of Mail-Order Sales of Computers After *Quill*: An Evaluation of MTC Bulletin 95-1, 11 State Tax Notes 177 (1996), excerpted in the chapter entitled, Use Taxes and Interstate Aspects of Sales, Use, and Gross Receipts Taxes.

11. See, e.g., Standard Pressed Steel v. Washington, 419 U.S. 560 (1975); General Trading Co. v. State Tax Commission, discussed in the chapter entitled, Use Taxes and Interstate Aspects of Sales, Use, and Gross Receipts Taxes.

---

12. For the leading state case, see Geoffrey, Inc. v. South Carolina Tax Comm'n, 437 S.E.2d 13 (1993); cert denied, 114 S. Ct. 550 (1993), in the chapter entitled, State Corporate Income Taxes: The Leading Cases.

13. Quill, supra note 5, at 306, quoting Moorman Mfg. Co. v. Bair, 437 U.S. 267, 273 (1978).

14. See, e.g., the fairly apportioned test set forth in Complete Auto, supra note 10, and the external consistency test set forth in Container v. Franchise Tax Board, 463 U.S. 159 (1983), in the chapter entitled, State Corporate Income Taxes: The Leading Cases.

15. Container, id. at 192.

Wisconsin v. J.C. Penney Co.
Supreme Court of the United States, 1940.
311 U.S. 435, 61 S. Ct. 246, 85 L. Ed. 267.

MR. JUSTICE FRANKFURTER delivered the opinion of the Court.

Whether the tax imposed by Wisconsin may apply to a foreign corporation licensed to do business in Wisconsin without offending the Fourteenth Amendment of the Constitution is the question before us. The statute is quoted in the margin.[1] . . .

_____

1. Section 3, Chapter 505, Laws of Wisconsin, 1935, as amended by Chapter 552, Laws of Wisconsin, 1935:

Section 3. Privilege Dividend Tax. (1) For the privilege of declaring and receiving dividends, out of income derived from property located and business transacted in this state, there is hereby imposed a tax equal to two and one-half per centum of the amount of such dividends declared and paid by all corporations . . . Such tax shall be deducted and withheld from such dividends payable to residents and non-residents by the payor corporation.

(2) Every corporation required to deduct and withhold any tax under this section shall, on or before the last day of the month following the payment of the dividend, make return thereof and pay the tax to the tax commission, reporting such tax on the forms to be prescribed by the tax commission.

(3) Every such corporation hereby made liable for such tax, shall deduct the amount of such tax from the dividends so declared.

(4) In the case of corporations doing business within and without the state of Wisconsin, such tax shall apply only to dividends declared and paid out of income derived from business transacted and property located within the state of Wisconsin. The amount of income attributable to this state shall be computed in accordance with the provisions of chapter 71. In the absence of proof to the contrary, such dividends shall be presumed to have been paid out of earnings of such corporation attributable to Wisconsin under the provisions of chapter 71, for the year immediately preceding the payment of such dividend. If a corporation had a loss for the year prior to the payment of the dividend, the tax commission shall upon application, determine the portion of such dividend paid out of corporate surplus and undivided profits derived from business transacted and property located within the state.

(5) Dividends paid by a subsidiary corporation to its parent shall not be subject to the tax herein imposed provided that the subsidiary and its parent report their income for taxation under the provisions of chapter 71 on a consolidated income return basis, or both corporations report separately.

(6) The provisions of this section shall not apply to dividends declared and paid by a Wisconsin corporation out of its income which it has reported for taxation under the provisions of chapter 71, to the extent that the business of such corporation consists in the receipts of dividends from which a privilege dividend tax has been deducted and withheld and the distribution thereof to its stockholders.

For many years, corporations chartered by other states but permitted to carry on business in Wisconsin have been subject to a general corporate income tax act on earnings attributable to their Wisconsin activities. The state has, of course, power to impose such a tax. "For the privilege of declaring and receiving dividends, out of income derived from property located and business transacted in" Wisconsin, an exaction "equal to two and one-half per centum of the amount of such dividends declared and paid by all corporations (foreign and local)" is the additional tax now before us. In the enforcement of this measure against foreign corporations, the amount of income attributable to Wisconsin is calculated according to the same formula as that employed in assessing the general corporate income tax paid by such foreign corporations. The practical operation of this legislation is to impose an additional tax on corporate earnings within Wisconsin but to postpone the liability for this tax until such earnings are paid out in dividends. In a word, by its general income tax Wisconsin taxes corporate income that is taken in; by the Privilege Dividend Tax of 1935 Wisconsin superimposed upon this income tax a tax on corporate income that is paid out.

As pressures for new revenues become more and more insistent, ways and means of meeting them present to a state not only the baffling task of tapping fresh sources of revenue but of doing so with due regard to a state's existing taxing system. The tax now assailed gains nourishing significance when placed in the context of the Wisconsin taxing system of which it became a part. Wisconsin relied heavily upon taxation of incomes and largely looked to this source to meet the increasing demands of the depression years. But a special Wisconsin feature was exemption of dividends from personal taxation. See Welch v. Henry, 305 U.S. at 142-43. This exemption persisted while regular and surtax rates against personal incomes were raised. Attempts at relief from the unfairness charged against this exemption of dividends, particularly advantageous to the higher brackets, were steadily pressed before the Wisconsin Legislature. To relieve local earnings of foreign corporations from a dividend tax would have had a depressive effect on wholly local enterprises.

_____

(7) For the purposes of this section dividends shall be defined as in section 71.02, except that the tax herein imposed shall not apply to stock dividend or liquidating dividends.

. . . .

The Privilege Dividend Tax was devised to reduce at least in part the state's revenue losses due to dividend exemptions, and also to equalize the burdens on all Wisconsin earnings, regardless of the formal home of the corporation.

Had Wisconsin, as part of its price for the privileges it afforded foreign corporations within its borders, explicitly provided for a supplementary tax on the Wisconsin earnings of such corporations, but postponed liability for the tax until such earnings were to be paid out in dividends, the power of Wisconsin to do so would hardly be questioned. But because the legislative language ran "For the privilege of declaring and receiving dividends, out of income derived from property located and business transacted in this state" the court below raised the barrier of the Fourteenth Amendment. Respondent is a Delaware corporation having its principal offices in New York; its meetings are held in the latter state where the dividends are voted and the dividend checks are drawn on New York bank accounts. Since the process for declaring dividends and the details attending their distribution among the stockholders transpired outside Wisconsin, although the exaction was apportioned to the earnings derived from Wisconsin, the state court concluded that the tax was an attempt by Wisconsin to levy an exaction on transactions beyond Wisconsin's borders.

The case thus reduces itself to the inquiry whether Wisconsin has transgressed its taxing power because its supreme court has described the practical result of the exertion of that power by one legal formula rather than another–has labeled it a tax on the privilege of declaring dividends rather than a supplementary income tax.

. . . .

The Constitution is not a formulary. It does not demand of states strict observance of rigid categories nor precision of technical phrasing in their exercise of the most basic power of government, that of taxation. For constitutional purposes the decisive issue turns on the operating incidence of a challenged tax. A state is free to pursue its own fiscal policies, unembarrassed by the Constitution, if by the practical operation of a tax the state has exerted its power in relation to opportunities which it has given, to protection which it has afforded, to benefits which it has conferred by the fact of being an orderly, civilized society.

Constitutional provisions are often so glossed over with commentary that imperceptibly we tend to construe the commentary rather than the text. We cannot, however, be too often reminded that the limits on the otherwise autonomous powers of the states are those in the Constitution and not verbal weapons imported into it. "Taxable event," "jurisdiction to tax," "business situs," "extra-territoriality," are all compendious ways of implying the impotence of state power because state power has nothing on which to operate. These tags are not instruments of adjudication but statements of result in applying the sole constitutional test for a case like the present one. That test is whether property was taken without due process of law, or, if paraphrase we must, whether the taxing power exerted by the state bears fiscal relation to protection, opportunities and benefits given by the state. The simple but controlling question is whether the state has given anything for which it can ask return. The substantial privilege of carrying on business in Wisconsin, which has here been given, clearly supports the tax, and the state has not given the less merely because it has conditioned the demand of the exaction upon happenings outside its own borders. The fact that a tax is contingent upon events brought to pass without a state does not destroy the nexus between such a tax and transactions within a state for which the tax is an exaction.

. . . .

Reversed.

MR. JUSTICE ROBERTS, Dissenting

. . . .

The respondent admittedly receives income in Wisconsin. No one questions the power of Wisconsin to lay a tax upon the receipt of that income. It has done so. It is said that the challenged exaction is merely an additional income tax–this, notwithstanding that the tax is not called an income tax, has been held by the highest court of Wisconsin not to be an income tax but an excise upon a privilege–in the view that in testing the constitutionality of an exaction this court examines for itself the nature and incidence of the tax and disregards mere names and descriptive epithets. With that principle I have no quarrel, but I think the opinion of the court demonstrates that the tax here in question is, and can be, sustained only by a disregard of it. Let me illustrate my meaning. Assuming that, by statute, an ad valorem tax on property is prohibited and an income tax permitted. The terms used in the statute necessarily have a conventional connotation. One cannot intelligently discuss things or actions except by using the names commonly employed to describe them. Concepts of ad valorem taxation on property and taxation of income are clear and easily discriminable. What would be said of a decision construing such a statutory provision so as to hold a tax of so many cents on the dollar upon property an income tax because, forsooth, all the property assessed has been received as the fruits of labor, of industry, or of capital, upon the theory that, as the property had come into existence at some remote date as income, the tax was an income tax? I think that is precisely what has been done in this case.

. . . .

Under the challenged statute, a presumption is created which is shown in the case of the assessment against the respondent for the years in question to be contrary to the fact–namely, that an arbitrarily assumed proportion if the dividend is paid out of the respondent's earnings in Wisconsin for the year immediately   preceding the payment of such dividend. By the very terms of the Act, the tax is laid not on the corporation but on the stockholder receiving the dividend and, by confession, thousands of such stockholders are not residents of Wisconsin. The corporation is the mere collector of the tax and the penalty for failure to collect it is that the corporation must pay it. If the exaction is an income tax in any sense it is such upon the stockholder and is obviously bad. It cannot, except by a perversion of the term and the affixing of an arbitrary label, be denominated a tax upon the income of the respondent.

The explanation of the reason and purpose for imposing the tax, disclosed in the opinion of the court, serves to condemn it. If Wisconsin found that dividend income of stockholders of domestic corporations escaped taxation, and should bear it, an effective way to reach the dividend receipts of the stockholders of such corporations was to place a tax upon the receipt of dividends by them. But such a levy upon the stockholders of a foreign corporation, not resident within Wisconsin, obviously was impossible although that is exactly what was attempted by the statute in question. We are now told that this is not a fair exposition of the law but that, on the contrary, and in the teeth of the known facts, what Wisconsin did was to lay a supplementary income tax upon foreign corporations. This is simply to take the name of a well understood concept and assign that name as a label to something which in ordinary understanding never fell within such concept. By this process any exaction can be tortured into something else and then justified under an assumed name.

The respondent owns property in various states of the Union. It is reasonable to suppose that much of that property has been purchased out of corporate surplus, that is, out of past earnings. An ad valorem tax by Wisconsin on property so acquired could be quite as easily justified under the label of an income tax because the property represented income once received, as the present tax, on the declaration and receipt of dividends out of earned surplus.

Upon the facts, the tax is levied on what lies outside the sovereignty of Wisconsin. Its attempted collection is a violation of the Due Process Clause of the Fourteenth Amendment and should be stricken down.

. . . .

Questions and Comments

1. Is Justice Roberts correct that the tax is laid on the stockholder receiving the dividend? What difference does it make whether the tax is laid on the corporation or on the shareholder? Does Justice Roberts explain why Wisconsin could not impose an income tax on nonresidents on their Wisconsin-source income?

2. The United States levies a withholding tax on dividends (and on other categories of income) paid to foreign corporations and foreign individuals. The tax is levied on that part of the dividend that constitutes U.S. source income. See I.R.C. §§ 871, 881, 1441, 1442. Is Wisconsin merely emulating the federal government with its Privilege Dividend Tax? Why didn't the Court talk about the source of the dividends that were being paid by the corporation?

3. Apparently, the Privilege Dividend Tax was intended to offset the exemption for dividends in the Wisconsin personal income tax. Does the Wisconsin approach make sense even in a state which does not exempt dividends? Consider the advantages and disadvantages of the Wisconsin approach in the following situations: dividends paid to foreign individuals or corporations, that is, persons resident abroad and corporations incorporated abroad; dividends paid to pension funds; dividends paid to residents of Wisconsin; dividends paid to residents of other states. States having a broad based personal income tax typically apply it to the worldwide income of their residents but provide a credit for income taxes paid to other states. Suppose Wisconsin levied its 2.5 percent tax on Wisconsin-source dividends paid to a resident of a state that had a three percent income tax. Would the shareholder

bear the economic burden of the Wisconsin tax?

4. Does the Wisconsin approach make good sense if applied to the payment of interest? Could Wisconsin use the same approach for determining interest subject to its withholding tax that it used for determining the amount of dividends subject to its withholding tax?

5. Suppose all states adopted a Dividend Privilege Tax such as Wisconsin's. Under what conditions would this approach raise revenue for a state? Under what conditions might it lose revenue for a state?

6. Is this opinion consistent with the highly formalistic approach that has characterized Justice Frankfurter's opinion in other cases?

7. After *J.C. Penney*, the Wisconsin courts interpreted the statute as taxing the shareholder and not the corporation. International Harvester brought suit charging that the statute violated the Due Process Clause because the dividends were declared in Illinois and over 98% of the shareholders were nonresidents of Wisconsin. The Court again upheld the tax:

"In determining whether a tax is within the state's constitutional power, we look to the incidence of the tax and its practical operation, and not its characterization by state courts ... Wisconsin may impose the burden of the tax either upon the corporation or upon the stockholders who derive the ultimate benefit from the corporation's Wisconsin activities. Personal presence within [Wisconsin] of the stockholder-taxpayers is not essential to the constitutional levy of a tax taken out of so much of the corporation's Wisconsin earnings as is distributed to them. A state may tax such part of the income of a non-resident as is fairly attributable either to property located in the state or to events or transactions which, occurring there, are subject to state regulation and which are within the protection of the state and entitled to the numerous other benefits which it confers." *International Harvester*, 322 U.S. at 441-42.

8. Can a state tax the distributed and undistributed income of an S corporation owned by a nonresident? Kulick v. Or., 624 P.2d 93, says yes, citing *J.C. Penney*. Both *Penney* and *Kulick* were pre-*Quill* decisions. What effect, if any, does *Quill* have on these cases? Cf. *Agley v. Ohio*, 719 N.E.2d 951 (1999); *Chase v. Conn.*, 733 A.2d 782 (1999); *Borden v. Ill.*, 726 N.E.2d 73 (2000).

Norfolk & Western Railway Co. v. Missouri State Tax Commission
Supreme Court of the United States, 1968.
390 U.S. 317, 88 S. Ct. 995, 19 L. Ed. 2d 1201.

MR. JUSTICE FORTAS delivered the opinion of the Court.

This case brings before us, once again, troublesome problems arising from state taxation of an interstate commercial enterprise. At issue is a tax assessment pursuant to a Missouri statute specifying the manner in which railroad rolling stock is to be assessed for the State's ad valorem tax on that property.[1]

In 1964 the Norfolk & Western Railway Co. (N & W), a Virginia corporation with interstate rail operations, leased all of the property of appellant Wabash Railroad Company. The Wabash owned substantial fixed property and rolling stock, and did substantial business in Missouri as well as in other States. Prior to the lease, N & W owned no fixed property and only a minimal amount of rolling stock in Missouri. N & W is primarily a coal-carrying railroad. Much of its equipment and all of its specialized coal-carrying equipment are generally located in the coal regions of Virginia, West Virginia, and Kentucky, and along the coal-ferrying routes from those regions to the eastern seaboard and the Great Lakes. Scarcely any of the specialized equipment ever enters Missouri. According to appellants, the Wabash property in Missouri was leased by N & W in order to diversify its business, not to provide the opportunity for an integrated through movement of traffic.

By the terms of the lease, the N & W became obligated to pay the 1965 taxes on the property of the Wabash in Missouri and elsewhere. . . .

I

The Missouri property taxable to the N & W was assessed by the State Tax Commission at $31,298,939. Of this sum, $12,177,597 relates to fixed property within the State, an assessment that is not challenged by appellants. Their attack is aimed only at that portion of the assessment relating to rolling stock, $19,981,757.

---

1. The tax in question applies to "all real property . . . [and] tangible personal property . . . owned, hired or leased by any railroad company . . . in this state." Intangible personal property is explicitly exempted from this tax.

With respect to the assessment of rolling stock, the Commission used the familiar mileage formula authorized by the Missouri statute. In relevant part, this provides:

". . . when any railroad shall extend beyond the limits of this state and into another state in which a tax is levied and paid on the rolling stock of such road then the said commission shall assess, equalize and adjust only such proportion of the total value of all the rolling stock of such railroad company as the number of miles of such road in this state bears to the total length of the road as owned or controlled by such company."

The Commission arrived at the assessment of rolling stock by first determining the value of all rolling stock, regardless of where located, owned or leased by the N & W as of the tax day, January 1, 1965. Value was ascertained by totaling the original cost, less accrued depreciation at 5% a year up to 75% of cost, of each locomotive, car, and other piece of mobile equipment. To the total value, $513,309,877, was applied an "equalizing factor" of 47%, employed in assessing all railroad property in an attempt to bring such assessments down to the level of other property assessments in Missouri. The Commission next found that 8.2824% of all the main and branch line road (excluding secondary and side tracks) owned, leased, or controlled by the N & W was situated in Missouri. This percentage was applied to the equalized value of all N & W rolling stock, and the resulting figure was $19,981,757.

There is no suggestion in this case that the Commission failed to follow the literal command of the statute. The problem arises because of appellants' contention that, in mechanically applying the statutory formula, the Commission here arrived at an unconscionable and unconstitutional result. It is their submission that the assessment was so far out of line with the actual facts of record with respect to the value of taxable rolling stock in the State as to amount to an unconstitutional attempt to exercise state taxing power on out-of-state property.

Appellants submitted evidence based upon an inventory of all N & W rolling stock that was actually in Missouri on tax day. The equalized value of this rolling stock, calculated on the same cost-less-depreciation basis employed by the Commission, was approximately $7,600,000, as compared with the assessed value of $19,981,000. Appellants also submitted evidence to show that the tax-day inventory was not unusual. The evidence showed that, both before and in the months immediately after the Wabash lease, the equalized value of the N & W rolling stock actually in Missouri never ranged

far above the $7,600,000 figure. In the preceding year, 1964, the rolling stock assessment against the Wabash was only $9,177,683, and appellants demonstrated that neither the amount of rolling stock in Missouri nor the Missouri operations of the N & W and Wabash had materially increased in the intervening period.[4] The assessment of the fixed properties (for which no mileage formula was applied) hardly increased between 1964 and 1965. In 1964, prior to the lease, the fixed properties in Missouri were assessed at $12,092,594; in 1965, after the lease, the assessment was $12,177,597.

The Supreme Court of Missouri concluded that the result reached by the Commission was justifiable. It pointed out that the statutory method used by the Commission proceeds on the assumption that "rolling stock is substantially evenly divided throughout the railroad's entire system, and the percentage of all units which are located in Missouri at any given time, or for any given period of time, will be substantially the same as the percentage of all the miles of road of the railroad located in Missouri." It then held that the evaluation found by the Commission could be justified on the theory of "enhancement," although the Commission had not referred to that principle. The court described the theory as follows:

"The theory underlying such method of assessment is that rolling stock regularly employed in one state has an enhanced or augmented value when it is connected to, and because of its connection with, an integrated operational whole and may, therefore, be taxed according to its value 'as part of the system, although the other parts be outside the State; in other words, the tax may be made to cover the enhanced value which comes to the property in the State through its organic relation to the system.' Pullman Co. v. Richardson, 261 U.S. at 338."

The court correctly noted, however, that "even if the validity of such methods be conceded, the results, to be valid, must be free of excessiveness and discrimination." It concluded that in the present case, the result reached by the Commission was justifiable. We disagree. In our opinion, the assessment violates the Due Process and Commerce Clauses of the Constitution.

---

4. Appellants further argue that the arbitrariness of the result reached here is shown by the fact that if the rolling stock in Missouri had been taxable to the Wabash in 1965, rather than to N & W, the application of the formula to the same rolling stock would have resulted in an assessment of little more than half of that which was actually levied ($10,103,340).

II

Established principles are not lacking in this much discussed area of the law. It is of course settled that a State may impose a property tax upon its fair share of an interstate transportation enterprise. That fair share may be regarded as the value, appropriately ascertained, of tangible assets permanently or habitually employed in the taxing State, including a portion of the intangible, or "going-concern," value of the enterprise. The value may be ascertained by reference to the total system of which the intrastate assets are a part. As the Court has stated the rule, "the tax may be made to cover the enhanced value which comes to the [tangible] property in the State through its organic relation to the [interstate] system." Pullman Co. v. Richardson, 261 U.S. at 338. Going-concern value, of course, is an elusive concept not susceptible of exact measurement. As a consequence, the States have been permitted considerable latitude in devising formulas to measure the value of tangible property located within their borders. Such formulas usually involve a determination of the percentage of the taxpayer's tangible assets situated in the taxing State and the application of this percentage to a figure representing the total going-concern value of the enterprise. A number of such formulas have been sustained by the Court, even though it could not be demonstrated that the results they yielded were precise evaluations of assets located within the taxing State.

On the other hand, the Court has insisted for many years that a State is not entitled to tax tangible or intangible property that is unconnected with the State. In some cases the Court has concluded that States have, in fact, cast their tax burden upon property located beyond their borders. The taxation of property not located in the taxing State is constitutionally invalid, both because it imposes an illegitimate restraint on interstate commerce and because it denies to the taxpayer the process that is his due. A State will not be permitted, under the shelter of an imprecise allocation formula or by ignoring the peculiarities of a given enterprise, to "project the taxing power of the state plainly beyond its borders." Any formula used must bear a rational relationship, both on its face and in its application, to property values connected with the taxing State.

Fargo v. Hart, 193 U.S. at 499-500.[6]

III

Applying these principles to the facts of the case now before us, we conclude that Missouri's assessment of N & W's rolling stock cannot be sustained. This Court has, in various contexts, permitted mileage formulas as a basis for taxation. A railroad challenging the result reached by the application of such a formula has a heavy burden. See Butler Brothers v. McColgan, 315 U.S. at 507; Norfolk & Western R. Co. v. North Carolina, 297 U.S. at 688. It is confronted by the vastness of the State's taxing power and the latitude that the exercise of that power must be given before it encounters constitutional restraints. Its task is to show that application of the mileage method in its case has resulted in such gross overreaching, beyond the values represented by the intrastate assets purported to be taxed, as to violate the Due Process and Commerce Clauses of the Constitution. Cf. Capitol Greyhound Lines v. Brice, 339 U.S. at 547. But here the appellants have borne that burden, and the State has made no effort to offset the convincing case that they have made.

Here, the record shows that rigid application of the mileage formula led to a grossly distorted result. The rolling stock in Missouri was assessed to N & W at $19,981,757. It was practically the same property that had been assessed the preceding year at $9,177,683 to the Wabash. Appellants introduced evidence of the results of an actual count of the rolling stock in Missouri. On the basis of this actual count, the equalized assessment would have been less than half of the value assessed by the State Commission. The Commission's mileage formula resulted in postulating that N & W's rolling stock in Missouri constituted 8.2824% of its rolling stock. But appellants showed that the rolling stock usually employed in the State comprised only about 2.71% by number of units (and only 3.16% by cost-less-depreciation value) of the total N & W fleet.

---

6. As the Court stated in Wallace v. Hines, 253 U.S. at 69: "The only reason for allowing a State to look beyond its borders when it taxes the property of foreign corporations is that it may get the true value of the things within it, when they are part of an organic system of wide extent, that gives them a value above what they otherwise would possess. The purpose is not . . . to open to taxation what is not within the State. Therefore no property of . . . an interstate road situated elsewhere can be taken into account unless it can be seen in some plain and fairly intelligible way that it adds to the value of the road and the rights exercised in the State."

Our decisions recognize the practical difficulties involved and do not require any close correspondence between the result of computations using the mileage formula and the value of property actually located in the State, but our cases certainly forbid an unexplained discrepancy as gross as that in this case. Such discrepancy certainly means that the impact of the state tax is not confined to intrastate property even within the broad tolerance permitted. The facts of life do not neatly lend themselves to the niceties of constitutionalism; but neither does the Constitution tolerate any result, however distorted, just because it is the product of a convenient mathematical formula which, in most situations, may produce a tolerable product.

The basic difficulty here is that the record is totally barren of any evidence relating to enhancement or to going-concern or intangible value, or to any other factor which might offset the devastating effect of the demonstrated discrepancy. The Missouri Supreme Court attempted to justify the result by reference to "enhanced" value, but the Missouri Commission made no effort to show such value or to measure the extent to which it might be attributed to the rolling stock in the State. In fact, N & W showed that it is chiefly a coal-carrying railroad, 70% of whose 1964 revenue was derived from coal traffic. It demonstrated that its coal operations require a great deal of specialized equipment, scarcely any of which ever enters Missouri. It showed that traffic density on its Missouri tracks was only 54% of traffic density on the N & W system as a whole. Finally, it proved that the overwhelming majority of its rolling stock regularly present in Missouri was rolling stock it had leased from the Wabash. As long ago as Pittsburgh, C., C. & St. L.R. Co. v. Backus, 154 U.S. 421 (1894), we indicated that an otherwise valid mileage formula might not be validly applied to ascertain the value of tangible assets within the taxing State in exceptional situations, for example, "where in certain localities the company is engaged in a particular kind of business requiring for sole use in such localities an extra amount of rolling stock." The Missouri Supreme

Court did not challenge the factual data submitted by the N & W. Its decision that these data did not place this case within the realm of "exceptional situations" recognized by this Court was apparently based on the conclusion that the lease transaction between Wabash and the N & W had increased the value of tangible assets formerly belonging to the two separate lines. This may be true, but it does not follow that the Constitution permits us, without evidence as to the amount of enhancement that may be assumed, to bridge the chasm between the formula and the facts of record. The difference between the assessed value and the actual value as shown by the evidence to which we have referred is too great to be explained by the mere assertion, without more, that it is due to an assumed and nonparticularized increase in intangible value. See Wallace v. Hines, 253 U.S. at 69.

As the Court recognized in Fargo v. Hart, 193 U.S. at 499-500, care must be exercised lest the mileage formula

"be made a means of unlawfully taxing the privilege, or property outside the State, under the name of enhanced value or good will, if it is not closely confined to its true meaning. So long as it fairly may be assumed that the different parts of a line are about equal in value a division by mileage is justifiable. But it is recognized in the cases that if for instance a railroad company had terminals in one State equal in value to all the rest of the line through another, the latter State could not make use of the unity of the road to equalize the value of every mile. That would be taxing property outside of the State under a pretense."

We repeat that it is not necessary that a State demonstrate that its use of the mileage formula has resulted in an exact measure of value. But when a taxpayer comes forward with strong evidence tending to prove that the mileage formula will yield a grossly distorted result in its particular case, the State is obliged to counter that evidence or to make the accommodations necessary to assure that its taxing power is confined to its constitutional limits. If it fails to do so and if the record shows that the taxpayer has sustained the burden of proof to show that the tax is so excessive as to burden interstate commerce, the taxpayer must prevail.

. . . .

Questions and Comments

1. What assumption underlies the Commission's formula for assessing the taxpayer's rolling stock?

2. Suppose the Commission considered intangible

values, such as goodwill and enhancement value, in assessing the rolling stock. Would such an assessment be consistent with the statute? See footnote 1.

3. The Court states that: "The income attributed to the State for tax purposes must be rationally related to values connected with the taxing State." Is this an early statement of what the Court later calls the "external consistency test"? See *Goldberg v. Sweet*, "The external consistency test asks whether a state has taxed only that portion of the revenues from the interstate activity which reasonably reflects the in-state component of the activity being taxed."

4. What does the taxpayer's assertion in footnote 4 prove? Why was the 1964 assessment against the Wabash relevant?

5. Was Missouri attempting to tax both Wabash—the lessor—and N & W—the lessee—on the same property?

6. Does every tax that is unfairly apportioned violate the Due Process Clause?

7. Which clause of the Constitution–Due Process or Commerce Clause–did the tax violate?

8. Did the State have sufficient due process connections with the coal equipment to justify including it in the taxpayer's preapportionment tax base?

9. Consider the application of the Missouri income tax to N & W. Would N & W be considered as conducting one or two unitary businesses? Could Missouri include in N & W's preapportionment tax base the income from the coal business?

National Bellas Hess

Quill Corp. v. North Dakota
Supreme Court of the United States, 1992.
504 U.S. 298, 112 S. Ct. 1904, 119 L. Ed. 2d 91.

JUSTICE STEVENS delivered the opinion of the Court.

This case, like National Bellas Hess, Inc. v. Department of Revenue of Ill., 386 U.S. 753 (1967), involves a State's attempt to require an out-of-state mail-order house that has neither outlets nor sales representatives in the State to collect and pay a use tax on goods purchased for use within the State. In Bellas Hess we held that a similar Illinois statute violated the Due Process Clause of the Fourteenth Amendment and created an unconstitutional burden on interstate commerce. In particular, we ruled that a "seller whose only connection with customers in the State is by common carrier or the United States mail" lacked the requisite minimum contacts with the State.

In this case the Supreme Court of North Dakota declined to follow Bellas Hess because "the tremendous social, economic, commercial, and legal innovations" of the past quarter-century have rendered its holding "obsole[te]." Having granted certiorari, we must either reverse the State Supreme Court or overrule Bellas Hess. While we agree with much of the State Court's reasoning, we take the former course.

I

Quill is a Delaware corporation with offices and warehouses in Illinois, California, and Georgia. None of

its employees work or reside in North Dakota and its ownership of tangible property in that State is either insignificant or nonexistent.[1] Quill sells office equipment and supplies; it solicits business through catalogs and flyers, advertisements in national periodicals, and telephone calls. Its annual national sales exceed $200,000,000, of which almost $1,000,000 are made to about 3,000 customers in North Dakota. It is the sixth largest vendor of office supplies in the State. It delivers all of its merchandise to its North Dakota customers by mail or common carrier from out-of-state locations.

As a corollary to its sales tax, North Dakota imposes a use tax upon property purchased for storage, use or consumption within the State. North Dakota requires every "retailer maintaining a place of business in" the

---

1. In the trial court, the State argued that because Quill gave its customers an unconditional 90-day guarantee, it retained title to the merchandise during the 90-day period after delivery. The trial court held, however, that title passed to the purchaser when the merchandise was received. The State Supreme Court assumed for the purposes of its decision that that ruling was correct. The State Supreme Court also noted that Quill licensed a computer software program to some of its North Dakota customers that enabled them to check Quill's current inventories and prices and to place orders directly. As we shall explain, Quill's interests in the licensed software does not affect our analysis of the due process issue and does not comprise the "substantial nexus" required by the Commerce Clause.

State to collect the tax from the consumer and remit it to the State. In 1987 North Dakota amended the statutory definition of the term "retailer" to include "every person who engages in regular or systematic solicitation of a consumer market in th[e] state." State regulations in turn define "regular or systematic solicitation" to mean three or more advertisements within a 12-month period. Thus, since 1987, mail-order companies that engage in such solicitation have been subject to the tax even if they maintain no property or personnel in North Dakota.

Quill has taken the position that North Dakota does not have the power to compel it to collect a use tax from its North Dakota customers. Consequently, the State, through its Tax Commissioner, filed this action to require Quill to pay taxes (as well as interest and penalties) on all such sales made after July 1, 1987. The trial court ruled in Quill's favor, finding the case indistinguishable from Bellas Hess; specifically, it found that because the State had not shown that it had spent tax revenues for the benefit of the mail-order business, there was no "nexus to allow the state to define retailer in the manner it chose."

The North Dakota Supreme Court reversed, concluding that "wholesale changes" in both the economy and the law made it inappropriate to follow Bellas Hess today. The principal economic change noted by the court was the remarkable growth of the mail-order business "from a relatively inconsequential market niche" in 1967 to a "goliath" with annual sales that reached "the staggering figure of $183.3 billion in 1989." Moreover, the court observed, advances in computer technology greatly eased the burden of compliance with a "'welter of complicated obligations'" imposed by state and local taxing authorities.

Equally important, in the court's view, were the changes in the "legal landscape." With respect to the Commerce Clause, the court emphasized that Complete Auto Transit, Inc. v. Brady, 430 U.S. 274 (1977), rejected the line of cases holding that the direct taxation of interstate commerce was impermissible and adopted instead a "consistent and rational method of inquiry [that focused on] the practical effect of [the] challenged tax." This and subsequent rulings, the court maintained, indicated that the Commerce Clause no longer mandated the sort of physical-presence nexus suggested in Bellas Hess.

Similarly, with respect to the Due Process Clause, the North Dakota court observed that cases following Bellas Hess had not construed "minimum contacts" to require physical presence within a State as a prerequisite to the legitimate exercise of state power. The State Court then concluded that "the Due Process requirement of a

'minimal connection' to establish nexus is encompassed within the Complete Auto test" and that the relevant inquiry under the latter test was whether "the state has provided some protection, opportunities, or benefit for which it can expect a return."

Turning to the case at hand, the State Court emphasized that North Dakota had created "an economic climate that fosters demand for" Quill's products, maintained a legal infrastructure that protected that market, and disposed of 24 tons of catalogs and flyers mailed by Quill into the State every year. Based on these facts, the court concluded that Quill's "economic presence" in North Dakota depended on services and benefits provided by the State and therefore generated "a constitutionally sufficient nexus to justify imposition of the purely administrative duty of collecting and remitting the use tax."[2]

II

As in a number of other cases involving the application of state taxing statutes to out-of-state sellers, our holding in Bellas Hess relied on both the Due Process Clause and the Commerce Clause. Although the "two claims are closely related," Bellas Hess, 386 U.S. at 756, the clauses pose distinct limits on the taxing powers of the States. Accordingly, while a State may, consistent with the Due Process Clause, have the authority to tax a particular taxpayer, imposition of the tax may nonetheless violate the Commerce Clause. See, e. g., Tyler Pipe Industries, Inc. v. Washington State Dept. of Revenue, 483 U.S. 232 (1987).

The two constitutional requirements differ fundamentally, in several ways. As discussed at greater length below, the Due Process Clause and the Commerce Clause reflect different constitutional concerns. Moreover, while Congress has plenary power to regulate commerce among the States and thus may authorize state actions that burden interstate commerce, see International Shoe Co. v. Washington, 326 U.S. at 315, it does not similarly have the power to authorize violations of the Due Process Clause.

Thus, although we have not always been precise in distinguishing between the two, the Due Process Clause and the Commerce Clause are analytically distinct. "'Due process' and 'commerce clause' conceptions are not always sharply separable in dealing with these

---

2. The court also suggested that, in view of the fact that the "touchstone of Due Process is fundamental fairness" and that the "very object" of the Commerce Clause is protection of interstate business against discriminatory local practices, it would be ironic to exempt Quill from this burden and thereby allow it to enjoy a significant competitive advantage over local retailers.

problems. . . . To some extent they overlap. If there is a want of due process to sustain the tax, by that fact alone any burden the tax imposes on the commerce among the states becomes 'undue.' But, though overlapping, the two conceptions are not identical. There may be more than sufficient factual connections, with economic and legal effects, between the transaction and the taxing state to sustain the tax as against due process objections. Yet it may fall because of its burdening effect upon the commerce. And, although the two notions cannot always be separated, clarity of consideration and of decision would be promoted if the two issues are approached, where they are presented, at least tentatively as if they were separate and distinct, not intermingled ones." International Harvester Co. v. Department of Treasury, 322 U.S. 340, 353 (1944) (Rutledge, J., concurring in part and dissenting in part).

Heeding Justice Rutledge's counsel, we consider each constitutional limit in turn.

III

The Due Process Clause "requires some definite link, some minimum connection, between a state and the person, property or transaction it seeks to tax," Miller Bros. Co. v. Maryland, 347 U.S. at 344-345, and that the "income attributed to the State for tax purposes must be rationally related to 'values connected with the taxing State.'" Moorman Mfg. Co. v. Bair, 437 U.S. at 273. Here, we are concerned primarily with the first of these requirements. Prior to Bellas Hess, we had held that that requirement was satisfied in a variety of circumstances involving use taxes. For example, the presence of sales personnel in the State,[3] or the maintenance of local retail stores in the State[4] justified the exercise of that power because the seller's local activities were "plainly accorded the protection and services of the taxing State." Bellas Hess, 386 U.S. at 757. The furthest extension of that power was recognized in Scripto, Inc. v. Carson, 362 U.S. 207 (1960), in which the Court upheld a use tax despite the fact that all of the seller's in-state solicitation was performed by independent contractors. These cases all involved some sort of physical presence within the State, and in Bellas Hess the Court suggested that such presence was not only sufficient for jurisdiction under the Due Process Clause, but also necessary. We expressly declined to obliterate the "sharp distinction . . . between mail order sellers with retail outlets, solicitors, or property within a State, and those who do no more than communicate with customers in the State by mail or common carrier as a

_____

3. Felt & Tarrant Mfg. Co. v. Gallagher, 306 U.S. 62 (1939).

4. Nelson v. Sears, Roebuck & Co., 312 U.S. 359 (1941).

part of a general interstate business."

Our due process jurisprudence has evolved substantially in the 25 years since Bellas Hess, particularly in the area of judicial jurisdiction. Building on the seminal case of International Shoe Co. v. Washington, 326 U.S. 310 (1945), we have framed the relevant inquiry as whether a defendant had minimum contacts with the jurisdiction "such that the maintenance of the suit does not offend 'traditional notions of fair play and substantial justice.'" Id., at 316 (quoting Milliken v. Meyer, 311 U.S. at 463). In that spirit, we have abandoned more formalistic tests that focused on a defendant's "presence" within a State in favor of a more flexible inquiry into whether a defendant's contacts with the forum made it reasonable, in the context of our federal system of government, to require it to defend the suit in that State. In Shaffer v. Heitner, 433 U.S. at 212 (1977), the Court extended the flexible approach that International Shoe had prescribed for purposes of in personam jurisdiction to in rem jurisdiction, concluding that "all assertions of state-court jurisdiction must be evaluated according to the standards set forth in International Shoe and its progeny."

Applying these principles, we have held that if a foreign corporation purposefully avails itself of the benefits of an economic market in the forum State, it may subject itself to the State's in personam jurisdiction even if it has no physical presence in the State. As we explained in Burger King Corp. v. Rudzewicz, 471 U.S. 462 (1985):

"Jurisdiction in these circumstances may not be avoided merely because the defendant did not _physically_ enter the forum State. Although territorial presence frequently will enhance a potential defendant's affiliation with a State and reinforce the reasonable foreseeability of suit there, it is an inescapable fact of modern commercial life that a substantial amount of business is transacted solely by mail and wire communications across state lines, thus obviating the need for physical presence within a State in which business is conducted. So long as a commercial actor's efforts are' purposefully directed' toward residents of another State, we have consistently rejected the notion that an absence of physical contacts can defeat personal jurisdiction there." Id., at 476 (emphasis in original).

Comparable reasoning justifies the imposition of the collection duty on a mail-order house that is engaged in continuous and widespread solicitation of business within a State. Such a corporation clearly has "fair warning that [its] activity may subject [it] to the jurisdiction of a foreign sovereign." Shaffer v. Heitner, 433 U.S. at 218 (Stevens, J., concurring in judgment). In "modern commercial life" it matters little that such solicitation is accomplished by a deluge of catalogs rather than a phalanx of drummers: the requirements of due process are met irrespective of a corporation's lack of physical presence in the taxing State. Thus, to the extent that our decisions have indicated that the Due Process Clause requires physical presence in a State for the imposition of duty to collect a use tax, we overrule those holdings as superseded by developments in the law of due process.

In this case, there is no question that Quill has purposefully directed its activities at North Dakota residents, that the magnitude of those contacts are more than sufficient for due process purposes, and that the use tax is related to the benefits Quill receives from access to the State. We therefore agree with the North Dakota Supreme Court's conclusion that the Due Process Clause does not bar enforcement of that State's use tax against Quill.

. . . .

IV

. . . .

Our interpretation of the "negative" or "dormant" Commerce Clause has evolved substantially over the years, particularly as that clause concerns limitations on state taxation powers. Our early cases, beginning with Brown v. Maryland, 12 Wheat. 419 (1827), swept broadly, and in Leloup v. Port of Mobile, 127 U.S. at 648, we declared that "no State has the right to lay a tax on interstate commerce in any form." We later narrowed that rule and distinguished between direct burdens on interstate commerce, which were prohibited, and indirect burdens, which generally were not. See, e. g., Sanford v. Poe, 69 F. 546 (CA6 1895), aff'd sub nom. Adams Express Co. v. Ohio State Auditor, 165 U.S. at 220. Western Live Stock v. Bureau of Revenue, 303 U.S. at 256-258, and subsequent decisions rejected this formal, categorical analysis and adopted a "multiple-taxation doctrine" that focused not on whether a tax was "direct" or "indirect" but rather on whether a tax subjected interstate commerce to a risk of multiple taxation. However, in Freeman v. Hewit, 329 U.S. at 256, we embraced again the formal distinction between direct and indirect taxation, invalidating Indiana's imposition of a gross receipts tax on a particular transaction because that application would "impos[e] a direct tax on interstate sales." Most recently, in Complete Auto Transit, we renounced the Freeman approach as "attaching constitutional significance to a semantic difference." We expressly overruled one of Freeman's progeny, Spector Motor Service, Inc. v. O'Connor, 340 U.S. 602 (1951), which held that a tax on "the privilege of doing interstate business" was unconstitutional, while recognizing that a differently denominated tax with the same economic effect would not be unconstitutional. Spector, as we observed in Railway Express Agency, Inc. v. Virginia, 358 U.S. at 441, created a situation in which "magic words or labels" could "disable an otherwise constitutional levy." Complete Auto emphasized the importance of looking past "the formal language of the tax statute [to] its practical effect," 430 U.S. at 279, and set forth a four-part test that continues to govern the validity of state taxes under the Commerce Clause.

Bellas Hess was decided in 1967, in the middle of this latest rally between formalism and pragmatism. Contrary to the suggestion of the North Dakota Supreme Court, this timing does not mean that Complete Auto rendered Bellas Hess "obsolete." Complete Auto rejected Freeman and Spector's formal distinction between "direct" and "indirect" taxes on interstate commerce because that formalism allowed the validity of statutes to hinge on "legal terminology," "draftsmanship and phraseology." 430 U.S. at 281. Bellas Hess did not rely on any such labeling of taxes and therefore did not automatically fall with Freeman and its progeny.

While contemporary Commerce Clause jurisprudence might not dictate the same result were the issue to arise for the first time today, Bellas Hess is not inconsistent with Complete Auto and our recent cases. Under Complete Auto's four-part test, we will sustain a tax against a Commerce Clause challenge so long as the "tax [1] is applied to an activity with a substantial nexus with the taxing State, [2] is fairly apportioned, [3] does not discriminate against interstate commerce, and [4] is fairly related to the services provided by the State." Bellas Hess concerns the first of these tests and stands for the proposition that a vendor whose only contacts with the taxing State are by mail or common carrier lacks the "substantial nexus" required by the Commerce Clause.

Thus, three weeks after Complete Auto was handed down, we cited Bellas Hess for this proposition and discussed the case at some length. In National Geographic Society v. California Bd. of Equalization, 430 U.S. at 559, we affirmed the continuing vitality of Bellas Hess' "sharp distinction . . . between mail-order sellers with [a physical presence in the taxing] State and those . . . who do no more than communicate with customers in the State by mail or common carrier as part of a general interstate business." We have continued to cite Bellas Hess with approval ever since. For example, in Goldberg v. Sweet, 488 U.S. at 263, we expressed "doubt that termination of an interstate telephone call, by itself, provides a substantial enough nexus for a State to tax a call. See National Bellas Hess . . . (receipt of mail provides insufficient nexus)." See also D. H. Holmes Co. v. McNamara, 486 U.S. at 33; Commonwealth Edison Co. v. Montana, 453 U.S. at 626; Mobil Oil Corp. v. Commissioner of Taxes, 445 U.S. at 437; National Geographic Society, 430 U.S. at 559. For these reasons, we disagree with the State Supreme Court's conclusion that our decision in Complete Auto undercut the Bellas Hess rule.

The State of North Dakota relies less on Complete Auto

and more on the evolution of our due process jurisprudence. The State contends that the nexus requirements imposed by the Due Process and Commerce Clauses are equivalent and that if, as we concluded above, a mail-order house that lacks a physical presence in the taxing State nonetheless satisfies the due process "minimum contacts" test, then that corporation also meets the Commerce Clause "substantial nexus" test. We disagree. Despite the similarity in phrasing, the nexus requirements of the Due Process and Commerce Clauses are not identical. The two standards are animated by different constitutional concerns and policies.

Due process centrally concerns the fundamental fairness of governmental activity. Thus, at the most general level, the due process nexus analysis requires that we ask whether an individual's connections with a State are substantial enough to legitimate the State's exercise of power over him. We have, therefore, often identified "notice" or "fair warning" as the analytic touchstone of due process nexus analysis. In contrast, the Commerce Clause, and its nexus requirement, are informed not so much by concerns about fairness for the individual defendant as by structural concerns about the effects of state regulation on the national economy. Under the Articles of Confederation, State taxes and duties hindered and suppressed interstate commerce; the Framers intended the Commerce Clause as a cure for these structural ills. See generally The Federalist Nos. 7, 11 (A. Hamilton). It is in this light that we have interpreted the negative implication of the Commerce Clause. Accordingly, we have ruled that that Clause prohibits discrimination against interstate commerce, see, e. g., Philadelphia v. New Jersey, 437 U.S. 617 (1978), and bars state regulations that unduly burden interstate commerce, see, e. g., Kassel v. Consolidated Freightways Corp. of Del., 450 U.S. 662 (1981).

The Complete Auto analysis reflects these concerns about the national economy. The second and third parts of that analysis, which require fair apportionment and non-discrimination, prohibit taxes that pass an unfair share of the tax burden onto interstate commerce. The first and fourth prongs, which require a substantial nexus and a relationship between the tax and State-provided services, limit the reach of State taxing authority so as to ensure that State taxation does not unduly burden interstate commerce.[6] Thus, the

"substantial-nexus" requirement is not, like due process' "minimum-contacts" requirement, a proxy for notice, but rather a means for limiting state burdens on interstate commerce. Accordingly, contrary to the State's suggestion, a corporation may have the "minimum contacts" with a taxing State as required by the Due Process Clause, and yet lack the "substantial nexus" with that State as required by the Commerce Clause.[7]

The State Supreme Court reviewed our recent Commerce Clause decisions and concluded that those rulings signaled a "retreat from the formalistic constrictions of a stringent physical presence test in favor of a more flexible substantive approach" and thus supported its decision not to apply Bellas Hess. Although we agree with the State Court's assessment of the evolution of our cases, we do not share its conclusion that this evolution indicates that the Commerce Clause ruling of Bellas Hess is no longer good law.

First, as the State Court itself noted, all of these cases involved taxpayers who had a physical presence in the taxing State and therefore do not directly conflict with the rule of Bellas Hess or compel that it be overruled. Second, and more importantly, although our Commerce Clause jurisprudence now favors more flexible balancing analyses, we have never intimated a desire to reject all established "bright-line" tests. Although we have not, in our review of other types of taxes, articulated the same physical-presence requirement that Bellas Hess established for sales and use taxes, that silence does not imply repudiation of the Bellas Hess rule.

Complete Auto, it is true, renounced Freeman and its progeny as "formalistic." But not all formalism is alike.

---

6. North Dakota's use tax illustrates well how a state tax might unduly burden interstate commerce. On its face, North Dakota law imposes a collection duty on every vendor who advertises in the State three times in a single year. Thus, absent the Bellas Hess rule, a publisher who included a subscription card in three issues of its magazine, a vendor whose radio advertisements were heard in North Dakota on three occasions, and a

corporation whose telephone sales force made three calls into the State, all would be subject to the collection duty. What is more significant, similar obligations might be imposed by the Nation's 6,000-plus taxing jurisdictions. See National Bellas Hess, Inc. v. Department of Revenue of Ill., 386 U.S. at 759-760 (noting that the "many variations in rates of tax, in allowable exemptions, and in administrative and record-keeping requirements could entangle [a mail-order house] in a virtual welter of complicated obligations") (footnotes omitted); see also Shaviro, An Economic and Political Look at Federalism in Taxation, 90 Mich. L. Rev. 895, 925-926 (1992).

7. We have sometimes stated that the "Complete Auto test, while responsive to Commerce Clause dictates, encompasses as well . . . Due Process requirement[s]." Trinova Corp v. Michigan Dept. of Treasury, 498 U.S. at 373. Although such comments might suggest that every tax that passes contemporary Commerce Clause analysis is also valid under the Due Process Clause, it does not follow that the converse is as well true: a tax may be consistent with Due Process and yet unduly burden interstate commerce. See, e. g., Tyler Pipe Industries, Inc. v. Washington State Dept. of Revenue, 483 U.S. 232 (1987).

Spector's formal distinction between taxes on the "privilege of doing business" and all other taxes served no purpose within our Commerce Clause jurisprudence, but stood "only as a trap for the unwary draftsman." In contrast, the bright-line rule of Bellas Hess furthers the ends of the dormant Commerce Clause. Undue burdens on interstate commerce may be avoided not only by a case-by-case evaluation of the actual burdens imposed by particular regulations or taxes, but also, in some situations, by the demarcation of a discrete realm of commercial activity that is free from interstate taxation. Bellas Hess followed the latter approach and created a safe harbor for vendors "whose only connection with customers in the [taxing] State is by common carrier or the United States mail." Under Bellas Hess, such vendors are free from state-imposed duties to collect sales and use taxes.[8]

Like other bright-line tests, the Bellas Hess rule appears artificial at its edges: whether or not a State may compel a vendor to collect a sales or use tax may turn on the presence in the taxing State of a small sales force, plant, or office. This artificiality, however, is more than offset by the benefits of a clear rule. Such a rule firmly establishes the boundaries of legitimate state authority to impose a duty to collect sales and use taxes and reduces litigation concerning those taxes. This benefit is important, for as we have so frequently noted, our law in this area is something of a "quagmire" and the "application of constitutional principles to specific state statutes leaves much room for controversy and confusion and little in the way of precise guides to the States in the exercise of their indispensable power of taxation." Northwestern States Portland Cement Co. v. Minnesota, 358 U.S. at 457-458.

Moreover, a bright-line rule in the area of sales and use taxes also encourages settled expectations and, in doing so, fosters investment by businesses and individuals.[9]

Indeed, it is not unlikely that the mail-order industry's dramatic growth over the last quarter-century is due in part to the bright-line exemption from state taxation created in Bellas Hess.

. . . .

In sum, although in our cases subsequent to Bellas Hess and concerning other types of taxes we have not adopted a similar bright-line, physical-presence requirement, our reasoning in those cases does not compel that we now reject the rule that Bellas Hess established in the area of sales and use taxes. To the contrary, the continuing value of a bright-line rule in this area and the doctrine and principles of stare decisis indicate that the Bellas Hess rule remains good law. For these reasons, we disagree with the North Dakota Supreme Court's conclusion that the time has come to renounce the bright-line test of Bellas Hess.

This aspect of our decision is made easier by the fact that the underlying issue is not only one that Congress may be better qualified to resolve,[10] but also one that Congress has the ultimate power to resolve. No matter how we evaluate the burdens that use taxes impose on interstate commerce, Congress remains free to disagree with our conclusions. Indeed, in recent years Congress has considered legislation that would "overrule" the Bellas Hess rule. Its decision not to take action in this direction may, of course, have been dictated by respect for our holding in Bellas Hess that the Due Process Clause prohibits States from imposing such taxes, but today we have put that problem to rest. Accordingly, Congress is now free to decide whether, when, and to what extent the States may burden interstate mail-order concerns with a duty to collect use taxes.

----

8. In addition to its common-carrier contacts with the State, Quill also licensed software to some of its North Dakota clients. See supra n. 1. The State "concedes that the existence in North Dakota of a few floppy diskettes to which Quill holds title seems a slender thread upon which to base nexus." We agree. Although title to "a few floppy diskettes" present in a State might constitute some minimal nexus, in National Geographic Society v. California Bd. of Equalization, 430 U.S. at 556, we expressly rejected a "'slightest presence' standard of constitutional nexus." We therefore conclude that Quill's licensing of software in this case does not meet the "substantial nexus" requirement of the Commerce Clause.

9. It is worth noting that Congress has, at least on one occasion, followed a similar approach in its regulation of state taxation. In response to this Court's indication in Northwestern States Portland Cement Co. v. Minnesota, 358 U.S. at 452, that, so long as the taxpayer has an adequate nexus with the taxing

State, "net income from the interstate operations of a foreign corporation may be subjected to state taxation," Congress enacted Pub. L. 86-272, codified at 15 U.S.C. § 381. That statute provides that a State may not impose a net income tax on any person if that person's "only business activities within such State [involve] the solicitation of orders [approved] outside the State [and] filled . . . outside the State." 15 U.S.C. § 381. As we noted in Heublein, Inc. v. South Carolina Tax Comm'n, 409 U.S. at 280, in enacting § 381, "Congress attempted to allay the apprehension of businessmen that 'mere solicitation' would subject them to state taxation. . . . Section 381 was designed to define clearly a lower limit for the exercise of [the State's power to tax]. *Clarity that would remove uncertainty was Congress' primary goal.*" (Emphasis supplied.)

10. Many States have enacted use taxes. An overruling of Bellas Hess might raise thorny questions concerning the retroactive application of those taxes and might trigger substantial unanticipated liability for mail-order houses. The precise allocation of such burdens is better resolved by Congress rather than this Court.

Indeed, even if we were convinced that Bellas Hess was inconsistent with our Commerce Clause jurisprudence, "this very fact [might] giv[e us] pause and counse[l] withholding our hand, at least for now. Congress has the power to protect interstate commerce from intolerable or even undesirable burdens." Commonwealth Edison Co. v. Montana, 453 U.S. at 637 (WHITE, J., concurring). In this situation, it may be that "the better part of both wisdom and valor is to respect the judgment of the other branches of the Government." Id., at 638.

JUSTICE SCALIA, with whom JUSTICE KENNEDY and JUSTICE THOMAS join, concurring in part and concurring in the judgment.

National Bellas Hess held that the Due Process and Commerce Clauses of the Constitution prohibit a State from imposing the duty of use-tax collection and payment upon a seller whose only connection with the State is through common carrier or the United States mail. I agree with the Court that the Due Process Clause holding of Bellas Hess should be overruled. Even before Bellas Hess, we had held, correctly I think, that state regulatory jurisdiction could be asserted on the basis of contacts with the State through the United States mail. See Travelers Health Assn. v. Virginia ex rel. State Corp. Comm'n, 339 U.S. at 646-650 (Blue Sky laws). It is difficult to discern any principled basis for distinguishing between jurisdiction to regulate and jurisdiction to tax. As an original matter, it might have been possible to distinguish between jurisdiction to tax and jurisdiction to compel collection of taxes as agent for the State, but we have rejected that. National Geographic Soc. v. California Bd. of Equalization, 430 U.S. at 558; Scripto, Inc. v. Carson, 362 U.S. at 211. I agree with the Court, moreover, that abandonment of Bellas Hess's due process holding is compelled by reasoning "[c]omparable" to that contained in our post-1967 cases dealing with state jurisdiction to adjudicate. I do not understand this to mean that the due process standards for adjudicative jurisdiction and those for legislative (or prescriptive) jurisdiction are necessarily identical; and on that basis I join Parts I, II, and III of the Court's opinion. Compare Asahi Metal Industry Co. v. Superior Court, 480 U.S. 102 (1987) with American Oil Co. v. Neill, 380 U.S. 451 (1965).

I also agree that the Commerce Clause holding of Bellas Hess should not be overruled. Unlike the Court, however, I would not revisit the merits of that holding, but would adhere to it on the basis of stare decisis. American Trucking Assns., Inc. v. Smith, 496 U.S. at 204 (SCALIA, J., concurring in judgment). Congress has the final say over regulation of interstate commerce, and it can change the rule of Bellas Hess by simply saying so. We have long recognized that the doctrine of stare decisis has "special force" where "Congress remains free

to alter what we have done." Patterson v. McLean Credit Union, 491 U.S. at 172-173 (1989). Moreover, the demands of the doctrine are "at their acme . . . where reliance interests are involved," Payne v. Tennessee, 501 U.S. 808 (1991). As the Court notes, "the Bellas Hess rule has engendered substantial reliance and has become part of the basic framework of a sizeable industry".

I do not share Justice White's view that we may disregard these reliance interests because it has become unreasonable to rely upon Bellas Hess. Even assuming for the sake of argument (I do not consider the point) that later decisions in related areas are inconsistent with the principles upon which Bellas Hess rested, we have never acknowledged that, but have instead carefully distinguished the case on its facts. See, e.g., D. H. Holmes Co. v. McNamara, 486 U.S. at 33 (1988); National Geographic Soc., supra, at 559. It seems to me important that we retain our ability–and, what comes to the same thing, that we maintain public confidence in our ability–sometimes to adopt new principles for the resolution of new issues without abandoning clear holdings of the past that those principles contradict. We seemed to be doing that in this area. Having affirmatively suggested that the "physical presence" rule could be reconciled with our new jurisprudence, we ought not visit economic hardship upon those who took us at our word. We have recently told lower courts that "[i]f a precedent of this Court has direct application in a case, yet appears to rest on reasons rejected in some other line of decisions, [they] should follow the case which directly controls, leaving to this Court the prerogative of overruling its own decisions." Rodriguez de Quijas v. Shearson/American Express, Inc., 490 U.S. at 484. It is strangely incompatible with this to demand that private parties anticipate our overrulings. It is my view, in short, that reliance upon a square, unabandoned holding of the Supreme Court is always justifiable reliance (though reliance alone may not always carry the day). Finally, the "physical presence" rule established in Bellas Hess is not "unworkable," to the contrary, whatever else may be the substantive pros and cons of the rule, the "bright-line" regime that it establishes is unqualifiedly in its favor. JUSTICE WHITE's concern that reaffirmance of Bellas Hess will lead to a flurry of litigation over the meaning of "physical presence," seems to me contradicted by 25 years of experience under the decision.

For these reasons, I concur in the judgment of the Court and join Parts I, II, and III of its opinion.

JUSTICE WHITE, concurring in part and dissenting in part.

Today the Court repudiates that aspect of our decision in National Bellas Hess which restricts, under the Due Process Clause of the Fourteenth Amendment, the power of the States to impose use tax collection responsibilities on out-of-state mail order businesses that do not have a "physical presence" in the State. The Court stops short, however, of giving Bellas Hess the complete burial it justly deserves. In my view, the Court should also overrule that part of Bellas Hess which justifies its holding under the Commerce Clause. I, therefore, respectfully dissent from Part IV.

I

In Part IV of its opinion, the majority goes to some lengths to justify the Bellas Hess physical presence requirement under our Commerce Clause jurisprudence. I am unpersuaded by its interpretation of our cases. In Bellas Hess, the majority placed great weight on the interstate quality of the mail order sales, stating that "it is difficult to conceive of commercial transactions more exclusively interstate in character than the mail order transactions here involved." As the majority correctly observes, the idea of prohibiting States from taxing "exclusively interstate" transactions had been an important part of our jurisprudence for many decades, ranging intermittently from such cases as Case of State Freight Tax, 15 Wall. 232, 279 (1873), through Freeman v. Hewit, 329 U.S. at 256, and Spector Motor Service, Inc. v. O'Connor, 340 U.S. 602 (1951). But though it recognizes that Bellas Hess was decided amidst an upheaval in our Commerce Clause jurisprudence, in which we began to hold that "a State, with proper drafting, may tax exclusively interstate commerce so long as the tax does not create any effect forbidden by the Commerce Clause," the majority draws entirely the wrong conclusion from this period of ferment.

The Court attempts to paint Bellas Hess in a different hue from Freeman and Spector because the former "did not rely" on labeling taxes that had "direct" and "indirect" effects on interstate commerce. Thus, the Court concludes, Bellas Hess "did not automatically fall with Freeman and its progeny" in our decision in Complete Auto. I am unpersuaded by this attempt to distinguish Bellas Hess from Freeman and Spector, both of which were repudiated by this Court. What we disavowed in Complete Auto was not just the "formal distinction between 'direct' and 'indirect' taxes on interstate commerce," but also the whole notion underlying the Bellas Hess physical presence rule–that "interstate commerce is immune from state taxation."

The Court compounds its misreading by attempting to show that Bellas Hess "is not inconsistent with Complete Auto and our recent cases." This will be news to commentators, who have rightly criticized Bellas Hess. Indeed, the majority displays no small amount of audacity in claiming that our decision in National Geographic Society, which was rendered several weeks after Complete Auto, reaffirmed the continuing vitality of Bellas Hess.

Our decision in that case did just the opposite. National Geographic held that the National Geographic Society was liable for use tax collection responsibilities in California. The Society conducted an out-of-state mail order business similar to the one at issue here and in Bellas Hess, and in addition, maintained two small offices in California that solicited advertisements for National Geographic Magazine. The Society argued that its physical presence in California was unrelated to its mail order sales, and thus that the Bellas Hess rule compelled us to hold that the tax collection responsibilities could not be imposed. We expressly rejected that view, holding that the "requisite nexus for requiring an out-of-state seller [the Society] to collect and pay the use tax is not whether the duty to collect the use tax relates to the seller's activities carried on within the State, but simply whether the facts demonstrate 'some definite link, some minimum connection, between (the State and) the person . . . it seeks to tax.'" 430 U.S. at 561 (citation omitted).

By decoupling any notion of a transactional nexus from the inquiry, the National Geographic Court in fact repudiated the free trade rationale of the Bellas Hess majority. Instead, the National Geographic Court relied on a due process-type minimum contacts analysis that examined whether a link existed between the seller and the State wholly apart from the seller's in-state transaction that was being taxed. Citations to Bellas Hess notwithstanding, it is clear that rather than adopting the rationale of Bellas Hess, the National Geographic Court was instead politely brushing it aside. Even were I to agree that the free trade rationale embodied in Bellas Hess' rule against taxes of purely interstate sales was required by our cases prior to 1967, therefore, I see no basis in the majority's opening premise that this substantive underpinning of Bellas Hess has not since been disavowed by our cases.[2]

---

2. Similarly, I am unconvinced by the majority's reliance on subsequent decisions that have cited Bellas Hess. In D.H. Holmes Co. v. McNamara, 486 U.S. at 33, for example, we distinguished Bellas Hess on the basis of the company's "significant economic presence in Louisiana, its many connections with the State, and the direct benefits it receives from Louisiana in conducting its business." We then went on to note that the situation presented was much more analogous to that in National Geographic Society v. California Bd. of Equalization, 430 U.S. 551 (1977). See id., at 33-34. In Commonwealth Edison Co. v. Montana, 453 U.S. at 626, the Court cited Bellas Hess not to revalidate the physical presence requirement, but rather to establish that a "nexus" must exist to justify imposition of a state tax. And finally, in Mobil Oil Corp. v. Commissioner of Taxes, 445 U.S. at 437, the Court cited Bellas Hess for the due process requirements necessary to sustain a tax. In my view, these citations hardly signal the continuing support of Bellas Hess that the majority seems to find persuasive.

II

The Court next launches into an uncharted and treacherous foray into differentiating between the "nexus" requirements under the Due Process and Commerce Clauses. As the Court explains, "[d]espite the similarity in phrasing, the nexus requirements of the Due Process and Commerce Clauses are not identical. The two standards are animated by different constitutional concerns and policies." The due process nexus, which the Court properly holds is met in this case, see ante, at Part III, "concerns the fundamental fairness of governmental activity." The Commerce Clause nexus requirement, on the other hand, is "informed not so much by concerns about fairness for the individual defendant as by structural concerns about the effects of state regulation on the national economy."

Citing Complete Auto, the Court then explains that the Commerce Clause nexus requirement is not "like due process' 'minimum-contacts' requirement, a proxy for notice, but rather a means for limiting state burdens on interstate commerce." This is very curious, because parts two and three of the Complete Auto test, which require fair apportionment and nondiscrimination in order that interstate commerce not be unduly burdened, now appear to become the animating features of the nexus requirement, which is the first prong of the Complete Auto inquiry. The Court freely acknowledges that there is no authority for this novel interpretation of our cases and that we have never before found, as we do in this case, sufficient contacts for due process purposes but an insufficient nexus under the Commerce Clause. See ante, n. 6.

The majority's attempt to disavow language in our opinions acknowledging the presence of due process requirements in the Complete Auto test is also unpersuasive. See ante, n. 7 (citing Trinova Corp. v. Michigan Dept. of Treasury, 498 U.S. at 373). Instead of explaining the doctrinal origins of the Commerce Clause nexus requirement, the majority breezily announces the rule and moves on to other matters. In my view, before resting on the assertion that the Constitution mandates inquiry into two readily distinct "nexus" requirements, it would seem prudent to discern the origins of the "nexus" requirement in order better to understand whether the Court's concern traditionally has been with the fairness of a State's tax or some other value.

The cases from which the Complete Auto Court derived the nexus requirement in its four-part test convince me that the issue of "nexus" is really a due process fairness inquiry. In explaining the sources of the four-part inquiry in Complete Auto, the Court relied heavily on Justice Rutledge's separate concurring opinion in Freeman v. Hewit, 329 U.S. 249 (1946), the case whose majority

opinion the Complete Auto Court was in the process of comprehensively disavowing. Instead of the formalistic inquiry into whether the State was taxing interstate commerce, the Complete Auto Court adopted the more functionalist approach of Justice Rutledge in Freeman. See Complete Auto, 430 U.S. at 280-281. In conducting his inquiry, Justice Rutledge used language that by now should be familiar, arguing that a tax was unconstitutional if the activity lacked a sufficient connection to the State to give "jurisdiction to tax," Freeman, supra, at 271; or if the tax discriminated against interstate commerce; or if the activity was subjected to multiple tax burdens. 329 U.S. at 276-277. Justice Rutledge later refined these principles in Memphis Natural Gas Co. v. Stone, 335 U.S. 80 (1948), in which he described the principles that the Complete Auto Court would later substantially adopt: "[I]t is enough for me to sustain the tax imposed in this case that it is one clearly within the state's power to lay insofar as any limitation of due process or 'jurisdiction to tax' in that sense is concerned; it is nondiscriminatory . . . ; [it] is duly apportioned . . .; and cannot be repeated by any other state." 335 U.S. at 96-97 (concurring opinion) (footnotes omitted).

By the time the Court decided Northwestern States Portland Cement Co. v. Minnesota, 358 U.S. 450 (1959), Justice Rutledge was no longer on the Court, but his view of the nexus requirement as grounded in the Due Process Clause was decisively adopted. In rejecting challenges to a state tax based on the Due Process and Commerce Clauses, the Court stated that "[t]he taxes imposed are levied only on that portion of the taxpayer's net income which arises from its activities within the taxing State. These activities form a sufficient 'nexus between such a tax and transactions within a state for which the tax is an exaction.'" Id., at 464. The Court went on to observe that "it strains reality to say, in terms of our decisions, that each of the corporations here was not sufficiently involved in local events to forge 'some definite link, some minimum connection' sufficient to satisfy due process requirements." Id., at 464-465 (quoting Miller Bros. v. Maryland, 347 U.S. at 344-345). When the Court announced its four-part synthesis in Complete Auto, the nexus requirement was definitely traceable to concerns grounded in the Due Process Clause, and not the Commerce Clause, as the Court's discussion of the doctrinal antecedents for its rule made clear. See Complete Auto, supra, at 281-282, 285. For the Court now to assert that our Commerce Clause jurisprudence supports a separate notion of nexus is without precedent or explanation.

Even were there to be such an independent requirement under the Commerce Clause, there is no relationship between the physical presence/nexus rule the Court retains and Commerce Clause considerations that allegedly justify it. Perhaps long ago a seller's "physical presence" was a sufficient part of a trade to condition imposition of a tax on such presence. But in today's economy, physical presence frequently has very little to do with a transaction a State might seek to tax. Wire transfers of money involving billions of dollars occur every day; purchasers place orders with sellers by fax, phone, and computer linkup; sellers ship goods by air, road, and sea through sundry delivery services without leaving their place of business. It is certainly true that the days of the door-to-door salesperson are not gone. Nevertheless, an out-of-state direct marketer derives numerous commercial benefits from the State in which it does business. These advantages include laws establishing sound local banking institutions to support credit transactions; courts to insure collection of the purchase price from the seller's customers; means of waste disposal from garbage generated by mail order solicitations; and creation and enforcement of consumer protection laws, which protect buyers and sellers alike, the former by ensuring that they will have a ready means of protecting against fraud, and the latter by creating a climate of consumer confidence that inures to the benefit of reputable dealers in mail order transactions. To create, for the first time, a nexus requirement under the Commerce Clause independent of that established for due process purposes is one thing; to attempt to justify an anachronistic notion of physical presence in economic terms is quite another.

III

The illogic of retaining the physical presence requirement in these circumstances is palpable. Under the majority's analysis, and our decision in National Geographic, an out-of-state seller with one salesperson in a State would be subject to use tax collection burdens on its entire mail order sales even if those sales were unrelated to the salesperson's solicitation efforts. By contrast, an out-of-state seller in a neighboring State could be the dominant business in the putative taxing State, creating the greatest infrastructure burdens and undercutting the State's home companies by its comparative price advantage in selling products free of use taxes, and yet not have to collect such taxes if it lacks a physical presence in the taxing State. The majority clings to the physical presence rule not because of any logical relation to fairness or any economic rationale related to principles underlying the Commerce Clause, but simply out of the supposed convenience of having a bright-line rule. I am less impressed by the convenience of such adherence than the unfairness it produces. Here, convenience should give way. Cf. Complete Auto, supra, at 289, n.15 ("We believe, however, that administrative convenience . . . is insufficient justification for abandoning the principle that 'interstate commerce may be made to pay its way'").

Also very questionable is the rationality of perpetuating a rule that creates an interstate tax shelter for one form of business–mail order sellers–but no countervailing advantage for its competitors. If the Commerce Clause was intended to put businesses on an even playing field, the majority's rule is hardly a way to achieve that goal. Indeed, arguably even under the majority's explanation for its "Commerce Clause nexus" requirement, the unfairness of its rule on retailers other than direct marketers should be taken into account. See ante, (stating that the Commerce Clause nexus requirement addresses the "structural concerns about the effects of state regulation on the national economy"). I would think that protectionist rules favoring a $180 billion-a-year industry might come within the scope of such "structural concerns."

IV

The Court attempts to justify what it rightly acknowledges is an "artificial" rule in several ways. First, it asserts that the Bellas Hess principle "firmly establishes the boundaries of legitimate state taxing authority and reduces litigation concerning state taxation." It is very doubtful, however, that the Court's opinion can achieve its aims. Certainly our cases now demonstrate two "bright-line" rules for mail order sellers to follow: under the physical presence requirement reaffirmed here they will not be subjected to use tax collection if they have no physical presence in the taxing State; under the National Geographic rule, mail order sellers will be subject to use tax collection if they have some presence in the taxing State even if that activity has no relation to the transaction being taxed. Between these narrow lines lies the issue of what constitutes the requisite "physical presence" to justify imposition of use tax collection responsibilities.

Instead of confronting this question head-on, the majority offers only a cursory analysis of whether Quill's physical presence in North Dakota was sufficient to justify its use tax collection burdens, despite briefing on this point by the State.[3] North Dakota contends that even should the Court reaffirm the Bellas Hess rule, Quill's physical presence in North Dakota was sufficient to justify application of its use tax collection law. Quill concedes it

---

3. Instead of remanding for consideration of whether Quill's ownership of software constitutes sufficient physical presence under its new Commerce Clause nexus requirement, the majority concludes as a matter of law that it does not. See ante, n. 8. In so doing, the majority rebuffs North Dakota's challenge without setting out any clear standard for what meets the Commerce Clause physical presence nexus standard and without affording the State an opportunity on remand to attempt to develop facts or otherwise to argue that Quill's presence is constitutionally sufficient.

owns software sent to its North Dakota customers, but suggests that such property is insufficient to justify a finding of nexus. In my view, the question of Quill's actual physical presence is sufficiently close to cast doubt on the majority's confidence that it is propounding a truly "bright-line" rule. Reasonable minds surely can, and will, differ over what showing is required to make out a "physical presence" adequate to justify imposing responsibilities for use tax collection. And given the estimated loss in revenue to States of more than $3.2 billion this year alone, it is a sure bet that the vagaries of "physical presence" will be tested to their fullest in our courts.

The majority next explains that its "bright-line" rule encourages "settled expectations" and business investment. Though legal certainty promotes business confidence, the mail order business has grown exponentially despite the long line of our post-Bellas Hess precedents that signaled the demise of the physical presence requirement. Moreover, the Court's seeming but inadequate justification of encouraging settled expectations in fact connotes a substantive economic decision to favor out-of-state direct marketers to the detriment of other retailers. By justifying the Bellas Hess rule in terms of "the mail order industry's dramatic growth over the last quarter-century," the Court is effectively imposing its own economic preferences in deciding this case. The Court's invitation to Congress to legislate in this area signals that its preferences are not immutable, but its approach is different from past instances in which we have deferred to state legislatures when they enacted tax obligations on the State's share of interstate commerce. See, e.g., Goldberg v. Sweet, 488 U.S. 252 (1989); Commonwealth Edison Co. v. Montana, 453 U.S. 609 (1981).

Finally, the Court accords far greater weight to stare decisis than was given to that principle in Complete Auto itself. As that case demonstrates, we have not been averse to overruling our precedents under the Commerce Clause when they have become anachronistic in light of later decisions. One typically invoked rationale for stare decisis—an unwillingness to upset settled expectations—is particularly weak in this case. It is unreasonable for companies such as Quill to invoke a "settled expectation" in conducting affairs without being taxed. Neither Quill nor any of its amici point to any investment decisions or reliance interests that suggest any unfairness in overturning Bellas Hess. And the costs of compliance with the rule, in light of today's modern computer and software technology, appear to be nominal. To the extent Quill developed any reliance on the old rule, I would submit that its reliance was unreasonable because of its failure to comply with the law as enacted by the North Dakota state legislature. Instead of rewarding companies for ignoring the studied judgments of duly-elected officials, we should insist that the appropriate way to challenge a tax as unconstitutional is to pay it (or in this case collect it and remit it or place it in escrow) and then sue for declaratory judgment and refund. Quill's refusal to comply with a state tax statute prior to its being held unconstitutional hardly merits a determination that its reliance interests were reasonable.

The Court hints, but does not state directly, that a basis for its invocation of stare decisis is a fear that overturning Bellas Hess will lead to the imposition of retroactive liability. See James B. Beam Distilling Co. v. Georgia, 501 U.S. 529 (1991). As I thought in that case, such fears are groundless because no one can "sensibly insist on automatic retroactivity for any and all judicial decisions in the federal system." Id., at 546. (WHITE, J., concurring in judgment). Since we specifically limited the question on which certiorari was granted in order not to consider the potential retroactive effects of overruling Bellas Hess, I believe we should leave that issue for another day. If indeed fears about retroactivity are driving the Court's decision in this case, we would be better served, in my view, to address those concerns directly rather than permit them to infect our formulation of the applicable substantive rule.

Although Congress can and should address itself to this area of law, we should not adhere to a decision, however right it was at the time, that by reason of later cases and economic reality can no longer be rationally justified. The Commerce Clause aspect of Bellas Hess, along with its due process holding, should be overruled.

Questions and Comments

1. What is the significance of this case on the constitutionality of federal legislation requiring out-of-state vendors to collect a use tax?

2. Does the Court explain why the due process standards for tax and personal jurisdiction should be similar? See Richard D. Pomp, *Are the Standards for Tax Jurisdiction and Personal Jurisdiction Identical?*, 54 Tax Notes 333 (1992); 2 State Tax Notes 86 (1992).

3. What is the relationship between this case and the others you read in this chapter?

4. If an out-of-state taxpayer is subject to suit under a

long-arm statute, does it follow that such a taxpayer can be made to collect that state's use tax?

5. Suppose one of Quill's products injures a North Dakota customer. Can Quill be sued in North Dakota? See *Burger King v. Rudzewicz*, 471 U.S. 462 (1985); *Keeton v. Hustler Magazine, Inc.*, 465 U.S. 770 (1977); *World-Wide Volkswagen Corp. v. Woodson*, 444 U.S. 286 (1980). If Quill could be sued in North Dakota, is it inconsistent not to make Quill collect and remit the North Dakota use tax on the sale of the product that injured the customer?

Does the ownership of property within a state allow the owner to be sued for a cause of action unrelated to the property? See *Rush v. Savchuk*, 444 U.S. 320 (1980); *Shaffer v. Heitner*, 433 U.S. 186 (1977). Does the ownership of property within a state mean that the owner must collect use tax on sales into that state even if the sales are unrelated to the property?

6. Examine *Complete Auto* in the Commerce Clause chapter. Was the Court in *Complete Auto* suggesting that "substantial nexus" had a different meaning for commerce clause purposes from its due process meaning? Indeed, was the *Complete Auto* Court careful in its use of "substantial nexus" or was it using that term as a synonym for "sufficient nexus," or for a "necessary connection?" Did *Complete Auto's* reference to nexus rely on due process cases or commerce clause cases?

7. As a matter of constitutional interpretation, is it sensible to argue that stare decisis has a greater role to play where Congress can reverse the holding of the Court, such as in commerce clause cases?

8. Is the opinion more of a political compromise than a principled interpretation of the Commerce Clause?9. Could North Dakota require Quill to provide the State with a list of its North Dakota customers? See Alice J. Davis, *State Jurisdiction to Compel Production of Documents and Witnesses After Quill*, 6 State Tax Notes 1343 (1994).

10. The Court did not grant certiorari on the issue of whether a reversal of *Bellas Hess* would apply retroactively. Nonetheless, during oral argument, in response to a question from the bench, the North Dakota Attorney General suggested that if the State were to win, it would pursue the issue of back use taxes from out-of-state vendors. Was this gratuitous statement a litigating blunder?

11. The comments supra address the due process issue in the case. The Commerce Clause aspect of *Quill*, which is more controversial than the Court's Due Process analysis, is considered in further detail in Chapter Nine.

12. For critical commentary on *Quill*, see Anna M. Hoti, *Finishing What Quill Started: The Transactional Nexus Test for State Use Tax Collection*, 59 Alb. L. Rev. 1449 (1996); Jerome R. Hellerstein, *'Geoffrey' and the Physical Presence Nexus Requirement of 'Quill'*, 66 Tax Notes 1015 (1995); Michael T. Fatale, *Geoffrey Sidesteps Quill: Constitutional Nexus, Intangible Property and the State Taxation of Income*, 23 Hofstra L. Rev. 407 (1994); David F. Shores, *State Taxation of Interstate Commerce: Quill, Allied Signal and a Proposal*, 72 Neb. L. Rev. 682 (1993); Shane D. Buntrock, *Quill Corporation v. North Dakota: Spawning the Physical Presence "Nexus" Requirement under the Commerce Clause*, 38 S.D. L. Rev. 130 (1993);Pamela M. Krill, *Quill Corp. v. North Dakota: Tax Nexus Under the Due Process and Commerce Clauses No Longer the Same*, 1993 Wis. L. Rev. 1405; Sylvia Dennen, *Nexus Determinations After the U.S. Supreme Court's Decisions in 'Quill' and 'Wrigley'*, 24 Tax Adviser 425 (1993); James John Jurinski, *Taxing Mail-Order Sales After Quill: Possible Solutions*, 12 J. St. Tax'n 53 (1993); Jerome R. Hellerstein, *The Quill Case: What the States Can Do To Undo the Effects of the Decision*, 58 Tax Notes 791 (1993); Rita Marie Cain, *Quill Corporation v. North Dakota: An Answer to the Taxing Problem Surrounding Mail-Order Sales*, 71 Taxes 3 (1993); Daniel L. Gaustad, *Constitutional Law-Implications of the Due Process Clause and the Commerce Clause When Imposing State Use-Tax Collection on Out-of-State Sellers: Settled Expectations?: Quill Corp. v. North Dakota*, 69 N.D. L. Rev. 445 (1993); Stewart L. Mandell, *Quill Clears the Way for Future State Taxation of Interstate Sales*, 71 Mich. Bar J. 946 (1992).

Chapter 4

Privileges & Immunities

"The Citizens of Each State shall be entitled to all Privileges and Immunities of Citizens in the several States." U.S. Const., art. IV, §2.

The United States Constitution contains two "Privileges and Immunities" Clauses, one in the Fourteenth Amendment and one in Article IV. The Fourteenth Amendment, which was adopted following the Civil War, provides in part: "No state shall make or enforce any law which shall abridge the privileges or immunities of citizens of the United States."[1] The Fourteenth Amendment's Privileges and Immunities Clause was, until recently, viewed as moribund because of the Supreme Court's widely condemned 1873 Slaughter-House cases. These cases dealt with an Act by the Louisiana Legislature, perhaps under carpetbagger influence, which created and granted to a Louisiana corporation a monopoly for slaughtering livestock. In an action brought by Louisiana butchers, the Court interpreted the Privileges or Immunities Clause of the Fourteenth Amendment as protecting the rights of *national* citizenship, rather than those of *state* citizenship. Because the Louisiana statute did not affect any privileges or immunities of United States citizenship,[2] it was immune from attack under the Fourteenth Amendment. According to this interpretation, the Privileges or Immunities Clause of the Fourteenth Amendment affords no protection against a state abridging rights, no matter how fundamental, unless these are rights of national citizenship.[3] With one short-lived exception,[4] no case has struck down a state taxing statute under the Privilege and Immunities Clause of the Fourteenth Amendment. Many commentators had come to view the Clause as

---

1. The Fourteenth Amendment refers to privileges *or* immunities whereas Article IV refers to privileges *and* immunities (emphasis added). Because the Privileges or Immunities Clause of the Fourteenth Amendment was rendered ineffective early in its life, this difference in terminology has gone unexplored.

2. The rights of national citizenship include the right to come to the seat of government, to assert claims against the government, to have free access to seaports and to courts, to transact business with the government, to demand the care and protection of the government over his or her life, liberty, and property when on the high seas or within the jurisdiction of a foreign government, Slaughter-House Cases, 83 U.S. at 79; the right to pass freely from state to state, to petition Congress for redress of grievances, to vote for national officers, to enter public lands, to be protected from violence while in the custody of a U.S. Marshal, Twining v. New Jersey, 211 U.S. at 97 and the right to carry on interstate commerce, Crutcher v. Kentucky, 141 U.S. 47 (1891).

3. To the extent that a right of national citizenship is sourced in the Constitution or in federal law, the Supremacy Clause of the Constitution would already protect it from state infringement, without the Fourteenth Amendment. Slaughter-House Cases, 83 U.S. at 96 (Field, J. dissenting).

4. The one exception was Colgate v. Harvey, 296 U.S. 404 (1935), which struck down a Vermont income tax exemption for interest income received by a resident on loans made within the State, whereas interest received by residents from out-of-state loans was taxable. Colgate v. Harvey characterized the right to lend money outside the state as a privilege of national citizenship. "The power to tax income here asserted by Vermont is, in the final analysis, the power to tax so heavily as to preclude loans outside the state altogether. It reasonably is not open to doubt that the discriminatory tax here imposed abridges the privilege of a citizen of the United States to loan his money and make contracts with respect thereto in any part of the United States." Id. at 433. Five years later, the case was expressly overruled in Madden v. Kentucky, 309 U.S. 83 (1940). Madden involved a Kentucky tax on bank deposits of its citizens; out-of-state deposits were taxed five times as heavily as in-state deposits. The Court upheld the statute under the Equal Protection Clause on the ground that enforcing the tax on out-of-state deposits is more difficult and more expensive than on in-state deposits. In upholding the tax under the Privileges and Immunities Clause, the Court stated that "we think it quite clear that the right to carry out an incident to a trade, business or calling such as the deposit of money in banks is not a privilege of national citizenship." Id. at 92-93. See Note, Privileges and Immunities of Citizens of the United States—Colgate v. Harvey Overruled, 9 Geo. Wash. L. Rev. 106 (1940). For non-tax cases, the Clause may serve as a source of inspiration "for the judicial articulation of rights which might otherwise have gone unprotected." Laurence H. Tribe, American Constitutional Law 558 (2nd ed. 1988).

a "dead letter for tax purposes."[5]

A recent non-tax case, however, Saenz v. Roe,[6] has focused attention on the Clause. In Saenz, the Court struck down a California statute limiting new residents' welfare benefits to the amount they would have received in their former state of residence. The decision was grounded on the right to travel, one component of which the Court held was protected by the 14th Amendment's Privileges and Immunities Clause. Some commentators regard Saenz as perhaps "foreshadow[ing] an era in which the clause acquires a modern significance. . ."[7] The course of constitutional law, however, has been notoriously unpredictable–and slow–and Saenz is unlikely to have any short-term impact on state taxation.

The second of the two Privileges and Immunities Clauses is set forth in Article IV, Section 2 of the Constitution: "The Citizens of each State shall be entitled to all Privileges and Immunities of Citizens in the several States."[8] Article IV is the successor to the same-numbered provision in the Articles of Confederation. This latter provision, the so-called states' relations article, was the origin of both the Privileges and Immunities Clause and the Commerce Clause.[9]

The states' relations article was required once the

colonies broke with England. Before independence, citizens of the several colonies were subjects of a common king.[10] No colony treated the inhabitants of other colonies as aliens.[11] This basis for unity among the colonies, and hence for non-discrimination by colonies against the citizens of other colonies, was destroyed by the Declaration of Independence and the Revolutionary War. Article IV of the Articles of Confederation filled this void and safeguarded the right to move freely among the colonies, and to be free of discrimination in commercial dealings.[12]

The Articles of Confederation provided no common sovereign for the states and their citizens. Consequently, the only basis for a "national" citizenship came through the privileges and immunities clause.[13] In chronicling the Constitutional Convention, James Madison described the states' relation article as "the Article . . . making the Citizens of one State citizens of all."[14] In The Federalist, Alexander Hamilton explained that the policy expressed in the clause "may be esteemed to be the basis of the Union."[15]

Disagreement over the clause's meaning and application continues two centuries after its adoption. The framers left a sparse record, with only scattered comments and early drafts illuminating its intended scope.[16] Further, the concept of privileges and immunities was evolving at the time of the framing of the Constitution.[17]

---

5. See, for example, P. Hartman, Federal Limitations on State and Local Taxation 162, 165 (1981); cf. Kurland, The Privileges or Immunities Clause: "Its Hour Come Round at Last"?, 1972 Wash. U. L.Q. 405. Some commentators have challenged the Court's restrictive reading of the Fourteenth Amendment's Privileges and Immunities Clause in the Slaughter-House cases. See Laurence H. Tribe, American Constitutional Law, 1303-1311 (3rd ed. 2000); but see A. Bickel, The Morality of Consent, 42-47 (1975).

6. 526 U.S. 489 (1999)

7. Tribe, supra note 5, at 1331.

8. The Privileges and Immunities Clause of Article IV served as the model for the Privileges or Immunities Clause of the 14th Amendment. Cong. Globe, 39th Cong., 1st Sess., pt. 2, at 1033-34 (1866). Unlike the 14th Amendment, Article IV's Privileges and Immunities Clause does not protect corporations. Paul v. Virginia, 75 U.S. (8 Wall.) 168, 177-82 (1869).

9. See Hicklin v. Orbeck, 437 U.S. at 531-34. The Privileges and Immunities Clause in Article IV was adopted with little debate. 2 Max Farrand, Records of the Federal Convention of 1787 at 173, 187, 443 (1911).

---

10. David S. Bogen, The Privileges and Immunities Clause of Article IV, 37 Case W. Res. L. Rev. 794 (1987).

11. Id. at 861.

12. 9 J. of the Continental Congress 908-909 (1977).

13. Id.

14. Notes of Debates in the Federal Convention of 1787 Reported By James Madison 441 (A. Koch ed. 1966).

15. The Federalist No. 80 at 575 (Modern Lib. Ed., 1937). Charles Pinckney is generally recognized as the author of the clause. See 5 L. Elliot, Debates on the Adoption of the Federal Constitution 128-29, 132 (rev. ed. 1845).

16. Bogen, supra note 10, at 795-96. See also Gary J. Simon, Discrimination Against Non-Residents and the Privileges and Immunities Clause of Article IV, 128 Pa. L. Rev. 379, 383 (1979).

17. Bogen, supra note 10, at 796.

Nonetheless, two points are clear. First, corporations are not "citizens" and are not covered by the Clause.[18] Second, the Clause covers only "fundamental" rights.[19] "Only with respect to those 'privileges and immunities' bearing upon the vitality of the Nation as a single entity must the State treat all citizens, resident and nonresident, equally."[20] "[O]ne of the privileges which the clause guarantees to citizens of State A is that of doing business in State B on terms of substantial equality with the citizens of that State."[21] The Privileges and Immunities Clause thus provides a much higher level of protection for economic activity than the Equal Protection Clause.

Of course, like the other constitutional provisions covered in this book–the Due Process Clause, the Equal Protection Clause, the Commerce Clause–the Privileges and Immunities Clause is not an absolute. It does not bar discrimination against nonresidents if there are substantial reasons for the differential treatment. As you read the cases that follow, determine whether these reasons exist and whether the degree of discrimination bears a close relation to them. "The inquiry must. . . be conducted with due regard for the principle that the States should have considerable leeway in analyzing local evils and in prescribing appropriate cures."[22]

---

18. Western Turf Ass'n. v. Greenberg, 204 U.S. 359 (1907).

19. Corfield v. Coryell, 6 F. Cas. 546 (No. 3, 230)(CC ED Pa. 1823)(on circuit) was one of the earliest cases interpreting the Privileges and Immunities Clause in Article IV. Corfield upheld a New Jersey law prohibiting nonresidents from gathering clams, oysters, or shells in that state's waters. The court described the Clause as covering those privileges "which are, in their nature, fundamental; which belong, of right, to the citizens of all free governments . . . "Id. at 551. These fundamental rights included "[p]rotection by the government; the enjoyment of life and liberty, with the right to acquire and possess property of every kind, and to pursue and obtain happiness and safety; subject nevertheless to such restraints as the government may justly prescribe for the general good of the whole. The right of a citizen of one state to pass through, or to reside in any other state, for purposes of trade, agriculture, professional pursuits, or otherwise; to claim the benefit of the writ of habeas corpus; to institute and maintain actions of any kind in the courts of the state; to take, hold and dispose of property, either real or personal; and an exemption from higher taxes or impositions than are paid by the other citizens of the state, . . ." Id. at 551-52.

Corfield has been described as "an attempt to import the natural rights doctrine into the Constitution by way of the privileges and immunities clause of article IV." Tribe, supra note 6, at 1252. Subsequent cases rejected this reading of the Clause. See id. at 530. The Clause came to be viewed as relieving state citizens of the disabilities of alienage in other states and of inhibiting discriminatory legislation against them by other states. Paul v. Virginia, 75 U.S. (8 Wall.) 168, 180 (1869).

Baldwin v. Montana Fish and Game Comm., 436 U.S. 371 (1978), upheld higher fees for nonresident elk-hunters than residents; recreational hunting was not a fundamental right.

20. Baldwin v. Mont. Fish and Game Comm., 436 U.S. at 383.

21. Toomer v. Witsell, 334 U.S. 385 (1948)(striking down higher license fees on shrimp fishing boats owned by nonresidents than on those owned by residents).

22. Id. at 395.

Shaffer v. Carter, State Auditor, et al.

Supreme Court of the United States, 1920.

252 U.S. 37, 40 S. Ct. 221, 64 L. Ed. 445.

MR. JUSTICE PITNEY delivered the opinion of the court.

. . . .

The [Oklahoma] act in question reads as follows:

"Each and every person in this state shall be liable to an annual tax upon the entire net income of such person arising or accruing from all sources during the preceding calendar year, and a like tax shall be levied, assessed, collected and paid annually upon the entire net income from all property owned, and of every business, trade or profession carried on in this state by persons residing elsewhere."

. . . .

Plaintiff, a nonresident of Oklahoma, being a citizen of Illinois and a resident of Chicago in that state, was at the time of the commencement of the suit and for several years theretofore (including the years 1915 and 1916) engaged in the oil business in Oklahoma, having purchased, owned, developed, and operated a number of oil and gas mining leases, and being the owner in fee of certain oil-producing land, in that state. From properties thus owned and operated during the year 1916 he received a net income exceeding $1,500,000 and of this he made, under protest . . . upon the ground that the act, in so far as it subjects the incomes of nonresidents to the payment of such a tax, takes their property without due process of law and denies to them the equal protection of the laws, burdens interstate commerce and discriminates against nonresidents in favor of residents, and thus deprives plaintiff and other nonresidents of the privileges and immunities of citizens and residents of the state of Oklahoma, in violation of § 2 of Art. IV. . . .

. . . .

The contention that a state is without jurisdiction to impose a tax upon the income of nonresidents, while raised in the present case, was more emphasized in Travis v. Yale & Towne Mfg. Co., decided this day, involving the Income Tax Law of the state of New York. There it was contended, in substance, that while a state may tax the property of a nonresident situated within its borders, or may tax the incomes of its own citizens and residents because of the privileges they enjoy under its constitution and laws and the protection they receive from the state, yet a nonresident although conducting a business or carrying on an occupation there, cannot be required through income taxation to contribute to the governmental expenses of the state whence his income is derived; that an income tax, as against nonresidents, is not only not a property tax, but is not an excise or privilege tax, since no privilege is granted; the right of the noncitizen to carry on his business or occupation in the taxing state being derived, it is said, from the provisions of the federal Constitution.

This radical contention is easily answered by reference to fundamental principles. In our system of government the states have general dominion, and, saving as restricted by particular provisions of the federal Constitution, complete dominion over all persons, property, and business transactions within their borders; they assume and perform the duty of preserving and protecting all such persons, property, and business, and, in consequence, have the power normally pertaining to governments to resort to all reasonable forms of taxation in order to defray the governmental expenses. Certainly they are not restricted to property taxation, nor to any particular form of excises. In well-ordered society property has value chiefly for what it is capable of producing, and the activities of mankind are devoted largely to making recurrent gains from the use and development of property, from tillage, mining, manufacture, from the employment of human skill and labor, or from a combination of some of these; gains capable of being devoted to their own support, and the surplus accumulated as an increase of capital. That the state, from whose laws property and business and industry derive the protection and security without which production and gainful occupation would be impossible, is debarred from exacting a share of those gains in the form of income taxes for the support of the government, is a proposition so wholly inconsistent with fundamental principles as to be refuted by its mere statement. That it may tax the land but not the crop, the tree but not the fruit, the mine or well but not the product, the business but not the profit derived from it, is wholly inadmissible.

Income taxes are a recognized method of distributing the burdens of government, favored because requiring contributions from those who realize current pecuniary benefits under the protection of the government, and because the tax may be readily proportioned to their ability to pay. Taxes of this character were imposed by several of the states at or shortly after the adoption of the federal Constitution. . . .

. . . .

And we deem it clear, upon principle as well as authority, that just as a state may impose general income taxes upon its own citizens and residents whose persons are subject to its control, it may, as a necessary consequence, levy a duty of like character, and not more onerous in its effect, upon incomes accruing to nonresidents from their property or business within the state, or their occupations carried on therein, enforcing payment, so far as it can, by the exercise of a just control over persons and property within its borders. . . .

That a state, consistently with the federal Constitution, may not prohibit the citizens of other states from carrying on legitimate business within its borders like its own citizens, of course is granted; but it does not follow that the business of nonresidents may not be required to make a ratable contribution in taxes for the support of the government. On the contrary, the very fact that a citizen of one state has the right to hold property or carry on an [o]ccupation or business in another is a very reasonable ground for subjecting such nonresident, although not personally yet to the extent of his property held, or his occupation or business carried on therein, to a duty to pay taxes not more onerous in effect than those imposed under like circumstances upon citizens of the latter state. Section 2 of art. IV of the Constitution entitles him to the privileges and immunities of a citizen, but no more; not to an entire immunity from taxation, nor to any preferential treatment as compared with resident citizens. It protects him against discriminatory taxation, but gives him no right to be favored by discrimination or exemption.

Oklahoma has assumed no power to tax nonresidents with respect to income derived from property or business beyond the borders of the state. The act, while imposing a tax upon inhabitants with respect to their entire net income arising from all sources, confines the tax upon nonresidents to their net income from property owned and business, etc., carried on within the state. A similar distinction has been observed in our federal income tax laws from one of the earliest down to the present. The acts of 1861 and 1864 confined the tax to persons residing in the United States and citizens residing abroad. But in 1866 there was inserted by amendment the

following: "And a like tax shall be levied, collected, and paid annually upon the gains, profits, and income of every business, trade, or profession carried on in the United States by persons residing without the United States, not citizens thereof." Similar provisions were embodied in the Acts of 1870 and 1894; and in the Act of 1913, after a clause imposing a tax upon the entire net income arising or accruing from all sources to every citizen of the United States, whether residing at home or abroad, and to every person residing in the United States though not a citizen thereof, the following appears: "And a like tax shall be assessed, levied, collected, and paid annually upon the entire net income from all property owned and of every business, trade, or profession carried on in the United States by persons residing elsewhere." Evidently this furnished the model for the Oklahoma statute.

[S]o far as the question of jurisdiction is concerned, the due process clause of the Fourteenth Amendment imposes no greater restriction in this regard upon the several States than the corresponding clause of the Fifth Amendment imposes upon the United States.

It is insisted, however, both by appellant in this case and by the opponents of the New York law in Travis v. Yale & Towne Mfg. Co., that an income tax is in its nature a personal tax, or a "subjective tax imposing personal liability upon the recipient of the income," and that as to a nonresident the state has no jurisdiction to impose such a liability. This argument, upon analysis, resolves itself into a mere question of definitions, and has no legitimate bearing upon any question raised under the federal Constitution. For, where the question is whether a state taxing law contravenes rights secured by that instrument, the decision must depend not upon any mere question of form, construction, or definition, but upon the practical operation and effect of the tax imposed. The practical burden of a tax imposed upon the net income derived by a nonresident from a business carried on within the state certainly is no greater than that of a tax upon the conduct of the business, and this the state has the lawful power to impose, as we have seen.

The fact that it required the personal skill and management of appellant to bring his income from producing property in Oklahoma to fruition, and that his management was exerted from his place of business in another state, did not deprive Oklahoma of jurisdiction to tax the income which arose within its own borders. The personal element cannot, by any fiction, oust the jurisdiction of the state within which the income actually arises and whose authority over it operates in rem. At most, there might be a question whether the value of the service of management rendered from without the state ought not to be allowed as an expense incurred in producing the income; but no such question is raised in the present case, hence we express no opinion upon it.

The contention that the act deprives appellant and others similarly circumstanced of the privileges and immunities enjoyed by residents and citizens of the state of Oklahoma, in violation of § 2 of art. IV of the Constitution, is based upon two grounds, which are relied upon as showing also a violation of the "equal protection" clause of the Fourteenth Amendment.

One of the rights intended to be secured by the former provision is that a citizen of one state may remove to and carry on business in another without being subjected in property or person to taxes more onerous than the citizens of the latter state are subjected to. Paul v. Virginia, 8 Wall. at 180; Ward v. Maryland, 12 Wall. at 430; Maxwell v. Bugbee, 250 U.S. at 537. The judge who dissented in Shaffer v. Howard, 250 Fed. at 883, concluded that the Oklahoma Income Tax Law offended in this regard, upon the ground that since the tax is as to citizens of Oklahoma a purely personal tax measured by their incomes, while as applied to a nonresident it is "essentially a tax upon his property and business within the state, to which the property and business of citizens and residents of the state are not subjected," there was a discrimination against the nonresident. We are unable to accept this reasoning. It errs in paying too much regard to theoretical distinctions and too little to the practical effect and operation of the respective taxes as levied; in failing

to observe that in effect citizens and residents of the state are subjected as [sic] least to the same burden as nonresidents, and perhaps to a greater, since the tax imposed upon the former includes all income derived from their property and business within the state and, in addition, any income they may derive from outside sources.

Appellant contends that there is a denial to noncitizens of the privileges and immunities to which they are entitled, and also a denial of the equal protection of the laws, in that the act permits residents to deduct from their gross income not only losses incurred within the state of Oklahoma but also those sustained outside of that state, while nonresidents may deduct only those incurred within the state. The difference, however, is only such as arises naturally from the extent of the jurisdiction of the state in the two classes of cases, and cannot be regarded as an unfriendly or unreasonable discrimination. As to residents it may, and does, exert its taxing power over their income from all sources, whether within or without the state, and it accords to them a corresponding privilege of deducting their losses, wherever these accrue. As to nonresidents, the jurisdiction extends only to their property owned within the state and their business, trade, or profession carried on therein, and the tax is only on such income as is derived from those sources. Hence there is no obligation to accord to them a deduction by reason of losses elsewhere incurred. It may be remarked, in passing, that there is no showing that appellant has sustained such losses, and so he is not entitled to raise this question.

. . . .

[Justice McReynolds dissented without an opinion.]

Questions and Comments

1. Both the United States and those states that have income taxes levy them on income earned within their boundaries by nonresidents (although the United States has generous rules that reduce the tax on investment income). Politically, not only is taxing the income earned by nonresidents attractive (unless, as in the case of the United States, preferential treatment is thought necessary in order to attract capital) but also in the case of business income, most persons would view giving nonresident competitors a tax advantage over U.S. or in-state businesses as

fundamentally unfair.

2. Politically, what protection do Shaffer and other nonresidents have against the Oklahoma Legislature increasing the rate of tax on income earned by nonresidents? What legal protection? What is the relationship between this case and Justice Brennan's concurrence in *Allied Stores*?

3. The appellant in *Shaffer* was a resident of Illinois. Illinois can tax the appellant's worldwide income,

including the income arising in Oklahoma. Does the appellant have a valid constitutional complaint because his income earned in Oklahoma is subject to an aggregate tax burden that exceeds that imposed by Oklahoma on his Oklahoma competitor doing business only in Oklahoma?

4. Does this case serve to equalize the tax burden of competitors in the oil business in Oklahoma, regardless of the state of which they are a resident? In other words, does the case create a level playing field between an Oklahoma resident who competes against an Illinois resident? In answering that question do you need to know how Illinois taxes an Illinois resident on income from Oklahoma sources?

5. Is it unfair for Oklahoma to levy a tax on Shaffer if his losses in other states were greater than his income from Oklahoma? Where would Shaffer get the money to pay the Oklahoma tax? If such losses exceed Oklahoma income, would Shaffer pay more in tax than a resident of Oklahoma having the same income and losses? If so, is that result constitutional?

6. In dictum, the Court suggests there might be a question whether the value of the services or management rendered outside Oklahoma ought to be allowed as an expense incurred in producing the income that is taxed by Oklahoma. No question was raised on this issue and so the Court did not address it. In normative terms, what should be the treatment of expenses incurred outside a state that are attributable to generating income within a state? More generally, how should a state decide how much income is appropriate for it to tax? How did Oklahoma calculate the amount of income upon which the nonresident was taxable?

7. Do any similarities exist between this case and *Michelin*, in the chapter entitled, Import-Export Clause, or *Complete Auto*, in the chapter entitled, Commerce Clause?

8. Would the opinion have been any different if the taxpayer were a corporation incorporated in Illinois?

9. Can Oklahoma tax a nonresident on her winnings from the Oklahoma lottery? See *Couchot v. State Lottery Commission*, 74 Ohio St. 3d 417 (1996).

Travis, as Comptroller of the State of N.Y., v. Yale & Towne Mfg. Co.
Supreme Court of the United States, 1920.
252 U.S. 60, 40 S. Ct. 228, 64 L. Ed. 460.

MR. JUSTICE PITNEY delivered the opinion of the court.

. . . .

The act imposes an annual tax upon every resident of [New York] with respect to his net income. . . A like tax is imposed [upon income] from all property owned and from every business, trade, profession or occupation carried on in this state by [non-residents]. "In the case of [non-residents], gross income includes only the gross income from sources within the state, but shall not include annuities, interest on bank deposits, interest on bonds, notes or other interest-bearing obligations or dividends from corporations, except to the extent to which the same shall be a part of income from any business, trade, profession or occupation carried on in this state subject to taxation under this article." [P]rovision is made for deducting in the computation of net income expenses, taxes, losses, depreciation charges, etc.; but "in the case of [non-residents], the deductions allowed in this section shall be allowed only if, and to the extent that, they are connected with income arising from sources within the state . . ." [C]ertain exemptions are allowed to any resident individual taxpayer, viz., in the case of a single person a personal exemption of $1,000, in the case of the head of a family or a married person living with husband or wife, $2,000; and $200 additional for each dependent person under 18 years of age or mentally or physically defective. . . "Credit for taxes in case of taxpayers other than residents of the state. Whenever a [non-resident] has become liable to income tax to the state or country where he resides upon his net income for the taxable year, derived from sources within this state and subject to taxation under this article, the comptroller shall credit the amount of income tax payable by him under this article with such proportion of the tax so payable by him to the state or country where he resides as his income subject to taxation under this article bears to his entire income upon which the tax so payable to such other state or country was imposed; provided that such credit shall be allowed only if the laws of said state or country grant a substantially similar credit to residents of this state subject to income tax under such laws." . . .

. . . .

That the state of New York has jurisdiction to impose a tax of this kind upon the incomes of nonresidents arising from any business, trade, profession, or occupation carried on within its borders, enforcing payment so far as it can by the exercise of a just control over persons and property within the state. . . is settled by our decision in Shaffer v. Carter, this day announced, involving the income tax law of the state of Oklahoma. That there is no unconstitutional discrimination against citizens of other states in confining the deduction of expenses, losses, etc., in the case of nonresident taxpayers, to such as are connected with income arising from sources within the taxing state, likewise is settled by that decision.

. . . .

The district court held that the act, in granting to residents exemptions denied to nonresidents, violated the provision of § 2 of Art. IV of the Federal Constitution: "The citizens of each state shall be entitled to all privileges and immunities of citizens in the several states"; and we affirm the ruling.

The purpose of the provision came under consideration in Paul v. Virginia, 8 Wall. 168, 180, where the court, speaking by Mr. Justice Field, said: "It was undoubtedly the object of the clause in question to place the citizens of each state upon the same footing with citizens of other states, so far as the advantages resulting from citizenship in those states are concerned. It relieves them from the disabilities of alienage in other states; it inhibits discriminating legislation against them by other states; it gives them the right of free ingress into other states, and egress from them; it insures to them in other states the same freedom possessed by the citizens of those states in the acquisition and enjoyment of property and in the pursuit of happiness; and it secures to them in other states the equal protection of their laws. It has been justly said that no provision in the Constitution has tended so strongly to constitute the citizens of the United States one people as this." And in Ward v. Maryland, 12 Wall. 418, holding a discriminatory state tax upon nonresident traders to be void, the court, by Mr. Justice Clifford, said (p. 430):

"Beyond doubt [privileges and immunities] are words of very comprehensive meaning, but it will be sufficient to say that the clause plainly and unmistakably secures and protects the right of a citizen of one state to pass into any other state of the Union for the purpose of engaging in lawful commerce, trade, or business without molestation; to acquire personal property; to take and hold real estate; to maintain actions in the courts of the state; and to be exempt from any higher taxes or excises than are imposed by the state upon its own citizens."

Of course the terms "resident" and "citizen" are not synonymous, and in some cases the distinction is important; but a general taxing scheme such as the one under consideration, if it discriminates against all nonresidents, has the necessary effect of including in the discrimination those who are citizens of other states; and, if there be no reasonable ground for the diversity of treatment, it abridges the privileges and immunities to which such citizens are entitled. . .

The nature and effect of the crucial discrimination in the present case are manifest. [Residents have a $1,000 exemption]; $2,000 in the case of a married person, and $200 additional for each dependent. A nonresident taxpayer has no similar exemption; but if liable to an income tax in his own state, including income derived from sources within New York and subject to taxation under this act, he is entitled to a credit upon the income tax otherwise payable to the state of New York by the same proportion of the tax payable to the state of his residence as his income subject to taxation by the New York Act bears to his entire income taxed in his own state; "provided that such credit shall be allowed only if the laws of said state . . . grant a substantially similar credit to residents of this state subject to income tax under such laws."

In the concrete, the particular incidence of the discrimination is upon citizens of Connecticut and New Jersey, neither of which states has an income tax law. A considerable number of complainant's employees, residents and citizens of one or the other of those states, spend their working time at its office in the city of New York, and earn their salaries there. The case is typical; it being a matter of common knowledge that from necessity, due to the geographical situation of that city, in close proximity to the neighboring states, many thousands of men and women, residents and citizens of those states, go daily from their homes to the city and earn their livelihood there. They pursue their several occupations side by side with residents of the state of New York, in effect competing with them as to wages, salaries, and other terms of employment. Whether they must pay a tax upon the first $1,000 or $2,000 of income, while their associates and competitors who reside in New York do not, makes a substantial difference. Under the circumstances as disclosed, we are unable to find adequate ground for the discrimination, and are constrained to hold that it is an unwarranted denial to the citizens of Connecticut and New Jersey of the privileges and immunities enjoyed by citizens of New York. This is not a case of occasional or accidental inequality due to circumstances personal to the taxpayer; but a general rule, operating to the disadvantage of all nonresidents including those who are citizens of the neighboring states, and favoring all residents including those who are citizens of the taxing state.

. . . .

In the brief submitted by the attorney general of New York in behalf of appellant, it is said that the framers of the act, in embodying in it the provision for unequal treatment of the residents of other states with respect to the exemptions, looked forward to the speedy adoption of an income tax by the adjoining states; in which event,

injustice to their citizens on the part of New York could be avoided by providing similar exemptions, similarly conditioned. This, however, is wholly speculative. New York has no authority to legislate for the adjoining states; and we must pass upon its statute with respect to its effect and operation in the existing situation. But besides, in view of the provisions of the Constitution of the United States, a discrimination by the state of New York against the citizens of adjoining states would not be cured were those states to establish like discriminations against citizens of the state of New York. A state may not barter away the right, conferred upon its citizens by the Constitution of the United States, to enjoy the privileges and immunities of citizens when they go into other states. Nor can discrimination be corrected by retaliation; to prevent this was one of the chief ends sought to be accomplished by the adoption of the Constitution.

Questions and Comments

1. What standard is the Court applying in interpreting the Privileges and Immunities Clause?

2. As a policy matter, why should a state grant exemptions to nonresidents and their dependents? How does the Internal Revenue Code treat nonresidents who earn taxable income within the United States? See McIntyre, The International Income Tax Rules of the United States, 2-7 - 2-82 (1989).

3. As a policy matter, should the state of source grant a credit for taxes paid by a resident to his or her state of residence, or should the state of residence grant a credit for taxes paid to the state of source? What approach does the United States use with respect to its residents and citizens receiving income from abroad? See McIntyre, supra, 4-5 - 4-107.

4. What is the relationship between the Attorney General's argument regarding the adoption of an income tax by other states and *Wheeling Steel* or *Western & Southern*, in the Equal Protection Clause chapter?

5. Neither New Jersey nor Connecticut, the two neighboring states that were mentioned by the Court probably because of the large number of their residents working in New York, had an income tax at the time of this case. Did that influence the Court's decision in any way?

6. Did the New York statute violate the Commerce Clause?

7. Suppose New York has a low-income tax credit, which reduces the tax burden on persons whose taxable income is less than a certain amount. Can New York limit that credit to New York residents? Suppose the credit is available to anyone having less than $5,000 of taxable income. How should taxable income be defined for purposes of the credit? Should a nonresident qualify if she has $1,000 of taxable income from New York sources but $50,000 of taxable income from non-New York sources? If the credit is viewed as a spending program to help alleviate poverty, should New York have to extend that program to nonresidents? Does New York have to provide welfare benefits to nonresidents?

8. New York has a progressive rate schedule, similar to that of the federal income tax. As income increases, the rate at which that income is taxed also increases. Should a nonresident with $5,000 of N.Y. source income but $200,000 of worldwide income be taxed at the same rate as a N.Y resident having worldwide income of $5,000? Or, should the rate applied to a nonresident's N.Y. source income be determined by the nonresident's total income? See *Brady v. State of New York*, 80 N.Y.2d 596, cert. denied, 509 U.S. 905 (1992); *Wheeler v. State*, 249 A.2d 887, appeal dismissed, 396 U.S. 4 (1969).

Austin et al. v. New Hampshire et al.
Supreme Court of the United States, 1975.
420 U.S. 656, 95 S. Ct. 1191, 43 L. Ed. 2d 530.

MR. JUSTICE MARSHALL delivered the opinion of the Court.

Appellants are residents of Maine who were employed in New Hampshire during the 1970 tax year and as such were subject to the New Hampshire Commuters Income Tax. On behalf of themselves and others similarly situated, they petitioned the New Hampshire Superior Court for a declaration that the tax violates the Privileges and Immunities and Equal Protection Clauses of the Constitutions of New Hampshire and of the United States. The cause was transferred directly to the New Hampshire Supreme Court, which upheld the tax. . . . [O]n the basis of the Privileges and Immunities Clause of Art. IV, we now reverse.

I

The New Hampshire Commuters Income Tax imposes a tax on nonresidents' New Hampshire-derived income in excess of $2,000. The tax rate is 4% except that if the nonresident taxpayer's state of residence would impose a lesser tax had the income been earned in that state, the New Hampshire tax is reduced to the amount of the tax that the state of residence would impose. Employers are required to withhold 4% of the nonresident's income, however, even if his home state would tax him at less than the full 4%. Any excess tax withheld is refunded to the nonresident upon his filing a New Hampshire tax return after the close of the tax year showing that he is entitled to be taxed at a rate less than 4%.

The Commuters Income Tax initially imposes a tax of 4% as well on the income earned by New Hampshire residents outside the state. It then exempts such income from the tax, however: (1) if it is taxed by the state from which it is derived; (2) if it is exempted from taxation by the state from which it is derived; or (3) if the state from which it is derived does not tax such income. The effect of these imposition and exemption features is that no resident of New Hampshire is taxed on his out-of-state income. Nor is the domestic earned income of New Hampshire residents taxed. In effect, then, the state taxes only the incomes of nonresidents working in New Hampshire;[3] it is on the basis of this disparate treatment

of residents and nonresidents that appellants challenge New Hampshire's right to tax their income from employment in that state.[4]

II

The Privileges and Immunities Clause of Art. IV, § 2, cl. 1, provides: "The Citizens of each state shall be entitled to all Privileges and Immunities of Citizens in the several states." The Clause thus establishes a norm of comity without specifying the particular subjects as to which citizens of one state coming within the jurisdiction of another are guaranteed equality of treatment. The origins of the Clause do reveal, however, the concerns of central import to the Framers. During the preconstitutional period, the practice of some states denying to outlanders the treatment that its citizens demanded for themselves was widespread. The fourth of the Articles of Confederation was intended to arrest this centrifugal tendency with some particularity. It provided:

"The better to secure and perpetuate mutual friendship and intercourse among the people of the different states in this Union, the free inhabitants of each of these states, paupers, vagabonds and

national banks and New Hampshire banks and thrift institutions) in excess of $600. Residents also pay a $10 annual "resident tax" for the use of their town or city of residence. Other state taxes, such as those on business profits, real estate transfers, and property, are paid by residents and nonresidents alike.

State income tax revenues from the tax on residents' unearned income in fiscal year 1970 were $3,462,000. In fiscal year 1971, the first in which the State taxed the earned income of nonresidents, total income tax revenues rose to $5,238,000.

4. Appellees challenge appellants' standing to maintain this action on the theory that their economic position was unchanged despite the imposition of the Commuters Income Tax because they received an offsetting credit under the tax laws of Maine, against income taxes owing to that State; the appellants' total tax liability, that is, was unaffected. We think the question is covered, however, by the holding of Allied Stores of Ohio, Inc. v. Bowers, 358 U.S. 522 (1959). In addition, appellants are affected by the requirements that they file a New Hampshire tax return and that their employers withhold 4% of their earnings; since the appellees do not suggest that appellants are subject to the tax at the 4% rate, at the very least the withholding requirement deprives them of the use value of the excess withheld over their ultimate tax liability, if any. These effects may not be substantial, but they establish appellants' status as parties "adversely affected" by the State's tax laws, giving them "a direct stake in the outcome" of this litigation. Sierra Club v. Morton, 405 U.S. at 740.

---

3. New Hampshire residents pay a 4.5% tax on interest (other than interest on notes and bonds of the State and on bank deposits) and dividends (other than cash dividends on stock in

fugitives from justice excepted, shall be entitled to all privileges and immunities of free citizens in the several states; and the people of each state shall have free ingress and regress to and from any other state, and shall enjoy therein all the privileges of trade and commerce, subject to the same duties, impositions and restrictions as the inhabitants thereof respectively."

The discriminations at which this Clause was aimed were by no means eradicated during the short life of the Confederation, and the provision was carried over into the comity article of the Constitution in briefer form but with no change of substance or intent, unless it was to strengthen the force of the Clause in fashioning a single nation. Thus, in the first, and long the leading, explication of the Clause, Mr. Justice Washington, sitting as Circuit Justice, deemed the fundamental privileges and immunities protected by the Clause to be essentially coextensive with those calculated to achieve the purpose of forming a more perfect Union, including "an exemption from higher taxes or impositions than are paid by the other citizens of the state." Corfield v. Coryell, 6 F. Cas. 546, 552 (No. 3,230) (CCED Pa. 1825).

In resolving constitutional challenges to state tax measures this Court has made it clear that "in taxation, even more than in other fields, legislatures possess the greatest freedom in classification." Madden v. Kentucky, 309 U.S. at 88. See Lehnhausen v. Lake Shore Auto Parts Co., 410 U.S. 356 (1973). Our review of tax classifications has generally been concomitantly narrow, therefore, to fit the broad discretion vested in the state legislatures. When a tax measure is challenged as an undue burden on an activity granted special constitutional recognition, however, the appropriate degree of inquiry is that necessary to protect the competing constitutional value from erosion.

. . . The Privileges and Immunities Clause, by making noncitizenship or nonresidence[8] an improper basis for locating a special burden, implicates not only the individual's right to nondiscriminatory treatment but also, perhaps more so, the structural balance essential to the concept of federalism. Since nonresidents are not represented in the taxing state's legislative halls, cf. Allied Stores of Ohio, Inc. v. Bowers, 358 U.S. at 532-533 (BRENNAN, J., concurring), judicial acquiescence in

taxation schemes that burden them particularly would remit them to such redress as they could secure through their own state; but "to prevent [retaliation] was one of the chief ends sought to be accomplished by the adoption of the Constitution." Travis v. Yale & Towne Mfg. Co., 252 U.S. at 82. Our prior cases, therefore, reflect an appropriately heightened concern for the integrity of the Privileges and Immunities Clause by erecting a standard of review substantially more rigorous than that applied to state tax distinctions among, say, forms of business organizations or different trades and professions.

The first such case was Ward v. Maryland 12 Wall. 418 (1871), challenging a statute under which nonresidents were required to pay $300 per year for a license to trade in goods not manufactured in Maryland, while resident traders paid a fee varying from $12 to $150, depending upon the value of their inventory. The state attempted to justify this disparity as a response to the practice of "runners" from industrial states selling by sample in Maryland, free from local taxation and other overhead expenses incurred by resident merchants. It portrayed the fee as a "tax upon a particular business or trade, carried on in a particular mode," rather than a discrimination against traders from other states. Although the tax may not have been "palpably arbitrary," see Allied Stores of Ohio, Inc. v. Bowers, supra, at 530, the discrimination could not be denied and the Court held that it violated the guarantee of the Privileges and Immunities Clause against "being subjected to any higher tax or excise than that exacted by law of . . . permanent residents."[9]

In Traveller's Insurance Co. v. Connecticut, 185 U.S. 364 (1902), the Court considered a tax laid on the value of stock in local insurance corporations. The shares of nonresident stockholders were assessed at their market value, while those owned by residents were assessed at market value less the proportionate value of all real estate held by the corporation and on which it had already paid a local property tax. In analyzing the apparent discrimination thus worked against nonresidents, the Court took account of the overall distribution of the tax burden between resident and nonresident stockholders. Finding that nonresidents paid no local property taxes, while residents paid those

---

8. For purposes of analyzing a taxing scheme under the Privileges and Immunities Clause the terms "citizen" and "resident" are essentially interchangeable. Travis v. Yale & Towne Mfg. Co., 252 U.S. at 79 ("a general taxing scheme . . . if it discriminates against all non-residents, has the necessary effect of including in the discrimination those who are citizens of other States"); Smith v. Loughman, 157 N.E. 753, 755, cert. denied, 275 U.S. 560 (1927); see Toomer v. Witsell, 334 U.S. at 397.

---

9. Accord, Toomer v. Witsell, supra, at 396, where the Court held invalid another disparate licensing-fee system, citing Ward v. Maryland for the proposition that "it was long ago decided that one of the privileges which the clause guarantees to citizens of State A is that of doing business in State B on terms of *substantial equality with the citizens of that State*." (Emphasis added.)

taxes at an average rate approximating or exceeding the rate imposed by the state on nonresidents' stock, the Court upheld the scheme. While more precise equality between the two classes could have been obtained, it was "enough that the state has secured a reasonably fair distribution of burdens, and that no intentional discrimination has been made against nonresidents." Their contribution to state and local property tax revenues, that is, was no more than the ratable share of their property within the state.

The principles of Ward and Travellers' were applied to taxes on nonresidents' local incomes in Shaffer v. Carter, 252 U.S. 37 (1920), and Travis v. Yale & Towne Mfg. Co., supra. Shaffer upheld the Oklahoma tax on income derived from local property and business by a nonresident where the state also taxed the income–from wherever derived–of its own citizens. Putting aside "theoretical distinctions" and looking to "the practical effect and operation" of the scheme, the nonresident was not treated more onerously than the resident in any particular, and in fact was called upon to make no more than his ratable contribution to the support of the state government. The New York tax on residents' and nonresidents' income at issue in Travis, by contrast, could not be sustained when its actual effect was considered. The tax there granted personal exemptions to each resident taxpayer for himself and each dependent, but it made no similar provision for nonresidents. The disparity could not be "deemed to be counterbalanced" by an exemption for nonresidents' interest and dividend income because it was not likely "to benefit nonresidents to a degree corresponding to the discrimination against them." Looking to "the concrete, the particular incidence" of the tax, therefore, the Court said of the many New Jersey and Connecticut residents who worked in New York:

> "They pursue their several occupations side by side with residents of the state of New York–in effect competing with them as to wages, salaries, and other terms of employment. Whether they must pay a tax upon the first $1,000 or $2,000 of income, while their associates and competitors who reside in New York do not, makes a substantial difference. . . . This is not a case of occasional or accidental inequality due to circumstances personal to the taxpayer . . . but a general rule, operating to the disadvantage of all nonresidents . . . and favoring all residents. . . ."

III

Against this background establishing a rule of substantial equality of treatment for the citizens of the taxing state and nonresident taxpayers, the New Hampshire Commuters Income Tax cannot be sustained. The overwhelming fact, as the state concedes, is that the tax falls exclusively on the income of nonresidents; and

it is not offset even approximately by other taxes imposed upon residents alone.[10] Rather, the argument advanced in favor of the tax is that the ultimate burden it imposes is "not more onerous in effect," Shaffer v. Carter, supra, on nonresidents because their total state tax liability is unchanged once the tax credit they receive from their state of residence is taken into account. See n. 4, supra. While this argument has an initial appeal, it cannot be squared with the underlying policy of comity to which the Privileges and Immunities Clause commits us.

According to the state's theory of the case, the only practical effect of the tax is to divert to New Hampshire tax revenues that would otherwise be paid to Maine, an effect entirely within Maine's power to terminate by repeal of its credit provision for income taxes paid to another state. The Maine Legislature could do this, presumably, by amending the provision so as to deny a credit for taxes paid to New Hampshire while retaining it for the other 49 states. Putting aside the acceptability of such a scheme, and the relevance of any increase in appellants' home state taxes that the diversionary effect is said to have,[11] we do not think the possibility that Maine could shield its residents from New Hampshire's tax cures the constitutional defect of the discrimination in that tax. In fact, it compounds it. For New Hampshire in effect invites appellants to induce their representatives, if they can, to retaliate against it.

---

10. The $10 annual resident tax and the tax on certain unearned income in excess of $600 would rarely equal, much less exceed, the 4% tax on nonresidents' incomes over $2,000. Appellant Logan, for example, with $33,000 of New Hampshire-derived income, paid $252 in taxes to that State; a resident with the same earned income would have paid only the $10 resident tax. Against this disparity and the disparities among nonresidents' tax rates depending on their State of residence, we find no support in the record for the assertion of the court below that the Commuters Income Tax creates no more than a "practical equality" between residents and nonresidents when the taxes paid only by residents are taken into account. "[S]omething more is required than bald assertion"–by the state court or by counsel here–to establish the validity of a taxing statute that on its face discriminates against nonresidents. Mullaney v. Anderson, 342 U.S. at 418.

11. The States of Maine and Vermont point out that at least $400,000 was diverted from Maine to New Hampshire by reason of the challenged tax and Maine's tax credit in 1971, and that the average Maine taxpayer, appellants included, thereby bore an additional burden of 40 cents in Maine taxes. While the inference is strong, we deem the present record insufficient to demonstrate that Maine taxes were actually higher than they otherwise would have been but for this revenue loss.

A similar, though much less disruptive, invitation was extended by New York in support of the discriminatory personal exemption at issue in Travis. The statute granted the nonresident a credit for taxes paid to his state of residence on New York-derived income only if that state granted a substantially similar credit to New York residents subject to its income tax. New York contended that it thus "looked forward to the speedy adoption of an income tax by the adjoining states," which would eliminate the discrimination "by providing similar exemptions similarly conditioned." To this the Court responded in terms fully applicable to the present case. Referring to the anticipated legislative response of the neighboring states, it stated:

"This, however, is wholly speculative; New York has no authority to legislate for the adjoining states; and we must pass upon its statute with respect to its effect and operation in the existing situation. . . . A state may not barter away the right, conferred upon its citizens by the Constitution of the United States, to enjoy the privileges and immunities of citizens when they go into other states. Nor can discrimination be corrected by retaliation; to prevent this was one of the chief ends sought to be accomplished by the adoption of the Constitution." 252 U.S. at 82.[12]

Nor, we may add, can the constitutionality of one state's statutes affecting nonresidents depend upon the present configuration of the statutes of another state.

. . . .

[Dissenting opinion by MR. JUSTICE BLACKMUN is omitted.]

---

12. Neither Travis nor the present case should be taken in any way to denigrate the value of reciprocity in such matters. The evil at which they are aimed is the unilateral imposition of a disadvantage upon nonresidents, not reciprocally favorable treatment of nonresidents by States that coordinate their tax laws.

Questions and Comments

1. Why was the rate of the New Hampshire tax a function of the rate of tax in the nonresident's home state?

2. Would New Hampshire tax a commuter who resided in a state that did not have an income tax?

3. The ultimate tax burden imposed on the plaintiffs was "not more onerous in effect on nonresidents because their total state tax liability is unchanged once the tax credit they receive from their state of residence is taken into account." Why, then, was a fundamental right of the plaintiffs infringed? Why did the taxpayers bring this suit? Who financed their litigation?

4. In examining the amount of taxes paid by residents, see footnote 10, why didn't the Court take into account property taxes?

5. New Hampshire argued that it was within Maine's ability to shield its residents from discrimination by repealing its credit for taxes paid to other states. How would repealing its credit shield Maine residents from the discrimination inherent in the New Hampshire statute?

6. Would the New Hampshire tax have been upheld if it had actually imposed a tax of 4 percent on the income of its residents earned outside the state?

7. Would the tax have been upheld if it approximated the other taxes imposed upon New Hampshire residents?

8. Did New Hampshire's tax violate the Commerce Clause?

9. The Court notes that Maine could have eliminated the problem in *Austin* by repealing its credit provision for income taxes paid to another state. Is the Court suggesting that Maine is not constitutionally required to grant a credit (or some other relief mechanism) for income taxes paid to other states? Would the tax be imposed if Maine did not provide a credit?

10. Consider a state that has a broad-based sales tax. The state currently exempts from the sales tax cars sold to nonresidents, even if they take delivery of the car in-state. The state is being advised to impose a sales tax on cars sold to nonresidents at a rate equal to the lower of either the state's normal rate or the rate of the state in which the purchaser is going to register the car. What would a state gain from this change? Would such a

change be constitutional?

11. If, as footnote 11 indicates, the effect of the tax was to transfer funds from one state treasury to another, why didn't this case come before the Supreme Court as a suit of original jurisdiction between the two states? In fact, one year after *Austin*, New York and Pennsylvania, two states neighboring New Jersey which also had at that time a discriminatory income tax on nonresidents, filed motions in the Supreme Court seeking permission to bring suits of original jurisdiction to recover the diverted taxes. Similarly, Maine, Massachusetts, and Vermont sought permission to sue New Hampshire. In *Pennsylvania v. New Jersey, Maine v. New Hampshire*, 426 U.S. 660 (1976), the Court denied the motions on two grounds: (1) the tax credit schemes that resulted in the transfers were of the plaintiff-states' own making; and (2) the Privileges and Immunities Clause and the Equal Protection Clause protect citizens and not states. That result left the New Jersey tax intact. Is the Court's first reason for dismissing the suit inconsistent with *Austin*?

Three New York residents who commuted to work in New Jersey challenged that State's discriminatory commuter tax in *Salorio v. Glaser*, 93 N.J. 447, 461 A.2d 1100 (1983), cert. denied 464 U.S. 993 (1983). The State court invalidated the tax prospectively. There was no refund of prior taxes paid:

In analyzing a statute challenged under the Privileges and Immunities Clause, it is necessary to determine if the statute discriminates against nonresidents, to identify the nature and extent of that discrimination, and to decide whether the discrimination is reasonably related to legitimate purposes that are the bases for the discrimination. If there is no substantial reason for the discrimination, the clause is violated and the inquiry is at an end. If there are one or more substantial reasons for the discrimination, then the discrimination must bear a close relationship to them. Put another way, the nonresident must 'constitute a peculiar source of the evil at which the statute is aimed,' and there must be a 'substantial relationship' between the evil and the discrimination practiced upon them.

When a state is exercising its taxing power, there should be substantial equality of treatment, unless a justification is advanced supportive of the discrimination. Such justifications must be linked to some evil or problem caused by the nonresident, and, if linked, the revenue derived from the tax should bear a substantial relationship to the cost of amelioration of the evil or the solution of the problem. The correlation need not be perfect and a state has 'considerable leeway in analyzing local evils and in prescribing appropriate cures.'

. . . .

The state's justification for the differential imposed on the nonresident is that his commuting has created a need for additional facilities to meet the commuting crunch between New York and New Jersey during certain peak hours in the morning and the afternoon. That being so, the expenditures attributable to the New York-to-New Jersey commuter should be borne by him. If true, it follows that the nonresident commuter could be required to pay up to an approximation of those expenditures. The charge imposed upon the commuter on the basis of benefits he derived from the use of those transportation facilities may have no relationship to the costs and would therefore violate the principle that there must be a 'substantial relationship' between the problem and the discrimination.

. . . .We find that the relationship between [taxes paid by nonresidents] and transportation costs allocable to New York-based commuters over the entire life of the tax and during recent years is too disparate to withstand the constitutional challenge. *Salorio v. Glaser*, 461 A.2d at 1103, 1105-1106, 1108.

12. For political reasons unique to New York, New York State residents who commuted to New York City were exempted from the New York City income tax; residents of other states were not. Blatantly unconstitutional? See *City of New York v. State*, 730 N.E.2d 920 (2000) (held unconstitutional under *Austin*).

13. For critical commentary on *Austin*, see Marilyn H. Elam, *Privileges and Immunities - Tax Discriminating Against Nonresidents Not Cured By Existing Tax Provisions of Neighboring States - Austin v. New Hampshire*, 29 Sw. L.J. 965 (1975-76).

Christopher H. Lunding v. New York Tax Appeals Tribunal
Supreme Court of the United States, 1998.
522 U.S. 287, 118 S. Ct. 766, 139 L. Ed.2d 717.

JUSTICE O'CONNOR delivered the opinion of the Court.

. . . .

I

A

New York law requires nonresident individuals to pay tax on net income from New York real property or tangible personalty and net income from employment or business, trade, or professional operations in New York. Under provisions enacted by the New York Legislature in 1987, the tax on such income is determined according to a method that takes into consideration the relationship between a nonresident taxpayer's New York source income and the taxpayer's total income, as reported to the Federal Government.

Computation of the income tax nonresidents owe New York involves several steps. First, nonresidents must compute their tax liability "as if" they resided in New York. The starting point for this computation is federal adjusted gross income, which, in accordance with the Internal Revenue Code, includes a deduction for alimony payments. After various adjustments to federal adjusted gross income, nonresidents derive their "as if" resident taxable income from which "as if" resident tax is computed, using the same tax rates applicable to residents. Once the "as if" resident tax has been computed, nonresidents derive an "apportionment percentage" to be applied to that amount, based on the ratio of New York source income to federal adjusted gross income. The denominator of the ratio, federal adjusted gross income, includes a deduction for alimony paid, by virtue of 26 U.S.C. § 215, as incorporated into New York law. The numerator, New York source income, includes the net income from property, employment, or business operations in New York, but specifically

disallows any deduction for alimony paid. In the last step of the computation, nonresidents multiply the "as if" resident tax by the apportionment percentage, thereby computing their actual New York income tax liability. There is no upper limit on the apportionment percentage. Thus, in circumstances where a nonresident's New York income, which does not include a deduction for alimony paid, exceeds federal adjusted gross income, which does, the nonresident will be liable for *more than* 100% of the "as if" resident tax.

[The disallowance of a deduction for alimony paid by nonresidents] was enacted as part of New York's Tax Reform and Reduction Act of 1987. Until then, nonresidents were allowed to claim a pro rata deduction for alimony expenses, pursuant to a New York Court of Appeals decision holding that New York tax law then "reflected a policy decision that nonresidents be allowed the same non-business deductions as residents, but that such deductions be allowed to nonresidents in the proportion of their New York income to income from all sources." *Friedsam v. State Tax Comm'n*, 64 N.Y.2d 76, 81, (1984) (internal quotation marks omitted); see also Memorandum of Governor, L.1961, ch. 68, N.Y. State Legis. Ann., 1961, p. 398 (describing former N.Y. Tax Law, which permitted nonresidents to deduct a pro rata portion of their itemized deductions, then including alimony, as "represent[ing] the fairest and most equitable solution to the problem of many years' standing" respecting the taxation of nonresidents working in New York). Although there is no legislative history explaining the rationale for its enactment, [the 1987 change disallowing a deduction for alimony paid by nonresidents] clearly overruled *Friedsam's* requirement that New York permit nonresidents a pro rata deduction for alimony payments.

B

In 1990, petitioners Christopher Lunding and his wife, Barbara, were residents of Connecticut. During that year, Christopher Lunding earned substantial income from the practice of law in New York. That year, he also incurred alimony expenses relating to the dissolution of a previous marriage. In accordance with New York law, petitioners filed a New York Nonresident Income Tax Return to report the New York earnings. Petitioners did not comply with the [1987 change], however, instead deducting a pro rata portion of alimony paid in computing their New York income based on their determination that approximately 48% of Christopher's business income was attributable to New York.

. . . .

II
A

. . . .

[W]hen confronted with a challenge under the Privileges and Immunities Clause to a law distinguishing between residents and nonresidents, a State may defend its position by demonstrating that "(i) there is a substantial reason for the difference in treatment; and (ii) the discrimination practiced against nonresidents bears a substantial relationship to the State's objective." Piper, 470 U.S. at 284.

Our concern for the integrity of the Privileges and Immunities Clause is reflected through a "standard of review substantially more rigorous than that applied to state tax distinctions, among, say, forms of business organizations or different trades and professions." Austin, supra, at 663. Thus, as both the New York Court of Appeals, and the State appropriately acknowledge, the State must defend [its 1987 change] with a substantial justification for its different treatment of nonresidents, including an explanation of how the discrimination elates to the State's justification.

B

Our review of the State's justification is informed by this Court's precedent respecting Privileges and Immunities Clause challenges to nonresident income tax provisions. In Shaffer v. Carter, the Court upheld Oklahoma's denial of deductions for out-of-state losses to nonresidents who were subject to Oklahoma's tax on in-state income. The Court explained that

"[t]he difference . . . is only such as arises naturally from the extent of the jurisdiction of the State in the two classes of cases, and cannot be regarded as an unfriendly or unreasonable discrimination. As to residents, it may, and does, exert its taxing power over their income from all sources, whether within or without the State, and it accords to them a corresponding privilege of deducting their losses, wherever these accrue. As to nonresidents, the jurisdiction extends only to their property owned within the State and their business, trade, or profession carried on therein, and the tax is only on such income as is derived from those sources. Hence there is no obligation to accord to them a deduction by reason of losses elsewhere incurred." 252 U.S. at 57.

In so holding, the Court emphasized the practical effect of the provision, concluding that "the nonresident was not treated more onerously than the resident in any particular, and in fact was called upon to make no more than his ratable contribution to the support of the state government." Austin, 420 U.S. at 664.

Shaffer involved a challenge to the State's denial of business-related deductions. The record in Shaffer discloses that, while Oklahoma law specified that nonresidents were liable for Oklahoma income tax on "the entire net income from all property owned, and of every business, trade or profession carried on in [Oklahoma]," there was no express statutory bar preventing nonresidents from claiming the same nonbusiness exemptions and deductions as were available to resident taxpayers.

In Travis v. Yale & Towne Mfg. Co., a Connecticut corporation doing business in New York sought to enjoin enforcement of New York's nonresident income tax laws on behalf of its employees, who were residents of Connecticut and New Jersey. In an opinion issued on the same day as Shaffer, the Court affirmed Shaffer's holding that a State may limit the deductions of nonresidents to those related to the production of in-state income. See Travis, 252 U.S. at 75-76 (describing Shaffer as settling that "there is no unconstitutional discrimination against citizens of other States in confining the deduction of expenses, losses, etc., in the case of non-resident taxpayers, to such as are connected with income arising from sources within the taxing State"). The record in Travis clarifies that many of the expenses and losses of nonresidents that New York law so limited were business-related, such as ordinary and necessary business expenses, depreciation on business assets, and depletion of natural resources, such as oil, gas, and timber. At the time that Travis was decided, New York law also allowed nonresidents a pro rata deduction for various nonbusiness expenses, such as interest paid (based on the proportion of New York source income to total income), a deduction for taxes paid (other than income taxes) to the extent those taxes were connected with New York income, and a deduction for uncompensated losses sustained in New York resulting from limited circumstances, namely nonbusiness transactions entered into for profit and casualty losses. Both residents and nonresidents were entitled to the same deduction for contributions to charitable organizations organized under the laws of New York. Thus, the statutory provisions disallowing nonresidents' tax deductions at issue in Travis essentially mirrored those at issue in Shaffer because they tied nonresidents' deductions to their in-state activities.

Another provision of New York's nonresident tax law challenged in Travis did not survive scrutiny under the Privileges and Immunities Clause, however. Evincing the same concern with practical effect that animated the Shaffer decision, the Travis Court struck down a provision that denied only nonresidents an exemption from tax on a certain threshold of income, even though New York law allowed nonresidents a corresponding credit against New York taxes in the event that they paid resident income taxes in some other State providing a similar credit to New York residents. The Court rejected the argument that the rule was "a case of occasional or accidental inequality due to circumstances personal to the taxpayer." Nor was denial of the exemption salvaged "upon the theory that non-residents have untaxed income derived from sources in their home States or elsewhere outside of the State of New York, corresponding to the amount upon which residents of that State are exempt from taxation [by New York] under this act," because "[t]he discrimination is not conditioned upon the existence of such untaxed income; and it would be rash to assume that non-residents taxable in New York under this law, as a class, are receiving additional income from outside sources equivalent to the amount of the exemptions that are accorded to citizens of New York and denied to them." Finally, the Court rejected as speculative and constitutionally unsound the argument that States adjoining New York could adopt an income tax, "in which event, injustice to their citizens on the part of New York could be avoided by providing similar exemptions similarly conditioned."

In Austin, a more recent decision reviewing a State's taxation of nonresidents, we considered a commuter tax imposed by New Hampshire, the effect of which was to tax only nonresidents working in that State. The Court described its previous decisions, including Shaffer and Travis, as "establishing a rule of substantial equality of treatment for the citizens of the taxing State and nonresident taxpayers," under which New Hampshire's one-sided tax failed.

Travis and Austin make clear that the Privileges and Immunities Clause prohibits a State from denying nonresidents a general tax exemption provided to

residents, while Shaffer and Travis establish that States may limit nonresidents' deductions of business expenses and nonbusiness deductions based on the relationship between those expenses and in-state property or income. While the latter decisions provide States a considerable amount of leeway in aligning the tax burden of nonresidents to in-state activities, neither they nor Austin can be fairly read as holding that the Privileges and Immunities Clause permits States to categorically deny personal deductions to a nonresident taxpayer, without a substantial justification for the difference in treatment.

III

. . . In attempting to justify the discrimination against nonresidents effected [in 1987], respondents assert that because the State only has jurisdiction over nonresidents' in-state activities, its limitation on nonresidents' deduction of alimony payments is valid. Invoking Shaffer and Travis, the State maintains that it should not be required to consider expenses "wholly linked to personal activities outside New York." We must consider whether that assertion suffices to substantially justify the challenged statute.

A

Looking first at the rationale the New York Court of Appeals adopted in upholding [the 1987 change], we do not find in the court's decision any reasonable explanation or substantial justification for the discriminatory provision. Although the court purported to apply the two-part inquiry derived from Toomer and Piper, in the end, the justification was based on rationales borrowed from another case, Goodwin v. State Tax Comm'n, 286 App.Div. 694, aff'd 1 N.Y.2d 680, appeal dism'd, 352 U.S. 805 (1956). There, a New Jersey resident challenged New York's denial of deductions for real estate taxes and mortgage interest on his New Jersey home, and his medical expenses and life insurance premiums. The challenge in that case, however, was to a provision of New York tax law substantially similar to that considered in Travis, under which nonresident taxpayers were allowed deductions " 'only if and to the extent that, they are connected with [taxable] income arising from sources within the state.'" 286 App.Div., at 695 (quoting then N.Y. Tax Law § 360(11)).

There is no analogous provision in [the current statute], which plainly limits nonresidents' deduction of alimony payments, irrespective of whether those payments might somehow relate to New York-source income. Although the Goodwin court's rationale concerning New York's disallowance of nonresidents' deduction of life insurance premiums and medical expenses assumed that such expenses, "made by [the taxpayer] in the course of his personal activities ... must be regarded as having taken place in ... the state of his residence," the court also found that those expenses "embodie[d] a governmental policy designed to serve a legitimate social end," namely "to encourage [New York] citizens to obtain life insurance protection and ... to help [New York] citizens bear the burden of an extraordinary illness or accident."

In this case, the New York Court of Appeals similarly described petitioners' alimony expenses as "wholly linked to personal activities outside the State," but did not articulate any policy basis for [the 1987 change], save a reference in its discussion of petitioners' Equal Protection Clause claim to the State's "policy of taxing only those gains realized and losses incurred by a nonresident in New York, while taxing residents on all income." Quite possibly, no other policy basis exists, given that, at the time Goodwin was decided, New York appears to have allowed nonresidents a deduction for alimony paid as long as the recipient was a New York resident required to include the alimony in income. And for several years preceding [the 1987 change], New York law permitted nonresidents to claim a pro rata deduction of alimony paid regardless of the recipient's residence. See Friedsam, 64 N.Y.2d, at 81-82 (1961).

In its reliance on Goodwin, the New York Court of Appeals also failed to account for the fact that, through its broad 1987 tax reforms, New York adopted a new system of nonresident taxation that ties the income tax liability of nonresidents to the tax that they would have paid if they were residents. Indeed, a nonresident's "as if" tax liability, which determines both the tax rate and total tax owed, is based on federal adjusted gross income from *all* sources, not just New York sources. In computing their "as if" resident tax liability, nonresidents of New York are permitted to consider every deduction that New York residents are entitled to, both business and personal. It is only in the computation of the apportionment percentage that New York has chosen to isolate a specific deduction of nonresidents, alimony paid, as entirely nondeductible under any circumstances. Further, after Goodwin but before this case, the New York Court of Appeals acknowledged, in Friedsam, that the State's policy and statutes favored parity, on a pro rata basis, in the allowance of personal deductions to residents and nonresidents. Accordingly, in light of the questionable relevance of Goodwin to New York's current system of taxing nonresidents, we do not agree with the New York Court of Appeals that "substantial reasons for the disparity in tax treatment are apparent on the face of [the statute]."

We also take little comfort in the fact, noted by the New

York Court of Appeals, that [the 1987 change] does not deny nonresidents all benefit of the alimony deduction because that deduction is included in federal adjusted gross income, one of the components in the nonresident's computation of his New York tax liability. That finding seems contrary to the impression of New York's Commissioner of Taxation and Finance as expressed in an advisory opinion, In re Rosenblatt, 1989-1990 Transfer Binder, CCH N.Y. Tax Rep. ¶252-998, p. 17,969 (Jan. 18, 1990), in which the Commissioner explained that "[t]he effect of [the statute's] allowance of the [alimony] deduction in the . . . denominator and disallowance in the numerator is that Petitioner cannot get the benefit of a proportional deduction of the alimony payments made to his spouse." In any event, respondents have never argued to this Court that [the statute] effects anything other than a denial of nonresidents' alimony deductions. Though the inclusion of the alimony deduction in a nonresident's federal adjusted gross income reduces the nonresident's "as if" tax liability, New York effectively takes the alimony deduction back in the "apportionment percentage" used to determine the actual tax owed, because the numerator of that percentage does not include any deduction for alimony paid, while the denominator does include such a deduction.

In summarizing its holding, the New York Court of Appeals explained that, because "there can be no serious argument that petitioners' alimony deductions are legitimate business expenses[,] . . . the approximate equality of tax treatment required by the Constitution is satisfied, and greater fine-tuning in this tax scheme is not constitutionally mandated." This Court's precedent, however, should not be read to suggest that tax schemes allowing nonresidents to deduct only their business expenses are per se constitutional, and we must accordingly inquire further into the State's justification for [the 1987 change] in light of its practical effect.

B

. . . .

In the context of New York's overall scheme of nonresident taxation, [the disallowance of a deduction for alimony paid by nonresidents] is an anomaly. New York tax law currently permits nonresidents to avail themselves of what amounts to a pro rata deduction for other tax-deductible personal expenses besides alimony. Before 1987, New York law also allowed nonresidents to deduct a pro rata share of alimony payments. The New York State Tax Commissioner's advisory opinion in In re Rosenblatt indicates that [the 1987 change] may have been intended to overrule Friedsam. See In re Rosenblatt, supra, ¶252-998, at 17,969 ([the 1987 change] "specifically reversed Friedson [sic] which had allowed an alimony deduction to a nonresident according to the formula for allocation of itemized deductions by the nonresident"). Certainly, as the New York Court of Appeals found, [the 1987 change] "had the effect of removing [the] impairment" imposed by Friedsam, thereby implying a disavowal of the State's previous policy of substantial equality between residents and nonresidents.

The policy expressed in Friedsam, which acknowledged the principles of equality and fairness underlying the Privileges and Immunities Clause, was not merely an "impairment," however. Although the State has considerable freedom to establish and adjust its tax policy respecting nonresidents, the end results must, of course, comply with the Federal Constitution, and any provision imposing disparate taxation upon nonresidents must be appropriately justified. As this Court has explained, where "the power to tax is not unlimited, validity is not established by the mere imposition of a tax." Mullaney v. Anderson, 342 U.S. at 418.

To justify [the 1987 change], the State refers to a statement, presented in 1959 by New York's then-Commissioner of Taxation and Finance before a Subcommittee of the House Judiciary Committee. In that statement, the Commissioner explained," '[s]ince legally we do not and cannot recognize the existence of [non-New York source] income, we have felt that, in general, we cannot recognize . . . other deductions, which, in the main, are of a personal nature and are unconnected with the production of income in New York.'" Brief for Respondent Commissioner of Taxation and Finance 14 (quoting statement of Hon. Joseph H. Murphy, Taxation of Income of Nonresidents, Hearing on H.J. Res. 33 et al. and H.R. 4174 et al. before Subcommittee No. 2 of the House Committee on the Judiciary, 86th Cong., 1st Sess., 98-99 (1959)). Yet there is good reason to question whether that statement actually is a rationale for [the 1987 change], given substantial evidence to the contrary, in both the history of the State's treatment of nonresidents' alimony deductions,[4] and its current treatment of other personal deductions.

---

4. See 1943 N.Y. Laws, ch. 245, § 3 (alimony deductions allowed only when recipient is subject to New York tax); 1944 N.Y. Laws, ch. 333, § 2 (alimony deduction allowed to all residents and to nonresidents only if recipient is subject to New York tax); 1961 N.Y. Laws, ch. 68, § 1 (itemized deductions, including alimony, generally allowed to nonresidents in proportion to New York source income).

Moreover, to the extent that the cited testimony suggests that no circumstances exist under which a State's denial of personal deductions to nonresidents could be constrained, we reject its premise. Certainly, as the Court found in Travis, 252 U.S. at 79-80, nonresidents must be allowed tax exemptions in parity with residents. And the most that the Court has suggested regarding nonresidents' nonbusiness expenses is that their deduction may be limited to the proportion of those expenses rationally related to in-state income or activities. See Shaffer, 252 U.S. at 56-57.

As a practical matter, the Court's interpretation of the Privileges and Immunities Clause in Travis and Shaffer implies that States may effectively limit nonresidents' deduction of certain personal expenses based on a reason as simple as the fact that those expenses are clearly related to residence in another State. But here, [the statute] does not incorporate such analysis on its face or, according to the New York Court of Appeals, through legislative history, see 89 N.Y.2d, at 290-291. Moreover, there are situations in which [the statute] could operate to require nonresidents to pay significantly more tax than identically situated residents. For example, if a nonresident's earnings were derived primarily from New York sources, the effect of [the 1987 change] could be to raise the tax apportionment percentage above 100%, thereby requiring that individual to pay *more* tax than an identically situated resident, solely because of the disallowed alimony deduction. Under certain circumstances, the taxpayer could even be liable for New York taxes approaching or even exceeding net income.

There is no doubt that similar circumstances could arise respecting the apportionment for tax purposes of income or expenses based on in-state activities without a violation of the Privileges and Immunities Clause. Such was the case in Shaffer, despite the petitioner's attempt to argue that he should be allowed to offset net business income taxed by Oklahoma with business losses incurred in other States. See 252 U.S. at 57. It is one thing, however, for an anomalous situation to arise because an individual has greater profits from business activities or property owned in one particular State than in another. An entirely different situation is presented by a facially inequitable and essentially unsubstantiated taxing scheme that denies only nonresidents a tax deduction for alimony payments, which while surely a personal matter, see United States v. Gilmore, 372 U.S. at 44, arguably bear some relationship to a taxpayer's overall earnings. Alimony payments also differ from other types of personal deductions, such as mortgage interest and property tax payments, whose situs can be determined based on the location of the underlying property. Thus, unlike the expenses discussed in Shaffer, alimony payments can not be so easily characterized as "losses elsewhere incurred." 252 U.S. at 57. Rather, alimony payments reflect an obligation of some duration that is determined in large measure by an individual's income generally, wherever it is earned. The alimony obligation may be of a "personal" nature, but it cannot be viewed as geographically fixed in the manner that other expenses, such as business losses, mortgage interest payments, or real estate taxes, might be.

Accordingly, contrary to the dissent's suggestion, we do not propose that States are required to allow nonresidents a deduction for all manner of personal expenses, such as taxes paid to other States or mortgage interest relating to an out-of-State residence. Nor do we imply that States invariably must provide to nonresidents the same manner of tax credits available to residents. Our precedent allows States to adopt justified and reasonable distinctions between residents and nonresidents in the provision of tax benefits, whether in the form of tax deductions or tax credits. In this case, however, we are not satisfied by the State's argument that it need not consider the impact of disallowing nonresidents a deduction for alimony paid merely because alimony expenses are personal in nature, particularly in light of the inequities that could result when a nonresident with alimony obligations derives nearly all of her income from New York, a scenario that may be "typical," see Travis, 252 U.S. at 80. By requiring nonresidents to pay more tax than similarly situated residents solely on the basis of whether or not the nonresidents are liable for alimony payments, [the disallowance of a deduction for the payment of alimony by nonresidents] violates the "rule of substantial equality of treatment" this Court described in Austin, 420 U.S. at 665.

C

Respondents also propose that [the 1987 statute] is "consistent with New York's taxation of families generally." Brief for Respondent Commissioner of Taxation and Finance 14-15. It has been suggested that one purpose of New York's 1987 tax law changes was to adopt a regime of "income splitting," under which each spouse in a marital relationship is taxed on an equal share of the total income from the marital unit. Ibid. (citing McIntyre & Pomp, State Income Tax Treatment of Residents and Nonresidents Under the Privileges and Immunities Clause, 13 State Tax Notes 245, 249 (1997)). A similar effect is achieved in the case of marital dissolution by allowing the payer of alimony to exclude the payment from income and requiring the recipient to report a corresponding increase in income. Such treatment accords with provisions adopted in 1942 by

the Federal Government as a means of adjusting tax burdens on alimony payers who, without a deduction for alimony paid, could face a tax liability greater than their remaining income after payment of alimony.

In the federal system, when one resident taxpayer pays alimony to another, the payer's alimony deduction is offset by the alimony income reported by the recipient, leading to parity in the allocation of the overall tax burden. [The 1987 change] however, disallows nonresidents' entire alimony expenses with no consideration given to whether New York income tax will be paid by the recipients. Respondents explain that such concerns are simply irrelevant to New York's taxation of nonresidents, because "[e]xtending the benefit of income splitting to nonresidents is inappropriate on tax policy grounds because nonresidents are taxed by New York on only a slice of their in-come—that derived from New York sources." Such analysis, however, begs the question whether there is a substantial reason for the difference in treatment, and is therefore not appreciably distinct from the State's assertion that no such justification is required because [the payment of alimony] does not concern business expenses.

Indeed, we fail to see how New York's disregard for the residence of the alimony recipient does anything more than point out potential inequities in the operation of [the statute]. Certainly, the concept of income splitting works when both former spouses are residents of the same State, because one spouse receives a tax deduction corresponding to the other's reported income, thereby making the state treasury whole (after adjustment for differences in the spouses' respective tax rates). The scheme also results in an equivalent allocation of total tax liability when one spouse is no longer a resident of the same State, because each spouse retains the burden of paying resident income taxes due to his or her own State on their share of the split income. The benefit of income splitting disappears, however, when a State in which neither spouse resides essentially imposes a surtax on the alimony, such as the tax increase New York imposes through [the non-deduction of alimony]. And, at the extreme, when a New York resident receives alimony payments from a nonresident New York taxpayer, [the 1987 change] results in a double-taxation windfall for the State: the recipient pays taxes on the alimony but the nonresident payer is denied any deduction. Although such treatment may accord with the Federal Government's treatment of taxpayers who are nonresident aliens, see 26 U.S.C. §§872 and 873, the reasonableness of such a scheme on a national level is a different issue that does not implicate the Privileges and Immunities Clause guarantee that individuals may migrate between States to live and work.

D

Finally, several States, as amici for respondents, assert that [the non-deduction of alimony] could not "have any more than a de minimis effect on the run-of-the-mill taxpayer or comity among the States," because States imposing an income tax typically provide a deduction or credit to their residents for income taxes paid to other States. Brief for State of Ohio et al. 8. Accordingly, their argument runs, "[a]ll things being equal . . . the taxpayer would pay roughly the same total tax in the two States, the only difference being that [the taxpayer's resident State] would get more and New York less of the revenue." There is no basis for such an assertion in the record before us. In fact, in the year in question, Connecticut imposed no income tax on petitioners' earned income. "Nor, we may add, can the constitutionality of one State's statutes affecting nonresidents depend upon the present configuration of the statutes of another State." Austin, 420 U.S. at 668; see also Travis, 252 U.S. at 81-82.

IV

In sum, we find that the State's inability to tax a nonresident's entire income is not sufficient, in and of itself, to justify the discrimination imposed by [the 1987 change]. While States have considerable discretion in formulating their income tax laws, that power must be exercised within the limits of the Federal Constitution. Tax provisions imposing discriminatory treatment on nonresident individuals must be reasonable in effect and based on a substantial justification other than the fact of nonresidence.

Although the Privileges and Immunities Clause does not prevent States from requiring nonresidents to allocate income and deductions based on their in-state activities in the manner described in Shaffer and Travis, those opinions do not automatically guarantee that a State may disallow nonresident taxpayers every manner of nonbusiness deduction on the assumption that such amounts are inevitably allocable to the State in which the taxpayer resides. Alimony obligations are unlike other expenses that can be related to activities conducted in a particular State or property held there. And as a personal obligation that generally correlates with a taxpayer's total income or wealth, alimony bears some relationship to earnings regardless of their source. Further, the manner in which New York taxes nonresidents, based on an allocation of an "as if" resident tax liability, not only imposes upon nonresidents' income the effect of New York's graduated tax rates but also imports a corresponding element of fairness in allowing nonresidents a pro rata deduction of

other types of personal expenses. It would seem more consistent with that taxing scheme and with notions of fairness for the State to allow nonresidents a pro rata deduction for alimony paid, as well.

Under the circumstances, we find that respondents have not presented a substantial justification for the categorical denial of alimony deductions to nonresidents. The State's failure to provide more than a cursory justification for [the disallowance of a deduction for the payment of alimony] smacks of an effort to "penaliz[e] the citizens of other States by subjecting them to heavier taxation merely because they are such citizens," Toomer, 334 U.S. at 408 (Frankfurter, J., concurring). We thus hold that [the denial of a deduction for alimony] is an unwarranted denial to the citizens of other States of the privileges and immunities enjoyed by the citizens of New York.

JUSTICE GINSBURG, with whom THE CHIEF JUSTICE and JUSTICE KENNEDY join, dissenting.

New York and other States follow the Federal Government's lead[1] in according an income tax deduction for alimony to resident taxpayers only.[2] That tax practice, I conclude, does not offend the nondiscrimination principle embodied in the Privileges and Immunities Clause. I therefore dissent from the Court's opinion.

I

To put this case in proper perspective, it is helpful to recognize not only that alimony payments are "surely a personal matter," ante; in addition, alimony payments are "unlike other . . . . personal obligation[s]," ante. Under federal tax law, mirrored in state tax regimes, alimony is included in the recipient's gross income, 26 U.S.C. §71(a), and the payer is allowed a corresponding deduction, §§215(a), 62(a)(10), for payments taxable to the recipient. This scheme "can best be seen as a determination with respect to choice of taxable person rather than as rules relating to the definition of income or expense. In effect, the [alimony payer] is treated as a conduit for gross income that legally belongs to the [alimony recipient]

---

1. See 26 U.S.C. §§872-873; McIntyre & Pomp, State Income Tax Treatment of Residents and Nonresidents Under the Privileges and Immunities Clause, 13 State Tax Notes 245, 248-249 (1997).

2. Four States in addition to New York—Alabama, California, West Virginia, and Wisconsin—expressly limit the alimony deduction to residents. Two other States—Illinois and Ohio—restrict nonresidents to specified deductions and adjustments in calculating in-state income, and do not list the alimony deduction as one available to nonresidents.

under the divorce decree." M. Chirelstein, Federal Income Taxation ¶9.05, p. 230 (8th ed.1997) (hereinafter Chirelstein); see also B. Bittker & M. McMahon, Federal Income Taxation of Individuals ¶36.7, p. 36-18 (2d ed. 1995) ("Unlike most other personal deductions, [the deduction for alimony payments] is best viewed as a method of designating the proper taxpayer for a given amount of income, rather than a tax allowance for particular expenditures. In combination, §71 [requiring the alimony recipient to include the payment in gross income] and §215 [allowing a deduction to the alimony payer] treat part of the [payer]'s income as though it were received subject to an offsetting duty to pay it to the payee."). New York applies this scheme to resident alimony payers. But New York Tax Law declares that, in the case of a nonresident with New York source income, the alimony deduction for which federal law provides "shall not constitute a deduction derived from New York sources."

Thus, if petitioner Christopher Lunding and his former spouse were New York residents, his alimony payments would be included in his former spouse's gross income for state as well as federal income tax purposes, and he would receive a deduction for the payments. In other words, New York would tax the income once, but not twice. In fact, however, though Lunding derives a substantial part of his gross income from New York sources, he and his former spouse reside in Connecticut. That means, he urges, that New York may not tax the alimony payments at all. Compared to New York divorced spouses, in short, Lunding seeks a windfall, not an escape from double taxation, but a total exemption from New York's tax for the income in question. This beneficence to nonresidents earning income in New York, he insists, is what the Privileges and Immunities Clause demands.

Explaining why New York must so favor Connecticut residents over New York residents, Lunding invites comparisons with other broken marriages–cases in which one of the former spouses resides in New York and the other resides elsewhere. First, had Lunding's former spouse moved from Connecticut to New York, New York would count the alimony payments as income to her, but would nonetheless deny him, because of his out-of-state residence, any deduction. In such a case, New York would effectively tax the same income twice, first to the payer by giving him no deduction, then to the recipient, by taxing the payments as gross income to her. Of course, that is not Lunding's situation, and one may question his standing to demand that New York take nothing from him in order to offset the State's arguably excessive taxation of others.

More engagingly, Lunding compares his situation to that of a New York resident who pays alimony to a former spouse living in another State. In such a case, New York would permit the New Yorker to deduct the alimony payments, even though the recipient pays no tax to New York on the income transferred to her. New York's choice, according to Lunding, is to deny the alimony deduction to the New Yorker whose former spouse resides out of state, or else extend the deduction to him. The Court apparently agrees. At least, the Court holds, New York "has not adequately justified" the line it has drawn.

The Court's condemnation of New York's law seems to me unwarranted. As applied to a universe of former marital partners who, like Lunding and his former spouse, reside in the same State, New York's attribution of income to *someone* (either payer or recipient) is hardly unfair. True, an occasional New York resident will be afforded a deduction though his former spouse, because she resides elsewhere, will not be chased by New York's tax collector. And an occasional New York alimony recipient will be taxed despite the nonresidence of her former spouse. But New York could legitimately assume that in most cases, as in the Lundings' case, payer and recipient will reside in the same State. Moreover, in cases in which the State's system is overly generous (New York payer, nonresident recipient) or insufficiently generous (nonresident payer, New York recipient), there is no systematic discrimination discretely against nonresidents, for the pairs of former spouses in both cases include a resident and a nonresident.

In reviewing state tax classifications, we have previously held it sufficient under the Privileges and Immunities Clause that "the State has secured a reasonably fair distribution of burdens, and that no intentional discrimination has been made against non-residents." Travellers' Ins. Co. v. Connecticut, 185 U.S. 364 (1902). In Travellers, the Court upheld a state tax that was facially discriminatory: Nonresidents who held stock in Connecticut corporations owed tax to the State on the full value of their holdings, while resident stockholders were entitled to a deduction for their proportionate share of the corporation's Connecticut real estate. But the State's tax system as a whole was not discriminatory, for although residents were entitled to deduct their share of the corporation's Connecticut real estate from their *state* taxes, they were required to pay *municipal* taxes on that property;* nonresidents owed no municipal taxes. See id.,

---

*. [Ed. Municipalities taxed residents on the fair market value of their shares in corporations, less a deduction for "capital of any such company as may be invested in real estate, on which it is

at 367. Municipal taxes varied across the State, so residents in low-tax municipalities might end up paying lower taxes than nonresidents. Nonetheless, "the mere fact that in a given year the actual workings of the system may result in a larger burden on the non-resident was properly held not to vitiate the system, for a different result might obtain in a succeeding year, the results varying with the calls made in the different localities for local expenses." Id., at 369.

Travellers held that tax classifications survive Privileges and Immunities scrutiny if they provide a rough parity of treatment between residents and nonresidents. See also Austin v. New Hampshire, 420 U.S. at 665 (Privileges and Immunities precedents "establis[h] a rule of substantial equality of treatment"). That holding accords with the Court's observation in Baldwin v. Fish and Game Comm'n of Mont., 436 U.S. at 383, that "[s]ome distinctions between residents and nonresidents merely reflect the fact that this is a Nation composed of individual States, and are permitted; other distinctions are prohibited because they hinder the formation, the purpose, or the development of a single Union of those States." A tax classification that does not systematically discriminate against nonresidents cannot be said to "hinder the formation, the purpose, or the development of a single Union." See McIntyre & Pomp, Post-Marriage Income Splitting through the Deduction for Alimony Payments, 13 State Tax Notes 1631, 1635 (1997) (urging that the Privileges and Immunities Clause does not require New York to forgo the income-splitting objective served by its alimony rules when both payer and recipient are residents of the same State simply because "results may be less than ideal" "when one of the parties to the alimony transaction is a resident and the other is a nonresident").[3]

_____

assessed and pay a tax." 364 U.S. at 365. Presumably, a deduction was allowed only for real estate subject to Connecticut property taxes. The average rate of local tax was 15 mills, which was the rate paid by nonresidents on the value of their stock in Connecticut corporations. The average rate of local tax in the larger towns was 21 mills. Id. at 368.]

3. Nor does it appear that New York gains "an unfair share of tax revenue" by denying nonresident alimony payers a deduction even when the recipient is a resident. McIntyre & Pomp, Post-Marriage Income Splitting through the Deduction for Alimony Payments, 13 State Tax Notes, at 1635. Alimony payments into and out of a State, it seems reasonable to assume, are approximately in balance; if that is so, then the revenue New York receives under its current regime is roughly equivalent to the revenue it would generate by granting a deduction to nonresident alimony payers with resident recipients and denying the deduction to resident payers with nonresident recipients. See ibid.

I would affirm the judgment of the New York Court of Appeals as consistent with the Court's precedent, and would not cast doubt, as today's decision does, on state tax provisions long considered secure.

II

Viewing this case as one discretely about alimony, I would accept New York's law as a fair adaptation, at the state level, of the current United States system. The Court notes but shies away from this approach, expressing particular concern about double taxation in the "extreme" case not before us—the "New York resident [who] receives alimony payments from a nonresident taxpayer," ante.[4] Instead, the Court treats alimony as one among several personal expenses a State makes deductible.

Significantly, the Court's approach conforms to no historic pattern. "Historically, both alimony and child support were treated as personal expenses nondeductible [by the payer] and not includable [in the recipient's income]. Successive [federal] statutory enactments beginning in 1942 allowed a deduction and corresponding inclusion for alimony payments while continuing the nondeductible-excludable treatment for child support payments."

Accepting, arguendo, the Court's "personal expense deduction" in lieu of "income attribution" categorization of alimony, however, I do not read our precedent to lead in the direction the Court takes. On Lunding's analysis, which the Court essentially embraces, the core principle is that "personal deductions, no matter what they are . . . must be allowed in the proportion that the New York State income bears to total income." Tr. of Oral Arg. 19. That has never been, nor should it be, what the Privileges and Immunities Clause teaches.

A

. . . In two companion cases—Shaffer v. Carter, 252 U.S. 37 (1920), and Travis v. Yale & Towne Mfg. Co., 252 U.S. 60 (1920)—the Court considered, respectively, Oklahoma's and New York's schemes of nonresident income taxation. Both had been challenged as violating the Privileges and

_____

4. As already observed, Lunding, who seeks to escape any state tax on the income in question (Connecticut, his State of residence, had no income tax in the year in issue), is hardly a fit representative of the individuals who elicit the Court's concern. See New York v. Ferber, 458 U.S. at 767 ("[A] person to whom a statute may constitutionally be applied may not challenge that statute on the ground that it may conceivably be applied unconstitutionally to others in situations not before the Court.").

Immunities Clause.

Upholding the Oklahoma scheme and declaring the New York scheme impermissibly discriminatory, the Court established at least three principles. First, "just as a State may impose general income taxes upon its own citizens and residents whose persons are subject to its control, it may, as a necessary consequence, levy a duty of like character, and not more onerous in its effect, upon incomes accruing to non-residents from their property or business within the State, or their occupations carried on therein." Shaffer, 252 U.S. at 52; accord, Travis, 252 U.S. at 75.

Second, a State may not deny nonresidents personal *exemptions* when such exemptions are uniformly afforded to residents. See id., at 79-81. Personal exemptions, which are typically granted in a set amount "to all taxpayers, regardless of their income," Nonresident's Personal Income, 72 Mich. L. Rev. 1309, 1343 (1974), effectively create a zero tax bracket for the amount of the exemption. Denial of those exemptions thus amounts to an across-the-board rate increase for nonresidents, a practice impermissible under longstanding constitutional interpretation. Because New York denied nonresidents the personal exemption provided to all residents, the Travis Court held the State's scheme an abridgment of the Privileges and Immunities Clause.

Finally, *deductions* for specific expenses are treated differently from the blanket exemptions at issue in Travis: A State need not afford nonresidents the same deductions it extends to its residents. In Shaffer, the Court upheld Oklahoma's rules governing deduction of business losses. Oklahoma residents could deduct such losses wherever incurred, while nonresidents could deduct only losses incurred within the State. The Court explained that the disparate treatment was "only such as arises naturally from the extent of the jurisdiction of the State in the two classes of cases, and cannot be regarded as an unfriendly or unreasonable discrimination." Shaffer, 252 U.S. at 57. A State may tax its residents on "their income from all sources, whether within or without the State," but it cannot tax nonresidents on their out-of-state activities. Ibid. "Hence there is no obligation to accord to [nonresidents] a deduction by reason of losses elsewhere incurred." Ibid. The Court stated the principle even more clearly in Travis, 252 U.S. at 75-76: "[T]here is no unconstitutional discrimination against citizens of other States in confining the deduction of expenses, losses, etc., in the case of non-resident taxpayers, to such as are connected with income arising from sources within the taxing State . . . ."

B

Shaffer and Travis plainly establish that States need not allow nonresidents to deduct out-of-state *business* expenses. The application of those cases to deductions for *personal* expenses, however, is less clear. On the one hand, Travis's broad language could be read to suggest that in-state business expenses are the only deductions States must extend to nonresidents. On the other hand, neither Shaffer nor Travis upheld a scheme denying nonresidents deductions for personal expenses. . . [5]

With rare exception, however, lower courts have applied Shaffer and Travis with equal force to both personal and business deductions. The New York court's decision in Goodwin v. State Tax Comm'n, exemplifies this approach. Goodwin concerned a lawyer who resided in New Jersey and practiced law in New York City. In his New York income tax return, he claimed and was allowed deductions for bar association dues, subscriptions to legal periodicals, entertainment and car expenses, and certain charitable contributions. But he was disallowed deductions for real estate taxes and mortgage interest on his New Jersey home, medical expenses, and life insurance premiums. Upholding the disallowances, the appeals court explained that the non-income-producing personal expenses at issue were of a kind properly referred to the law and policy of the State of the taxpayer's residence. That State, if it had an income tax, might well have allowed the deductions, but the New York court did not think judgment in the matter should be shouldered by a sister State.

Goodwin further reasoned that a State may accord certain deductions "[i]n the exercise of its general governmental power to advance the welfare of its residents." But it does not inevitably follow that the State must "extend similar aid or encouragement to the residents of other states." A

---

5. The New York law before the Court in Travis allowed residents to deduct non-business-related property losses wherever incurred, but allowed nonresidents such deductions only for losses incurred in New York. See Tr. of Records in Travis v. Yale & Towne Mfg. Co., O.T.1919, No. 548 (State of New York, The A, B, C of the Personal Income Tax Law, pp. 12, 14, ¶¶42, 44). Although Travis held New York's law infirm, the Court rested its decision solely on the ground that denying personal exemptions to nonresidents violated the Privileges and Immunities Clause. See Travis, 252 U.S. at 79-82. The Court did not extend its ruling to New York's differential treatment of residents and nonresidents with regard to personal-loss deductions. See id., at 75-76 ("no unconstitutional discrimination" in confining deductions for nonresidents' losses "to such as are connected with income arising from sources within the taxing State").

State need not, in short, underwrite the social policy of the Nation.

Other lower courts, upholding a variety of personal expense deductions for residents only, have agreed with Goodwin's analysis. Challenges to such rulings, like the appeal in Goodwin, have been disposed of summarily by this Court. See, e.g., Lung v. O'Chesky, 94 N.M. 802 (1980) (upholding denial to nonresidents of grocery and medical tax rebates allowed residents where rebates served as relief for State's gross receipts and property taxes), appeal dismissed for want of a substantial federal question, 450 U.S. 961 (1981); Anderson v. Tiemann, 182 Neb. 393, 407-408 (1967) (upholding denial to nonresidents of a deduction allowed residents for sales taxes paid on food purchased for personal use), appeal dismissed for want of a substantial federal question, 390 U.S. 714 (1968); Berry v. State Tax Comm'n, 241 Ore. 580, 582 (1964) (upholding denial to nonresidents of deductions allowed residents for medical expenses, interest on home-state loans, and other personal items; court stated that the legislature could legitimately conclude that "personal deductions are so closely related to the state of residence that they should be allowed only by the state of residence and not by every other state in which some part of a taxpayer's income might be found and taxed"), appeal dismissed for want of a substantial federal question, 382 U.S. 16 (1965). But see Wood v. Department of Revenue, 305 Ore. 23, 32-33 (1988) (State may not deny alimony deduction to nonresidents).

C

. . . .

Alimony payments (if properly treated as an expense at all) are a personal expense, as the Court acknowledges. They "ste[m] entirely from the marital relationship," United States v. Gilmore, 372 U.S. 39, 51 (1963), and, like other incidents of marital and family life, are principally connected to the State of residence. Unlike donations to New York-based charities or mortgage and tax payments for second homes in the State, Lunding's alimony payments cannot be said to take place in New York, nor do they inure to New York's benefit. They are payments particularly personal in character, made by one Connecticut resident to another Connecticut resident pursuant to a decree issued by a Connecticut state court. Those payments "must be deemed to take place in" Connecticut, "the state of [Lunding's] residence, the state in which his life is centered." Goodwin, 286 A.D., at 701. New York is not constitutionally compelled to subsidize them.

The majority is therefore wrong to fault the Court of

Appeals for insufficient articulation of a "policy basis for [the 1987 change]." The Court of Appeals recalled Goodwin, characterizing it as the decision that "definitively addressed" the disallowance of personal life expenses. The court concluded that alimony payments were no less referable to the law and policy of the taxpayer's residence than "the expenditures for life insurance, out-of-State property taxes and medical treatment at issue in Goodwin." That policy-based justification for [the disallowance of an alimony deduction] needed no further elaboration.

III

Although Lunding's alimony payments to a Connecticut resident surely do not facilitate his production of income in New York or contribute to New York's riches, the Court relies on this connection: "[A]s a personal obligation that generally correlates with a taxpayer's total income or wealth, alimony bears some relationship to earnings regardless of their source." See also ante (alimony payments "arguably bear some relationship to a taxpayer's overall earnings," and are "determined in large measure by an individual's income generally, wherever it is earned"). But all manner of spending similarly relates to an individual's income from all sources. Income generated anywhere will determine, for example, the quality of home one can afford and the character of medical care one can purchase. Under a "correlat[ion] with a taxpayer's total income" approach, ante, it appears, the nonresident must be allowed to deduct his medical expenses and home state real estate taxes, even school district taxes, plus mortgage interest payments, if the State allows residents to deduct such expenses. And as total income also determines eligibility for tax relief aimed at low-income taxpayers, notably earned income tax credits, a State would be required to make such credits available to nonresidents if it grants them to residents.[6]

The Court does not suggest that alimony correlates with a taxpayer's total income more closely than does the run of personal life expenses. Indeed, alimony may be more significantly influenced by other considerations, for example, the length of the marriage, the recipient's earnings, child custody and support arrangements, an

---

6. New York currently allows low-income nonresident taxpayers to use the State's Earned Income Tax Credit to offset their income tax liability, but does not refund any excess credits to nonresidents as it does to residents. N.Y. Tax Law §§606(d)(1)-(d)(2); see also §§606(c)(1)-(c)(2) (residents entitled to a refund of excess credit for certain household and dependent care services; nonresidents may use the credit only to offset tax liability).

antenuptial agreement.[7] In short, the Court's "related-to-income" approach directly leads to what Christopher Lunding candidly argued: Any and every personal deduction allowed to residents must be allowed to nonresidents in the proportion that New York income bears to the taxpayer's total income. If that is the law of this case, long-settled provisions and decisions have been overturned, beyond the capacity of any legislature to repair. . .

. . . .

---

7. Connecticut, where Lunding was divorced, lists as factors relevant to alimony determinations "the length of the marriage, the causes for the annulment, dissolution of the marriage or legal separation, the age, health, station, occupation, amount and sources of income, vocational skills, employability, estate and needs of each of the parties . . . and, in the case of a parent to whom the custody of minor children has been awarded, the desirability of such parent's securing employment." Conn. Gen. Stat. § 46b-82.

Questions and Comments

1. The majority was influenced by the fact that a nonresident who pays alimony and who earns all of his income in New York would pay more income tax than an equivalent New York resident. Did the same result occur in *Shaffer*? When is it constitutional for a nonresident to pay more income tax than an equivalent resident?

2. The majority raises the possibility that a nonresident could pay New York income taxes approaching or exceeding his or her net income (N.Y. taxable income less alimony). Assume a nonresident has $100,000 of New York taxable income prior to the payment of alimony and that all of this income is earned in New York. Assume that the payment of alimony is deductible for residents but not for nonresidents. Assume also a flat 10% tax rate. How much alimony would the nonresident have to pay before the New York income tax would equal the nonresident's New York taxable income less the alimony payment?

3. Is it unconstitutional for a state to have a rebuttable presumption that the payment of alimony by nonresidents is not a cost of generating in-state income?

4. What would Justice O'Connor have accepted as an "adequate justification" by New York for its treatment of nonresidents?

5. The majority acknowledges that "*Shaffer* and *Travis* establish that States may limit nonresidents' deductions of business expenses and nonbusiness deductions based on the relationship between those expenses and in-state property or income." Why isn't denying nonresidents a deduction for alimony consistent with this principle?

6. The majority seems to accept that a state could deny nonresidents a deduction of mortgage interest payments or real estate taxes because these expenditures are "geographically fixed." Could a state deny a nonresident a charitable deduction? Is a charitable contribution "geographically fixed?" Can New York continue to deny a N.J. resident a deduction for real estate taxes on his or her N.J. property?

7. Suppose a nonresident sells shoes in New York. The nonresident purchases the shoes and takes possession of the shoes in Connecticut, where they are manufactured. Are the payments for the shoes "geographically fixed?" Should the nonresident be allowed a deduction for the cost of the shoes, regardless of whether the payments are "geographically fixed?"

Why should whether a payment is "geographically fixed" have anything to do with whether that payment should be deductible?

8. The majority describes "the concept of income splitting [as working] when both former spouses are residents of the same State, because one spouse receives a tax deduction corresponding to the other's reported income, thereby making the state treasury whole. . . The scheme also results in an equivalent allocation of total tax liability when one spouse is no longer a resident of the same State, because each spouse retains the burden of paying resident income taxes due to his or her own State on their [sic] share of the split income." For this second statement to be true, does the recipient of the alimony have to be subject to an income tax in his or her State of residence?

9. Is it per se unconstitutional for a state to deny nonresidents a deduction for the payment of alimony while allowing residents the deduction?

10. If a state allows its residents to deduct their itemized deductions, does it have to allow nonresidents to deduct their property taxes and interest payments associated with second homes in New York, or charitable contributions to New York charities?

11. Suppose the Connecticut courts determined Lunding's alimony payment at a time when he had no New York income. In what sense could it then be said that the payment of alimony relates to his New York source income? Does *Gilmore*, cited by the Court, support New York's position that alimony is not an expense of generating New York source income?

12. *Austin* involved New Hampshire's attempt to tax *only* nonresidents. Do you agree with the Court's description of *Austin* as a case in which nonresidents were denied "a general tax exemption provided to residents?"

13. The majority distinguishes alimony from the losses that were denied nonresidents in *Shaffer* on the grounds that "unlike the expenses discussed in *Shaffer*, alimony payments can not be so easily characterized as 'losses elsewhere incurred.'" Suppose *Shaffer* had described the losses "as not related to generating New York source income, regardless of where incurred." Could the same thing then be said of the payment of alimony?

14. The majority describes alimony as reflecting "an

obligation of some duration that is determined in large measure by an individual's income generally, wherever it is earned." Could the same thing be said about the interest Lunding pays on his home in Connecticut?

15. Alaska charges a resident $30 per year for a commercial fishing license, whereas a nonresident pays $90 per year for the same license. Constitutional? See *Carlson et al. v. Alaska*, 919 P.2d 1337 (Alaska 1996); cert. den. 117 S. Ct. 789 (1997).

16. Could New York give a homestead exemption (a form of property tax abatement) for an individual's principal residence but not for a second home if the effect is to favor New York residents? See *Markham v. Comstock*, 708 N.Y.S.2d 674 (2000); *Reinish v. Clark*, 765 So.2d 197 (Fl. 2000); *Rubin v. Glaser*, 416 A.2d 382 (1980).

17. Can a state give an income tax credit for the sales taxes paid on food to only residents? What if many nonresidents work in the state and spend substantial amount of money eating lunch out? See *Anderson v. Tiemann*, 155 N.W.2d 322 (1967), appeal dismissed, 390 U.S. 714 (1968) (upholding a sales tax credit limited to residents).

18. For critical commentary on *Lunding*, see Amy Royal, *The Parameters of the Substantial Justification Test as Established by the Supreme Court in Lunding v. New York Tax Appeals Tribunal*, 63 Alb. L. Rev. 657 (1999); Gene Matthew Eckel, *The New Standard Applicable to State Taxation of a Nonresident – An Analysis of the Supreme Court's Treatment of the Privileges and Immunities Clause in Lunding v. New York Tax Appeals Tribunal*, 32 Creighton L. Rev. 1311 (1999); Michel P. Cassier and Andrew Sobol, *Recent Developments in New York Taxation* 48 Syracuse L. Rev. 843 (1998); James Michael Dailey, *The Thin Line Between Acceptable Disparate Tax Treatment of Nonresidents and Unconstitutional Discrimination under the Article IV Privileges and Immunities Clause: Lunding v. New York Appeals Tribunal, 118 S. Ct. 766 (1998)*, 21 Hamline L. Rev. 563 (Spring, 1998); *The Supreme Court 1997 Term Leading Cases*, 112 Harv. L. Rev. 122 (1998); Carolyn Joy Lee, *Lunding: The Supreme Court Debates Discrimination*, 98 STN 197-6 (October 13, 1998); Michael J. McIntyre and Richard D. Pomp, *Post-Marriage Income Splitting through the Deduction for Alimony Payments: A Reply to Professor Schoettle's Free-Trade Analysis of New York v. Lunding*, 13 State Tax Notes 1631 (1997); Michael J. McIntyre and Richard D. Pomp, *State Income Tax Treatment of Residents and Nonresidents Under the Privileges and Immunities Clause*, 13 State Tax Notes 245 (1997).

Post-Marriage Income Splitting through the Deduction for Alimony Payments
by Michael J. McIntyre & Richard D. Pomp
13 State Tax Notes 1631(1997)

. . . .

Alimony, Income Splitting, and the Alleged
Discrimination Against Nonresidents under the Privileges and Immunities Clause

As we noted in our earlier article, New York adopted the alimony rule complained of in Lunding in 1987 as part of a major overhaul of the family taxation features of its personal income tax. The most fundamental change was the replacement of its separate filing regime, which it had employed since 1919, with a marital income splitting regime. Marital income splitting was necessarily limited to residents because both marital partners must be taxable in New York on their total income for the goals of income splitting to be fully implemented. For much the same reason, the 1987 legislation eliminated the deduction for alimony payments made by nonresident individuals.

To appreciate the policy justification for denying nonresidents a deduction for alimony, it is necessary to see how the deduction for the payer, in conjunction with the taxation of alimony to the recipient, operates as an income-splitting mechanism. As discussed below, the effectiveness of the deduction in achieving the tax policy goal of income splitting depends in part on the residence of the payer and the recipient. Because formerly married couples tend to live in the same state, the two most important patterns to discuss are when both former spouses are residents of New York and when both are nonresidents. The difference in the treatment of these two pairs of taxpayers under New York law is being challenged in Lunding under the Privileges and Immunities Clause. For completeness, nevertheless, it is useful to consider two additional patterns—(1) when the payer is a resident and the recipient is a nonresident and (2) when the payer is a nonresident and the recipient is a resident.

Payments of Alimony from One Resident to Another

Under New York law, the alimony deduction operates best as an income-splitting mechanism when the payer and the recipient are both resident in New York. Assume, for example, that FH is the former spouse of FW, that both are New York residents, and that FH has income of $100,000 and is paying alimony of $40,000 to FW. If FH is allowed to deduct the alimony payment of $40,000 and FW is taxable on that amount, then the obvious result is the shifting of income from FH to FW.

When income is shifted between former spouses and both former spouses are New York residents, the income out of which the alimony is presumed to be paid ends up being taxed at the tax rate of the recipient rather than the tax rate of the payer. This result is desirable in a state that has adopted the tax principle that income is properly taxable to the person who enjoys the consumption and savings that it finances. Marital income splitting for New York residents was adopted by New York in 1987 to implement that principle. The application of that principle to former spouses is a logical extension of the marital income splitting rule.

The fundamental point to note is that the deduction for alimony in the above example does not change the amount of income taxable by New York. New York taxes the same $100,000 of income that it would have taxed if no alimony payment had been made. What is changed is the rate at which that income is taxed. Given the graduated rate structure of New York, the effective tax rate on that income is reduced, assuming, as would be typical, that the recipient of the alimony is in a lower tax bracket than the payer.

Alimony Payments Between Nonresidents

When both former spouses are nonresidents, which is the situation in Lunding, New York denies an alimony deduction to the payer and exempts the recipient of the alimony payment from New York tax. The result is that the income presumed to be deflected to the alimony recipient is taxed once and only once by New York. The tax is formally imposed on the payer through the increased tax that results from the denial of the deduction.[6]

---

6. Some of the burden of that tax, however, is likely to be shifted to the recipient because tax burdens imposed on alimony payments are usually taken into account in setting the level of such payments.

In theory, New York could grant a deduction for alimony to the nonresident payer and tax that amount to the nonresident recipient. By adopting that approach, New York presumably could avoid having to confront the Privileges and Immunities Clause issue presented in Lunding. It would still end up taxing 100 percent of the New York source income out of which the alimony is presumed to be paid. Leaving aside constitutional issues, that approach is less desirable than the approach actually followed by New York because of the administrative problems that would arise in taxing the nonresident recipients of alimony payments. Those alimony recipients typically do not file a New York tax return. In practice, therefore, New York would need to establish an information reporting system or some type of withholding system to collect its tax, thereby turning thousands of ordinary individuals paying alimony into reporting or collecting agents for the tax department.

New York's current system, which denies a deduction to a nonresident payer and exempts the nonresident recipient, is firmly grounded on tax principles. An alternative system that would grant the deduction to a nonresident payer and taxed the nonresident recipient also would be justified on tax policy grounds, notwithstanding the administrative problems it would pose. Both systems recognize that a state should tax income used to pay alimony once and only once. In sharp contrast, the system argued for by the taxpayer in Lunding is unprincipled, for it would allow some portion of the New York income used to pay alimony to escape New York taxation entirely.

To illustrate the defect in the system proposed by the taxpayer in Lunding, assume that FH and FW in the above example are both nonresidents. FH earns his entire income of $100,000 from New York sources. As a nonresident, FW is not taxable by New York on the alimony payment of $40,000 received from FH. If the deduction for alimony were to be granted to FH, therefore, New York would collect tax on only $60,000 of income, notwithstanding that FH and FW have together derived $100,000 of income from New York sources.

As noted above, the Court's constitutional jurisprudence would allow New York to impose tax on a nonresident individual receiving an alimony payment that was paid out of income properly traceable to New York sources. By imposing that tax and granting the payer a deduction, the State would have an easy statutory fix if the Court were to decide Lunding against it. If it is constitutional to tax a nonresident recipient of alimony directly, however, it should also be constitutional to do so indirectly by denying an alimony deduction to the person making the payment. We do not believe that the Privileges and

Immunities Clause should be interpreted so as to elevate form over substance.

. . . .

In summary, the New York rule of denying a deduction for alimony payments between nonresidents results in the full taxation of New York source income out of which the alimony is presumed to be paid. The same amount of income is taxable by New York when the alimony payments are made between residents. Thus there is no discrimination under New York law in the rules defining taxable income between a pair of formerly married individuals who are New York residents and an equivalent pair of former spouses who are nonresidents.

Alimony Payments Between a Resident and a Nonresident

The above discussion has focused on alimony payers and recipients when both are residents of New York or when both are nonresidents, as is the case of Mr. Lunding and his former spouse. New York policy makers could plausibly have believed that these two situations account for the overwhelming majority of former spouses with New York ties who are receiving or paying alimony. Two other situations can arise, however, that merit some discussion. Neither of these situations would properly invoke the Privileges and Immunities Clause because they do not entail a systematic discrimination against nonresident individuals.

In the first of these situations, the payer is a resident of New York and the recipient is a nonresident. Under certain normative tax principles, New York's alimony rules are overly generous to former spouses in this situation because the payer receives an alimony deduction and the recipient is not taxable on the alimony payment. Thus the income shifted from the resident to the nonresident recipient is not subject to New York tax at all.

The seemingly overly generous treatment of a resident payer and nonresident recipient will be mitigated by the treatment of the recipient in his or her state of residence, assuming that the resident state imposes an income tax comparable to the New York tax. As discussed above, nearly all states would tax the alimony recipient, thereby removing some or all of the benefit the former spouses would obtain from the New York rule. New York's overly generous treatment of the recipient thus inures primarily to the benefit of that individual's state of residence.

In the second situation, the payer of alimony is a nonresident and the recipient is a resident. Here the New York rules are insufficiently generous under normative tax policy criteria because they deny the payer an alimony deduction and also tax the recipient of the alimony payment. The New York rules may be viewed as subjecting the former spouses to a tentative double tax on income used to pay alimony in this situation.

The insufficiently generous treatment of former spouses in this second situation is likely to be mitigated or eliminated by the harmonization of the New York rules with the tax rules of most sister states. All states imposing an income tax give a credit to their residents for taxes paid to sister states on income that is treated as arising in those states. Thus the tentative double tax on the former spouses will be eliminated, in whole or in part, when the state of residence gives the alimony payer a credit for the New York tax. Accordingly, New York's insufficiently generous treatment of the payer is unlikely to impact substantially on his or her after-tax position; its primary effect will be on the amount of taxes collected by the payer's state of residence.[11]

Rather than relying on widely accepted principles of comity to solve the equity problem in the second situation involving a nonresident payer and a resident recipient, New York might attempt to give relief directly by allowing nonresidents making alimony payments to New York residents to take the deduction. That rule, of course, would not help Mr. Lunding, who pays alimony to a nonresident and who suffers no hardship from the current New York rule. It would give appropriate relief, however, to that presumably small number of nonresident alimony payers whose former spouses reside in New York.

The apparently simply solution suggested above is anything but simple in practice. The suggested rule would work acceptably well only if most nonresident payers of alimony could be expected to know the residency of the alimony recipient. In fact, they often would not. Residency is one of the most litigated issues

---

11. If payers were to receive a deduction for the payment of alimony in calculating their New York taxable income, their New York taxes would be less than what they are under current law; such a reduction in New York taxes would reduce the credit they would otherwise receive against the income tax in their state of residence. Consequently, although the deduction would reduce their New York income taxes, it would increase the income taxes paid in their state of residence. Thus a decision by New York to allow or disallow an alimony deduction is likely to have its primary effect on the way the tax base is shared between New York and the state of residence of the payer and to have relatively little effect on the tax burdens imposed on those payers, unless of course the payer is resident in one of the handful of states that does not have a personal income tax.

in a state income tax, oftentimes turning on factors of which the payer may have no knowledge and which may change from year to year. In a contentious divorce, the payer may know only the mailing address of the recipient, which is not terribly relevant in determining residency. The New York tax department, moreover, would face problems of administration in determining whether a nonresident alimony payer was entitled to the deduction. In auditing individual taxpayers, the department depends very heavily on information received from the federal tax authorities. The state residency of taxpayers is of no interest to federal authorities, and that information does not appear on a taxpayer's federal tax return.

In theory, New York could adopt a rule that was neutral toward resident and nonresident payers of alimony by denying the alimony deduction to all New York taxpayers, whether resident or nonresident, whenever the alimony payments were made to a nonresident former spouse. This rule would present formidable administrative problems because it would require payers of alimony to know the state of residency of the recipient. As noted above, that information is often not available to them or to the tax department.

The hypothetical replacement rule described above would not be neutral on its face with respect to resident and nonresident *recipients* of alimony. Nonresident recipients of alimony can fairly claim that they would be affected adversely by the rule because they are likely to bear some or all of the tax burden imposed on the payer with respect to alimony payments. Whether nonresident alimony recipients would receive support in the courts for a constitutional challenge to that rule is unknown. In our view, the tax policy arguments that can be advanced in its favor are significantly less persuasive than the arguments offered above in defense of the current New York rule.

The only difference between the hypothetical replacement rule and the current New York rule is in the treatment of resident payers of alimony. New York currently allows residents payers to deduct alimony payments to nonresidents, whereas the replacement rule would not allow the deduction. As discussed in detail above, the current New York rule is far simpler to administer than the hypothetical replacement, and it harmonizes better with the alimony rules of sister states. Nonresident alimony recipients would be treated unfairly under the replacement rule if they were taxable on the receipt of alimony in their state of residence and also paid indirectly some or all of the New York tax imposed on the payer. This implicit double taxation would occur most frequently when the payer was a New

York resident because nonresident payers typically would receive a credit in their state of residence for the New York tax, whereas New York residents obviously would not get a credit.[13]

Lack of Systematic Bias

Under the Court's long-standing constitutional jurisprudence, a tax rule is not suspect under the Privileges and Immunity Clause simply because a nonresident happens to be denied a tax benefit enjoyed by certain other taxpayers. The burden on the taxpayer making a case under that clause is to show that some identifiable class of nonresident individuals is systematically disadvantaged under the challenged rule. Certainly no proof of such systematic bias was offered by the taxpayer in Lunding.

Nor could the taxpayer in the Lunding case make that proof. Because New York's alimony rules implement the goal of income splitting, they should be evaluated for tax policy purposes and for constitutional purposes by reference to the combined tax consequences to the payer of alimony and the recipient. As discussed above, the New York system gets the correct tax policy result when both the payer and the recipient are New York residents and when both individuals are nonresidents. These cases are far and away the most important ones.

The New York system typically gets reasonable results when one of the parties to the alimony transaction is a resident and the other is a nonresident. Those latter results may be less than ideal, but the overly generous and insufficiently generous results sometimes achieved are typically ameliorated by the comparable tax rules of other states. Most importantly from the perspective of the Privileges and Immunities Clause, those results are not biased against any identifiable class of nonresidents. The potential bias is against certain pairs of former spouses, one a resident and the other a nonresident.

Notwithstanding the lack of systematic bias, a question legitimately arises as to whether New York obtains an unfair share of tax revenue from the interplay of its alimony deduction rules with the comparable rules of other states. The answer is clearly no, on the reasonable assumption that the inflows and outflows of alimony payments among the states are approximately in balance.
. . . .

---

13. By giving a credit to resident payers for their New York taxes paid with respect to New York income used to pay alimony, New York would effectively convert the suggested replacement rule into the current New York rule.

Chapter 5

Import-Export Clause

"No State shall. . .lay any Imposts or Duties on Imports or Exports. . ." U.S. Const., art I, §10, cl. 2.

The Articles of Confederation did not provide for Congress to regulate foreign and interstate commerce. Each state had the power to regulate such commerce and often did so in a way that was detrimental to a unified national government. Seaboard states with good harbor facilities levied heavy taxes on goods imported from abroad, thereby undermining the ability of the national government to exploit fully what was contemplated to be one of its principal sources of revenue. The state levies also irritated and disadvantaged the states lacking ports and provoked their retaliation. In addition, state taxation of imports and exports undercut the national government's ability to regulate commercial relations with foreign governments.

To eliminate these weaknesses in the Articles of Confederation and to form a more cohesive union, the Constitution of the new federal government incorporated both the Commerce Clause and the Import-Export Clause. The Import-Export Clause, contained in Article I, Section 10, clause 2, states:

No State shall, without the Consent of the Congress, lay any Imposts or Duties on Imports or Exports, except what may be absolutely necessary for executing its inspection Laws: and the net Produce of all Duties and Imposts, laid by any State on Imports or Exports, shall be for the Use of the Treasury of the United States; and all such Laws shall be subject to the Revision and Controul [sic] of the Congress.

"The Import-Export Clause has long been overshadowed by the Commerce Clause, but their roles were reversed at the Philadelphia Convention, where commercial strife among the states occupied center stage and evoked the passion and eloquence of the delegates, including the Convention's most memorable metaphors–New Jersey, the 'cask tapped at both ends' by New York and Philadelphia; and North Carolina, the 'patient bleeding from both arms' because it was located between Virginia and South Carolina. The remedy for this exploitation of the inland states by the seaboard states was to be the Import-Export Clause." Bittker On The Regulation of Interstate and Foreign Commerce, p. 12-4 (1999).

The following case, *Michelin Tire v. Wages*, provides a useful summary of the political and economic considerations leading to the adoption of the Import-Export Clause. In *Michelin* the Court abandons more than 100 years of precedent and adopts a fundamentally new approach to interpreting that Clause.

A. Taxation of Imports

Michelin Tire Corp. v. Wages, Tax Commissioner, et al.
Supreme Court of the United States, 1976.
423 U.S. 276, 96 S. Ct. 535, 46 L. Ed. 2d 495.

MR. JUSTICE BRENNAN delivered the opinion of the Court.

Respondents, the Tax Commissioner and Tax Assessors of Gwinnett County, Ga., assessed ad valorem property taxes against tires and tubes imported by petitioner from France and Nova Scotia that were included on the assessment dates in an inventory maintained at its wholesale distribution warehouse in the county. Petitioner brought this action for declaratory and injunctive relief in the Superior Court of Gwinnett County, alleging that with the exception of certain passenger tubes that had been removed from the original shipping cartons, the ad valorem property taxes assessed against its inventory of imported tires and tubes were prohibited by Art. I, § 10, cl. 2, of the Constitution, which provides in pertinent part: "No State shall, without the Consent of the Congress, lay any Imposts or Duties on Imports or Exports, except what may be absolutely necessary for executing its inspection Laws. . . ." [T]he only question presented is whether the Georgia Supreme Court was correct in holding that the tires were subject to the ad valorem property tax.[2] We affirm without addressing the question whether the Georgia Supreme Court was correct in holding that the tires had lost their status as imports. We hold that, in any event, Georgia's assessment of a nondiscriminatory ad valorem property tax against the imported tires is not within the constitutional prohibition against laying "any Imposts or Duties on Imports . . ." and that insofar as Low v. Austin, 13 Wall. 29 (1872) is to the contrary, that decision is overruled.

I

Petitioner, a New York corporation qualified to do business in Georgia, operates as an importer and wholesale distributor in the United States of automobile and truck tires and tubes manufactured in France and Nova Scotia by Michelin Tires, Ltd. . . . Some 25% of the tires and tubes are manufactured in and imported from Nova Scotia, and are brought to the United States in tractor-driven, over-the-road trailers packed and sealed at the Nova Scotia factory. The remaining 75% of the imported tires and tubes are brought to the United States by sea from France and Nova Scotia in sea vans packed and sealed at the foreign factories. Sea vans are essentially over-the-road trailers from which the wheels are removed before being loaded aboard ship. Upon arrival of the ship at the United States port of entry, the vans are unloaded, the wheels are replaced, and the vans are tractor-hauled to petitioner's distribution warehouse after clearing customs upon payment of a 4% import duty.

The imported tires, each of which has its own serial number, are packed in bulk into the trailers and vans, without otherwise being packaged or bundled. They lose their identity as a unit, however, when unloaded from the trailers and vans at the distribution warehouse. When unloaded they are sorted by size and style, without segregation by place of manufacture, stacked on wooden pallets each bearing four stacks of five tires of the same size and style, and stored in pallet stacks of three pallets each. This is the only processing required or performed to ready the tires for sale and delivery to the franchised dealers.

_____

2. The respondents did not cross-petition from the affirmance of the holding of the Superior Court that the tubes in the corrugated shipping cartons were immune from the tax, and that holding is therefore not before us for review.

II

. . . .

Low v. Austin is the leading decision of this Court holding that the States are prohibited by the Import-Export Clause from imposing a nondiscriminatory ad valorem property tax on imported goods until they lose their character as imports and become incorporated into the mass of property in the State. The Court there reviewed a decision of the California Supreme Court that had sustained the constitutionality of California's nondiscriminatory ad valorem tax on the ground that the Import-Export Clause only prohibited taxes upon the character of the goods as imports and therefore did not prohibit nondiscriminatory taxes upon the goods as property. This Court reversed on its reading of the seminal opinion construing the Import-Export Clause, Brown v. Maryland, 12 Wheat. 419 (1827), as holding that "[w]hilst retaining their character as imports, a tax upon them, in any shape, is within the constitutional prohibition." 13 Wall., at 34.

Scholarly analysis has been uniformly critical of Low v. Austin. It is true that Mr. Chief Justice Marshall, speaking for the Court in Brown v. Maryland, said that "while [the thing imported remains] the property of the importer, in his warehouse, in the original form or package in which it was imported, a tax upon it is too plainly a duty on imports to escape the prohibition in the constitution." Commentators have uniformly agreed that Low v. Austin misread this dictum in holding that the Court in Brown included nondiscriminatory ad valorem property taxes among prohibited "imposts" or "duties," for the contrary conclusion is plainly to be inferred from consideration of the specific abuses which led the Framers to include the Import-Export Clause in the Constitution.

Our independent study persuades us that a nondiscriminatory ad valorem property tax is not the type of state exaction which the Framers of the Constitution or the Court in Brown had in mind as being an "impost" or "duty" and that Low v. Austin's reliance upon the Brown dictum to reach the contrary conclusion was misplaced.

III

One of the major defects of the Articles of Confederation, and a compelling reason for the calling of the Constitutional Convention of 1787, was the fact that the Articles essentially left the individual States free to burden commerce both among themselves and with foreign countries very much as they pleased. Before 1787 it was commonplace for seaboard States with port facilities to derive revenue to defray the costs of state and local governments by imposing taxes on imported goods destined for customers in other States. At the same time, there was no secure source of revenue for the central government. . . .

. . . .

The Framers of the Constitution thus sought to alleviate three main concerns by committing sole power to lay imposts and duties on imports in the Federal Government, with no concurrent state power: the Federal Government must speak with one voice when regulating commercial relations with foreign governments, and tariffs, which might affect foreign relations, could not be implemented by the States consistently with that exclusive power; import revenues were to be the major source of revenue of the Federal Government and should not be diverted to the States; and harmony among the States might be disturbed unless seaboard States, with their crucial ports of entry, were prohibited from levying taxes on citizens of other States by taxing goods merely flowing through their ports to the other States not situated as favorably geographically.

Nothing in the history of the Import-Export Clause even remotely suggests that a nondiscriminatory ad valorem property tax which is also imposed on imported goods that are no longer in import transit was the type of exaction that was regarded as objectionable by the Framers of the Constitution. For such an exaction, unlike discriminatory state taxation against imported goods as imports, was not regarded as an impediment that severely hampered commerce or constituted a form of tribute by seaboard States to the disadvantage of the other States.

It is obvious that such nondiscriminatory property taxation can have no impact whatsoever on the Federal Government's exclusive regulation of foreign commerce, probably the most important purpose of the Clause's prohibition. By definition, such a tax does not fall on imports as such because of their place of origin. It cannot be used to create special protective tariffs or particular preferences for certain domestic goods, and it cannot be applied selectively to encourage or discourage any importation in a manner inconsistent with federal regulation.

Nor will such taxation deprive the Federal Government of the exclusive right to all revenues from imposts and duties on imports and exports, since that right by definition only extends to revenues from exactions of a particular category; if nondiscriminatory ad valorem taxation is not in that category, it deprives the Federal Government of nothing to which it is entitled. Unlike imposts and duties, which are essentially taxes on the commercial privilege of bringing goods into a country, such property taxes are taxes by which a State apportions the cost of such services as police and fire protection among the beneficiaries according to their respective wealth; there is no reason why an importer should not bear his share of these costs along with his competitors handling only domestic goods. The Import-Export Clause clearly prohibits state taxation based on the foreign origin of the imported goods, but it cannot be read to accord imported goods preferential treatment that permits escape from uniform taxes imposed without regard to foreign origin for services which the State supplies. . . . [Nondiscriminatory property taxes] cannot be selectively imposed and increased so as substantially to impair or prohibit importation.

Finally, nondiscriminatory ad valorem property taxes do not interfere with the free flow of imported goods among the States, as did the exactions by States under the Articles of Confederation directed solely at imported goods. Indeed, importers of goods destined for inland States can easily avoid even those taxes in today's world. Modern transportation methods such as air freight and containerized packaging, and the development of railroads and the Nation's internal waterways, enable importation directly into the inland States. Petitioner, for example, operates other distribution centers from wholesale warehouses in inland States. Actually, a quarter of the tires distributed from petitioner's Georgia warehouse are imported interstate directly from Canada. To be sure, allowance of nondiscriminatory ad valorem property taxation may increase the cost of goods purchased by "inland" consumers.[8] But as already noted, such taxation is the quid pro quo for benefits actually conferred by the taxing State. There is no reason why local taxpayers should subsidize the services used by the importer; ultimate consumers should pay for such services as police and fire protection accorded the goods just as much as they should pay transportation

---

8. Of course, depending on the relevant competition from domestic goods, an importer may be forced to absorb some of these ad valorem property assessments rather than passing them on to consumers.

costs associated with those goods. An evil to be prevented by the Import-Export Clause was the levying of taxes which could only be imposed because of the peculiar geographical situation of certain States that enabled them to single out goods destined for other States. In effect, the Clause was fashioned to prevent the imposition of exactions which were no more than transit fees on the privilege of moving through a State. A nondiscriminatory ad valorem property tax obviously stands on a different footing, and to the extent there is any conflict whatsoever with this purpose of the Clause, it may be secured merely by prohibiting the assessment of even nondiscriminatory property taxes on goods which are merely in transit through the State when the tax is assessed.

Admittedly, the wording of the prohibition of the Import-Export Clause does not in terms except nondiscriminatory taxes with some impact on imports or exports. But just as clearly, the Clause is not written in terms of a broad prohibition of every "tax." The prohibition is only against States laying "Imposts or Duties" on "Imports." By contrast, Congress is empowered to "lay and collect Taxes, Duties, Imposts, and Excises," which plainly lends support to a reading of the Import-Export Clause as not prohibiting every exaction or "tax" which falls in some measure on imported goods. Indeed, Professor Crosskey makes a persuasive demonstration that the words "imposts" and "duties" as used in 1787 had meanings well understood to be exactions upon imported goods as imports. "Imposts" were like customs duties, that is, charges levied on imports at the time and place of importation. "Duties" was a broader term embracing excises as well as customs duties, and probably only capitation, land, and general property exactions were known by the term "tax" rather than the term "duty." 1 W. Crosskey, Politics and the Constitution in the History of the United States 296-297 (1953). The characteristic common to both "imposts" and "duties" was that they were exactions directed at imports or commercial activity as such and, as imposed by the seaboard States under the Articles of Confederation, were purposefully employed to regulate interstate and foreign commerce and tax States situated less favorably geographically.

In any event, since prohibition of nondiscriminatory ad valorem property taxation would not further the objectives of the Import-Export Clause, only the clearest constitutional mandate should lead us to condemn such taxation. The terminology employed in the Clause– "Imposts or Duties"–is sufficiently ambiguous that we decline to presume it was intended to embrace taxation that does not create the evils the Clause was specifically intended to eliminate.

IV

The Court in Low v. Austin nevertheless expanded the prohibition of the Clause to include nondiscriminatory ad valorem property taxes, and did so with no analysis, but with only the statement that Brown v. Maryland had marked the line "where the power of Congress over the goods imported ends, and that of the State begins, with as much precision as the subject admits." 13 Wall., at 32. But the opinion in Brown v. Maryland cannot properly be read to propose such a broad definition of "imposts" or "duties."

. . . .

The Court [in Brown v. Maryland]* stated that there were two situations in which the prohibition would not apply. One was the case of a state tax levied after the imported goods had lost their status as imports. The Court devised an evidentiary tool, the "original package" test, for use in making that determination. The formula was: "It is sufficient for the present to say, generally, that when the importer has so acted upon the thing imported, that it has become incorporated and mixed up with the mass of property in the country, it has, perhaps, lost its distinctive character as an import, and has become subject to the taxing power of the State; but while remaining the property of the importer, in his warehouse, in the original form or package in which it was imported, a tax upon it is too plainly a duty on imports to escape the prohibition in the constitution." Id., at 441-442. "It is a matter of hornbook knowledge that the original package statement of Justice Marshall was an illustration, rather than a formula, and that its application is evidentiary, and not substantive. . . ." Galveston v. Mexican Petroleum Corp., 15 F.2d 208 (SD Tex. 1926).

The other was the situation of particular significance to our decision of this case, that is, when the particular state exaction is not a prohibited "impost" or "duty.". . . The Court illustrated the kinds of state exactions that in its view fell without the prohibition as examples of neutral and nondiscriminatory taxation: a tax on itinerant peddlers, a service charge

---

*. [Ed. *Brown* involved a Maryland fee that importers had to pay for a license before they could sell in that State; the license applied to those selling imports by bale or package.]

for the use of a public auctioneer, a property tax on plate or furniture personally used by the importer. These could not be considered within the constitutional prohibition because they were imposed without regard to the origin of the goods taxed. In contrast, the Maryland exaction in question was a license fee which singled out imports, and therefore was prohibited because "the tax intercepts the import, *as an import*, in its way to become incorporated with the general mass of property."

Thus, it is clear that the Court's view in Brown was that merely because certain actions taken by the importer on his imported goods would so mingle them with the common property within the State as to "lose their distinctive character as imports" and render them subject to the taxing power of the State, did not mean that in the absence of such action, no exaction could be imposed on the goods. Rather, the Court clearly implied that the prohibition would not apply to a state tax that treated imported goods in their original packages no differently from the "common mass of property in the country"; that is, treated it in a manner that did not depend on the foreign origins of the goods.

. . . .

It follows from the foregoing that Low v. Austin was wrongly decided. That decision therefore must be, and is, overruled.

V

Petitioner's tires in this case were no longer in transit. They were stored in a distribution warehouse from which petitioner conducted a wholesale operation, taking orders from franchised dealers and filling them from a constantly replenished inventory. The warehouse was operated no differently than would be a distribution warehouse utilized by a wholesaler dealing solely in domestic goods, and we therefore hold that the nondiscriminatory property tax levied on petitioner's inventory of imported tires was not interdicted by the Import-Export Clause of the Constitution. The judgment of the Supreme Court of Georgia is accordingly

Affirmed.

MR. JUSTICE STEVENS took no part in the consideration or decision of this case.

MR. JUSTICE WHITE, concurring in the judgment.

Being of the view that the goods involved here had lost their character as imports and that subjecting them to ad valorem taxation was consistent with the Constitution as interpreted by prior cases, including Low v. Austin, 13 Wall. 29 (1872), I would affirm the judgment. There is little reason and no necessity at this time to overrule Low v. Austin. None of the parties has challenged that case here, and the issue of its overruling has not been briefed or argued.

Questions and Comments

1. Justice Brennan's opinion has been described as "exud[ing] the spirit of constitutional originalism. Ten years later Justice Brennan was to assert that doctrinaire reliance on the intent of the framers 'is little more than arrogance cloaked in humility.' William J. Brennan, *The Constitution of the United States: Contemporary Ratification*, 27 S. Tax. L.J. 433, 435 (1986)." Bittker On The Regulation of Interstate and Foreign Commerce, p. 12-12 n.41 (1999).

2. No doubt the original package doctrine encouraged taxpayers to retain their imports in their original packaging, even if that were not required for business reasons. In *Low v. Austin*, referred to in *Michelin*, an importer of French champagne successfully avoided a nondiscriminatory ad valorem property tax because he had not yet taken the champagne out of their original cases, even though the champagne was being

held for sale in competition with domestically produced goods. The effect of *Low* was to discriminate against domestically produced goods, which were subject to a tax that could not be applied to imported goods. In this sense, the interpretation of the Import-Export Clause had the same effect as cases holding that interstate commerce was immune from taxation: a lack of neutrality or level playing field among competitors.

3. Predictably, the definition of "original package" became the focus of much litigation with unsatisfying results. See, for example, *May v. New Orleans*, 178 U.S. 496 (1900) (European goods packed in separate parcels or bundles but offered for sale in opened shipping boxes were taxable under an ad valorem property tax); *Anglo-Chilean Nitrate Sales Corp. v. Alabama*, 288 U.S. 218 (1933) (100 pound bags of

Chilean nitrates stored in a warehouse in their original packages until sold were immune from state taxation); *Hooven & Allison Co. v. Evatt*, 324 U.S. 652 (1945) (bales of Philippine hemp stored in a warehouse awaiting use in manufacturing were immune from state taxation), *reh'g denied*, 325 U.S. 892 (1945), *overruled* by *Limbach v. Hooven & Allison Co.*, 466 U.S. 358 (1984); *Youngstown Sheet & Tube Co. v. Bowers*, 358 U.S. 534 (1959) (piles of foreign ore and plywood awaiting use in manufacturing were taxable under an ad valorem property tax). As the original package doctrine stood prior to *Michelin*, it was sometimes easier for a taxpayer to invoke successfully Import-Export Clause immunity for goods purchased from abroad that were held for resale than for goods purchased from abroad that were used by the taxpayer in manufacturing. See Early & Weitzman, *A Century of Dissent: The Immunity of Goods Imported for Resale from Nondiscriminatory State Personal Property Taxes*, 7 Sw. U. L. Rev. 247, 265 (1975); Dakin, *The Protective Cloak of the Export-Import Clause: Immunity for the Goods or for the Process*, 19 La. L. Rev. 747 (1959).

4. Are there similarities between the Court's analysis in this case and its analysis in *Swaggert*? *Minneapolis Star*? Is this opinion philosophically akin to *Complete Auto*?

5. Prior to this case, would it be fair to say that all taxes levied on imports were considered to be imposts? After this case, is every exaction that constitutes an impost or a duty unconstitutional?

6. How did the Court resolve the issue of whether the taxed goods were still in their original package? What role does the original package doctrine play after *Michelin*?

7. Does the original package doctrine have its origins in Chief Justice Marshall's opinion in *McCulloch*?

8. What is the definition of an "impost" or "duty"? How would the Court have proceeded if it had held that the Georgia property tax were an impost or duty?

9. Was the Court acting properly in overruling *Low v. Austin*? In "The Unpublished Decisions of the Burger Court," Professor Schwartz explains that the *Michelin* Court's decision to reexamine *Low* sua sponte was in response to one of Justice Brennan's earlier drafts of the Court's opinion, which questioned *Low* but did not reexamine it. Id. at 342.

10. When does an import cease to be in transit?

11. Should Congress' power to regulate the scope of state taxation under the Import-Export Clause affect the way a court interprets that Clause? In close cases, should a court err in favor of a state tax, leaving it to Congress to intervene if it disagrees with the result?

12. Can a state levy a fairly apportioned, nondiscriminatory property tax on goods in transit, including goods from other states and goods from abroad?

13. Suppose the same tires subject to the property tax upheld in *Michelin* were shipped to State X, where they were subject to that State's property tax. Would the imposition of State X's property tax be constitutional if the same tires were previously subject to Georgia's property tax?

14. What is the relationship between the protections offered by the Import-Export Clause and those offered by the Commerce Clause?

15. Can a state favor imports over domestic goods? Why might it want to do so?

16. Is the Import-Export Clause anachronistic? Suppose a court thought that the Import-Export Clause is less important today because of modern transportation alternatives. Should that influence the way a court interprets the Clause?

17. As indicated in *Michelin*, the first case interpreting the Import-Export Clause was *Brown v. Maryland*. In dictum, Chief Justice Marshall suggested that the Clause applied to state taxes on goods imported from other states and was not limited to taxes on imports from abroad, 25 U.S. at 449 ("we suppose the principles laid down in this case, to apply equally to importations from a sister state"). Chief Justice Taney accepted this construction in *Almy v. California*, 65 U.S. 169 (1861). This interpretation, however, was rejected in *Woodruff v. Parham*, 75 U.S. (8 Wall.) 123 (1868). The Clause does not apply to goods shipped to other states. *Coe v. Errol*, 116 U.S. 517 (1886). Professor Crosskey, upon whom the Court relied for the historical meaning of duties and imposts, believed that contrary to the Court's holding in *Woodruff*, the Import-Export Clause applied to goods imported from other states. 1 Crosskey, *Politics and the Constitution in the History of the United States*, 296-304 (1953). "[I]t would be fantastic to suggest that the Americans of the time could have read the [Import-Export] Clause as applying to 'foreign imports' and 'foreign exports' only." Id at 304. Compare Justice Thomas' dissent in *Camps Newfound/Owatonna* in the Commerce Clause

chapter.

18. *Michelin* has been applied in *R.J. Reynolds Tobacco Co. v. Durham County*, 479 U.S. 130 (1986) (imported tobacco stored in customs warehouse pending domestic use is subject to state ad valorem tax); *Los Angeles v. Marine Wholesale Co.*, 15 Cal. App. 4th 1834 (1993) (goods stored in federally-regulated customs bonded warehouses are subject to city's nondiscriminatory tax on gross receipts and payroll); *Blue Star Line v. San Francisco*, 77 Cal. App. 3d 429 (1978) (steamship lines and stevedore firms engaged in foreign maritime commerce are subject to San Francisco payroll tax).

19. For critical commentary on *Michelin Tire*, see Leonard A. Carlson, *Michelin Tire Corp v. Wages: Impact on State and Local Ad Valorem Taxation*, 6 Cap. U. L. Rev. 651 (1977); Frank M. Keesling, *Michelin Tire Corp v. Wages: The Demise of the Original Package Doctrine*, 50 S. Cal. L. Rev. 719 (1977); Walter Hellerstein, *Michelin Tire Corp v. Wages: Enhanced State Power to Tax Imports*, 1976 Sup. Ct. Rev. 99; Mary O'Boyle II, *Original Package Doctrine - Assessment of a Nondiscriminatory Ad Valorem Property Tax*, 11 Tex. Int'l L.J. 369 (1976); Jeanne A. Carpenter, *States' Power to Assess Nondiscriminatory Ad Valorem Property Taxes on Imported Goods: Michelin Tire Corp. v. Wages*, 8 Law & Pol'y Int'l Bus. 243 (1976); James H. Peters, *Supreme Court Sets New Test for Local Taxation of Imports in Michelin Tire*, 44 J. Tax'n 244 (1976); Graham G. Clark, *Constitutional Law - Ad Valorem Taxation as an "Impost or Duty" Under the Import Clause: Michelin Tire Corp. v. Wages*, 12 Wake Forest L. Rev. 1055 (1976); C. Grigsby Scifres, *Michelin Tire Corp. v. Wages: A Limitation Upon the Traditional Tax-Exempt Status of Imports*, 1976 Det. C.L. Rev. 359.

B. Taxation of Exports

The original package doctrine was never applied in the context of exports. Presumably the explanation is that goods destined for use within the state of manufacture, use within other states, or use abroad might well be packed in identical containers. All these goods would be part of the general mass of property in the state so that the original package doctrine would not be helpful in identifying the goods to be exported.

Instead, the test for exports was whether the good had sufficiently entered the stream of commerce for transportation abroad. *See Coe v. Errol*, 116 U.S. 517 (1886) (upholding under the Commerce Clause an ad valorem property tax levied on logs stored in New Hampshire for eventual processing and sale in Maine; the mere intent to export without any physical movement of the goods does not trigger any constitutional protection); *A.G. Spalding & Bros. v. Edwards*, 262 U.S. 66 (1923) (striking down a N.Y. sales tax imposed on the sale of baseballs and bats to a Venezuelan company with a N.Y. purchasing agent; delivery of the goods to the ship constituted a significant step in the exportation process and thus invoked the Import-Export Clause); *Richfield Oil Corp. v. State Board of Equalization*, 329 U.S. 69 (1946) (invalidating a sales tax on sale of oil f.o.b. Los Angeles to a New Zealand navy vessel; because the ship was going abroad, delivery of the oil from the vendor's tanks at the dock into the hold marked the commencement of the movement of the oil abroad, and it was clear that the oil was headed to sea); *Empresa Siderurgica, S.A. v. County of Merced*, 337 U.S. 154 (1949) (sustaining an ad valorem property tax on the remaining portion of a cement factory prepared for shipment to South America; despite the virtual certainty of the factory being exported, the Court held it had not entered into the export stream); *Kosydar v. National Cash Register Co.*, 417 U.S. 62 (1974) (sustaining an ad valorem property tax on cash registers notwithstanding that they were custom designed for foreign purchasers and unsuitable for sale in the United States).

The Court's approach in the export area has been criticized as "overly wooden or mechanistic," *id.* at 71, but has been defended as "an instance, however, where we believe that simplicity has its virtues." *Id.* The rule these cases seem to set forth is that immunity extends only to goods that have already entered the export stream, the final and continuous journey out of the country; immunity applies only once the journey abroad has actually begun. For cases dealing with the interruption of an interstate journey, see *Coe v. Errol*, supra, *Independent Warehouses, Inc. v. Scheele*, 331 U.S. 70 (1947); *Carson Petroleum Co v. Vial*, 279 U.S. 95 (1929); *Champlain Realty Co. v. Town of Brattleboro*, 260 U.S. 366 (1922); and *Bacon v. Illinois*, 227 U.S. 504 (1913). See Leslie W. Abramson, *State Taxation of Exports: The Stream of Constitutionality*, 54 N.C. L. Rev. 59 (1975).

The Court's approach to determining whether exportation has begun is similar to determining whether goods are in interstate commerce for purposes of the Commerce Clause. At one time, determining whether goods were in interstate commerce was highly significant, but after *Complete Auto*, the older cases discussing when interstate commerce begins and ends, and what constitutes interstate commerce have little significance for

Commerce Clause purposes. See the discussion after *Commonwealth Edison* in the Commerce Clause chapter.

How do *Complete Auto, Michelin,* and the following opinion affect the preceding cases?

Department of Revenue of Washington
v. Association of Washington Stevedoring Companies et al.
Supreme Court of the United States, 1978.
435 U.S. 734, 98 S. Ct. 1388, 55 L. Ed. 2d 682.

Mr. JUSTICE BLACKMUN delivered the opinion of the Court.

For the second time in this century, the State of Washington would apply its business and occupation tax[*] to stevedoring. The State's first application of the tax to stevedoring was unsuccessful, for it was held to be unconstitutional as violative of the Commerce Clause of the United States Constitution. Puget Sound Stevedoring Co. v. State Tax Comm'n, 302 U.S. 90 (1937). The Court now faces the question whether Washington's second attempt violates either the Commerce Clause or the Import-Export Clause.[2]

I

Stevedoring is the business of loading and unloading cargo from ships.[3] Private stevedoring companies

constitute respondent Association of Washington Stevedoring Companies; respondent Washington Public Ports Association is a nonprofit corporation consisting of port authorities that engage in stevedoring activities. . .

. . . .

Consistent with Complete Auto [430 U.S. 274 (1977)], then, we hold that the Washington business and occupation tax does not violate the Commerce Clause by taxing the interstate commerce activity of stevedoring. To the extent that Puget Sound Stevedoring Co. v. State Tax Comm'n and Joseph v. Carter & Weekes Stevedoring Co. stand to the contrary, each is overruled.

. . . .

III
The Import-Export Clause

Having decided that the Commerce Clause does not per se invalidate the application of the Washington tax to stevedoring, we must face the question whether the tax contravenes the Import-Export Clause. Although the parties dispute the meaning of the prohibition of "Imposts or Duties on Imports or Exports," they agree that it differs from the ban the Commerce Clause erects against burdens and taxation on interstate commerce. The Court has noted before that the Import-Export Clause states an absolute ban, whereas the Commerce Clause merely grants power to Congress. On the other hand, the Commerce Clause touches all state taxation and regulation of interstate and foreign commerce, whereas the Import-Export Clause bans only "Imposts or Duties on Imports or Exports." Michelin Tire Corp. v. Wages, 423 U.S. 276, 279, 290-294 (1976). The resolution of the Commerce Clause issue, therefore, does not dispose of the

---

[*]. [Ed. The tax is measured by gross receipts. The tax is identical to the one at issue in *Tyler Pipe*, infra Chapter Nine.]

2. "No State shall, without the Consent of the Congress, lay any Imposts or Duties on Imports or Exports, except what may be absolutely necessary for executing its inspection Laws: and the net Produce of all Duties and Imposts, laid by any State on Imports or Exports, shall be for the Use of the Treasury of the United States; and all such Laws shall be subject to the Revision and Controul of the Congress." U.S. Const., Art. I, § 10, cl. 2.

3. . . . This Court explained the activities of the appellant stevedoring company in Puget Sound as follows: "What was done by this appellant in the business of loading and unloading was not prolonged beyond the stage of transportation and its reasonable incidents. . . . True, the service did not begin or end at the ship's side, where the cargo is placed upon a sling attached to the ship's tackle. It took in the work of carriage to and from the 'first place of rest,' which means that it covered the space between the hold of the vessel and a convenient point of discharge upon the dock. . . . The fact is stipulated, however, that no matter by whom the work is done or paid for, 'stevedoring services are essential to waterborne commerce and always commence in the hold of the vessel and end at the "first

place of rest," and vice versa.'" 302 U.S. at 93.

Import-Export Clause question.

A

In Michelin the Court upheld the application of a general ad valorem property tax to imported tires and tubes. The Court surveyed the history and purposes of the Import-Export Clause to determine, for the first time, which taxes fell within the absolute ban on "Imposts or Duties." Previous cases had assumed that all taxes on imports and exports and on the importing and exporting processes were banned by the Clause. Before Michelin, the primary consideration was whether the tax under review reached imports or exports. With respect to imports, the analysis applied the original package doctrine . . . . So long as the goods retained their status as imports by remaining in their import packages, they enjoyed immunity from state taxation. With respect to exports, the dispositive question was whether the goods had entered the "export stream," the final, continuous journey out of the country. Kosydar v. National Cash Register Co., 417 U.S. 62, 70-71 (1974); Empresa Siderurgica v. County of Merced, 337 U.S. 154, 157 (1949); A. G. Spalding & Bros. v. Edwards, 262 U.S. 66, 69 (1923); Coe v. Errol, 116 U.S. 517, 526, 527 (1886). As soon as the journey began, tax immunity attached.

Michelin initiated a different approach to Import-Export Clause cases. It ignored the simple question whether the tires and tubes were imports. Instead, it analyzed the nature of the tax to determine whether it was an "Impost or Duty." Specifically, the analysis examined whether the exaction offended any of the three policy considerations leading to the presence of the Clause. . . .

. . . .

A similar approach demonstrates that the application of the Washington business and occupation tax to stevedoring threatens no Import-Export Clause policy. First, the tax does not restrain the ability of the Federal Government to conduct foreign policy. As a general business tax that applies to virtually all businesses in the State, it has not created any special protective tariff. The assessments in this case are only upon business conducted entirely within Washington. No foreign business or vessel is taxed. Respondents, therefore, have demonstrated no impediment posed by the tax upon the regulation of foreign trade by the United States.

Second, the effect of the Washington tax on federal import revenues is identical to the effect in Michelin.

The tax merely compensates the State for services and protection extended by Washington to the stevedoring business. Any indirect effect on the demand for imported goods because of the tax on the value of loading and unloading them from their ships is even less substantial than the effect of the direct ad valorem property tax on the imported goods themselves.

Third, the desire to prevent interstate rivalry and friction does not vary significantly from the primary purpose of the Commerce Clause. The third Import-Export Clause policy, therefore, is vindicated if the tax falls upon a taxpayer with reasonable nexus to the State, is properly apportioned, does not discriminate, and relates reasonably to services provided by the State. . . .

Under the analysis of Michelin, then, the application of the Washington business and occupation tax to stevedoring violates no Import-Export Clause policy and therefore should not qualify as an "Impost or Duty" subject to the absolute ban of the Clause.

B

The Court in Michelin qualified its holding with the observation that Georgia had applied the property tax to goods "no longer in transit." 423 U.S. at 302. Because the goods were no longer in transit, however, the Court did not have to face the question whether a tax relating to goods in transit would be an "Impost or Duty" even if it offended none of the policies behind the Clause. Inasmuch as we now face this inquiry, we note two distinctions between this case and Michelin. First, the activity taxed here occurs while imports and exports are in transit. Second, however, the tax does not fall on the goods themselves. The levy reaches only the business of loading and unloading ships or, in other words, the business of transporting cargo within the State of Washington. Despite the existence of the first distinction, the presence of the second leads to the conclusion that the Washington tax is not a prohibited "Impost or Duty" when it violates none of the policies.

In Canton R. Co. v. Rogan, 340 U.S. 511 (1951), the Court upheld a gross-receipts tax on a steam railroad operating exclusively within the Port of Baltimore. The railroad operated a marine terminal and owned rail lines connecting the docks to the trunk lines of major railroads. It switched and pulled cars, stored imports and exports pending transport, supplied wharfage, weighed imports and exports, and rented a stevedoring crane. Somewhat less than half of the company's 1946 gross receipts were derived from the transport of imports or exports. The company contended that this income was immune, under the Import-Export Clause, from the state tax. The Court rejected that argument primarily on the ground that immunity of services incidental to importing and exporting was not so broad as the immunity of the goods themselves:[21]

The difference is that in the present case the tax is not on the *goods* but on the *handling* of them at the port. An article may be an export and immune from a tax long before or long after it reaches the port. But when the tax is on activities connected with the export or import the range of immunity cannot be so wide.

. . . . The broader definition which appellant tenders distorts the ordinary meaning of the terms. It would lead back to every forest, mine, and factory in the land and create a zone of tax immunity never before imagined. Id., at 514-515 (emphasis in original).

In Canton R. Co. the Court did not have to reach the question about taxation of stevedoring because the company did not load or unload ships. As implied in the opinion, however, id., at 515, the only distinction between stevedoring and the railroad services was that the loading and unloading of ships crossed the waterline. This is a distinction without economic significance in the present context. The transportation services in both settings are necessary to the import-export process. Taxation in neither setting relates to the value of the goods, and therefore in neither can it be considered taxation upon the goods themselves. The force of Canton R. Co. therefore prompts the conclusion that the Michelin policy analysis should not be discarded

merely because the goods are in transit, at least where the taxation falls upon a service distinct from the goods and their value.[23]

C

Another factual distinction between this case and Michelin is that here the stevedores load and unload imports and exports whereas in Michelin the Georgia tax touched only imports. As noted in Part III-A, supra, the analysis in the export cases has differed from that in the import cases. In the former, the question was when did the export enter the export stream; in the latter, the question was when did the goods escape their original package. The questions differed, for example, because an export could enter its export package and not secure tax immunity until later when it began its journey out of the country. Until Michelin, an import retained its immunity so long as it remained in its original package.

Despite these formal differences, the Michelin approach should apply to taxation involving exports as well as imports. The prohibition on the taxation of exports is contained in the same Clause as that regarding imports. The export-tax ban vindicates two of the three policies identified in Michelin. It precludes state disruption of the United States foreign policy. It does not serve to protect federal revenues, however, because the Constitution forbids federal taxation of exports. U.S. Const., Art. I, § 9, cl. 5;[25] see United States v. Hvoslef, 237 U.S. 1 (1915). But it does avoid friction and trade barriers among the States. As a result, any tax relating to exports can be tested for its conformance with the first and third policies. If the constitutional interests are not disturbed, the tax should not be considered an "Impost or Duty" any more than should a tax related to imports. This approach is consistent with Canton R. Co., which permitted taxation of income from services connected to both imports and exports. The respondents' gross receipts from loading exports, therefore, are as

---

21. The Court distinguished the Maryland tax from others struck down by the Court. 340 U.S. 513-514, distinguishing Richfield Oil Corp. v. State Board, 329 U.S. 69 (1946); Thames & Mersey Ins. Co. v. United States, 237 U.S. 19 (1915); and Fairbank v. United States, 181 U.S. 283 (1901). In these cases the State had taxed either the goods or activity so connected with the goods that the levy amounted to a tax on the goods themselves. In Richfield, the tax fell upon the sale of goods and was overturned because the Court had always considered a tax on the sale of goods to be a tax on the goods themselves. See Brown v. Maryland, 12 Wheat. 419, 439 (1827). The sale had no value or significance apart from the goods. Similarly, the stamp tax on bills of lading in Fairbank effectively taxed the goods because the bills represented the goods. The basis for distinguishing Thames & Mersey is less clear because there the tax fell upon marine insurance policies. Arguably, the policies had a value apart from the value of the goods. In distinguishing that case from the taxation of stevedoring activities, however, one might note that the value of goods bears a much closer relation to the value of insurance policies on them than to the value of loading and unloading ships.

23. We do not reach the question of the applicability of the Michelin approach when a State directly taxes imports or exports in transit.

Our Brother Powell, as his concurring opinion indicates, obviously would prefer to reach the issue today, even though the facts of the present case, as he agrees, do not present a case of a tax on goods in transit. As in Michelin, decided less than three years ago, we prefer to defer decision until a case with pertinent facts is presented. At that time, with full argument, the issue with all its ramifications may be decided.

25. "No Tax or Duty shall be laid on Articles exported from any State."

subject to the Washington business and occupation tax as are the receipts from unloading imports.

D

None of respondents' additional arguments convinces us that the Michelin approach should not be applied in this case to sustain the tax.

First, respondents contend that the Import-Export Clause effects an absolute prohibition on all taxation of imports and exports. The ban must be absolute, they argue, in order to give the Clause meaning apart from the Commerce Clause. They support this contention primarily with dicta from Richfield Oil, 329 U.S. at 75-78, and with the partial dissent in Carter & Weekes. Neither, however, provides persuasive support because neither recognized that the term "Impost or Duty" is not self-defining and does not necessarily encompass all taxes. The partial dissent in Carter & Weekes did not address the term at all. Richfield Oil's discussion was limited to the question whether the tax fell upon the sale or upon the right to retail. The State apparently conceded that the Clause precluded all taxes on exports and the process of exporting. The use of these two cases, therefore, ignores the central holding of Michelin that the absolute ban is only of "Imposts or Duties" and not of all taxes. Further, an absolute ban of all taxes is not necessary to distinguish the Import-Export Clause from the Commerce Clause. Under the Michelin approach, any tax offending either of the first two Import-Export policies becomes suspect regardless of whether it creates interstate friction. Commerce Clause analysis, on the other hand, responds to neither of the first two policies. Finally, to conclude that "Imposts or Duties" encompasses all taxes makes superfluous several of the terms of Art. I, § 8, cl. 1, of the Constitution, which grants Congress the "Power To lay and collect Taxes, Duties, Imposts and Excises." In particular, the Framers apparently did not include "Excises," such as an exaction on the privilege of doing business, within the scope of "Imposts" or "Duties." See Michelin, 423 U.S. at 291-292, n. 12, citing 2 M. Farrand, The Records of the Federal Convention of 1787, p. 305 (1911), and 3 id., at 203-204.[26]

---

26. But see 1 W. Crosskey, Politics and the Constitution in the History of the United States 296-297 (1953), cited in 423 U.S. at 290-291, in which the author argues that the concept of "Duties" encompassed excises. He does not explain, however, why Art. I, § 8, cl. 1, enumerated "Taxes, Duties, Imposts and Excises" if the Framers intended duties to include excises.

Second, respondents would distinguish Michelin on the ground that Georgia levied a property tax on the mass of goods in the State, whereas Washington would tax the imports themselves while they remain a part of commerce. This distinction is supported only by citation to the License Cases, 5 How., at 576 (opinion of Taney, C.J.). The argument must be rejected, however, because it resurrects the original-package analysis. Rather than examining whether the taxes are "Imposts or Duties" that offend constitutional policies, the contention would have the Court explore when goods lose their status as imports and exports. This is precisely the inquiry the Court abandoned in Michelin. Nothing in the License Cases, in which a fractioned Court produced nine opinions, prompts a return to the exclusive consideration of what constitutes an import or export.

Third, respondents submit that the Washington tax imposes a transit fee upon inland consumers. Regardless of the validity of such a toll under the Commerce Clause, respondents conclude that it violates the Import-Export Clause. The problem with that analysis is that it does not explain how the policy of preserving harmonious commerce among the States and of preventing interstate tariffs, rivalries, and friction, differs as between the two Clauses. After years of development of Commerce Clause jurisprudence, the Court has concluded that interstate friction will not chafe when commerce pays for the governmental services it enjoys. Requiring coastal States to subsidize the commerce of inland consumers may well exacerbate, rather than diminish, rivalries and hostility. Fair taxation will be assured by the prohibition on discrimination and the requirements of apportionment, nexus, and reasonable relationship between tax and benefits. To the extent that the Import-Export Clause was intended to preserve interstate harmony, the four safeguards will vindicate the policy. To the extent that other policies are protected by the Import-Export Clause, the analysis of an Art. I, § 10, challenge must extend beyond that required by a Commerce Clause dispute. But distinctions not based on differences in constitutional policy are not required. Because respondents identify no such variation in policy, their transit-fee argument must be rejected.

E

The Washington business and occupation tax, as applied to stevedoring, reaches services provided wholly within the State of Washington to imports, exports, and other goods. The application violates none of the constitutional policies identified in Michelin. It is, therefore, not among the "Imposts or Duties" within the prohibition of the Import-Export Clause.

. . . .

MR. JUSTICE POWELL, concurring in part and concurring in the result.

I join the opinion of the Court with the exception of Part III-B. As that section of the Court's opinion appears to resurrect the discarded "direct-indirect" test, I cannot join it.

In Michelin Tire Corp. this Court abandoned the traditional, formalistic methods of determining the validity of state levies under the Import-Export Clause and applied a functional analysis based on the exaction's relationship to the three policies that underlie the Clause: (i) preservation of uniform federal regulation of foreign relations; (ii) protection of federal revenue derived from imports; and (iii) maintenance of harmony among the inland States and the seaboard States. The nondiscriminatory ad valorem property tax in Michelin was held not to violate any of those policies, but the Court suggested that even a nondiscriminatory tax on goods merely in transit through the State might run afoul of the Import-Export Clause.

The question the Court addresses today in Part III-B is whether the business tax at issue here is such a tax upon goods in transit. The Court gives a negative answer, apparently for two reasons. The first is that Canton R. Co. v. Rogan, 340 U.S. 511 (1951), indicates that this is a tax "not on the *goods* but on the *handling* of them at the port." Id., at 514 (emphasis in original). While Canton R. Co. provides precedential support for the proposition that a tax of this kind is not invalid under the Import-Export Clause, its rather artificial distinction between taxes on the handling of the goods and taxes on the goods themselves harks back to the arid "direct-indirect" distinction that we rejected in Complete Auto Transit, Inc. v. Brady, 430 U.S. 274 (1977), in favor of analysis framed in light of economic reality.

The Court's second reason for holding that the instant tax is not one on goods in transit has the surface appearance of economic-reality analysis, but turns out to be the "direct-indirect" test in another guise. The Court likens this tax to the one at issue in Canton R. Co. and declares that since "[t]axation in neither setting relates to the value of the goods, . . . in neither can it be considered taxation upon the goods

themselves." That this distinction has no economic significance is apparent from the fact that it is possible to design transit fees that are imposed "directly" upon the goods, even though the amount of the exaction bears no relation to the value of the goods. For example, a State could levy a transit fee of $5 per ton or $10 per cubic yard. These taxes would bear no more relation to the value of the goods than does the tax at issue here, which is based on the volume of the stevedoring companies' business, and, in turn, on the volume of goods passing through the port. Thus, the Court does not explain satisfactorily its pronouncement that Washington's business tax upon stevedoring–in economic terms–is not the type of transit fee that the Michelin Court questioned.

In my view, this issue can be resolved only with reference to the analysis adopted in Michelin. The Court's initial mention of the validity of transit fees in that decision is found in a discussion concerning the right of the taxing state to seek a quid pro quo for benefits conferred by the State:

> There is no reason why local taxpayers should subsidize the services used by the importer; ultimate consumers should pay for such services as police and fire protection accorded the goods just as much as they should pay transportation costs associated with those goods. An evil to be prevented by the Import-Export Clause was the levying of taxes which could only be imposed because of the peculiar geographical situation of certain States that enabled them to single out goods destined for other States. In effect, the Clause was fashioned to prevent the imposition of exactions which were no more than transit fees on the privilege of moving through a State. [The tax at issue] obviously stands on a different footing, and to the extent there is any conflict whatsoever with this purpose of the Clause, it may be secured merely by prohibiting the assessment of even nondiscriminatory property taxes on goods which are merely in transit through the State when the tax is assessed. 423 U.S. at 289-290. (Footnotes omitted.)

In questioning the validity of "transit fees," the Michelin Court was concerned with exactions that bore no relation to services and benefits conferred by the State. Thus, the transit fee inquiry cannot be answered by determining whether or not the tax relates to the value of the goods; instead, it must be answered by inquiring whether the State is simply making the imported goods pay their own way, as opposed to exacting a fee merely for "the privilege of moving through a State." Ibid.

The Court already has answered that question in this case. In Part II-C, the Court observes that "nothing in the record suggests that the tax is not fairly related to services and protection provided by the State." Since the stevedoring companies undoubtedly avail themselves of police and fire protection, as well as other benefits Washington offers its local businesses, this statement cannot be questioned. For that reason, I agree with the Court's conclusion that the business

tax at issue here is not a "transit fee" within the prohibition of the Import-Export Clause.

Questions and Comments

1. In what way is this case similar to *Goldberg v. Sweet*?

2. How did the Court resolve the issue of whether the Washington tax was imposed on imports or exports?

3. Will any tax that survives a Commerce Clause attack also survive an Import-Export Clause attack?

4. The case involved a tax on the service of handling imported and exported goods. Could a property tax be levied on those goods which were being loaded for export? Similarly, when could the imported goods become subject to a property tax? See Note, Nondiscriminatory, Fairly Apportioned Excise Tax As Applied to Stevedoring Companies Loading and Unloading Goods and Import and Export Transit Does Not Constitute an Import or Duty Within the Prohibition of the Import-Export Clause, 9 Ga. J. Int'l & Comp. L. 445 (1979); Lockhart, *A Revolution in State Taxation of Commerce?*, 65 Minn. L. Rev. 1025, 1045-47 (1981).

5. Does the Court's analysis in Part B of its opinion violate the spirit of *Complete Auto*?

6. Why does the Constitution prohibit Congress from taxing exports?

7. How would Justice Powell decide whether a state was "making the imported goods pay their own way" or was exacting a fee for the privilege of moving the goods through the state? Like the stevedores, do goods in transit "avail themselves of police and fire protection, as well as other benefits Washington offers its local businesses?"

8. How would the majority analyze Justice Powell's transit fee of $5 per ton?

9. In *Virginia Indonesia Company, Inc. v. Harris County Appraisal District*, 910 S.W.2d 905 (1995), cert. denied, 116 S. Ct. 2523 (1996), the Texas Supreme Court held that an ad valorem property tax imposed on goods exported to a foreign country that were temporarily located in Texas violated the Export Clause. Under the same facts would the Commerce Clause be violated? See *Vinmar Inc. v. Harris County Appraisal District*, Texas

Supreme Court, No. 95-0243 (6/20/97). The Court in *Virginia Indonesia* opined that the "rejection of the original package doctrine does not compel the conclusion that the *Michelin* court abandoned the rule of immunity for in-transit goods. To the contrary, by explicitly articulating an exception for in-transit goods, *Michelin* appears to preserve the bright-line immunity for goods in the stream of export." 910 S.W.2d at 911.

10. In *Louisiana Land & Exploration v. Pilot Petroleum*, 900 F. 2d 816 (5th Cir. 1990), cert. denied, sub nom. *Dept. Rev. v. Pilot Petroleum Corp.*, 498 U.S. 897 (1990), a nondiscriminatory Alabama sales tax was struck down under the Export Clause. The tax was applied to the sale of jet fuel oil, delivered to a foreign oil tanker in Mobile for export to Canada. The tax was held to be "an impost upon an export within the meaning of the Import-Export Clause. . ." 900 F. 2d at 821.

11. For a case holding the Export Clause prohibits assessment of nondiscriminatory *federal* taxes on goods in transit for export, see *U.S. v. IBM*, 116 S. Ct. 1793 (1996). The Court cited *Virginia Indonesia*, supra, in rejecting the Government's position that "our Import-Export Clause jurisprudence now permits a State to impose a nondiscriminatory tax directly on goods in import or export transit." Id. at 1803-04.

12. How is the "in-transit" exemption affected by *Itel Containers*, discussed in the Commerce Clause chapter?

13. Revisit Justice Thomas' dissent in *Camps Newfound/Owatonna*, discussed in the Commerce Clause chapter.

14. For critical commentary on *Association of Washington Stevedoring Companies*, see James W. Sargent, *State Taxation Under the Commerce and Import-Export Clauses: Department of Revenue v. Association of Washington Stevedoring Companies*, 32 Sw. L.J. 1373 (1979); Anthony J. Ceravolo, *State Taxation of Interstate Commerce: An Analysis of Current Standards Promulgated by the United States Supreme Court–Department of Revenue v. Association of Washington Stevedoring Cos.*, 28 DePaul L. Rev. 205 (1978).

Chapter 6

Sales Taxes: Introduction

Historical Developments, Federal Analogues, and Policy Analysis

Consumption-type taxes are a major source of tax revenue for state governments in the United States. In 2000, state general sales taxes raised $180.7 billion, albeit less than the $204.5 billion raised by the personal income tax. If selective sales taxes are included (e.g., excise taxes on alcohol, amusements, motor fuels, public utilities, tobacco) however, the total of consumption taxes is $255.3 billion, far exceeding the personal income tax.[1] The personal income tax overtook the general sales tax (excluding excise taxes) as the leading state revenue producer in 1998. That year was the first time in the last half century that the sales tax was not the number one revenue raiser.[2]

In 2000, the states on average raised about 33% of their tax revenue from the general retail sales tax (the personal income tax accounted for 37%). If the selective sales taxes are taken into account, the states raised nearly half of their tax revenue from consumption-type taxes, but there is considerable variation among states.[3]

The mean of state tax rates as of April, 2000 is 5.119%,[4] compared with 4.861% a decade earlier.[5] Much of the increase in rates occurred before 1995 and the mean rate has remained relatively flat since then.[6]

The rate increases in the early 90's helped maintain the sales tax as a primary state revenue source. Without these rate increases, the sales tax would not have kept up with the growth in the economy. The base of the sales tax actually grew more slowly than the increase in personal consumption.[7]

The only states still without a sales tax are Delaware,

---

1. U.S. Bureau of Census, State Government Tax Collections : 1999, www.census.gov/govs/qtax. It is unclear from the technical documentation provided by the Bureau of Census whether the figure includes any revenue from the state use tax. The figure does not include local sales and use taxes. The Bureau of the Census places gross receipts taxes in the same category as sales taxes. To be sure, some gross receipts taxes are functionally equivalent to sales taxes, but many gross receipts taxes are intended to fall on businesses and not consumers. In the latter case, gross receipts is being used as a proxy for business activity. For a discussion of the differences between sales taxes and gross receipts taxes, see Walter Hellerstein, Michael J. McIntyre, and Richard D. Pomp, Commerce Clause Restraints on State Taxation after Jefferson Lines, 51 Tax Law Rev. 47 (1995).

2. In 1944, the sales tax replaced the motor fuel tax as the revenue leader. John L. Mikesell, The Future of American Sales and Use Taxation, in The Future of State Taxation 15 (D. Brunori ed. 1998).

3. John L. Mikesell, Retail Sales Taxes, 1995-98: An Era Ends, 18 State Tax Notes 583 (2000) (hereinafter Mikesell). In states that do not have a broad-based income tax, such as Florida,

Tennessee, Texas, South Dakota, and Nevada, the sales tax contributes the majority of state tax revenues. Reliance on the sales tax fell in Connecticut in the 1990s after its adoption of a broad-based personal income tax. States in the Northeast tend to rely less heavily on the sales tax than the nation as a whole. Reliance is low, for example, in Massachusetts and New York. Mikesell, State Retail Sales Taxation: A Quarter-Century Retrospective, State Tax Today, June 30, 1997. Generalizations always have exceptions. Wyoming, for example, does not have an income tax but does not overly rely on the sales tax, having the luxury of being able to tax natural resources. Mississippi has an income tax but still relies heavily on the sales tax.

Per capita sales tax collections are highest in Hawaii, the District of Columbia, Nevada, Washington, and New Mexico, states that have a broad sales tax base and a vibrant tourist economy. Per capita collections are lowest in Colorado, Alabama, Louisiana, Virginia, and Oklahoma, states that have low rates.

4. This calculation includes the District of Columbia and takes into account only state-level rates. Where a state has more than one rate, the more general rate was used in the calculation.

5. The mean was 3.94% in 1980.

6. Mikesell, supra note 3.

7. Mikesell, State Retail Sales Taxation: A Quarter Century Retrospective, State Tax Today, June 30, 1997.

New Hampshire, Montana, Oregon and Alaska[8] – states that together comprise less than 3% of the nation's population. As a small state, Delaware has used tax and regulatory policies (notably its corporation law) to enhance its competitive position in many ways and the lack of a sales tax is part of this overall strategy. New Hampshire, well-known for its powerful anti-tax political leanings, is the only state to lack a broad-based income tax as well as a sales tax.[9] New Hampshire is currently in the midst of litigation over the financing of public schools, which may result in changes to its tax structure. Montana, similar to Alaska, relies heavily on its taxation of natural resources for government revenue. Its voters periodically reject proposals for a sales tax.

Oregon is the odd member of this group. The absence of a sales tax is explained more by its referendum requirement for adopting new taxes than by its general tax and spending policies. Oregon voters have rejected proposals for a sales tax at least nine times, most recently in 1993. Not surprisingly, Oregon has compensated for the lack of a sales tax by its heavy reliance upon income and property taxation. In 1997, Oregon voters amended the State constitution to reduce their property tax burdens.

The sales tax faces serious challenges from the growth of remote vendors (mail order companies, electronic commerce), the continued difficulties of obtaining voluntary compliance with the use tax, and the shift in the economy from tangible personal property to services. These themes are more fully developed below and throughout the casebook.[10]

---

8. Alaska does not have a state sales tax but does have an extensive system of local sales taxes. These taxes apply to most of the populated areas. Many of the local governments rely heavily on the sales tax and would be expected to oppose a state sales tax.

9. In 23 of the 45 sales tax states, the sales tax produced more revenue than the individual income tax. Mikesell, supra note 2. In the 39 states with both retail sales and individual income taxes, the retail sales tax was a bigger revenue-producer in only 13, which is a marked decline from earlier periods. Id.

---

10. For a perceptive and very readable overview of the issues in this Chapter by one of the most refreshing voices in the field, see David Brunori, State Tax Policy 67-87 (2001).

A. Historical Development

Various types of sales taxes have a long history throughout the world. Ancient Athens laid taxes upon the sale of real property and selected goods. The taxation of specific commodities, especially salt, was common in China, India, and Egypt, where the Ptolemies imposed a general sales tax of five percent. During the reign of Augustus, a Roman tax of one percent was levied on all articles, movable goods, and fixtures sold in the markets or by auction. The rate was two percent upon slaves. Under the Romans the sales tax spread to France and Spain, where, revealing a tenacity that would characterize it throughout history, the tax persevered long after the end of Roman rule. One commentator described these ancient and medieval sales taxes as "iniquitous in their collection, unjust in their burdens, and unpopular with taxpayers."[11] The most notorious of the medieval sales taxes was the infamous *alcavala* of Spain, a cascading gross receipts or turnover tax, often blamed for that country's economic decline.[12]

At the conclusion of World War I the sales tax existed in only a few underdeveloped countries (for example, both Mexico and the Philippines had sales taxes because of Spain's influence) and in Germany, which levied a tax on all commodity transfers. Many European nations subsequently adopted the sales tax in order to aid fiscal systems suffering the drain of war, post-war expenditures, and uncontrolled inflation. In this context, taxes that were hidden in prices, collected through relatively convenient business channels, and paid in small installments offered obvious advantages. In addition, the need to finance government in a time of rapid inflation enhanced the attractiveness of a tax that was responsive to price increases. In the two decades following World War I, the sales tax became an important fiscal element throughout most of Europe, South America, Australia, and Canada.

In the United States, the Great Depression of the 1930's led to widespread adoption of the sales tax at the state level. Before that time, Mississippi and several mid-Atlantic states had experimented with taxes upon business that had some similarity–superficial in some cases–to taxes on consumption. In 1921, West Virginia adopted a general levy on the gross receipts of virtually all businesses and professions–often considered the first sales tax in the United States[13]–although it is unclear whether the Legislature intended it to be a consumer levy, whether it had the features commonly associated with consumption taxes, or whether it should not be viewed as a type of gross receipts tax.

These early business taxes, which developed from lump-sum occupation or license taxes, were levied for the privilege of doing business or were imposed in lieu of a property tax upon merchants' inventories. Their rates were typically one-fifth to one-fifteenth as high as the retail sales taxes adopted during the Depression. These experiments with taxes that might have had some features of a tax on consumption remained the exception rather than the rule until the Depression. The plummeting revenues and escalating social needs of the 1930's provided a powerful impetus for a new and stable source of government funds.

The sales taxes of the 1930's were generally considered emergency or temporary measures, which reflects the ambivalence with which they were adopted. "Rejected by most economists as medieval anachronisms, the taxes were drawn up hastily, with little thought to their exact aims beyond raising money, their economic effects, or the best structures in terms of the desired purposes. States introducing [them] subsequently copied the law of the pioneers in the movement. Typically the taxes were regarded as temporary expedients, designed to raise money quickly, and destined for elimination once the depression was over."[14]

Sales taxes were supported by those seeking reduced reliance upon the property tax, a group including real estate owners, farmers, and public utilities. The desire

---

11. Alfred G. Buehler, General Sales Taxation: Its History and Development 5 (1932).

12. See John F. Due, The Evolution of Sales Taxation, 1915-1972, in Modern Fiscal Issues: Essays in Honor of Carl S. Shoup 318-19 (Richard M. Bird and John Head eds. 1972).

13. Id. at 324. Mikesell credits Mississippi with originating the tax in 1932 by converting its general business tax into a 2% tax on retail sales. John L. Mikesell, The Future of American Sales and Use Taxation, in the Future of State Taxation 15 (D. Brunori ed. 1998).

14. John F. Due, Retail Sales Taxation in Theory and Practice, 3 Nat'l Tax J. 314, 314-315 (1950).

to reduce the property tax partially explains why the sales taxes did not explicitly apply to real estate. (The tax implicitly applied because the purchase of many of the business inputs that went into the construction of real estate were sales taxable.) Others championed the sales tax because they desired a new source of educational financing; these groups included schoolteachers and educational associations.

Some advocated the tax to protect existing revenue sources. The highway lobby, for example, sometimes supported the sales tax in order to preserve gasoline taxes, motor license taxes, or similar fees for spending on transportation projects.

The tax was opposed by organized labor, on grounds of its alleged regressivity, and also by retailers who feared that they could not shift the tax completely to consumers. Retailers also stressed the unfair competition that would result with mail order houses and out-of-state merchants, a complaint even more relevant today. Farmers, who supported the sales tax in some states, resisted it in others if the revenue would not reduce reliance on the property tax but would instead be used for relief programs.

Over time, this opposition failed to stymie the sales tax movement and was never strong enough to repeal permanently a sales tax. Following the Great Depression, the expanding public sector needs of the post-World War II period and the failure of other taxes to keep pace with inflationary trends in wages and costs, as well as continued pressure for property tax relief, led to a new set of sales tax enactments.

Number of States Adopting Permanent General Retail Sales Taxes[15]	
1932	1
1933	9
1934	3
1935	7
1937[16]	2
1942	1
1947	4
1949	2
1951	3
1955	1
1956	1
1960	1
1961	1
1962	1
1963	1
1965	2
1966	3
1967	2
1969	1

By 1970, the sales tax had spread throughout the country. The ensuing story is one of increasing the rate and expanding the base of the tax. In addition, some anecdotal evidence suggests that states are becoming increasingly aggressive in administering their sales taxes.

The state sales tax has no federal counterpart. The states have come to view the sales tax as their exclusive domain and oppose suggestions about the adoption of a national sales tax, or what is essentially the same thing, a national value added tax. The states also vehemently oppose any restrictions by Congress on their ability to tax electronic commerce, such as

---

15. John F. Due and John L. Mikesell, Sales Taxation: State and Local Structure and Administration (2d ed. 1994), p. 3. Hawaii adopted a sales tax in 1935 and is counted as a state for purposes of the Table, although it did not become a state until 1959. The District of Columbia adopted a sales tax in 1949 and is counted as a state for purposes of the Table. Alaska is counted as a state without a sales tax, although it has an extensive system of local sales taxes.

16. Between 1933 and 1936, Pennsylvania, New York, Kentucky, New Jersey, Idaho, and Maryland let their sales taxes expire, typically within 2 years (or less) of their enactment. All of these states subsequently reinstated their sales taxes between 1947 and 1966. Louisiana repealed its sales tax in 1940, but reinstated it in 1942. See supra note 15.

those imposed by the Internet Tax Freedom Act.[17] Similarly, the states have been caustic critics of the U.S. Supreme Court's *Quill* decision, which limits their ability to require a remote vendor to collect the destination state's use tax.[18]

17. See the chapter entitled "The Taxation of Electronic Commerce", infra Chapter 13.

18. Quill is discussed supra Chapter Three and infra Chapters Nine and Eleven.

B. Federal Consumption Taxes

Taxes on consumption have played an important role in the fiscal history of the United States. Before the Civil War, customs duties were a major source of federal revenue. From the Civil War to World War I, customs duties and excise taxes (sales taxes limited to specific commodities) were equally important.

Over the years, Congress has periodically considered imposing a federal sales tax. The first movement for a general federal sales tax in the United States arose during the Civil War and reflected dissatisfaction with the new wartime income tax and the wide range of excises that had also been imposed. Congress rejected a proposed one percent sales tax in 1862. A second movement occurred immediately after World War I, motivated again by opposition to high wartime income taxes. A bill providing for a federal sales tax was defeated in 1918. In 1921, a proposal for a personal consumption tax was rejected as were proposals for various forms of sales taxes.

Proposals for a federal sales tax were renewed, again unsuccessfully, during the Great Depression, with newspaper publisher William Randolph Hearst the most outspoken proponent. From 1933 to 1936 excise taxes again became a major source of federal revenue, but their relative importance later declined with increasing reliance upon the income tax. To finance World War II, the government considered–but rejected–a sales tax and an expenditure tax; instead, the war was financed by income, excess-profits taxes, and excise taxes. Excise taxes were similarly used to finance the Korean War. The last vestiges of these wartime excises were generally eliminated in 1965, although the United States still imposes a wide variety of excise taxes on certain goods, services, and occupations. Commodities and services subject to federal excise taxes include alcoholic beverages, tobacco products, motor fuels, heavy tires and trucks, coal, pistols and revolvers, sports and fishing equipment, and domestic air transportation. Excise taxes also apply to certain businesses, such as breweries.[19]

President Nixon considered a value added tax, a type of sales tax, as a partial substitute for the Social Security tax and corporate income tax in the early 1970's. His proposal was vehemently opposed by mayors and governors, who realized that a value added tax was just a different means of administering a sales tax, which they coveted as their exclusive revenue source.[20] Proposals for a federal value added tax were considered by the Treasury in the early 1970's, and formed a major part of the Treasury's 1984 tax reform study that led to the 1986 revision of the federal income tax.

In 1995 and 1996, proposals for some kind of consumption tax, sales tax, or value added tax figured prominently in the inevitable political jockeying preceding the presidential election. Many of these, if enacted, would have forced the states to have overhauled radically their tax structures. None of the sweeping proposals generated any depth of support in the 2000 presidential campaign.

---

19. See United States General Accounting Office, Revenue Potential of Restoring Excise Taxes to Past Levels, p. 8 (1989).

20. Is it a coincidence that subsequent proposals for federal value added taxes have been careful to shun this label in favor of "flat rate taxes," "consumed income taxes," or "business transfer taxes"?

C. Policy and Design Considerations

1. Introduction

A retail sales tax is intended to be borne by individuals who acquire goods or services for personal consumption. In principle, the tax should not be imposed upon the acquisition of goods or services for use in a trade or business ("business inputs") or for use with regard to investment activities. The tax should apply to only the last transaction in the chain of production and distribution, i.e., the sale of the final good to the person who plans to consume it. In practice, deviations from these principles abound and state retail sales taxes fail to reach some items of personal consumption while taxing various business and investment inputs.

Reform proposals calling for modifying the federal income tax by removing the savings component so that the base becomes essentially consumption have some relevance to retail sales taxation as well. In theory, both a federal personal consumption tax and a retail sales tax are levied on consumption and in that sense raise similar issues about defining the appropriate tax base. Unlike a retail sales tax, however, which is levied at the time of each sale, the types of federal taxes on personal consumption that are discussed by reformers would be levied annually on the basis of a tax declaration filed by the individual. An annual tax upon consumption can take into account an individual's income, total consumption, and family circumstances and, most importantly, can apply a graduated rate.

More relevant to a study of the sales tax is the interest in some quarters in the adoption of a federal value added tax (VAT). Long a feature of European tax systems, a value added tax has only recently been seriously debated in the United States. Defining the base of a value added tax raises issues that are similar to defining the base of a retail sales tax.

2. Evaluating a Retail Sales Tax

A widespread consensus exists that an income tax, which is grounded on the concept of ability to pay, is superior to other forms of individual taxation. Sales taxation has never enjoyed that same support. The retail sales tax was not adopted out of any strong philosophical movement, but rather to address an acute need for revenue. Once the tax became an accepted feature of most state fiscal structures, legislators did not have to provide any justification for

its existence. Like the proverbial reason to climb that mountain, the sales tax "was just there."[21]

If pressed, most legislators would defend the tax on pragmatic rather than philosophical grounds. The tax raises substantial revenue in most states (some of it from businesses and nonresidents) in a visible manner that most voters apparently find acceptable. The collection of small amounts of money from consumers (and businesses) on each of hundreds of thousands of transactions makes the sales tax less painful than other sources of revenue, although some would cite this feature as a disadvantage rather than an advantage.

Unlike the income tax, the sales tax provides states with an independent source of revenue that Congress has not yet tapped and allows property taxation, also untapped federally, to be ceded to the local jurisdictions. Compared to other sources of revenue, the tax can be relatively stable during economic downturns[22] and revenue elastic during inflationary periods (depending, of course, on what is included in the base),[23] providing additional revenue when the

---

21. "The state retail sales tax in America can be likened to an illegitimate child that was not wanted but that came anyway. Being unwanted is not really unusual and it is certainly no bar to normal growth. It is even possible for the illegitimate to gain respectability." Daniel C. Morgan, Jr., Retail Sales Tax: An Appraisal of New Issues 3 (1964).

22. The sales tax tends to be less volatile than the income tax. Richard F. Dye and Therese J. McGuire, Block Grants and the Sensitivity of State Revenues to Recession, Proceedings of the 90th Annual Conference in Taxation, National Tax Association (1998). The income tax is more revenue elastic in part because of the progressive rates that most states use. However, even if a state uses a flat rate with no exemptions, or a rate adjusted for inflation, the income tax can still be elastic if real incomes rise annually. A tax that is revenue elastic can be volatile, with revenues increasing rapidly during periods of boom, and falling rapidly during downturns. During upswings, taxable income can increase faster than wage income, reflecting the growth in capital gains and other forms of so-called unearned income. Capital gains are more volatile than wages.

23. People are likely to defer nonessential consumption during a recession; if a state tends to exempt essentials and tax discretionary spending, the tax will be rather revenue elastic in a downturn.
   A study of the Connecticut tax structure concluded that the sales tax grew at an average annual inflation-adjusted rate of 4.1% (after eliminating the effects of legislative changes) from 1978 to 1990. The income elasticity of the tax was 1.16, that is,

cost of government is likely to be increasing. Revenue elasticity, however, is not welcomed by those advocating a smaller role for the public sector (nor do these advocates welcome the "painlessness" of the sales tax. If you prefer a smaller role for government, taxes should "hurt" in order to increase voter awareness of the cost of the public sector.)

The significant revenue raised by the sales tax reduces the pressure on other taxes. Consequently, a state can have lower nominal rates for all of its other taxes than would be possible without a sales tax. A broad-based state tax structure with low nominal rates is generally believed by policy analysts to be superior to one that relies on fewer taxes and higher nominal rates. This same broad-base, low-rate philosophy motivated the federal 1986 Tax Reform Act, which greatly expanded the base of the federal income tax and used the resulting revenue to lower nominal rates.

Notwithstanding these pragmatic justifications for the sales tax,[24] academics have long argued over the philosophical underpinnings of the tax and the recent interest in a federal personal consumption tax and a value added tax has rekindled this debate. Much of this debate, however, has taken place in the context of a national tax, and some of the issues discussed at that level are less relevant in the context of a state sales tax.[25]

More relevant for our present purposes is the defense of consumption taxation based on considerations of equity. The case in defense of a retail sales tax is that it taxes persons based on their standard of living, as exhibited by their consumption of goods and services. Using terminology usually associated with the income tax, this defense is sometimes formulated in terms of ability to pay. Taxpayers have demonstrated an ability to pay by their decision to consume rather than save, at least with respect to discretionary items.

A consumption tax is sometimes described as levying a tax on the claims that a taxpayer makes on society's resources for his or her own consumption purposes. A taxpayer who saves rather than consumes, the argument goes, is putting resources back into society's productive pool. By consuming, the taxpayer is withdrawing resources from the pool–an appropriate transaction to tax. One of the earliest formulations of this argument was made by Thomas Hobbes.[26]

Nicholas Kaldor, a well-known British economist, held the view that "each individual [measures taxpaying ability] for himself when, in light of all his present circumstances and future prospects, he decides on the scale of his personal living expenses. Thus a tax based on actual spending rates each individual's spending capacity according to the yardstick which he applies to himself."[27]

To avoid confusion, the term ability to pay will be used to refer to the equity defense of the income tax; the term standard of living will be used to refer to the equity defense of a sales tax. For the purposes of this introduction and overview, debating the relative merits of the concepts of ability to pay or standard of living is unnecessary. More important is being aware of which concept is being applied by critics or supporters of sales taxation. Too often, commentators fail to articulate the evaluative criteria they are applying, or do not acknowledge that if they applied alternative criteria, different conclusions might be drawn.[28]

---

on average every ten percent increase in personal income generated an 11.6% increase in revenue. This responsiveness is explained by the degree to which Connecticut has exempted items such as food, clothing, gasoline, and residential utilities, while taxing consumer durables. See KPMG Peat Marwick, Final Report–Sales Tax 1991, pp. 47-57 (prepared for the Task Force on State Tax Revenue). The Connecticut sales tax base is typical of that of many states.

24. Some legislators defend the sales tax on the basis that every citizen should "feel" the responsibility of government by contributing to the upkeep of the state. But is a sales tax, which is paid indirectly, in piecemeal fashion, and often without much awareness of the amount, a particularly good response to this argument? Others defend the sales tax as reaching persons who are part of the underground economy and presumably outside the income tax net, but should this group be the tail that wags the dog?

25. For example, part of the recent discussion in the United States compares a consumption tax with the existing federal income tax and concludes that the former avoids many problems of measuring income from business and capital, does not require indexing adjustments for inflation, and provides a better solution to the problem of tax arbitrage–issues that are less germane at the state level.

---

26. See Thomas Hobbes, Leviathan, p. 298 (Alexander D. Lindsay ed. 1959).

27. Nicholas Kaldor, An Expenditure Tax 47 (1955).

28. As an illustration, consider a criticism of the sales tax on the grounds that it is perverse because the amount of sales tax paid increases with family size (at comparable income levels). See Daniel C. Morgan, Jr., Reappraisal of Sales Taxation: Some

The rest of this Section analyzes the sales tax in the context of three traditional measures used to evaluate any tax: horizontal equity, vertical equity, and neutrality. The text focuses on considerations of horizontal and vertical equity because they play a prominent role in attacks on the sales tax and it is here that much misunderstanding can result from unarticulated premises. Neutrality is discussed for an opposite reason–it does not figure prominently enough in legislative debate over expanding the base of the sales tax. For a similar reason, administrative considerations are interspersed throughout the presentation.

a. Horizontal Equity

The principle of horizontal equity dictates that taxpayers in the same situation should be taxed identically. The principle itself is not controversial; the difficulty is in determining which taxpayers are in the "same situation." Standard-of-living advocates would argue that consumption should be the measure of "sameness." Residents with the same amount of consumption are in the same situation and should pay the same amount of sales tax. Ability-to-pay supporters assume that income should be the measure of sameness.

As a practical matter, it is difficult to incorporate ability-to-pay criteria into a transactional tax levied upon individual purchases rather than upon a resident's annual consumption. A retail sales tax can attempt to respond to ability-to-pay concerns through two primary techniques: exemptions and differential rates. Each approach has its weaknesses. An exemption can reduce or eliminate tax upon items purchased predominantly by lower-income persons but not without also conferring the same benefit upon middle- and upper-income consumers. Differential rates can increase the tax upon goods favored by

upper-income groups, but not without also increasing the tax upon some lower-and middle-income consumers who purchase the same goods.

Consider, for example, the nearly universal efforts to reduce the regressivity of a sales tax (or value-added tax) by exempting necessities, such as food and medicine, or the less common attempts to foster progressivity through higher taxes upon luxury items. These approaches lead to several problems:

(1) An exemption for food applies to all purchasers, regardless of their income, making the reduction in regressivity costly to the taxing jurisdiction. In addition, the exemption may bias consumer choices toward food and away from taxed items. Further, the exemption may be capitalized into higher food prices;

(2) Any classification of commodities incurs serious administrative and compliance costs to ensure that the correct rate is applied to a particular purchase. As discussed below, it is not easy to define the precise limits of a category such as "food" or "medicine;"

(3) What constitutes a "luxury"? "It has well been said that 'luxuries' are commodities that poor people 'should not buy, but do buy.'"[29] Purchases by persons in the lower income groups may consist not so much of different articles from those bought by other income groups, but rather of the same articles bought in smaller quantities or of inferior quality.[30]

One commentator has written:

If articles are classed as luxuries because of the nature of the article, its workmanship, or the materials used in its manufacture, all available substitutes will have to be taxed or they will be consumed instead of the taxed luxury. . . . Furthermore, it may be argued that superior quality is not a test of luxury, for superior quality in a purchase may mean real economy and not simply extravagance. Since the so-called luxuries are frequently consumed by others than the wealthy, a luxury tax will not be paid exclusively by the richer classes.

. . . .

If price be taken as the standard of luxury consumption, similar difficulties develop. When prices are rising the luxury classification will have to be revised frequently, or many articles will become luxuries for tax purposes without any change in the intent of the law. If prices are falling, on the other hand, the articles subject to the luxury tax will decrease in number, and the standard of

---

Recent Arguments, 16 Nat'l Tax J. 89, 94 (1963). This criticism is based on two implicit premises. First, that income should be the measure of "sameness" or equality. Second, that in the case of a family, aggregate income rather than the income of each member of the family is relevant. Standard-of-living advocates, however, would reject the first premise because consumption, not income, is the relevant measure of sameness. The second premise would be rejected because per capita consumption is presumably what should be compared, not family consumption, although there is little discussion of this issue in the literature. For a rejection of the use of family income as the measure of sameness in the context of a personal income tax, see Michael J. McIntyre and Oliver Oldman, Taxation of the Family in a Comprehensive and Simplified Income Tax, 90 Harv. L. Rev. 1573 (1977).

---

29. Neil H. Jacoby, Retail Sales Taxation (1938), at 197.

30. Due, supra note 12, at 378-379.

definition is again defective.[31]

No state or local sales tax uniformly taxes all consumption, which violates the principle of horizontal equity. Professor Ronald Fisher has estimated that general sales taxes at the state level reach only 54% of personal consumption; Professor Mikesell estimates that from 1970 to 1995 the coverage of the sales tax declined from almost two-thirds of personal income to one-half; Professor Fox estimates that in 1998 the tax base declined to 42% of personal income, down from 51.4% in 1979.[32] Only some of this decline is likely to be attributable to a legislative narrowing of the base.

The sale or use of tangible personal property is much more likely to be taxed than is the sale or use of services. Even in the case of tangible personal property, however, violations of uniformity are not only common but often involve the drawing of rarefied distinctions. In New York, for example, the sales tax is paid on the purchase of baseball tickets, Prell shampoo, non-sterilized cotton and hot nuts, but not on the purchase of Broadway tickets, Head & Shoulders shampoo, sterilized cotton, or cold nuts (until recently, large marshmallows were taxable whereas small marshmallows were exempt).

Legislatures do not always articulate their motivation or rationale in exempting certain goods or services from sales taxation, and explanations will vary depending on the provision at issue. Nonetheless, putting aside well-organized and sharply focused political pressure, the following seven considerations underlie most exemptions and thus explain why the principle of horizontal equity is difficult to implement: (1) reducing the regressivity of the sales tax if measured by income; (2) reducing the absolute burden of the tax on the poor; (3) providing relief for a special hardship; (4) providing an incentive (even if only symbolic) for socially or economically desirable behavior; (5) reducing the administrative difficulty or expense of taxing a particular good or service; (6) responding to an exemption adopted by a neighboring state; or (7) reducing the sales tax burden on specific goods or services already subject to a selective excise or gross receipts tax, such as cigarettes, alcohol, or gasoline.

The first two considerations permeate much of the political and academic discussion of the sales tax. Because of their importance, both are treated more fully below in the specific setting of the food exemption.[33] The third consideration best explains the exemption for drugs and medicines and is also discussed below.[34]

The fourth consideration is a familiar one to students of the federal income tax because of the frequent use of that tax as a tool of social engineering; the sales tax has not escaped the same temptation. Exemptions that might reflect incentives for desirable behavior are those provided for textbooks sold to students, Bibles (an exemption of questionable constitutionality), and flags of the United States or of the taxing state. Some critics might include exemptions for research and development or manufacturing in this category but these provisions are normatively correct because the activities exempted are business inputs, which should not be taxable.

The fifth consideration explains the near universal exemption for casual sales, such as the sale of a used camera or stereo to a friend.[35] The sixth consideration explains why certain exemptions (and more recently, tax holidays), such as a clothing exemption, often spread (sometimes within a short time period) among neighboring states. For example, Massachusetts, Connecticut, New Jersey, New York and Pennsylvania all have favorable rules for taxing clothing (and New Hampshire does not have a sales tax).

The seventh consideration addresses items such as

---

31. Buehler, supra note 11, at 156-57.

32. Ronald Fisher, State and Local Public Finance, 169 n. 4 (1988); Mikesell, supra note 2; William F. Fox, Can the State Sales Tax Survive a Future Like Its Past, in The Future of State Taxation (David Brunori ed. 1998), p. 34; Donald Bruce and William F. Fox, E-Commerce in the Context of Declining State Sales Tax Bases, Center for Business and Economic Research, U. of Tenn., 2000. Professor Mikesell attributes the decline in coverage to the spread of the exemption for food. Id. Professor Fisher points out that total personal consumption in 1986 was $2762.4 billion, while state government general sales tax revenue was $74.8 billion. At a median sales tax rate of 5%, this amount would convert to a sales tax base of $1496 billion, substantially less than $2762.4 billion.

33. See subsection (d), infra.

34. See subsection (d), infra.

35. For an argument that the exemption for casual sales is required by normative considerations, see Richard D. Pomp and Oliver Oldman, A Normative Inquiry into the Base of a Retail Sales Tax, 43 Nat. Tax J. 427 (1990), reprinted in 1 State Tax Notes 170 (1991).

cigarettes, alcohol, and gasoline, which are subject to special excise taxes. The exemption for such items from the sales tax is presumably to avoid their double taxation, that is, their taxation under both the special excise tax and the more generally applicable sales tax. Although industries subject to excise taxes argue that the general sales tax should not also be imposed, the better view, as many writers have observed, is that no justification exists for such an exemption. If the amount of the excise taxes was appropriate before the imposition of the sales tax, then the adoption of a sales tax should not reduce the relative burden on these goods. If the absolute amount of both the excise tax and the general sales tax is considered too high, the preferred solution is to reduce the level of the excise tax.

Excise taxes on cigarettes and alcohol are known as sin taxes and are often defended as discouraging the consumption of a harmful item. This result is difficult to achieve, however, if demand for such goods is relatively inelastic, which historically might have described goods that were commonly subject to sin taxes. Accordingly, a sin tax will raise more revenue than will an excise tax imposed upon a good having greater price elasticity. Perhaps it was this feature of sin taxes that traditionally made them attractive to legislators. In the case of cigarettes, however, the combination of high taxes and anti-smoking sentiment may have finally had a significant impact on consumer demand, at least among some socio-economic groups.[36]

Even sin taxes that do not discourage consumption may be justified if they recover some of the social costs incurred by the use of alcohol and tobacco. Alcohol-related accidents commonly injure persons other than the user, and, second-hand smoke can also damage non-smokers. The costs of treating those who drink and smoke excessively are borne by non-smokers and non-drinkers, who help finance Medicare, Medicaid, hospitals, private insurance programs, and public health services. This rationale provided important support for the success of California's "Proposition 99," approved by the voters in 1988, which raised the tax upon cigarettes from ten cents to thirty-five cents per pack in order to fund county hospitals and public health programs.[37] Excise taxes on products that pollute or on pollutants can also be defended as a charge for social costs.[38]

The excise tax on gasoline rests on a different footing from sin taxes. The system of state excise taxes on gasoline was pioneered by Oregon in 1919 and has been popularly viewed as implementing the benefit principle of taxation. The excise tax is sometimes defended as a method of "metering" the benefits provided by public roads and streets because the quantity of gasoline purchased is, in a rough but politically acceptable sense, a gauge of road use (although the amount raised by the excise tax will not automatically increase as the cost of maintaining the roads increases). Under this view a motorist receives a definite benefit in exchange for the gasoline excise tax.

Retail sales taxes, by contrast, are neither paid by, nor expended for, a particular class of users. Consequently, no reason exists why persons using gasoline should not also bear their share of the general sales tax burden.[39] As discussed below,

36. In 1990, sixteen states passed excise tax legislation that was expected to raise $2.1 billion in fiscal year 1991; more than half the legislatures raised rates on two or more types of sin taxes. Governing, Dec. 1990, p. 21. The ability of a state to levy excise taxes can be affected by the level of any existing federal excise taxes applicable to that same item. In 1990, for example, some states, such as California rushed to raise their gasoline taxes before Congress raised its federal gasoline excise tax. Id.

   Some evidence suggests that the demand curve of teenagers for cigarettes has become relatively price elastic. See United States General Accounting Office, Teenage Smoking: Higher Excise Tax Should Significantly Reduce the Number of Smokers, p. 8 (1989).

   One commentator succinctly summed up the issue of taxing cigarettes as follows: "the seven out of ten adults who don't smoke don't mind when legislators sock it to the three out of ten who do." Governing, Dec. 1990, p.22.

37. Many excise taxes are imposed on a per quantity basis, such as a tax imposed on a pack of cigarettes or on a bottle of beer, which makes them easy to collect but unresponsive to increases (or decreases) in the price of the underlying good. Consequently, such excise taxes do not rise with inflation.

38. Florida imposed an excise tax on automobiles that fell more heavily on newcomers to that State. Those who registered cars that added to the total volume of automobiles already on the road paid $295 per car. The tax did not apply to Florida families who replaced a car they already owned; only those who added an additional car to their fleet paid it. That exclusion did not apply to new arrivals. Governing, Dec. 1990, p.22. The tax was held to violate the Commerce Clause in Dep't of Rev. v. Kuhnlein, 646 So.2d 717 (1994).

39. Jacoby, supra note 29, at 108-109, 112. For a general discussion of excise taxes, see Thomas F. Pogue, Excise Taxes, in Reforming State Tax Systems 259 (Steven Gold ed. 1986). The exemption of motor fuel from the sales tax entails revenue losses second only to the food exemption. Mikesell, supra note 2, at 25.

gasoline that constitutes a business input–for example, gasoline used by a commercial trucking enterprise–should in theory not be taxed, but that consideration has not affected the application of the tax in practice.

The preceding has focused on the violations of horizontal equity arising from exemptions. Another type of violation is more subtle but equally significant and arises from the taxation of business inputs, discussed below.

b. Vertical Equity

Vertical equity refers to how a tax treats persons who are not in the same situation, whatever the measure of "sameness." If, for example, the measure of sameness is income, as it is for purposes of an income tax, vertical equity describes how the tax burden changes as income changes. The policy issue is whether the tax should be: (1) the same percentage of income regardless of the amount of income (a proportional tax); (2) an increasing percentage of income as income increases (a progressive tax); or (3) a decreasing percentage of income as income increases (a regressive tax). A tax upon an individual, such as a personal income tax or a personal consumption tax, can achieve whatever degree of vertical equity is desired through the use of graduated rates. A personal consumption tax, for example, could have rates that increase as the amount of an individual's consumption increases, a feature that many would support. Vertical equity is a harder issue to address in a transaction tax. A retail sales tax, for example, can levy different rates on different goods or services, but this is a poor mechanism for achieving vertical equity.

Debate over the regressivity of the sales tax probably reflects one of the sharpest clashes between the ability-to-pay and standard-of-living views of the tax. Because of the importance of this issue, a fuller discussion is presented below in the context of the food exemption.

c. Neutrality

A tax that does not change the economic behavior of individuals and businesses is described as neutral. A truly neutral tax would not interfere with decisions that would be made in a pre-tax world to work or to play, to save or to consume, to consume one good or service over another, or to use one production process rather than another. Neutrality is a worthwhile goal if preserving the status quo ante is desirable.

Obviously, any tax tends to discourage the type of activity upon which it is levied. A personal income tax, for example, may discourage some persons from working, although others may be encouraged to forgo leisure and to work harder in order to offset the "cost" of the tax. Similarly, a retail sales tax theoretically discourages some persons from spending (or less directly, perhaps from working) and encourages them to save. Others may be encouraged to work harder in order to maintain their prior level of consumption. These effects, if they materialize, would follow from the initial decision to levy a particular type of tax and would violate the principle of neutrality.

Once that decision is made, however, the neutrality principle asserts that the tax should be designed to interfere as little as possible with the choice of what is purchased or produced in the marketplace, unless the tax is specifically being used for that purpose.

Most taxes, including the sales tax, may purposely be used to change consumer behavior, redistribute resources, or alter private decision making. Large increases in cigarette excise taxes in recent years, for example, are intended to discourage tobacco consumption. Absent such extra-fiscal considerations, the neutrality principle states that a sales tax designed to raise revenue should interfere as little as possible with economic decisions concerning production and consumption.

Unless all consumption is taxed uniformly, a retail sales tax may distort choices among purchases. If two goods or services are similar in the satisfaction or utility they provide, but one is taxable whereas the other is exempt, the change in relative prices can be expected to alter some consumers' purchasing decisions and to increase sales of the exempt good or service.

The concepts of horizontal equity and neutrality are related. Deviations from horizontal equity can result in a lack of economic neutrality. In some situations, a violation of neutrality is an unintentional consequence of a conscious legislative decision to exempt certain goods and services from the sales tax; other times, a violation of horizontal equity is an unintended result of a decision to deviate purposely from neutrality. For example, New York's sales tax exemption for Broadway tickets is intended as an economic incentive for New York City theaters and represents a purposeful violation of neutrality. It can be presumed that the unfairness of exempting Broadway tickets while taxing, for example, baseball tickets was not purposely intended. By contrast, the exemptions for Head & Shoulders shampoo and hot nuts are unintended deviations from neutrality. The New York Legislature did not intend to distort a consumer's decision about what kinds of shampoo or nuts to purchase. Other considerations drive these exemptions as the following discussion suggests.

d. The Exemptions for Food, Clothing, and Drugs and Medicines

Many of the themes discussed above are nicely illustrated in the context of sales tax exemptions for food, clothing, and drugs and medicines. Consider, for example, the food exemption. Twenty-five years ago, 28 states taxed food. Today, 17 states fully tax food, whereas 26 (including the District of Columbia) fully exempt it and five tax it at a reduced rate,[40] but all states tax at least some restaurant meals. The exemption for food, like many other exemptions, responds to criticism that the sales tax is regressive if measured against income and imposes too high an absolute burden upon the poor.

Recall that a tax is generally characterized as regressive, proportional, or progressive depending upon whether it comprises a decreasing, constant, or increasing percentage of some base, as that base increases. In the context of the income tax, the

relevant base is some measure of income (e.g., economic income, adjusted gross income, taxable income). More generally, the regressivity or progressivity of any tax can be determined by forming a fraction whose denominator is some base, such as income, consumption, or wealth, and whose numerator is the amount of taxes paid for any specified amount of the base, and examining how that fraction changes as the base changes.

The issue of how best to measure the distribution of a retail sales tax presents a sharp clash between the standard-of-living and the ability-to-pay rationales of the tax. The numerator of the relevant fraction is obviously the amount of retail sales tax paid (whether annually or over some longer period). Some measure of income is normally used as the denominator of the fraction,[41] which implicitly adopts an ability-to-pay criterion. Consumption is a declining percentage of income as income rises, which is not surprising because low-income persons tend to consume all of their incomes (or even dissave), whereas high-income persons tend to save part of their incomes. Consequently, even a pure retail sales tax levied uniformly on all consumer expenditures would be regressive if measured against income.

If, however, a retail sales tax is viewed as implementing a standard-of-living criterion, consumption would be a more logical choice for the denominator of the fraction.[42] Using consumption as the denominator, the relevant distributional inquiry would be how the amount of sales tax varies as consumption varies. A flat rate, retail sales tax on all consumer expenditures would be neither progressive

---

40. Mikesell, supra note 2. In 1998, Georgia became the first state in more than a decade to enact an exemption for food. In 1999, North Carolina also exempted food. In 1997, Missouri reduced its sales tax on food from 4.225 percent to 1.225 percent. Illinois also taxes food at a lower rate. Nicholas Johnson and Iris J. Lav, Should States Tax Food? Examining the Policy Issues and Options, 14 State Tax Notes 1785 (1998). Prior to 1945, only California, Ohio, and North Carolina exempted food. John F. Due, Retail Sales Taxation in Theory and Practice, 3 Nat. Tax J. 314, 324. States that adopted the sales tax during the Great Depression were not in a position to incur the revenue loss that would have resulted from the exemption of food or other non-discretionary purchases. One of the reasons that the sales tax reaches a smaller percentage of personal income today than it did 25 years ago is because of the expanding exemption for food. Mikesell, supra note 2. Instead of exempting food, some states refund to low-income persons part or all the sales tax that they are assumed to have paid on their food purchases. This credit often takes the form of a credit against the income tax. Is limiting the credit to only residents constitutional? What if the state is one like New York, which has a lot of nonresidents working in New York City who eat out lunch. Should they be excluded from the credit?

41. Should the income measure used in the denominator include transfer payments (social security, welfare, unemployment compensation, and worker's compensation)? Whose income should be measured, an individual's or, if the individual lives at home, the family's? How should students be treated? How should persons who are only "temporarily" poor (due to illness, unemployment, or retirement) be treated?

42. Cf. Organization for Economic Cooperation & Development (OECD), Taxing Consumption, p. 126 (1988): "Consumption tax paid may be related to gross income, disposable income or the consumption of households. The choice between these different denominators depends upon the question being addressed. If the intention is to compare a VAT and an income tax, then the appropriate basis for the comparison would seem to be the gross income of households since this is the base used to measure the progressivity of the income tax. If the intention is to examine how the structure of a consumption tax can be made more or less progressive, then the appropriate base is consumption."

nor regressive under this measure, but rather proportional. Standard of living advocates would applaud such a tax for its horizontal equity rather than lament it for its regressivity as would ability-to-pay advocates.

In practice, retail sales taxes do not tax all consumption so that depending on the denominator of the fraction, the tax may be progressive over some ranges of the denominator and proportional or regressive over other ranges. Much of the consumption of low-income persons consists of housing, food, utilities and medical services, items that many states exempt. Consequently, it is possible for low-income persons to pay only nominal amounts of sales tax, which achieves a degree of progressivity.

As income increases, more taxable items, such as restaurant meals, electronic goods, and durable consumer items will be purchased, making it possible for a retail sales tax to be progressive if measured against either income or consumption over some lower ranges of consumption or income. As income continues to increase, at some point the percentage that is consumed will decrease. The sales tax will then become regressive if measured by income. Whether it will become regressive if measured by consumption will depend on whether a change occurs in the composition of taxable and exempt goods and services that are purchased. If, for example, half of all purchases are taxable independent of the absolute level of consumption, a sales tax will be proportional over broad ranges of consumption. If, however, as consumption increases, its composition shifts toward more exempt goods and services, the sales tax will become regressive even if measured by consumption. As this brief discussion suggests, whether and to what extent a sales tax should be viewed as regressive is a more complex question than is generally recognized.

Even after the proper frame of reference is resolved, determining the distribution of the sales tax requires information about who actually bears the economic burden of the tax and the discussion above implicitly assumed that this is the consumer. Of course, the legal incidence of a tax, that is, who is the designated taxpayer under the statute, has no bearing on economic incidence, that is, who actually bears the economic effects of the tax. Furthermore, the common statutory requirement that the sales tax be separately stated from the purchase price will not necessarily determine the economic effects of the tax. The merchant may lower the base price to keep the consumer's total payment no higher than before the

tax, thus absorbing its actual burden. A merchant that left base prices unchanged and merely added on the sales tax may face a loss in sales and profits, and also end up bearing part of the burden of the sales tax.

The extent to which the sales tax may be shifted depends upon the nature of supply and demand. The more price elastic the demand for a particular item, the more the amount demanded will fall as the tax is added to its price. Moreover, if the demand for various goods and services is interdependent, a tax upon one item will affect demand for others. In addition, a tax upon business inputs may alter the way businesses are organized or the way they produce their goods. Empirical research is further complicated if shifting occurs not through price changes but through alterations in quantity or quality, as when a restaurant reduces the size of its portions or uses less expensive ingredients without changing its prices.

Isolating price changes in order to measure economic incidence is exceedingly difficult even when a sales tax is first imposed; after it has been in existence for many years, with corresponding changes in general price levels, consumer tastes, and substitute products, the task may be hopeless. A complete analysis must also examine how the government spends the sales tax revenue (or how spending would be changed if the sales tax were repealed). Two commentators have concluded, "An analysis of tax shifting can easily become discouraging . . . . Depending on the conditions assumed, it is possible to reach conclusions that the imposition of a sales tax results in an increased, decreased or unchanged price and that some or all of the burden of the tax is borne by the consumer. . . . Under various conditions, some or all of the burden may be borne by factors of production. Depending on the responsiveness of productive effort to tax burden, the result may be an increase, a decrease, or no change in output."[43] Considering this uncertainty, what should a legislator assume about the regressivity of the sales tax?

However the regressivity issue is resolved, a sales tax is only one component of a state revenue system, and progressivity in other taxes may outweigh, or at least offset, any perceived regressivity of the sales tax. For example, a state that utilizes a progressive income

---

43. Harold Somers and Joseph J. Launie, The Sales Tax, in Part 4 of a Major Tax Study for the California Legislature, Vol. 4, No. 11, Assembly Interim Committee on Revenue and Taxation, p. 24 (Dec. 1964).

tax might be able to achieve a politically acceptable distribution of its overall tax burden even if the sales tax is assumed to be regressive if measured against income. Some states offset the perceived regressivity of the sales tax with targeted rebates administered through the income tax.[44] In addition, the regressivity of the sales tax can be offset through the spending and welfare programs that a sales tax helps to finance or that the federal government sponsors.

More fundamentally:

The relation of the sales tax to the problem of social balance is admirably direct. The community is affluent in privately produced goods. It is poor in public services. The obvious solution is to tax the former to provide the latter–by making private goods more expensive, public goods are made more abundant. Motion pictures, electronic entertainment and cigarettes are made more costly so that schools can be more handsomely supported. We pay more for soap, detergents and vacuum cleaners in order that we may have cleaner cities and less occasion to use them. We have more expensive cars and gasoline so that we may have more agreeable highways and streets on which to drive them. Food being relatively cheap, we tax it in order to have better medical services and better health in which to enjoy it.[45]

The problem of regressivity is similar to, but not identical with, another concern that is often asserted in defense of the exemption of food: the absolute tax burden imposed upon the lowest income groups on their non-discretionary purchases. For example, the 1984 Treasury Report on federal tax reform estimated on the basis of 1980-1981 data that families earning less than $10,000 spent 32% of their before-tax income on food consumed at home. Accordingly, a sales tax on food can impose a non-trivial burden on the poor regardless of whether overall the tax is progressive, proportional, or regressive. Both ability-to-pay and standard-of-living advocates would likely agree that a sales tax should not exact money needed for maintaining a minimum subsistence level. An exemption for food (and exemptions for housing, medical care, utilities, heating oil, clothing, drugs, and medicines and so forth) is roughly the sales tax equivalent of the deductions used in the income tax to exempt subsistence income from taxation.

Exempting "necessities" from sales taxation while taxing "luxuries" and other non-necessities produces many arbitrary classifications. A state that views food purchased for home consumption as a necessity that should be exempt will typically tax candy, which is viewed as a non-essential, discretionary item; distinguishing between the two, however, often requires an inordinate expenditure of administrative resources. New York, for example, for many years exempted small marshmallows as food because they could be used in baking whereas large marshmallows were taxable as candy. In 1998, New York announced that large marshmallows would henceforth be exempt as food! Can hot nuts, currently taxable whereas cold nuts are exempt, be next on New York's list of burning social issues? Similar problems arise in distinguishing taxable candy from exempt baked goods, exempt fruit drinks from taxable soft drinks, and taxable prepared meals from exempt grocery items. The last problem is particularly troublesome at a time when take-out food from restaurants and prepared items in grocery stores and supermarkets grow ever more similar.

Sometimes the number of items purchased is used as a measure of whether the items are intended for immediate consumption, and thus taxable like restaurant meals, or are intended for home consumption, and exempt like groceries. In Massachusetts, six or fewer items purchased from a bakery are considered a sale for immediate consumption and taxed; seven or more items are exempt. Some states tax warm food and exempt unheated food; others tax food sold by establishments with tables and trays, but exempt the same food if sold by other establishments. In Ohio, ice cream bars are exempt as food, but popsicles are not. Vitamin preparations and health foods have raised endless questions.[46]

Since 1950, the California tax administration has issued rulings on over five hundred products, beginning with the unexceptional (lemon juice and noodles), quickly moving to the exotic ("figs stuffed with cherries in port wine"), the mysterious–or defunct?–("Borden's Hemo," "Ralph's Cloud 900"), and the typically Californian ("Health-A-Whey"). The purported healthfulness of an item is apparently no guarantee of exemption. California has denied an exemption to lecithin protein and kelp, while exempting "Scarlett O'Hara Cocktail Mix," "Old World Pecan Fudge Brownies" and chocolate-flavored

---

44. See infra notes 59-61.

45. John Kenneth Galbraith, The Affluent Society 238 (Boston, Houghton Mifflin Company, 4th Edition, 1984).

46. Morgan, supra note 21, at 137.

marshmallows.[47]

Nor are such definitional problems limited to the food exemption. Consider, for example, the exemption for drugs and medicines. Administratively, this exemption poses few problems if limited to prescription items, which nearly all states exempt, (New Mexico being one exception). Sometimes, however, the exemption is applicable to over-the-counter, non-prescription items.[48] Exemption of non-prescription medicine avoids a sales tax incentive to obtain a prescription if an over-the-counter remedy would be sufficient and also avoids penalizing those who fail to seek professional care. Exempting non-prescription drugs and medicines, however, creates formidable administrative problems similar to those encountered in defining exempt "food." In New York, for example, sterilized cotton and Head & Shoulders shampoo are exempt but non-sterilized cotton and Prell shampoo are taxable; foot powders that eliminate excessive perspiration are exempt because they prevent athlete's foot, but foot powders that only deodorize are taxable; lip balm that prevents chapped lips is exempt, but suntan lotions that presumably prevent "chapped bodies" are taxable—even though products used to treat sunburn are exempt.[49]

Distinctions of this sort aggravate tax administrators, who are called upon to draw up regulations addressing them. But consider their effect upon shopkeepers who must insure that the proper amount of sales tax is collected. Any vendor's nightmare is to be audited two years after a sale and be assessed additional taxes after the consumer is long gone. As a result, in ambiguous cases stores may err on the side of caution and collect tax, even if legally the sale is exempt. A 1984 study by the New York Consumer Protection Board, for example, found that 82% of the drug stores and 54% of the food stores surveyed charged tax upon various exempt items.[50] New York pharmacy owners have asserted that they cannot afford to hire employees who are capable of interpreting that State's drug and medicine exemptions. Some found it cheaper to negotiate a settlement if they were to be audited; others charged that the statute's complexity merely constituted a disguised means of raising additional revenue.[51] The lesson to be learned is that complexity may result in an unlegislated tax on consumers.

In all likelihood, most legislators are not aware of the fine distinctions that can exist in their sales taxes. After all, legislators voted to exempt food and medicine from the sales tax, not to tax big marshmallows or Prell shampoo. The administrative burden upon tax officials and the compliance costs for businesses may not be evident until after the exemption has been enacted.

Some states exempt clothing, motivated in part by concern for the poor and in part by the perceived need to match similar exemptions adopted by neighboring states. Pennsylvania exempts most clothing, but not formal day or evening wear, fur, accessories, or sports clothing. Connecticut exempts items of clothing or footwear priced under $50 (excluding athletic clothing and accessories). Massachusetts exempts up to $175 of clothing (excluding athletic clothing),[52] and New Jersey

---

47. CCH California State Tax Reporter, ¶ 60-201.82(d). In 1991, California adopted the so-called "Twinkie Tax," or snack tax, which essentially extended the sales tax to snack foods (candy and confectionery). Confusion about what constituted snack food raised howls of protest from vendors and consumers. Candy, potato chips, and cupcakes were clearly taxable; imitation pork rinds were taxable, but real pork rinds were not. Ritz brand crackers were taxable but not Saltines, Graham crackers, or animal crackers. Glazed fruit was exempt if sold for baking but not if sold for candy. Granola bars were taxed, granola was not. A spokesperson for then Gov. Pete Wilson, who proposed the snack tax, offered the following rationale: true snacks have no appreciable nutritional value or come in certain kinds of packaging. A banana is not taxed, but if you dip it in chocolate and put it on a stick, it's taxed. The spokesperson had no explanation for why Ritz crackers were taxable but Saltines were not. Wall St. J., July 18, 1991, p. B1. Did California create a situation where a lobbyist's spread for legislators of brie, caviar, and French bread was exempt but a lower-scale reception of cookies, chips, and pretzels was taxable? In any event, this extension of the sales tax was rescinded in a 1992 referendum.

48. See, e.g., N.Y. Tax Laws, § 1115 (a)(3) (McKinney 1987).

49. See Richard D. Pomp, State Tax Reform for the Eighties, 16 Conn. L. R. 925, 932, 933 n.25.

50. Keeney, Sales Tax Inconsistencies Tax Merchants, Shoppers, Sunday Times Union, April 15, 1984, at D1, col. 1.

51. See Pomp, supra note 49, at 932-933.

52. The Massachusetts exemption does not extend to clothing or footwear primarily designed for athletic activity or protective use, which is not normally worn except when so used. Mass. Gen. Laws, Ch. 64H, Sec. 6.

In Massachusetts, can a consumer save sales tax on the purchase of a suit if the vendor bills the suit jacket separately from the suit pants, with the charge for each being less than $175?

Massachusetts also exempts the sale of wearing materials or cloth made of natural or synthetic fibers used for clothing

exempts all clothing except those articles for which fur is the component of greatest value. New York recently joined this regional group by also exempting clothing during select periods of the year. Unfortunately, the limited evidence that exists suggests that a clothing exemption makes a sales tax more regressive if measured by income, not less.[53]

The clothing exemption also illustrates how an exemption distorts geographic neutrality. The problem is not that consumers are encouraged to purchase an exempt item (clothing) instead of a taxable one; rather an exemption offered by one state may divert sales from neighboring states unless they adopt competing exemptions.[54] One of the reasons, for example, that New York has experimented with tax holidays for clothing is the fear that its residents were shopping for exempt clothing in New Jersey, or that New Jersey residents were discouraged from shopping for clothing in New York. Connecticut also offers a sales tax holiday on clothing and footwear costing less than $300 for one week in August right before the start of school.

Besides increasing administrative and compliance costs, exemptions are an extremely expensive response to concerns of regressivity because their benefits are not limited to lower-income consumers. The food exemption, for example, is not limited to inexpensive staples, but applies to exotic and out-of-season fruits and vegetables, prime meats, and

imported delicacies. A food exemption is estimated to produce a loss of between 20% and 25% of a state's total potential sales tax revenue and to provide twice as much relative tax reduction to families in the highest income quintile than to those in the lowest quintile.[55] A state with a 5% rate and no food exemption would have to increase its rate by around one percentage point, to 6%, to offset the revenue loss resulting from the adoption of a food exemption. Some of the tax savings realized by low-income families because of the food exemption will be offset because the higher rate will be imposed upon their non-exempt purchases, unless the loss in revenue is made up by increasing (or adopting) other taxes that will have less impact on them.

Consider, for example, a low-income family that purchases in one year $5,000 of food in a state with a 5% sales tax and no exemption. This family pays $250 (5% of $5,000) in sales tax on their food purchases. Assume the state now exempts food. To offset the aggregate loss in revenue from the exemption, the state increases its sales tax to 6%. Some of the family's $250 savings would thus be eroded because it would now pay one percentage point more on all of its taxable purchases. More fundamentally, to save this family $250, the state must forgo sales tax revenue on all purchases of food, including those made by the non-poor. The most glaring defect is that the exemption provides no benefit to low-income persons who because of their special social and housing circumstances may have few choices but to eat their meals in restaurants. Exemptions for necessities or non-discretionary items also reduces the stability of the sales tax during economic downturns, which can adversely affect the financing of spending programs directed at the poor.

Finally, it is possible that the exemption for food has been capitalized into higher prices. That is, the cost of food in a state might be higher because of the exemption than it otherwise might be. Merchants might appropriate some of the benefits of the exemption so that the full amount does not inure

---

purposes. Are thread, buttons, zippers, hooks and eyes exempt if bought for use in wearing materials? What if you plan to use these items for making curtains or drapes? Is the vendor supposed to cross-examine you about the purchase? Are jewelry, handbags, luggage, wallets, hairnets, wigs, aprons, scarves, belts, ear muffs, gloves, and watches exempt from tax in Massachusetts?

Is the approach in the sales tax similar to, or different from, the approach used in determining whether a taxpayer can take a federal income tax deduction for the purchase of clothing? See, e.g., Pevsner v. Comm'r, 628 F.2d 467 (5th Cir. 1980), reh'g denied, 636 F.2d 1106 (5th Cir. 1981).

53. Jeffrey M. Schaefer, Sales Tax Regressivity Under Alternative Tax Bases and Income Concepts, 22 Nat. Tax J. 516, 521-22 (1969); Jeffrey M. Schaefer, Clothing Exemptions and Sales Tax Regressivity, 59 Amer. Econ. Rev. 596 (1969); David G. Davies, Clothing Exemptions and Sales Tax Regressivity, 61 Amer. Econ. Rev. 187 (1971).

54. In theory, the use tax should prevent this geographical distortion, but the administrative difficulties of collecting it makes the use tax ineffective except in specific circumstances. See the chapter entitled, Use Taxes and Interstate Aspects of Sales, Use, and Gross Receipts Taxes.

---

55. Due and Mikesell, supra note 15, at 75; John L. Mikesell, Should Grocery Food Purchases Bear a Sales Tax, 11 State Tax Notes 751 (1996). The large loss in revenue that accompanies an exemption for food explains why states typically phase-in the exemption. The 20% to 25% range cited in the text may mask the actual dollar amounts at stake. Johnson and Lav, supra note 40, at 1789, state that the share of state and local tax revenue provided by sales taxes ranged from less than 15% in Maryland, Massachusetts, New Jersey, and Vermont, to more than 40% in Washington, Tennessee, and New Mexico.

exclusively to the consumer. Whether this occurs or not is yet one more tricky econometric question.

The political motivation for various exemptions extends beyond a desire to minimize regressivity. The common exemption for newspapers has been defended on the grounds of furthering public information and education.[56] A more cynical view is that the exemption helped secure editorial support for introducing a sales tax.[57]

Proponents of an exemption are often able to cloak their proposals with politically attractive rhetoric. The Association of American Publishers opened a campaign (ultimately unsuccessful) in 1985 to exempt book purchases from the New York sales tax, equating that tax with a "tax on knowledge . . . at odds with the state's effort to combat illiteracy."[58] The Association did not explain how the proposed exemption would be a cost-effective weapon in the State's battle to combat illiteracy. The State's 4% tax raised $8.6 million from book sales in 1984. If the New York Legislature had voted to appropriate $8.6 million dollars to combat illiteracy, what is the likelihood that a sales tax exemption for books would have been a high priority for the use of those funds?

e. The Use of Credits Instead of Exemptions

Some states have replaced specific exemptions with a sales tax credit against their state income taxes. This approach allows a legislature the flexibility of setting the terms of the credit to achieve a given level of sales tax relief, which can be tied to the amount of sales tax estimated to be paid by various income groups on their purchases of food, their purchases of all necessities (however defined), or on all of their consumption. Various refinements are possible. For example, the credit can diminish as income increases and can vary with the number of family members.

Some states offer a refundable credit, which grants relief to the very poor who pay no income tax.[59] To be successful, a refundable credit must extend to persons who do not normally file income tax returns and who may have difficulty completing a return in order to receive a credit, or who may be apprehensive about the consequences of doing so. A state must also be able to process a large number of returns that are filed only to obtain the rebate.[60] Moreover, like any state assistance program, a credit requires decisions regarding eligibility and the determination of need; for example, whether taxable income is to be the exclusive measure of eligibility, or whether assets as well as income are to be considered. Should the measure of income, for example, take into account tax-exempt income, such as municipal bond interest or transfer payments?

Compared with a sales tax exemption that benefits all persons, whether needy or not, a credit focuses relief on a targeted group of state residents and minimizes erosion of the sales tax base. Another approach would adjust the rate structure of a broad-based state income tax to reduce the total tax burden upon low-income persons to offset their sales tax burdens. Again, cash payments would be necessary in order to reach the most needy who would have no income tax liability. A rate adjustment, however, would not provide as much explicit annual information about the amount and distribution of the benefit as would be available from analyzing returns that claimed a credit. Also, over time, a rate adjustment originally intended as sales tax relief may lose its identity, especially if rates subsequently change for reasons independent of the sales tax. Being more visible, a credit may also prove more effective in countering political pressure to erode the sales tax with an ever-increasing number of exemptions, at least when such pressure is based upon concerns about the impact of the tax upon the poor. Conversely, a credit may facilitate broadening the sales tax base; objections

---

56. Jacoby, supra note 29, at 114.

57. Jacoby, supra note 29, at 114-115.

58. N.Y. Times, August 10, 1985, § I, at 9, col. 1. The effort to rescind the sales tax on books was backed by the Authors League, the American Booksellers Association, the American Library Association and a half-dozen other related groups. The campaign was supported by John Irving, Norman Mailer, and Erica Jong. Id.

59. Six states–Hawaii, Idaho, Kansas, Oklahoma, South Dakota, and Wyoming—tax groceries but provide credits or rebates to offset some of the taxes paid by certain segments of the population. Georgia provides both a partial exemption and a credit. See Johnson and Lav, supra note 40, at 1786, who criticize these programs for not being generous enough.

60. One commentator reported that New Mexico, which offered rebates for taxpayers with family income less than $16,000, processed over 220,000 rebate returns out of a total filing population of 660,000. Laird Graeser, Sales Taxes on Services: An Idea Whose Time Has Come?, (paper prepared for the Federation of Tax Administrators, Charleston, S.C., p. 11, 1990).

(real or feigned) based on considerations of regressivity and the impact on the poor can now be addressed through adjustments in the credit.

Implementing a credit is more difficult when a state lacks a broad-based income tax. These states, such as Nevada or Florida, would require an independent and refundable credit program. Programs of this type have been utilized both in states with an income tax, such as Kansas, and in states without an income tax, such as South Dakota.[61] An alternative, although one requiring federal legislation, would be for the Internal Revenue Service to take into account a state credit in the computation of federal tax liability, with the state then reimbursing the federal government for the aggregate credits claimed by its residents.[62]

Other possibilities of targeting relief measures include exempting food purchased with food stamps, or an exemption by the state contingent upon a certificate that would be issued to welfare recipients, needy senior citizens, or other specific groups. Exemption certificates are already common in the sales tax. For example, charitable institutions or businesses making purchases for resale most often use a certificate to establish their right to an exemption. The use of exemption certificates by the purchaser, however, places a burden upon the seller for record-keeping and verification, and has obvious potential for abuse. In addition, some eligible purchasers might find such identification objectionable, although favorable experience with other forms of senior-citizen discounts and with food stamps diminishes this concern somewhat. The important question is whether a given alternative would, on balance, be an improvement over the existing system of broad-based exemptions.

Ultimately, the most that any tax system can do for the poor is not to tax them. Issues of poverty must be addressed through transfer payments and social programs directed at root causes and systemic problems. The effect of the tax system upon low-income residents must be evaluated through an integrated analysis of the means of raising revenue and the ways in which it is spent. A state that has enacted programs addressing the needs of the poor (e.g., welfare, medical indigency payments, job training or unemployment benefits) can adjust this spending to mitigate the impact of a tax. On balance, advocates for the poor might be better off supporting a broad-based retail sales tax raising sufficient revenues for these programs rather than a tax rife with well-intentioned exemptions for their constituents.

f. Sales Tax Holidays

One of the recent political contributions to the sales tax has been the use of so-called tax holidays, where a tax exemption is granted for particular items for a short time only.[63] New York offered one of the first, a tax holiday on clothing, and many other states have jumped in. If sales increase during this period, as they are likely to do, the holiday is declared a success in a frenzy of self-congratulations and favorable press.

The announcement of a tax holiday will affect consumer behavior. Some persons will delay until the holiday period the purchase of an item they otherwise would have made earlier. Others will accelerate a purchase they otherwise would have waited to make. And still others, like the editors of this book, will buy what they need regardless of the tax holiday. The question is not whether sales increase during the holiday but whether there is an overall, net increase in sales because of the holiday. Such an increase could come from residents who would have shopped elsewhere,[64] including through the mails or over the Internet, or from nonresidents attracted to the state because of the holiday. A net increase in sales might also result if persons bought items they would not have purchased except for the holiday. In the latter case, the state may not have an increase in net sales if the exempt item is simply substituting for the in-state purchase of a taxable item.[65]

---

61. South Dakota restricts its refunds to persons 65 or older and to the disabled. S.D. Codified Laws Ann. § 10-45A-2.

62. See by analogy the Federal-State Tax Collection Act of 1972, P.L. 92-512.

63. Typical items include clothing, computers, and school supplies.

64. New Jersey exempts clothing from its income tax and one of the arguments for N.Y.'s holiday on clothing was to compete with New Jersey. One of the authors of this book lived in New York for more than 6 years and is convinced he could shop more cheaply for clothing in New York, notwithstanding the sales tax, than in New Jersey (or anywhere else in the region).

65. One study showed that while sales increased during the holiday week, sales during the quarter showed normal growth. N.Y. State Department of Taxation and Finance, Office of Tax Policy Analysis, The Temporary Clothing Exemption (Nov. 1997).

In addition, depending on market conditions, some of the benefits of the holiday may be appropriated by the merchant. More technically, the benefit of the exemption may be capitalized into the price of the good through less generous markdowns, discounts, or sales.[66]

Moreover, not all merchants even favor tax holidays because of their administrative costs. Electronic cash registers are often programmed to take into account the tax status of the items sold by the store. To reprogram the register for the holiday and then reprogram it again once the holiday expires can be a costly and time-consuming task.[67]

For yet a different spin on tax holidays, consider the following piece by Mike Madsen, a leading state tax practitioner with Vickers Madsen and Goldman in Tallahassee, Florida:

LESSON IN REFINING TAX POLICY: THE FANNY PACK EXEMPTION IN FLORIDA.

"Is this booming economy great, or what? Here in the Sunshine State, the 1998 Legislature happened to be looking at more tax revenues than even it could spend, given that we have a Republican majority in both houses that won't admit to spending anything. Anyway, in a fit of public spiritedness, and being that it was an election year and all, the Legislature declared "Tax Freedom Week," during which articles of "clothing" that cost less than $50 could be purchased free of sales tax.

The Legislature defined "clothing" as "any article of wearing apparel, including footware, intended to be worn on or about the human body," but specifically excluded ties, belt buckles (but not whole belts that happened to include an otherwise-illicit buckle), and similar, unworthy items. This left plenty of details to be worked out by our faithful Department of Revenue before the scheduled buying bonanza less than 90 days away.

Showing that it was easily up to the task, the

Department quickly adopted "emergency" rules filling the gaps in the Legislature's brilliantly conceived pronouncement. In almost no time, we had a *huge*, detailed list of items that were declared either taxable or exempt. Examples: My fishing vest was exempt, but my waders were taxable, yet both were intended to be worn on or about the human body. Boat shoes and tennis shoes were exempt, but not golf shoes or football shoes. Golf shirts and golf dresses were exempt, though. Lobster bibs–no kidding, the list included "lobster bibs–were, of course (?!), exempt. As far as I know, our unflappable public servants did all this without even cracking a smile.

My legal mind grappled to find some rationale for the distinction between the taxable and the exempt, but to no avail. Thinking that the Legislature's definition of "clothing" to mean "apparel" must have been based on a profound insight, I looked up "apparel" in the dictionary only to find that it means..... "clothing." My next hypothesis was that perhaps the only exempt "clothing" would be that which a fairly sane human would be seen wearing in public, such as to a movie. This might explain the distinction between golf shoes and boat shoes, for example. But then I realized that I wouldn't voluntarily be seen at a shopping center wearing either a fishing vest or waders. Perhaps the test was one of degree, as to *how silly* one would feel seen in public wearing a particular item. I'd certainly rather be seen in a fishing vest than in waders at my nearest barbecue restaurant. But, then a friend pointed out (quite correctly, upon further reflection) that either of those items seemed perfectly okay to him as everyday apparel.

Alas, the first tax-free week was history before I formulated any more theories. The week went off with nary a hitch as far as I could tell, but a trip to Panama City Beach (a.k.a., the "Redneck Riviera," a.k.a. "L.A.," which stands for "Lower Alabama") revealed some shrewd tax planning by the local merchants. In that part of the State, little shops that specialize in cheap souvenirs and airbrush t-shirts are thicker than Starbucks coffee shops in the *real* L.A. One of the popular souvenir items is those HUGE belt buckles, like the one worn by Richard Petty (pronounced "Ree-sherd Pa-ay-tee"). They're not cheap (in price, anyway), but many did come in under the fifty dollar limit. Seems that during tax-free week, you could get your brass Harley Davidson emblem, or steam locomotive, or whatever, attached to a cheap, vinyl (but nevertheless exempt) *belt*, which

---

66. See Richard R. Hawkings, The Tax Cut a Mother Might not Love: Short-run Incidence and Temporary Sales Tax Exemptions on Clothing, State Tax Notes, July 19, 1999, p. 199.

67. David Brunori, the well-known author and columnist for State Tax Notes, quotes a practitioner who refers to sales tax holidays as "dumber than a bag of hammers." See David Brunori, Dumber Than a Bag of Hammers, State Tax Notes Magazine, March 12, 2001.

avoided the problem with "belt buckles" not being exempt. Nobody ever said you've gotta have all your teeth to be clever.

Another election year is upon us, and the economy still booms. Our latest crop of legislators has presented the Citizens of Florida with the "Florida Residents' Tax Relief Act of 2000." Thank Heaven for term limits, which kicked in this year in Florida.

Seriously, though, the new Act is a shining example of refining tax policy to deal with weighty issues of public policy. Given that the Consumer Price Index has gone up by at *least* four percent over the past two years, the Legislature wisely increased the tax-free limit per clothing item from $50 to $100. Not only that, but instead of only seven blissful, tax-free days, we now have no less than NINE days to purchase our tax-free apparel, including two full weekends. Glorious! And belt buckle tax avoidance is no longer necessary in L.A., as the Legislature saw fit to include belt buckles within the exempt class of "clothing."

What's more, the Legislature also clarified that the exemption now applies to "*all* footwear," except skis, skates, and fins, which eliminates the problem with football shoes and golf shoes. And, the exemption applies not only to "clothing," but now applies also to "wallets, or bags, including handbags, backpacks, fanny packs, and diaper bags." With absolutely no research, I'm willing to wager that this is the only tax statute anywhere in the world that contains the phrase, "fanny packs."

The ink is hardly dry on the Governor's signature, and already we have this year's "emergency rule." How disappointing to see that "lobster bibs" didn't make this year's list, presumably encompassed within the more generic exemption for "bibs." The new, clarified statute has helped to shorten the list, I suppose. We still find that fishing vests and hunting vests are exempt, but not ski vests (or waders, for that matter). "Hats" are exempt as long as they're not "hard hats." "Leather gloves" are exempt, but the diligent reader will discover that "golf gloves" and "batting gloves" (both of which were made of leather the last time I looked) are taxable. I've given up trying to figure out why; I've just accepted that golf shoes are "footwear," but golf gloves are not "leather gloves." Acceptance of such paradoxes is taught in the first year of law school.

The astute tax practitioner may wonder if the title, "Florida Residents' Tax Relief Act," portends a questionable discrimination against interstate transactions. Nope; the word "resident" appears nowhere in the text of the Act. In its wisdom, however, the Legislature decreed that clothing sales at any "theme park or entertainment complex" would remain taxable. This caused me to abandon that weekend shopping trip to Disney World I'd planned for late July. Guess I'll leave it to the tourists, or anyone else silly enough to stand around in the central Florida summer sun. Maybe legislators, come to think of it."

3. Taxation of Services

The common statutory pattern in most states is to tax tangible personal property unless specifically exempted, but to exclude services unless specially enumerated.[68] This distinction is not inherent in the nature of a consumption tax itself, as the widespread coverage of services under various forms of the value-added tax demonstrates. Rather, it is the result of a number of historical and political factors: introduction of the tax as a limited and temporary measure; the relatively greater economic importance of sales of tangible personal property at the time the tax was adopted;[69] and the equation of a tax on services with a wage tax or a tax upon labor.[70] Moreover, the most financially significant services,

---

68. The approach of the states is quite different from that of most countries that levy a value added tax, in which both goods and services are generally taxable unless specifically exempt.

69. In 1960, each point of the sales tax in the median state produced $0.69 of revenue per $100 of personal income; by 1988, that figure had fallen to $0.56. Part of that erosion is due to increased exemptions, but part is also due to the faster growth in the consumption of exempt services rather than taxable goods. Governing, Dec. 1990, p.23. Presumably, during the Great Depression when many states adopted a sales tax, services played a more minor role in the economy then they did in 1960. See infra note 77.

70. Because sales taxes were adopted during the Great Depression, at a time of widespread unemployment, legislators must have been skittish about enacting any provision that could be characterized as discouraging jobs. The most notable exception apparently was New Mexico, which adopted an "emergency school tax" in 1934 that applied broadly to tangible personal property and services. Laird Graeser, Sales Taxes on Services: An Idea Whose Time Has Come?, (paper prepared for the Federation of Tax Administrators, Charleston, S.C., p. 1, 1990). Hawaii and South Dakota also tax a wide array of services.

such as legal,[71] accounting, housing, medical,[72] and educational were politically difficult to tax, whereas the less significant ones, such as home repair, music lessons, lawn mowing, and baby-sitting, would not yield revenue sufficient to justify the corresponding administrative costs. (As these examples suggest, many small vendors are brought into the tax base when services are taxed.)[73] Because legislatures have a tendency to model their taxes upon those adopted in other states, the initial exemption of services soon became a general pattern. The widespread exemption of at least some services increases the regressivity of the sales tax if measured by either income or consumption, for the proportion of consumption represented by services rises with both income and consumption.

The exemption for services also helps eviscerate the base of the tax. Services are an increasing percentage of consumption. For example, services grew from 47.4% of personal consumption in 1979 to 57.7% in 1996.[74] One reason for this shift is inflation, which affected services more than tangible personal property. Another reason is a change in consumption patterns, favoring services over tangible property. More than half of the increase was for medical care (typically exempt).[75]

The philosophy of a retail sales tax, which dictates the taxation of all consumer expenditures, does not justify any distinction between property and services. Furthermore, because personal property embodies both capital and labor, services are in fact already taxed under all state sales taxes whenever they are employed in the production of taxable property. In the context of a retail sales tax, differences between tangible personal property and services are usually one of degree rather than of kind.

Put differently, consumption expenditures can be placed upon a continuum, arranged by the percentage of the sales price that represents the non-capital component of the item. Some transactions are predominantly labor intensive whereas others are capital intensive. Which transactions are considered to fall on the property end of the continuum and which fall on the service end is more a matter of custom than of logic.[76] After all, as a matter of logic a vendor of tangible personal property can be considered as performing the service of selling, rather than selling property.

This casebook, for example, is traditionally viewed as tangible property, yet the cost of the paper, ink, and binding represents only a minor portion of the purchase price, most of which is attributable to the labor of the authors and others involved in the production and distribution chain. A more extreme example involves a famous painting or a set of blueprints for a home, for which the materials involved (canvas, paint, and stretchers in the former case and blueprint paper in the latter) represent a trivial percentage of the sales price. Conceptually, what is the difference between the purchase of a painting for a home, taxable as tangible personal property in all states, and the purchase of the blueprints to build that home, exempt in most states as a service? Or between buying a painting and commissioning the artist to produce a painting, which in many states would be exempt as a service? Similarly, what is the difference between buying a newspaper, taxable as the purchase of tangible personal property, and reading that same newspaper on a computer screen, which would be exempt in some states as a service?

As the amount spent on services grows, attributable in part to the more rapid increase in prices of services than goods, and in part to changes in relative

---

71. Perhaps the large number of lawyers who are legislators may explain the difficulty many states have had in taxing legal services. A normative sales tax should not tax, however, legal services that constitute business inputs.

72. Although medical services are usually exempt, what should the treatment be of an ophthalmologist who sells glasses to their patients? Most states have exempted the sale, viewing it as incidental to the provision of an exempt medical service. Opticians, however, have been held subject to the sales tax on their sale of eyeglasses. Why have states been blind to this obvious competitive inequity?

73. Iowa, for example, found that the number of vendors rose 60% when it expanded its base to cover new services, and the average tax liability per vendor was low. Fox, infra note 74, at 38.

74. William F. Fox, Can the State Sales Tax Survive a Future Like its Past, in The Future of State Taxation 33, 35 (D. Brunori ed. 1998). The data are based on the personal consumption of services and excludes business purchases of services.

75. Id.

---

76. The discussion in the text focuses on transactions in which the labor or service is performed in producing the item. Other situations can involve the performance of a service before, with, or after, the transfer of the item; for example, the application of nail polish as part of a manicure.

consumption patterns,[77] legislators have reexamined the traditional statutory demarcation between personal property and services. In response to mounting financial pressures, states have slowly expanded their sales taxes to encompass a greater number of specified services,[78] with Hawaii, New Mexico and South Dakota having a history of broadly taxing services.[79] Depending upon the services taxed, incremental changes may or may not enhance progressivity and revenue stability,[80] but they may introduce economic distortions by taxing business inputs that will be subject to tax again as they are passed forward into the price of the final retail sale.[81]

Common business inputs that are taxed include engineering and information processing. Other taxable services might be purchased by either businesses or consumers, such as the repair of tangible property, architectural services, landscaping, dry cleaning services, utilities,[82] and hotel and transient room rentals.[83] Personal services commonly taxed include barbers and beauticians and admissions, whereas private school tuition, household services, and legal and accounting fees typically remain exempt. The result of this pattern may be to increase the progressivity of the sales tax (if measured by income) for the middle class without significantly affecting the distribution of the tax among upper-income groups.[84]

If a service is an alternative to the purchase of a tangible good, taxation of both is required for neutrality. To some extent, car repairs may serve as alternatives to car purchases, and laundry services may serve as alternatives to the purchase of washing machines.[85] Taxing the car repair and the laundry

---

77. In 1965, 67.3% of the gross national product excluding government purchases came from commodities; by 1989, that share had declined to 55.3%. As a share of personal consumption expenditure, services increased from 42.1% to 54.0%. Mikesell, Sales Tax Coverage for Services–Policy for a Changing Economy, 9 J. of State Taxation 31 (1991). By 1997, total personal consumption expenditures were $5.5 trillion, of which durable and nondurable goods represented 41% and services represented 59%. Economic Report of the President, at 300 Table B-16. By comparison, in 1945, 67% of personal consumption was for goods and 33% for services. Id. at 239 Table B-10. In terms of the impact on sales tax revenue, more than half of the increase in services was for medical care, exempt in nearly all states. One of the declines in the consumption of tangible personal property was for food purchased for home consumption, exempt in many states. See Fox, supra note 74, at 35. In 1960, the average U.S. family spent 17¢ of each consumption dollar on food for home consumption; by 1995 the average family spent only 8¢. Johnson and Lav, supra note 40, at 1705.

78. States recently expanding their coverage of services include Arkansas, Connecticut, Minnesota, Ohio, and Texas. Some states added selective services to their sales tax; others, such as Florida and Massachusetts, made abortive attempts at taxing a broad array of services. For a discussion of the Florida experience, see the chapter entitled, Sales Taxation of Services and of Intellectual Property, infra.

79. Haw. Rev. Stat. § 237-13(6); N.M. Stat. Ann. §§ 7-9-3(B), (F), 7-9-5; S.D. Codified Laws Ann. § 10-4-4,5. Other states that are generally viewed as liberally taxing services include Washington, West Virginia, and Iowa.

80. Although the evidence is only preliminary and tentative, revenue from a broad-based tax on services can be more stable over the business cycle and can grow somewhat more rapidly over time than revenue from the tax on tangible goods. See Charles E. Rockwood, Edgar A. Fresen, and James Francis, Broadening the Sales Tax Base to Include Services: The Florida Experience, Proceedings of the 1987 NTA-TIA Annual Conference, p. 165 (1987).

81. Some evidence exists suggesting that the largest revenue gain from taxing services is attributable the taxation of business inputs. William F. Fox and Matthew Murray, Economic Aspects

of Taxing Services, 41 Nat. Tax J. 19 (1988).

82. Some states exempt utility services from the sales tax but levy a special tax on public utilities, using the same base and rate that would apply under the sales tax. Some states exempt residential use of certain utility services, either generally or within certain consumption limits. Other states exempt utility purchases for agricultural, manufacturing, or similar uses in a production process. See infra Chapter Thirteen.

83. Some states, e.g., Alabama, Illinois, Massachusetts, Texas, and Vermont, exempt transient accommodations from their state sales tax, but cover them under a companion occupancy or lodging tax. Some states tax transient accommodations under a selective excise tax.

84. High-income households spend relatively more on services than others, but the question is whether such services are the types that a state typically taxes when it expands its sales tax base and whether these services are purchased domestically. Some evidence indicates that by taxing a broad array of services, a state's sales tax will be regressive if measured by income to levels of around $30,000, and will become roughly proportional thereafter. William F. Fox and Matthew Murray, Economic Aspects of Taxing Services, 41 Nat. Tax. J. 19 (1988).

Services whose taxation might make the sales tax less regressive if measured by income include accounting and legal services, boat slips and moorings, hotel and motel lodging, private school tuition, and country club and health club dues. Services having the opposite effect might include coin operated laundries.

85. The examples in the text involve consumer goods and services and not business inputs. It would be improper to argue that because the purchase of a washing machine by a consumer

services will enhance neutrality.[86] Moreover, what is the logic in taxing the purchase of an appliance but not its repair? Or in failing to tax the purchase of a warranty on the appliance? Further, although extending the tax to services carries obvious administrative costs, especially in the multistate context,[87] exemptions can burden administrative resources as well, particularly if fine distinctions must be drawn.

By now it should be clear that no state attempts to tax all consumption. During the 1980's and 1990's, extensive debate took place over expanding the sales tax base to include a broad range of services. Florida, Indiana, Massachusetts, and North Dakota seriously debated this issue. Florida actually passed sweeping legislation that was short-lived, and Massachusetts enacted legislation that never became effective. Instead of sweeping reforms, the states made incremental changes. All states now tax canned software; other services commonly taxed include cable television, pet grooming, amusements, and lawn care.[88] Clearly, major items remain exempt, including housing and medical care.[89] As the following section indicates, however, even items that are exempt from the sales tax may nonetheless bear an implicit or hidden tax arising from the taxation of business inputs that contributed to the production of the nominally exempt item.

4. Exclusion of Business Inputs and Investment-Related Activities

A normative retail sales tax would exempt all goods and services used in producing consumer goods and services (business inputs) and all goods and services related to investment activities. Just as no state sales tax covers all consumption, none excludes all business inputs, although the trend is toward broader exclusions.[90]

The taxation of business inputs has several major consequences. First, if part or all of the tax on business inputs is passed forward to consumers, they will pay an implicit and hidden sales tax, even if the sale of the item is exempt. Consider, for example, an exemption for food. Although the food itself may be statutorily exempt from tax, in all likelihood various elements in its production have borne some sales tax. A farmer may have paid sales tax upon the purchase of livestock, feed, farm tools, tractors, or trucks, while the processors, distributors, wholesalers, and retailers may have paid tax upon the purchase of equipment, machinery, delivery trucks, display cases, wrapping materials, light bulbs, utilities, cash registers, boxes or bags. The sales tax will "pyramid" as firms calculate their markup as a percentage of total costs, including any tax paid on their inputs. The difficulty of estimating the tax upon business inputs is evident, but such information is necessary for an accurate picture of the absolute burden of the sales tax or its distribution among income groups.[91]

Second, to the extent the tax on business inputs is passed forward and reflected in the final cost to the consumer, relative prices of comparable goods will change according to their percentage of taxable components, undermining uniformity in taxation and violating the goal of horizontal equity.

Third, this change in relative prices will affect methods of production. An incentive exists to minimize the use of taxable inputs even if they would permit greater efficiency in a tax-free world. A tax upon business inputs encourages firms to produce intermediate goods in-house rather than procuring

---

is taxable, the use of a commercial laundry by a business should also be taxable. The latter situation involves a business input that should be exempt under a normative sales tax.

86. Economists would describe the failure to tax services as imposing a deadweight or welfare loss because the resulting distortions would mean that scarce economic resources (capital and labor) would not be used as productively as they would if the sales tax were more neutral.

87. See the article by Jim Francis on Florida's experience in Chapter Eight.

88. Fox, supra note 74, at 37.

89. See also supra note 32 and accompanying text.

90. Ohio and West Virginia are two of the states having the broadest exclusion of business inputs. The sales taxes adopted during the Great Depression have been described as broadly exempting business inputs. See Graeser, supra note 60, at 1-2. Business inputs are referred to by economists as intermediate goods or producer's goods. For an attempt to quantify the taxation of business inputs, see Raymond J. Ring, Jr., Consumer's Share and Producer's Share of the General Sales Tax, 52 Natn'l Tax J. 79 (1999).

91. A principal reason for the widespread support by business of value added taxes (VAT), with their high rates on personal consumption of 10% to 20%, is that most business inputs are exempt. The gap between the rates of retail sales tax in the United States and the rates of value added taxes would narrow if the hidden tax on business inputs were taken into account.

them from outside suppliers.[92] Because larger firms are more likely to produce intermediate goods themselves, a tax on business inputs discriminates against small businesses.

Fourth, even if a tax upon business inputs does not affect methods of production, it violates what might be called competitive horizontal equity because two firms producing identical goods pay different amounts of sales tax depending on their production processes. No economic justification exists for placing the firm with more taxable inputs at a disadvantage. This disadvantage may be especially serious if the business competes internationally against vendors in countries levying value added taxes. Such taxes do a much better job of exempting business inputs than does the retail sales tax.

Fifth, even among firms utilizing the same means of production, those located in states taxing fewer inputs will enjoy a competitive advantage, and those in other states may feel pressure to relocate (or at least threaten to do so).

All of these defects would be minimized if states broadened the base of their sales taxes in a normatively acceptable manner and used the resulting revenue to lower the rate or to exclude more business inputs.

Despite these defects, no state exempts all business inputs. Such a broad-based exemption would pose formidable administrative problems in ensuring that the purchase of items such as personal computers, pencils, cars, electronic goods, and furniture was not simply disguised as business purchases in order to evade tax, although an exemption could be made dependent upon the purchase being treated as a business outlay for purposes of the federal income tax.[93] The revenue loss from exempting legitimate

business purchases is another significant factor in retaining the present system. Politically, revenue that is raised through the multiple application of a low nominal rate is often preferable to raising the same amount of revenue through a higher rate, even if that higher rate is applied only once to the purchase by the consumer. Presented with a choice, many legislators will opt for the taxation of some business inputs, raising more money from the sales tax at a given rate, even if the consumer ultimately bears a higher effective burden because of pyramiding.

Some legislators view a tax on inputs as falling not upon consumers but rather upon businesses. Legislators who favor shifting the sales tax burden from consumers to businesses might view the taxation of business inputs favorably. Others who suspect that the tax will ultimately be passed forward in whole or in part to consumers may find the "hidden" nature of the tax attractive. If key businesses feel that they can pass the tax forward without undue competitive consequences, perhaps because the tax represents a small percentage of the total cost of their products, and if consumers are unaware of the implicit sales tax inherent in their purchase of goods and services, a legislator might well be charmed by this "no lose" political situation. Some legislators might view the taxation of business inputs as a convenient way of exporting their state's sales tax to consumers in other states. Finally, some legislators might view the exclusion of business inputs as a "loophole," rather than a normatively required adjustment.

All states address the more blatant aspects of the business inputs problem and make some efforts to prevent multiple taxation, especially if administrative considerations are manageable. At a minimum, nearly all states with a retail sales tax exempt purchases made for resale, which eliminates the multiple taxation of inventory.[94] All states also grant an exemption for materials or parts that are physically incorporated as components or ingredients of items to be resold. Many states go even further and exempt inputs directly used in the production of goods for sale, even if such inputs are not components or ingredients, such as machinery or equipment used in the production process; exact rules in this area vary widely among the states. Generally speaking, more than 30 states exempt from the sales tax the purchase of manufacturing equipment and other

---

92. A properly designed use tax could reduce this advantage. For example, suppose a state taxed legal services. Without a use tax, a business with an in-house legal staff would avoid the tax. A use tax could be levied, however, on the payroll cost of the legal department, reducing the advantage that an integrated firm would otherwise have over an unintegrated firm that purchased legal services from third parties. (In the context of a value added tax, the use tax in this situation would be known as a tax on self supply or self production.)

93. Not surprisingly, states will tend to exempt items that are not likely to be purchased by consumers, such as industrial equipment and machinery, farm livestock, industrial fuel, display cases, lubricants, and abrasives.

94. Hawaii and Mississippi, however, tax sales to retailers, although at lower rates than the retail sales themselves.

states apply preferential rates. Some states limit the exemption to purchases made for new or expanded production. The trend is in the direction of broader exclusions for business inputs.

Business inputs are sometimes taxed as a quid pro quo for exempting the good or service they are used to produce. Mortuary services provide a somber illustration. Legislators might conclude that levying a sales tax on mortuary services is politically unacceptable (or they might be unwilling to oppose the introduction of such an exemption by a trade association), even if they believe that a retail sales tax should be imposed on these services. Having excluded mortuary services, however, a legislature might decide that the coffin purchased by a mortician should not be exempt under the usual rules as a "purchase for resale." A legislature might also conclude that other business input exemptions (e.g., an exemption for machinery, or an ingredients and components exemption) should not apply to morticians. Assuming that the sales tax on all inputs is fully passed forward, the consumer of the exempt mortuary services is subject to an implicit sales tax on the mortician's business inputs, which is buried in the price paid for the funeral. The net effect is that only the labor component of the mortician's services is tax free. In the same vein, many of the business inputs in the chain of production of food are taxable, even though (or because) the ultimate sale of food for home consumption is exempt.

Similarly, if a service, such as auto repair, is not itself taxed, the service provider will sometimes be required to treat the transfer of any related tangible property, such as automotive parts, as a taxable retail sale.[95] In such a case, the auto repairer should be able to buy the parts free of sales tax. Alternatively, if the transfer of the parts to the customer is not taxable, the shop's purchase would not be considered a purchase for resale, and would be subject to tax. Lawyers, for example, who provide exempt services cannot buy their legal stationery tax free under a purchase for resale exemption.

These examples raises the issue of bundling. When should a transaction be disaggregated into its parts, i.e., the purchase of property and the purchase of a service, and when should the entire transaction be treated as either the purchase of a service or the purchase of property. If both property and services were taxable, the issue would not arise. The exemption of either, the property or the service component, forces the issue, which can appear in many different contexts. For example, should a restaurant meal be viewed as the purchase of food, exempt in many states, and the service of preparing and serving that food, taxable in many states? Should the purchase of this book be viewed as the purchase of paper, taxable in all states, and the purchase of intellectual property, exempt in all states?

The nearly universal exemption of sales of real property poses a parallel question. How should a contractor's purchases of tangible items such as lumber, fixtures, bricks and mortar, be taxed if they are to be incorporated in a building, the sale of which is exempt from tax?[96] The issue is further complicated because some contractors also act as retailers of tangible personal property themselves, and in this capacity are similar to other retailers that are allowed to purchase their inventory tax free but charge tax on their sales. In addition, many materials bought by contractors are also purchased by "do-it-yourself" consumers. Finally, many small contractors are notorious for poor bookkeeping and lax attention to details of tax reporting. The majority of states deal with this situation by treating contractors as the ultimate consumer, taxing their purchase of materials as a retail sale and collecting the tax from their suppliers.[97] Presumably, the sales tax is then passed forward to the property owner, which has the effect of imposing tax on homeowners, as well as property constructed for state and local governments and nonprofits, such as hospitals, schools, and religious organizations, which are generally exempt from the

---

95. Similarly, morticians could be required to itemize their bills, segregating services from materials and collect the sales tax only with respect to the latter. Apparently, they have resisted this approach, arguing that it would be difficult to explain to their clientele the relative magnitude of the "service element" in their total charges. Jacoby, supra note 29, at 211 n.13. Have mechanics, in those states in which they must itemize their bills because their labor is an exempt service whereas the parts they supply are taxable as tangible personal property, had the same problem that the morticians fear?

96. Sales and use taxes do not generally apply to the sale or use of real property. The exemption reflects in part the reason that led to the adoption of the sales tax, which was to reduce the pressure on the property tax; this rationale would have been undercut if real property were to have been subject to the newly enacted sales tax. Definitional problems can exist in some circumstances over whether the purchase of an item constitutes exempt real property or taxable personal property.

97. Contractors operating retail stores must separately account for sales made there as normal taxable retail transactions. See Due and Mikesell, supra note 15, at 97.

sales tax on their purchases.[98]

5. Use Taxes

Use taxes are a necessary backstop to a retail sales tax. Use taxes are typically levied upon the use, storage, or consumption of tangible personal property within the state if such property had not already been subject to the state's sales tax. The rate of the use tax is the same as the rate of the sales tax. Property that would have been exempt from the retail sales tax if purchased in the state of use is typically exempt from the use tax. (If not, would the use tax be constitutional?) A credit is allowed for any sales taxes (and some states allow credits for use taxes) paid to other states upon purchase (or use) of the goods. If the credit exceeds the use tax no additional tax is due, but if the credit is less than the use tax the state of use collects the difference.

The use tax responds to four situations. The first involves an item not initially subject to sales tax on its purchase because of the customer's intended use; subsequently, the good is used for a taxable purpose. For example, a merchant might make a tax-free purchase of an item for resale, which is later removed from inventory for personal use.[99] Second, the use tax applies when a sales tax should have been charged upon the original purchase but was not collected, for whatever reason. Third, the use tax applies when a taxpayer produces property for itself for use in its own business. Taxing this situation helps maintain parity between those persons able to self-produce (typically larger corporations), and those that buy the same goods in a taxable transaction.

The fourth and most significant situation concerns the purchase of property in a jurisdiction at a rate lower than the rate that would have applied had the good been purchased in the taxpayer's state of use. The use tax helps ensure that goods purchased for consumption will be subject to the same rate of tax, whether purchased in-state or out-of-state. Without the use tax, merchants in the taxpayer's state of use would face a competitive disadvantage because consumers could purchase similar goods without tax, or with a lower rate of tax, in another jurisdiction. The

use tax guards against erosion of the sales tax by maintaining tax parity between in-state and out-of-state purchases–provided, of course, that a state can collect it.

Erosion of the base can result if shoppers can drive to nearby sales tax havens or purchase goods through the mail, by telephone, television, or over the Internet and not pay the use tax because of ignorance, neglect, or outright evasion. For example, merchants in New York City, where the combined rate of state and local taxes is 8-1/4%, with no exemption for clothing, face competition from retailers in New Jersey, where clothing is exempt. These pressures led New York to experiment with a moratorium on the sales tax on clothing. Similar border problems exist wherever tax savings are a short drive away. For example, residents of Connecticut, Maine, Massachusetts, and Vermont are within driving distance of New Hampshire, which does not have a sales tax; similarly, residents of Maryland can drive to Delaware, which also does not have a sales tax. Theoretically, the use tax should apply when the goods are brought into the home state, but to the extent the use tax is not paid, the differential in sales tax rates will not be offset and residents will have an incentive to purchase out-of-state.

The common sales tax exemption for goods shipped out-of-state greatly magnifies the need for, and the difficulty of, enforcing the use tax.[100] In many cases a

---

98. A minority of states exempt building materials used in construction projects for governments and certain nonprofits. Id. at 103.

99. This situation is an example of what is described in a value added tax as a "self supply."

100. This exemption probably reflects two separate considerations. First, before Complete Auto, a sales tax on an interstate sale was likely viewed as unconstitutional. Second, no state wanted to put their merchants at a disadvantage by

consumer who orders by mail, telephone, or over the Internet can avoid both the sales and use taxes. No sales tax is due in the seller's state because of the exemption for out-of-state sales. The use tax, while legally applicable, is unlikely to be paid voluntarily by the purchaser or collected by the seller.

The potential for abuse was dramatically illustrated when five exclusive New York City jewelry stores, including Van Cleef & Arpels, Cartier, and Bulgari, pleaded guilty in 1986 and 1987 to evasion of sales taxes by falsely reporting taxable over-the-counter sales as exempt out-of-state shipments. In some cases empty boxes were mailed out-of-state to provide documentation of shipment. These jewelers would commonly alter business records and encourage customers to submit false out-of-state addresses to avoid sales tax. Van Cleef & Arpels was ordered to pay more than $5 million in taxes, penalties, and interest, the largest sales tax recovery ever made by New York State, while Cartier paid $2.2 million.[101] Two-thirds of all Cartier sales went untaxed and no taxes were paid on more than 90 percent of jewelry worth at least $10,000.[102] A similar investigation of luxury fur retailers led, in 1987, to a $2 million recovery from Revillon Inc. after auditors noticed that the shipping weight of coats purportedly sent out-of-state was only one to two pounds, suggesting that the customers took their purchases with them.

An effective use tax collection mechanism would insure that consumers in cases such as these would pay a tax equivalent to the rate of sales tax that would have applied in their own states. For practical reasons, however, enforcement is generally feasible in only

select circumstances. If the out-of-state seller has sufficient contacts (nexus) with the purchaser's state, the seller can be required to collect the use tax. Many mail order sellers purposely arrange their activities in order to avoid having nexus with most states.

Use tax can be collected upon vehicles, such as cars, planes or boats, which have to be registered in the consumer's home state.[103] The home state will allow the consumer a credit for sales (or use) taxes paid to other states, and collect as use tax any additional amount due. Sometimes, in the case of cars, no use tax will be due if any sales tax was paid on its out-of-state purchase.

The bulk of consumer goods, including cameras, computers, books, software, stereos, CDs, and clothing, obviously are not registered with the state, and voluntary compliance with the use tax is likely to be low, either from ignorance or from the knowledge that the risk of discovery is nearly nonexistent. Probably no tax obligation is more ignored than the requirement to pay the use tax.[104] The state of use can cajole, coax, and exhort its residents to pay the use tax but the tax is easiest collected with the cooperation of the out-of-state vendor. One recent estimate is that the states and local governments lose $23.9 billion in uncollected use taxes.[105] The stakes

---

discouraging sales to nonresidents. To be sure, the nonresident was subject to a use tax in the state of residency, but realistically it was rare for the use tax to be paid.

101. N.Y. Times, Jan. 9, 1987, §B, at 3, col. 4. The average price of items purchased for which sales taxes were not paid was $40,000. The City Finance Commissioner estimated that the State and the City each lost $400 million a year in unpaid sales taxes from the underground economy. Id.

102. N.Y. Times, Mar. 20, 1985, §A, at 1, col. 1. Van Cleef & Arpels claimed on its state tax returns for 1980 through 1984 that about 90 percent of its sales at its Fifth Avenue store were nontaxable. By comparison, a typical retailer of luxury goods reported about 45 percent of its sales were nontaxable. Van Cleef & Arpels' problems were not confined to state taxes; in 1977, both the president and the controller of Van Cleef & Arpels pleaded guilty to bribery in connection with offering gifts to an Internal Revenue agent auditing their tax returns. N.Y. Times, Dec. 17, 1985, §B, at 3, col. 4.

103. Congress has intervened with respect to one type of interstate sale: cigarettes. Persons selling cigarettes in interstate commerce to non-licensed distributors must notify the taxing authority of the destination state. 15 U.S.C. §375. Would it be sensible to expand this requirement to other types of goods?

104. In an attempt to increase consumer awareness of use tax liability, a coalition of retail associations and government groups filed a complaint in June 1996 with the Federal Trade Commission. The complaint sought to require a warning from direct marketers on their order forms of potential use tax liability. The coalition stated that many order forms mislead consumers into thinking tax is owed only in the states indicated on the form; only the states with which the vendor has nexus are listed on the form. In response, The Direct Marketing Association contended that any consumer confusion is the result of a failure by state government to educate their own citizens. Warning labels would consume valuable space and telephone time. 6 Sales & Use Tax Alert 1 (1996). Apparently, nothing came of this complaint. The FTC does, however, have a policy of sending "cease and desist" letters to retailers that advertise "No Sales Tax."

105. Donald Bruce and William F. Fox, E-Commerce in the Context of Declining Sales Tax Bases, 53 National Tax Journal 1373 (2000). For a suggestion that the $23.9 billion in use tax might not materialize if Bellas Hess were overturned, see

are likely to grow even larger with the increase in telemarketing, television shopping channels, television infomercials, and greater use of the Internet. Many states have become increasingly aggressive in requiring out-of-state vendors to collect the use tax.[106] Although individual consumers rarely volunteer to pay the use tax, business purchasers, especially the larger ones, have a higher degree of compliance. Auditors are trained to look for unpaid use taxes when dealing with businesses that purchase out-of-state.

States have started to use their state income taxes as a vehicle for collecting the use tax from the individual consumer. The income tax instructions may contain information about the use tax, or include a use tax return, or the income tax return may have a line added for the use tax. Maine goes further than most states. Taxpayers are told to either report the exact amount owed on taxable purchases made without paying the use tax or to multiply their adjusted gross income by 0.04% and report that amount plus the tax on items that cost $1,000 or more.[107]

Some border states have entered into bilateral agreements whereby participating vendors in each state voluntarily collect the other state's use tax. In addition, both states' tax agencies agree to share information on possible use tax violations, and offer merchants incentives to participate in the program. For example, the New Jersey-New York agreement provides an immunity from prior violations of the neighboring state's use tax law and reduces paperwork by limiting registration, tax filing and

remittances to the state of location, with consequent exposure to only one coordinated sales and use tax audit for the two states. These inducements are coupled with the threat of increased audit for non-participating vendors and actions against their customers to recover unpaid use taxes along with fines and penalties. Literature distributed to retailers as part of the New York-New Jersey program suggests that they would benefit from "certainty as to responsibilities as to both states, and continued customer goodwill." The New York-New Jersey agreement has inspired others.[108]

6. Local Sales Taxes

Historically, local governments have relied upon a combination of state aid and property taxation as their major revenue sources. Local sales taxes were first introduced in the 1930's, but were relatively uncommon until World War II. New York City and New Orleans are often cited as two of the earliest jurisdictions to have imposed local sales taxes. Local sales taxes became widespread following World War II. Initially, local sales and use taxes had low rates and were uniform within a state.[109] At first, the revenue was used to support general purpose activities, but now it is often earmarked.[110] Today, approximately 6,500 local jurisdictions, including cities, counties, school districts, transit districts and special taxing districts in over thirty states, impose local sales taxes,[111] with sales tax revenue outweighing property tax collections in a few instances. Overall, the percentage of local tax revenue contributed by sales and gross receipts taxes increased from 7% in 1957[112]

Richard D. Pomp, Determining the Boundaries of a Post Bellas Hess World, 44 Nat. Tax J. 237 (1991). Professor Jacoby speculated in 1938 that the initial growth of mail order merchandising was significantly encouraged by the adoption of state sales taxes. Jacoby, supra note 29, at 329-330.

The OECD estimates that electronic commerce might generate $330 billion in revenue by 2001 and perhaps reach $1 trillion by 2005. OECD Division for Fiscal Affairs, Will There be Uniform International Tax Rules for E-Commerce? (1999).

106. See the chapter entitled "Use Taxes and Interstate Aspects of Sales, Use, and Gross Receipts Taxes."

107. For a fuller discussion, see John L. Mikesell, Administering Use Taxes as Direct Collection Through Income Tax Reports, State Tax Notes, May 26, 1997. It is widely understood that L.L. Bean was instrumental in getting the change made to the Maine return. L.L. Bean, which had an obvious stake in the outcome of Quill, wanted the Court in hearing that case to know that the states could—and were—able to collect the use tax from the consumer without help from the mail order vendor.

108. Some states, especially those in the Northeast, have sent special teams to conduct joint audits on companies in other parts of the country, including Silicon Valley, the Washington Beltway, Southern California, and Florida.

109. Gary C. Cornia, Kelly D. Edmiston, David L. Sjoquist, and Steven M. Sheffrin, An Analysis of the Feasibility of Implementing a Single-Rate Sales Tax, State Tax Today, May 14, 2001.

110. Id.

111. ACIR, Significant Features of Fiscal Federalism, 1995 Ed., Budget Processes and Tax Systems, Table 27.

112. ACIR, Significant Features of Fiscal Federalism 1994, Vol. 2, Table 60.

to nearly 11% in 1996.[113] In 1996, local governments collected nearly 30 billion in sales taxes.[114]

Of the 200 cities with populations above 100,000, 116 levy retail sales taxes. Cities and counties raise more revenue from these taxes than from any tax except for the property tax.[115]

Except in Alaska, which has no state sales tax, a local sales tax is in addition to the state tax. Typically, the local rate is less than the state rate, but in a few cases, like New York City, the local rate may be equal to or even exceed the state rate.

Local sales taxes are often popular with state legislators as a means of reducing the burden of local aid upon the state budget while leaving the responsibility for imposing a new tax upon local officials. Local sales taxes raise many complex administrative issues, including the level of government that should be responsible for collection and enforcement, whether the local tax base should be permitted to deviate from the state base, how a local use tax should be enforced, what latitude should be permitted in setting local rates, and at what point a combined local/state rate will prove so high as to be detrimental to local business. Moreover, the use tax issues examined above with regard to interstate sales arise in the intrastate context if the sales tax is not uniform throughout the state.

In states where the local jurisdictions are small in size, with porous borders, and suburban malls compete with urban shopping areas, the rates of local sales taxes are likely to fall within a narrow range; otherwise, merchants in relatively high tax regions might suffer from a shift in cross-border shopping. Where the size of the local jurisdiction increases so that shoppers have less ability to avoid the local tax by shopping in nearby jurisdictions, a wider range in rates can be tolerated.

7. Sales Tax Reform: The Streamlined Sales Tax Project

One of the brightest rays of hope for state sales tax reform involves the streamlined sales tax project (SSTP). Instituted by state governments in 1999 with the assistance of the Multistate Tax Commission, the Federation of Tax Administrators, the National Governors' Association, the National Conference of State Legislatures (NCSL), local governments, and the private sector, the SSTP's goal is to modernize sales and use tax collection and administration. The states will assume the responsibility for implementing the entire Streamlined Sales Tax System. Participation in the system by vendors and states will be voluntary.

Thirty-eight states are involved. Thirty-two states are voting participants; six states are non-voting participants (California, Colorado, Connecticut, Georgia, Idaho and Pennsylvania.)

At the end of 2000, the participating states adopted the Uniform Sales and Use Tax Administration Act (Act) and the Streamlined Sales and Use Tax Agreement (Agreement). By adopting the Act, a state authorizes its tax officials to negotiate with other states in implementing the Agreement. The Agreement establishes the specific framework of a uniform set of rules and procedures that participating states agree to adopt. To become a participant member in the System, an adopting State must bring its law into compliance with the requirements of the Agreement. In recognition of individual state sovereignty, the Agreement has no enforcement mechanism against participating States for non-compliance other than the risk of expulsion from the System. The Agreement takes effect when five states have signed it.

The National Conference on State Legislatures reviewed the SSTP and adopted many of its recommendations as the basis for its own version, which it has likewise recommended to state legislatures. The NCSL Act is less comprehensive than the SSTP version; for example, it does not contain any of the uniform definitions contained in the Act. The NCSL version provides more flexibility for a state and more power to local jurisdictions. States are divided on which version they prefer.[116]

---

113. Based on information supplied the authors by Robert Tannenwald of the Federal Reserve Bank of Boston. If selective sales taxes are taken into account, the percentage rises to nearly 16%.

114. Id.

115. John L. Mikesell, The Future of American Sales and Use Taxation, in The Future of State Taxation (David Brunori, ed. 1998), p. 16.

---

116. See Doug Sheppard, "NCSL Executive Panel Approves Amended Streamlined Legislation," State Tax Notes, Jan. 29, 2001.

The Agreement sets forth its goals as follows: state level administration of sales and use tax collections; uniformity in state and local tax bases; a central, electronic registration system for all member states; simplification of state and local rates; uniform sourcing rules for all taxable transactions; uniform definitions for key elements of the tax bases; simplified administration of exemptions; simplified tax returns; uniform rules for deductions of bad debts; simplification of tax remittances; and protection of consumer privacy.

The Agreement contains uniform definitions for the sales tax base, as well as other key terms of the sales and use tax. The Agreement allows a state to choose what is taxable and what is exempt, in accordance with the uniform definitions established in the Agreement. The Agreement contains definitions of food, prepared food, clothing, soft drinks, and candy. There are ongoing efforts to develop uniform definitions of tangible personal property, digital products, software, medical equipment, purchase price, retail sale, and sales price. The Act also sets forth sourcing rules for the sale of tangible and intangible property and services.

Sales tax administration will also be simplified. A state will require only one return per taxing period and provide the option of filing electronically. A vendor registering with one participating state will be deemed to be registered in all participating states. Once a seller registers, it must collect tax in all participating states, whether it has nexus with those states or not. But registering will not have any effect on whether nexus exists for other taxes.

Under the Agreement, sellers will be relieved of the "good faith" requirements that exist in current law when a seller accepts an exemption certificate from a purchaser; accordingly, they will not be liable for uncollected tax. Instead, purchasers will be responsible if their claim for an exemption is unfounded. There will be uniform tax returns, and uniform rules on the deduction for bad debts, remittances of funds, and confidentiality and privacy protections.

The vast array of local sales and use taxes will be simplified. States will be responsible for the administration of all state and local sales and use taxes. The states will collect these taxes and distribute them to their local governments. Sellers will register only with the state and not with local governments. Sellers will be subject to state-level audits only.

The Agreement requires that local jurisdictions in a state must have the same tax base, but it can be different within limited parameters from that of the state. After 2005, the local tax base must be identical to the state base.

Three models for calculating and collecting the tax will be provided. Under Model One, a seller can select a Certified Service Provider (CSP). A CSP will be a third-party vendor, certified under the Project, to perform all of the seller's sales and use tax functions (other than the seller's obligation to pay the use tax on its own purchases). Provided the seller does not mislead the CSP, the seller cannot be held liable for failure to collect the sales or use tax and is not subject to audit on sales for which the CSP is responsible.

Under Model Two, the seller will install a Certified Automated System (CAS), which is software authorized by the SSTP to calculate the tax imposed by a jurisdiction on a transaction, determine the amount to remit, and maintain all required records. The software company is liable to Member States for errors in the software. The seller retains the responsibility to remit the tax.

Under Model Three, a multistate vendor selling into a minimum of five states, with total revenue of at least $500 million, can apply to have its in-house software certified by the SSTP as a CAS. Vendors adopting one of these three models will either not be audited by participating states or be subject to a reduced audit.

To encourage remote sellers to register voluntarily to collect the tax, the Agreement provides an amnesty for previously uncollected or unpaid taxes. In addition, the Agreement mandates that a monetary allowance be paid to vendors to compensate them for collecting the tax. Currently, about half the states allow vendors to keep a percentage of the tax collected. The amount of compensation mandated by the Agreement will be determined in the future. Compensation will be provided to CSP's, as well as sellers that use a CAS or a proprietary system.

Kansas, Michigan, North Carolina, and Wisconsin are already participating in a Streamlined Sales Tax Pilot, testing currently available technology that allows third-parties to calculate the tax, and collect and report it. These states have contracted with third parties that act as certified service providers (CPS) for the Pilot. These CSPs contract with sellers to perform their sales tax functions, including registration, exemption, administration, computation, filing, and remittance in the Pilot states. The CSP links its software to the seller. The CSP calculates the amount of tax due on the seller's remote sales over the Internet, by telephone, or mail order, or at its physical stores. The CSP then debits the seller's bank account for the amount of tax collected on the sales by the seller in the Pilot states. Compensation cannot exceed the total tax collected. Participation will result in a reduced sales tax audit exposure for any transaction processed by the CSP.

Besides the obvious advantages for all parties of simplifying the sales and use taxes, the SSTP, if enacted by a sufficient number of key states will make it more likely that the courts will uphold the states in cases involving challenges over nexus. If one of the considerations in determining whether nexus exists is the burden imposed on interstate commerce, adoption of the Act and Agreement could result in more favorable decisions for the states. Another positive feature, addressing concerns expressed in Quill, is that the SSTP only applies prospectively. A simplified sales and use tax may also encourage Congress to adopt legislation requiring remote vendors to collect the destination state's use tax.

There have been unsuccessful efforts in the past by the states and the remote sellers at simplifying the sales and use tax. The SSTP holds out the promise of succeeding where these prior efforts failed. One change in the political dynamics has been the increased participation of Main Street retailers. For whatever reason, these retailers have finally become more active in protecting their interests. They represent a potentially powerful force at state legislatures and the Congress.

Allies of the states, such as Senator Byron Dorgan, a former state tax commissioner from North Dakota, have introduced bills giving the states the power to require remote sellers to collect the use tax if the sales and use tax is simplified, thus mirroring the SSTP's efforts. As this book goes to press in July, 2001, a number of states have adopted either the SSTP or the NCSL versions. Passing either version is easier than making the conforming changes to existing state law that will be required. A legislature will have to overcome the very political forces that lobbied for the many exemptions that must now be eliminated in the interest of uniformity and simplification. In addition, local governments have already started to object to their potential loss of control.

The situation at both the state and Congressional fronts is extremely fluid. Interested readers should check for the latest developments at www.streamlinedsalestax.org.

Questions and Comments

1. Consider how a normative retail sales tax would treat the following transactions:

(a)   A gift of a stereo;

(b)   The payment of tuition to a private elementary school, or to a law school;

(c)   A business making a gift of a pocket calculator to a valued client with the name of the business on the calculator;

(d)   The cutting of the lawn of your personal residence by a professional landscaping company;

(e)   The purchase of meals by a lawyer while away from home overnight in the pursuit of a client's business;

(f)   The purchase of work clothes;

(g)   The purchase of a car that will be used 50% for business and 50% for personal purposes;

(h)   The owner of a women's apparel store withdrawing from inventory clothes for her own personal use;

(i)   The purchase of a refrigerator;

(j)   Rent paid for an apartment used solely for personal purposes;

(k)   The purchase of stock;

(l)   Commissions paid to a stockbroker on the purchase of stock;

(m)   Premiums paid on an ordinary life insurance policy;

n)   The purchase of a residence;

(o)   The purchase of an apartment building by an investor; and

(p)   The purchase of a factory for use by the purchaser.

2. Suppose the preceding question had asked whether the transactions would have been deductible in a normative income tax. Would your thought process have been very different in answering that question?

<table>
<tr><td>**Chapter 7**</td><td># Taxable Sales
**Identifying the Taxable Event and
Discussion of Various Exemptions from Tax**</td></tr>
</table>

A. Statutory Overview

To prepare the reader for the cases that follow, this section sketches the statutory framework that is generally found in most states having a retail sales tax. Obviously, the exact pattern varies from state to state, as well as the terminology that is used. Further, many statutes, especially the older ones, are not as "clean" as they could be. Nonetheless, because all states must resolve similar generic problems, generalizing about statutory frameworks is useful. Moreover, the cases usually deal with interdependent issues that require seeing the "big picture" in order to grasp the narrower issue before the court.

For any sales tax, one of the conceptual building blocks is the definition of a sale. Without a sale there will be no tax. A sale is to a sales tax what a realization is to an income tax. The definition of a sale will typically encompass barter, exchanges, rentals, and sometimes licenses.[1]

Not all sales should—or will—trigger a tax, however. Levying a sales tax on all sales would be contrary to the theory underlying a retail sales tax, which is to exempt business or investment inputs and tax only the ultimate consumer on personal consumption. Statutorily, this philosophy is implemented in part through the definition of a retail sale. Retail sales are a subset of all sales and thus the definition of "retail sale" first requires the existence of a "sale." The usual approach is to sweep all sales into the retail sales net, but then exclude specifically designated transactions. At a minimum, most states will define a retail sale as a sale of tangible personal property for any purpose except for resale. In this manner, the definition of retail sale incorporates the "purchase for resale" exemption, almost everywhere referred to more clumsily as the "sale for resale" exemption, which eliminates from taxation one major class of business inputs: inventory. Other exemptions might also be set forth as part of the definition of retail sale, especially if they address the issue of business inputs. In any event, a panoply of exemptions will usually be found in other provisions of the statute.

The sales tax is typically levied on the sales price or receipts from a retail sale. The definition of "sales price" will oftentimes deal with trade-ins, refunds, installment sales, methods of accounting and the like. These issues are commonly referred to under the rubric of "the measure of the tax." Sometimes a statute will be silent on these issues, leaving their resolution initially to the tax administration, then to the courts, and if important enough, eventually to the legislature.

Every state sales tax applies, at a minimum, to all tangible personal property unless specifically exempted. Accordingly, all statutes define "tangible personal property," although the usual definition–personal property that may be seen, weighed, measured, felt, or touched or which is in any manner perceptible to the senses–is not helpful in resolving borderline cases. The statute will also enumerate whatever services are taxable. This difference in statutory treatment–all tangible personal property is taxable unless specifically exempted but only selected services are taxable–ensures that the statutory definition of taxable services will often be more useful to administrators, taxpayers, and the courts than will the definition of tangible personal property. As discussed in Chapter 6, however, this difference is explained more by historical rather than conceptual considerations.

In some states, the sales tax is considered a vendor levy and liability is imposed on the retailer for the "privilege" of engaging in business as a retailer or on the privilege of selling or leasing at retail. In these states the measure of the sales tax is typically gross

---

1. Countries imposing a value added tax do not define "sale" but levy the tax on the delivery or supply of the taxable goods or services. As you read the U.S. cases, consider whether significant differences exist between these approaches.

receipts from retail sales.[2] Some states impose the tax on the gross proceeds from the business of selling at retail.[3] In other states, liability is imposed on the consumer and the measure of the tax is generally the sales price (although gross receipts will be the measure in the case of rentals or services).[4] In yet other states, the statute may be unclear whether the tax is legally imposed on the vendor or on the consumer.

If the tax is levied on the consumer the statute usually provides that it must be collected by the vendor and the vendor is liable if it fails to do so.[5] If the tax is levied on the vendor, the law usually provides that it can be collected from the consumer by the vendor and responsibility for sending the proceeds to the state falls on the vendor.[6] In practice, only a few situations turn on whether the tax is legally imposed on the vendor or on the consumer. One involves a vendor's bankruptcy; a state might have a higher priority over other claimants if the tax is imposed on the vendor and not the consumer. Another involves sales to the federal government. Imposing the tax on the vendor and not on the federal government, which is immune from certain types of state taxation, allows a state to collect the tax on sales to the federal government and federal instrumentalities.

Nearly every state prohibits vendors from advertising that they will absorb the sales tax or refund it after it is paid.[7] This prohibition is consistent with the underlying philosophy of the tax, which is that the economic burden of the sales tax should fall on the consumer. In practice, however, any vendor that wishes to absorb the tax can do so simply by lowering the base price of the item to which the tax will apply. In other words, a vendor who sold an item for $100 prior to the imposition of a 5% sales tax can now sell the item for $95.24 ($95.24 x 1.05 = $100).

---

2. See, e.g., Wis. Stat. Ann § 77.52(1) (West 1989); Cal. Rev. & Tax Code § 6051 (West 1987).

3. See, e.g., Ark. Rev. Stat. § 42-1312(A) (1991).

4. See, e.g., Utah Code Ann. § 59-12-103(1)(Supp. 1990); Ind. Code Ann. § 6-2.5-2-1 (Burns 1989).

5. See, e.g., Utah Code Ann. § 59-12-107(6)(Supp. 1990); Ind. Code Ann. § 6-2.5-2-1(b) (Burns 1989).

6. See, e.g., Ala. Code § 40-23-26 (Supp. 1990).

7. See, e.g., Md. Tax-Gen. Code Ann. § 11-402 (1988); Vt. Stat. Ann. tit. 32, § 9708(a) (1981 and Supp. 1990). Query whether such restrictions are constitutional under the First Amendment.

To encourage the shifting of the tax to purchasers, many states require that it be separately quoted, which appears to be the nationwide practice anyway, regardless of whether required by the law. Internationally, however, the separate stating of the sales tax (value added tax) is far less common. Does separately stating the sales tax make it more likely that consumers will bear the economic burden of the tax? Do you think that retailers were in favor of or against laws requiring mandatory shifting, separate quotation of the sales tax, and prohibitions against advertising that the tax will be absorbed?

All states that levy a sales tax also levy a use tax. The cases in this Chapter present two of the three different contexts in which use tax cases arise. In the first, although the case formally involves a use tax assessment, the use tax per se is not at the heart of the issue before the court. For example, the issue before the court might be whether the item purchased out-of-state and brought into the state was for "resale?" If so, the use tax would not apply, just the way the sales tax would not apply if the same good were bought in-state. Because the item was purchased out-of-state, the use tax rather than the sales tax is formally implicated. But the same issue would have been raised even if the item were purchased in-state because the case essentially involves the purchase for resale exemption. By contrast, the issue raised in the second of the three contexts is inherent in a use tax: what is the definition of "use"?

The third context involves interstate sales and raises jurisdictional and constitutional problems. For example, does sufficient nexus exist between the state of use and the out-of-state vendor so that the vendor can be required to collect the use tax? These issues are pursued in Chapter Nine.

Every statute contains detailed administrative provisions on the collection and remission of the sales and use tax, the filing of returns, audits, penalties and so forth. These provisions apply to vendors (or whatever the equivalent term, such as retailers). Typically, a person must be engaged in business in order to be considered a vendor. Sufficient contacts (nexus) must exist between the vendor and the taxing state to satisfy the Due Process and Commerce Clauses. A business with an office in the taxing state has sufficient nexus and would be subject to the various reporting and collection responsibilities under the law. As connections with the state become more attenuated, however, the statutory definition of vendor (or the equivalent term) must be examined carefully to determine not only whether it is satisfied by a particular fact pattern, but also whether a state can constitutionally assert jurisdiction over the vendor in such circumstances. Just because a fact

pattern satisfies a statutory definition does not necessarily mean that a state can constitutionally assert jurisdiction over the vendor.

B. Defining a Sale

The statutory heart of a retail sales tax statute is the definition of a "sale." The occurrence of a sale is a precondition to the imposition of the tax. Obviously, not all sales are taxable because of exemptions and so forth, but there can be no tax without a sale.

States tend to use fairly similar definitions of a sale. A typical modern definition is:

Any transfer of title or possession or both, exchange or barter, rental, lease or license to use or consume, conditional or otherwise, in any manner or by any means whatsoever for a consideration, or any agreement therefor, including the rendering of any service, taxable under this act, for a consideration or any agreement

therefor. N.J. Stat. Ann. §54:32B-2(f); N.Y. Tax Laws, § 1101(b)(5).[8]

Some states provide explicitly that the sale must occur within the state. The definitions above do not provide this limitation but it is implicit in the statutory framework and required by constitutional constraints. See *McLeod v. J.E. Dilworth*, infra Chapter 9.

Some states make it clear that a sale includes the transfer of possession if the seller retains title as security for the payment of the price. Va. Code Ann. § 58.1-602.

---

8. Some states define transfer of possession to include only transactions in lieu of transfers of title. See, e.g., Cal. Rev. & Tax. Code §6006(a). Some state definitions do not include a transfer of possession but only a transfer of title. See, e.g., Conn. Stat. §12-407(2).

Questions and Comments

1. Using the above definitions, consider whether a sale occurs in the following situations:

(a) The rental of a car;

(b) A tax-free exchange of business property under Section 1031 of the Internal Revenue code;

(c) Diapers supplied by a baby diaper service;[9]

(d) The giving of blood for a consideration;[10]

(e) The rental of lockers in a railroad station;[11]

(f) Newspapers that are distributed free of charge (all of the newspaper's revenue is derived from advertising);

(g) Bats given away for free to persons attending a baseball game on "bat day";

(h) Clothes transferred to a laundry for dry cleaning;

(i) The leasing of computer time;

(j) A new car given as a bonus by an insurance company to its employee selling the most insurance;

(k) A toaster given by a bank to a customer for opening a savings account;

(l) Personal tangible property transferred to a pawnbroker as collateral for a loan;

(m) The rental of a motion picture to a theater;

(n) The rental of space on a billboard;[12]

(o) A charitable contribution of inventory by a dealer;

(p) The sale of cocaine;[13]

(q) You call up a merchant in another state and place an order for a good that will be sent to you through the mail;

(r) You walk into a neighborhood store and order a gift to be sent by the store to your friend in another state;

(s) The out-of-state purchase of a gift by a nonresident who has the store send the item to a resident of the taxing state.[14]

2. Can title be transferred in one state and possession transferred in another? If so, can each state levy a sales tax on the transaction?

3. Is the above definition of a sale "internally consistent"?

4. Is it consistent with the goals of a retail sales tax to levy a tax on the purchase of an asset and also on the rental of that asset? Should Hertz, for example, pay a sales tax on the purchase of its cars in a state that also levies a sales tax on the rental of such cars?

5. Should the sales tax apply to sales between a parent corporation and its wholly-owned subsidiary?

---

9. See Saverio v. Carson, 208 S.W.2d 1018 (1948).

10. See Parkridge Hosp. v. Woods, 561 S.W.2d 754 (1978).

11. See American Locker v. Nye, 125 N.E.2d 421 (1955); Ariz v. Peck, 476 P.2d 849 (1970).

12. See Federal Sign & Signal v. Ohio, 174 N.E.2d 91 (1961); Register Mobile Advertising v. Ga., 250 S.E.2d 468 (1978).

13. See Greer v. Department of Treasury, 377 N.W.2d 836 (1985). Suppose a sales tax exempts prescription medicines. Can someone illegally selling quaaludes claim the benefit of the exemption? See Zimmerman v. Commonwealth, 449 A.2d 103 (1982).

14. See Bloomingdale Brothers v. Chu, 513 N.E.2d 233 (1987).

Alabama v. Delta Air Lines, Inc.
Court of Civil Appeals of Alabama, 1978.
356 So. 2d 1205.

A final assessment for sales tax in the amount of $57,178.30 was entered against Delta Air Lines by the Revenue Department, State of Alabama. The basis of the assessment was that Delta sold meals, snacks and other foods to its passengers when they purchased their tickets in Alabama. According to the State, the purchase of the ticket from Delta was the taxing event, a retail sale.

The undisputed facts are: Delta sells tickets to passengers departing on its flights from Alabama. On certain flights meals, snacks and other foods are served. None of such meals, snacks and other foods are served while the aircraft is in airspace over Alabama. All flights are in interstate commerce. The transaction relating to the purchase of tickets is subject to cancellation by either the purchaser or the airline. The price of the ticket is the same on such flights whether a meal is served or not. If for some reason a meal, though scheduled, is not served there is no right to a refund or a chit for a comparable meal at destination. There is no agreement or commitment concerning serving of meals except as provided by the ticket or appropriate tariff. Delta has control over meals and there is no assurance of or right to a meal until it is served. The assessment of taxes was computed by the Revenue Department through use of a mathematical formula. That formula was as follows:

$$\frac{\text{Ticket Sales in Alabama}}{\text{Total Ticket Sales in Delta System}} \times \frac{\text{All Catered}}{\text{Food Costs}} = \frac{\text{Alabama Food}}{\text{Sales to be Taxed at 4\%}}$$

. . . .

Alabama sales tax applies only to sales that are "closed" within the State. For tax purposes, sales are closed when title to the goods passes to the purchaser. Actual delivery is of great importance in determining when title passes. Title passes, unless otherwise explicitly agreed, at the time and place of completion of performance by physical delivery of the goods.

Under the stated facts delivery of a meal, if at all, occurs outside Alabama and in interstate commerce. Delta has no contractual obligation to deliver a meal at all. It maintains possession until actually served. Therefore, the trial court did not improperly conclude that the alleged sale was closed and title passes at the time of delivery without the State and was not subject to Alabama sales tax.

. . . .

Questions and Comments

1. In *Republic Airlines, Inc. v. Dep't of Revenue*, 464 N.W.2d 62 (1990), the Wisconsin Court of Appeals reversed a lower court's holding that the Wisconsin sales tax could be imposed on the in-flight sales of liquor, as well as the consumption of complimentary beverages served on commercial flights that flew over Wisconsin. The State used a formula to determine which sales were subject to its sales tax. Wisconsin sales were determined by the ratio of Wisconsin revenue passenger miles to total revenue passenger miles. After the lower court's decision, Congress passed legislation preventing a state from levying any tax on or with respect to any flight in a commercial aircraft or any activity or service on board such aircraft unless such aircraft takes off or lands in such state as part of such flight. 49 USC Section 1513 (f).

2. Why didn't the Revenue Department assess Delta on the full price of the ticket? The relevant section of Alabama law, Section 40-23-2(1), referred to in the opinion reads as follows: There is hereby levied . . . a privilege or license tax against the person on account of the business activities . . . as follows: (1) upon every person, firm, or corporation . . . in business of selling at retail any tangible personal property whatsoever . . . .

3. If all sales tax statutes were identical to Alabama's

and interpreted as in this case, which state would tax in-flight meals? As a normative matter, should any state tax the meals?

4. Would the opinion be the same if the price of the ticket varied depending on whether a full meal was served rather than only a snack? What if the airline gave a refund if a scheduled meal was not served?

5. Should the Alabama Legislature change its statute to reverse the result in this case? How?

6. Suppose an Alabama resident orders goods through the mail from L.L. Bean. L.L. Bean mails the goods to the Alabama resident and has no other contact with the State whatsoever. Under Alabama law, has a sale occurred in Alabama?

7. Suppose Alabama amended its statute to levy a sales tax on the purchase of all airline tickets that provide for transportation out of or into Alabama. Would such a tax have to be apportioned under *Complete Auto Transit*, supra Chapter One. Suppose the Alabama Legislature decided to apportion the tax. How should it do so? Compare *Jefferson Lines*.

8. What were the sales tax consequences on the sale by the caterer to Delta? Why is that relevant?

9. Suppose Alabama had prevailed in this case and buoyed by its success the State next assesses American Airlines. American can prove that no meals are served on any flights departing or landing in Alabama. Could Alabama assess the sales tax under such circumstances?

What if American Airlines could show that it served some meals on flights departing or landing in Alabama but far fewer than what was implied by the formula?

What if Alabama used a formula for apportioning its income tax and a taxpayer could show through accounting records that it earned no profits in Alabama. Could Alabama use its formula and assess tax against such a taxpayer?

10. For purpose of the federal income tax, if a deduction for transportation is otherwise available, the taxpayer can deduct the entire amount of the ticket, even though that part allocable to any meals might not be deductible if purchased separately. For example, a lawyer who leaves Hartford in the morning for a flight to Chicago, who eats breakfast on the plane, and returns from Chicago that same day eating dinner on the plane, will be able to deduct the entire cost of the ticket even though another lawyer, also on a one day trip to Chicago, who eats both lunch and dinner in a restaurant in Chicago, would not be able to deduct the cost of either meal. See IRC Section 162 (a); *U.S. v. Correll*, 389 U.S. 299 (1967). Is that approach consistent with this case?

11. Review this case after your discussion of the purchase for resale exemption. Could Delta have claimed that the purchase of the meals were exempt as a purchase for resale? See *Air Jamaica v. Fla.*, 374 So.2d 575 (1979) (purchase of meals is taxable); *Ala. v. Hertz Skycenter*, 317 So.2d 324 (1975) (purchase of meals is exempt).

12. A law adopted by Pennsylvania on June 22, 2001 exempts the purchase of airline food from the State sales and use tax. The Governor supported the exemption as part of a package of incentives to encourage United Airlines to expand in Pennsylvania as part of its proposed merger with U.S. Air. The exemption is estimated to provide U.S. Air, which has hubs in Philadelphia and Pittsburgh, with more than $3 million in benefits.

Frisch, Dudek and Slattery, Ltd v. Wisconsin Department of Revenue
Court of Appeals of Wisconsin, 1986.
133 Wis. 2d 444, 396 N.W.2d 355.

. . . .
The issue is whether the law firm is required to pay sales tax on photocopy charges it bills to clients. We are satisfied that this practice does not involve any taxable sale and that the firm is not a "retailer" within the meaning of the statute. . . .

. . . .
Frisch bills clients only for photocopies made for the clients' benefit. Frisch elected to include these

charges in its itemization of out-of-pocket costs and disbursements, billing them separately from the legal fees, in order to fairly distribute the costs among all clients. Copies billed to clients represent roughly one-half of all copies made by the firm. The billed copies are those made for opposing counsel, courts, government agencies, and for the firm's own internal use. The clients themselves receive only a small portion of the billed copies. All decisions on photocopy billing are made by the attorney handling the case. It is conceded that during the tax years in question, Frisch charged first 20 cents and then 25 cents per copy and that the average cost to the firm for each copy made is approximately 23 cents.

Section 77.52(1) requires retailers to pay a sales tax on the gross receipts from sales of tangible personal property. Neither party seriously argues that photocopies are not tangible personal property as defined by sec. 77.51(5). The dispute is whether the law firm is a "retailer" and whether it makes "sales" of photocopies to its clients.

The commission concluded that, because of its billing practice, Frisch was "selling" the photocopies to its clients within the meaning of sec. 77.51(4)(h). That section defines "sale" as "[a] transfer for a consideration of the title or possession of tangible personal property which has been produced, fabricated or printed to the special order of the customer. . . ."

The great majority of the copies for which Frisch's clients are billed are for use of the court or government agency in which the case is pending or for transmission to opposing parties. Only a very few copies ever find their way to the client, and when they do, it is only as an incident to their use in the firm's representation of the client. In addition, the copies are not "produced . . . to the special order of the [client]"; the decision to copy is the firm's alone.

Even if it could be said that a "sale" occurred as to those copies provided to clients, we are satisfied that the firm is not a "retailer" as that term appears in sec. 77.52(1).

"Retailer" is defined as "[e]very seller who makes any sale of tangible personal property or taxable service." Sec. 77.51(7)(a). In Kollasch v. Adamany, 313 N.W.2d 47, 54 (1981), the supreme court adopted the commonly-understood conception of a retailer as "one who transacts business with a consumer in hopes of making a profit on the transaction." In the court's view, "[t]he type of transactions which make one a . . . retailer are mercantile ones." Applying these principles, the Kollasch court held that a group of nuns who sold meals to the public at cost in order to promote their religious beliefs were not "retailers"

for sales tax purposes.

Even though Frisch may charge a client a penny or two per page more than its estimated average cost of making the copies, it has not been established that when it bills those charges it "hopes [to make] a profit on the transaction." It is not a "mercantile" transaction.

The department argues, however, that the absence of profit or a profit motive is immaterial, because photocopying should not be "isolated" or "analyzed independently" from the firm's law practice which, undoubtedly, is expected by its members to reap a profit. The department's own rules, however–notably Wis. Adm. Code, sec. Tax 11.67, which was adopted to explain the sales tax statutes–provide that:

When a transaction involves the transfer of tangible personal property along with the performance of a service, the true objective of the purchaser must be considered to determine whether such transaction is a sale of tangible personal property or the performance of a service with the transfer of property being merely incidental to the performance of the service. If the objective of the purchaser is to obtain the personal property, a taxable sale of that property is involved. However, if the objective of the purchaser is to obtain the service, a sale of a service is involved even though, as an incidence to the service, some tangible personal property may be transferred.

Frisch's clients do not patronize the firm to purchase photocopies. The need to make copies is wholly dependent upon the provision of legal services. We agree with the department's assertion that "a law firm does not exist solely for charitable purposes." But we also agree with the supreme court's statement that "[t]he taxability of a sale depends on the specific circumstances of the transaction to which it relates rather than of the parties to it." Kollasch, 313 N.W.2d at 53. Here, the purpose of separate itemization was not to make a profit, but only to fairly distribute photocopying costs among clients in fair proportion. Charges to clients for photocopying, whether done by the firm or, where large amounts of copies were needed, an outside photocopying service, always approximated actual costs of production. The firm did not make photocopies for the general public but only for its clients.

. . . .

[W]e conclude the firm is not a "retailer" of photocopies and thus no sales tax may be imposed on its client photocopying charges.

Questions and Comments

1. As a matter of sales tax policy, is the result in this case correct? Should the Legislature amend the statute to change the result? If the result in the case is correct, how might the statute be amended to avoid future litigation?

2. If the law firm never itemized its photocopying expenses, but simply built them into the fees it charged, the issue in the case would never have arisen. Wisconsin does not tax the provision of legal services and thus no sales tax would be paid on that part of the fee that was attributable to photocopying expenses. In essence, the case holds that the result will be no different regardless of whether a firm itemizes its bill or not. But suppose the client made its own copies using an outside photocopying service. Presumably, the client would then pay the sales tax. Why should the result be any different because it used a law firm to make the copies?

The court mentioned that the firm sometimes used an "outside photocopying service" for large jobs. Was a sales tax paid on that transaction? Should any sales tax be paid again when the firm bills the client for that service? Does your answer depend on whether the firm bills the client only for the amount it paid the outside photocopier or whether the firm added a mark up? Would the case have arisen if the firm did all of its copying through outside firms and billed its clients only for the actual costs incurred?

Alternatively, what if the client could have done the photocopying in-house, using its own machines? Would any use tax be due on its in-house copies? If not, why should the result be different just because the law firm did the photocopying?

3. If the State had won this case, a firm that increased its unitemized "fee for legal services rendered" by the amount of its reproduction costs would not charge sales tax but a firm that itemized such costs would charge sales tax. Is it so unusual that a firm's billing practices should have tax consequences? In the case of meals and entertainment expenses incurred on behalf of a client, whether a law firm itemizes its bills can also have very different federal income tax consequences. Suppose a firm performs legal services related to a client's business. If the firm submits an itemized bill the client can deduct only 50% of the

meals and entertainment expense that the firm incurred on its behalf. If, however, the law firm does not itemize such expenses but rather builds them into its fee for legal services, the law firm can deduct only 50% of the expenses. See I.R.C. Section 274.

4. Does the law firm pay any sales tax on its purchase of the paper, toner, and other supplies that are used for making the photocopies? If so, what is really at stake in this case? Was the State merely being greedy or was the law firm attempting to avoid all sales taxes with respect to its photocopying?

5. Should it make any difference that the clients physically received only a small portion of the photocopied materials? Can't the clients be viewed as having constructively received all of the copies and then having their agent–the law firm–distribute them to the various parties? If so, is the statutory definition of "sale" satisfied?

6. Would the court have reached a different result if the law firm added a substantial mark-up to its photocopying costs?

7. In effect, does the court characterize the law firm as essentially performing a service and not as selling personal property? If so, was the definition of "retailer" relevant to the analysis?

8. Do you think the Department's rule, cited by the court, was meant to apply to a situation in which the service provider separately billed for tangible personal property?

9. Can a putative service provider separately bill for the cost of tangible personal property that is transferred, albeit incidentally to the performance of the service, and charge a sales tax? In other words, can a service provider turn itself into a provider of tangible personal property through its method of billing? If the law firm had charged sales tax, would there be any reason to apply the tax department's rule that if the objective of the purchaser is to obtain a service, the incidental sale of tangible personal property will be ignored?

10. Would this case have arisen if Wisconsin taxed legal services?

Columbia Pictures Industries, Inc. v. Tax Commissioner
Supreme Court of Connecticut, 1979.
176 Conn. 604, 410 A.2d 457.

The plaintiffs appealed from the payment under protest of a sales tax imposed on the rental of a film from the plaintiff distributor to the plaintiff motion picture exhibitor. . . .

The parties are in accord on the facts and have stipulated substantially as follows: The plaintiff Columbia Pictures Industries, Inc., hereinafter designated as Columbia, distributes motion pictures owned by producers whose ownership and benefit to be thereby derived are protected by copyright. On or about January 14, 1976, the plaintiff Columbia licensed a motion picture entitled "Hard Times" to the plaintiff, doing business as Cheshire Cinema. The producer of "Hard Times" had licensed Columbia to grant to exhibitors the right to possess and exhibit it. In the ordinary transaction, the distributor grants such rights in a motion picture to the exhibitor for a definite time and for a definite number of showings, after which the film print is returned to the distributor. In the present case, the film was shown at Cheshire Cinema from January 14, 1976, through January 20, 1976.

. . . The actual cost of the film print material for one print of "Hard Times" was $595. The production cost for the film was approximately $3,500,000, which consisted primarily of payment for the personal services of actors, directors, composers, musicians, authors, cameramen and other technicians. The value or cost of the actual film bears little or no relation at all to the payments contracted for pursuant to the agreement between the exhibitor and the distributor. The payments are based upon the number of persons expected to view the motion picture.

Pursuant to General Statutes § 12-407(2) "'Sale' and 'selling' mean and include . . . (k) the leasing or rental of tangible personal property of any kind whatsoever, including but not limited to motor vehicles, linen or towels, machinery or apparatus, office equipment and data processing equipment." The term "tangible personal property" is defined in § 12-407 (13) as "personal property which may be seen, weighed, measured, felt or touched or which is in any other manner perceptible to the senses." By virtue of these statutes, the defendant imposed a sales and use tax on the rental of films.

. . . .

The plaintiffs claim that their agreement is a license. The defendant, however, claims the agreement is a lease or rental. The issues presented by this appeal are: (1) does the license agreement[1] constitute a "leasing or rental of tangible personal property" within the statute and, (2) if the transaction does constitute a leasing or rental of tangible personal property within the statute, is the transaction exempt under General Statutes § 12-412 (k) which exempts from the sales and use tax "professional. . . or personal service transactions. . . which involve sales as inconsequential elements for which no separate charges are made."

The plaintiffs' argument is that the ownership of the copyright of the film is distinct and separate from the ownership of the film and that the license agreement is a license to exhibit publicly what is on the film and, therefore, is the transfer of an intangible right for a limited period of time and not a leasing or rental of tangible personal property under the provisions of General Statutes § 12-407(2)(k).

The agreement between the two plaintiffs is entitled "License Agreement" and is in the form of a license. In determining what the transaction is, the character of the agreement rather than the phrasing of the contract involved is examined. It is true, as claimed by the plaintiffs, that a copyright may be an incorporeal right to publish and does exist detached from the personal property out of which it arises. The agreement in the present case does not involve a transfer of the copyright itself unrelated to the film but is the leasing of the film in its finished state. The plaintiffs agree that the possession of the film was transferred to the exhibitor but contend that the agreement was for a limited license to reproduce the performance of the actors. They claim that possession was transferred so that the exhibitor could exercise that right and that without the right to reproduce the

---

1. "1. LICENSE: Exhibitor is granted and accepts a limited license under the copyright of the motion picture or pictures designated in the Schedule (herein individually and collectively called 'the picture') to exhibit the picture publicly by use of the print furnished by Distributor, without cuts or alterations of any kind, without any intermission unless otherwise provided, and only at the theatre, and only on the consecutive days specified in the Schedule or otherwise determined as provided herein (which consecutive days are herein called the 'license period'), and for no other purposes."

value of the film was inconsequential. See Washington Times-Herald, Inc. v. District of Columbia, 213 F.2d 23 (D.C. Cir. 1954); Watson Industries, Inc. v. Shaw, 69 S.E.2d 505 (1952).

Further, the plaintiffs urge that the licensing of "Hard Times" was exempt under General Statutes § 12-412(k) because the agreement was a service contract and the film was at most only incidental to the service rendered. Therefore, the transfer of possession of the film itself to the exhibitor was inconsequential and not taxable as a lease of tangible property.

In contrast, the defendant commissioner argues that even if a copyright does exist in this case, it is the film, that is, the finished product, which was leased and not the copyright itself. As was stated in one of the early cases involving this issue, "[t]he license to exhibit without the transfer of possession would be valueless. Together they are one transaction and constitute a sale." United Artists Corporation v. Taylor, 7 N.E.2d 254, 256 (1937).

The plaintiffs' reliance on such cases as Dun & Bradstreet, Inc. v. City of New York, 11 N.E.2d 728 (1937), to support their argument that the transfer of the film was not a transfer of tangible personal property is misplaced. In Dun & Bradstreet, Inc., an information service was sold to its subscriber. Books were furnished to the subscribers with title retained by Dun & Bradstreet. No charge was made for the use of these books. In that case it was concluded that the books that were given to subscribers were only incidental to providing information and hence were not taxable. In a later case, Moody's Investors Service v. Taylor, 5 N.Y.S.2d 765 (1938), it was held that if the information furnished was not confidential, so that the subscriber may assign or exhibit for his own profits the reports which he received as a service, then it apparently loses its character as essentially a service to its subscriber and becomes taxable.

In examining the character of the present agreement, although called a license, it is evident that under it the plaintiffs' object was to acquire possession of the film in its finished state in order to reproduce it for profit rather than to acquire the services performed in producing the film. See Federated Department Stores, Inc. v. Kosydar, 340 N.E.2d 840 (1976). Although, as the plaintiffs argued, the performances could have been telecast without the film or could have been performed live on stage, the fact is, that was not the case. Rather, the performances were shown on film, which is tangible personal property. The transaction was therefore a lease of tangible personal property.

The plaintiffs state that even if it is determined that there was a transfer of tangible personal property, General Statutes § 12-412 exempts the transaction from taxation. Under § 12-412(k), the sale or lease of personal services are not taxable: "Personal Services. Professional, insurance or personal services transactions. . . which involve sales as inconsequential elements for which no separate charges are made." The plaintiffs point to the fact that the cost of producing and printing "Hard Times" was $3,500,000. Most of this was for personal services and the film print itself was worth only $595.

Since this state's sales and use tax is based substantially on the Ohio statutes, the decisions of that court have more than passing interest in the examination and applicability of our sales and tax statutes. In Recording Devices Co. v. Porterfield, 283 N.E.2d 626, 629 (1972), it was held that "'[p]ersonal service' means an act done personally by a particular individual; it is, in effect, an economic service involving either the intellectual or manual personal effort of an individual, not the saleable product of his skill." In Columbus Coated Fabrics Division v. Porterfield, 285 N.E.2d 50 (1972), the plaintiffs claimed that artistic designs which could be translated into wall covering designs were the product of an artist's skill and talent and that the value of the design was determined by its quality and merit and not by the inconsequential cost of the paper and paint used to convey the design. The court held that the fact that an artist's skill and professional knowledge go into the creation of a design does not mean that a subsequent sale of that design is an incident to a personal service transaction, regardless of the inconsequentiality of the tangible personal property. It held that the transaction involved the sale of an end product rather than the service rendered.

In Accountants Computer Services, Inc. v. Kosydar, 298 N.E.2d 519 (1973), the test laid down for determining whether a consequential service rendered is taxable or not under the exemption (which is similar to the exemption under question here) was to examine the real object sought by the buyer, i.e., the service per se or the property produced by the service, and to determine if it was the buyer's object to obtain an act done personally by the individual as an economic service involving either the intellectual or manual effort of the individual, or if it was the buyer's object to obtain only the saleable end product of some individual's skill.

An examination of the cases on the issues raised in this action makes clear that there is a split of authority. Taking into consideration these opposing views, this court is persuaded by the reasoning in the more recent decisions which is advanced by the defendant commissioner. The test suggested by the Ohio case of Accountants Computer Services, Inc. v. Kosydar, supra, is the correct standard for determining the taxability under our tax statutes when consequential services are entwined with tangible personal property. The critical factor is whether the buyer intended to buy an individual's skills or a tangible end product of those skills. Based on the stipulated facts, it is clear that the plaintiff

exhibitor's object in this case was to obtain possession of the saleable end product, the film. This is especially true in this instance where the rental fee or "license" cost is dependent on how many persons were estimated to view the film.

The rental or license to exhibit the motion picture "Hard Times" was a taxable "sale" under the Sales and Use Tax Act. Moreover, since the film is a saleable end product, the personal service exemption of General Statutes § 12-412(k) is inapplicable.
. . . .

Questions and Comments

1. What were the sales tax consequences when the producer of "Hard Times" licensed Columbia to grant to exhibitors the right to possess and exhibit the film?

2. Some states define a sale to include a license. See, e.g., N.J. Stat. Ann. § 54:32B-2(f). If Connecticut had defined a sale to include a license, would this case have arisen? Could the taxpayer have offered the court a principled reason why the definition of a sale covered leases but not licenses? How is a license different from a lease?

3. Connecticut's definition of tangible personal property as personal property which may be seen, weighed, measured, felt, or touched or which is in any other manner perceptible to the senses, is a common one. Consider some items that are typically considered to be intangible property: stocks, bonds, insurance policies, copyrights, patents, and so forth. Does Connecticut's definition appear to embrace some of these items? Did the taxpayer argue that a film was not tangible personal property?

4. How is this case any different from one in which the plaintiff rented a car for a few days? Would that rental be treated as a sale? Should any different result be reached where the asset being rented is a film rather than a car?

5. The plaintiffs argued that the performances depicted on the film could have been telecast without the film or could have been performed live on stage. In such a case, no sales tax would presumably be due. According to the plaintiffs, the same result should prevail where the performances are captured on film. Does that argument prove too much?

6. Suppose you go to an accountant to have your tax

return prepared. What have you bought–the accountant's skills or a tangible end-product of those skills, i.e., the return? Does it depend on what the accountant actually did? What if the accountant had you fill out a data sheet, which was then keypunched into a computer that prepared the return and all the accountant did was skim and sign the return?

7. Two ingredients were necessary for the transaction in *Columbia Pictures* to be of value. The theater needed possession of the film and the right to show that film. When two ingredients are necessary, is it possible as a matter of logic to view one but not the other as the object of the transaction?

8. When you rent a video for the night, can you argue that no sales tax is due because you are acquiring an exempt license to see the images contained on the tape, and that the tape is inconsequential? What if you downloaded the same movie from the Internet? Is your argument now stronger?

9. As a normative matter, is it relevant whether Connecticut taxed admission to movie theaters?

10. Did the distributor have nexus with the State?

11. To bolster its conclusion that the exhibitors wanted to obtain possession of the saleable end-product–the film–the court notes that the rental fee or "license" cost is dependent on how many persons were estimated to view the film. What is the relevance of this observation? Suppose you are a part of a dance troupe whose compensation is a percentage of the gross receipts paid for the performance. Why does the method of compensation have anything to do with whether a transaction is characterized as tangible personal property or as services?

12. Suppose that technological advances allow the movie theater to obtain a copy of a movie electronically, by downloading it from a satellite. How would that technological advance affect the analysis in this case?

13. For other cases dealing with licenses to exhibit motion pictures, television films, or videos, see *WDKY-TV v. Ky.*, 838 S.W.2d 431 (1992); *Mount Mansfield Television v. Vt.*, 336 A.2d 193 (1975); *Boswell v. Paramount Television Sales, Inc.*, 282 So.2d 892 (Ala. 1973); *American Television Co. v. Hervey*, 490 S.W.2d 796 (Ark. 1972) infra; *Universal Images, Inc. v. Missouri Dep't of Revenue*, 608 S.W.2d 417 (Mo. 1980).

C. Sale For Resale (Purchase For Resale) Exemption

As was discussed earlier, a normative retail sales tax would exempt all business inputs. No state has adopted this approach. Typical exemptions include sales for resale (found in every state with a sales tax), the purchase of machinery used in manufacturing, and the purchase of items that will become ingredients or component parts of manufactured products.

Statutorily, the sale for resale exemption is almost always embodied in the definition of a retail sale, that is, a retail sale is defined to exclude sales for resale. Probably the largest single category of business inputs covered by the sale for resale exemption is inventory. The definition of a retail sale may also incorporate other exemptions as well, or these may be set forth in explicit statutory provisions. A combination of approaches is also common, whereby the definition of a retail sale incorporates some exemptions whereas others are found in various parts of the statute.

Statutory Snippets

"Retail sale" or a *"sale at retail"* means a sale to any person for any purpose *other than for resale in the form of tangible personal property or [taxable] services*. . . and shall include any such transaction as the Tax Commissioner upon investigation finds to be in lieu of a sale . . . Va. Code Ann. § 58.1-602 (emphasis added).

Retail Sale. (1) A sale of tangible personal property to any person for any purpose, *other than (A) for resale either as such or as converted into or as a component part of a product produced for sale by the purchaser*, or (B) for use by that person in performing the services subject to tax . . . where the property so sold becomes a physical component part of the property upon which the services are performed or where the property so sold is later actually transferred to the purchaser of the service in conjunction with the performance of the service subject to tax. N.J. Stat. Ann. § 54:32B-2(e)(emphasis added).

(E) "Retail sale" and "sales at retail" include all sales except those in which the purpose of the consumer is:

(1) *To resell the thing transferred or benefit of the service provided, by a person engaging in business, in the form in which the same is, or is to be, received by him;*

(2) To incorporate the thing transferred as a material or a part, into tangible personal property to be produced for sale by manufacturing, assembling, processing, or refining . . . This paragraph does not exempt or except from "retail sale" or "sales at retail" the sale of tangible personal property that is to be incorporated into a structure or improvement to real property.
. . . .
(7) To incorporate the thing transferred as a material or a part into, or to use or consume the thing transferred directly in the production of, magazines distributed as controlled circulation publications;
(8) To use or consume the thing transferred in the production and preparation in suitable condition for market and sale of printed, imprinted, overprinted, lithographic, multilithic, blueprinted, photostatic, or other productions or reproductions of written or graphic matter; [Ohio Rev. Code Ann. § 5739.01 (emphasis added)].

(4) Retail sale. (i) A sale of tangible personal property to any person for any purpose, *other than (A) for resale as such or as a physical component part of tangible personal property*, or (B) for use by that person in performing the services subject to tax . . . where the property so sold becomes a physical component part of the property upon which the services are performed or where the property so sold is later actually transferred to the purchaser of the service in conjunction with the performance of the service subject to tax. Notwithstanding the preceding provisions of this subparagraph, a sale of any tangible personal property to a contractor, subcontractor or repairman for use or consumption in erecting structures or buildings, or building on, or otherwise adding to, altering, improving, maintaining, servicing or repairing real property, property or land, as the terms real property, property or land are defined in the real property tax law, is deemed to be a retail sale regardless of whether the tangible personal property is to be resold as such before it is so used or consumed. . . . N.Y. Tax Law § 1101(b)(4)(emphasis added).

* * *

Examine the above definitions. Does the sale for resale exemption apply if the person purchasing the property is in the business of providing exempt services? Taxable services? Does the exemption apply if the goods are to be sold in another state? Does the exemption apply if the resold good is not taxable? Can a taxpayer whipsaw a state by buying a good under a purchase for resale exemption but sell it as part of an exempt transaction, such as an exempt service transaction for which the good is merely incidental or inconsequential.

Does the purchase for resale exemption apply if the good is first used by the purchaser in its business and later resold? Cf. *Baltimore Foundry and Machine Corp. v. Md.*, 127 A.2d 368 (1956) with *Law Lincoln Mercury v. Strickland*, 271 S.E.2d 152 (1980). As the above definitions indicate, in some states the sale for resale

exemption applies when the purchased property is used in performing a taxable service and is transferred to the end user (i.e., the customer of the purchaser). The exemption will also apply to services purchased for resale. See, e.g., N.Y. Tax Law §1105(c)(sales tax on "receipts from every sale, except for resale, of the following services. . .).

Bullock v. Cordovan Corporation
Court of Appeals of Texas, Austin, 1985.
697 S.W.2d 432.

Cordovan Corporation filed suit to recover $19,116.66 in use taxes paid under protest. The Comptroller filed a counterclaim for sales taxes allegedly due from Cordovan's sale of its publications.

. . . .

The Comptroller sought to impose a use tax on certain supplies, materials and services such as printing, photography, and other processes in the physical preparation of two of Cordovan's publications. A use tax is imposed on the storage, use, or other consumption of a taxable item purchased from a retailer for storage, use or other consumption. In district court, Cordovan argued successfully that its operation was entitled to the benefit of the Tex. Tax Code Ann. § 151.302 exemption, [which] provides:

The sale for resale of a taxable item is exempted from the taxes imposed by this chapter.

The facts underlying this dispute may be described as follows. Cordovan is a publishing company located in Houston. Cordovan publishes several periodicals, "controlled subscription" publications, aimed primarily at certain industry groups. Among such publications are Jet Cargo News and Western Outfitter. The readers of Jet Cargo News consist primarily of persons with decision-making authority in industries which often use air freight. The readers of Western Outfitter are primarily retailers who make large and frequent purchases of western wear and leather goods. The qualified readers pay nothing for the publications they receive. A de minimis number of copies of each of these publications is distributed on a paid circulation basis.

It is the quality of Cordovan's mailing lists, which contain frequent users of air freight and frequent purchasers of large orders of western goods, that encourages airlines and manufacturers of western goods to place advertisements with Cordovan. Cordovan updates these lists frequently and accepts subscriptions only from those whom it considers

qualified readers. Persons not likely to use the products and services of Cordovan's advertisers in its controlled circulation publications are deleted from the list of qualified readers.

. . . .

The rates paid by advertisers in these publications reflect the promised volume of circulation of Jet Cargo News and Western Outfitter, as well as the audience of qualified readers promised by Cordovan. In the publishing and advertising industry, rates for advertisements placed in controlled circulation publications are much higher per thousand circulation than for those placed in other publications because of the promise that the tangible magazine will be delivered to only a specified category of readers.

Cordovan's staff assembles the monthly draft of articles, features and advertisements. Cordovan then sends the draft to an independent printer who prints the requested number of copies. Upon delivery of the copies from the printer, Cordovan mails them to the readers on its mailing list. Except for a very small number of subscription sales, Cordovan distributes the publications free of charge.

. . . .

The Comptroller's position is that in order for there to be a "resale," Cordovan must receive from someone, "consideration valued in money." We observe that the definition of a "sale for resale" does not contain a requirement that the "consideration be valued in money." That definition provides:

§ 151.006. "Sale for Resale"
"Sale for resale" means a sale of:
(1) tangible personal property or a taxable service to a purchaser who acquires the property or service for the purpose of reselling it in the United States of America or a possession or territory of the United States of America in the normal course of business in the form or condition in which it is acquired or as an attachment to or integral part of other tangible personal property or taxable service.

The source of the Comptroller's contended-for definition is found in the definition of "sales price" or "receipts" in § 151.007:

§ 151.007. "Sales Price" or "Receipts"
(a) "Sales price" or "receipts" means the total amount for which a taxable item is sold, leased, or rented, valued in money, without a deduction for the cost of:
(1) the taxable item sold, leased, or rented;
(2) the materials used, labor or service employed, interest, losses, or other expenses;
(3) the transportation of tangible personal property before the sale; or
(4) transportation incident to the performance of a taxable service.

This Court has no difficulty in concluding that the definition of "sales price" or "receipts" has little or no relevance in defining "sale for resale."

On the other hand, § 151.005(1) appears helpful and provides:

§ 151.005. "Sale" or "Purchase"
"Sale" or "purchase" means any of the following when done or performed for consideration:
(1) a transfer of title or possession of tangible personal property;

Cordovan points out that there are two elements of this definition. First, title or possession must be transferred, and second, there must be consideration for the transfer. With respect to the facts in this appeal, the first element is indisputably satisfied as Cordovan transfers possession of the publications to the readers. At issue is whether or not Cordovan receives consideration. The Comptroller admits in his brief: "[t]he Comptroller agrees that in certain situations consideration can be paid by a third party.

Nothing in the statutory definition of "sale" requires the consideration to be paid by the consumer (or reader in this case)." As no consideration was received from the readers except for a de minimis number of subscriptions, the principal issue is whether the advertisers gave consideration for the transfer by Cordovan to the readers. This consideration is distinct from their payments for the publication of their advertisements.

The most significant element of the transaction between Cordovan and its advertisers is that Cordovan guarantees distribution of its controlled circulation publications only to qualified readers likely to use the advertiser's products. The advertising rates for such controlled circulation publication are much higher than for regular publications because of the promise that the magazine will be delivered to only a specified category of readers. Accordingly, the advertisers do not pay merely to have their advertisements published, but also pay an additional amount to have the magazines distributed to a certain group. As such, the advertisers do pay additional consideration to have the magazines delivered to a special group of readers.

. . . .

The district court properly concluded that the transaction between the printer and Cordovan was exempt from use taxation pursuant to the "sale for resale" exemption of § 151.302.

. . . .

[The Court held that the Comptroller's counterclaim for sales taxes was barred by the statute of limitations.]

Questions and Comments

1. The Comptroller filed a counterclaim for sales taxes due from Cordovan's sale of its publications. How did the Comptroller calculate the amount of sales tax due? Suppose you work for the Comptroller. What would your argument be for assessing sales taxes on Cordovan?

2. Examine the definition of "sales price." Suppose a supermarket uses milk as a loss leader and sells it below cost. What amount is subject to the sales tax (assuming food is taxable)?

3. Unless a sales tax is paid on the distribution of the publications, or on the payments for the production, Cordovan will neither pay any sales or use taxes on its purchases because of the sale for resale exemption

nor collect any sales taxes on the "sale" of its publications. Does this pervert the rationale underlying the purchase for resale exemption?

4. After *Cordovan*, the Comptroller amended the regulations to provide that publishers of controlled circulation magazines must collect sales tax from persons who advertise in their magazines based upon the "sales price" of the magazine. A controlled circulation magazine is defined as a magazine which is paid for by advertisers rather than by recipients of the magazines. In *Sharp v. Cox Texas Publications*, 943 S.W.2d 206 (1997), the court held that, to the extent the regulation provides that a taxable sale occurs whenever retailers pay to advertise in a magazine that is distributed for free, the regulation is invalid

because it violates *Cordovan*.

5. Can the case be viewed as if the advertisers had purchased the publication from Cordovan, and Cordovan then distributed the publication on behalf of the advertisers? If the case were viewed in this manner, what would be the sales and use tax consequences?

6. Would a sales or use tax apply if a telephone company purchased materials for use in its printing of a telephone directory, which contained no advertising, and which was distributed "free" to all telephone subscribers? See *Princeton Community Phone Book*, 368 A.2d 933, cert. den., 372 A.2d 331 (1977). Similar issues arise with "pennysavers," which are typically given away for free and financed entirely from advertising revenue. See, e.g., *Fairlawn Shopper v. N.J.*, 484 A.2d 659 (1984).

7. The "sale for resale" definition employed by Texas requires that the tangible personal property be resold in the United States (or in a possession or territory of the United States). Why? Is the Texas Legislature unwilling to exempt a sale for resale unless there is the possibility that another state will tax the consumer? If the purchased good is resold to a purchaser in another state, that state's sales or use tax y be applicable. What is the likelihood of the use tax

being paid if the good is sold to a purchaser in a state that has a sales and use tax? Is there any difference, however, between a sale to a purchaser who will resell the item abroad and a sale to a purchaser who will resell the item in a state that does not have a sales tax? Or a sale to a purchaser who will resell the item in a state that has a sales and use tax but the likelihood of either being paid is minimal? Or is Texas simply worried about consumers who live near the border going into Mexico to buy Texas goods free of Texas sales tax?

Is Texas' discrimination against items to be resold outside the U.S. constitutional?

8. Should a state ever grant a sale for resale exemption for items that are intended for purchasers in other states? Why should it give up any revenue by allowing an exemption if it will not offset this loss with a tax on the sale? Constitutionally, could a purchase for resale exemption be denied for goods purchased for sale outside Texas? See *Don McCullagh v. Mich.*, 93 N.W. 2d 252 (1958), appeal dismissed, 359 U.S. 343 (1959).

9. Constitutionally, could Texas levy a use tax on those magazines which are distributed for free in Texas?

State of Alabama v. Tri-State Pharmaceutical
Court of Civil Appeals of Alabama, 1979.
371 So. 2d 910, writ denied, 371 So. 2d 914 (1979).

The State Department of Revenue appeals from a decree holding that Tri-State Pharmaceutical's sales of pharmaceutical drugs to hospitals were sales for resale or wholesale sales and therefore not subject to tax [under the City of Enterprise, Alabama's local use tax]. We reverse.

. . . .

The facts as set forth in the pre-trial order are as follows:

Tri-State Pharmaceutical was, during the relevant taxable period, engaged in the business of selling pharmaceutical drugs to hospitals in Alabama. . . . Tri-State made sales of drugs to Coffee General Hospital in Enterprise, Alabama, which hospital the parties agree to be representative of the vendees in question in all cases presently before this court. . . . (Coffee General, like all of the hospital vendees in question in these appeals, is a private hospital; public hospitals are exempt from payment of sales and use taxes in Alabama). Following the sale of those drugs to Coffee General the drugs were administered to patients in that hospital. Those drugs

were dispensed to patients by hospital personnel pursuant to either specific or standing orders of an attending physician. No prescription drugs of the type sold by Tri-State to Coffee General were dispensed to hospital patients without specific prescription or order from an attending physician. A charge for all drugs so prescribed and administered to each patient by Coffee General is listed as a separate item on each bill rendered by the hospital to the patient or the third party payor responsible for payment of the patient's medical care bills. Included in the itemized charges to patients made by Coffee General for prescription drugs administered to patients are (a) the wholesale cost of the drugs (b) a charge to cover the costs of operation of the hospital pharmacy (including the pharmacist's salary), (c) a charge to cover a contribution to general hospital overhead and (d) a return on the equity interest of the owners of the hospital. No sales tax is added by Coffee General to the charge made by it for drugs administered to patients.

[The trial court framed the issue as whether the sales of drugs by Tri-State to Coffee General Hospital are subject to sales or use taxation as "retail sales" or "sales for use or consumption," or whether such sales are "wholesale sales" or "sales for resale."]

The trial court correctly stated the applicable law as follows:

The City of Enterprise Use Tax is levied upon all storages, uses or consumptions of tangible personal property in the City of Enterprise. . . . [T]he tax is parallel to the State Use Tax; therefore the question reduces to one of applicability of the State Use Tax. That tax is properly laid when there is a purchase of personal property at *retail* and that property is brought into the City of Enterprise and stored for use or other consumption but not for resale. Pursuant to Section 40-23-60(4) of the Code, all purchases of tangible personal property are deemed to be at retail, and therefore taxable, unless the purchase is a wholesale sale. If the purchase is at wholesale, the Use Tax is, by definition, inapplicable.

The Use Tax, as a complement of the Sales Tax, is a tax levied on, and is to be paid by or in respect of, the ultimate consumer of a product. In defining what constitutes use or "consumption," the Legislature has provided under Section 40-23-60(4)(a) that wholesale sales are not subject to the Sales Tax. Section 40-23-60(4)(a) further states that a wholesale sale "does not include a sale by wholesalers to users or consumers not for resale."Applying these principles to the stipulated facts, the trial court concluded that:

Tri-State made wholesale sales of drugs (as opposed to retail sales of those items) to Coffee General, since, as a matter of law, Coffee General, did not itself use or consume the drugs, but rather resold them to its patients. Therefore, no sales or use tax would be due to be collected by Tri-State from Coffee General . . . .The State contends that the sales by Tri-State to Coffee General

Hospital were taxable retail sales because Coffee General uses or consumes the drugs in rendering services to its patients. In support of its contentions the State cites Sales and Use Tax Regulation H15-021 which provides in relevant part:

Hospitals, infirmaries, sanitariums and like institutions are primarily engaged in the business of rendering services. They are not liable for sales tax with respect to their gross receipts from meals, bandages, dressings, drugs, X-ray photographs or other tangible personal property when such items of tangible property are used in the rendering of a hospital service. This is true irrespective of whether or not such tangible items are billed separately to their patients. Hospitals, infirmaries, and sanitariums are deemed to be the purchasers for use or consumption of such tangible personal property, and the sellers of these items to hospitals, infirmaries or sanitariums are required to collect the tax on sales of such property to hospitals.

. . . .

After careful consideration we have concluded that the State's position is the better reasoned view. Hospitals are not in the business of selling drugs or other tangible personal property, but are primarily in the business of *rendering services* to their patients. Drugs and other items are purchased by them for use or consumption in the rendition of these professional services, and any transfer of the drugs by a hospital to its patients is but an incident to the services rendered. Consequently, the sales by Tri-State to Coffee General Hospital are "retail sales," and sales tax is due to be collected by Tri-State as the retail seller.

. . . .

Questions and Comments

1. The exemption for sales made for resale did not require that the resale be taxable for the exemption to apply. Most states do not condition the exemption on the taxability of the item when it is resold. Should they?

2. Why didn't the Tax Department assess the hospitals for the sales tax due on their sale of the drugs? Wouldn't that have generated a larger assessment because the charge for drugs included not only the wholesale cost of the drugs (which presumably was the subject of the assessment in the case), but also charges to cover the operation of the hospital pharmacy, overhead, and an element for profit?

3. After this case, would you advise the hospital to charge tax on the sale of its drugs?

4. Alabama does not impose a sales tax on the

provision of medical and hospital services. If a legislature believed that hospital and medical services were properly part of the base of a normative retail sales tax, but for political reasons could not be taxed, might taxing the business inputs be a palatable compromise, much the way some states exempt mortuary services but do not grant a sale for resale exemption on the items purchased by the mortician? Is the court's holding consistent with this view?

5. After this case, patients will presumably pay a hidden sales tax because the hospital is likely to increase the wholesale cost of its drugs by the amount of its sales tax. Suppose the hospital increases the wholesale cost of its drugs by 50 percent to cover all of its additional costs (operation of the pharmacy, overhead, and the return on equity). Suppose, further, that the hospital is able to fully pass forward all of its costs for drugs. Is there any difference in the sales tax

(explicit or hidden) in what a patient would pay in the following two situations:

(a) The hospital buys a drug for $100, pays a 10 percent sales tax on its purchase, adds on a 50 percent charge for all of its other costs, and calculates this charge on a base that includes both the cost of the drug, and the sales tax on its purchase. The patient pays the resulting amount without any additional sales taxes;

(b) The hospital buys the drug for $100 sales tax free, adds on a 50 percent charge, and charges the patient the resulting amount, but now the sale is subject to the 10 percent sales tax. Is there any difference in the amount of sales tax the state would collect? In the amount a patient would pay? In the hospital's bottom line?

6. Ideally, the hospital would like to buy its drugs tax free and not have to levy a tax on their sale to patients. This situation is no longer possible after *Tri-State*. Is the hospital indifferent between: (a) buying drugs tax-free and levying a sales tax on their resale to patients; and (b) paying a sales tax on the purchase of the drugs and selling them tax fee to the patients?

7. As a statutory matter, was there any way for the court to avoid deciding whether the hospital was primarily in the business of rendering services to patients?

Sta-Ru Corporation v. Mahin
Supreme Court of Illinois, 1976.
64 Ill. 2d 330, 356 N.E.2d 67, 1 Ill. Dec. 67.

[The Plaintiff operated six Dairy Queen-Brazier restaurants in Illinois, which sell ice cream, custard, beverages, hamburgers, and other foods].

The principal question on this appeal is whether sales to the plaintiff, the Sta-Ru Corporation, of paper and plastic containers used by it to contain foods and beverages consumed by the plaintiff's customers on its premises are "sale[s] at retail" and thus taxable under the Illinois Retailers' Occupation Tax Act (hereafter ROTA) and the Illinois Use Tax Act.

The ROTA provides:

"'Sale at retail' means any transfer of the ownership of or title to tangible personal property to a purchaser, for the purpose of use or consumption, and not for the purpose of resale in any form as tangible personal property to the extent not first subjected to a use for which it was purchased, for a valuable consideration. Ill. Rev. Stat. 1975, ch. 120, par. 440.

. . . .

[Rule 51 of the Department of Revenue] provides. . . :

"Sales of paper napkins, drinking straws, paper cups and paper plates to restaurants (including drive-in restaurants) and other vendors of food or beverages for use on the premises as serving equipment in lieu of more durable kinds of serving equipment (such as linen napkins, metal drinking straws, glass or porcelain cups and plates) are taxable retail sales. Sales of paper napkins, drinking straws, paper cups and paper plates to food and beverage vendors are nontaxable sales for resale if the items are resold for a direct and specific charge, or if the items are employed as containers for food or beverages contained therein and are transferred with the food or beverages to the purchaser thereof either by being

delivered by the food or beverage vendor away from his premises to his customers or by being delivered on the premises of the food or beverage vendor to customers who take the packaged food or beverages away from such premises with them for consumption elsewhere (i.e., the so-called 'carry-out trade')."
. . . .

. . . Sta-Ru's president . . . testified that its customers may consume their purchases either on or off the premises, and that all foods are sold in nonreusable plastic or paper containers whether they are consumed on or off Sta-Ru's premises. He considered that the ownership of the disposable containers was transferred to customers at the time of sales. There was no separate charge for the containers, but their cost was included in the price set for the food or beverage. . . .
. . . .

Sta-Ru's contention is that the ownership of the disposable paper and plastic containers is passed to the customer when he purchases beverage or food. Therefore it argues, Sta-Ru's purchase of the containers from its suppliers is not a taxable "sale at retail" within the meaning of the ROTA, but instead is a purchase for resale which is exempt from taxation. The defendants, however, say that these paper and plastic products used by customers for on-premises consumption are not purchased by Sta-Ru for resale, since they are not resold by Sta-Ru for a separate consideration as required by the ROTA to be tax exempt. Since the plaintiff could use permanent or reusable dishes and glasses to serve customers on the premises the defendants contend that the use of the disposable containers for on-premises consumption is part of the cost of doing business.

We consider that there is a "sale at retail" when Sta-Ru purchases disposable containers from its suppliers for on-premises use by its customers and that the taxes assessed pursuant to Rule 51 are authorized under the ROTA and the Use Tax Act.

. . . .

. . . No separate charge is made by Sta-Ru for the disposable containers furnished its customers. Obviously, Sta-Ru is in the business of selling food and beverages, not disposable containers, and it is the food or beverage which its customers come to purchase . . . . Sta-Ru provides the plastic and paper containers as a part of its standard method of doing business. There is no resale of the containers to the customers within the meaning of the ROTA. Rather, the cost of the containers used to serve food on its premises is a cost of doing business as would be the cost of permanent dinnerware.

Sta-Ru's contention that the containers are resold since their ownership is transferred to the customer with no right in Sta-Ru to reclaim possession is hardly convincing. Beyond the fact that no separate consideration is paid for the containers, it is conceded that the containers are not reusable. The customer acquires nothing of permanent benefit. The containers are consumed or used by Sta-Ru in a business sense when it serves the food or beverage. . . .The appellate court's reliance on Belleville Dr. Pepper v. Korshak, 221 N.E.2d 635, in holding that the disposable containers were resold within the meaning of the statutes was erroneous. In that case the plaintiff brought an action to enjoin the Department of Revenue from imposing and collecting the tax on its purchase of bottles, cartons and shells. The stipulation of facts showed that the plaintiff's customers paid a deposit on the bottles and containers, which was admittedly less than the cost of the containers. Possession of the containers was turned over to the customer without any right of reclamation. It was further stipulated that many of the bottles and containers were never returned, but instead were retained and used by customers for various household purposes. This court upheld the circuit court's injunction, holding that the sale of the containers was not a sale for use or consumption and that the purchases were not taxable.

Belleville Dr. Pepper is clearly distinguishable. There a separate consideration, the "deposit," was made for the containers. It is true, as Sta-Ru says, that the deposit was less than the actual cost of the bottles and the balance of the cost was included in the price charged for the beverage. But this factor was immaterial to the holding in Belleville Dr. Pepper, for courts generally will not inquire into the adequacy of consideration. There was, in fact, a separate consideration given. Too, unlike the case here, the bottles and other containers in Belleville Dr. Pepper were reusable by the customers. For the reasons given, the judgments of the circuit and appellate courts are reversed.

Questions and Comments

1. What is the rationale underlying the distinction between on-premises sales and off-premises sales?

2. How is the plaintiff supposed to determine which of its paper or plastic napkins, straws, cups and plates were used on its premises and which were used off its premises? Do you suppose the plaintiff had been previously rebuked on the methodology it used for determining its on-premises and off-premises use of napkins and the like and was therefore attempting to moot that issue entirely by arguing that the exemption should apply regardless of where the food was consumed? Or, perhaps the Department had never focused on the plaintiff's methodology. Perhaps the plaintiff's fallback position if it were to lose the case would be to take a more aggressive stand on the apportionment issue.

3. How would the Sta-Ru court have decided Tri-State?

4. The court states that no separate charge was made by Sta-Ru for the disposable containers furnished to its customers. Does this prove too much? Was any separate charge made for the hamburger bun that was transferred as part of the purchase of a hamburger? What about the condiments? What about the hamburger itself?

5. Suppose a health food store charges a lower price for a taxable good if a customer brings his or her own bags or containers. Would the store now be able to purchase its own bags and containers sales tax free?

6. The court characterizes Sta-Ru as in the business of selling food and beverages, not disposable containers, and it is the food or beverage that its customers come to purchase. But would its customers purchase a beverage if it did not also come with a container? Is the analysis advanced at all by describing Sta-Ru as in

the business of selling food and beverages and not disposable containers? Aren't there many ways in which to describe Sta-Ru's business? For example, why can't Sta-Ru be described as in the business of selling food and beverages, with accompanying condiments, in containers that allow such food to be eaten wherever convenient by the customer? Does rephrasing Sta-Ru's business in these terms shed any light on the underlying issues in the case?

7. The court notes that Sta-Ru provides the plastic and paper containers as a part of its standard method of doing business. No doubt, the same can be said of the hamburgers, the ice cream, and so forth. What is the relevance of the court's comment?

8. In response to Sta-Ru's contention that the containers are sold to the customers because their ownership is transferred with no rights in Sta-Ru to reclaim possession, the court focuses on the containers not being reusable. "The customer acquires nothing of permanent benefit." Isn't this also true of the food and beverages? What is a "permanent" benefit anyway?

9. The Tax Department argued that because the plaintiff could use permanent or reusable dishes and glasses to serve customers on the premises, the use of disposable containers is part of the cost of doing business. Isn't Sta-Ru's purchase of inventory part of its cost of doing business, but yet isn't such inventory the quintessential example of what is covered by the sale for resale exemption?

10. Conceptually, is there any difference for sales tax purposes between the hamburgers, the buns, or the condiments that Sta-Ru sells, and the container in which the whole soggy mess is placed? Yet if some line must be drawn, where should it be? Representing a taxpayer in a state that has not resolved this issue, how would you argue the case? As a legislator in a state adopting a new sales tax, how would you handle this problem?

11. What was the relevance in *Belleville Dr. Pepper* that the deposit was less than the cost of the containers?

Celestial Food of Massapequa Corporation v. New York State Tax Commission
Court of Appeals of New York, 1984.
63 N.Y.2d 1020, 484 N.Y.S.2d 509, 473 N.E.2d 737.

MEMORANDUM.

. . . .

The issue before us is whether the purchase of certain paper and plastic items by a fast food restaurant is a "retail sale of tangible personal property" subject to sales tax under 1105(a) of the Tax Law, or is subject to an exclusion from sales tax. In Matter of Burger King v. State Tax Comm., 51 N.Y.2d 614, we held that a restaurant's purchases of materials for packaging or containing the food it sells came within section 1101(b)(4)(i)(A) of the Tax Law, which excludes from the definition of retail sales subject to tax purchases of tangible personal property "for resale as such." Wrappers for hamburgers, sleeves for french fries, and cups for beverages, while not actually component parts of the food and drink sold, were recognized as items purchased "for resale as such" because they form a critical element of the product sold, consumers ultimately paying sales tax on these items as part of their food purchases (Matter of Burger King, supra, 51 N.Y.2d p. 623). We are now asked by respondent to enlarge our holding in Burger King to declare invalid a regulation of appellant Tax Commission which subjects a restaurant's purchases of napkins, straws, stirrers, plastic utensils and other similar items to sales tax (20 NYCRR 528.20[d][2])[2]. . . .

Unlike the packaging in Burger King, the items re-spondent here seeks to exclude from sales tax are not a critical element of the product sold and thus are not purchased "for resale as such." Whereas a cup of coffee cannot be purchased without a container, the same cannot be said of napkins, stirrers and utensils, which are more akin to items of overhead, enhancing the comfort of restaurant patrons consuming the food products. The Appellate Division's reasoning in this case, that because "the fast food customer expects to be provided with a stirrer for coffee, a straw for soft drinks, plastic utensils for food, and napkins for cleanliness" such items are purchased "for resale as such" has potentially limitless application. Although the cost of such items may well be taken into account by the restauranteur [sic] when setting the price of food, so are other amenities a restaurant patron expects, such as service, utilities and fixtures, which do not become a part of the product being sold merely because their cost is a factor in determining the price a customer pays. Only when, as in Burger King, such items are necessary to contain the product for delivery can they be considered a critical element of the product sold, and excluded from sales tax. Accordingly, the items referred to in 20 NYCRR 528.20(d)(2) were not purchased "for resale as such" by respondent and the challenged regulation requiring payment of sales tax on its purchases of such items is not at odds with the Tax Law.

. . . .

---

2. In Burger King, the taxpayer conceded sales tax liability as to outer bags, straws and coffee stirrers (Matter of Burger King, 51 N.Y.2d 614, 618-619, n. 1).

Questions and Comments

1. Representing the taxpayer, how would you have characterized *Burger King*?

2. As *Burger King* and *Celestial Food* suggest, once a state decides to exempt a subset of business inputs, it is not at all apparent where the line should be drawn. Unless a state is willing to exempt all business inputs, it must draw a line that is administratively convenient even if it results in the taxation of some business inputs. Is there anything in the logic of a sales tax that would defend the exemption for wrappers for hamburgers but not for napkins or stirrers? Can you suggest an approach that might tax a tablecloth bought by a restaurant but not paper napkins? Can you explain why there should be any tax difference between the two? Does a risk exist that tablecloths, like cars, computers, and so forth, might be used for either business or personal purposes and that policing this problem is too difficult? Are there similar problems in the personal income tax?

3. Suppose that after this case, the plaintiff changed its prices so that a customer would pay one cent less if he or she did not want any stirrers, napkins, plastic utensils, etc. Would that change have any sales tax consequences?

4. Which state has a more sensible approach in this area—Illinois (*Sta-Ru*) or New York?

5. *In the Matter of Dunking' Donuts Mid-Atlantic Distribution Center, Inc. v. Tax Appeals Tribunal of New York*, 639 N.Y.S.2d 168 (1996), the court held that the purchase for resale exemption did not extend to the sale of wax tissue paper to the well-known donut chain. The wax paper is used to pick up individual donuts or muffins and place them in bags or boxes such that the good is partially covered and separated from other donuts or muffins in the same container. "Unlike the situation in Burger King, where the wax paper served as the product's 'container,' at Dunking' donut shops the obvious function of the paper tissue is to provide a hygienic means of handling the food products."

6. Suppose a hotel provides a complimentary breakfast. Can it buy the food under a purchase for resale exemption? See *Nashville Clubhouse Inn v. Tenn.*, 27 S.W.3d 542 (2000) (purchase of food for a complimentary breakfast is exempt as a purchase for resale). What about the hotel's purchase of toilet paper and soap? See *Adamar of N.J. v. N.J.*, 18 N.J. Tax 70 (1999) (purchase is taxable).

Darien Lake Fun Country, Inc. v. State Tax Commission of New York
Supreme Court, Appellate Division, Third Department, 1986.
118 A.D.2d 945, 499 N.Y.S.2d 511.

. . . .

The pertinent facts are undisputed. Petitioner operates an amusement park located midway between Rochester and Buffalo. It sold two kinds of admission tickets to its customers: one entitled the holder to enter the park and enjoy various attractions, and the other enabled the holder to also enjoy unlimited use of specified carnival-like rides. Although the appropriate sales taxes on revenues received from customers for both types of tickets were paid, petitioner did not pay sales tax on the amounts it had expended to purchase or lease its various amusement rides. Petitioner held the view that, under the Tax Law, the rides had been purchased for resale to its customers; hence, their acquisition was exempt from taxation and petitioner paid no sales tax thereon. Respondent, after an audit and hearing, concluded

otherwise and assessed a deficiency against petitioner.

Petitioner's contention that the admission charge constitutes a sale of its amusement facilities and equipment to its patrons underlies petitioner's argument that it purchases or leases these rides for resale, a nontaxable event. However, in Matter of Shanty Hollow Corp. v. New York, lv. denied 489 N.E.2d 256, this court very recently professed continued adherence to the long-standing principle that "only transactions involving passage of title or of actual exclusive possession constitute sales". Here, there is no gainsaying the correctness of respondent's finding that the sale of an admission ticket does not transfer title to, or exclusive possession of, the amusement rides to the ticket holder. Since there is no sale of the rides, there is no resale. Respondent's conclusion that petitioner's purchases and leases of rides constitute transactions taxable as the sale of tangible personal property rationally follows.

Roller Coaster at Darien Lake Fun Country

As for petitioner's suggestion that taxability of its receipts from customer admissions results in the pyramiding of taxes, a practice proscribed by Matter of Burger King v. State Tax Comm'n. [Ed. see supra this chapter], that prohibition is limited to instances unlike

that presented herein where there has been a transfer of exclusive possession of the item allegedly taxed twice (see, id.; see also, Celestial Food of Massapequa v. New York State Tax Comm'n., 473 N.E.2d 737).

KANE, Justice (dissenting).

Tax Law § 1101(b)(5) defines the terms "sale, selling or purchase" as:

Any transfer of title or possession or both, exchange or barter, rental, lease or license to use or consume, conditional or otherwise, in any manner or by any means whatsoever for a consideration, or any agreement therefor, including the rendering of any service, taxable under this article, for a consideration or any agreement therefor.

In addition, 20 NYCRR 526.7(a)(4) provides that the term "sale" includes, among other things, "the transactions enumerated in subdivision (d), (e) or (f) of section 1005 of the Tax Law". Tax Law § 1105(f)(1) concerns "admission charges". Accordingly, petitioner's sale of a ticket constitutes a "sale" of the facilities to its patrons as a transaction "enumerated in subdivision (f) of section 1105 of the Tax Law". Since petitioner is "selling" its facilities to its customers, its acquisition of the facilities in question is for resale and thus nontaxable. The facilities in question here were not incidental to the taxpayer's primary business (see, Matter of Albany Calcium Light Co. v. State Tax Comm'n., 380 N.E.2d 165).

Questions and Comments

1. N.Y. Tax Laws §1101(b)(4)(i)(A) defines a retail sale, inter alia, as a sale of tangible personal property to any person for any purpose other than for resale as such. The taxpayer was arguing that its purchase or lease of its various amusement rides was not a retail sale because it resold the rides to its customers. The definition of sale includes any transfer of possession or any lease or license to use or consume, conditional or otherwise. When a customer purchases the right to occupy a seat on an amusement ride, is possession of that seat being transferred? Is the customer leasing that seat, albeit only on a short-term basis? Could a movie theater wishing to buy its seats tax free under a sale for resale exemption argue that it transfers possession of the seats to its customers? Is the taxpayer's argument undercut because admission to amusement parks is taxable under a specific statutory provision (N.Y. Tax Laws § 1105(f)) and not as the sale of tangible personal property?

2. How is the lease of a ride for one minute any different from the lease of a car for one hour? Would the latter situation constitute a sale? What is the difference between a lease and a license to use or consume?

3. Why should the proscription against pyramiding apply only to the transfer of items the exclusive possession of which is transferred to the customer?

4. What is the dissent's definition of "facilities"? What is the taxpayer's definition of "rides"? What is the majority's definition of "rides"?

5. How would this court treat the rental of a locker? When you rent a locker do you obtain possession of it? See *American Locker v. City of New York*, 125 N.E.2d 421 (1955) (rental of locker not a transfer of title or possession and thus exempt from sales taxation). Is the leasing of an advertising sign, like a billboard, exempt because the advertiser does not obtain possession? See *Federal Sign & Signal v. Ohio*, 174 N.E.2d 91 (1961) (leasing of advertising signs exempt); *Register Mobile Advertising v. Georgia*, 250 S.E.2d 468 (1978) (contra). Does it advance the analysis of these situations to describe them as involving a service rather than the rental of tangible personal property?

6. A rental or license to use or consume is commonly included within the definition of a sale. In states

adopting this definition, it is common to treat a purchase of property for the purpose of subsequently leasing it as a sale for resale. See, for example, N. J. Rev. Stat. Section 54:32B-2(e)-1. Some states provide a purchaser of property that will be leased with the option of either: (1) paying sales tax on the purchase and exempting the lease payments; or (2) exempting the purchase and collecting

sales tax on the rental payments. See, for example, Cal. Rev. & Tax. Code Section 6006(g). Some states tax both the purchase and the subsequent rental payments, a position that is difficult to defend on normative grounds. See, for example, *Ryder Truck Rental, Inc. v. Bryant*, 170 So.2d 822 (1964).

Wisconsin Department of Revenue v. Milwaukee Brewers Baseball Club
Court of Appeals of Wisconsin, 1982.
108 Wis. 2d 553, 322 N.W.2d 528.

. . . .

The Milwaukee Brewers Baseball Club is a partnership with its principal place of business in Milwaukee. It owns a professional baseball franchise. [T]he club purchased promotional items, such as baseball bats and jackets, from out-of-state vendors for about $243,000. It transferred the promotional items to its customers in connection with the purchase of paid admission tickets to its home games in Milwaukee. During the same periods, the club purchased printed tickets from out-of-state vendors for use in selling admissions to its Milwaukee games. The tickets cost the club about $108,000 at a unit cost of one cent each.

The commission found that the promotional items and tickets were included in the price of admission and were not transferred by separate retail sales. The commission also concluded that because a sales tax was paid on game admissions, and the admission price included the promotional items and tickets, no use tax liability was incurred.

. . . .

We start with the purpose of the use tax: to prevent a buyer from avoiding sales tax in this state by purchasing goods in other states. The use tax supplements the sales tax by levying a tax on property purchased in another state for the storage, use or other consumption in this state of personalty or certain services, "the sale of which has not been reached by the sales tax."

Spelled out, the statutory framework is as follows: Section 77.53(1) levies a use tax on the storage, use or other consumption in this state of tangible personal property "purchased from any retailer." A "retailer," for our purposes, is defined by sec. 77.51(7)(a) as "[e]very seller who makes any sale of tangible personal property. . . ." "Sale" is defined by sec. 77.51(4) as including "the transfer of the ownership of, title to, possession of, or enjoyment of tangible personal property or services for use or consumption *but not* for resale . . . ." (Emphasis added.) Consequently, if the taxpayer's acquisitions were "not for resale," and if the

taxpayer stored, used or consumed the property in this state, then it is liable for a use tax.

1. Promotional Items

The club contends that a retail sale of its promotional items occurs when they are transferred to ticket holders. Because admission price to its games is taxed as a service under sec. 77.52(2)(a)2, and because promotional items are tied to the price of admission, the club contends the promotional items are already subject to sales tax and should not be doubly taxed. It claims that the price of admission offsets the cost of the goods and their transfer is therefore a retail sale.

Section 77.51(24) provides, "With respect to the services covered by s. 77.52(2), no part of the charge for the service may be deemed a sale or rental of tangible personal property." The plain meaning of this provision is that no part of the Brewers' admission charge, for purposes of the sales or use tax, is allocable to a sale of the promotional items. The taxpayer contends that the purpose of sec. 77.51(24) is to prevent avoidance of a sales tax on a service rendered in connection with nontaxable personal property, a purpose not involved in this case because the service–admission to an athletic event–is taxable under sec. 77.52(2)(a)2. Perhaps a purpose of sec. 77.51(24) is as the club contends. The statutory language, however, is unambiguous as applied to the question before us. "When the statutory language is clear and unambiguous no judicial rules of construction are permitted, and the court must arrive at the intention of the legislature by giving the language its ordinary and accepted meaning."

Because sec. 77.51(24), Stats., prevents the club from characterizing transfer of its promotional products to a game patron as a sale of an admission plus a sale of a promotional item–a "two for one sale" as the club puts it–no resale occurs.

Nor does transfer of the promotional items result in a

sales tax on those and therefore a double tax if a use tax is imposed on their acquisition. The sales and use taxes are separate and cover different events. The sales tax is on the sale of an admission, unaffected by the accompanied promotional item. The use tax is on the acquisition of the promotional items.

The club asserts that the transfer of promotional items to game patrons is nevertheless a retail sale because sec. 77.51(4)(k) recognizes that goods may be transferred as a part of the sale of a service. Section 77.51(4)(k) includes the following within the definition of "sale," etc., as a transfer for use or consumption but not for resale:

Any sale of tangible personal property to a purchaser even though such property may be used or consumed by some other person to whom such purchaser transfers the tangible personal property without valuable consideration, such as gifts, and advertising specialties distributed gratis apart from the sale of other tangible personal property or service.

Noting that sec. 77.51(4)(k) refers to goods transferred "gratis apart from the sale of other tangible personal property or service," the club finds a negative implication that promotional items may be tied to an admission price and resold. The claimed negative implication does not exist. The purpose of subsec. (4)(k) is to clarify that an acquisition of personal property is not for resale if it is acquired for the purpose of making a gift to a person who will be its ultimate user or consumer. In other words, a person who acquires property to give it away is a user or consumer as opposed to a reseller, and is liable for the use tax.

The term "promotional items" itself indicates that the club uses those items to enhance the attractiveness of its home games to baseball fans. Because the club purchased the promotional items for use in this state and not for resale, the use tax applies to those acquisitions.

2. Tickets

The trial court found that a ticket is part of an admission and is already subject to sales tax under sec. 77.52(2). The department argues that, under sec. 77.51(24), the one cent unit cost cannot be allocated to admission charge. We agree with the department. Despite the apparent identification of an admission ticket with an admission, and the small unit cost, a consistent interpretation of sec. 77.51(24) requires us to assess the use tax against the cost of the tickets. Because a ticket is used by its vendor, as well as its purchaser, to identify its holder as having a right to watch a home game, the club must pay a use tax on the acquisition of the tickets.

The concern that imposing a use tax on the tickets results in a double tax is unwarranted. Under sec. 77.51(24), Stats., the cost of the ticket is not included in the admission price.

. . . .

Questions and Comments

1. What would the result in the case have been if the Brewers had sold the bats for one cent? For 50 cents? Is there any normative reason why the bats should not have been bought tax free?

If the Philadelphia Phillies sold bats for one cent, the Pennsylvania Department of Revenue would be authorized to increase the price upon which the sales tax would be levied to take into account the true, or fair price, of the bat. Pa. Stat. Ann. 72, §7201(g)(3). How would you determine the fair market price of the bat when you must pay admission to the game in order to get one?

2. After this case, would the Brewers be well-advised to sell the bats to customers at cost and reduce the price of the admission ticket by that same amount? In other words, if the Brewers would normally charge $3.50 for the ticket and give a bat away for free, should they print on the ticket that $2.00 is for the bat (assume that to be the cost of the bat) and $1.50 is the price of admission? Alternatively, should they sell the ticket for $1.50 and sell bats inside the stadium for $2.00? Or, should they sell bats outside the stadium for $2.00 and provide a coupon with every sale that allows the holder to obtain admission for $1.50? Can they engage in these strategies and sell the bats for less than cost?

3. Is the court correct in stating that its opinion does not result in a double tax?

4. In what sense is the cost of the ticket not included in the admission price, as the court states at the conclusion of its opinion?

5. Why isn't the taxpayer viewed as reselling the tickets that it purchased?

6. Should there be a tax difference between "gifts" in a business context and gifts in a personal context? Does the personal income tax make such a distinction?

7. Suppose Wisconsin exempted printing services from the sales and use tax. Could the taxpayer now characterize the acquisition of its tickets as the purchase of an exempt printing service?

8. What would be the court's response to the double taxation argument if the bats were bought in-state?

9. If the use tax is separate from the sales tax and covers different events as the court states, does the use tax violate the Commerce Clause?

10. Did the taxpayer properly interpret Section 77.51(24)?

11. The Minnesota Twins struck out on issues similar to the Brewers, 587 N.W.2d (1998), but the Kansas City Royals hit a home run, 32 S.W.2d 560, 563 (2000) ("Although the promotional items are ostensibly given away, the cost of purchasing these items is factored into the price charged for each ticket of admission to a Royal game. This is sufficient consideration to find that a resale had occurred"). This reasoning, which is eminently correct, lays the groundwork for arguing that all business inputs should be exempt.

D. Definition of Tangible Personal Property

Dine Out Tonight Club, Inc. v. Department of Revenue Services
Supreme Court of Connecticut, 1989.
210 Conn. 567, 556 A.2d 580.

This is a declaratory judgment action brought by the plaintiff Dine Out Tonight Club, Inc., to determine whether it is liable for Connecticut sales taxes on the sale of its membership privileges to Connecticut residents . . . . The plaintiff is a Rhode Island corporation with its sole office and place of business in that state. The plaintiff solicits memberships in its club from Connecticut residents by newspaper and direct mail advertising. In consideration of the payment of a membership fee an applicant receives a membership card that entitles such person to one free meal with the purchase of a second meal of equal or greater value at restaurants that participate in the plaintiff's plan. A member also receives a directory of participating restaurants and supplements to the directory as new restaurants enroll in the plan. . . . A participating restaurant receives no remuneration from the plaintiff for furnishing free meals to its members. Restaurants apparently agree to participate in the plan for the exposure it provides them to the dining public.

All a member has to do to obtain the free meal available to club members is to present a membership card where dining. The card is then punched by the restaurateur to whom the card is presented in order to indicate that the club member has exhausted the privilege at that particular restaurant. . . .

Prior to January 15, 1985, the defendant department of revenue services did not tax the sale of dining club cards. It did, however, require a restaurant serving a free meal to a club member to collect the sales tax on the value of that meal. On December 20, 1984, the defendant issued Bulletin No. 24 that effectively eliminated the sales tax on free meals as of January 15, 1985. Thereafter, on February 20, 1985, the defendant informed the plaintiff that "the sale of the Dine Out Tonight Club Card [was] a sale of tangible personal property." On January 13, 1986, the defendant in a letter to plaintiff's counsel affirmed its position that the sale of the plaintiff's membership card constituted "the sale of tangible personal property and as such is subject to the Connecticut Sales and Use Tax."

On February 7, 1986, the plaintiff brought this action in the Superior Court wherein it contended that it was not engaged in the sale of tangible personal property and asked the court to render a declaratory judgment to that effect. Subsequently, on September 22, 1986, the defendant issued a revised Bulletin No. 24 that reiterated its position that the value of free meals provided by restaurants involved in plans such as the plaintiff's were not taxable but that sales of dining out cards were taxable. The trial court deferred "to the commissioner's interpretation of 'dining out' cards as tangible personal property" and ruled that the sale of the cards constituted "a sale of tangible personal property." We disagree.

Only the sale of tangible personal property at retail is subject to the imposition of the Connecticut sales tax. Tangible personal property is defined as "personal property which may be seen, weighed, measured, felt or touched or which is in any other manner perceptible to the senses." Therefore, if what the plaintiff sells, and what its members purchase, is a membership card and a restaurant directory, the plaintiff is engaged in the retail sale of tangible personal property and its transactions are subject to the imposition of a sales tax. The Connecticut sales tax does not, however, extend to the sale of intangible rights. If, therefore, what the plaintiff sells, and what its members purchase, is the intangible right to free meals and knowledge of the restaurants that provide them, the club membership fees are not subject to the imposition of the Connecticut sales tax.[7]

A conclusion as to whether the sales tax is applicable to the plaintiff's membership fees requires a determination of the true object of the transaction between the club and its members. We must therefore ascertain whether the true object of that transaction is to provide club members with a card and a directory or to bestow upon them the intangible right to free meals under specified conditions. The determinant is the intention of the parties. We think that intention is evident. Obviously, prospective club members are not enticed to pay the plaintiff for the prospect of obtaining a card and a directory, items that would be of little or no value without the concomitant right to receive free meals. Conversely, the plaintiff could not expect to stay in business by offering for sale only a card and a directory. Manifestly, the sine qua non of the transaction between the club and its members is the intangible right to receive free meals and access to the knowledge of an expanding list of restaurants that provide them. The membership card and directory are merely indicia of that intangible right and incidental aids to its exercise. Because the transaction between the plaintiff club and its members is essentially the conveyance of an intangible right to free meals, the plaintiff's membership fees are not subject to the imposition of the Connecticut sales tax.

. . . .

---

7. Because the question posed by this case concerns the imposition of a tax, the taxing statute must be strictly construed against the taxing authority and in favor of the taxpayer. Further, any ambiguity should be resolved in favor of the taxpayer and against the taxing authority.

Questions and Comments

1. Would it be accurate to paraphrase the court's opinion by stating that the cards were only the means to an end: the consumption of a meal? If so, should sales tax be due at some point in time? Should the purchaser of a card be entitled to consume a meal without the imposition of a sales tax? If not, what is the appropriate time at which to levy the tax–the sale of the card or the consumption of the meal?

Does it help in analyzing *Dine Out* to first determine how much sales tax should be properly collected and then determine where in the chain of transactions that amount can be easiest levied upon?

What if the card is never used?

2. Why did the Department of Revenue Services change its position from levying a sales tax on the free meal to levying a sales tax on the purchase of the card?

3. What would be the treatment if a restaurant, instead of participating in the Dine Out plan, simply had a "two-for-one" sale from time to time? In other words, you pay $20 instead of $40 and receive two meals. How much sales tax should you pay? What if you had to buy a two-for-one coupon for $5?

4. Should the State have characterized the purchase of the coupon as a "deposit" for future consumption or perhaps as prepaid consumption? Under this approach, when should a sales tax theoretically be imposed? Is the card like the purchase of a gift certificate in that both represent prepaid consumption? When should the sales tax be imposed in the latter case? What distinguishes *Dine Out* from the purchase of a gift certificate from a store selling both taxable and exempt goods?

5. How should the State respond to this case? Should the sales tax be levied on the value of both meals consumed, including the free meal?

6. Suppose the cost of a meal is $25 and you tip $4. Should the sales tax be levied on $25 or $29?

7. Suppose you charge the meal and tip and pay interest to the credit card company because you do not pay your account in full. Should the sales tax be levied on the interest?

8. Would it be constitutional to tax the card if it were sold in Connecticut but all the meals were consumed in other states?

9. Why did Dine Out have nexus with Connecticut?

10 Barnes & Noble sells a card entitling customers to a discount on books. The Tennessee tax department taxed the sale of the card on the theory that it was tangible property, or alternatively, that the sale represented the prepayment of merchandise. The Tennessee Court of Appeals affirmed the lower court's decision that because a purchaser has no obligation to purchase any merchandise in the future, the card is merely documentation of the intangible right to receive a discount. *Barnes & Noble Superstores, Inc. v. Huddleston*, 1996 Tenn. App. Lexis 670.

11. **Prepaid telephone calling cards**. These raise issues that are conceptually similar to that raised by *Dine Out*, although the administrative aspects are different. Prepaid calling cards can be sold directly to the end user, can be given away as a promotional device, or may be purchased in bulk by businesses for the use of their employees.

The majority approach is not to treat the card as tangible personal property. Accordingly, in most states the card is not taxable under the sales tax at the point of sale. Given *Dine Out*, it is not surprising that Connecticut treats the sale of a telephone card as the purchase of an intangible right to purchase a future service. States that exempt the sale of the card from the sale tax may instead tax the use of the card as a telecommunications service. The telecommunications provider is responsible for remitting the appropriate taxes that are imposed on the use of the card. (A state that does not tax telephone calls is unlikely to tax the sale of the card.)

The states that tax the sale of the card as tangible personal property tend not to also tax the use of the card as a telecommunications service. A minority of states, however, tax both the sale of the card and its use. The rules vary among the states, however, and administrative complexities abound. If a card is purchased in a state that taxes it as tangible personal property, but is subsequently used in a state that taxes it as a telecommunications service, double taxation is likely to result. Conversely, if a card is purchased in a state that taxes the use (but not the purchase) of the card, but the card is used in a state that taxes the purchase (but not the use), the call will be exempt.

Administratively, the simplest route is to tax the card at the point of sale, the way that some other types of prepaid consumption are taxed. For a concise treatment of the issues, see Walter Nagel, Linda P. Holman, and Douglas A. Richards, One Approach to State and Local Taxation of Prepaid Calling Cards, 11 State Tax Notes 1747 (1996). Although administratively attractive, one weakness in taxing the purchase of the card arises if the user of the card makes calls that would not be taxable under the state's telecommunications tax. For example, a state may tax only intrastate calls, yet the purchaser of the card may make only interstate calls (or not use the card at all). In this case, taxing the purchase of the card is an imperfect proxy for taxing the use of the card.

12. Suppose your membership in the AAA allows you to purchase a variety of goods at a discount. How should your membership fee be taxed? What about your membership in the ABA, which also provides a discount on the purchase of goods? What about your membership in a wholesale buying club, such as Sams, or BJ's?

13. Suppose a supermarket normally sells detergent for $3.00 a box. If the supermarket runs a "two for one" sale, what is the proper amount of sales tax that should be collected? What if you can get the second one "free" only if you have a coupon issued by the store? What if you must have a coupon issued by the manufacturer and that the store will be reimbursed by the manufacturer for the cost of the second box of detergent?

14. **The Normative Treatment of Coupons.** For sales tax purposes, nearly all states (Texas and Massachusetts being two major exceptions) distinguish between store coupons and manufacturers' coupons. The nearly universal rule throughout the country is that taxable items purchased with store coupons are taxed net of the face value of the coupon (i.e., only the amount of cash paid is taxable and the face value of the coupon is excluded) but that taxable items bought with manufacturers' coupons are taxed on the aggregate of the cash paid and the face value of the coupon. In contrast to this pattern, Texas and Massachusetts exclude both store and manufacturers' coupons from tax.

From the consumer's perspective, a 20 cent manufacturers' coupon is identical in benefit to a 20 cent store coupon. In the case of the former, however, the manufacturer will pay the face amount of the coupon–20 cents–to the store.[1] This apparent difference in the amount the vendor receives that is attributable to the sale has presumably led states to include the face value of manufacturers' coupons in the base of their sales taxes.[2]

Conceptually, the normative sales tax treatment of coupons is most easily approached by first considering the purchase of an item on sale. We start with the widely accepted proposition that an ideal retail sales tax would tax the fair market value of consumption that occurs in market exchanges once and only once.[3] As an application of that proposition, assume that an item normally priced at $1.50 is purchased on sale for $1.30. All states would charge sales tax on $1.30. That the item would normally sell for $1.50 would be irrelevant just as would the fact that the item was currently selling for $1.50 at nearby stores.[4]

This same analysis applies if a consumer buys the item

---

1. In addition, manufacturers typically pay vendors 8 cents per redeemed coupon as a handling fee. 64 Progressive Grocer 44 (1985). For sales tax purposes, the 8 cents would presumably be characterized as a fee received for the provision of a service and not for the sale of tangible personal property. If a state had a sales tax that broadly covered services, presumably the 8 cents would be taxable. In an ideal sales tax, the 8 cents would be properly exempt as a business input.

2. "The tax typically applies to undiscounted price if the coupon is issued by the manufacturer because the vendor receives the coupon value from that source. Receipts from the sale thus come partly from the purchaser and partly from the manufacturer. Store coupons are treated simply as price reductions, so the tax applies to the net of coupon price." Due and Mikesell, Sales Taxation: State and Local Structure and Administration 38 (1983).

3. McDaniel and Surrey (eds.), International Aspects of Tax Expenditures 63-69 (1985); Due and Mikesell, Sales Taxation: State and Local Structure and Administration 23-24 (1983); Due, State and Local Sales Taxation: Structure and Administration 24-28 (1971).

4. The IRS' approach is apparently consistent with this position. In a situation involving a merchant transferring goods to customers in exchange for store coupons, the IRS ruled that the federal excise tax is based on the fair market value of the goods at the time of the transfer. The ruling, however, does not discuss how fair market value is to be determined nor does it discuss the treatment of manufacturers' coupons. Rev. Rul. 62-90, 1962-1 C.B. 190. See also Southern Premium Stamp Co., 289 F.2d 319 (1961).

using a 20 cent store coupon. Essentially, the store has stratified the market by running a mini-sale. For shoppers willing to clip a coupon, the item is available at a sales price of $1.30; all other shoppers pay $1.50.[5] Two prices for the item coexist.[6]

Although the preceding discussion involved a store coupon, from the economic perspective of the purchaser (tax considerations aside) whether the 20 cent coupon is a store coupon or a manufacturers' coupon is irrelevant–the item still costs the purchaser $1.30 in either case, which is its fair market value to anyone having a coupon. The states have apparently been mislead in their treatment of this issue by focusing on the amount the vendor receives from the manufacturer and viewing that amount as part of the consideration paid for the item. As argued below, it is preferable to view the 20 cents as a rebate from the manufacturer to the retailer that should be characterized as an inventory adjustment.[7]

The fallacy in treating the amount received from the manufacturer as part of the base of the sales tax can be illustrated by considering three situations that have the same economic impact on both the consumer and the retailer as either a store sale or a store coupon. Suppose a manufacturer is willing to

forgo 20 cents in revenue by reducing the price of an item to the consumer by 20 cents in order to increase sales. Assume the manufacturer has three alternatives: (1) issue a 20 cent manufacturers' coupon; (2) reduce the price of the item to the store by 20 cents from say $1.00 to 80 cents and have the store reduce the price to the consumer by 20 cents through a sale;[8] or (3) reduce the price of the item to the store by 20 cents from $1.00 to 80 cents and have the store reduce the price to the consumer by 20 cents by issuing a store coupon.[9]

Under the first alternative, the store receives $1.30 from the consumer and clears 50 cents on the sale ($1.50[10] - $1.00). Under the second alternative, the store receives $1.30 from the consumer and clears 50 cents on the sale ($1.30 - $.80), and under the third alternative the store again receives $1.30 from the consumer and again clears 50 cents on the sale ($1.30 - $.80). In all three cases, both the consumer, who pays the same amount out-of-pocket, and the store, which clears the same amount, are in the same economic position, yet in the first situation, sales tax is paid on $1.50 in nearly all states, rather than on $1.30 as in the second and third situations. No normative justification exists for treating these economically equivalent transactions differently. Accordingly, a manufacturers' coupon is best viewed not as additional consideration that is properly included in the base of the tax, but rather as an inventory adjustment, exactly how a rebate received by a dealer from a manufacturer is treated by the IRS under the federal income tax.[11]

The arbitrariness of a rule that taxes a consumer on $1.30 if the purchase is made with a 20 cent store

---

5. One court equated a store coupon with a cash discount and held that sales tax was properly chargeable on only the cash amount received from the customer. Burger King v. Division of Taxation, 541 A.2d 241 (1988). A sale price could also be conceptualized as a cash discount. For example, using the figures in the text, the consumer could be viewed as paying $1.50 for the item and receiving a cash discount of $.30. Some courts have equated trading stamps to a cash discount.

6. The existence of two prices–one for coupon clippers and one for all other shoppers is conceptually equivalent to the two prices that exist when an item is on sale at one store but not at another store.

7. That the 20 cents is paid by a third party (the manufacturer) rather than the consumer is not dispositive of whether it should be included within the base of a sales tax. The relevant issue is how to characterize the payment by the third party. For example, if a consumer purchased a car for $10,000 by paying $8,000 cash and by having his employer pay $2,000 directly to the dealer, the sales tax would then be properly paid on $10,000, exactly as if the $2,000 were first paid by the employer to the employee who then used it to pay for the car. The question posed in the text, however, is whether the 20 cents received from the manufacturer is best viewed as consideration for the sale or, as we proceed to argue, as an inventory adjustment. See also Rev. Rul. 84-41, 1984-1 C.B. 130, holding that a rebate received by a dealer from a manufacturer is treated as an inventory adjustment and not as income to the dealer.

8. For simplicity, assume the manufacturer is dealing directly with the store rather than through a distributor.

9. From a marketing perspective, the situations are obviously different. A manufacturer that reduces the inventory cost of the item by 20 cents has no assurance that the store will pass this savings onto the consumer. A manufacturers' coupon allows the manufacturer to reduce the price to the consumer directly and can play a key role in a manufacturers' national advertising campaign. A store can, of course, frustrate the manufacturers' goal by raising the store price of the item by some or all of the 20 cents; in effect, the store can attempt to appropriate some of the revenue the manufacturer is willing to forgo.

10. $1.30 from the consumer plus a rebate of $.20 from the manufacturer = $1.50.

11. Rev. Rul. 84-41, 1984-1 C.B. Accord, Rev. Rul. 85-30, 1985-1 C.B. 20.

coupon but on $1.50 if the purchase is made with a 20 cent manufacturers' coupon can be illustrated in yet a different way. Suppose the manufacturer of an item offers the store a rebate of 20 cents for every item the store sells and that the store runs a sale by reducing the price of the item to $1.30 from $1.50. At the time of the purchase, all states would tax only $1.30, the amount of cash the consumer pays. The economic effect of this situation (sales tax considerations aside) is the same as one in which the consumer purchases the good with a 20 cent manufacturers' coupon, in which case all states but Texas would have taxed the consumer on $1.50. By restructuring the transaction in the form of a rebate from the manufacturer to the store, it should be more obvious that the 20 cents the store subsequently receives is an inventory price adjustment.

All the preceding examples assumed that the store or the manufacturer did not try to recover the revenue forgone through the coupon (or rebate) by an increase in price. The analysis would not change, however, even if prices were increased so that a consumer implicitly pays for the putatively free coupon.

Consider, for example, a taxable item that previously sold for $8. Assume the item now sells for $10 because a consumer receives as part of the purchase a $2 manufacturers' coupon that can be used on a subsequent purchase of the same (or another) item. When the consumer bought the first item, he paid sales tax on $10. Accordingly, because part of the $10 is attributable to the value of the coupon, sales tax has already been paid on that amount. Because the state has received sales tax on the value attributable to the coupon, the consumer has prepaid sales tax on that amount of future consumption. When the consumer uses the coupon plus $8 cash to buy the next item, no reason exists to impose a sales tax a second time on the value of the coupon.[12]

Consequently, only $8 should be taxed on the second purchase, exactly the result reached if only the cash price of the item is taxed, net of the face value of the coupon, notwithstanding that the coupon is issued by the manufacturer.

Whether the price of the item was increased to reflect the coupon or not is irrelevant to our analysis.[13] If the price was not increased, a consumer now obtains the item and the coupon at the same price–$8–that previously paid for only the item. In effect, the price of the item has been reduced by the value of the coupon (and it is irrelevant whether the coupon is issued by the store or by the manufacturer). The $8 represents the fair market value of the package of "item plus coupon."

This last example can be approached in yet a different manner by assuming the manufacturer agrees to rebate $2 to the store for every two of the taxable $10 items that are sold, and the store then issues its own $2 coupon to a customer who purchases the first of the $10 items. A consumer who uses the store coupon to purchase a second of the two items pays the same $18 ($10 + $8) as he would have if he had used a $2 manufacturers' coupon on the purchase of the second item. The store would clear the same amount on the sale of the two items as in the situation involving a manufacturers' coupon. If a consumer had purchased the second item for $8 cash and had presented a $2 store coupon, all states would have levied sales tax on $8. The result will be the same if a consumer who purchases the second item for $8 cash plus a $2 manufacturers' coupon pays sales tax on only $8.

The analysis can be generalized to many other areas where the purchase of one item gives the consumer the right to some other item in the future. Consider, for example, a warranty that accompanies the purchase of a new car. Suppose the purchaser of the new car discovers that one of the tires is defective and subsequently receives for free a new tire under the warranty. No sales tax is properly due on the receipt of the new tire because the possibility of receiving the free tire was already paid for as part of the purchase

---

12. A consumer who does not use the coupon has expressed a willingness to pay $10 for only the first item. In a sense, a bifurcated market exists: some consumers are willing to pay $10 for the first item, and are properly charged sales tax on that amount, whereas others are implicitly willing to pay $8 for the first item and purchase a coupon for $2. Of course, there will always be some consumers who planned on using the coupon but could not because of circumstances beyond their control. They can be analogized to those who pay sales tax on a restaurant meal that they don't enjoy (i.e., they value the meal at an amount less than that which they paid), or pay sales tax on a movie they don't enjoy. These cases of frustration are ignored in a sales tax (unless a refund is available, in which case the sales tax is refunded along with the ex tax price of the good). More conceptually, the price of any item in part already reflects the possibility of frustration.

13. In reality, the pricing decision is exceedingly complicated. A merchant might increase the price of an item whose purchase triggers receipt of the coupon, or might increase the price of an entirely different set of goods. Alternatively, the merchant might not increase the price of any goods whatsoever, in which case he is relying on increased sales volume and increased profits to cover the cost of the coupon. A merchant's pricing strategy might vary by product, by market, or by innumerable other factors.

of the car.

The analysis is independent of whether a retail sales tax is formally levied on the vendor or the consumer. In either case the normative inquiry should be the same: what is the value of consumption that should be included in the base of the tax. Superficially, if a retail sales tax is levied on a vendor's gross receipts, the amount received under a manufacturers' coupon would appear to be part of such receipts. As the above analysis suggests, however, the normative issue is best resolved by viewing the reimbursement as an inventory adjustment reducing the vendor's cost of goods sold and not as part of the vendor's gross receipts.

The proper sales tax treatment of rebates is closely akin to that of coupons. A store rebate is indistinguishable from a store coupon or a storewide sale, and sales tax should be paid on the price of an item reduced by the amount of the rebate. A manufacturers' rebate is also indistinguishable from a manufacturers' coupon, except for an administrative complication. Suppose a consumer who buys a $10 item can receive a $2 rebate from the manufacturer by sending in proof of purchase. If the consumer receives the rebate, the sales tax should theoretically be levied on only $8, exactly as if he bought the item on sale for that amount. Realistically, however, the consumer has to pay sales tax on $10 because at the time of the purchase whether he will receive the rebate is unknown.

A refund mechanism could be provided, however, whereby a state would reimburse a consumer for the sales tax paid on the amount of the price that was refunded through the rebate. A manufacturer could, for example, be authorized by a state to increase its rebate by the sales tax on that amount. The manufacturer would verify that sales tax had been paid by examining the purchaser's proof of purchase, which presumably has to be submitted anyway to obtain the rebate. The manufacturer would then receive a refund of the tax from the appropriate state.

Obviously, in many cases the sales tax refund due the consumer will be too small to justify this added administrative complication.

If the rebate is substantial, however, so that the consumer is certain to claim it, a state should tax at the time of the sale only the price net of the rebate. For example, manufacturers periodically offer substantial rebates on the sale of cars. Because of the amount involved, all purchasers can be assumed to receive the rebate (and in some cases they actually receive the benefit of the rebate at the time of purchase by assigning it to the dealership). In this situation, sales tax should be levied on the price of the car excluding the amount of the rebate, exactly as if the manufacturer lowered the cost of the car to the dealer who passed that savings onto the consumer.

State practices comport with the proposition that a rebate should be viewed the same as a coupon. The treatment of rebates in each state generally tracks that state's treatment of coupons. Most states that have explicit rules on rebates exclude from taxation rebates offered by a store, thus mirroring the treatment of a store coupon. Manufacturers' rebates are improperly included within the tax base, the same as manufacturers' coupons.[14] Utah and a few other states provide the normatively correct rule by excluding from sales taxation any "rebate that is certain and the amount has been determined."[15]

---

14. See, e.g., CCH, State Tax Reporter for Ala. ¶ 64-337; Conn. ¶ 63-824; Ga. ¶ 60-079; Ind. ¶64-062a; Miss. ¶64-014a. Rhode Island is the exception to the rule that the treatment of rebates tracks that of coupons: Rhode Island excludes manufacturers' rebates from the sales tax, R.I., ¶ 60-070, even though manufacturers' coupons are taxed. Wyoming excludes a manufacturers' rebate only if the purchaser assigns it to the dealer as a contractual condition in the sales contract. Wyo. ¶ 60-362.20. Presumably, all purchasers would assign it, even without sales tax considerations, in order to receive the benefit of the rebate without waiting. Idaho exempts a manufacturer's rebate on the purchase of a motor vehicle if the rebate is "used to reduce the retail sales price of the vehicle, or is used as a down payment on the purchase." The customer's invoice must show the manufacturer's rebate as a deduction to, or down payment on, the price of the motor vehicle. Id.

15. See CCH, State Tax Reporter, Utah, ¶ 61-565 (citing Bulletin of the State Tax Commission, Feb. 15, 1975). Louisiana recently amended its sales tax to exclude cash discounts or rebates given by either a vendor or a manufacturer on any new motor vehicle. This exclusion does not apply, however, to the Louisiana Recovery District 1% tax. Louisiana Act 350, amending and reenacting La. Rev. Stat. 47:301(13).

Idaho State Tax Commission v. Boise Cascade Corporation
Supreme Court of Idaho, 1975.
97 Idaho 312, 543 P.2d 865.

. . . .

The single issue on appeal is whether the district court was correct in determining that the construction and sale of prefabricated homes, pursuant to an existing contract with the landowner [required] the payment of a use tax on the value of materials used. Appellant contends that these were retail sales under I.C. § 63-3609, requiring the payment of a sales tax on the sales price of the homes.[1]

The Tax Commission, in support of its contention that Boise Cascade was involved in the sale of tangible personal property, refers to the House Revenue and Taxation Committee Report in Support of House Bill 222 (the Idaho Sales Tax Act) and a series of examples contained in that report to show the intent of the legislature in enacting I.C. § 63-3609(a). The Board of Tax Appeals examined these examples and made the following determination:

"The Tax Commission relied on Example 4 of the House Revenue and Taxation Committee Report in support of House Bill 222 under Section 63-3609(a), Idaho Code, to support its contention that the contractor constructing prefabricated buildings can never be regarded as improving the real property.

That example reads as follows:

"'Subcontractor agrees to furnish labor and materials for the erection of a shell home (a home which is prefabricated and later transported and affixed to a lot) for contractor. The contractor intends to sell the shell home to a purchaser who will have it installed on the purchaser's lot either by contractor or someone else. So the contractor may give a resale certification on those materials which are incorporated into the "shell home"; he will pay tax on those supplies which he uses in his operations which do not become a part of the "shell home". The subcontractor will take a resale certificate from contractor on the sale of materials as part of the contract.'

"'Contractor will collect a sales tax from owner (the ultimate purchaser) on the entire sales price of the "shell home". If contractor erects the home, sales tax will be imposed on the entire price; if the price of the "shell home" is segregated from installation charges in the contract, that part of the contract which represents charges for installation will not be taxed. (See Sec. 13(b) (4)).'

"A reading of the examples shows that Example 4 was dealing with the special situation where a contractor was constructing a prefabricated building in the expectation and in the hopes that he would sell the prefabricated building to an owner of a site who would then transport it to his lot and have it installed. That this is the situation Example 4 deals with is shown by the language of the example. It is the *purchaser* who installed the prefabricated building. The second sentence of the example, which reads 'contractor intends to sell. . .', conclusively shows that the contractor is not obligated to build and affix the prefabricated building to the real property. Whoever subsequently purchases the building arranges for its fixation to the real property. Title to the prefabricated building passes to such person as personalty and the purchaser is the improver of the real property and not the contractor in the example given. Hence, in the example, the contractor collects a sales tax on the sales price of personalty.

"Example 5 of the same section of such report, illustrating the operation of Section 63-3609(a), is also revealing. That example reads as follows:

"'Subcontractor agrees to provide services and materials in the construction of a "shell home" (as defined in Example 4) for contractor. Contractor intends to place the "shell home" on a lot which he owns and sell the house and lot. Subcontractor will give a resale certificate for those materials which will become a component part of the "shell home". Subcontractor is selling both labor (services) and material to the contractor. Contractor is a consumer as defined in Section 9(a). Subcontractor will collect a sales tax on the materials from contractor. If contractor later alters his intention and sells the "shell home" for installation on a lot owned by the purchaser, he will offset the sales tax he paid as illustrated by Section 13(a)(1).'

---

1. "63-3609. Retail sale–Sale at retail.– The terms 'retail sale' or 'sale at retail' mean a sale of tangible personal property for any purpose other than resale in the regular course of business or the rental of tangible personal property in the regular course of business.

(a) All persons engaged in constructing, altering, repairing or improving real estate are consumers of the material used by them; all sales of tangible personal property to such persons are taxable whether or not such persons intend resale of the improved property."

"63-3619. Imposition and rate of the sales tax.–An excise tax is hereby imposed upon each sale at retail at the rate of three per centum (3%) of the sales price of all property subject to taxation under this act and such amount shall be computed monthly on all sales at retail within the preceding month."

"63-3621. Imposition and rate of the use tax.–An excise tax is hereby imposed on the storage, use, or other consumption in this state of tangible personal property acquired on or after July 1, 1965, for storage, use, or other consumption in this state at the rate of three per centum (3%) of the value of the property, and a recent sales price shall be presumptive evidence of the value of the property."

"It is clear from this example that under some circumstances contractor engaged in constructing a prefabricated building is engaged in improving real property and hence is taxed, but only on the materials used in the construction. If the contractor constructing a prefabricated home which he intends to place on a lot which he owns is the consumer under Section 63-3609(a), Idaho Code, certainly it should follow that a contractor engaged in constructing a prefabricated house which he is obliged to place on the lot of another and then attach it to its foundation is engaged in improving the real property to that person and to be treated as a consumer of the materials used and is taxed only on such materials, and not the selling price of the completed building. Similarly, the fact that under Example 5 if the contractor changes his intention and later sells the house to another for installation, he loses his status as a consumer under Section 63-3609(a), is clear evidence that Example 4 of the House Report relied upon by the Tax Commission applies to a situation where the contractor is constructing a prefabricated building, hoping to sell the house to a purchaser when completed, who will, himself, arrange for installation and hence the contractor is not engaged in improving real property."

We find the Board's analysis to be well reasoned and applicable to the facts of this case. Boise Cascade did not build any prefabricated homes without a contract and then offer them for sale. Rather, the course of business in all such transactions was as follows: The customer, an owner of a tract of land on which he wished a structure to erected, entered into a contract with Boise Cascade Corporation which required Boise Cascade Corporation to construct a building according to plans and specifications of the customer, who could and did frequently modify basic model designs. Boise Cascade Corporation then proceeded to construct the building in one of its three factories. When Boise Cascade Corporation completed the structure, it was required by the contract to, and did, transport the completed

building to the site of the owner, and place it on a foundation on the site, shim and level the building, attach the building to the foundation (which may or may not have been constructed by Boise Cascade Corporation), and perform other tasks. In all cases where Boise Cascade constructed a prebuilt or prefabricated building and attached it to a foundation at the site of the customer, the title to such building did not pass to the customer until Boise Cascade placed the building on the site of the customer, and attached it to its foundation.

Thus, the examples certainly support the lower court's finding that Boise Cascade was improving real property and not making retail sales of personalty. In addition, the Idaho Sales Tax Act defines "sale" as "any transfer of title, exchange or barter, conditional or otherwise, in any manner or by any means whatsoever, of tangible personal property." Since title to the home does not pass to the buyer until the home is fixed to the lot foundation there has been no sale of personalty, as defined by I.C. § 63-3612, but rather the improvement of real estate.

The only distinction between Boise Cascade's method of construction and that of the traditional on-site contractor is that Boise Cascade does a majority of its construction at their plant while a majority of the traditional contractor's work is done at the homeowner's lot. The legislature considered the process of construction to be a service and enacted I.C. § 63-3609(a) to tax the contractor for the materials consumed in the building process. The fact that Boise Cascade's method of construction involves hauling the nearly completed home to the buyer's lot does not change the end result, that is, the landowner having a home on his previously unimproved lot.

It is the Court's opinion that the method employed by Boise Cascade does not alter the normal application of the use tax to contractors. Affirmed. Costs to respondent.

Questions and Comments

1. Does the court's opinion help to maintain neutrality between someone who purchases a prefabricated home and someone who purchases traditional housing?

2. How would the court treat the sale of a mobile home?

3. Is there any reason for treating the sale of prefabricated houses or mobile homes differently from the sale of traditional homes?

4. Several states exclude specified percentages of the purchase price of mobile homes from sales taxation. See Due and Mikesell, *Sales Taxation: State and Local Structure and Administration* (2d. ed. 1994), p. 99. What is the rationale behind this approach?

5. In a normative sales tax, would examples 4 and 5 in the House Revenue and Taxation Committee Report in Support of House Bill 222 be treated differently?

E.   Ingredient and Component Exemption

Conceptually, the ingredient or component exemption is akin to the sale (purchase) for resale exemption. Both exempt a subset of business inputs. In general, if an item is purchased and will be resold without changing its form or without becoming part of another object, the sale for resale exemption applies. The quintessential item covered by this exemption is the purchase of inventory (e.g., the purchase of CDs by a music store). If the purchased item becomes part of another item, the ingredient or component exemption is likely to apply. In this sense, the ingredient or component exemption is a kind of sale for resale exemption.

Consider, for example, an automotive dealership. No sales tax (or use tax) is due on its purchase of cars because of the sale for resale exemption. Suppose, however, that the dealership provides its customers certain options, including a CD player. Assume these players are purchased from suppliers and are installed by the dealership. The component or ingredient rule would exempt the CD players from the sales (or use) tax. Although the substance of the transaction is that the dealership bought the CD players for resale, the "sale for resale" exemption is not applicable to the transaction, as it would be, for example, if an electronics store bought the CD players as part of its inventory. Instead, the ingredient or component rule is the operative provision, although the result is the same: the purchase of the CD players by the dealer is exempt. Similarly, from the perspective of the car manufacturer, the steel that becomes the body of the car is a component of the product that it sells. accordingly, the steel is purchased sales tax free under an ingredient or component exemption. Tech-

nically, the sale for resale exemption would not apply. The difference between the sale for resale exemption and the ingredient or component exemption is conceptually blurry. A car, for example, can be viewed as the aggregation of its components. Whether its sale is viewed as that of a car or as "tires, seats, engine, body, windshield, trunk, CD player," and so forth, is more a matter of custom than of substance. Without an ingredient or component rule, much meaningless litigation would occur over silly metaphysical issues. As it is, enough issues remain to please both metaphysicians and tax lawyers and to annoy taxpayers and administrators.

Statutory Snippets

[An exemption from the sales tax is provided for] [i]ndustrial materials for future processing, manufacturing, refining, or conversion into articles of tangible personal property for resale *where such industrial materials . . . become a component part of the finished product.* Va. Code Ann. §58.1-608(3)(b)(i)(emphasis added).

"Retail sale" and "sales at retail" include all sales except those in which *the purpose of the consumer is . . . to incorporate the thing transferred as a material or a part, into tangible personal property. . .* Ohio Rev. Code Ann. §5739.01 (emphasis added).

Sales of tangible personal property, which property, to the extent not first subjected to a use for which it was purchased, *as an ingredient or constituent, goes into and forms a part of tangible personal property* subsequently the subject of a "Sale at retail," are not sales at retail . . . Ill. Ann. Stat. ch. 35, para 120/1 §1 (emphasis added).

(2) Retail sale or sale at retail shall not mean:
(a) The sale of: (1) *[p]roperty which will enter into and become an ingredient or component part of property manufactured, processed, or fabricated* for ultimate sale at retail; Neb. Rev. Stat. §77-2702.13(2)(a)(i) (emphasis added).

American Stores Packing Co. v. Peters
Supreme Court of Nebraska, 1979.
203 Neb. 76, 277 N.W.2d 544.

The issue in this case is whether cellulose casings used in the manufacture of skinless meat products such as frankfurters is subject to payment of the use tax. . . .

Section 77-2703(2), R.R.S.1943, provides in part:

"A use tax is hereby imposed on the storage, use, or other consumption in this state of tangible personal property purchased, leased or rented from any retailer for storage, use, or other consumption in this state . . . . Every person storing, using, or

otherwise consuming in this state tangible personal property purchased from a retailer or leased or rented from another person for such purpose is liable for the use tax. Use shall mean the exercise of any right or power over tangible personal property incident to the ownership or possession of that tangible personal property, except that it does not include . . . personal property in the regular course of business or the exercise of any right or power over tangible personal property *which will enter into or become an ingredient or component part of tangible personal property* manufactured, processed or fabricated *for ultimate sale at retail.*" (Emphasis supplied.)

The precise issue is whether the casing is used so that it "will enter into or become an ingredient or component part" of the finished meat product and thus not subject to the use tax.

The evidence pertinent to the issue was introduced by stipulation of the parties and the explanatory testimony of a chemist called by American Stores. The testimony of the chemist was founded upon the facts and evidence contained in the stipulation and his observation of the manufacturing process. He conducted no chemical or other tests.

From the evidence, the Tax Commissioner could arrive at the following as fact. American Stores is a meat packer and manufacturer of finished meat products with a plant located in Nebraska. Its products are sold to retail food markets for ultimate resale to consumers. In the process of manufacturing "skinless" frankfurters and certain luncheon meats, it uses cellulose casings purchased from makers outside the state and brings the casings into this state for use in the process of manufacture of the mentioned meat products. Into the cellulose casing have been "absorbed" (the language of the chemist) glycerine and moisture. . . .

The casing is in long, tubular form. In the course of manufacture of the skinless meat products, the casing is utilized in the following fashion. It is stuffed mechanically with the prepared meat product. The casing, after being tied in segments, then moves onto a conveyor belt and is subjected to a series of processes, among which are a vinegar shower, liquid smoke shower, cooking, and a series of chill showers. The testimony is that, during the vinegar shower, an undetermined amount of the glycerine with which the casing is impregnated, moves by osmosis from the casing into the meat and penetrates the meat slightly. At the end of the process, the cellulose casing is slit by a device with a razor-like edge and the casing is blown off. The casing is still recognizable as a casing, but it is without economic value and is discarded.

The glycerine and moisture in the casing serve several functions. In the words of the chemist, they make the cellulose manageable so that it can be stuffed, shaped, and conveyed. The glycerine permits the casing to be peeled easily from the frankfurter or other product after slitting. The glycerine also coats the outer surface of the product, improves its appearance, and inhibits drying out of the product, thus increasing its shelf life. Two and one-tenth percent of the casings contain dye which moves into the meat with the glycerine and improves the coloration of the product. The chemist testified it would be excessively expensive to conduct tests to determine the amount of glycerine moving from the casing into the meat because there is already glycerine in the meat and the testing would be complex.

The position of American Stores, stated in the briefest form, is that "enough [of the glycerine] goes in [to the product] to make a difference" and this should be the test of whether the casing enters into or becomes an ingredient or component part of the product. The Tax Commissioner emphasizes that the casings as such do not enter into or become components or ingredients of the product in any real sense and American Stores is the ultimate consumer of the casings. He points out the general plan of the sales and use tax is that every item of personal property, not specifically excluded, is to be subject to either one or the other of the taxes at some point of the chain of commerce. Unless, therefore, the tax is imposed on the use of the casings in the hands of American Stores, the casings escape taxation completely.

We do not propose to discuss in any detail American Stores' highly refined semantic arguments. Nor do we think it necessary to discuss rules of construction of statutes. We find the precedents cited by the Tax Commissioner the most persuasive.

American Stores argues that this case is governed by State v. United States Steel Corporation, 206 So.2d 358; and State v. Southern Kraft Corporation, 8 So.2d 886. In State v. United States Steel Corporation, supra, the issue was whether the sales of oxygen to a manufacturer of steel were retail sales subject to tax, or wholesale sales not subject to tax. The determination of the issue depended upon language of the Alabama statute defining wholesale sales as including those of tangible personal property "'which enters into and becomes an ingredient or component part'" of the product which is manufactured for sale. In that case, the oxygen was acquired from a seller in the state. This would be the same situation in our case had American Stores purchased the casings from a supplier in this state. The issue in the two cases is therefore essentially identical although one involves use tax and the other sales tax. In our judgment, however, the difference in facts makes the Alabama precedent inapplicable to the issue here. In the Alabama case, the oxygen was injected into the molten metal in the furnaces. The purpose of putting the oxygen in the steel was to control the carbon content of the steel and contribute to its hardness and smoothness. Clearly in that case the oxygen was an essential component that entered into the chemical process of making steel. The oxygen did not in any degree serve the function of a mold or substitute for any mechanical device. It was in any view an ingredient even though most of the oxygen escaped or remained in the slag which was the waste product remaining after the process was completed. State v. Southern Kraft Corporation, supra, involved paper manufacture and the issue was whether or not various chemicals, such as lime, sulphur, and others used in the process, became "'ingredient or component part of the finished product.'" The court held as fact that the chemicals did become a substantial "ingredient or component part," even though only a small percentage remained in the finished product. State v. Southern Kraft Corporation, supra, in our view, involves essentially the same situation as that in State v. United States Steel Corporation, supra.

. . . .

The determination of whether or not tangible property enters into or becomes an ingredient or component part of other property does not ordinarily offer any difficulty. The lumber which goes into the manufacture of a piece of furniture obviously becomes a component part of that furniture, i.e., the function of the lumber is that of being a component and it serves no other purpose. In the case before us, the casing served the apparently indispensable function of a mold. In the end, the casing is discarded. It does not become an ingredient or component in any real sense, as it does not reach the ultimate consumer of the eat product. If one judges solely by the physical evidence, i.e., a sample of unused casing and a sample of used casing, the answer seems almost obvious. The casing remains after the manufacture. The principal function of the glycerine and moisture is to enable the casing to serve its function. The transfer of some part of the glycerine into meat which already contains glycerine appears incidental. The Tax Commissioner's determination that the cellulose casing did not enter into or become an ingredient or component part of the meat products was correct and was properly sustained by the District Court.

Questions and Comments

1. In deciding a case like *American Stores Packing*, what latitude does the judge have in considering the normative principle that business inputs should not be taxed?

2. The Tax Commissioner argued that if the casings were not taxed in the hands of American Stores, they would escape taxation completely. Is the Commissioner right? How could the taxpayer respond to this argument?

3. In *U.S. Steel*, the oxygen was viewed by the court as entering into the chemical process of making steel, even though most of the oxygen escaped or remained in the slag, which was the waste product remaining after the steel had been made. In *Southern Kraft*, only a small percentage of the chemicals remained in the finished product. Why should those situations be viewed as falling within the "ingredient or component" exemption, but not the casings? Can a catalyst in a chemical reaction ever be a physical ingredient of the item that it helped produce?

4. Would the case have been different if the casings were destroyed during the manufacturing of the hot dogs? What if the casings had evaporated once the

glycerine was used up? If the casings were destroyed, would the case be more similar to *U.S. Steel* and *Southern Kraft*? What if the casings had some resale value?

5. What if the casings were seasoned with spices and those spices entered the hot dogs during manufacturing?

6. In support of its statement that the ingredient or component rule does not ordinarily present any difficulties the court offers the example of lumber being used in the manufacture of furniture. How would the court treat the lumber that goes to waste in the making of furniture?

7. At best, should the plaintiffs be allowed to buy the casings sales tax free, or purchase tax free only that portion of the casings attributable to the glycerine and dye?

8. If Nebraska had a manufacturer's exemption, would the casings qualify? Would a mold?

9. Would the case have been different if the hot dogs were not skinless?

10. Should barrels used to age bourbon whiskey be eligible for the ingredient or component exemption? See *American Distilling Co. v. Department of Revenue*, 368 N.E.2d 541 (Neb. 1977). Cf. *Container Corp. v. Ill.*, 689 N.E.2d 259 (1997).

11. Is *American Stores Packing* consistent with *Carlisle Engineered Products v. Alabama*, No. U-99-524 (Admin. Law Div. Aug. 28, 2000)? That case held that the purchase of molds, barrels, and screws used in the

manufacturing process were exempt from the use tax under the ingredient or component exemption. The Chief ALJ, Judge Bill Thompson, one of the well-known tax jurists in the country, found that minute portions of these business inputs broke off in the manufacturing process and ended up in the finished products. The fact that their presence was incidental was irrelevant. The decision is clearly right in normative terms, see Chapter Six, and should lead to more business inputs being exempt in Alabama.

Al-Tom Investment, Inc. v. Director of Revenue
Supreme Court of Missouri, 1989.
774 S.W.2d 131.

. . . .

I

Kentucky Fried Chicken of Spanish Lake, Inc., Al-Tom Investment, Inc., doing business as Kentucky Fried Chicken, and Scott Marshall Enterprises, Inc., (appellants), are corporations licensed to do business in Missouri and have their principal places of business in Missouri. For preparing the fried foods at their restaurants, mainly chicken, fish and potatoes, the appellants purchased vegetable cooking oil, and issued blanket exemption certificates to their vendors which allowed appellants to avoid paying sales taxes on their purchases of the oil. . .

The Director contended that only that part of the oil that was actually absorbed into the food product would qualify for the tax exemption. The Director assessed a sales tax on 50 percent of appellants' purchases of cooking oil in line with "the policy of the Department of Revenue", which considered only 50 percent of the oil to be absorbed into the final product.

At the hearing, Allen Scott of Scott Marshall Enterprises, Inc., testified that his estimated rate of incorporation of oil into the food products was 82 percent. His estimate was based upon figures supplied by both his oil supplier and his renderer, as well as Kentucky Fried Chicken personnel who had determined when the oil in present use should be discarded in order to guarantee proper flavor and cooking qualities. . . .

Thomas J. Slater, Jr., of Kentucky Fried Chicken of Spanish Lake, Inc., and Al-Tom Investment, Inc., also testified that the 82 percent testified to by Allen Scott

was similar to the overall absorption rate in his businesses.

The Director offered no evidence in any way contradicting or refuting the evidence offered by appellants, nor did the Director offer any evidence to support his imposition of a tax on 50 percent of the oil purchased by appellants.

The Commission determined that appellants had not satisfied their burden of proof as to the content of the oil that was absorbed into the foods and upheld the Director's assessment of the tax on 50 percent of the purchases of cooking oil, finding:

petitioner presented no evidence as to how much cooking oil was absorbed into the fish and french fries. Petitioner's evidence as to how much cooking oil was absorbed into chicken was based on hearsay, gross approximations and speculation. We find the evidence unpersuasive, inconclusive and incompetent. Petitioner did not establish that more than 50 percent of the cooking oil was absorbed.

The Commission's decision was based on Blueside Companies, Inc. v. Director of Revenue, 2 Mo.Tax Rep. (CCH) Para. 200-973 (Mo. Admin. Hearing Comm., Oct 5, 1984) . . . 12 CSR 10-3.292,[2] and 12 CSR 10-3.294.[3]

_____

2. 12 CSR 10-3.292 states, in part: (1) In order to be considered as ingredients or component parts of the new personal property resulting from manufacturing, or otherwise, the materials must be purchased by the manufacturer for the purpose of becoming a recognizable, essential and basic ingredient or component part of the new personal property which is to be ultimately sold for final use or consumption. Materials qualify for this exemption only to the extent that they become an ingredient or component part of the new personal property.

3. 12 CSR 10-3.294 states, in part: (1) Sellers of parts to manufacturers or other producers who sell component parts or substances or who physically incorporate such property as an ingredient or constituent of other tangible personal property

Following the Commission's decision, this appeal followed.

. . . .

III

. . . .

The 1984 Administrative Hearing Commission opinion that the Director alluded to was the Blueside Companies opinion. The case involved all of the chemicals utilized in the process of tanning leather. The Commission held that if the products were not detectable in the finished product, they were fully taxable, and that if they were detectable in the finished product, they were exempted only to the extent that the taxpayer could prove that they physically existed (and could be measured) in the finished product. The cause was remanded to the Director and no further appeal was later made. Blueside Companies cited and relied on the Commission's Leduc Packing Companies opinion rendered in 1980 and dealing with casings for meat products such as bologna and frankfurters. The Commission there had held that the dye contained in the casings was eligible for exemption, but that on the record there was no showing of how much of the dye was retained in the finished product.

The "50 percent policy" of the Director referred to by the Commission in the findings of fact herein apparently harks back to a 1985 unappealed Commission opinion in Hardee's of Springfield, Inc. v. Director of Revenue, 2 Mo.Tax Rep. (CCH) Para. 200-987 (Admin. Hearing Comm., June 11, 1989), where a 50 percent exemption was allowed.

In [Ceramo Company, Inc. v. Goldberg, 650 S.W.2d 303 (Mo. App. 1983)], our Court of Appeals held that the fuel oil mixed with clay to give it a shiny finish after baking constituted a component part or an ingredient of the final product. The court of appeals believed this to be true even though little if any of the fuel oil remained after the cooking process was completed, saying:

[t]he fact that the fuel oil was consumed in the process is irrelevant because it was initially a "component part or ingredient" of the final product and was necessary to produce a high quality product.

Our Court declined transfer thereby permitting the court of appeals opinion to stand.

. . . .

[W]e have examined the rulings of our sister states, and we find [our cases] to be totally compatible with what we believe to be the better reasoned rule. States such as Alabama, Georgia, Nebraska, New York, Texas, and Washington follow the rule that if any part of a material is intended to and does remain as an essential or necessary element of the finished product then the entire purchase is exempt. This includes the material that is used or consumed in the manufacturing process. The other rule, followed in states such as Arkansas, California, Illinois, Maryland, Ohio, Tennessee, Colorado, and found in 12 CSR 10-3.292 and 12 CSR 10-3.294 as the official policy of the Director, is that materials are exempt only to the extent that the taxpayer can prove that they are physically incorporated into the finished product. This rule requires measurement of the pro rata part of each material remaining in the final product.

We do not believe that the legislature either intended or believed that the Director should or could go into the field and make such measurements and computations. In the establishments herein, the cooking oil would be but the first step. Only a portion of the flour and spices end up in the final product. Only a portion of the potatoes end up as finished product. Chicken trimmings are consigned to the garbage. The same is true for the component parts of the salad. Accurately measuring the amount of material physically remaining in the final product is neither feasible nor possible. Our court of appeals [decisions] have followed and applied the appropriate rule and have reached the result we believe intended by the legislature.

. . . .

---

which they manufacture or otherwise produce and sell, are not subject to the sales tax. This exemption is applicable to the extent that such property or its reduced component substances are resold or incorporated into tangible personal property intended to be ultimately sold at retail for use or consumption. Property which is used or consumed in the manufacturing or other production process, but not physically incorporated into tangible personal property for ultimate retail sales as a product which the producer or manufacturer produces or sells, is subject to the sales tax.

Questions and Comments

1. The Director of Revenue contended that only that part of the business input that actually became an ingredient of the tangible personal property should qualify for a sales tax exemption. Could such a rule be administered evenhandedly? Was the "50 percent" rule consistent with the Director's contention?

2. The Tax Commission determined that the appellants had not satisfied their burden of proof regarding the content of the oil that was absorbed. What kinds of evidence should the appellants have introduced?

3. Missouri's sales tax contained the normal exemp-
tion for sales for resale. Would the chicken bought by the appellants qualify for an exemption under the sale for resale exemption, under the ingredient or component exemption, or under both? What about the tomatoes, lettuce, and so forth that entered into salads that they might have sold? What about scraps, waste, and so forth, which like the frankfurter casings in *American Stores*, are never sold?

4. Under the Missouri statute, as interpreted by the Director of Revenue before this case, was it necessary to determine which of the two exemptions–a sale for resale or ingredient or component–covers a particular item?

F. Manufacturing-Related Exemptions

Sales tax statutes often contain special exemptions (or special rates)[1] for manufacturing-related business inputs, which allow these to be bought sales tax free. In some states the exemptions apply to machinery or equipment used in manufacturing; other states limit the exemption to items used or consumed directly in the production of tangible personal property by manufacturing. Some states extend the exemption beyond manufacturing and explicitly include processing or fabricating, as well as assembling, extracting, and refining. The manufacturing exemption is motivated less by normative principles, which dictate that business inputs should be exempted, and more by attempts to remove possible tax barriers to economic development and to make in-state businesses more competitive in interstate and international markets. The business community often misses an opportunity to cloak itself in normative principles by lobbying for these exemptions on the grounds that they are an inherent feature of the sales tax. Instead of seizing the high ground, business lobbyists typically argue for these exemptions as if they were tax incentives.

The amount of money that turns on these exemptions is large and so, not surprisingly, litigation abounds over what constitutes manufacturing. Processing scrap metal? Quarrying stone? Raising mice for use in medical research? Publishing casebooks? Performing

administrative or distribution functions? An accountant told one of the authors of this book that he paid no sales tax on the purchase of his PC because he used it to "manufacture" tax returns.

There are various stages to manufacturing and states might choose to exempt all or few of these stages. Some of the phases include research and design, the actual processing, manufacturing, or assembling, and the distribution and sale of the finished good.

To minimize revenue loss, an exemption might be limited to items used only "directly" or "predominantly" (or sometimes both) in manufacturing, requirements that invite litigation. Where, for example, should the line be drawn between "direct" and "indirect" use? How would you classify a forklift used to bring materials from a warehouse to an assembly line? A forklift used to store the manufactured goods in a warehouse? A truck used to convey raw materials to a plant? What percentage of time must a machine be used in manufacturing to satisfy the "predominantly" test? 40 percent? 50 percent? More than 50 percent? How can an auditor verify a company's claim regarding the percentage of use?

There are hundreds of cases involving the manufacturing exemption. Some of the more unusual ones involve chemicals used to ripen bananas, food fed to laboratory rats, equipment used to wax apples, computers used to send your voice through cellular telephones, computers used to convert tax returns to electronic returns, equipment used to put labels on

---

1. See, e.g., Conn. Gen. Ann. § 12-408 (providing inter alia for a lower rate on the sale of repair or replacement parts exclusively for use in machinery used directly in a manufacturing or agricultural production process).

beer bottles, machinery used to place CD's into their cases, and dry ice placed upon already packaged poultry.

The following statutory excerpts and cases provide a very small sampling of the kinds of issues implicated in manufacturing-related exemptions.

Statutory Snippets

[Receipts from the sale of the following are exempted from the sales and use tax]: *Machinery or equipment for use or consumption directly and predominantly in the production of tangible personal property . . . by manufacturing* . . . but not including parts with a useful life of one year or less or tools or supplies used in connection with such machinery . . . N.Y. Tax Law § 1115(a)(12) (emphasis added).

[Receipts from the following are exempted from the sales and use tax]: Sales of and the storage, use or other consumption of *machinery used directly in a manufacturing production process*. The word "machinery". . . means the basic machine itself, including all of its component parts and contrivances, such as belts, pulleys, shafts, moving parts, operating structures and all equipment or devices used or required to control, regulate or operate the machinery, but excluding office equipment or data processing equipment other than numerically controlled machinery used directly in the manufacturing process.[Conn. Gen. Stat. Ann. §12-412(34) (emphasis added).

Receipts from the following are exempt from the tax imposed under the Sales and Use Tax Act:
  a. *Sales of machinery, apparatus or equipment for use or consumption directly and primarily in the production of tangible personal property by manufacturing, processing, assembling, or refining*. . . N.J. Stat. Ann. § 54:32B-8.13 (emphasis added).

[The following is exempt from the sales and use tax]: (9) *Machinery for new and expanded industry*; Ky. Rev. Stat. Ann. §139.480 (emphasis added).

"Machinery for new and expanded industry" shall mean that *machinery used directly in the manufacturing or processing production*, which is incorporated for the first time into plant facilities established in this state, and which does not replace machinery in such plants. The term "processing production" shall include: the processing and packaging of raw materials, in-process materials, and finished products; the processing and packaging of farm and dairy products for sale; and the extraction of minerals, ores, coal, clay, stone and natural gas. Ky. Rev. Stat. Ann. §139.170 (emphasis added).

There are hereby specifically exempted [from sales tax] the following:
27. The gross receipts from the sale or rental . . . of industrial machinery, equipment and computers, including replacement parts which are depreciable for state and federal income tax purposes, if. . . *machinery, equipment and computers shall be directly and primarily used in . . . processing tangible personal property or in research and development of new products or processes of manufacturing* . . . . Iowa Code Ann. § 23-422.45(27)(a) (emphasis added).

* * *

Compare these statutes. What do they share in common and how do they differ? If you were a manufacturer, would you prefer one of these definitions over the others? Would your preference be the same if you were a producer of software? An artist producing paintings, sculpture, or stone carvings? For a state-by-state review of the exemption for machinery and equipment, see Jordan Goodman, Fred O. Marcus, and David A. Hughes, Sales and Use Taxes: The Machinery and Equipment exemption, 1330 T.M. (2001) (BNA Multistate Tax Portfolio Series).

Oamco v. Lindley
Supreme Court of Ohio, 1987.
27 Ohio St. 3d 7, 500 N.E.2d 1379.

(On Rehearing)

There is no dispute of fact in this case. The Tax Commissioner, appellee herein, assessed OAMCO, appellant herein, sales and use taxes, plus penalties, on the purchase and operation of an asphalt manufacturing plant. OAMCO's manufacturing process involves the combination under carefully controlled circumstances of coarse and fine aggregate and asphalt cement. The manufacturing process commences once the taxpayer begins combination of the aggregates. After the aggregate is blended it is transferred to storage bins where it can be dropped onto conveyor belts, which are used to regulate the further mixing of the various aggregates and to transport them to a drum mixer. A belt scale is used to control the amount of asphalt cement to be mixed with the aggregate. During this mixing process, the bag house draws air through the drum mixer, reinjects fine dust particles and causes oxygen to be introduced into the drum mixer. The finished product then exits the drum, is placed on the heated main conveyor belt and is transferred to a heated surge bin. This bin is elevated to allow trucks to pull underneath for purposes of loading. A truck scale, located directly beneath the surge bin, is used to weigh the amount of the loaded product. The entire process is controlled by computer.

The commissioner's assessment was applied to the whole of the plant as described above. The assessment and penalties were paid, whereupon the taxpayer perfected an appeal to the Board of Tax Appeals (hereinafter "board"). In its decision and order, the board concluded that a refund should be limited to the drum mixer.

The cause is now before this court on rehearing of OAMCO v. Lindley (1986), 493 N.E.2d 1345.

PER CURIAM.

At issue in this case is whether the various parts of the manufacturing process are directly related to, or used in, the manufacture of appellant's product. For the reasons which follow, we affirm in part and reverse in part the board's decision.

Initially, appellant would have this court adopt the integrated plant theory. This theory views all the components of the manufacturing process as a single unit for tax purposes, and would allow no inquiry beyond whether the whole plant was purchased at the same time. It further implies that every component of the plant is directly used in manufacturing. However, "[t]his theory has never been accepted in Ohio * * *." Southwestern Portland Cement Co. v. Lindley (1981), 424 N.E.2d 304, citing Youngstown Bldg. Material & Fuel Co. v. Bowers (1958), 149 N.E.2d 1, and Ohio Ferro-Alloys Corp. v. Kosydar (1973), 296 N.E.2d 533. While there is much to be said from a public policy standpoint for the integrated plant theory, its adoption would prevent a part-by-part analysis, which we think is essential. Likewise, we reject the commissioner's rigid application of the "direct use" exemption contained within R.C. 5739.01(E)(2).*

It is readily apparent that equipment used in the manufacturing of products is exempt from sales and use taxes. R.C. 5741.02(C)(2), 5739.01(E)(2), and 5739.02(B)(15) and (16). To qualify for such exemption, a particular component must be "used directly in manufacturing." Southwestern Portland Cement Co., supra, citing Tri-State Asphalt Corp. v. Glander (1950), 90 N.E.2d 366. To determine whether the component is used directly in manufacturing, we must ask, "'*when* does the actual manufacturing activity begin and end.'" Southwestern Portland Cement Co., supra. "Manufacturing" has been statutorily defined to mean, "*transformation or conversion* of material or things into a different state or form from that in which they originally existed and the adjuncts used during and in, and necessary to

carry on and continue, production." (Emphasis added) R.C. 5739.01(R).**

In the context of this case, it is readily apparent that the transformation or conversion of material or things into a different state or form occurs primarily in the drum mixer. There, the various ingredients are heated and mixed so that they become the product ultimately sold. However, the manufacture of the product is, in no sense, either initiated or ended in the drum mixer.

As a matter of factual determination, the materials utilized are prepared before they reach the drum mixer. A precise, computerized mixing system composed of various small conveyor belts regulates the flow of aggregates from the bins. The result is a uniform size and weight of aggregate, which is essential to the required standardization of product. Likewise, the feed belt conveyor and scale are utilized to regulate the amount of asphalt cement to be added to a particular weight/volume of aggregate. Without these pieces of equipment, there could be no mix specifications, nor constancy of finished product. Without doubt, they are "adjuncts used during and in, and necessary to carry on and continue, production." R.C. 5739.01(R).

The heated main conveyor belt and surge bin are utilized to carefully remove the freshly mixed asphalt from the dryer drum and load it into the trucks. The product, although complete in the dryer drum, is nevertheless not capable of maintaining itself in the form required for delivery. The heated conveyor belt moves the material in small batches to maintain the aggregate consistency. Without this heated equipment, the material would harden after exiting from the dryer drum. Thus, far from merely transporting the product, these machines maintain the product in heated, usable form until delivery. As such, they are crucial for this manufacturing process. Further, in Hawthorn Mellody v. Lindley (1981), 417 N.E.2d 1257, the tax-exempt equipment was for the refrigeration of raw milk and ice cream. Such refrigeration was said to be "essential to prevent spoilage during the processing ." Id. at 48. The heated main conveyor belt and surge bin are utilized in the very same sense by appellant. Without the

---

*. [Ed. Ohio Rev. Code Ann. Sec. 5739.01(E)(2) reads in part: a retail sale does not include those in which the purpose of the consumer is to use or consume the thing transferred directly in the production of tangible personal property.]

**. [Ed. Ohio Rev. Code Ann. Sec. 5739.01(R)(2) defines manufacturing to include the "...adjuncts used during and in, and necessary to carry on and continue, production to complete a product at the same location after such transforming or converting has commenced."]

heat, and special handling, the asphalt will quickly become an unmarketable, solid mass. Consequently, the equipment utilized to preserve the required product state is an adjunct to property used or consumed directly in the production of tangible personal property. See R.C. 5739.01(E)(2), and Hawthorn Mellody, supra, at 49-50.

The unlicensed front-end loading vehicle as well as the holding bins are asserted to be tax-exempt under the holding of National Lime & Stone Co. v. Kosydar (1974), 311 N.E.2d 899. In that case, the front-end loading vehicles were utilized to load and blend piles of stone aggregate as part of the processing of raw stone into special sizes of crushed stone. The holding bins were used to keep the materials categorized. Id. at 207. In the present case, the same equipment is put to the same use. Also, appellant's finished product similarly requires special mixes of particular sizes of stone. We must therefore conclude that the bins and front-end loader herein were as directly involved in transforming materials into the finished product as was the equipment in National Lime & Stone Co., and thus subject to the exemption in R.C. 5739.01(R).

The control house, which functions to control all of the equipment and therefore regulate all variables, is exempted to the extent and in the direct proportion that it controls equipment subject to an exemption. Also, repair parts allocable to exempt equipment are also entitled to an exemption. However, we are unable to find any exception applicable to the truck scales, since they are used outside the manufacturing process.

Finally, we conclude that in view of the strong public policy considerations supporting the finality of judicial and quasi-judicial pronouncements, today's decision shall, with the exception of the subject litigants, only receive prospective application. Accordingly, the validity of other decisions by the Board of Tax Appeals, rendered prior to the date of this decision, shall not be affected. Accord Schucker v. Metcalf (1986), 488 N.E.2d 210; Hoover v. Bd. of Franklin Cty. Commrs. (1985), 482 N.E.2d 575.

For all of the foregoing reasons, the decision of the Board of Tax Appeals is affirmed in part and reversed in part.

CELEBREZZE, C.J., concurs in part and dissents in part.
. . . .

Further, I re-emphasize that the majority's draft ruling is a transparent exercise in judicial legislation. Like the amateur magician who is unable to perform a trick without revealing his sleight of hand, no one in this audience will be fooled by the majority's pretension that it is not adopting the integrated plant theory.

The premise of this theory is that the items of property involved are part of an integrated plant and that each item is essential to manufacturing or processing. Adoption of it "would in many instances except from taxation the sales of practically all instrumentalities used by manufacturers or processors, since it could always be said that each instrumentality plays *some* part in the manufacturing or processing." Youngstown Bldg. Material & Fuel Co. v. Bowers (1958), 149 N.E.2d 1. Time and again, this court has wisely rejected judicial adoption of the integrated plant theory because it is based on an interpretation of R.C. 5739.01(R) and 5739.01(E)(2) which has been found to be contrary to the General Assembly's intent. See, e.g. Bowers, supra; Ohio Ferro-Alloys Corp. v. Kosydar (1973), 296 N.E.2d 533; Southwestern Portland Cement Co. v. Lindley (1981), 424 N.E.2d 304.

The General Assembly has defined manufacturing, in R.C. 5739.01(R), as "the transformation or conversion of material or things into a different state or form from that in which they originally existed." The Tax Code further provides that adjuncts used directly during and in production after manufacturing has commenced will be exempt from taxation. R.C. 5739.01(R).

In the instant case, the majority exempts equipment in a self-contradictory manner which spurns the mandates of R.C. 5739.01(R) and 5739.01(E)(2). While acknowledging that "it is readily apparent that the transformation or conversion of material or things into a different state or form occurs primarily in the drum mixer," the majority also posits in its statement of the case that "[t]he manufacturing process commences once the taxpayer begins combination of the aggregates," that is, at a stage which is preparatory to the change in state or form which occurs in the drum mixer. There is no way that equipment used exclusively to *prepare* material *prior* to a change in state or form can also be classified as equipment used in manufacturing or an adjunct directly used in the manufacturing process pursuant to R.C. 5739.01(R) and 5739.01(E)(2). By exempting equipment which is used in activities either preparatory or subsequent to the manufacturing process in the instant case, on grounds that this equipment is "essential" or "crucial" to manufacturing, the court has abandoned the statutory "change in state or form" test in favor of one based solely on essentiality. Thus, since it can always be said that each instrumentality is in some way essential to the overall manufacturing process, the majority has junked R.C. 5739.01(R) and 5739.01(E)(2) and gratuitously granted unforeseen and sweeping exceptions to Ohio's Tax Code by rout of judicial enactment. In so doing, the majority has shaken our tripartite system of government by usurping a legislative function.

. . . .

Questions and Comments

---

1. Most states that exempt from the sales or use tax the sale of equipment used in manufacturing require that the machinery be directly used or consumed in manufacturing. Cases interpreting the exemption often struggle with the definition of "manufacturing" and of "directly." Generally, manufacturing is defined as the production, whether by hand or machinery, of a new and different article or product from raw or prepared materials. The manufactured articles must have new forms, qualities, or properties. There must be some material, substantial, or significant change in the basic material. See 17 A.L.R. 3d 7. Obviously, statutory provisions may broaden or modify this general approach.

2. *Oamco* addresses the issue of whether the various parts of the manufacturing process are directly related to or used in the manufacture of asphalt. The court must first establish when the manufacturing process begins and ends. The dissent complains that the majority has replaced the statutory "change in state or form" test with a test based solely on essentiality. Is that a fair analysis of what the majority has done?

3. The majority concedes that the mixing of the asphalt is completed inside the drum, but that the manufacturing process nevertheless continues on the heated conveyor belts and in the storage bin. If these pieces of equipment had been unheated, would the result have been different? One test sometimes applied to determine whether equipment is used directly in the production of tangible personal property is the "intermediate agency test," that is, does the equipment come into direct contact with the manufactured property without the use of any intervening agent. See 3 A.L.R. 4th 1129. If such equipment operates through an intermediate agency, it is not considered part of manufacturing. In *Blackmon v. Screven County Industrial Dev. Auth.*, 131 Ga. App. 265, 205 S.E.2d 497 (1974) equipment used to heat and humidify an area to allow the smooth handling of synthetic fibers failed the intermediate agency test. The court held that the equipment functioned to heat and humidify the air that circulated around the synthetic fibers.

4. The dissent argues that the manufacturing process takes place entirely inside the heated drum; presumably, the dissent would characterize the conveyor belts that draw the aggregate to the drum as merely providing transportation. The majority would have the manufacturing process begin at an earlier point. What is

that point? Can a component that merely provides transportation from A to B ever be said to change the state or form of an item in the manufacturing process? Examine the Ohio statutes. Why is it relevant, regarding the conveyor belts, to determine when the manufacturing process begins and ends?

Is there something special about the aggregates that are conveyed that might distinguish this case from a conveyor belt used to transport lumber to where it will be cut? Even though in some cases transportation equipment might not have a direct effect on changing the state or form of the manufactured item, the cases tend to allow the exemption where the transportation activity occurs after the beginning but before the end of the manufacturing process provided the activity is perceived as "essential." See 30 A.L.R. 2d 1439 and 3 A.L.R. 4th 1129. See *Cromwell-Collier Pub. Co. v. Glander*, 155 Ohio St. 511, 44 Ohio Op. 460, 99 N.E.2d 649 (1951), holding that a conveyor belt used to transport magazines from the room where they were assembled and bound to awaiting trucks was not used in the manufacturing process.

5. The majority deems a portion of the controlling computer to be tax exempt. What statutory provision allows such proportional treatment? Consider the New York statute. Would the words "directly and predominantly" necessitate a different result in New York? What about a statute requiring the equipment to be used "directly and primarily" in manufacturing?

6. Equipment used in the installation, repair, or replacement of equipment that is directly used in manufacturing will normally not be considered to be directly used in the manufacturing process. In *Standard Oil Co. v. Peck*, 163 Ohio St. 63, 56 Ohio Op. 56, 125 N.E.2d 342 (1955), a crane used to maintain pipe lines and valves at an oil refinery was held not to be used directly in the production of tangible personal property. A legislature may obviously expand the exemption to include such equipment. See 11 A.L.R. 2d 926.

7. Is machinery that packages or bottles goods "used in manufacturing"? If a state does not statutorily address the issue (see, e.g., the Kentucky statute above) the issue defaults to the tax administration and the courts. The court in *Oklahoma Tax Comm. v. Oklahoma Coca-Cola Bottling Co.*, 494 P.2d 312 (Okla. 1972) held a bottle washing machine to be part of the manufacturing

process of a soft drink bottler. Is the bottle an item that is manufactured for sale? What if the bottle is returnable?

8. Do construction activities constitute manufacturing? Presumably, a lumber mill that transforms trees into building materials is a "manufacturer," but what about a contractor who transforms the building materials into a structure? See 17 A.L.R. 3d

9. In terms of the policies that underlie an exemption for equipment used in manufacturing, might a legislature distinguish construction activities from similar activities and not grant any special treatment to the former?

10. Suppose Oamco bought a truck to transport the asphalt from the factory to a work site. Is the purchase exempt?

11. Should a legislature grant an exemption for machinery used to produce an item the sale of which is exempt from tax?

12. In its treatment of the control room, did the court abandon Ohio's primary use test?

13. The Ohio Department of Taxation predicted that the application of the OAMCO rule would result in a $600 million revenue loss. In response, the State amended the definitions of manufacturing and processing to narrow the effect of the case. See Ohio Tax Review, September/October, 1990.

14. Missouri courts have adopted an integrated plant approach to its manufacturing exemption. See *Floyd Charcoal Co. v. Director of Revenue*, 599 S.W.2d 173 (Mo. 1980). Kansas has recently moved toward a modified integrated plant theory. See HB 2011, effective July 1, 2000.

Connecticut Water Company v. Barbato
Supreme Court of Connecticut, 1988.
206 Conn. 337, 537 A.2d 490.

. . . .

The plaintiff sells drinking water. [I]t constructed two water treatment plants, one in Clinton and the other in Chester. At these facilities, untreated or raw water that is unsuitable for drinking is drawn from reservoirs and collected in rapid mixing tanks in which hydrated lime and other agents that assist in the removal of suspended solids are added. Thereafter, the water passes through a pulsator clarifier unit (Clinton facility only) and certain filtration media, both of which serve to remove significant amounts of organic solids and other foreign material. In addition, this process assists in the correction of the water's odor and taste. A number of chemical compounds not present in the untreated water are added and thereafter remain present through to consumption. The entire process involves the use of basins, tanks, buildings, structures, pipes and a variety of machinery. Among the structures are certain water tanks known as "clearwells" in which finished water is held prior to its distribution by gravity feed through mains and pipes to the plaintiff's customers.

. . . .

The questions reserved for the advice of this court are: (1) Is the transformation of raw water into finished, potable water at the company's treatment plants a process that constitutes "manufacturing"?

. . . .

I

§12-412 (hh), which was in effect at the time of the defendant's assessment, provided an exemption from the sales and use tax for "[s]ales of and the storage, use or other consumption of machinery used directly in a manufacturing or agricultural production process." The plaintiff argues that its water treatment equipment is machinery used in a manufacturing process.

While there is no statutory definition of "manufacturing," §12-426-11b(a)(10) of the regulations of Connecticut state agencies provides that "'[m]anufacturing' shall mean the performance as a business of an integrated series of operations which places personal property in a *form, composition or character* different from that in which it was acquired for sale in the regular course of business by the manufacturer. The change in form, composition, or character must be a substantial change, and it must result in a transformation of property into a different product having a distinctive name, nature and use. Operations such as compounding or fabricating are illustrative of the types of operation which may result in such a change. 'Manufacturing' is an activity which shall occur *solely at an industrial plant*." (Emphasis added.)

Section 12-426-11b(a)(7) of the regulations of Connecticut state agencies in turn provides that an "'[i]ndustrial plant' shall mean a manufacturing facility at which a *manufacturing production process is occurring*. . . ." (Emphasis added.) A "manufacturing production process" is defined by these same regulations as "any one of a series of production activities, beginning with the movement of the raw materials after their receipt, inspection and storage, to the first production machine and ending with the completion of the finished product, including any packaging operations, for its sale to the ultimate consumer. . . ." Regs., Conn. State Agencies §12-426-11b(a)(11).

The plaintiff claims that the present controversy should be resolved in its favor based upon the ruling in Ziperstein v. Tax Commissioner, 423 A.2d 129 (1979). In that case, we held that electricity used in the preparation of various ice milk and frozen slush products was exempt from sales tax, having been used in "a process of manufacturing tangible personal property for sale in the regular course of business" as then provided in §12-426-11(g) of the regulations of Connecticut state agencies. The ice milk in issue was "produced by taking a commercially prepared liquid mixture of sugar, corn syrup and other items, and whipping air into the mixture and passing it through refrigerating machinery . . . . The . . . 'slush' . . . drink [was] made by mixing water, sugar, flavoring and chemical additives in a walk-in cooler where the product is stored until pumped from a machine."

Since a "process of manufacturing" had neither a statutory nor regulatory definition at the time, we applied the commonly understood meaning of the phrase and found the production of the plaintiff's products to be a "process of manufacturing" because "raw materials are transformed from an intrinsically valueless state into a finished product which has an *enhanced value and use* . . . ." (Emphasis added.) Id., at 500.[5] Relying on Ziperstein's emphasis on enhanced value and use, the plaintiff claims that its conversion of raw water to potable water is analogous to the production of the dairy bar products in that case.

The defendant argues that after the Ziperstein ruling, §12-426-11b(a)(10) of the regulations of Connecticut state agencies was promulgated, defining "manufacturing" in a narrower context with a different focus. The defendant claims that the processing of potable water does not place personal property in "a form, composition or character different from that in which it was acquired for sale" as the regulation now requires. The defendant further claims that the plaintiff's process does not meet this regulation's requirement that "[t]he change in form, composition, or character must be a substantial change, and it must result in a *transformation of property into a different product having a distinctive name, nature and use*." (Emphasis added) . . . We agree.

"It is a settled rule of law that statutes which exempt from taxation are to be strictly construed against the party claiming an exemption.". . . .

This regulation's requirement for a change in "form, composition, or character" to the end that there has been a "transformation of property" is consistent with our holding in American Sumatra Tobacco Corporation v. Tone, 15 A.2d 80 (1940). There, we concluded that the numerous steps required in preparing shade grown tobacco for market did not constitute a manufacturing operation even though stopping the operation "short of completion would result in spoiled and valueless tobacco." Despite the fact that "[t]he production and preparation for market of . . . shade grown tobacco is a complicated, intricate and unique process"; we reasoned that "[it was] still a leaf of tobacco." Similarly, despite the complexity of the equipment and procedures used by the plaintiff to render its water potable, the fact remains that the plaintiff's eventual product is still water and it does not carry the "distinctive name [and] nature" required by the regulation. Therefore, the transformation of raw water into finished, potable water at the company's treatment plant is not a process that constitutes "manufacturing" within the meaning of General Statutes §12-412(34).[7]

. . . .

---

5. In the present case, there is really only one raw material, i.e., the water. There is, therefore, a significant factual distinction between this case and Ziperstein v. Tax Commissioner, 423 A.2d 129 (1979).

7. We conclude that the test of "enhanced value and use" set forth in Ziperstein v. Tax Commissioner, 178 Conn. 493, 500, 423 A.2d 129 (1979), has been superseded and replaced by the later, more comprehensive regulation defining manufacturing, §12-426-11b(a)(10) of the regulations of Connecticut state agencies.

Questions and Comments

1. Was the court correct in assuming that only one raw material was involved–water?

2. Is the court claiming that water that is safe for drinking has the same character as untreated, unsafe water?

3. Was the chemical composition of the treated water different from that of the untreated water? Does water that is safe for drinking have a different use from water that is not fit for drinking? If so, why did the plaintiffs lose?

4. In representing the plaintiffs, how would you have distinguished *American Sumatra Tobacco*?

5. How would this court treat quarrying? Compare *Chilvis v. Marble Products Co.*, 217 S.E.2d 441 (1975).

6. Under Connecticut law, would a taxpayer qualify for the manufacturing exemption for equipment used in producing raisins by drying grapes? For pasteurizing and homogenizing milk? For producing orange juice?

Burger King, Inc. v. State Tax Commission
Court of Appeals of New York, 1980.
51 N.Y.2d 614, 416 N.E.2d 1024, 435 N.Y.S.2d 689.

[I]n the context of the "fast food" restaurant business, this appeal poses issues that test the scope of section 1105(a) of the Tax Law, which imposes taxes on retail sales of "tangible personal property". The focus is on whether the taxpayers come within the exceptions to this impost articulated in either section 1101(b)(4)(i)(A), which excludes a sale "for resale as such *or* as a physical component part of tangible personal property"* (emphasis added), or section 1115(a)(12), which exempts the sale of machinery and equipment used to produce "tangible personal property".

The operative facts are undisputed.

Burger King, a nationwide "fast food" chain, refused to pay sales tax on its purchases of certain paper or plastic packaging materials. The materials consisted of wrappers for hamburgers, cups for beverages and "sleeves" for french fries.[1] The taxpayer insists that it bought these articles for the purpose of resale and that, accordingly, their purchase was tax free.

Davmor Industries, Inc., a wholly owned subsidiary of

Burger King, manufactures restaurant equipment for sale to Burger King establishments. [I]t did not collect taxes on such sales of ovens, fryers, broilers, coffee urns, milk shake machinery and other similar equipment. It claims exemption because the equipment was used exclusively and directly to manufacture and otherwise process the food and beverages Burger King sells.

. . . .

In sustaining the Burger King assessment, the commission's rationale was that the taxpayer's patrons received the paper products "only as an incident to the purchase of food and drink" and thus, rather than being bought by Burger King for resale "as such", were consumed by Burger King in the course of consummating the "hybrid" transactions involved in the delivery of its combined food and service. It also asserts that the food and drink is not "tangible personal property" within the meaning of that phrase as it is used in subdivision (a) of section 1105.** On this basis, it then also reasoned, consistently, that the machinery and equipment in the Davmor and Edgmor cases, even if the processing of the restaurant food and drink could be said to be manufacturing, was not used for the "production of tangible personal property".

In the ensuing court proceedings, Special Term confirmed the determination as to Burger King, but on a different theory. Though it held the food and drink was tangible personal property, it decided that the packaging did not

---

*. [Ed. Sec. 1101(b)(4)(i) defines a retail sale as a "sale of tangible personal property to any person for any purpose, other than (A) for resale as such or as a physical component part of tangible personal property . . ."]

1. Only so much of these items as were used by Burger King for on-premises consumption of meals are at stake on this appeal. The commission is not pursuing a like assessment as to off-premises consumption only because it failed to give the taxpayer notice that taxes due on such sales were also to be the subject matter of his hearing. At the hearing, the taxpayer conceded liability as to outer bags, straws and coffee stirrers.

**. [Ed. Sec. 1101(b)(4)(i) defines a retail sale as a "sale of tangible personal property to any person for any purpose, other than (A) for resale as such or as a physical component part of tangible personal property . . ."]

qualify for the exclusion because it was neither a physical component part of the product nor sold by Burger King for resale as such and so served "only to facilitate the sale of the product". As to the equipment sold by Davmor, having held the food was tangible personal property, the court rejected the commission's conclusion that the machinery was not exempt under section 1115(a)(12). For its part, the Appellate Division, two Justices dissenting, annulled the assessments in toto. For the reasons which follow, we agree with the result it reached as to Burger King, but not as to Davmor.

For this purpose, we first look at whether Burger King's packaging material is excepted from the tax on the theory that it is a "physical component part" of the "tangible personal property" Burger King sells to its patrons (§ 1101(b)(4)(i)(A)). To arrive at an answer, preliminarily we address the subissue of whether food sold by restaurants is "tangible personal property" within the reasonable intendment of the Tax Law.

On that score, both courts below simply applied the broad definition of "tangible personal property" contained in the definitional section of the sales tax statute, i.e., "[c]orporeal property of any nature" (§ 1101(b)(6)). This interpretation, however, creates an ambiguity in the statutory scheme. If restaurant food is merely "tangible personal property", then section 1105(a), which imposes a tax on such retail sales, would seem to suffice. Nevertheless, there is a separate section (§ 1105(d)), which imposes a tax on the sale of restaurant food. Nowhere in this section is reference made to "tangible personal property". It is a familiar and salutary canon of construction that courts, in construing apparently conflicting statutory provisions must try to harmonize them.

This principle in mind, the commission's assertion that restaurant food, within the meaning of the Tax Law, is distinct from "tangible personal property", provides a ready means to reconcile the differing statutory sections. For the purchase of restaurant food is more than the mere receipt of an edible or a potable. Surely, it requires no impermissible outreach of the imagination to see it as a delivery of food and service in combination. Whether the proportion of the combination is 90% of service and 10% of food, as it might be in a gourmet restaurant which features pheasant under glass, or whether it is 10% of service and 90% of food, as it might be at a hot dog stand, it is difficult to see why the commission could not view the totality, as it did, as a "hybrid" transaction rather than as the sale of "tangible personal property". In so saying, we recognize that where the interpretation of a statute or its application involves a special knowledge, courts regularly defer to administrative expertise.

Indeed, it is appropriate here to comment on the modern-day economic and social phenomenon which, not without cause, has come to be known as the "fast food restaurant". Its universal proliferation on our national scene has made it common knowledge that such restaurants, for better or worse, are designed to mass-produce uniform, popular-priced food and drink products for consumption on ready demand on a conveyor-like, assembly-line basis. The amount of service it incorporates in its operation may be different from that of other types of restaurants, but, if anything, may be more significant. For its method of doing business requires that the food and drink it serves be in a form available for delivery whenever the unheralded patron chooses to arrive. The goal is streamlined movement of bagged food in sanitary form from restaurant to customer, who takes it in its ready-to-eat state without pause to wherever, on or off the premises, she or he wishes to consume it. Key to imparting these vaunted service features–of speed, sanitation and portability–is the use of paper or plastic goods in its preparation, storage and delivery.

Turning now to the applicability of the sale "for resale as such" exclusion. . . . decisional guidance is to be found in the so-called "container cases" (Matter of American Molasses Co. v McGoldrick, 22 N.E.2d 369; Matter of Colgate-Palmolive-Peet Co. v. Joseph, 125 N.E.2d 857; Matter of Dairylea Co-op. v. State Tax Comm., 342 N.Y.S.2d 761. The nub of these cases is that a sale is not one at retail when a supplier sells containers to a wholesaler or manufacturer, who then sells his product packed in these containers either to a retailer or to an ultimate consumer. The courts reasoned that the containers, although bought to be resold as "an incident to the sale of the contents" (Matter of American Molasses Co. v. McGoldrick, supra, p. 274, 22 N.E.2d 369), were nonetheless sales for resale as such. The cartons, although "*not inseparable*" from the contents, were, in this context, being resold "*as containers*" (see Matter of Colgate-Palmolive-Peet Co. v. Joseph, supra, 125 N.E.2d 857 [emphasis in original]).

All the more is this so in the case of Burger King, whose packaging, as we have seen, is such a critical element of the final product sold to customers. So regarded, the packaging material is as much a part of the final price as is the food or drink item itself. It would be exalting form over substance, therefore, to hold that a resale of these paper products does not take place merely because Burger King does not list a separate price.

Now, though the relative delicacy of the paper goods employed in Burger King's "fast food" operation is qualitatively much different from the grosser and coarser containers (pails, wooden barrels, metal drums, wooden crates, burlap sacks and three-gallon ice cream containers) with which the courts treated in the cited cases, and though the containers in these cases were largely confined to conventional delivery functions rather than the far more intimate product association afforded to Burger Kings' wrappings, in the present case, as in the cited ones, the containers and their contents at no time become "inseparably connected" (Matter of American Molasses Co. v. McGoldrick, 22 N.E.2d 369, supra). It follows that Burger King purchases its packaging from its suppliers for "resale as such" to its customers and thus is entitled to the exclusion of section 1101(b)(4)(i)(A).

This holding also brings that statute within the spirit underlying our sales tax law, which is to impose the tax only upon the sale to the ultimate consumer, at which time the price paid for the taxable item would presumably be at its highest. (See Matter of Dairylea Co-op. v. State Tax Comm., 342 N.Y.S.2d 761.) Yet if Burger King were required to pay sales tax on its purchases of packaging, the consumer would end up paying a tax on the sales tax. Clearly, this pyramiding of taxes would distort the original legislative intent and is to be avoided.

Lastly, we now treat Edgmor's contention that section 1115(a)(12) exempted the sale of machinery used to process food and drink. That section, as it existed during the assessment periods at issue provided:

"(a) Receipts from the following shall be exempt from the tax * * *

"(12) Machinery or equipment for use or consumption directly and exclusively *in the production of tangible personal property* * * * for sale, by manufacturing [or] processing" (emphasis added).

In effect, we have already rejected the taxpayers' claim of an exemption under this legislation. As its plain language tells us, necessary to a conclusion that the provision applies is a finding that the machinery is used to produce "tangible personal property". While in another context (e.g., the production of a frozen food product to be sold in a grocery store) these machines might be said to be so used, we have already demonstrated that here the production efforts are geared to the processing and delivery of restaurant food—a category distinct from tangible personal property. Certainly, the commission is not to be faulted because, in refusing to classify restaurant food as tangible personal property, it did not allow the particular stage at which its products were being "serviced" to result in an inconsistent conceptualization of their nature. Consequently, we are compelled to conclude that the sales of the machinery and equipment at issue are not exempt.

JONES, Judge (dissenting).

I would transpose the conclusions reached by the majority. The purchases by Burger King of the paper products (e.g., wrappers for sandwiches, cups to contain coffee, soda and other drinks, and sleeves for holding french fries) should be held to be subject to the sales tax (to that extent I would agree with the State Tax Commission), and the purchases by Burger King of equipment for processing food and drink (e.g., ovens, fryers, broilers, coffee urns and milk shake machinery) should be held to be exempt from the sales tax (to that extent I would disagree with the commission).

With reference to the paper products, the commission was surely justified in determining that their purchase was a retail sale within the definition of section 1101(b)(4) and did not come within the exception set forth in subclause (A) of clause (i) of that paragraph as a purchase "for resale as such or as a physical component part of tangible personal property". . . . Burger King did not sell the paper products as such to their customers and that the paper products did not become physical component parts of the food and drink which were sold to their customers.

As to the processing equipment, I am persuaded that the purchase of this equipment, as a matter of law, falls within the exemption provided in section 1115 (a)(12). That paragraph provided that receipts from the sale of "[m]achinery or equipment for use or consumption directly and exclusively [since 1974, 'predominantly'] in the production of tangible personal property" were exempt from the tax imposed by section 1105(a). I can agree with the contention of the commission that, under the design of the sales tax law, receipts from sales of food and drink by this taxpayer were taxable under section 1105(d) as a hybrid sale of tangible personal property with associated service incident to their delivery to the customer, rather than under subdivision (a) as a sale of tangible personal property, and to that extent that restaurant food subject to the tax under subdivision (d) does not fall within the definition of "tangible personal property" set out in section 1101(b)(6).

The matter does not end there, however. The exemption provision of section 1115 (a)(12) on which the taxpayer relies is entirely independent of section 1105(d) which imposes a tax on the "hybrid" sales. The exemption granted is from the tax imposed section 1105(a), not from the tax imposed by subdivision (d) of that section. No reason appears why the explicit definition of "tangible personal property" as "[c]orporeal personal property of any nature" (§ 1101(b)(6)) should not be applied in accordance with the plain meaning of the words used. Food and drink as such would clearly fall within the sweep of that definition.[2] The hybrid concept of the taxation of sales of restaurant food and drink as a combination of tangible personal property and services within the contemplation of section 1105(d) on which the commission would rely, is irrelevant.

Even if that concept were thought to be relevant, however, it would not be applicable. The equipment in question processed only food and drink—the tangible personal property component of the hybrid—and had nothing whatsoever to do with the services component of the hybrid. It could not be concluded, therefore, that the sales of the processing equipment did not enjoy the benefits of the paragraph (12) exemption on the theory that the equipment was acquired for use in the production of the hybrid; it was not.

. . . .

---

2. Were this not the case there would have been no occasion for the express exemption from the tax on "tangible personal property" under subdivision (a) of section 1105 of "[f]ood, food products and beverages" found in section 1115 (a)(1).

Questions and Comments

1. New York Tax Law § 1115(a)(1) exempts *inter alia* food, food products and beverages from the sales tax. Does that provision undercut the court's analysis?

2. The majority opinion describes restaurant meals as a hybrid and uses that characterization as an explanation for excluding restaurant meals from tangible personal property. Does the majority opinion prove too much?

3. The court bolsters its holding on the "sale for resale" issue by appealing to the legislative intent of the sales tax, which is to avoid pyramiding. Is its holding regarding the manufacturing exemption consistent with its view of legislative intent?

4. In holding that the purchase of the wrapping material was a "sale for resale," did the court have to determine whether the food sold by Burger King was tangible personal property? Is its holding on the sale for resale exemption consistent with its holding on the manufacturing exemption?

5. Were the so-called "container cases" really on point? Did any of those cases involve items that were not undeniably tangible personal property?

6. If the machinery in question had been used to produce frozen food products, the court would have held them exempt as being used to produce tangible personal property. Why does the court reach a different result because they are used to produce hot food rather than frozen food?

7. The Tax Commission held that the restaurant food was not tangible personal property and thus the machinery was not used to produce tangible personal property. At what point in the production process has Burger King created "restaurant food"?

8. What if Burger King sold in supermarkets exactly what it was selling at its restaurants? In other words, suppose you could buy in a supermarket a Styrofoam box containing a Burger King hamburger and fries, which you would take home and microwave. Would such a purchase be exempt as food?

9. If Burger King liquidated Davmor and operated it as a manufacturing division, would any sales or use tax apply on Burger King's manufacturing of its restaurant equipment?